Scott Foresman · Addison Wesley

enVisionMATH™ California

Scott Foresman • Addison Wesley
enVisionMATH™ California

Authors

Randall I. Charles
Professor Emeritus
Department of Mathematics
San Jose State University
San Jose, California

Mary Cavanagh
Mathematics Consultant
San Diego County Office of Education
San Diego, California

Juanita V. Copley
Professor
College of Education
University of Houston
Houston, Texas

Warren D. Crown
Associate Dean for Academic Affairs
Graduate School of Education
Rutgers University
New Brunswick, New Jersey

Francis (Skip) Fennell
Professor of Education
McDaniel College
Westminster, Maryland

Alma B. Ramirez
Sr. Research Associate
Math Pathways and Pitfalls WestEd
Oakland, California

Kay B. Sammons
Coordinator of Elementary Mathematics
Howard County Public Schools
Ellicott City, Maryland

Jane F. Schielack
Professor of Mathematics
Associate Dean for Assessment and
Pre K-12 Education, College of Science
Texas A&M University
College Station, Texas

William Tate
Edward Mallinckrodt Distinguished
University Professor in Arts & Sciences
Washington University
St. Louis, Missouri

John A. Van de Walle
Professor Emeritus, Mathematics Education
Virginia Commonwealth University
Richmond, Virginia

Consulting Mathematicians

Edward J. Barbeau
Professor of Mathematics
University of Toronto
Toronto, Canada

Sybilla Beckmann
Professor of Mathematics
Department of Mathematics
University of Georgia
Athens, Georgia

David Bressoud
DeWitt Wallace Professor of Mathematics
Macalester College
Saint Paul, Minnesota

Gary Lippman
Professor of Mathematics and Computer Science
California State University East Bay
Hayward, California

Editorial Offices: Glenview, Illinois • Parsippany, New Jersey • New York, New York
Sales Offices: Boston, Massachusetts • Duluth, Georgia • Glenview, Illinois
Coppell, Texas • Sacramento, California • Mesa, Arizona

Consulting Authors

Stuart J. Murphy
Visual Learning Specialist
Boston, Massachusetts

Jeanne Ramos
Secondary Mathematics Coordinator
Los Angeles Unified School District
Los Angeles, California

Verónica Galván Carlan
Private Consultant Mathematics
Harlingen, Texas

EL Consultants/Reviewers

Alma B. Ramirez
Sr. Research Associate
Math Pathways and Pitfalls WestEd
Oakland, California

California Reviewers

Martha Borquez
Teacher
Los Angeles USD

Elsa M. Campos
Teacher
Corona-Norco USD

Lynn Cevallos
K-12 Mathematics Consultant
Los Angeles, CA

Jann Edwards
Teacher, GATE Coordinator
Los Angeles USD

Katherine J. Jones
Teacher, District Math Coach
Newark USD

Kevin M. Kazala
Math Specialist K-6
Corona-Norco USD

Karen Jae Ko
Teacher
Long Beach USD

Kristin Leidig-Sears
Teacher
Los Angeles USD

Ariana R. Levin
Teacher
Los Angeles USD

Patrick A. McCormack
Special Education Teacher
Los Angeles USD

Stefani Maida
Teacher
Berkeley USD

Misook Park-Kimura
Professional Development Mentor
Long Beach USD

Elgin Michael Scott
Educator
Los Angeles USD

Doris L. Sterling
Teacher/Math Facilitator
Sacramento City USD

Amy N. Tindell
Math Coach
Los Angeles USD

Rachel M. Williams
Math Curriculum Associate/Teacher
North Sacramento School District

ISBN-13: 978-0-328-27289-1
ISBN-10: 0-328-27289-2

6 7 8 9 10 V064 12 11 10 09

CC: 2

Scott Foresman • Addison Wesley

enVisionMATH™ California

Topic Titles

Table of Contents

MATH STRAND COLORS

Number Sense

Algebra and Functions

Measurement and Geometry

Statistics, Data Analysis, and Probability

Problem Solving

Mathematical Reasoning, which includes problem solving, is infused throughout all lessons.

Topic 1 Numeration NS 1.0, 1.1, 1.2, 1.3, 1.5, AF 1.2, MR 1.1

Topic 2 Rounding NS 1.4, 2.1, MR 2.0, 2.6

Topic 3 Adding Whole Numbers NS 1.4, 2.0, 2.1, MR 2.1, 2.5, 3.1

Subtracting Whole Numbers

NS 1.4, 2.0, 2.1, MR 2.1, 2.3, 2.5, 3.2

Topic 5

Solids and Shapes

MG 2.0, 2.1, 2.2, 2.3, 2.4, 2.5, 2.6, MR 3.3

Topic 6

Multiplication Concepts

NS 3.1, Grade 2; NS 2.0, AF 1.2, 1.3, 1.5, 2.1, MR 2.4

Topic 7 Multiplication Facts: Use Patterns NS 2.2, 2.6, 2.8, AF 1.0, 1.3, MR 1.1, 2.0

Topic 8 Multiplication Facts: Use Known Facts NS 2.1, 2.2, 2.8, AF 1.5, MR 1.2

Topic 9 Division Concepts NS 3.0 Grade 2, NS 3.2 Grade 2, MG 2.0, MR 1.1, 2.3

Topic 10 Division Facts NS 2.3, 2.6, MR 2.0

Topic 11 Patterns and Relationships

NS 2.0, AF 1.0, 1.1, 1.3, 2.1, 2.2, MR 1.1, 2.0, 2.3

Topic 12 Fraction Concepts

NS 3.0, 3.1, AF 2.0, MR 2.3, 3.0

Topic 13 Adding and Subtracting Fractions

NS 3.1, 3.2, MR 2.3

Topic 14 Multiplying Greater Numbers

NS 2.4, MR 1.2, 2.0, 2.1, 2.3

Topic 15 Dividing by 1-Digit Numbers
NS 2.0, 2.3, 2.5, MR 1.2, 2.1, 2.2, 2.3

Topic 16 Customary Measurement
NS 2.8, AF 1.0, 1.4, MG 1.0, 1.1, 1.4, AF 1.4, MR 1.0; MG 1.5, Grade 2

Topic 17 Metric Measurement
NS 2.8, MG 1.1, 1.4, AF 1.4, 2.0, 2.1, MR 2.3

Topic 18 Perimeter, Area, and Volume
MG 1.2, 1.3, 2.3, MR 2.2

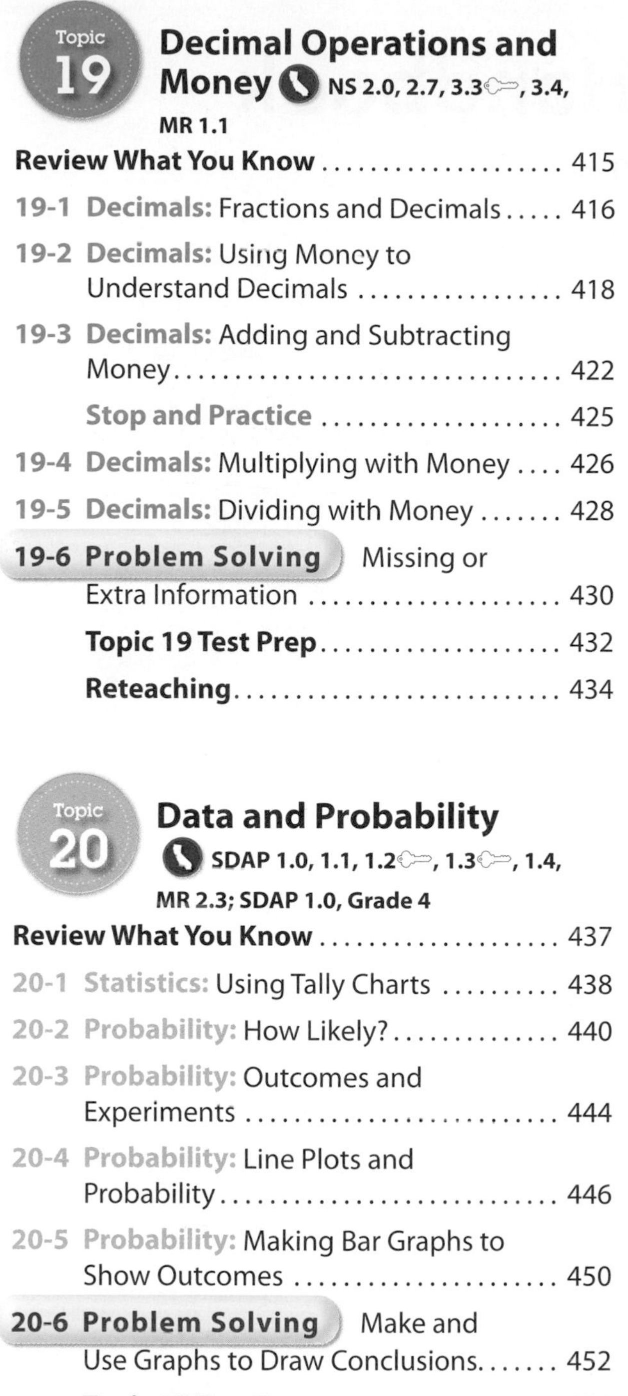

Topic 19 Decimal Operations and Money NS 2.0, 2.7, 3.3, 3.4, MR 1.1

Topic 20 Data and Probability SDAP 1.0, 1.1, 1.2, 1.3, 1.4, MR 2.3; SDAP 1.0, Grade 4

Student Resources

Problem-Solving Handbook

Use this Problem-Solving Handbook throughout the year to help you solve problems.

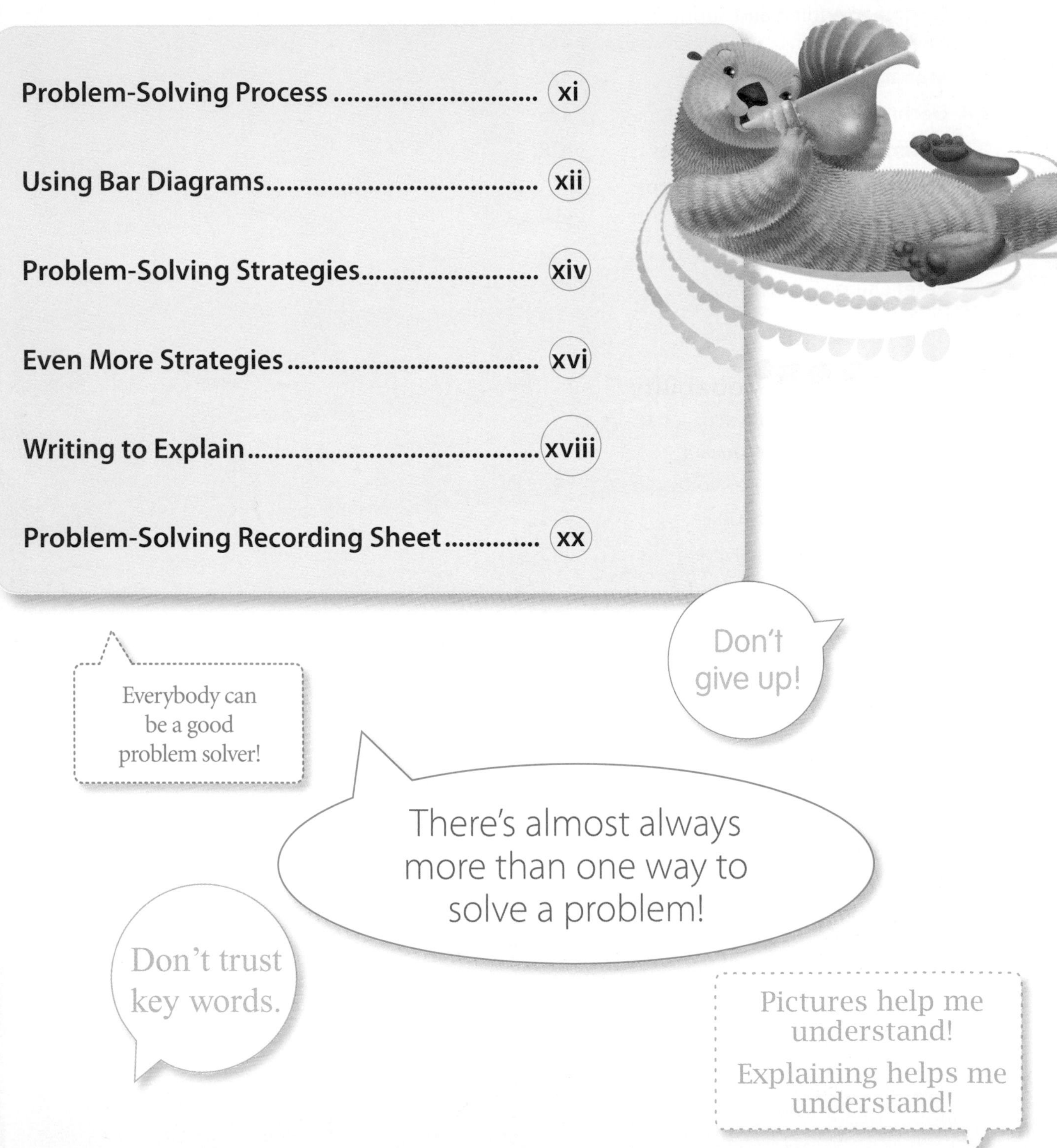

Problem-Solving Process

Read and Understand

What am I trying to find?
- Tell what the question is asking.

What do I know?
- Tell the problem in my own words.
- Identify key facts and details.

Plan and Solve

What strategy or strategies should I try?

Can I show the problem?
- Try drawing a picture.
- Try making a list, table, or graph.
- Try acting it out or using objects.

How will I solve the problem?

What is the answer?
- Tell the answer in a complete sentence.

Strategies

- Show What You Know
  - Draw a Picture
  - Make an Organized List
  - Make a Table
  - Make a Graph
  - Act It Out/ Use Objects
- Look for a Pattern
- Try, Check, Revise
- Write a Number Sentence
- Use Reasoning
- Work Backward
- Solve a Simpler Problem

Look Back and Check

Did I check my work?
- Compare my work to the information in the problem.
- Be sure all calculations are correct.

Is my answer reasonable?
- Estimate to see if my answer makes sense.
- Make sure the question was answered.

Using Bar Diagrams

Use a bar diagram to show how what you know and what you want to find are related. Then choose an operation to solve the problem.

Problem 1

Carrie helps at the family flower store in the summer. She keeps a record of how many hours she works. How many hours did she work on Monday and Wednesday?

Carrie's Work Hours

Days	Hours
Monday	5
Tuesday	3
Wednesday	6
Thursday	5
Friday	5

Bar Diagram

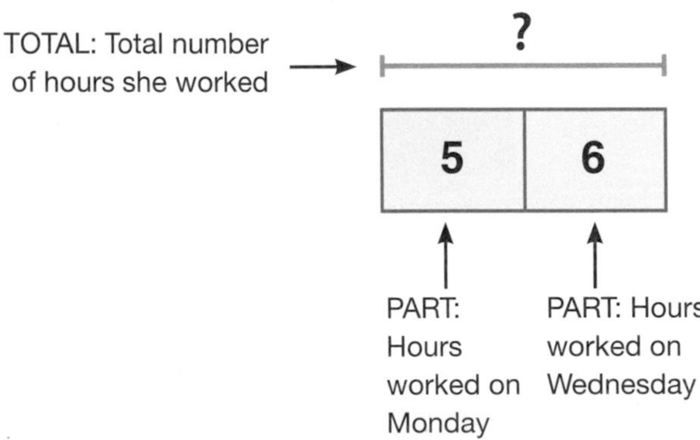

5 + 6 = ?

I can add to find the total.

Problem 2

Kim is saving to buy a sweatshirt for the college her brother attends. She has \$9. How much more money does she need to buy the sweatshirt?

Bar Diagram

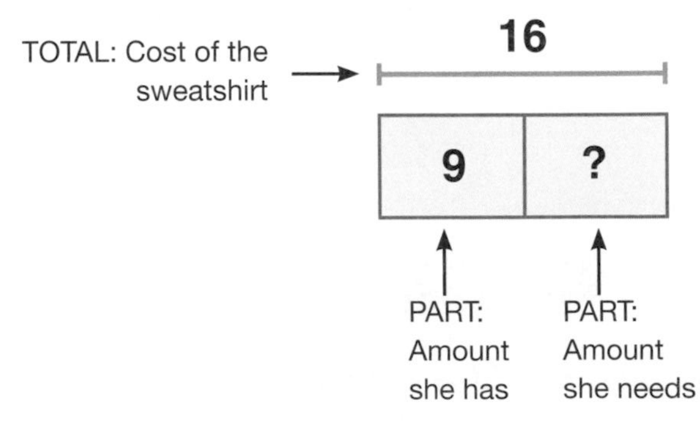

16 − 9 = ?

I can subtract to find the missing part.

Pictures help me understand!

Don't trust key words!

Problem 3

Tickets to a movie on Saturday cost only $5 each no matter what age you are. What is the cost of tickets for a family of four?

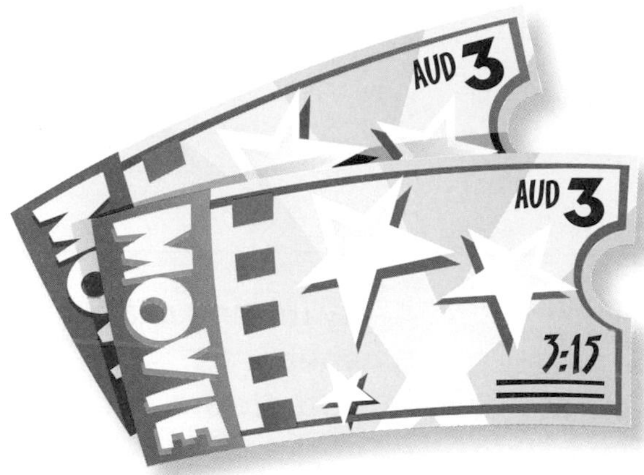

Bar Diagram

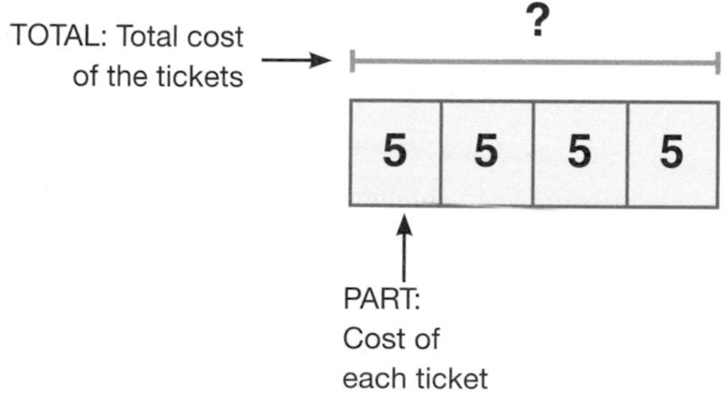

4 × 5 = ?

I can multiply because the parts are equal.

Problem 4

Twelve students traveled in 3 vans to the zoo. The same numbers of students were in each van. How many students were in each van?

Bar Diagram

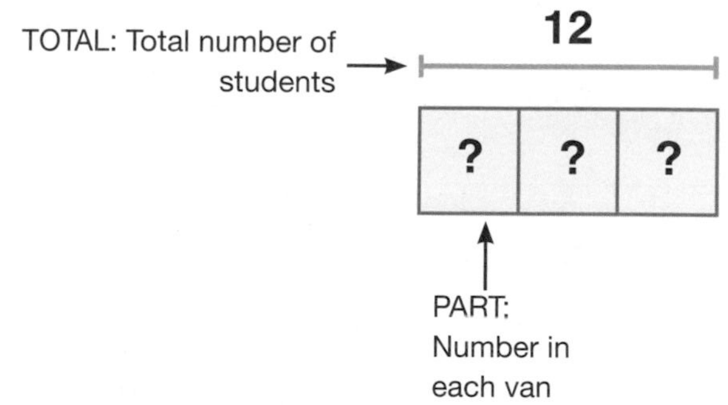

12 ÷ 3 = ?

I can divide to find how many are in each part.

Problem-Solving Strategies

Strategy	Example	When I Use It
Draw a Picture	The race was 5 kilometers. Markers were at the starting line and the finish line. Markers showed each kilometer of the race. Find the number of markers used. Start Line — Finish Line Start Line, 1 km, 2 km, 3 km, 4 km, Finish Line	Try drawing a picture when it helps you visualize the problem or when the relationships such as joining or separating are involved.
Make a Table	Phil and Marcy spent all day Saturday at the fair. Phil rode 3 rides each half hour and Marcy rode 2 rides each half hour. How many rides had Marcy ridden when Phil rode 24 rides?	Try making a table when: • there are 2 or more quantities, • amounts change using a pattern.
Look for a Pattern	The house numbers on Forest Road change in a planned way. Describe the pattern. Tell what the next two house numbers should be. 3, 6, 10, 15, ?, ?	Look for a pattern when something repeats in a predictable way.

Rides for Phil	3	6	9	12	15	18	21	24
Rides for Marcy	2	4	6	8	10	12	14	16

Everybody can be a good problem solver!

Strategy	Example	When I Use It
Make an Organized List	How many ways can you make change for a quarter using dimes and nickels? 1 quarter = 1 dime + 1 dime + 1 nickel 1 dime + 1 nickel + 1 nickel + 1 nickel 1 nickel + 1 nickel + 1 nickel + 1 nickel + 1 nickel	Make an organized list when asked to find combinations of two or more items.
Try, Check, Revise	Suzanne spent \$27, not including tax, on dog supplies. She bought two of one item and one of another item. What did she buy? \$8 + \$8 + \$15 = \$31 \$7 + \$7 + \$12 = \$26 \$6 + \$6 + \$15 = \$27	Use Try, Check, Revise when quantities are being combined to find a total, but you don't know which quantities. **Dog Supplies Sale!** Leash .... \$8 Collar .... \$6 Bowls .... \$7 Medium Beds .... \$15 Toys \$12
Write a Number Sentence	Maria's new CD player can hold 6 discs at a time. If she has 54 CDs, how many times can the player be filled without repeating a CD? Find 54 ÷ 6 = ■.	Write a number sentence when the story describes a situation that uses an operation or operations.

Even More Strategies

Strategy	Example	When I Use It
Act It Out	How many ways can 3 students shake each other's hand?	Think about acting out a problem when the numbers are small and there is action in the problem you can do.
Use Reasoning	Beth collected some shells, rocks, and beach glass. **Beth's Collection** 2 rocks ●● 3 times as many shells as rocks ●● ●● ●● 12 objects in all How many of each object are in the collection?	Use reasoning when you can use known information to reason out unknown information.
Work Backward	Tracy has band practice at 10:15 A.M. It takes her 20 minutes to get from home to practice and 5 minutes to warm up. What time should she leave home to get to practice on time? Time Tracy leaves home ? ← 20 minutes ← Time warm up starts ← 5 minutes ← Time practice starts **10:15**	Try working backward when: • you know the end result of a series of steps, • you want to know what happened at the beginning.

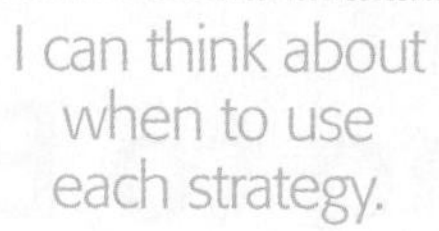

Strategy	Example	When I Use It
Solve a Simpler Problem 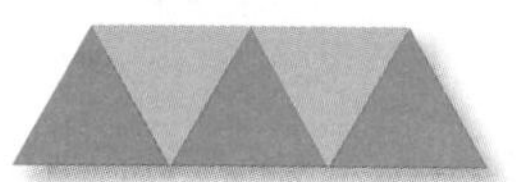	Each side of each triangle in the figure at the left is one centimeter. If there are 12 triangles in a row, what is the perimeter of the figure? I can look at 1 triangle, then 2 triangles, then 3 triangles. 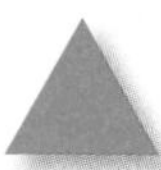 perimeter = 3 cm 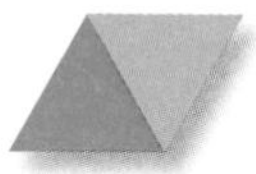 perimeter = 4 cm  perimeter = 5 cm	Try solving a simpler problem when you can create a simpler case that is easier to solve.
Make a Graph	Mary was in a jump rope contest. How did her number of jumps change over the five days of the contest? 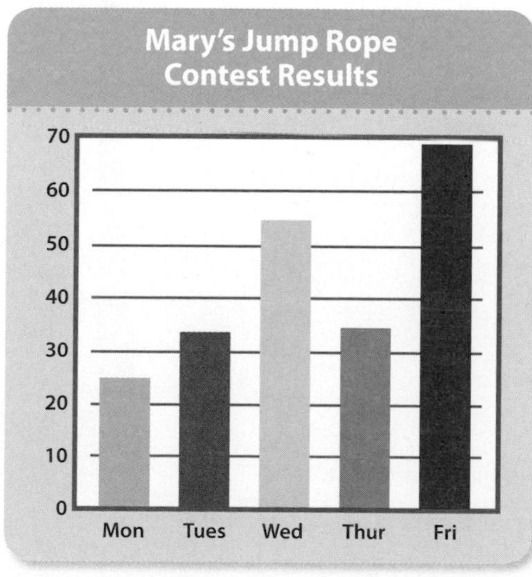	Make a graph when: • data for an event are given, • the question can be answered by reading the graph.

Writing to Explain

Here is a good math explanation.

Writing to Explain What happens to the area of the rectangle if the lengths of its sides are doubled?

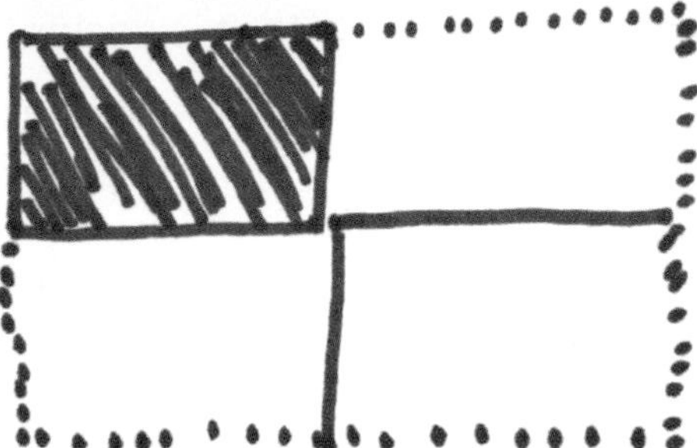

■ = $\frac{1}{4}$ of the whole rectangle

The area of the new rectangle is 4 times the area of the original rectangle.

Tips for Writing Good Math Explanations....

A good explanation should be:

- correct
- simple
- complete
- easy to understand

Math explanations can use:

- words
- pictures
- numbers
- symbols

Explaining helps me understand!

This is another good math explanation.

Writing to Explain Use blocks to show 3 × 24.
Draw a picture of what you did with the blocks.

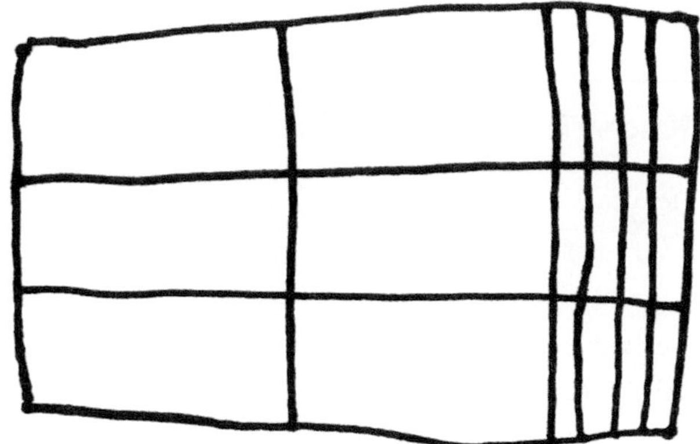

First we made a row of 24 using 2 tens and 4 ones. Then we made 2 more rows. Then we said 3 rows of 2 tens is 3 x 2 tens = 6 tens or 60. Then we said 3 rows of 4 ones is 3 x 4 = 12. Then we added the parts 60 + 12 = 72 So, 3 x 24 = 72.

Problem-Solving Recording Sheet

Name Jane

Teaching Tool 1

Problem-Solving Recording Sheet

Problem:
On June 14, 1777, the Continental Congress approved the design of a national flag. The 1777 flag had 13 stars, one for each colony. Today's flag has 50 stars, one for each state. How many stars were added to the flag since 1777?

Find?

Number of stars added to the flag

Know?

Original flag
13 stars

Today's flag
50 stars

Strategies?

Show the Problem
- ☑ Draw a Picture
- ☐ Make an Organized List
- ☐ Make a Table
- ☐ Make a Graph
- ☐ Act It Out/Use Objects

- ☐ Look for a Pattern
- ☐ Try, Check, Revise
- ☑ Write an Equation
- ☐ Use Reasoning
- ☐ Work Backwards
- ☐ Solve a Simpler Problem

Show the Problem?

50	
13	?

Solution?

I am comparing the two quantities.
I could add up from 13 to 50. I can also subtract 13 from 50. I'll subtract.

$$\begin{array}{r} 50 \\ -\ 13 \\ \hline 37 \end{array}$$

Answer?

There were 37 stars added to the flag from 1777 to today.

Check? Reasonable?

37 + 13 = 50 so I subtracted correctly.

50 − 13 is about 50 − 10 = 40
40 is close to 37. 37 is reasonable.

Teaching Tools • 1

Here's a way to organize my problem-solving work

Name Benton

Teaching Tool 1

Problem-Solving Recording Sheet

Problem:

Suppose your teacher told you to open your math book to the facing pages whose page numbers add to 85. To which two pages would you open your book?

Find?

Two facing page numbers

Know?

Two pages.
Facing each other.
Sum is 85.

Strategies?

Show the Problem
- ☑ Draw a Picture
- ☐ Make an Organized List
- ☐ Make a Table
- ☐ Make a Graph
- ☐ Act It Out/Use Objects

- ☐ Look for a Pattern
- ☑ Try, Check, Revise
- ☑ Write an Equation
- ☐ Use Reasoning
- ☐ Work Backwards
- ☐ Solve a Simpler Problem

Show the Problem?

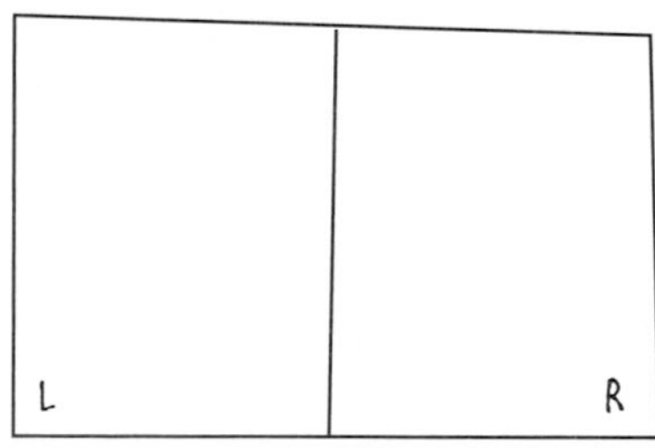

L + R = 85
L is 1 less than R

Solution?

I'll try some numbers in the middle.
40 + 41 = 81, too low
How about 46 and 47?
46 + 47 = 93, too high
Ok, now try 42 and 43.
42 + 43 = 85.

Answer?

The page numbers are 42 and 43.

Check? Reasonable?

I added correctly.
42 + 43 is about 40 + 40 = 80
80 is close to 85.
42 and 43 is reasonable.

Topic 1

Numeration

1 How many dominos were used to set the world record for domino-toppling? You will find out in Lesson 1-3.

2 How much did the world's largest pumpkin weigh? You will find out in Lesson 1-2.

3 How many grooves, or reeds, do coins have around their edges? You will find out in Lesson 1-5.

Review What You Know!

Vocabulary

Choose the best term from the box.

- hundreds
- numbers
- ones
- tens

1. The number 49 has 4 __?__.
2. The number 490 has 4 __?__.
3. The number 54 has 4 __?__.

Place Value

Write each number.

4. 3 tens 5 ones **5.** 9 tens

6. forty-six **7.** ninety-eight

8. fifty-two **9.** seventy-six

Addition and Subtraction

Find the sum or difference.

10. 6 + 5 **11.** 7 + 2 **12.** 8 + 9

13. 8 − 2 **14.** 7 − 5 **15.** 9 − 6

16. 7 + 6 **17.** 7 + 9 **18.** 9 − 1

Compare Numbers

19. **Writing to Explain** Which is greater, 95 or 59? How do you know?

20. Write these numbers in order from least to greatest:
14 54 41

Lesson
1-1

NS 1.1 Count, read, and write whole numbers to 10,000.
Also **NS 1.3** Identify the place value for each digit in numbers to 10,000.

Hundreds

Hands-On
place-value blocks

How can you read and write a number in the hundreds?

All numbers are made from the digits, 0, 1, 2, 3, 4, 5, 6, 7, 8, and 9.

Place value is the value of the place a digit has in a number.

Bicycles with chains have been used for more than 125 years.

Another Example

How can you show 850 on a place-value chart?

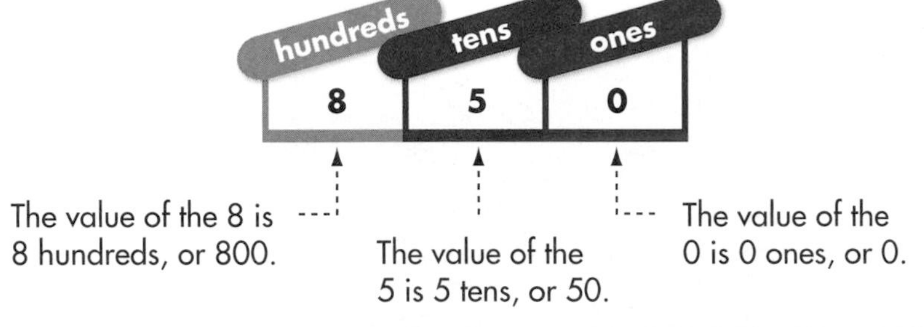

Guided Practice*

Do you know HOW?

For **1–3**, write each number in standard form.

1. 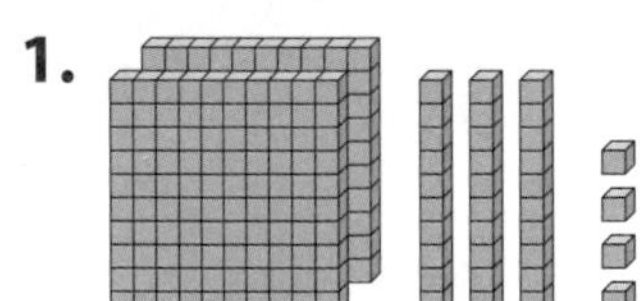

2. 600 + 50 + 3

3. eight hundred seventy-nine

4. Write 156 in expanded form.

Do you UNDERSTAND?

5. How does a place-value chart show the value of a number?

6. When 850 is written in expanded form, why are there only two addends?

7. How do you know that 37 and 307 do not name the same number?

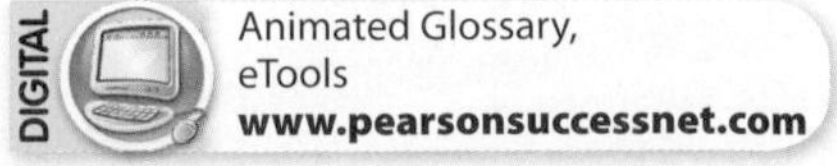

*For another example, see Set A on page 20.

You can show 125 in different ways.

place-value blocks:

standard form: **125**

expanded form: **100 + 20 + 5**

word form: **one hundred twenty-five**

Independent Practice

Write each number in standard form.

8. 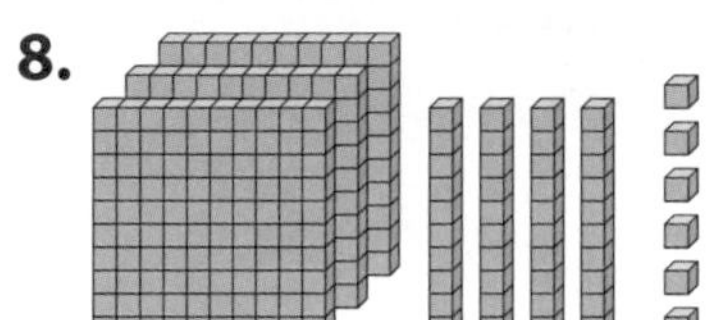

9. 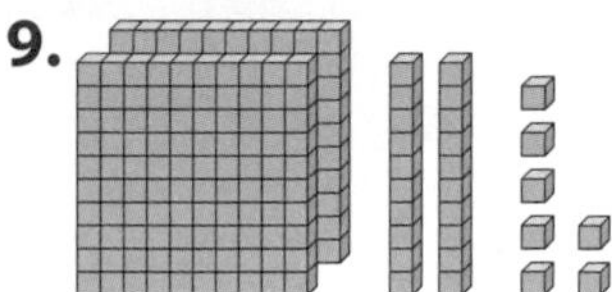

10. 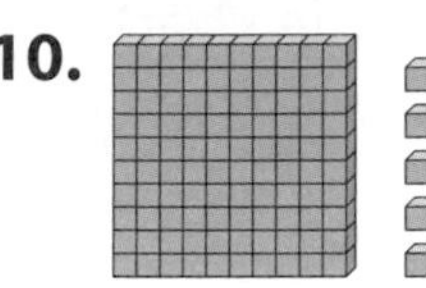

11. 900 + 80 + 5

12. 400 + 70 + 8

13. three hundred four

Write each number in expanded form and word form.

14. 707

15. 683

16. 894

17. 520

18. 251

19. 402

Problem Solving

20. Reasoning The sum of the digits in a three-digit number is 4. The ones digit is 3. What is the number?

21. Algebra Find the value of the missing number.
389 = ▢ + 80 + 9

22. Writing to Explain Which digit has the greatest value in 589?

23. Which is the standard form of 700 + 50?

A 570

B 705

C 750

D 1,200

Lesson
1-2

NS 1.1 Count, read, and write whole numbers to 10,000.
Also NS 1.3 Identify the place value for each digit in numbers to 10,000.

Thousands

Hands-On
place-value blocks

How can you read and write 4-digit numbers?

Ten hundreds equal one thousand.

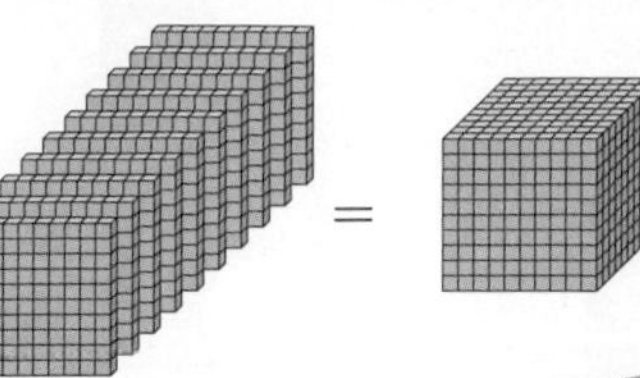

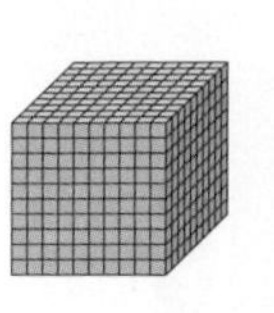

Did you know that a two-humped camel weighs between 1,000 and 1,450 pounds?

This camel weighs 1,350 pounds.

Another Example

You can also show 1,350 on a place-value chart.

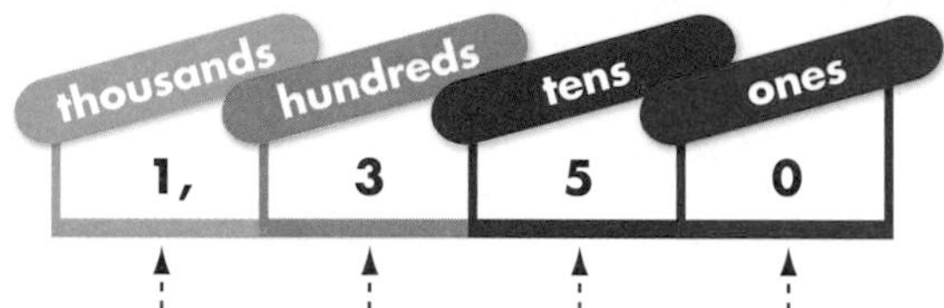

The value of the 1 is 1 thousand, or 1,000.

The value of the 3 is 3 hundred, or 300.

The value of the 5 is 5 tens, or 50.

The value of the 0 is 0 ones, or 0.

Guided Practice*

Do you know HOW?

Write each number in standard form.

1.

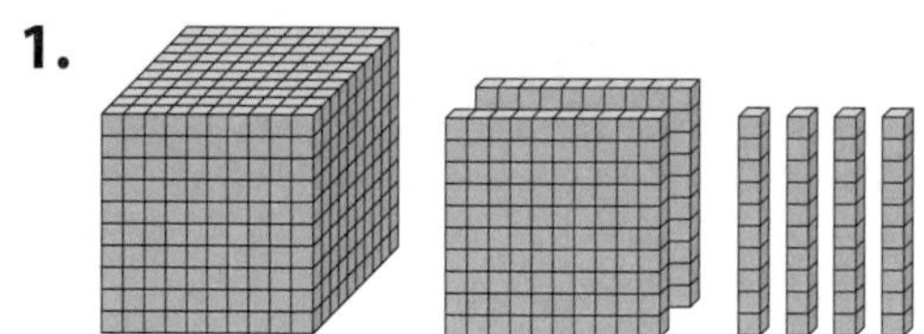

2. 8,000 + 500 + 30 + 9

3. two thousand, four hundred sixty-one

Do you UNDERSTAND?

4. Explain the value of each digit in 6,802.

5. Write a 4-digit number that has a tens digit of 5, a hundreds digit of 2, and 6 for each of the other digits.

6. Suppose another animal is three hundred pounds heavier than the camel in the photo. How would you write that weight in expanded form?

7. How could you show 1,350 with place-value blocks if you do not have a thousand block?

*For another example, see Set B on page 20.

You can show 1,350 in different ways.

place-value blocks:

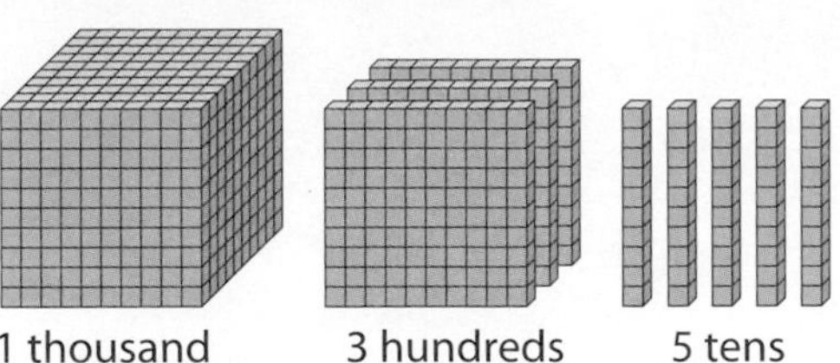

expanded form: 1,000 + 300 + 50

standard form: 1,350

Write a comma between the thousands and the hundreds.

word form: one thousand, three hundred fifty

Write a comma between the thousands and the hundreds.

Independent Practice

For **8–10**, write each number in standard form.

8.

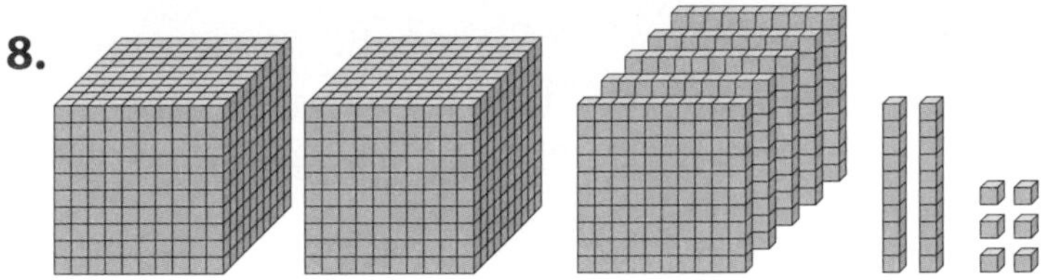

9. 4,000 + 600 + 50 + 8

10. 7,000 + 200 + 1

For **11** and **12**, write each number in expanded form.

11. six thousand, two hundred four

12. 5,033

For **13–17**, write the place of the underlined digit. Then write its value.

13. 4,<u>8</u>65 **14.** 3,2<u>4</u>5 **15.** <u>9</u>,716 **16.** 5,3<u>0</u>9 **17.** <u>7</u>,240

Problem Solving

18. **Writing to Explain** Is one thousand, four hundred the same as fourteen hundred? Explain why or why not.

19. In 2005, the world's largest pumpkin weighed 1,469 pounds. Write that number in word form.

20. Which is the word form of 2,406?

A twenty four thousand, six

B two thousand, four hundred six

C two thousand, forty-six

D two hundred forty-six

21. **Number Sense** Write the greatest possible number and the least possible number using the four digits 5, 2, 8, and 1.

Lesson

1-3

NS 1.5 Use expanded notation to represent numbers (e.g., 3,206 = 3,000 + 200 + 6). Also **NS 1.0** Understand the place value of whole numbers.

Greater Numbers

How can you read and write greater numbers?

Capitol Reef National Park in Utah covers 241,904 acres of land.

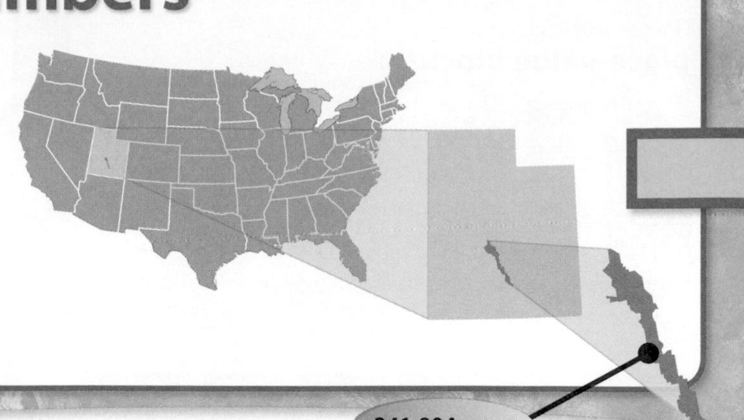

Guided Practice*

Do you know HOW?

Write each number in standard form.

1. three hundred forty-two thousand, six hundred seven
2. ninety-eight thousand, three hundred twenty
3. 500,000 + 40,000 + 600 + 90 + 3
4. What is the value of the 9 in the number 379,050?

Do you UNDERSTAND?

5. **Number Sense** Ramos says the value of the digit 7 in 765,450 is 70,000. Do you agree? Why or why not?
6. **Writing to Explain** Describe how 130,434 and 434,130 are alike and how they are different.

Independent Practice

Write each number in standard form.

7. twenty-seven thousand, five hundred fifty
8. 800,000 + 20,000 + 6,000 + 300 + 50

Write each number in expanded form.

9. 46,354
10. 395,980

Write the place of the underlined digit. Then write its value.

11. 404,705   12. 163,254   13. 45,391   14. 983,971   15. 657,240

*For another example, see Set C on page 20.

How can you show 241,904 in different ways?

place-value chart:

hundred thousands	ten thousands	thousands	hundreds	tens	ones
2	4	1,	9	0	4

thousands period / ones period

A period is a group of 3 digits in a number, starting from the right. Two periods are separated by a comma.

standard form:
241, 904

expanded form:
200,000 + 40,000 + 1,000 + 900 + 4

word form: two hundred forty-one thousand, nine hundred four

Algebra Find each missing number.

16. 26,305 = 20,000 + ▢ + 300 + 5

17. 801,960 = 800,000 + 1,000 + ▢ + 60

18. 400,000 + ▢ + 30 + 2 = 470,032

19. 618,005 = ▢ + 10,000 + 8,000 + 5

20. 300,000 + ▢ + 600 + 3 = 304,603

21. 200,000 + 4,000 + 60 + 3 = ▢

Problem Solving

For **22–24**, use the table.

22. Write the population of each city in the table in expanded form.

23. Write the population of Columbus, OH in word form.

24. Which cities listed have fewer than eight hundred thousand people?

City Populations (Data)

City	Number of People
Fresno, CA	841,400
Jacksonville, FL	777,704
Columbus, OH	730,008

25. A new world record was set when 303,628 dominos fell. Write 303,628 in expanded form.

26. Which is the word form of 805,920?

A eighty-five thousand, ninety-two

B eight hundred five thousand, ninety-two

C eight thousand, five hundred ninety-two

D eight hundred five thousand, nine hundred twenty

Lesson
1-4

NS 1.2 Compare and order whole numbers to 10,000.
Also **AF 1.2** Solve problems involving numeric equations or inequalities.

Comparing Numbers

How do you compare numbers?

When you compare two numbers you find out which number is greater and which number is less.

Which is taller, the Statue of Liberty or its base?

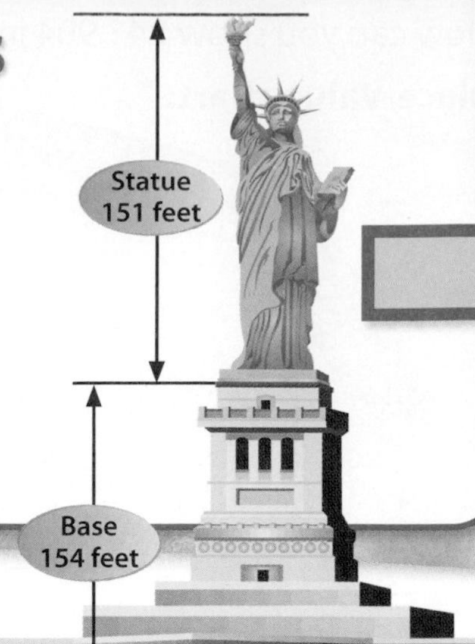

Another Example How can you use place value to compare numbers?

Compare 3,456 and 3,482 using a place-value chart.

Line up the digits by place value.
Compare the digits starting from the left.

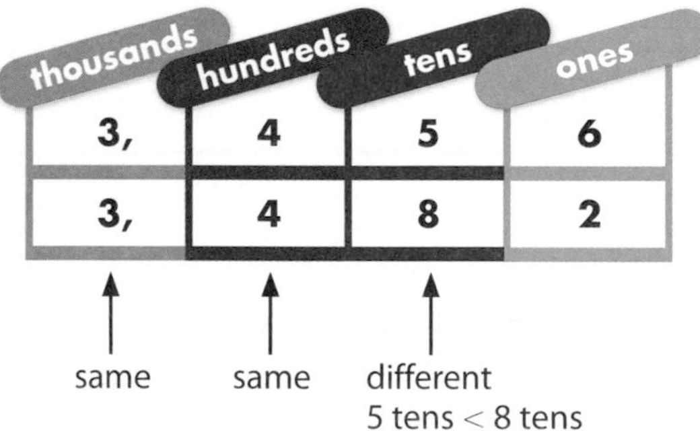

thousands	hundreds	tens	ones
3,	4	5	6
3,	4	8	2

So 3,456 **is less than** 3,482.

$3,456 < 3,482$

Explain It

1. In this example, why don't you need to compare the digits in the ones place?
2. Why can't you tell which number is greater by just comparing the first digit in each number?

Animated Glossary
www.pearsonsuccessnet.com

You can use symbols.

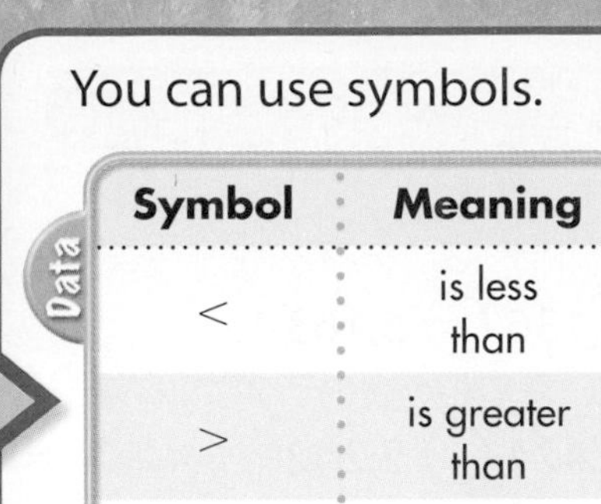

Symbol	Meaning
<	is less than
>	is greater than
=	is equal to

You can compare 151 and 154 with place value.

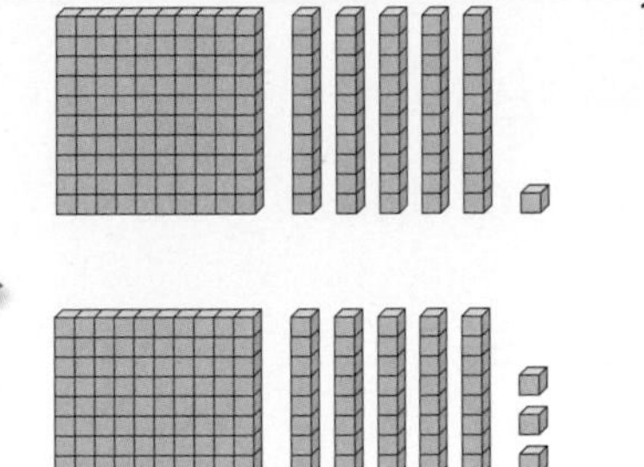

154 is greater than 151.

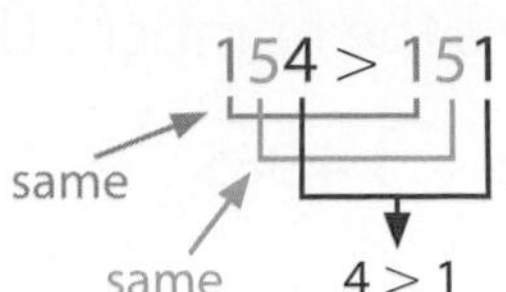

The place-value blocks also show that 151 is less than 154.

151 < 154

So, the base is taller than the statue.

Guided Practice*

Do you know HOW?

Compare the numbers. Use <, >, or =.

1.

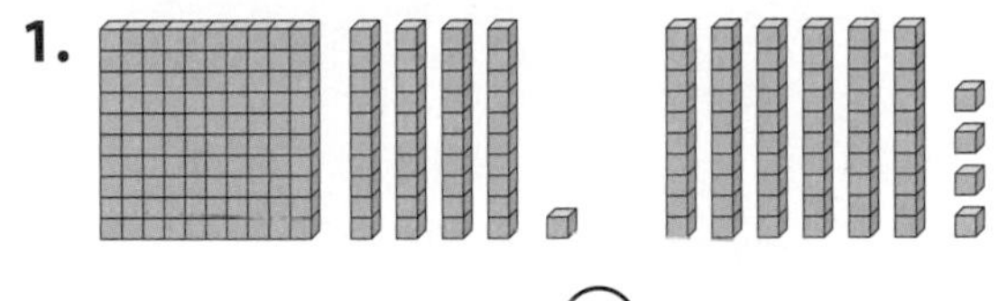

141 ◯ 64

2.

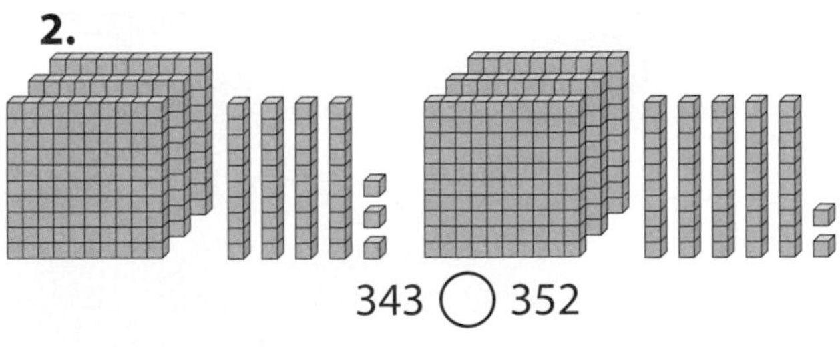

343 ◯ 352

3. 2,561 ◯ 2,261

4. 6,807 ◯ 6,807

Do you UNDERSTAND?

5. **Number Sense** Cara says that since 4 is greater than 1, the number 496 is greater than 1,230. Do you agree? Why or why not?

6. **Writing to Explain** The total height of the Statue of Liberty is 305 feet. The height of the Washington Monument is 555 feet. Which is taller? Explain how you know.

Independent Practice

Compare the numbers. Use <, >, or =.

7.

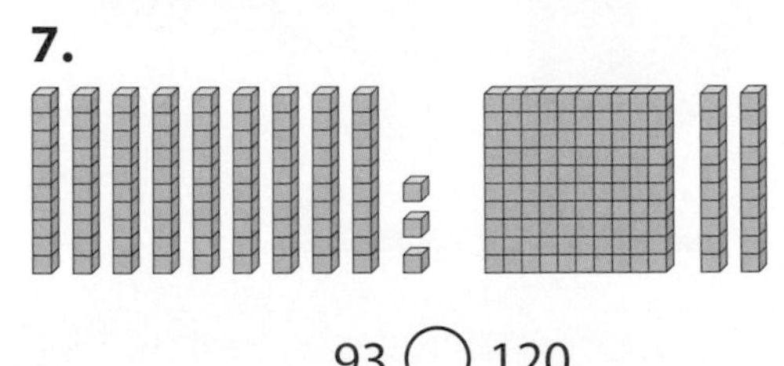

93 ◯ 120

8.

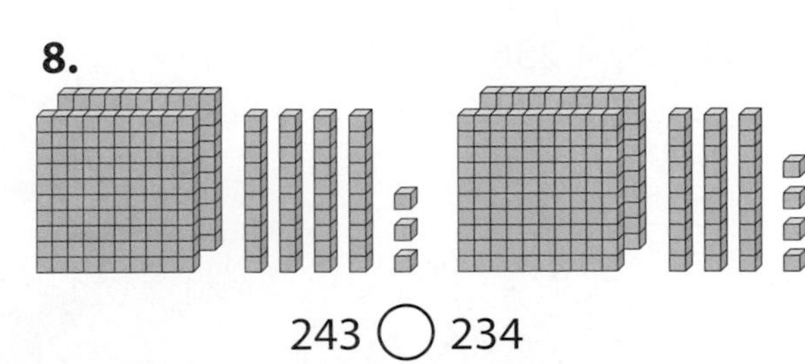

243 ◯ 234

For another example, see Set D on page 21.

Independent Practice

Compare the numbers. Use <, >, or =.

9. 679 ○ 4,985 **10.** 9,642 ○ 9,642 **11.** 5,136 ○ 5,163

12. 8,204 ○ 8,402 **13.** 3,823 ○ 3,853 **14.** 2,424 ○ 2,242

Number Sense Write the missing digits to make each number sentence true.

15. □24 > 896 **16.** 6□7 < 617 **17.** 29□ = 2□0

18. □,000 < 1,542 **19.** 3,□12 > 3,812 **20.** 2,185 > 2,□85

Problem Solving

Use the pictures for **21** and **22**.

21. Writing to Explain Which is taller, the Washington Monument or the General Sherman tree? How do you know?

22. Which is taller, the Gateway Arch or the Space Needle?

23. Reasoning Mark is thinking of a 3-digit number. Rory is thinking of a 4-digit number. Whose number is greater? How do you know?

24. Number Sense Suppose you are comparing 1,272 and 1,269. Do you need to compare the ones digits? Explain.

25. Which number sentence is true if the number 537 replaces the box?

A 456 > □

B □ = 256

C 598 < □

D □ > 357

Algebra Connections

Number Patterns

Remember that skip counting can be used to make a number pattern. Skip counting can also be used to find missing numbers in a given pattern.

Copy and complete. Write the number that completes each pattern.

Examples: 2, 4, 6, 8, ▢, 12

Can you skip count by a certain number to get each number in the pattern?

Skip count by 2s for this pattern.

2, 4, 6, 8, 10, 12

1. 3, 6, 9, 12, ▢, 18

2. 14, ▢, 18, 20, 22, 24

3. 20, 30, ▢, 50, 60, 70

4. 25, 50, 75, 100, 125, ▢

5. 3, 8, 13, 18, 23, ▢

6. 9, 19, 29, ▢, 49, 59

7. 7, 9, 11, ▢, 15, 17

8. 12, ▢, 20, 24, 28

9. 90, 80, 70, ▢, 50, 40

10. 22, 20, 18, 16, ▢, 12

11. 86, 81, ▢, 71, 66, 61

12. 150, ▢, 100, 75, 50, 25

For **13** and **14**, copy and complete each pattern. Use the pattern to help solve the problem.

13. Rusty saw that the house numbers on a street were in a pattern. First he saw the number 101. Then he saw the numbers 103, 105, and 107. There was a missing number, and then the number 111. What was the missing number?

101, 103, 105, 107, ▢, 111

14. Alani was skip counting the pasta shapes she made. The numbers she said were 90, 95, 100, 105, 110, 115. She needed to say one more number in the count to finish counting the pasta. How many pasta shapes did Alani make?

90, 95, 100, 105, 110, 115, ▢

15. Write a Problem Copy and complete the number pattern below. Write a problem to match the number pattern.

5, 10, 15, 20, 25, 30, ▢

Lesson
1-5

NS 1.2 Compare and order whole numbers to 10,000.
Also **NS 1.3** Identify the place value for each digit in numbers to 10,000.

Ordering Numbers

How can you order numbers?

When you order numbers, you write them from greatest to least or from least to greatest.

Three rivers are shown on the map. Write their lengths in order from greatest to least.

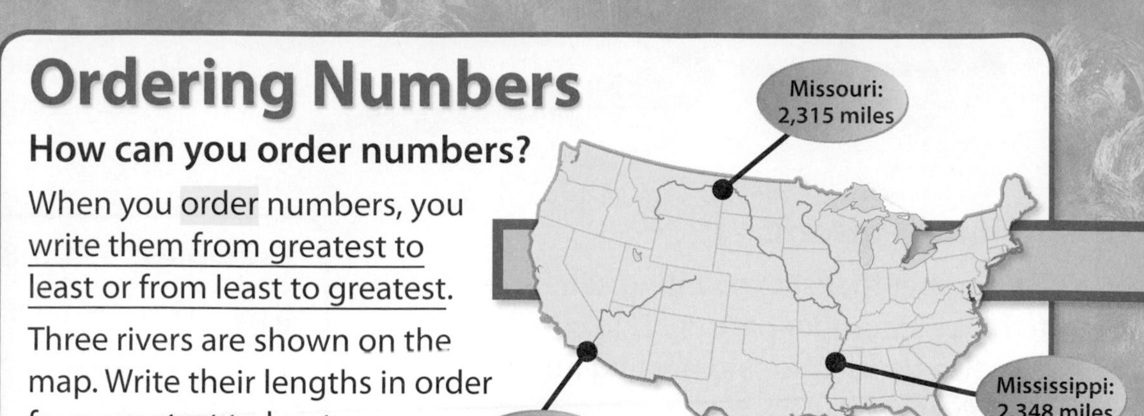

Guided Practice*

Do you know HOW?

For **1** and **2**, order the numbers from least to greatest.

1. 769 679 697

2. 359 368 45

For **3** and **4**, order the numbers from greatest to least.

3. 4,334 809 4,350

4. 1,137 1,573 1,457

Do you UNDERSTAND?

5. Writing to Explain The length of another river has a 2 in the hundreds place. Can this river be longer than the Colorado? Why or why not?

6. Draw a place-value chart showing hundreds, tens, and ones. Write the numbers 315, 305, and 319 in the place-value chart. Use the place-value chart to write the numbers in order from greatest to least.

Independent Practice

Order the numbers from least to greatest.

7. 6,743 6,930 6,395 **8.** 995 1,932 1,293 **9.** 8,754 8,700 8,792

Order the numbers from greatest to least.

10. 2,601 967 2,365 **11.** 3,554 3,454 3,459 **12.** 5,304 5,430 5,403

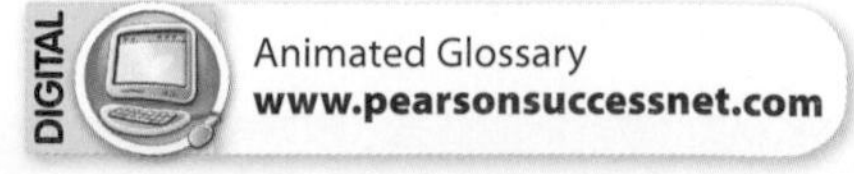

*For another example, see Set E on page 21.

You can use a place-value chart to help you.

thousands	hundreds	tens	ones
1,	4	5	0
2,	3	4	8
2,	3	1	5

$1 < 2$ So 1,450 is the least number.

$3 = 3$

$4 > 1$ So 2,348 is the greatest number.

The lengths of the rivers in order from greatest to least are:

Mississippi: 2,348 miles;
Missouri: 2,315 miles;
Colorado: 1,450 miles.

Problem Solving

Use the pictures for **13–16**.

13. Which animal weighs 100 pounds more than a moose?

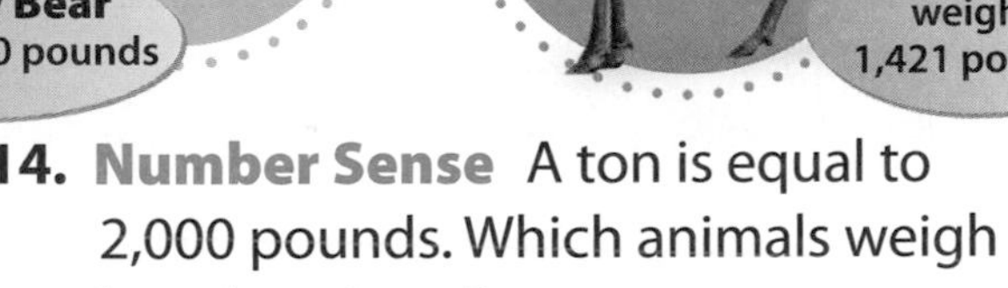

14. **Number Sense** A ton is equal to 2,000 pounds. Which animals weigh less than 1 ton?

15. Write the names of the animals in the order of their weights from least to greatest.

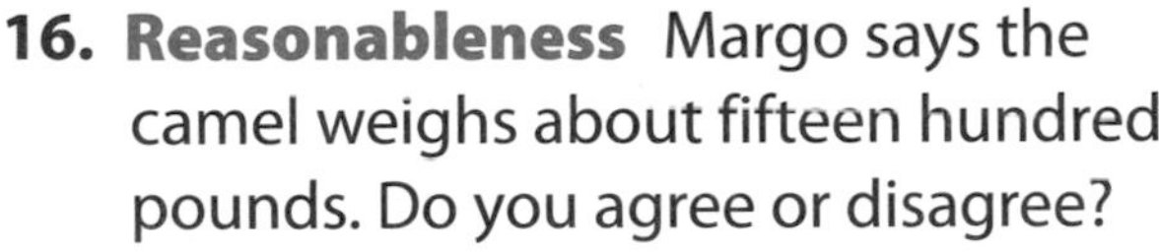

16. **Reasonableness** Margo says the camel weighs about fifteen hundred pounds. Do you agree or disagree?

17. **Writing to Explain** Describe how you would write the numbers below from least to greatest.

3,456   3,654   2,375

18. The grooves around the outside of some coins are called reeds. List the coins in the table in order from least to greatest number of reeds.

Data

Coin	Number of Reeds
Dime	118
Dollar	133
Half dollar	150
Quarter	119

19. Which number is between 5,695 and 6,725?

A 5,659 **B** 6,735 **C** 6,632 **D** 6,728

5,695		6,725

Lesson
1-6

MR 1.1 Analyze problems by identifying relationships, distinguishing relevant from irrelevant information, sequencing and prioritizing information, and observing patterns. Also **NS 1.0**

Problem Solving

Make an Organized List

Randy is playing a game called *Guess the Number*. What are all the possible numbers that fit the clues shown at the right?

You can make an organized list to find all the possible numbers.

Clues

- It is a 3-digit even number.
- The digit in the hundreds place is greater than 8.
- The digit in the tens place is less than 2.

Guided Practice*

Do you know HOW?

Make an organized list to solve.

1. Rachel has a quarter, a dime, a nickel, and a penny. She told her brother he could take two coins. List all the different pairs of coins her brother can take.

Do you UNDERSTAND?

2. **Writing to Explain** How did making an organized list help you solve Problem 1?

3. **Write a Problem** Write and solve a real-world problem by making an organized list.

Independent Practice

For **4** and **5**, make an organized list to solve.

4. List all the 4-digit numbers that fit these clues.
   - The thousands digit is less than 2.
   - The hundreds digit is greater than 5.
   - The tens digit and ones digit both equal 10 − 5.

5. Jen, Meg, and Emily are standing in line at the movies. How many different ways can they line up? List the ways.

Stuck? Try this....

- What do I know?
- What am I asked to find?
- What diagram can I use to help understand the problem?
- Can I use addition, subtraction, multiplication, or division?
- Is all of my work correct?
- Did I answer the right question?
- Is my answer reasonable?

*For another example, see Set F on page 21.

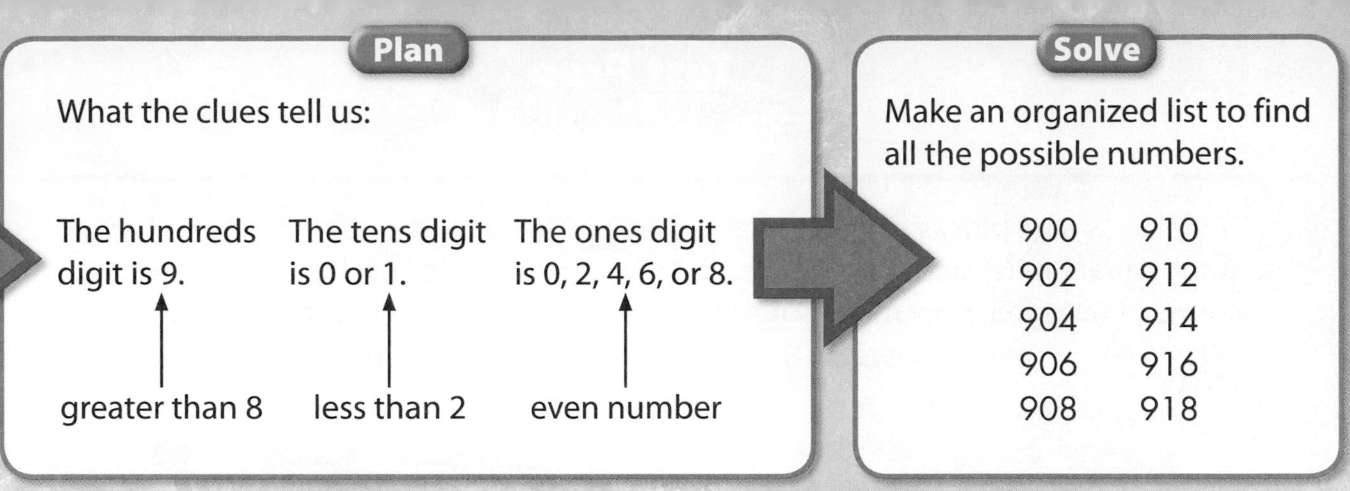

For **6–8**, use the table.

Sandwich Choices	
Bread Choices	**Filling Choices**
White	Ham
Rye	Tuna
	Turkey

6. How many different kinds of sandwiches can you choose if you want white bread?

7. How many different kinds of sandwiches can you choose if you don't want turkey?

8. Suppose wheat bread was added as a bread choice. How many different kinds of sandwiches could you choose then?

9. Jeremy has tan pants and black pants. He also has three shirts: blue, green, and red. List all the different outfits that Jeremy can wear.

10. Dennis bought a 3-pound bag of apples for $3. He also bought some grapes for $4. How much did Dennis spend?

11. How many different ways can you make 15 cents using dimes, nickels, or pennies?

A 15 ways
B 9 ways
C 6 ways
D 3 ways

12. Carla bought 4 sheets of poster board. Each sheet cost $2. She paid with a $10 bill. Carla cut each sheet into 2 pieces. How many pieces does Carla have?

13. **Reasoning** What is this 3-digit number?

- The hundreds digit is 3 less than 5.
- The tens digit is greater than 8.
- The ones digit is 1 less than the tens digit.

Test Prep

1. The place-value blocks show how many square miles are in Alpine County, California. How many square miles are in Alpine County? (1-1)

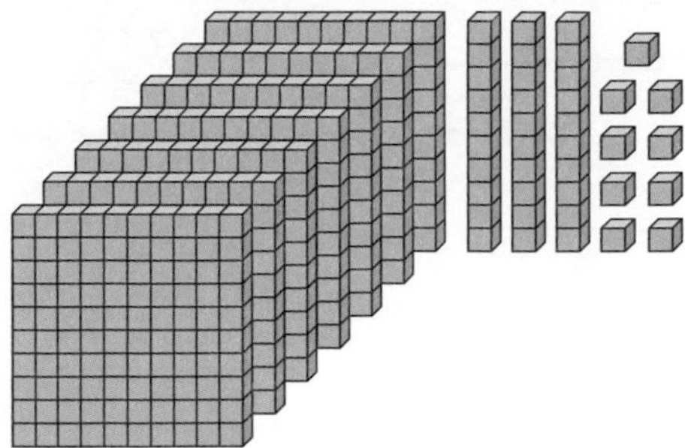

A 7,039

B 739

C 730

D 729

2. On Friday, 1,593 people watched the play *Cinderella*. On Saturday, 1,595 people watched, and on Sunday, 1,586 people watched. Which lists these numbers in order from least to greatest? (1-5)

A 1,586 1,593 1,595

B 1,586 1,595 1,593

C 1,593 1,595 1,586

D 1,595 1,593 1,586

3. In 295,463 what is the value of the 9? (1-3)

A 90

B 9,000

C 90,000

D 900,000

4. The place-value chart shows how many miles of shoreline California has. Which is another way to write the number in the place-value chart? (1-2)

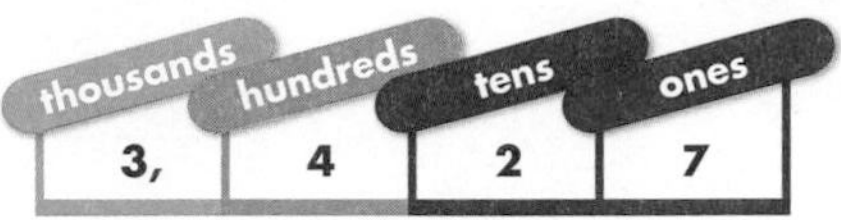

thousands	hundreds	tens	ones
3,	4	2	7

A 300 + 400 + 20 + 7

B 3,000 + 40 + 20 + 9

C 3,000 + 400 + 7

D 3,000 + 400 + 20 + 7

5. Which of the following is the word form of 6,450? (1-2)

A Six thousand, forty-five

B Six thousand, four hundred fifty

C Six, four fifty

D Six thousand, four hundred five

6. Mike's school had 4,324 people attend the school carnival. Tiffany said her school had a greater attendance. Which of these numbers is greater than 4,324? (1-4)

A 4,342

B 4,314

C 4,322

D 3,424

Test Prep

7. One of the games at the *Test Your Estimation* Olympics was to estimate how many beans were in a large glass jar. Keira guessed 34,003 beans. Which is another way to write 34,003? (1-3)

A Three thousand four hundred three

B Thirty-four hundred, three

C Thirty-four thousand, three

D Thirty-four and three

8. Which number is between 3,674 and 5,628? (1-5)

3,674		5,628

A 5,629

B 3,673

C 3,629

D 5,575

9. Which of the following has a 7 in the thousands place and a 3 in the ones place? (1-2)

A 7,403

B 6,937

C 5,743

D 5,271

10. Which equals $700 + 8$? (1-1)

A 78

B 708

C 780

D 7,008

11. The school sold 2,346 concert tickets for Thursday's performance, 2,356 for Friday's, and 2,364 for Saturday's. Which statement is true? (1-4)

A $2,346 > 2,356$

B $2,346 = 2,364$

C $2,356 < 2,346$

D $2,356 > 2,346$

12. Alex, Eric, Josh, and Tony are playing tennis. How many different groups of 2 can they make? (1-6)

A 12

B 8

C 6

D 2

13. The table shows the number of people who went to the fair each night.

Data

Night	People
Wednesday	346
Thursday	326
Friday	354
Saturday	349

More than 347 but fewer than 352 people went to the fair on which night? (1-4)

A Wednesday

B Thursday

C Friday

D Saturday

Set A, pages 4–5

Write the number in expanded form, standard form, and word form.

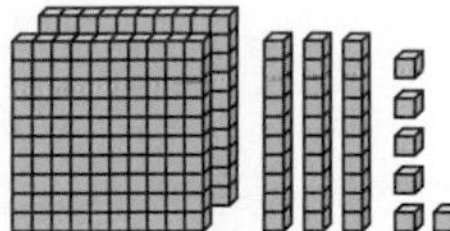

Standard form: 236

Expanded form: 200 + 30 + 6

Word form: two hundred thirty-six

Remember that, in some numbers, the digit 0 is needed to hold a place.

Write each number in standard form.

1. 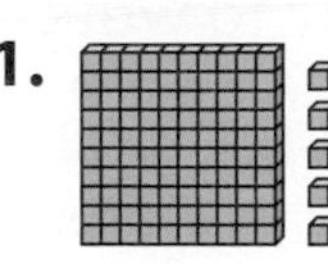

2. 300 + 20 + 7

Write each number in expanded form and word form.

3. 456 **4.** 620

Set B, pages 6–7

Write four thousand, sixteen in standard form and expanded form.

Standard form: 4,016

Expanded form: 4,000 + 10 + 6

Remember to use a comma to separate thousands from hundreds.

Write each number in standard form and expanded form.

1. Two thousand, one hundred four
2. Six thousand, seven hundred twenty-two

Set C, pages 8–9

Find the value of the 4 in 847,193.

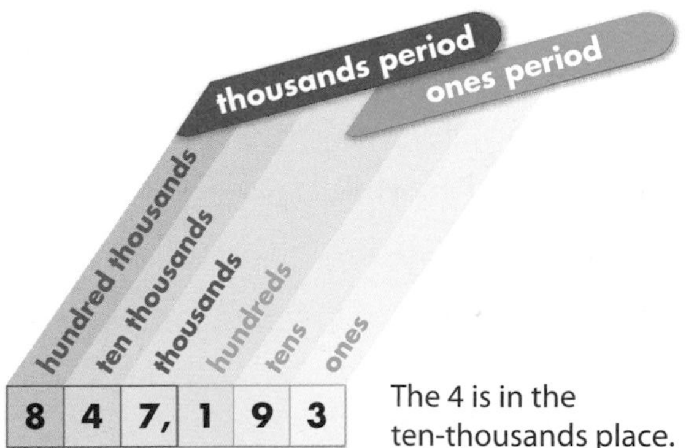

The 4 is in the ten-thousands place.

The value is 40,000.

Remember that 10 thousands equal 1 ten thousand.

Write the place of each underlined digit. Then write its value.

1. $\underline{3}41{,}791$ **2.** $82\underline{9}{,}526$

3. $570{,}\underline{8}90$ **4.** $2\underline{1}5{,}003$

5. $\underline{1}97{,}206$ **6.** $4\underline{7}3{,}069$

7. $628{,}\underline{1}74$ **8.** $78\underline{2}{,}413$

Topic 1

Reteaching

Set D, pages 10–12

Compare 7,982 and 7,682.
Line up the digits by place value.
Compare the digits starting from the left.

7,	9	8	2
7,	6	8	2
↑ same	↑ different: 9 hundreds > 6 hundreds		

7,982 > 7,682

Remember, when ordering numbers, compare one place at a time.

Compare the numbers.
Use <, >, or =.

1. 479 ◯ 912 **2.** 3,187 ◯ 837

3. 1,156 ◯ 156 **4.** 271 ◯ 2,175

Set E, pages 14–15

Write the numbers in order from least to greatest.

3,446 3,459 2,865

Use a place-value chart.

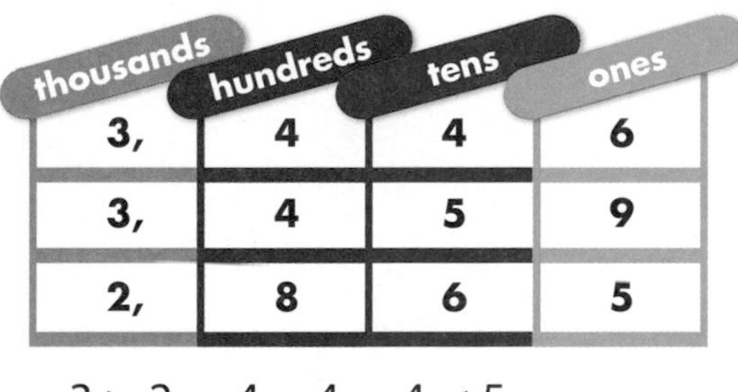

thousands	hundreds	tens	ones
3,	4	4	6
3,	4	5	9
2,	8	6	5

3 > 2 4 = 4 4 < 5

The numbers from least to greatest:
2,865; 3,446; 3,459

Remember to compare only two numbers at a time.

Write the numbers in order from greatest to least.

1. 393 182 229

2. 1,289 2,983 1,760

3. 916 1,916 196

4. 5,201 5,120 5,210

5. 816 8,160 8,016

6. 2,485 2,458 2,845

Set F, pages 16–17

When you make an organized list to solve problems, follow these steps.

Step 1

Carefully read the clues or information from the problem.

Step 2

Choose one clue or piece of information and use it to start your list.

Step 3

Repeat Step 2 as often as needed until you have used all of the clues or information to make an organized list.

Remember to make sure each item matches all of the clues.

1. Pedro has a red marble, a blue marble, a yellow marble, and a green marble. He told Frank to take two marbles. How many different pairs of marbles can Frank take? List the pairs.

Topic 2

Rounding

3 The world's largest American flag is 255 feet wide. Each star is 17 feet high. How long is the flag? You will find out in Lesson 2-1.

1 How many different kinds of alligators and crocodiles are there? You will find out in Lesson 2-4.

2 How many feet long is the Golden Gate Bridge? You will find out in Lesson 2-3.

4

How many steps lead to the top of the Leaning Tower of Pisa? You will find out in Lesson 2-2.

Review What You Know!

Vocabulary

Choose the best term from the box.

- hundreds
- sum
- ones
- tens

1. In 259, the 2 is in the ? place.
2. In 259, the 9 is in the ? place.
3. The answer in addition is the ?.

Place Value

Copy and complete.

4. 35 = ▢ tens ▢ ones
5. 264 = ▢ hundreds ▢ tens ▢ ones
6. 302 = ▢ hundreds ▢ tens ▢ ones

Addition Facts

Write each sum.

7. 3 + 5	8. 1 + 8	9. 6 + 4
10. 4 + 3	11. 8 + 2	12. 6 + 6
13. 7 + 6	14. 8 + 6	15. 9 + 9

16. Janika bought 3 books on Monday and 6 books on Tuesday. How many books did she buy in all?

17. **Writing to Explain** Derrick has 4 red, 2 blue, 2 green, 2 yellow, and 2 orange balloons. Explain how to skip count to find how many balloons he has in all.

Lesson

2-1

NS 1.4 Round off numbers to 10,000 to the nearest ten, hundred, and thousand.

Finding the Halfway Number

How can you find the number halfway between two numbers?

What number is halfway between 80 and 90?

85 is halfway between 80 and 90.

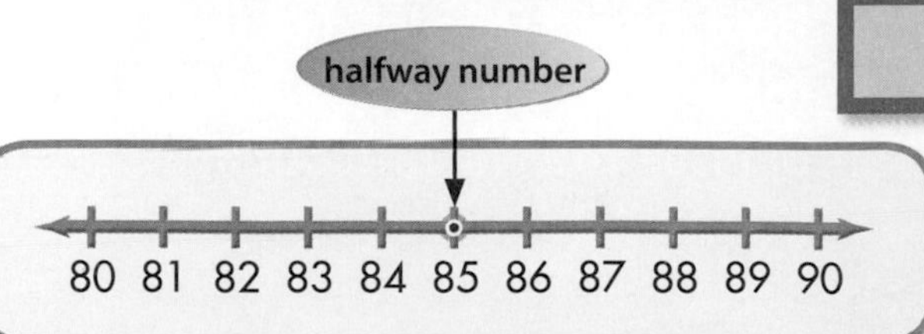

Guided Practice*

Do you know HOW?

Find the number halfway between each pair of numbers.

1. 40 and 50

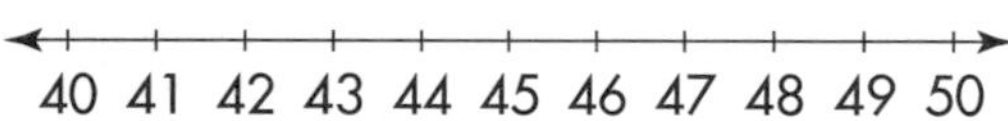

2. 9,000 and 10,000

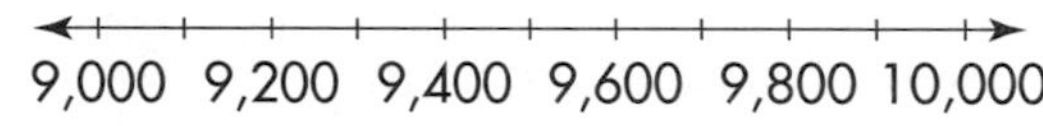

Do you UNDERSTAND?

3. **Writing to Explain** Look at the number line above that shows 6,000 and 7,000. How do you know that 6,800 is not the halfway number?

4. A road has a mile marker every mile. Marge has stopped at a rest area at mile marker 60. There is a gas station at mile marker 70. What mile marker is halfway between Marge and the gas station?

Independent Practice

Find the number halfway between each pair of numbers. You may draw number lines to help.

5. 20 and 30
6. 40 and 50
7. 90 and 100
8. 700 and 800
9. 300 and 400
10. 800 and 900
11. 4,000 and 5,000
12. 8,000 and 9,000
13. 8,800 and 8,900
14. 6,300 and 6,400
15. 2,000 and 3,000
16. 7,600 and 7,700

*For another example, see Set A on page 36.

What is the number halfway between 400 and 500?

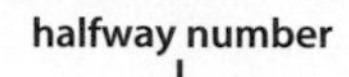

450 is halfway between 400 and 500.

What is the number halfway between 6,000 and 7,000?

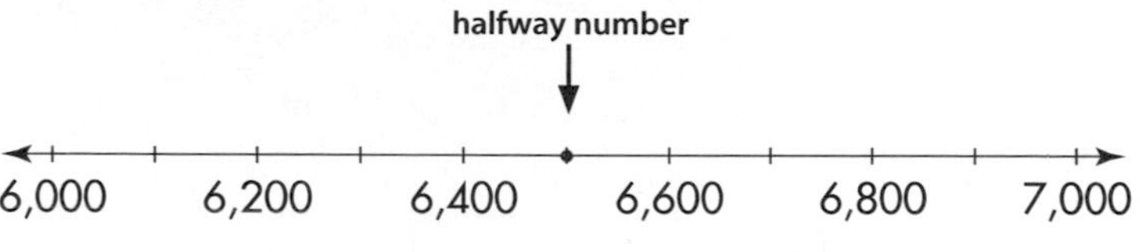

6,500 is halfway between 6,000 and 7,000.

When you find the number that is halfway between two numbers, you find the number that is the same distance from both of the other numbers.

Problem Solving

For **17–19**, find the halfway number for each number line.

17. 10 11 12 13 14 15 16 17 18 19 20

18. 200 220 240 260 280 300

19. 3,000 3,200 3,400 3,600 3,800 4,000

20. Look back at your answers for problems **17–19**. How are they alike?

21. Jack read 132 pages in one week. Jim read 125 pages in the same week. Who read more pages? Explain how you know?

22. The length of the world's largest American flag is halfway between 500 feet and 510 feet. How many feet long is this flag?

23. Ricardo says that 5,600 is halfway between 5,000 and 6,000. Is he correct? Why or why not?

24. **Writing to Explain** Explain how to find the number halfway between 500 and 600.

25. The number 650 is halfway between which pair of numbers?

A 65 and 6,500

B 500 and 600

C 600 and 700

D 6,000 and 7,000

26. Which set of numbers is in order from least to greatest?

A 121, 119, 118, 115

B 115, 119, 121, 118

C 118, 115, 121, 119

D 115, 118, 119, 121

Lesson

2-2

NS 1.4 Round off numbers to 10,000 to the nearest ten, hundred, and thousand.

Rounding 2- and 3-Digit Numbers

How can you round numbers?

To the nearest 10, about how many rocks does Tito have?

Round 394 to the nearest ten. To round, replace a number with a number that tells about how many.

Another Example How can you round to the nearest hundred?

To the nearest hundred, about how many rocks does Donna have? Round 350 to the nearest hundred.

One Way You can use a number line.

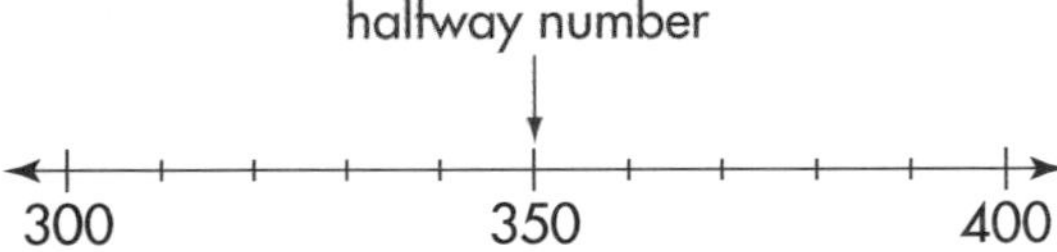

If a number is halfway between, round to the greater number.

350 is halfway between 300 and 400, so 350 rounds to 400.

Another Way You can use place value.

Find the digit in the rounding place. Then look at the next digit to the right.

hundreds place

Since 5 = 5, increase the digit in the hundreds place by one. Then change all the digits to the right to zero.

So, 350 rounds to 400. Donna has about 400 rocks.

Explain It

1. If you round 350 to the nearest ten, would you still say that Donna has about 400 rocks? Why or why not?
2. Explain why 350 is the least number that rounds to 400.

One Way

You can use a number line.

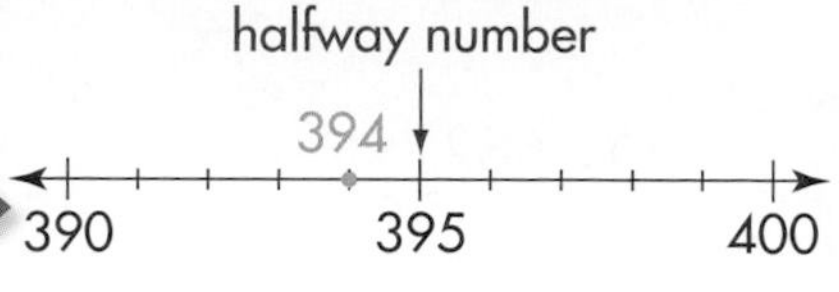

394 is closer to 390 than 400, so 394 rounds to 390.

Tito has about 390 rocks.

Another Way

You can use place value.

- Find the digit in the rounding place.
- Look at the next digit to the right. If it is 5 or greater, increase the digit in the rounding place by 1. If it is less than 5, leave the rounding digit alone.
- Change all digits to the right of the rounding place to 0.

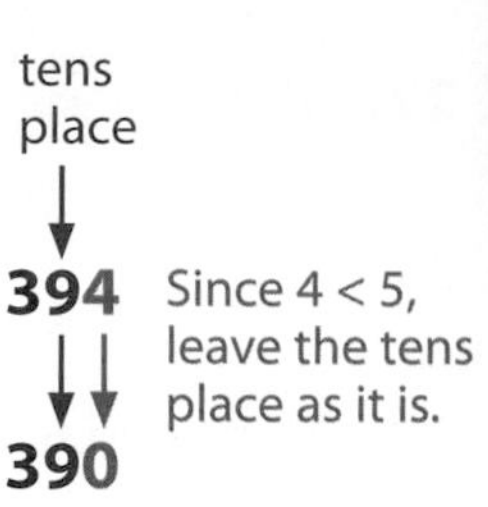

So, 394 rounds to 390.

Tito has about 390 rocks.

Guided Practice*

Do you know HOW?

Round to the nearest ten.

1. 37 **2.** 63 **3.** 85

4. 654 **5.** 305 **6.** 752

Round to the nearest hundred.

7. 557 **8.** 149 **9.** 461

10. 207 **11.** 888 **12.** 835

Do you UNDERSTAND?

13. Number Sense What number is halfway between 250 and 260?

14. Reasoning Tito adds one more rock to his collection. Now about how many rocks does he have, rounded to the nearest ten? rounded to the nearest hundred? Explain your answer.

15. Writing to Explain Tell what you would do to round 46 to the nearest ten.

Independent Practice

Round to the nearest ten.

16. 45 **17.** 68 **18.** 98 **19.** 24 **20.** 55

21. 249 **22.** 732 **23.** 235 **24.** 805 **25.** 703

26. Reasoning Round 996 to the nearest ten. Explain your answer.

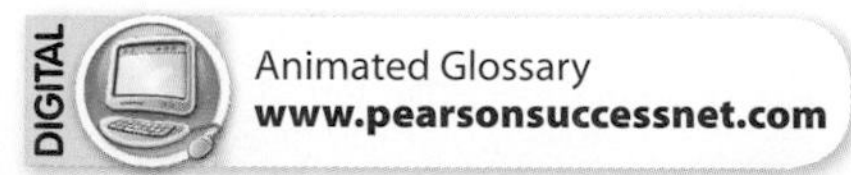

**For another example, see Set B on page 36.*

Independent Practice

Round to the nearest hundred.

27. 354 **28.** 504 **29.** 170 **30.** 839 **31.** 682

32. 945 **33.** 585 **34.** 850 **35.** 702 **36.** 270

37. **Reasoning** Round 954 to the nearest hundred. Explain your answer.

Problem Solving

38. **Number Sense** Give a number that rounds to 200 when it is rounded to the nearest hundred.

39. **Writing to Explain** Describe the steps you would follow to round 439 to the nearest ten.

40. **Number Sense** If you are rounding to the nearest hundred, what is the greatest number that rounds to 600? What is the least number that rounds to 600?

41. **Number Sense** A 3-digit number has the digits 2, 5, and 7. To the nearest hundred, it rounds to 800. What is the number?

42. To the nearest hundred dollars, a computer game costs \$100. Which could **NOT** be the actual cost of the game?

A \$89 **C** \$95

B \$91 **D** \$150

43. What is the standard form of 700 + 40?

A 740 **C** 470

B 704 **D** 407

44. There are 293 steps to the top of the Leaning Tower of Pisa in Italy. To the nearest hundred, about how many steps are there?

Algebra Connections

Greater, Less, or Equal

Remember that the two sides of a number sentence can be equal or unequal. A symbol >, <, or = tells how the sides compare. Estimation or reasoning can help you tell if one side is greater.

Example: $6 + 2 \bigcirc 8 + 1$

Think Is 6 + 2 more than 8 + 1?

Since 6 + 2 = 8, 8 is already less than 8 + 1. Write "<."

$6 + 2 < 8 + 1$

>	<	=
is greater than	*is less than*	*is equal to*

Copy and complete. Replace the circle with >, <, or =. Check your answers.

1. $3 + 4 \bigcirc 2 + 7$	**2.** $9 + 1 \bigcirc 5 + 4$	**3.** $5 + 3 \bigcirc 6 + 3$
4. $2 + 9 \bigcirc 1 + 8$	**5.** $4 + 6 \bigcirc 4 + 7$	**6.** $8 + 6 \bigcirc 9 + 5$
7. $18 + 2 \bigcirc 16 + 4$	**8.** $15 + 5 \bigcirc 10 + 8$	**9.** $14 + 4 \bigcirc 12 + 4$
10. $17 + 3 \bigcirc 20 + 1$	**11.** $21 + 2 \bigcirc 19 + 2$	**12.** $27 + 3 \bigcirc 26 + 4$

For **13** and **14**, copy and complete each number sentence. Use it to help solve the problem.

13. Al and Jiro had some toy animals. Al had 8 lizards and 3 frogs. Jiro had 11 lizards and 2 frogs. Who had more toy animals?

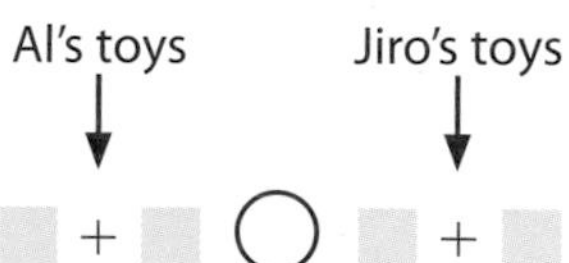

14. Look at the number of blocks that come in a set below. Val used all of the small and large cylinders. Jen used all of the small and large cubes. Who used more blocks?

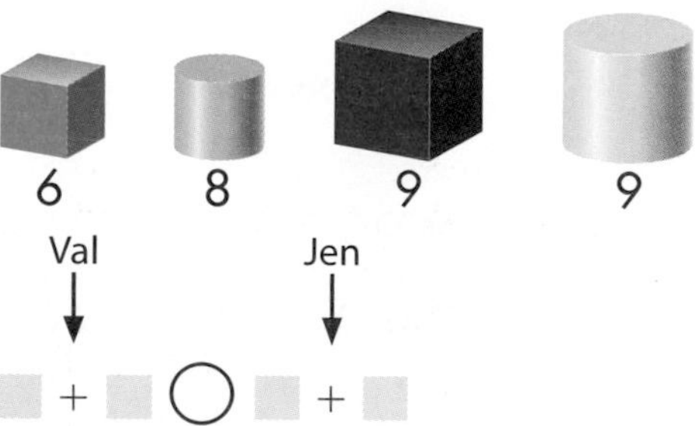

15. Write a Problem Write a problem using this number sentence: $9 + 2 > 4 + 5$.

Lesson
2-3

NS 1.4 Round off numbers to 10,000 to the nearest ten, hundred, and thousand.

Rounding 4-Digit Numbers

How can you round four-digit numbers?

The table shows ticket sales for two sports games. To the nearest thousand, about how many tickets were sold for the baseball game?

Data

Tickets Sold

Game	Number
Baseball	2,379
Football	2,653

Round 2,379 to the nearest thousand to find out.

Guided Practice*

Do you know HOW?

Round to the nearest hundred.

1. 4,569 **2.** 2,310 **3.** 9,992

Round to the nearest thousand.

4. 4,737 **5.** 8,333 **6.** 4,099

7. 3,914 **8.** 1,111 **9.** 6,274

Do you UNDERSTAND?

10. How does the halfway number on the number line help you round 2,379?

11. **Writing to Explain** Describe how to round 2,379 to the nearest hundred.

12. In the example above, about how many tickets were sold for the football game, to the nearest hundred? to the nearest thousand?

Independent Practice

For **13–22**, round to the nearest hundred.

13. 3,708 **14.** 5,542 **15.** 7,356 **16.** 8,929 **17.** 6,991

18. 4,008 **19.** 7,890 **20.** 6,555 **21.** 3,945 **22.** 9,961

For **23–32**, round to the nearest thousand.

23. 2,774 **24.** 3,870 **25.** 5,077 **26.** 7,299 **27.** 8,603

28. 6,905 **29.** 8,500 **30.** 4,099 **31.** 2,495 **32.** 9,573

*For another example, see Set C on page 37.

One Way

You can use a number line to round.

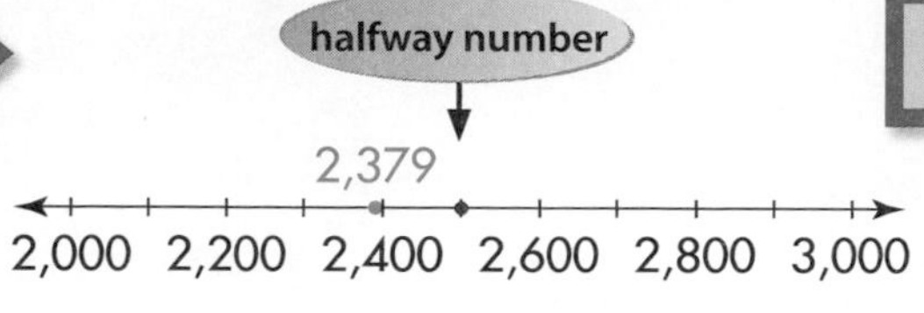

2,379 is closer to 2,000 than to 3,000.
2,379 rounds to 2,000.

About 2,000 tickets were sold for the baseball game.

Another Way

You can use place value to round.

- Find the digit in the rounding place.
- If the next digit to the right is 5 or greater, increase the digit in the rounding place by 1. If the next digit is less than 5, keep the digit in the rounding place as it is.
- Change all the digits to the right of the rounding place to zero.

thousands place

Since $3 < 5$, the thousands place is not changed.

So, 2,379 rounds to 2,000.

About 2,000 tickets were sold for the baseball game.

Problem Solving

In **33–36**, write a number that rounds to the number given. Use all four of the digits at the right once in each answer.

33. 4,000 **34.** 6,000

35. 5,500 **36.** 5,400

37. The Golden Gate Bridge is 4,200 feet long. What is 4,200 rounded to the nearest thousand?

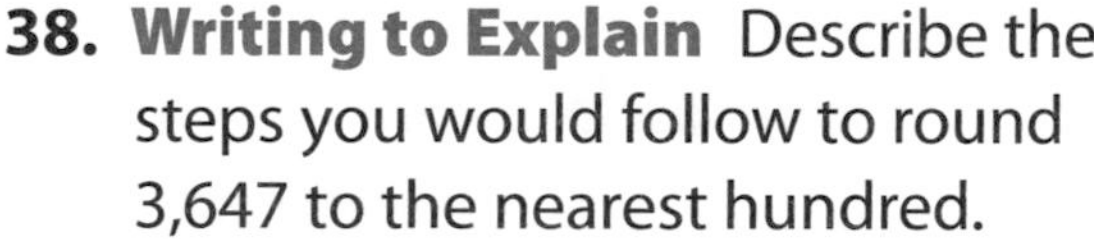

38. Writing to Explain Describe the steps you would follow to round 3,647 to the nearest hundred.

39. Number Sense Write a number that rounds to 7,000 when it is rounded to the nearest thousand.

40. In 1 hour, an adult's heart beats about 4,320 times.

a To the nearest thousand, about how many times does an adult's heart beat in one hour?

b To the nearest hundred, about how many times does an adult's heart beat in one hour?

41. Which number rounds to 5,000 when it is rounded to the nearest thousand or to the nearest hundred?

A 4,895

B 5,029

C 5,170

D 5,956

Lesson

2-4

MR 2.0 Use strategies, skills, and concepts in finding solutions. Also **MR 2.6** Make precise calculations and check the validity of the results from the context of the problem. Also **NS 2.1** Find the sum or difference of two whole numbers between 0 and 10,000.

Problem Solving

Try, Check, and Revise

Tad, Holly, and Shana made 36 posters all together. Shana made 3 more posters than Holly. Tad and Holly made the same number of posters. How many posters did Shana make?

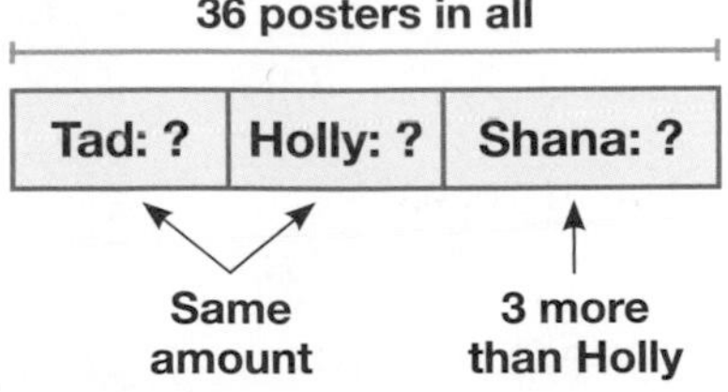

Guided Practice*

Do you know HOW?

1. Peg and Pat are sharing 64 crayons. Pat has 10 more crayons than Peg. How many crayons does each girl have?

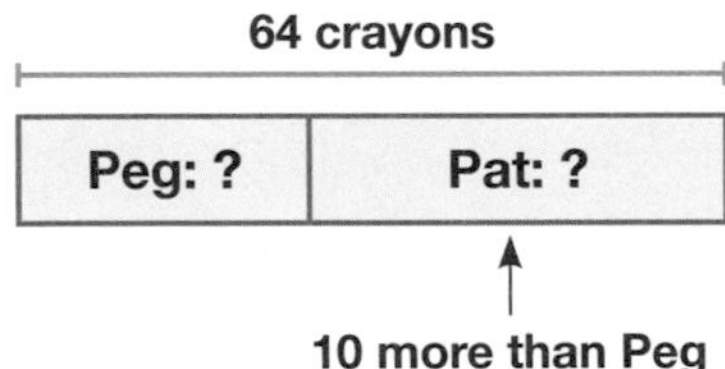

Do you UNDERSTAND?

2. Look at the diagram for Problem 1. Why aren't Peg's part and Pat's part of the rectangle the same size?

3. **Write a Problem** Write a problem that can be solved by using reasoning to make good tries.

Independent Practice

4. All together, Rod has 38 crayons, markers, and pencils. He has 5 more crayons than markers. He has the same number of markers and pencils. How many markers does he have?

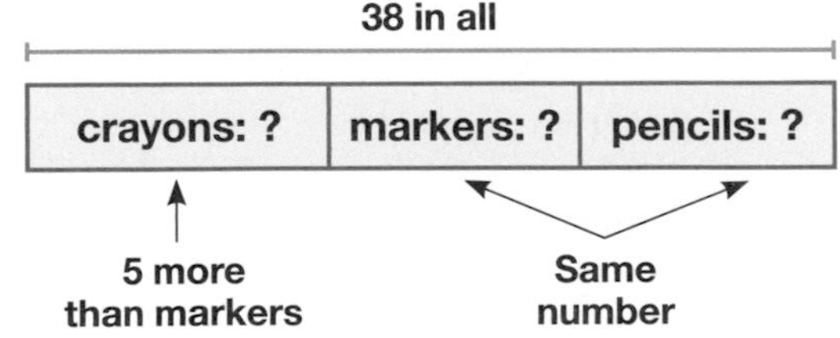

Stuck? Try this....

- What do I know?
- What am I asked to find?
- What diagram can I use to help understand the problem?
- Can I use addition, subtraction, multiplication, or division?
- Is all of my work correct?
- Did I answer the right question?
- Is my answer reasonable?

For another example, see Set D on page 37.

Plan

Use reasoning to make good tries. Then check.

Try: $10 + 10 + 13 = 33$
Check: $33 < 36$
Too low, I need 3 more.

Try: $12 + 12 + 15 = 39$
Check: $39 > 36$
Too high, I need 3 less.

Solve

Revise, using what you know.

Try: $11 + 11 + 14 = 36$
Check: $36 = 36$
This is correct.

Shana made 14 posters.

Use the pictures at the right for **5** and **6**.

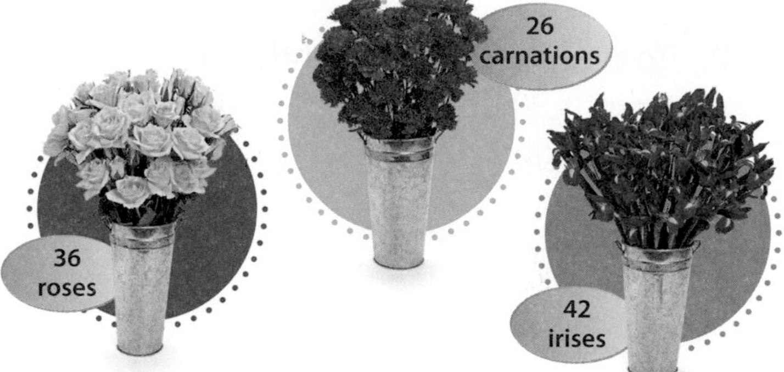

5. The clerk at the flower store puts all the roses into two vases. One vase has 2 more roses than the other vase. How many roses are in each vase?

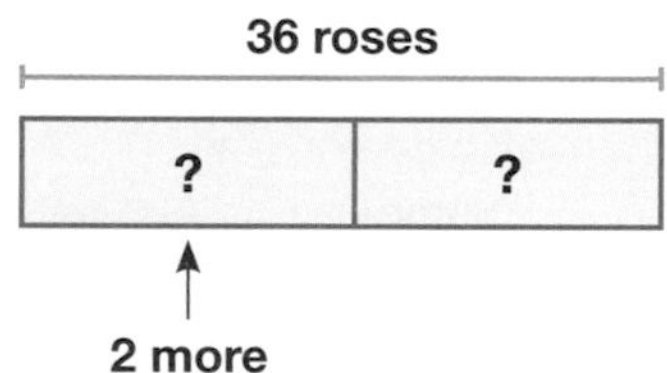

6. Edna, Jay, and Bob bought all of the carnations in the flower store. Edna bought 2 more than Jay. Bob and Jay bought the same number. How many carnations did Edna buy?

7. Mr. Tyler bought one iris for \$1.25 and 3 roses for \$3 each. How much did Mr. Tyler spend for the roses?

8. Cam bought an iris for \$1.25. He paid with 6 coins. What coins did he use?

9. Jared is thinking of two numbers. They have a sum of 12 and a difference of 6. What are the two numbers?

A 11 and 1

B 10 and 2

C 9 and 3

D 8 and 4

10. Hanna read that there are 22 types of crocodiles and alligators in all. There are 6 more types of crocodiles than alligators. How many types of crocodiles are there? How many types of alligators are there?

Test Prep

1. What number is halfway between 1,000 and 2,000? (2-1)

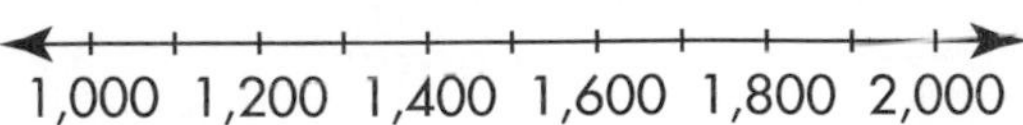

A 500

B 1,050

C 1,500

D 1,600

2. To the nearest ten pounds, Riley weighs 90 pounds. Which could be her weight? (2-2)

A 84

B 86

C 95

D 98

3. Each of the 26 students in Carrie's class chose either drums or horns to play during music. If 4 more students chose drums than horns, how many chose each? (2-4)

A 16 chose drums and 10 chose horns

B 15 chose drums and 11 chose horns

C 14 chose drums and 12 chose horns

D 14 chose drums and 10 chose horns

4. The Nile River in Africa is the world's longest river. It is 4,160 miles long. What is 4,160 to the nearest hundred? (2-3)

A 4,000

B 4,100

C 4,200

D 5,000

5. Interstate 40 runs from Barstow, California, to Wilmington, North Carolina. It is 2,554 miles long. What is 2,554 to the nearest thousand? (2-3)

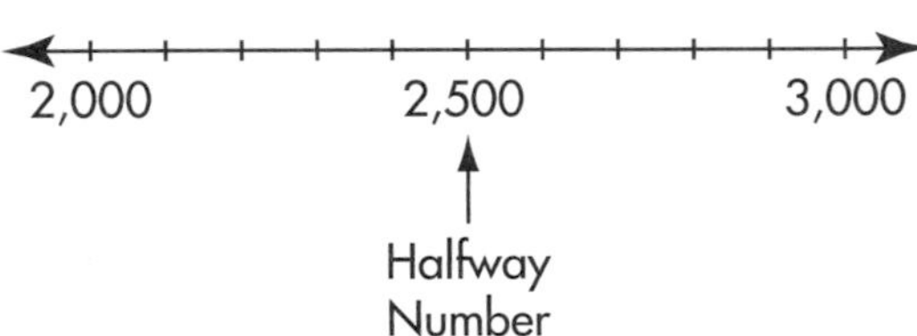

A 2,000

B 2,500

C 2,600

D 3,000

6. Zoe saw a 268 pound ostrich at the zoo. What is 268 rounded to the nearest ten? (2-2)

A 200

B 260

C 270

D 300

7. Mr. Kipper's class collected $453 for the local animal shelter. What is $453 to the nearest hundred? (2-2)

A $500

B $460

C $450

D $400

8. The number 950 is halfway between which pair of numbers? (2-1)

A 900 and 1,000

B 900 and 910

C 940 and 950

D 800 and 900

9. Deception Island in Antarctica is still considered an active volcano. It is 1,890 feet tall. What is 1,890 to the nearest thousand? (2-3)

A 1,000

B 1,800

C 1,900

D 2,000

10. Party favors come in packages of 10, 20, or 25. Cristina bought 50 favors in 3 packages. Which sizes of packages could she have bought? (2-4)

A 20, 10, and 10

B 20, 20, and 10

C 25 and 25

D 25 and 20

11. The trees below are found in Sequoia and Kings Canyon National Parks. (2-2)

Data

Name of Tree	Height (in ft)
General Grant	268
General Sherman	274
Lincoln	255
Boole	269

Which tree is 260 feet tall to the nearest ten?

A General Grant

B General Sherman

C Lincoln

D Boole

12. Callahan Tunnel is an underwater tunnel for cars and trucks in Boston, Massachusetts. The tunnel is 5,070 feet long. What is 5,070 to the nearest thousand? (2-3)

A 6,000

B 5,200

C 5,100

D 5,000

13. What is 7,248 to the nearest ten? (2-3)

A 7,000

B 7,200

C 7,240

D 7,250

Reteaching

Set A, pages 24–25

What is the number halfway between 800 and 900?

Use a number line.

Find the number that is the same distance from the beginning number and the ending number.

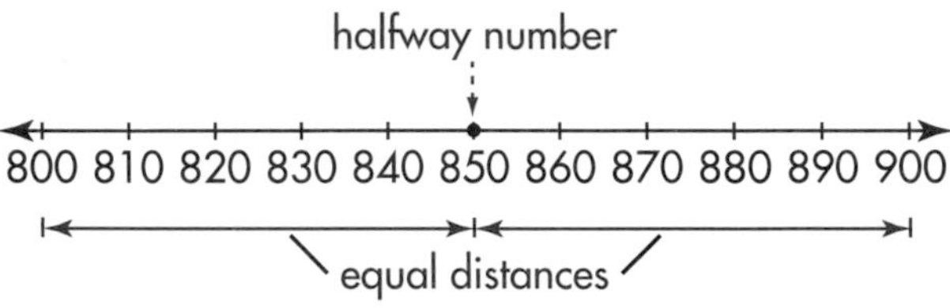

The number that is halfway between 800 and 900 is 850.

Remember to check that your number is the same distance from the beginning number and the ending number on a number line.

Find the number halfway between each pair of numbers.

1. 60 and 70

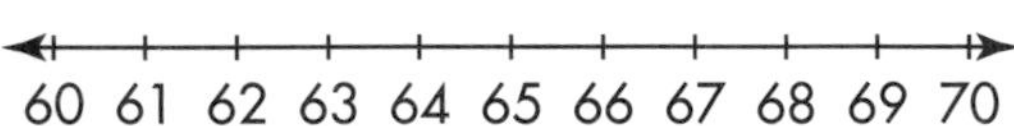

2. 2,000 and 3,000

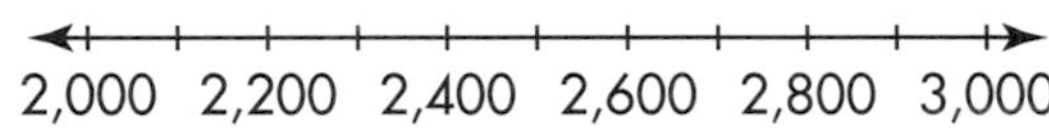

3. 900 and 1,000

4. 3,300 and 3,400

5. 860 and 870

Set B, pages 26–28

Round 867 to the nearest hundred.

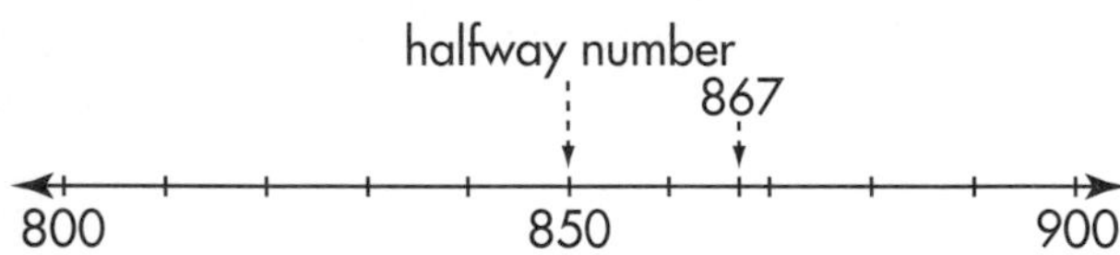

On the number line, 867 is closer to 900 than to 800.

You can also use place value.

hundreds place

867 → 900

Since $6 > 5$, increase the digit in the hundreds place by one. Then change all the digits to the right to zero.

To the nearest hundred, 867 rounds to 900.

Remember to think of the halfway number when rounding.

Round to the nearest ten.

1. 65 **2.** 813 **3.** 489

4. 24 **5.** 78 **6.** 942

Round to the nearest hundred.

7. 229 **8.** 349 **9.** 651

10. 856 **11.** 109 **12.** 783

Set C, pages 30–31

Round 2,613 to the nearest thousand.

You can use place value.

- Find the digit in the rounding place. That digit is 2.
- If the next digit to the right is 5 or greater, increase the digit in the rounding place by 1. If the next digit is less than 5, keep the digit in the rounding place as it is. Since 6 > 5, increase the 2 to 3.
- Change all the digits to the right of the rounding place to zero.

To the nearest thousand, 2,613 rounds to 3,000.

Remember to compare the correct digit to 5 to find if the digit in the rounding place should change.

Round to the nearest thousand.

1. 3,817 **2.** 6,495 **3.** 8,562

4. 1,709 **5.** 2,500 **6.** 7,248

7. 5,692 **8.** 3,178 **9.** 9,714

Round to the nearest hundred.

10. 2,136 **11.** 5,624 **12.** 4,449

13. 7,751 **14.** 6,275 **15.** 8,941

16. 4,307 **17.** 9,768 **18.** 3,549

Set D, pages 32–33

Follow these steps for using Try, Check, and Revise to solve problems.

Think to make a reasonable first try.

Check using information from the problem.

Step 3

Revise. Use your first try to make a reasonable second try. Check.

Continue trying and checking until you find the correct answer.

Remember to check each try.

Use Try, Check, and Revise to solve.

1. Mark and Tony have 32 markers. Mark has 2 more markers than Tony. How many markers does each boy have?

2. There are 28 players in the soccer club. There are 4 more girls than boys. How many boys are in the soccer club?

3. Jason and Dave have 45 baseball cards together. Jason collected 7 fewer cards than Dave. How many baseball cards does Dave have?

Topic 3

Adding Whole Numbers

1 This statue of Abraham Lincoln is 19 feet tall. How tall would the statue be if President Lincoln were standing? You will find out in Lesson 3-5.

2 How many spines does a lionfish have? You will find out in Lesson 3-1.

3 The desert tortoise is the state reptile of California. How long can it live? You will find out in Lesson 3-2.

4 The Kingda Ka is the tallest roller coaster in the world. How tall is it? You will find out in Lesson 3-6.

Review What You Know!

Vocabulary

Choose the best term from the box.

- addends
- estimate
- hundreds
- sum

1. In the problem 56 + 42, 56 and 42 are called __?__.
2. The answer in addition is the __?__.
3. If you don't need an exact answer, you can __?__.

Comparing

Compare. Write >, <, or =.

4. 24 ◯ 26
5. 81 ◯ 80
6. 156 ◯ 156
7. 654 ◯ 546
8. 478 ◯ 478
9. 639 ◯ 693

Estimating

Round to the nearest ten to estimate.

10. 13 + 25
11. 253 + 47
12. 129 + 482

Round to the nearest hundred to estimate.

13. 613 + 325
14. 253 + 347
15. 629 + 252

Addition Properties

16. **Writing to Explain** Is 24 + 16 the same as 16 + 24? How do you know?

Lesson

3-1

NS 2.1 Find the sum or difference of two whole numbers between 0 and 10,000.

Addition Meaning and Properties

What are some ways to think about addition?

You can use addition to join groups.

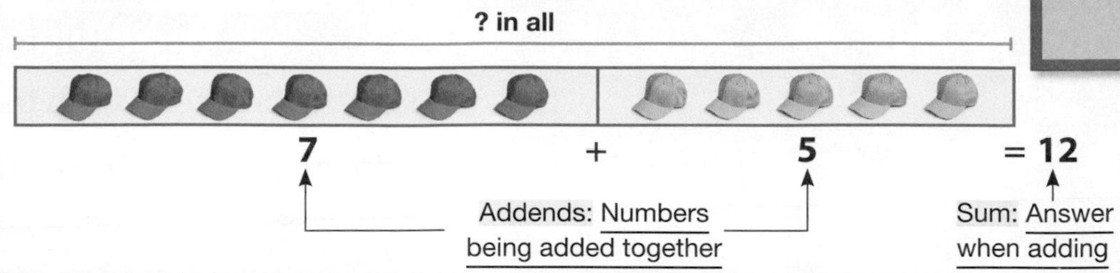

Another Example What is another way to think about addition?

Marda has two pieces of ribbon. One is 4 inches long and the other is 3 inches long. How many inches of ribbon does Marda have all together?

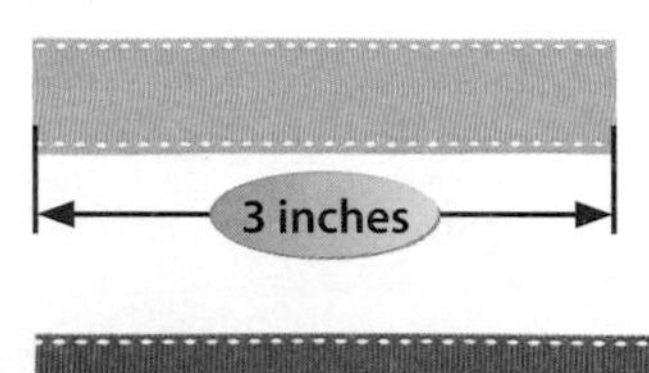

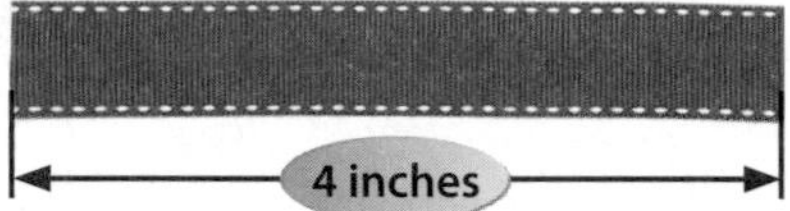

You can use a number line to think about addition.

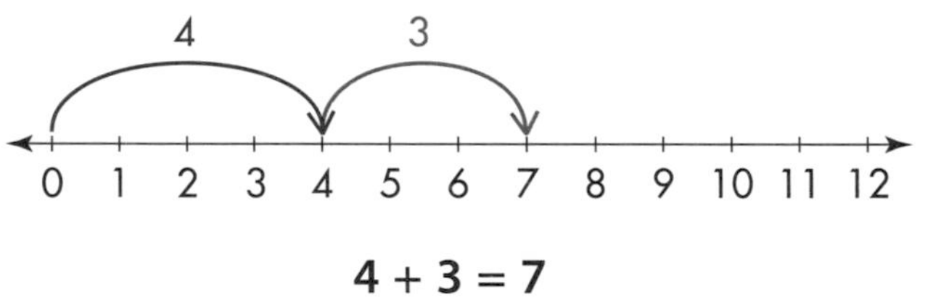

4 + 3 = 7

All together, Marda has 7 inches of ribbon.

Guided Practice*

Do you know HOW?

Write each missing number.

1. ▢ + 9 = 9

2. 4 + 6 = 6 + ▢

3. (2 + ▢) + 6 = 2 + (3 + 6)

Do you UNDERSTAND?

4. Why does it make sense that the Commutative Property is also called the Order property?

5. **Writing to Explain** Ralph says you can rewrite (4 + 5) + 2 as 9 + 2. Do you agree? Why or why not?

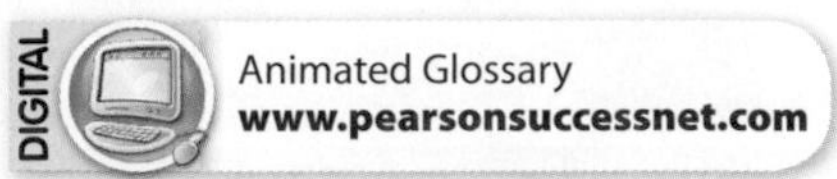

*For another example, see Set A on page 62.

Commutative (Order) Property of Addition: You can add numbers in any order and the sum will be the same.

7 + 5 = 5 + 7

Identity (Zero) Property of Addition: The sum of zero and any number is that same number.

5 + 0 = 5

Associative (Grouping) Property of Addition: You can group addends in any way and the sum will be the same.

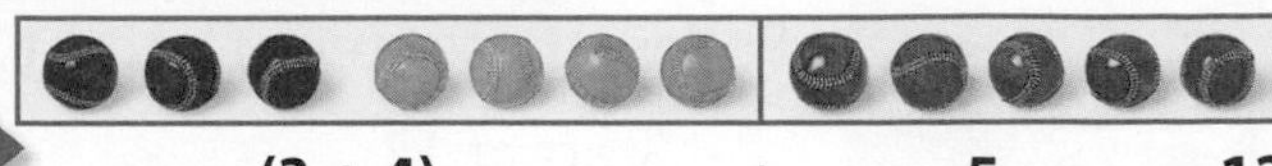

(3 + 4) + 5 = 12

3 + (4 + 5) = 12

(3 + 4) + 5 = 3 + (4 + 5)

Parentheses, (), show what to add first.

Independent Practice

Write each missing number.

6. ☐ + 8 = 8 + 2

7. 19 + ☐ = 19

8. (3 + ☐) + 2 = 2 + 8

9. 4 + (2 + 3) = 4 + ☐

10. 7 + 3 = ☐ + 7

11. ☐ + 25 = 25

12. (3 + ☐) + 6 = 3 + (4 + 6)

13. (6 + 2) + ☐ = 8 + 7

Problem Solving

14. Reasoning What property of addition is shown in the number sentence 3 + (6 + 5) = (6 + 5) + 3? Explain.

15. Draw objects of 2 different colors to show that 4 + 3 = 3 + 4.

16. A lionfish has 13 spines on its back, 2 near the middle of its underside, and 3 on its underside near its tail. Write two different number sentences to find how many spines a lionfish has in all. What property did you use?

17. Which number sentence matches the picture?

A 3 + 8 = 11

B 11 + 0 = 11

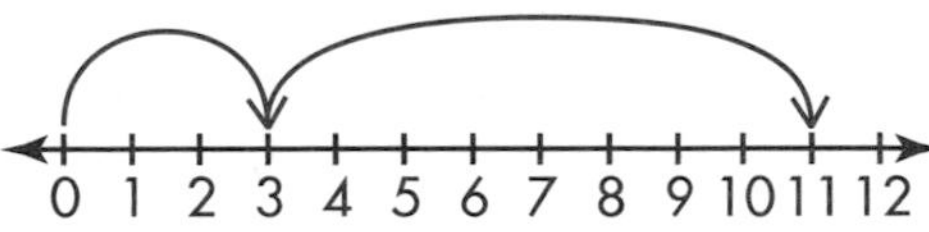

C 11 − 8 = 3

D 11 − 3 = 8

Lesson

3-2

NS 2.1 Find the sum or difference of two whole numbers between 0 and 10,000.

Adding on a Hundred Chart

How can you add on a hundred chart?

Follow these steps to add 17 + 30.

- Start at 17.
- Count down three rows to add 30.
- You end up at 47.

So, 17 + 30 = 47.

1	2	3	4	5	6	7	8	9	10
11	12	13	14	15	16	17	18	19	20
21	22	23	24	25	26	27	28	29	30
31	32	33	34	35	36	37	38	39	40
41	42	43	44	45	46	47	48	49	50

Another Example How can you add on a hundred chart by counting backward?

Follow these steps to add 44 + 29:

- Start at 44.
- Move down 3 rows to add 30. You added 30 to 44. But you only needed to add 29, so you need to subtract 1.
- Move left 1 space.
- You end up at 73.

So, 44 + 29 = 73.

1	2	3	4	5	6	7	8	9	10
11	12	13	14	15	16	17	18	19	20
21	22	23	24	25	26	27	28	29	30
31	32	33	34	35	36	37	38	39	40
41	42	43	44	45	46	47	48	49	50
51	52	53	54	55	56	57	58	59	60
61	62	63	64	65	66	67	68	69	70
71	72	73	74	75	76	77	78	79	80
81	82	83	84	85	86	87	88	89	90
91	92	93	94	95	96	97	98	99	100

Guided Practice*

Do you know HOW?

Use a hundred chart to add.

1. 34 + 20

2. 78 + 19

3. 53 + 26

4. 68 + 18

5. 37 + 16

6. 44 + 29

7. 26 + 38

8. 57 + 35

Do you UNDERSTAND?

9. Reasoning Look at the examples at the top of this page and the next. Compare the steps used to find each sum. How are they the same? How are they different?

10. Allie's mom bought 21 red apples and 18 green apples. How many apples did she buy in all?

*For another example, see Set B on page 62.

Follow these steps to add 56 + 35.

- Start at 56.
- Move down 3 rows to add 30.
- Move right 4 spaces to add 4 more. So far you have added 34 to 56.
- Go down to the next row and move right 1 space to add 1 more.

51	52	53	54	55	56	57	58	59	60
61	62	63	64	65	66	67	68	69	70
71	72	73	74	75	76	77	78	79	80
81	82	83	84	85	86	87	88	89	90
91	92	93	94	95	96	97	98	99	100

You end up at 91.

56 + 35 = 91

Independent Practice

Use a hundred chart to add.

11. 48 + 50 **12.** 75 + 15 **13.** 73 + 20 **14.** 55 + 34

15. 38 + 15 **16.** 22 + 17 **17.** 68 + 16 **18.** 55 + 29

Number Sense Compare. Use <, >, or =.

19. 23 + 50 ◯ 23 + 65 **20.** 37 + 40 ◯ 47 + 30 **21.** 65 + 34 ◯ 65 + 43

22. 25 + 35 ◯ 35 + 45 **23.** 71 + 20 ◯ 61 + 20 **24.** 82 + 16 ◯ 72 + 26

Problem Solving

25. A desert tortoise lived for 87 years. To the nearest ten, about how many years did the desert tortoise live?

26. **Reasoning** You have learned to add 9 to a number by first adding 10 and then subtracting 1. How could you add 99 to a number using mental math? Try using your method to find 24 + 99.

27. Which number is missing in the pattern below?

0, 50, 100, ▢, 200

A 190 **C** 175

B 180 **D** 150

Lesson

3-3

NS 2.1 Find the sum or difference of two whole numbers between 0 and 10,000.

Using Mental Math to Add

How can you add with mental math?

Dr. Gomez recorded how many whales, dolphins, and seals she saw. How many whales did she see during the two weeks?

Find 25 + 14.

Data

Marine Animals Seen

Animal	Week 1	Week 2
Whales	25	14
Dolphins	28	17
Seals	34	18

Another Example How can you make tens to add mentally?

How many dolphins did Dr. Gomez see during the two weeks?

You can make a ten to help you find 28 + 17.

- Break apart 17.
  17 = 2 + 15
- Add 2 to 28
  2 + 28 = 30
- Add 15 to 30.
  30 + 15 = 45

? dolphins in all

28	17

So, 28 + 17 = 45.

Dr. Gomez saw 45 dolphins during the two weeks.

Explain It

1. How does knowing that 17 = 2 + 15 help you find 28 + 17 mentally?
2. Can you find another way to make a 10 to add 28 + 17?
3. How many whales and seals did Dr. Gomez see in the second week?

One Way

Break apart one of the addends.

- Break apart 14.
  14 = 10 + 4
- Add 10 to 25.
  25 + 10 = 35
- Add 4 to 35.
  35 + 4 = 39

So, 25 + 14 = 39.

Dr. Gomez saw 39 whales.

Another Way

Break apart both addends.

- Break apart both addends.
  25 = 20 + 5   14 = 10 + 4
- Add the tens. Then add the ones.
  20 + 10 = 30   5 + 4 = 9
- Add the tens and ones together.
  30 + 9 = 39

So, 25 + 14 = 39.

Dr. Gomez saw 39 whales.

Guided Practice*

Do you know HOW?

1. Make a ten to add 38 + 26.

38 + 26
26 = 2 + 24
38 + ☐ = 40
40 + ☐ = 64
So, 38 + 26 = ☐.

2. Use breaking apart to add 25 + 12.

25 + 12
12 = 10 + 2
25 + 10 = ☐
☐ + 2 = 37
So, 25 + 12 = ☐.

Do you UNDERSTAND?

3. **Reasoning** Compare the two examples at the top of the page. How are they the same? How are they different?

4. **Number Sense** To find 37 + 28 you could add 37 + 30 = 67. Then what should you do next?

5. Use breaking apart or making tens to find how many seals Dr. Gomez saw during the two weeks. Explain which method you used.

Independent Practice

Leveled Practice Use breaking apart to add mentally.

6. 72 + 18
18 = 10 + ☐
72 + ☐ = 82
82 + ☐ = 90
So, 72 + 18 = ☐.

7. 34 + 25
25 = 20 + ☐
34 + ☐ = 54
☐ + 5 = 59
So, 34 + 25 = ☐.

8. 53 + 36
36 = ☐ + 6
53 + ☐ = 83
☐ + 6 = 89
So, 53 + 36 = ☐.

*For another example, see Set B on page 62.

Independent Practice

Leveled Practice Make a ten to add mentally.

9. 47 + 9
9 = ☐ + 6
47 + ☐ = 50
☐ + 6 = 56
So, 47 + 9 = ☐.

10. 55 + 37
37 = 5 + ☐
☐ + 5 = 60
60 + ☐ = 92
So, 55 + 37 = ☐.

11. 49 + 29
29 = ☐ + 28
49 + ☐ = 50
50 + ☐ = 78
So, 49 + 29 = ☐.

Find each sum using mental math.

12. 35 + 26 **13.** 50 + 42 **14.** 43 + 4 **15.** 71 + 13

16. 52 + 44 **17.** 7 + 54 **18.** 63 + 12 **19.** 62 + 34

20. 37 + 9 **21.** 5 + 38 **22.** 65 + 15 **23.** 33 + 23

Problem Solving

24. How long can a python be?

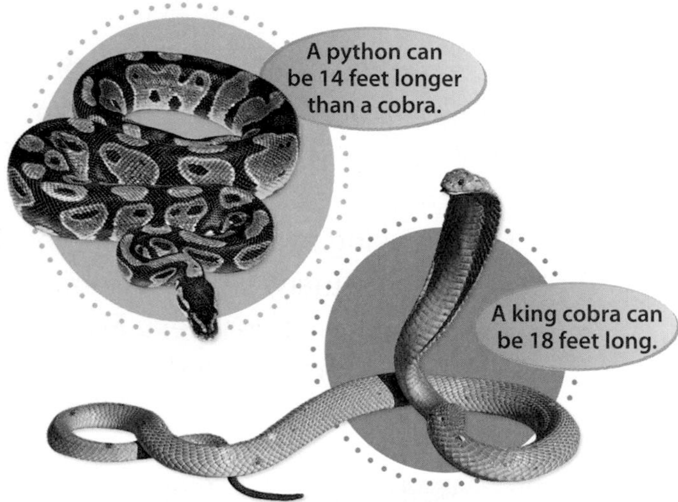

25. What is the total length of the iguana?

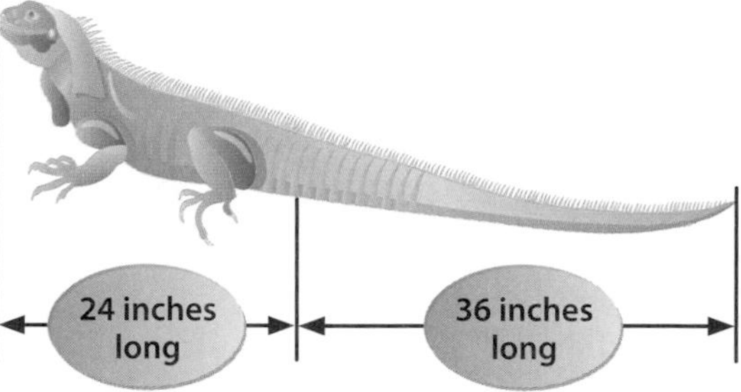

26. Writing to Explain Bill's work is shown below. Is it correct? If not, tell why and write a correct answer.

Find 38 + 7.
I'll think of 7 as 2 + 5.
38 + 2 = 40
40 + 7 = 47
So, 38 + 7 is 47.

27. How is the number 4,038 written in word form?

A four hundred thirty-eight
B four thousand, three hundred eight
C four thousand, thirty-eight
D forty thousand, thirty-eight

Stop and Practice

Write each number in standard form.

1. 300 + 70 + 4

2. 6,000 + 50 + 8

3. 900,000 + 2,000 + 100 + 60 + 7

Compare the numbers. Use $<$, $>$ or $=$.

4. 209 ◯ 213 **5.** 1,146 ◯ 799 **6.** 4,687 ◯ 4,805

Round to the nearest ten.

7. 58 **8.** 45 **9.** 213 **10.** 905 **11.** 672

Round to the nearest hundred.

12. 736 **13.** 550 **14.** 3,827 **15.** 9,256 **16.** 4,193

Use a hundred chart to add.

17. 26 + 30 **18.** 53 + 22 **19.** 39 + 50 **20.** 76 + 23

Error Search Find each sum that is not correct.
Write it correctly and explain the error.

21. 45 + 14 = 58 **22.** 63 + 25 = 88 **23.** 28 + 30 = 31 **24.** 33 + 46 = 89

Number Sense

Estimating and Reasoning Write true or false for each statement.
If it is false, explain why.

25. The sum 2 + 7 is greater than 7 + 2.

26. The sum 2 + 0 is equal to 2.

27. The sum 5 + 8 is greater than 4 + 8.

28. The sum (2 + 3) + 5 is less than 1 + (3 + 5).

29. The sum 0 + 9 is greater than 9.

30. The sum (4 + 2) + 2 is equal to 4 + (2 + 2).

Lesson
3-4

NS 1.4 Round off numbers to 10,000 to the nearest ten, hundred, and thousand.
NS 2.1 Find the sum or difference of two whole numbers between 0 and 10,000.
Also MR 2.1, 2.5

Estimating Sums

How can you estimate sums?

Do the two pandas together weigh more than 500 pounds?

You can estimate to find out about how much the two pandas weigh.

Estimate 255 + 322.

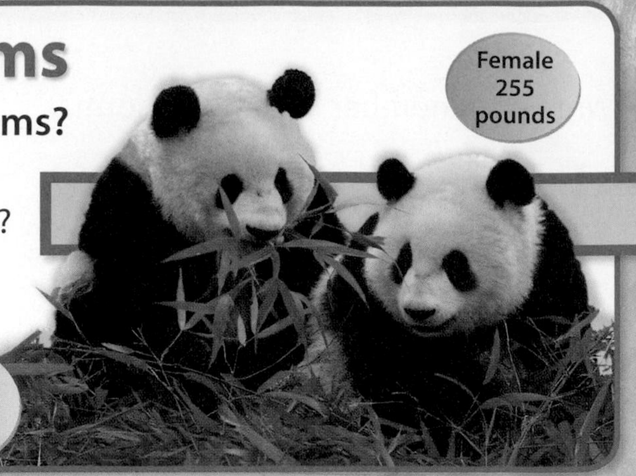

Other Examples

Estimate 3,646 + 1,253.

One Way

Round to the nearest thousand.

$$\begin{array}{r} 3,646 \\ +\ 1,253 \\ \hline \end{array} \longrightarrow \begin{array}{r} 4,000 \\ +\ 1,000 \\ \hline 5,000 \end{array}$$

3,646 + 1,253 is about 5,000.

Another Way

Round to the nearest hundred.

$$\begin{array}{r} 3,646 \\ +\ 1,253 \\ \hline \end{array} \longrightarrow \begin{array}{r} 3,600 \\ +\ 1,300 \\ \hline 4,900 \end{array}$$

3,646 + 1,253 is about 4,900.

Guided Practice*

Do you know HOW?

Round to the nearest ten to estimate.

1. 28 + 46
2. 175 + 307

Round to the nearest hundred to estimate.

3. 114 + 58
4. 2,198 + 1,426

Round to the nearest thousand to estimate.

5. 2,142 + 986
6. 1,924 + 2,345

Do you UNDERSTAND?

7. **Writing to Explain** Which estimate in the example at the top of page 49 is closer to the actual sum? Explain.
8. How could you use rounding to estimate 487 + 354?
9. **Number Sense** If both addends are rounded down, will the estimate be greater or less than the actual sum?

*For another example, see Set C on page 62.

One Way

Round to the nearest hundred.

$$\begin{array}{r} 255 \\ +\ 322 \\ \hline \end{array} \longrightarrow \begin{array}{r} 300 \\ +\ 300 \\ \hline 600 \end{array}$$

255 + 322 is about 600.
600 > 500

The pandas together weigh more than 500 pounds.

Another Way

Round to the nearest ten.

$$\begin{array}{r} 255 \\ +\ 322 \\ \hline \end{array} \longrightarrow \begin{array}{r} 260 \\ +\ 320 \\ \hline 580 \end{array}$$

255 + 322 is about 580.
580 > 500

The pandas together weigh more than 500 pounds.

Independent Practice

In **10–13**, round to the nearest ten to estimate.

10. 18 + 43 **11.** 75 + 72 **12.** 39 + 102 **13.** 376 + 295

In **14–17**, round to the nearest hundred to estimate.

14. 403 + 179 **15.** 462 + 3,251 **16.** 64 + 403 **17.** 1,539 + 399

In **18–21**, round to the nearest thousand to estimate.

18. 1,429 + 8,294 **19.** 4,826 + 1,106 **20.** 2,347 + 865 **21.** 987 + 5,687

Problem Solving

Reasonableness Estimate to decide if each answer is reasonable. Write *yes* or *no*. Then explain your thinking.

22. 32 + 58 = 70 **23.** 83 + 46 = 129 **24.** 55 + 64 = 99

In **25** and **26**, use the table at the right.

25. Which city is farthest from Los Angeles?

26. Mr. Tyson drove from Los Angeles to Monterey and back again. To the nearest ten miles, about how many miles did he drive?

A 320 **C** 640
B 600 **D** 660

Data

Distance from Los Angeles, CA

City	Miles Away
Monterey	324 miles
Palm Springs	115 miles
Sacramento	388 miles
Santa Barbara	91 miles

Lesson
3-5

NS 2.1 Find the sum or difference of two whole numbers between 0 and 10,000.
MR 2.1 Use estimation to verify the reasonableness of calculated results.
Also MR 2.5.

Adding 2-Digit Numbers

Hands-On
place-value blocks

How can you use addition to solve problems?

How many ears of corn are there in all?

- Add to find the total. **58 + 47 = ▢**

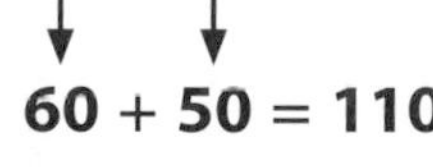

- Estimate first. **60 + 50 = 110**
  58 + 47 is about 110.

Guided Practice*

Do you know HOW?

Estimate. Then find each sum. Place-value blocks may help.

1. $42 + 59$
2. $64 + 22$
3. $93 + 28$
4. $57 + 52$
5. 47 + 9
6. 84 + 28

Do you UNDERSTAND?

7. **Estimation** Look at the problem in the example above about ears of corn. Why is an estimate not enough?
8. Look at the pumpkins above.
   a Estimate the total weight of the pumpkins.
   b Write and solve a number sentence to find the actual total weight of the pumpkins.

Independent Practice

Estimate. Then find each sum.

9. $77 + 52$
10. $19 + 24$
11. $57 + 8$
12. $72 + 26$
13. $75 + 39$

14. 33 + 45
15. 88 + 16
16. 24 + 54
17. 17 + 37
18. 59 + 13
19. 83 + 9
20. 71 + 19
21. 45 + 34

DIGITAL eTools
www.pearsonsuccessnet.com

*For another example, see Set D on page 63.

What You Think

58 + 47 = ▢

- Add the ones.
  8 ones + 7 ones = 15 ones and 15 ones = 1 ten 5 ones.
- Add the tens.
  1 ten + 5 tens + 4 tens = 10 tens and 10 tens = 1 hundred.

What You Write

```
   1
   5 8
+  4 7
 1 0 5
```

105 is close to 110, so 105 is reasonable.

There are 105 ears of corn in all.

Problem Solving

In **22 and 23**, use the table at the right.

22. Follow the steps below to find how many points the Hoop Troop scored all together in Games 1 and 2.

- **a** Write a number sentence to show how to solve the problem.
- **b** Estimate the answer.
- **c** Solve the problem.
- **d** Is your answer reasonable? Explain.

The Hoop Troop

Games	Points Scored
Game 1	66
Game 2	57
Game 3	64

23. List the Hoop Troop's scores in order from the fewest to the most points.

24. Reasonableness Stan added 36 + 29 and got 515. Explain why his answer is not reasonable.

25. A statue of President Lincoln standing would be 9 feet taller than the statue in the picture. How tall would that statue be?

26. Number Sense What is the greatest possible sum of two 2-digit numbers? Explain.

27. Colleen ran 18 miles last week. She ran 26 miles this week. She plans to run 28 miles next week. Which number sentence shows how many miles she has run so far?

A 18 + 28 = ▢ **C** 18 + 26 + 28 = ▢

B 18 + 26 = ▢ **D** 28 − 18 = ▢

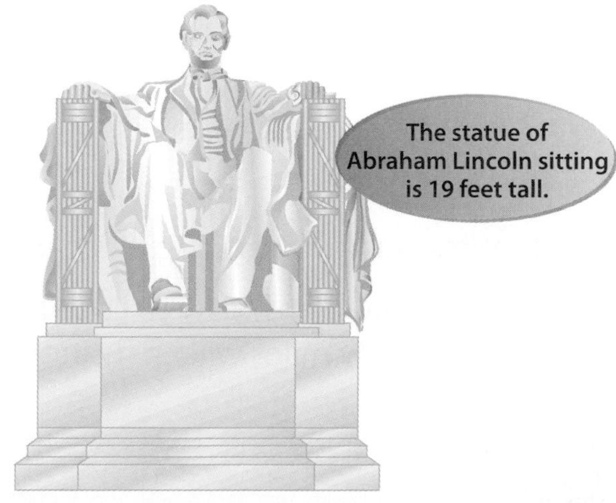

Lesson

3-6

NS 2.1 Find the sum or difference of two whole numbers between 0 and 10,000.

Adding 3- and 4-Digit Numbers

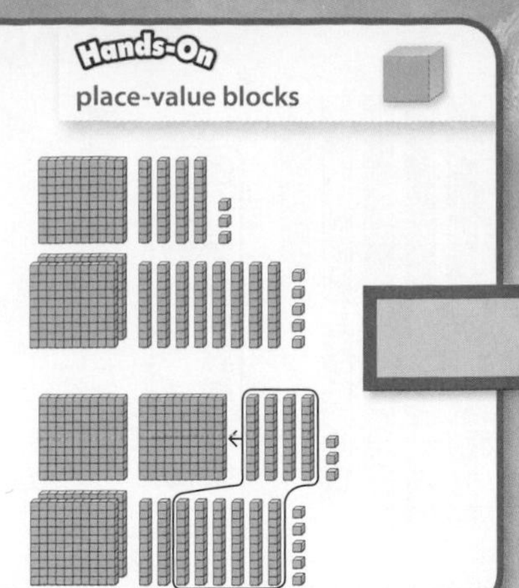

How can you add greater numbers?

Jason drove 143 miles on Monday and 285 miles on Tuesday. How far did he drive in all?

Find 143 + 285. Estimate: 100 + 300 = 400

Use place-value blocks or drawings.

Another Example How can you add 4-digit numbers?

Last week, Mr. Figaro flew from Chicago to Los Angeles. The trip was 1,745 miles each way. How many miles did he fly round trip?

? miles in all

1,745	1,745

Choose an Operation Since you are finding the total number of miles, you add. Find 1,745 + 1,745.

Step 1

Add the ones.

Regroup 10 ones as 1 ten 0 ones.

$$\begin{array}{r} {\scriptstyle 1} \\ 1{,}745 \\ +\ 1{,}745 \\ \hline 0 \end{array}$$

Step 2

Add the tens.

$$\begin{array}{r} {\scriptstyle 1} \\ 1{,}745 \\ +\ 1{,}745 \\ \hline 90 \end{array}$$

Step 3

Add the hundreds.

Regroup 14 hundreds as 1 thousand 4 hundreds.

$$\begin{array}{r} {\scriptstyle 1\ \ 1} \\ 1{,}745 \\ +\ 1{,}745 \\ \hline 3{,}490 \end{array}$$

Step 4

Add the thousands.

$$\begin{array}{r} {\scriptstyle 1\ \ 1} \\ 1{,}745 \\ +\ 1{,}745 \\ \hline 3{,}490 \end{array}$$

Mr. Figaro flew 3,490 miles round trip.

Explain It

1. Why must you regroup twice in this example?
2. Mr. Figaro plans to fly to Los Angeles and back again this week. How many miles will he fly in the two round trips?

Step 1

Add the ones.

3 ones + 5 ones = 8 ones

```
  143
+ 285
    8
```

Step 2

Add the tens.

4 tens + 8 tens = 12 tens

Regroup.
12 tens = 1 hundred 2 tens

```
  1
  143
+ 285
   28
```

Step 3

Add the hundreds.

1 hundred + 1 hundred + 2 hundreds = 4 hundreds

```
  1
  143
+ 285
  428
```

Jason drove 428 miles.

Guided Practice*

Do you know HOW?

For **1–6**, estimate and then find each sum. You may use place-value blocks or drawings to help.

1. 126 + 171

2. 415 + 168

3. 2,574 + 3,674

4. 3,528 + 349

5. 394 + 97

6. 753 + 2,449

Do you UNDERSTAND?

In **7** and **8**, use the example above.

7. Why did you regroup tens?

8. **Reasonableness** Is the answer reasonable? Explain.

9. Mrs. Lane drove 268 miles on Monday, 278 miles on Tuesday, and 342 miles on Wednesday. Write and solve a number sentence to show how far she drove on Tuesday and Wednesday.

Independent Practice

For **10–19**, estimate. Then find each sum.

10. 347 + 325

11. 136 + 252

12. 564 + 283

13. 499 + 484

14. 347 + 587

15. 3,382 + 5,587

16. 5,302 + 4,591

17. 3,555 + 462

18. 2,736 + 6,274

19. 8,424 + 589

DIGITAL eTools **www.pearsonsuccessnet.com**

For another example, see Set D on page 63.

Independent Practice

For **20–27**, find each sum.

20. 324 + 465 **21.** 709 + 94 **22.** 381 + 57 **23.** 492 + 288

24. 4,136 + 5,342 **25.** 5,083 + 641 **26.** 2,196 + 3,374 **27.** 7,526 + 697

Problem Solving

For **28–31**, use the table at the right.

Data

Labels from Soup Cans

Grade	Number Collected
1	385
2	704
3	2,488
4	2,239

28. a Write a number sentence to find how many labels the first and second grade collected in all.

b Estimate the answer.

c Solve the problem.

d Use the estimate to explain why your answer is reasonable.

29. Reasonableness Without finding the actual sum, how do you know that the second and fourth grades together collected more labels than the third grade?

30. Writing to Explain How many times would you regroup to find the labels collected in all by the third and fourth grades? Explain.

31. Which describes the total number of labels collected?

A Fewer than 5,000

B Exactly 5,000

C Between 5,000 and 6,000

D More than 6,000

32. Which number is the same as six thousand, twenty-six?

A 626 **C** 6,026

B 662 **D** 6,206

33. The tallest roller coaster in the world is called Kingda Ka. It is 192 feet higher than the first Ferris wheel. How tall is Kingda Ka?

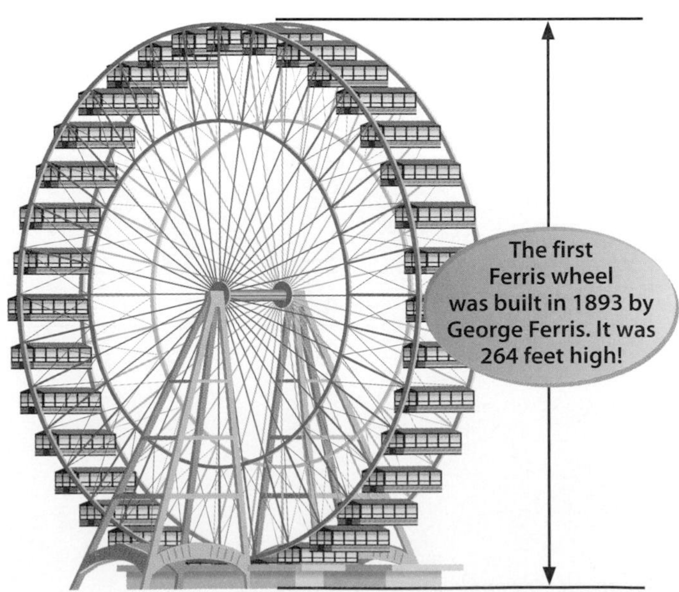

Mixed Problem Solving

Read the story and then answer the questions.

We Can't Wait!

Jamie and her sisters stared out of the front window of their home. They were talking about all the good stories their grandmother always tells them when she visits. About 10 minutes ago, their dad had called home from the airport. He said that he was exactly 26 blocks away. He needed to make one more stop 12 blocks farther away. Then he would come home.

When Dad finally came around the street corner, the sisters jumped off the sofa and ran to the door. Dad arrived at the door with some grocery bags, a suitcase, and a special visitor. Soon the family would be hearing many good stories.

1. What conclusion can you draw?

2. About 10 minutes ago, while the sisters were staring out of the window, their dad called. Write a number of minutes that rounds to 10 minutes.

3. To the nearest 10 blocks, about how many blocks away from home was Dad when he called home?

4. To the nearest 10 blocks, about how many blocks did Dad travel from his last stop to home?

---

5. Look at the table below.

Write the distances in order from least to greatest.

Data

Place	Distance from Home
Bakery	38 blocks
Bank	12 blocks
Grocery Store	21 blocks
Toy Store	26 blocks

6. **Strategy Focus** Solve the problem. Use the strategy Make an Organized List.

Jamie earned some money doing chores. She wants to put 70 cents in her bank. What are two different ways she could use coins to make 70 cents?

Lesson

3-7

NS 2.0 Calculate and solve problems involving addition, subtraction, multiplication and division.

Adding 3 or More Numbers

How can you use addition to solve problems?

Different kinds of birds are for sale at a pet store. How many birds are for sale in all?

- Find 137 + 155 + 18.
- Estimate: 140 + 160 + 20 = 320.

Guided Practice*

Do you know HOW?

Find each sum.

1.
```
   36
   47
 + 35
```

2.
```
  247
  362
 +  49
```

3.
```
  273
   82
+ 124
```

4.
```
   59
  506
  302
+  24
```

5. 9 + 46 + 24

6. 385 + 97 + 34

Do you UNDERSTAND?

For **7–9**, look at the example above.

7. Why is there a 2 above the tens place in Step 2?

8. **Reasonableness** How can you tell that 310 birds is a reasonable answer?

9. Suppose the pet store gets 46 lovebirds to sell. Write and solve a number sentence to show how many birds are for sale now.

Independent Practice

Find each sum.

10.
```
   64
   42
 + 88
```

11.
```
  307
   37
+ 234
```

12.
```
  602
  125
+ 231
```

13.
```
  246
   54
  233
+ 205
```

14.
```
  303
  128
   63
+ 149
```

15. 164 + 68 + 35

16. 32 + 9 + 46 + 8

17. 125 + 36 + 124 + 239

**For another example, see Set E on page 63.*

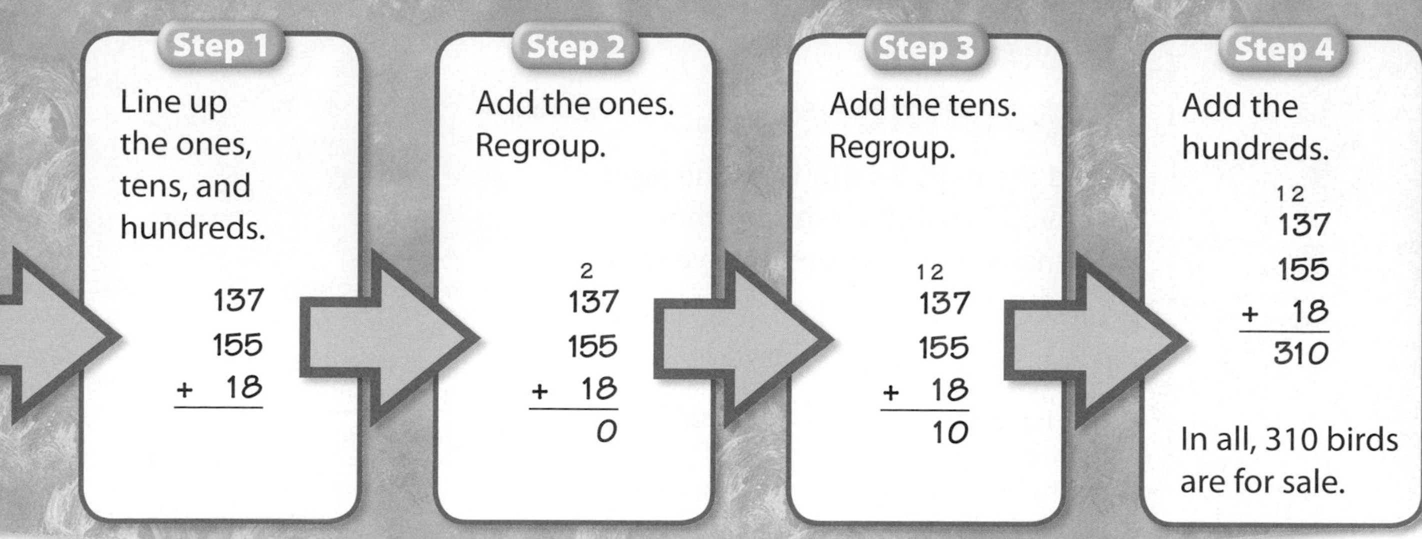

Problem Solving

Calories are used to measure the energy in food. Use the pictures for **18–20**.

18. Karin had cereal, a glass of milk, and a banana for breakfast. Follow these steps to find how many calories were in the food she ate.

a Write a number sentence to show how to solve the problem.

b Estimate the answer.

c Solve the problem.

d Use the estimate to explain why your answer is reasonable.

19. Stan put 2 tablespoons of maple syrup on the stack of two pancakes he ate for breakfast. Then he had an apple. How many calories were in the food he ate?

20. Compare the number of calories in an apple with the number of calories in a banana. Use $>$, $<$, or $=$.

21. **Reasonableness** Meg said that $95 + 76 + 86$ is greater than 300. Explain why her answer is not reasonable.

22. Ramos has 225 pennies, 105 nickels, and 65 dimes. How many coins does he have?

A 385 coins

B 395 coins

C 980 coins

D 3,815 coins

Lesson

3-8

MR 3.1 Evaluate the reasonableness of the solution in the context of the original situation. Also **NS 2.0** Calculate and solve problems involving addition, subtraction, multiplication, and division.

Problem Solving

Reasonableness

Al had the marbles shown at the right. He gave 18 marbles to his brother. How many marbles does Al have left?

After you solve a problem, ask yourself:

- Is the answer reasonable?
- Did I answer the right question?

53 marbles in all

18 marbles	?

Guided Practice*

Do you know HOW?

1. Rosita is reading a book that is 65 pages long. She has 27 pages left to read. How many pages has she already read?

65 pages in all

?	27

Do you UNDERSTAND?

2. **Writing to Explain** Describe how to check that your answer is reasonable and that you have answered the right question.

3. **Write a Problem** Write and solve a problem. Check that your answer is reasonable.

Independent Practice

Solve. Then check that your answer is reasonable.

4. James is reading a book that is 85 pages long. He read 35 pages yesterday and 24 pages today. How many pages did James read in the two days?

? pages in all

35	24

5. Kyle had 56 model cars. He gave his brother 36 of them. How many model cars does Kyle have now?

- What do I know?
- What am I asked to find?
- What diagram can I use to help understand the problem?
- Can I use addition, subtraction, multiplication, or division?
- Is all of my work correct?
- Did I answer the right question?
- Is my answer reasonable?

*For another example, see Set F on page 63.

Jim's Answer

53 − 18 = 35
Al's brother has 35 marbles.

53 − 18 is about 50 − 20, or 30.

35 is close to 30, so 35 is reasonable.

The number 35 is reasonable, but Jim did not answer the right question.

Sally's Answer

53 − 18 = 45
Al has 45 marbles left.

53 − 18 is about 50 − 20, or 30.

45 is not close to 30, so 45 is not reasonable.

Sally answered the right question, but the number 45 is not reasonable.

Pablo's Answer

53 − 18 = 35
Al has 35 marbles left.

53 − 18 is about 50 − 20, or 30.

35 is close to 30, so 35 is reasonable.

The number 35 is reasonable, and Pablo did answer the right question.

Use the table to solve **6–8**. Estimate, then check that your answer is reasonable.

Data

Total Points Scored	
Games	**Points**
Game 1	68
Game 2	74
Game 3	89

6. How many points were scored all together in Games 1 and 2?

? points in all

68	74

7. There were 39 points scored in the first half of Game 1. How many points were scored in the second half?

68 points in all

39	?

8. **Estimation** About how many points were scored all together in the three games?

? points in all

70	70	90

9. Carl practices the piano 45 minutes each day. Today, he practiced 15 minutes after school and 10 minutes before dinner. How much time does he still need to practice?

A 70 minutes
B 60 minutes
C 35 minutes
D 20 minutes

10. Carrie has 15 pennies. Her brother has 10 more pennies than Carrie. How many pennies do they have in all?

A 40 pennies
B 25 pennies
C 10 pennies
D 5 pennies

Test Prep

1. Which number sentence can be used to find how many erasers in all? (3-1)

A $8 + 6 = 14$

B $9 + 6 = 15$

C $9 + 5 = 14$

D $3 + 6 = 9$

2. When using a hundred chart to find $43 + 25$, you start at 43. Which of the following steps should you do next? (3-2)

21	22	23	24	25	26	27	28	29	30
31	32	33	34	35	36	37	38	39	40
41	42	43	44	45	46	47	48	49	50
51	52	53	54	55	56	57	58	59	60
61	62	63	64	65	66	67	68	69	70

A Count down 2 rows.

B Count to the right 2 squares.

C Count to the left 2 squares.

D Count up 2 rows.

3. What is $86 + 47$? (3-5)

A 123

B 132

C 133

D 143

4. Mary brought 23 bananas and 13 oranges for the third grade picnic. How many pieces of fruit did she bring? Use mental math to solve. (3-3)

A 36

B 33

C 26

D 10

5. Jupiter has 63 moons, Saturn has 56, and Uranus has 27. How many moons do these 3 planets have together? (3-7)

A 119

B 136

C 146

D 149

6. The United States has 389 kinds of endangered animals and 599 kinds of endangered plants. How many is this in all? (3-6)

A 878

B 888

C 978

D 988

7. Marty's Toy Store has 36 teddy bears and 28 stuffed horses. How many of these toys does it have in all? (3-5)

A 8

B 12

C 54

D 64

8. The bakery sold 225 blueberry bagels on Saturday and 171 blueberry bagels on Sunday. Which picture models how to find the total number of blueberry bagels sold during the weekend? (3-6)

A

?

225	171

B

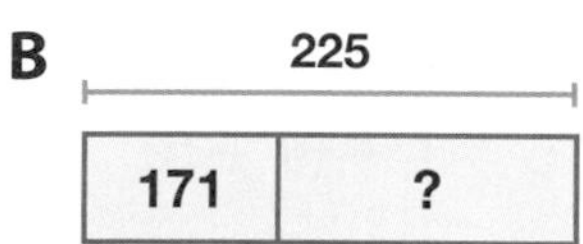

C

171

225	?

D

225

171	171	?

9. To find 39 + 49, Ava made a ten, as shown below. What is the missing number? (3-3)

$39 + 49 = 40 + \square = 88$

A 29

B 30

C 47

D 48

10. The population of Jackson is 4,068, and the population of Hidden Hills is 1,993. What is the total population of Jackson and Hidden Hills? (3-6)

A 5,961

B 6,061

C 10,661

D 15,061

11. Which number makes the number sentence true? (3-1)

$\square + 6 = 6 + 3$

A 9

B 4

C 3

D 0

12. Fossil Butte in Wyoming is about 8,198 acres. Devil's Tower is about 1,346 acres. Which is a reasonable total size for these two national monuments combined? (3-8)

A 10,044, because 1,346 + 8,198 is about 2,000 + 8,000 = 10,000

B 9,544, because 1,346 + 8,198 is about 1,300 + 8,200 = 9,500

C 9,044, because 1,346 + 8,198 is about 1,000 + 8,000 = 9,000

D 8,544, because 1,346 + 8,198 is about 1,000 + 7,500 = 8,500

13. In a survey, 1,491 third grade students said they had flown in a plane, and 3,609 said they had not flown in a plane. How many students answered the survey? (3-6)

A 5,110

B 5,100

C 5,000

D 4,090

Reteaching

Set A, pages 40–41

Write the missing number.

(2 + ☐) + 1 = 2 + (5 + 1)
The Associative Property of Addition states that you can group addends in any way and the sum will be the same.
(2 + 5) + 1 = 2 + (5 + 1)

7 + ☐ = 6 + 7
The Commutative Property of Addition states that you can add numbers in any order and the sum will be the same.
7 + 6 = 6 + 7

Remember the Identity Property of Addition states that the sum of any number and zero is that same number.

Write each missing number.

1. 8 + 4 = 4 + ☐
2. (2 + 3) + 5 = 2 + (3 + ☐)
3. ☐ + 0 = 6
4. (1 + ☐) + 6 = 1 + (4 + 6)

Set B, pages 42–46

Use mental math to find 38 + 21.

Break apart both numbers into tens and ones.

38 = 30 + 8 21 = 20 + 1

Add the tens.
30 + 20 = 50

Add the ones.
8 + 1 = 9

Add the tens and ones together.
50 + 9 = 59
So, 38 + 21 = 59.

Remember that to add on a hundred chart, first add the tens. Then move to the right or left if necessary to adjust the ones.

Use a hundred chart or mental math to find each sum.

1. 37 + 20
2. 52 + 17
3. 83 + 11
4. 52 + 30
5. 25 + 16
6. 36 + 39

Set C, pages 48–49

Estimate 478 + 134.

One Way

Round each number to the nearest ten.

```
  478 ──►   480
+ 134 ──► + 130
            610
```

Remember to check place value when rounding.

1. Estimate 367 + 319 by rounding to the nearest hundred.
2. Estimate 98 + 42 by rounding to the nearest ten.
3. Estimate 1,527 + 3,256 by rounding to the nearest thousand.

Set D, pages 50–54

Find 276 + 189.

Estimate: 300 + 200 = 500

Then, add.

```
  1 1
  2 7 6
+ 1 8 9
-------
  4 6 5
```

6 + 9 = 15 ones
Regroup into 1 ten 5 ones.

1 ten + 7 tens + 8 tens = 16 tens
Regroup into 1 hundred 6 tens.

1 hundred + 2 hundreds +
1 hundred = 4 hundreds

465 is close to 500, so 465 is reasonable.

Remember to regroup 10 ones as 1 ten, 10 tens as 1 hundred, and 10 hundreds as 1 thousand.

Estimate. Then find each sum.

1. $\begin{array}{r} 77 \\ +\ 56 \\ \hline \end{array}$

2. $\begin{array}{r} 213 \\ +\ 538 \\ \hline \end{array}$

3. $\begin{array}{r} 1{,}652 \\ +\ 2{,}184 \\ \hline \end{array}$

4. $\begin{array}{r} 4{,}386 \\ +\ 766 \\ \hline \end{array}$

5. 311 + 289

6. 371 + 283

7. 3,046 + 98

8. 495 + 63

Set E, pages 56–57

Find 43 + 187 + 238.

Estimate: 40 + 190 + 240 = 470

```
  1 1
    4 3
  1 8 7
+ 2 3 8
-------
  4 6 8
```

Line up ones, tens, and hundreds. Then add each column. Regroup as needed.

468 is close to 470, so 468 is reasonable.

Remember to estimate so you can check if your answer is reasonable.

Find each sum.

1. 25 + 67 + 132
2. 139 + 209 + 55
3. 328 + 381 + 42
4. 56 + 167 + 35

Set F, pages 58–59

Carla is reading a book that has 87 pages. She has read 49 pages. How many pages does she have left to read?

Estimate: 87 − 49 is about 90 − 50, or 40.
Subtract: 87 − 49 = 38

Carla has 38 pages left to read. The answer is reasonable because 38 is close to the estimate of 40.

Remember that you can use an estimate to check if your answer is reasonable.

1. Lucy has 45 tulips. There are 27 red tulips. The rest are yellow. How many yellow tulips does Lucy have?

Topic 4

Subtracting Whole Numbers

1 How much longer was a *Brachiosaurus* than a *Tyrannosaurus rex*? You will find out in Lesson 4-4.

2 The world's largest "basket" is really a building in Newark, Ohio. How big is this basket? You will find out in Lesson 4-7.

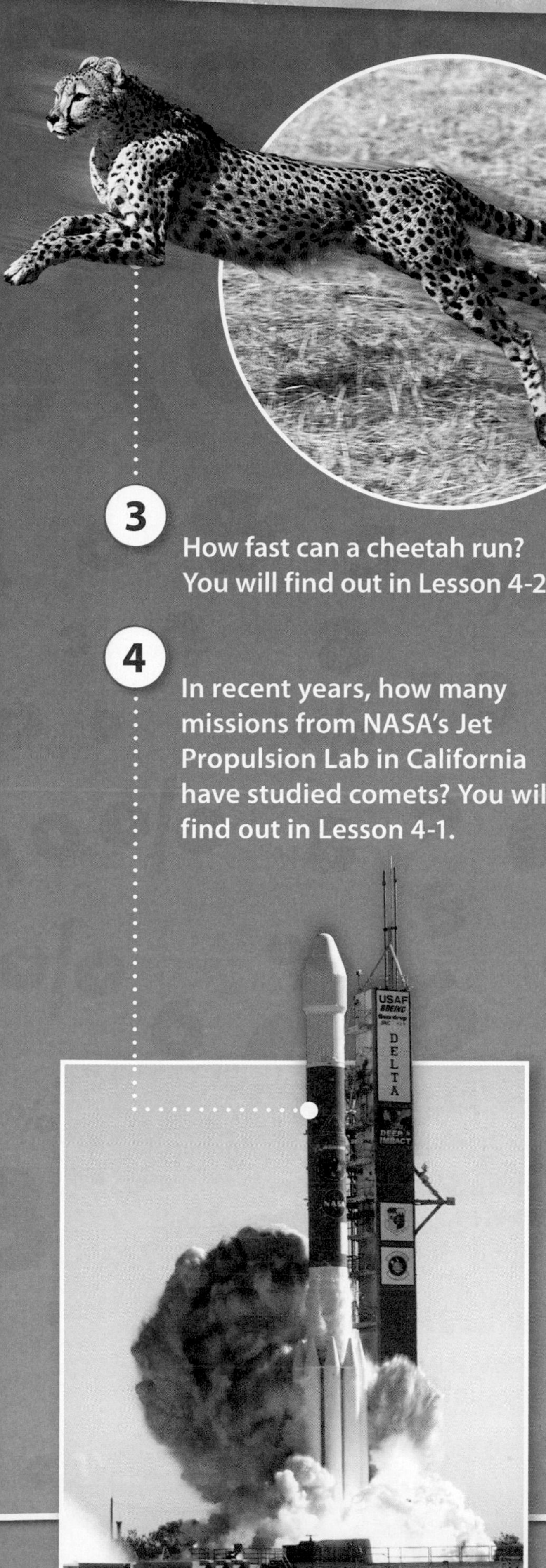

3 How fast can a cheetah run? You will find out in Lesson 4-2.

4 In recent years, how many missions from NASA's Jet Propulsion Lab in California have studied comets? You will find out in Lesson 4-1.

Review What You Know!

Vocabulary

Choose the best term from the box.

- add
- round
- skip count
- subtract

1. To take away a part from a whole, you can __?__.
2. You can __?__ to find a number that is close to the actual number.
3. To join parts together, you can __?__.

Subtraction Facts

Find each difference.

4. 9 − 5 **5.** 11 − 3 **6.** 16 − 7

Addition Facts

Find each sum.

7. 4 + 8 **8.** 9 + 8 **9.** 6 + 7

Rounding

Writing to Explain

10. To what two numbers can you round 78? Explain why there is more than one way to round 78.

11. Is the sum of 5 + 8 the same as or different from the sum of 8 + 5? Explain.

Lesson

4-1

NS 2.1 Find the sum or difference of two whole numbers between 0 and 10,000.

Subtraction Meanings

When do you subtract?

Ms. Aydin's class is making school flags to sell at the school fair.

The table shows how many flags several students have made so far.

Data

Flags for School Fair

Student	Number Made
Brent	12
Devon	9
Keisha	11
Ling	14
Pedro	7
Rick	8

Another Example **You subtract to find a missing addend.**

Rick plans on making 13 flags. How many more flags does he need?

The parts and the whole show how addition and subtraction are related.

13 flags in all

8	?

$8 + \square = 13$

You can write a fact family when you know the parts and the whole.

A fact family is a group of related facts using the same numbers.

$5 + 8 = 13$ $\quad$ $13 - 8 = 5$

$8 + 5 = 13$ $\quad$ $13 - 5 = 8$

The missing part is 5. This means Rick needs to make 5 more flags.

Guided Practice*

Do you know HOW?

Use the table to write and solve a number sentence.

1. How many more flags has Ling made than Devon?
2. How many more flags must Pedro make to have 15 in all? to have the same number as Ling?

Do you UNDERSTAND?

3. Ling sold 8 of the flags she had made. Write a number sentence to find how many flags she has left. Then solve the problem.
4. **Write a Problem** Write and solve a word problem that can be solved by subtracting.

*For another example, see Set A on page 96.

Subtract to take some away and find how many are left.

Brent sold 5 of the flags he made. How many flags did he have left?

12 flags in all	
5	?

$12 - 5 = 7$

Brent had 7 flags left.

Subtract to compare amounts.

How many more flags did Keisha make than Pedro?

Keisha	11	
Pedro	7	?

$11 - 7 = 4$

Keisha made 4 more flags than Pedro.

Independent Practice

Write a number sentence for each situation. Solve.

5. Pat has 15 pins. Chris has 9 pins. How many more pins does Pat have than Chris?

Pat	15	
Chris	9	?

6. How many more orange flags than green flags are there?

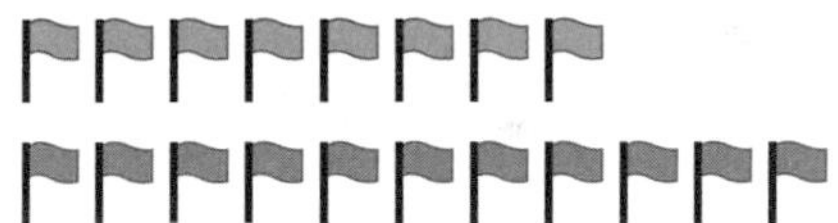

Problem Solving

7. Ching had 12 pies to sell. After she sold some of the pies, she had 4 pies left. How many pies had Ching sold?

8. A pole holding a state flag is 10 feet tall. The height of the flag is 4 feet. How many feet taller is the pole than the flag?

9. The Jet Propulsion Lab had 9 missions between 2003 and 2006. Two of these missions were to study comets. How many of these missions did not study comets?

10. Rob had 17 pens. After he gave some of them to his friend, he had 8 pens. Which number sentence shows one way to find how many pens Rob gave to his friend?

A $17 + 8 = \square$

B $8 - 1 = \square$

C $17 - 1 = \square$

D $17 - \square = 8$

Lesson

4-2

NS 2.1 Find the sum or difference of two whole numbers between 0 and 10,000.

Subtracting on a Hundred Chart

How can you subtract on a hundred chart?

Find 38 − 20 on a hundred chart.

Start at 38. To count back 2 tens, move up 2 rows.

38 − 20 = 18

1	2	3	4	5	6	7	8	9	10
11	12	13	14	15	16	17	(18)	19	20
21	22	23	24	25	26	27	28	29	30
31	32	33	34	35	36	37	(38)	39	40
41	42	43	44	45	46	47	48	49	50

Another Example How can you count on to find the difference on a hundred chart?

The difference is the answer to a subtraction problem.

Find 43 − 19.

Think 19 + ▢ = 43.

Start at 19.
Move right one square to count on to the next ten.
20

Count on by tens by moving down two rows.
30, 40

Then count on by ones until you reach 43.
41, 42, 43

You counted on: 1 + 20 + 3 = 24.

So, 43 − 19 = 24.

1	2	3	4	5	6	7	8	9	10
11	12	13	14	15	16	17	18	(19)→	20
21	22	23	24	25	26	27	28	29	30
31	32	33	34	35	36	37	38	39	40→
41→	42→	(43)	44	45	46	47	48	49	50
51	52	53	54	55	56	57	58	59	60
61	62	63	64	65	66	67	68	69	70
71	72	73	74	75	76	77	78	79	80
81	82	83	84	85	86	87	88	89	90
91	92	93	94	95	96	97	98	99	100

Explain It

1. Why do you stop at 20 when you first count on from 19?
2. Why do you add 1 + 20 + 3?

Find 85 − 19.

Think 85 − 20 = ▢

Start at 85 on the hundred chart.

Count back 2 tens to subtract 20.
To do this, move up two rows.
75, 65

Since you subtracted 1 more than 19, add 1 by moving to the right one square.
65 + 1 = 66

So, 85 − 19 = 66.

51	52	53	54	55	56	57	58	59	60
61	62	63	64	65	66	67	68	69	70
71	72	73	74	75	76	77	78	79	80
81	82	83	84	85	86	87	88	89	90
91	92	93	94	95	96	97	98	99	100

Guided Practice*

Do you know HOW?

Use a hundred chart to subtract.

1. 72 − 40
2. 86 − 30
3. 54 − 29
4. 95 − 39
5. 37 − 18

Do you UNDERSTAND?

6. **Writing to Explain** When you move up 2 rows on a hundred chart, how many are you subtracting? Explain.
7. How is subtracting ten on a hundred chart different from adding ten on a hundred chart?
8. Janey has 75 cents. She wants to buy a sticker that costs 39 cents. How much money would she have left? Explain how to use a hundred chart to find the answer.

Independent Practice

Use a hundred chart to subtract.

9. 75 − 30 **10.** 53 − 20 **11.** 68 − 40 **12.** 27 − 10

13. 84 − 50 **14.** 96 − 60 **15.** 47 − 19 **16.** 53 − 28

17. 65 − 39 **18.** 81 − 58 **19.** 76 − 29 **20.** 94 − 38

21. 96 − 17 **22.** 79 − 15 **23.** 81 − 26 **24.** 77 − 48

DIGITAL Animated Glossary
www.pearsonsuccessnet.com

*For another example, see Set B on page 96.

Use the table for **25–27**.

25. A cottonwood tree in Max's yard is 30 feet shorter than an average cottonwood tree. How tall is the tree in his yard?

26. Write the average heights of the trees from shortest to tallest.

Data

State Trees

State	Kind of Tree	Average Height
Kansas	Cottonwood	75 feet
Michigan	Eastern white pine	70 feet
New York	Sugar maple	80 feet

27. A sugar maple tree in the local park is 92 feet tall. How many feet taller is the tree in the park than an average sugar maple tree?

28. Writing to Explain A white pine tree is 52 feet tall. If it grows 10 feet in 7 years, how tall will it be in 7 years? Explain how you found your answer.

29. Reasonableness Liam used a hundred chart to find 92 − 62. He said the difference is 40. Is his answer reasonable? Why or why not?

Tip *What addition sentence can help?*

30. The workers in the lunchroom made 234 ham sandwiches and 165 tuna sandwiches. They also made 150 cheese pizzas and 125 veggie pizzas. How many sandwiches did they make in all?

31. For short distances, an elephant can run as fast as 15 miles per hour. How much faster can a cheetah run than an elephant? Write and solve a number sentence.

A cheetah can run short distances as fast as 70 miles an hour.

32. John is 56 inches tall. John's father is 72 inches tall. How much taller is John's father than John? Explain how you found your answer.

33. Maya had 15 small rocks. She had 9 large rocks. Which number sentence shows one way to find how many more small rocks than large rocks Maya had?

A 15 − 9 = ▢

B 15 + 6 = ▢

C 15 + 9 = ▢

D 24 − 15 = ▢

Algebra Connections

Addition and Subtraction Number Sentences

The symbol = means "is equal to."
In a number sentence, the symbol = tells you that the value on the left is equal to the value on the right.

Examples: $29 = 20 + 9$

$6 = 11 - 5$

$9 + 4 = 13$

The value on the left side of the number sentence is equal to the value on the right side.

Copy and complete. Write the number that makes the number sentence true.

1. 9 + ▢ = 11 **2.** 10 = 3 + ▢ **3.** 17 − ▢ = 9

4. 5 + ▢ = 13 **5.** 8 = 12 − ▢ **6.** 14 = 5 + ▢

7. 10 = 10 + ▢ **8.** 6 + ▢ = 26 **9.** 19 + ▢ = 29

10. 50 + ▢ = 60 **11.** 30 = 40 − ▢ **12.** 25 = 5 + ▢

13. 10 + ▢ = 17 **14.** 42 = 45 − ▢ **15.** 13 − ▢ = 0

For **16** and **17**, copy and complete the number sentence below each problem. Use it to solve the problem.

16. Nate had 10 river stones. Chen had 26 river stones. How many more river stones did Chen have than Nate?

10 + ▢ = 26

17. Tania collected 10 more leaves than Gwen. Tania collected 37 leaves. How many leaves did Gwen collect?

▢ + 10 = 37

18. **Write a Problem** Write and solve a problem to match the number sentence below.

48 = 20 + ▢

Lesson
4-3

NS 2.1 Find the sum or difference of two whole numbers between 0 and 10,000. Also MR 3.2.

Using Mental Math to Subtract

How can you subtract with mental math?

The store is having a sale on jackets. A jacket is on sale for $17 less than the original price. What is the sale price?

You can use mental math to subtract and solve this problem.

Guided Practice*

Do you know HOW?

In **1–8**, find each difference using mental math.

1. 26 − 18
2. 34 − 19
3. 73 − 16
4. 45 − 27
5. 67 − 28
6. 83 − 39
7. 42 − 14
8. 49 − 19

Do you UNDERSTAND?

9. **Writing to Explain** In the One Way example above, why do you add 3 to 32 instead of subtract 3 from 32?

10. Suppose a coat has an original price of $74 and it is on sale for $18 less than the original price. What is the sale price of the coat? How can you use mental math to solve this problem?

Independent Practice

In **11–30**, find each difference using mental math.

11. 28 − 19
12. 46 − 18
13. 39 − 17
14. 68 − 11
15. 52 − 9
16. 75 − 12
17. 29 − 18
18. 49 − 18
19. 64 − 15
20. 43 − 16
21. 97 − 14
22. 86 − 13
23. 31 − 14
24. 98 − 17
25. 57 − 18
26. 72 − 19
27. 53 − 39
28. 27 − 19
29. 82 − 27
30. 73 − 39

*For another example, see Set C on page 96.

One Way

52 − 17 = ☐

It is easier to subtract 20.
52 − 20 = 32

If you subtract 20, you subtract 3 more than 17. You must add 3 to the answer.

32 + 3 = 35

52 − 17 = 35

The sale price is $35.

Another Way

52 − 17 = ☐

Make a simpler problem by changing each number in the same way.

You can change 17 to 20 because it is easy to subtract 20. So, add 3 to both 17 and 52.

$$\begin{array}{ccccc} 52 & - & 17 & = & \square \\ \downarrow +3 & & \downarrow +3 & & \\ 55 & - & 20 & = & 35 \end{array}$$

52 − 17 = 35

Problem Solving

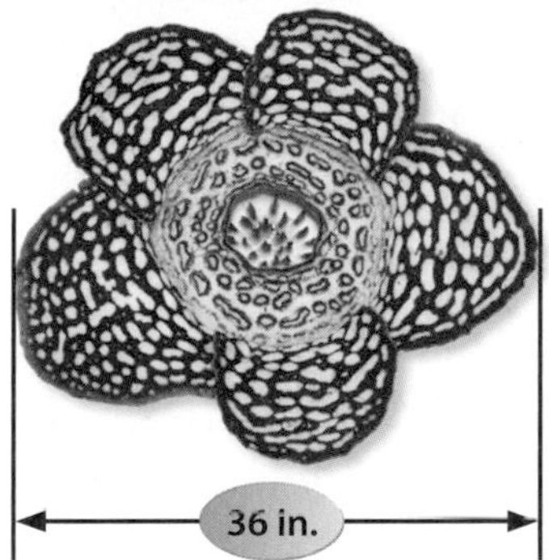

31. Number Sense The giant Rafflesia flower can be as wide as what is shown at the right. One petal can be 18 inches wide. How can you use mental math to find how much wider the whole flower is than one petal?

32. Writing to Explain To subtract 57 − 16, Tom added 4 to each number, while Saul added 3 to each number. Will both methods work to find the correct answer? Explain.

In **33** and **34**, use the photo below.

33. a What is the sale price of the jeans? Describe one way you can use mental math to find the answer.

b Maria bought two pairs of jeans. What was the total sale price of the jeans Maria bought?

34. Which number sentence shows the original price of two pairs of jeans?

A 46 + 46 = ☐

B 46 + 18 = ☐

C 18 + 18 = ☐

D 46 − 18 = ☐

35. Eva had $38. She bought a book for $17. Which number sentence shows one way to find how much money Eva had left?

A 38 + 17 = ☐

B 38 − 17 = ☐

C ☐ − 38 = 17

D ☐ − 17 = 38

Lesson
4-4

NS 1.4 Round off numbers to 10,000 to the nearest ten, hundred, and thousand.
NS 2.1 Find the sum or difference of two whole numbers between 0 and 10,000.
Also **MR 2.1, 2.5**

Estimating Differences

How can you estimate differences?

All of the tickets for a concert were sold. So far, 126 people have arrived at the concert. About how many people who have tickets have not arrived?

Since you need to find *about* how many, you can estimate.

493 tickets sold

Estimate 493 − 126 by rounding.

Another Example How can you use compatible numbers to estimate differences?

Compatible numbers are numbers that are close and easy to work with.

The Perry family is taking a car trip. The trip is 372 miles long. So far, the family has traveled 149 miles. About how many miles are left to travel?

Use compatible numbers to estimate 372 − 149.

$$\begin{array}{r} 372 \\ -\ 149 \\ \hline \end{array} \longrightarrow \begin{array}{r} 375 \\ -\ 150 \\ \hline 225 \end{array}$$

The Perry family still has about 225 miles to travel.

Explain It

1. How are the numbers 375 and 150 easy to work with?
2. Use a different pair of compatible numbers to estimate 372 − 149.
3. Is an estimate enough to solve this problem? Why or why not?
4. What numbers would you use to estimate 372 − 149 to the nearest ten? to the nearest hundred?

One Way

You can round each number to the nearest hundred.

$$\begin{array}{r} 493 \\ -\ 126 \\ \hline \end{array} \longrightarrow \begin{array}{r} 500 \\ -\ 100 \\ \hline 400 \end{array}$$

About 400 people have not yet arrived.

Another Way

You can round each number to the nearest ten.

$$\begin{array}{r} 493 \\ -\ 126 \\ \hline \end{array} \longrightarrow \begin{array}{r} 490 \\ -\ 130 \\ \hline 360 \end{array}$$

About 360 people have not yet arrived.

Guided Practice*

Do you know HOW?

In **1** and **2**, round to the nearest hundred to estimate each difference.

1. 321 – 112 **2.** 255 – 189

In **3** and **4**, round to the nearest ten to estimate each difference.

3. 579 – 214 **4.** 216 – 97

In **5** and **6**, use compatible numbers to estimate each difference.

5. 328 – 207 **6.** 472 – 148

Do you UNDERSTAND?

7. **Writing to Explain** In the problem above, which way of rounding gives an estimate that is closer to the actual difference? Explain why.

8. The theater sold 415 tickets to the comedy show. So far, 273 people have arrived at the show. About how many more people are expected to arrive? Tell which estimation method you used and how you found your answer.

Independent Practice

In **9–11**, round to the nearest hundred to estimate each difference.

9. 186 – 75 **10.** 704 – 369 **11.** 291 – 93

In **12–17**, round to the nearest ten to estimate each difference.

12. 88 – 32 **13.** 149 – 95 **14.** 361 – 117

15. 75 – 41 **16.** 86 – 38 **17.** 227 – 121

*For another example, see Set C on page 96.

Independent Practice

In **18–23**, use compatible numbers to estimate each difference.

18. 77 − 28 **19.** 202 − 144 **20.** 611 − 168

21. 512 − 205 **22.** 342 − 153 **23.** 904 − 31

Problem Solving

Use the table for **24–27**.

Data

Grand Concert Hall	
Day of Concert	**Number of Tickets Sold**
Wednesday	506
Thursday	323
Friday	251
Saturday	427
Sunday	

24. The concert hall sold 28 fewer tickets for the Sunday concert than for the Friday concert. About how many tickets were sold for the Sunday concert?

25. About how many tickets in all were sold for Thursday and for Friday?

26. **Think About the Process** About how many more tickets were sold for the Wednesday concert than for the Friday concert? Write a number sentence that uses numbers rounded to the nearest ten to estimate. Explain your answer.

27. Which number sentence shows the best way to estimate how many fewer tickets were sold for the Friday concert than for the Thursday concert?

A 400 − 200 = 200

B 300 − 300 = 0

C 325 − 200 = 125

D 325 − 250 = 75

28. **Writing to Explain** About how many feet longer was a *Brachiosaurus* than a *T. rex*? Use compatible numbers to estimate. Explain why you chose the numbers you used.

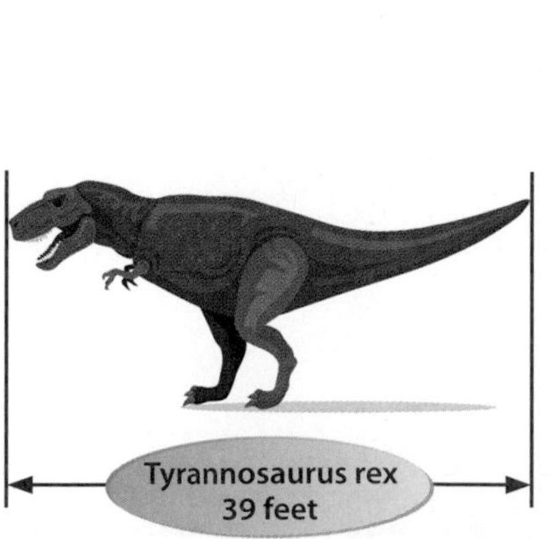

Mixed Problem Solving

The length of one year on a planet is the total time for the planet to make one complete trip around the Sun.

1. About how many fewer Earth days is a year on Mercury than a year on Earth?

2. About how many more Earth days is a year on Mars than a year on Earth?

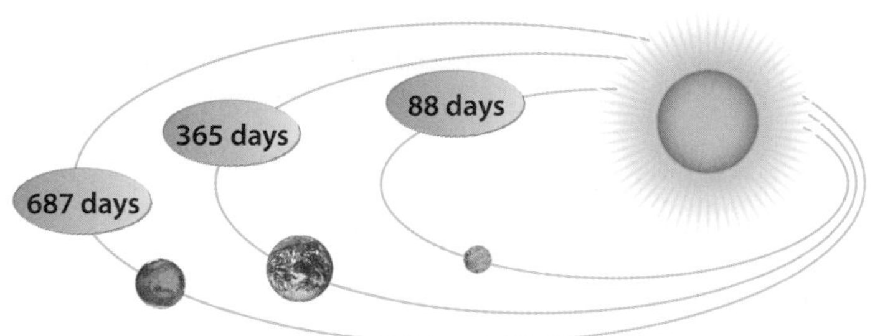

Data

Length of Year

Planet	Length of Year (in Earth Days)
Mercury	88
Venus	225
Earth	365
Mars	687
Jupiter	4,330
Saturn	10,756
Uranus	30,687
Neptune	60,190

3. Which planet has a digit 6 with a value of sixty thousand in the length of its year?

4. Which planet has a year that is about six thousand Earth days more than Jupiter's?

5. Which space object listed in the table at the right has an average surface temperature closest to Mercury's?

6. Write the average surface temperatures in order from least to greatest.

Data

Space Object	Average Surface Temperature
Mercury	332°F
Earth	59°F
Moon	225°F
Venus	854°F

7. **Strategy Focus** Solve. Use the strategy Make an Organized List.

Meg's favorite planet has at least 5 letters in its name. The length of its year is less than 10,000 Earth days. List all the planets that fit these clues.

Lesson

4-5

NS 2.1 Find the sum or difference of two whole numbers between 0 and 10,000.
Also **MR 2.1** Use estimation to verify the reasonableness of calculated results.

Subtracting 2-Digit Numbers

How can you use subtraction?

Animal rescue workers have released 16 of the eagles they have cared for. How many eagles are left?

Find 34 − 16. Use compatible numbers to estimate.
35 − 15 = 20

16 eagles released

34 eagles cared for

Guided Practice*

Do you know HOW?

In **1–8**, subtract.

1. 35 − 19

2. 42 − 17

3. 54 − 26

4. 61 − 38

5. 47 − 9

6. 73 − 25

7. 62 − 34

8. 47 − 25

Do you UNDERSTAND?

9. In the example above, why is regrouping needed? What was regrouped?

10. Workers at the park have cared for 52 falcons. If 28 falcons are still at the park, how many of the falcons have left?

a Write a number sentence.

b Estimate the answer.

c Solve the problem.

d Use the estimate to explain why your answer is reasonable.

Independent Practice

In **11–20**, subtract.

11. 26 − 19

12. 45 − 17

13. 37 − 18

14. 56 − 38

15. 83 − 61

16. 75 − 48

17. 22 − 13

18. 31 − 14

19. 53 − 6

20. 48 − 29

For another example, see Set D on page 97.

Subtract the ones.

6 ones > 4 ones
Regroup 1 ten 4 ones into 14 ones.

14 − 6 = 8 ones

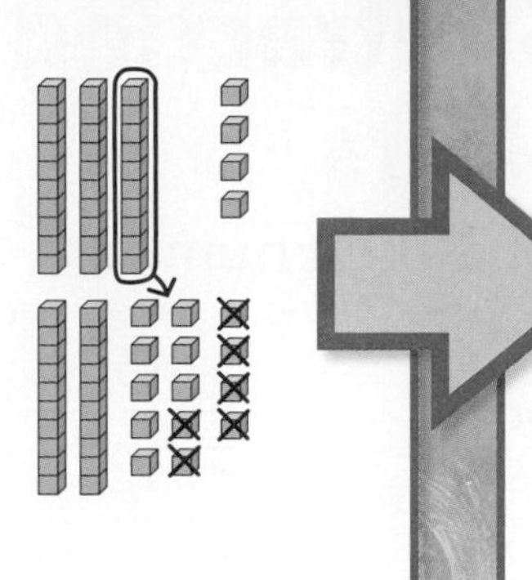

```
  2 14
  3̸ 4̸
- 1 6
-----
    8
```

Subtract the tens.

2 tens − 1 ten = 1 ten

34 − 16 = 18

```
  2 14
  3̸ 4̸
- 1 6
-----
  1 8
```

18 eagles are left.

The answer is reasonable because 18 is close to the estimate of 20.

Problem Solving

For **21** and **22**, use the table at the right.

21. Follow the steps below to find how many owls are left at the animal rescue park.

a Write a number sentence that can be used to solve the problem.

b Estimate the answer.

c Solve the problem.

d Use the estimate to explain why your answer is reasonable.

Data: Animal Rescue Park

Kind of Bird	Number Taken In	Number Released
Hawk	51	34
Kite	32	19
Owl	43	27

22. How many fewer kites than hawks have been released from the animal rescue park?

23. **Writing to Explain** Do you need to regroup to find 64 − 37? Explain your answer.

24. **Reasonableness** Trista subtracted 75 − 48 and got 37. Explain why her answer is not reasonable.

25. Andy's family bought two pumpkins. One pumpkin weighed 17 pounds, and the other pumpkin weighed 26 pounds.

a What was the total weight of the two pumpkins?

b What was the difference of their weights?

26. A sweater costs \$29. A shirt costs \$18. Meg has \$36. Which number sentence can be used to find how much money Meg would have left if she bought the sweater?

A 29 + 36 = ☐ **C** 36 − 29 = ☐

B 29 − 18 = ☐ **D** 36 − 18 = ☐

Lesson
4-6

NS 2.1 Find the sum or difference of two whole numbers between 0 and 10,000.

Models for Subtracting 3-Digit Numbers

Hands-On place-value blocks

How can you subtract 3-digit numbers with place-value blocks?

Use place value to subtract the ones first, the tens next, and then the hundreds.

Find 237 − 165.

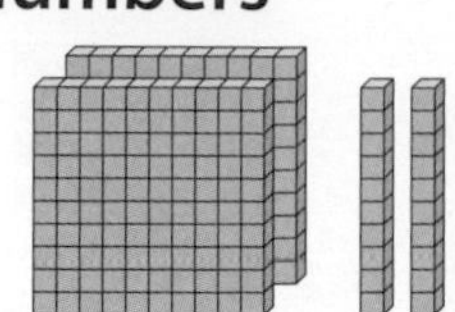

Show 237 with place-value blocks.

Guided Practice*

Do you know HOW?

In **1–6**, use place-value blocks or draw pictures to subtract.

1. 249 − 187

2. 261 − 134

3. 158 − 76

4. 384 − 182

5. 173 − 158

6. 325 − 213

Do you UNDERSTAND?

7. In the example above, why do you need to regroup 1 hundred into 10 tens?

8. Colby saved $256 doing jobs in the neighborhood. He bought a computer printer for $173. How much money did he have left? Draw a picture to help you subtract.

Independent Practice

In **9–18**, use place-value blocks or draw pictures to subtract.

You can draw squares to show hundreds, lines to show tens, and Xs to show ones. This picture shows 127.

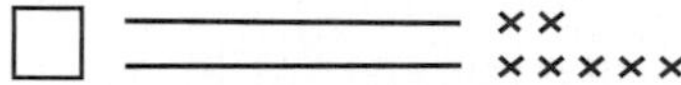

9. 347 − 263

10. 196 − 149

11. 218 − 117

12. 251 − 132

13. 423 − 291

14. 123 − 81

15. 265 − 84

16. 539 − 275

17. 376 − 153

18. 417 − 308

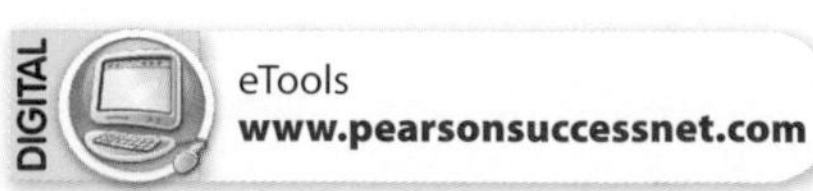

DIGITAL eTools www.pearsonsuccessnet.com

*For another example, see Set D on page 97.

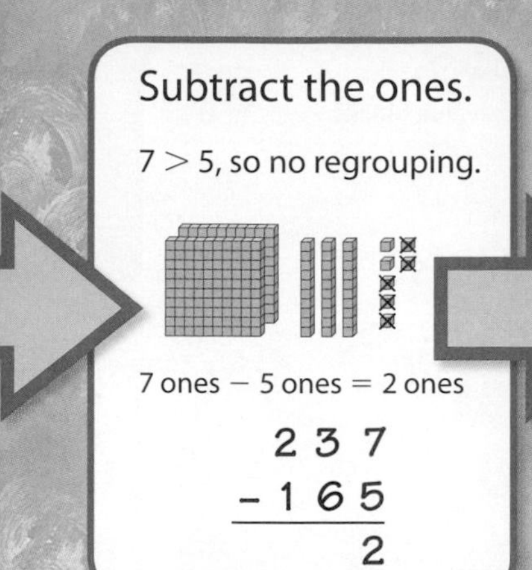

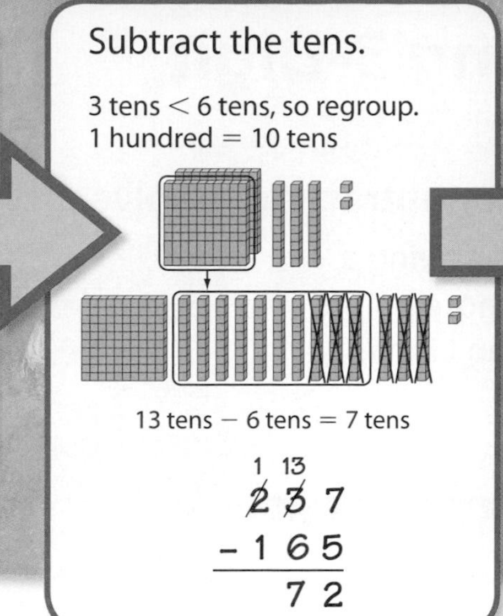

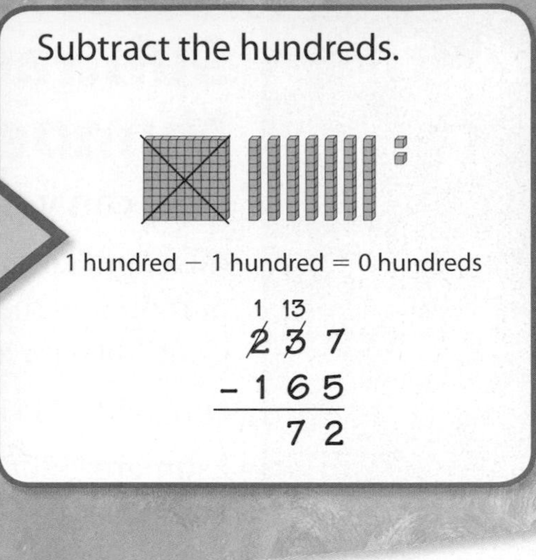

Problem Solving

For **19** and **20**, use the table at the right.

19. The Wen family drove from Cincinnati to Cleveland. Then the family drove to Chicago. How many miles did the family drive in all?

20. The Miller family is driving from Washington D.C. to Cleveland and then to Cincinnati. So far the Millers have traveled 127 miles. How many miles are left in their trip?

Trip Distances

Trip	Miles
Cleveland to Chicago	346
Cincinnati to Cleveland	249
Washington, D.C., to Cleveland	372

21. **Estimation** Round to the nearest hundred to estimate how many more musicians are in the world's largest accordion band than in the world's largest trombone band.

World's Largest Bands

Trombone	289 musicians
Accordion	625 musicians

22. An amusement park ride can hold 120 people. There were 116 people on the ride and 95 people waiting in line. Which number sentence can be used to find how many people in all were on the ride or waiting in line?

A 116 − 95 = ▢

B 120 + 116 + 95 = ▢

C 116 + 95 = ▢

D 120 − 95 = ▢

Lesson 4-7

NS 2.1 Find the sum or difference of two whole numbers between 0 and 10,000.
Also MR 2.1 Use estimation to verify the reasonableness of calculated results.

Subtracting 3-Digit Numbers

Hands-On
place-value blocks

How can you use subtraction to solve problems?

Mike and Linda are playing a game. How many more points does Mike have than Linda?

Find 528 − 341.

Estimate: 530 − 340 = 190

Another Example How do you subtract with two regroupings?

Find 356 − 189.

Estimate: 400 − 200 = 200

Step 1

Subtract the ones. Regroup if needed.

6 ones < 9 ones. So, regroup 1 ten into 10 ones.

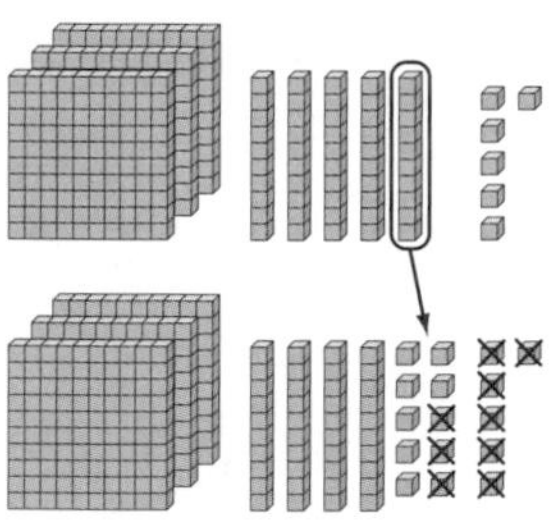

$$\begin{array}{r} \overset{4}{\cancel{5}}\,\overset{16}{\cancel{6}} \\ 3\ \ \ \ \ \ \ \\ -\,1\,8\,9 \\ \hline 7 \end{array}$$

Step 2

Subtract the tens. Regroup if needed.

4 tens < 8 tens. So, regroup 1 hundred into 10 tens.

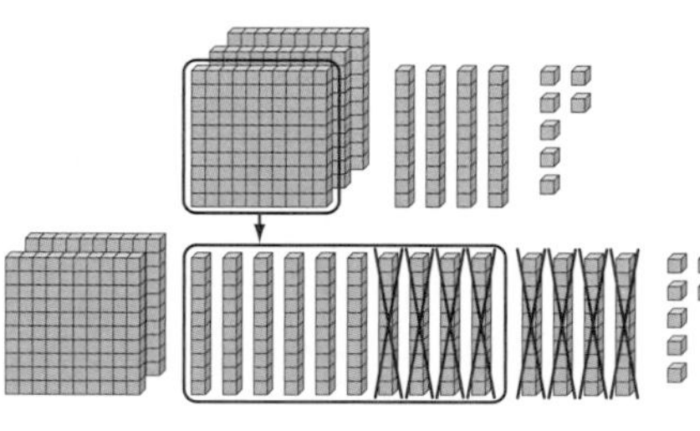

$$\begin{array}{r} \overset{2}{\cancel{3}}\,\overset{\overset{14}{\cancel{4}}}{\cancel{5}}\,\overset{16}{\cancel{6}} \\ -\,1\,8\,9 \\ \hline 6\,7 \end{array}$$

Step 3

Subtract the hundreds.

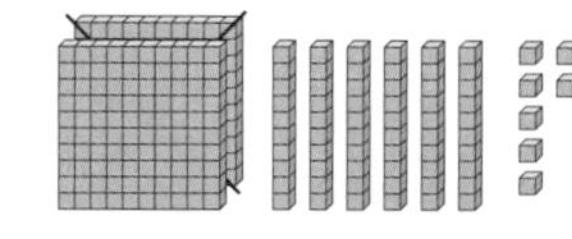

$$\begin{array}{r} \overset{2}{\cancel{3}}\,\overset{\overset{14}{\cancel{4}}}{\cancel{5}}\,\overset{16}{\cancel{6}} \\ -\,1\,8\,9 \\ \hline 1\,6\,7 \end{array}$$

The answer 167 is reasonable because it is close to the estimate.

Explain It

1. Why do you need to regroup both a ten and a hundred?
2. How is 3 hundreds 5 tens 6 ones the same as 3 hundreds 4 tens 16 ones? How is 3 hundreds 4 tens 16 ones the same as 2 hundreds 14 tens 16 ones?

Subtract the ones.

8 ones > 1 one
You do not regroup.

8 ones − 1 one = 7 ones

$$\begin{array}{r} 528 \\ -\ 341 \\ \hline 7 \end{array}$$

Subtract the tens.

Since 2 tens < 4 tens, regroup 1 hundred into 10 tens.

12 tens − 4 tens = 8 tens

$$\begin{array}{r} \scriptstyle 4\ 12 \\ \not{5}\,\not{2}\,8 \\ -\ 341 \\ \hline 87 \end{array}$$

Subtract the hundreds.

4 hundreds − 3 hundreds = 1 hundred

$$\begin{array}{r} \scriptstyle 4\ 12 \\ \not{5}\,\not{2}\,8 \\ -\ 341 \\ \hline 187 \end{array}$$

Mike has 187 more points.

187 is close to the estimate of 190. The answer is reasonable.

Guided Practice*

Do you know HOW?

In **1–6**, subtract. Use place-value blocks to help.

1. $\begin{array}{r} 374 \\ -\ 176 \\ \hline \end{array}$ **2.** $\begin{array}{r} 431 \\ -\ 145 \\ \hline \end{array}$

3. $\begin{array}{r} 568 \\ -\ 269 \\ \hline \end{array}$ **4.** $\begin{array}{r} 327 \\ -\ 238 \\ \hline \end{array}$

5. 574 − 86 **6.** 410 − 257

Do you UNDERSTAND?

7. In the example above, explain how to decide if regrouping is needed.

8. At the end of their game, Lora had 426 points, and Lou had 158 points. Complete **a–d** to find how many more points Lora had than Lou.

a Write a number sentence.

b Estimate the answer.

c Solve the problem.

d Explain why your answer is reasonable.

Independent Practice

Estimate and then find each difference. Check that your answers are reasonable.

9. $\begin{array}{r} 385 \\ -\ 296 \\ \hline \end{array}$ **10.** $\begin{array}{r} 276 \\ -\ 97 \\ \hline \end{array}$ **11.** $\begin{array}{r} 516 \\ -\ 238 \\ \hline \end{array}$ **12.** $\begin{array}{r} 629 \\ -\ 453 \\ \hline \end{array}$ **13.** $\begin{array}{r} 948 \\ -\ 569 \\ \hline \end{array}$

***For another example, see Set D on page 97.**

Independent Practice

Subtract. Estimate and check answers for reasonableness.

14. $392 - 195$

15. $754 - 476$

16. $819 - 652$

17. $123 - 84$

18. $435 - 367$

19. 236 − 78

20. 568 − 362

21. 147 − 58

22. 952 − 794

Problem Solving

For **23–25**, use the table at the right.

23. How many more swimmers signed up for the 1st session at Oak Pool than for the 1st session at Park Pool?

a Write a number sentence that you can use to solve the problem.

b Estimate the answer.

c Solve the problem.

d Explain why your answer is reasonable.

Swim Class Enrollment

Data

Pool	Number of Swimmers	
	1st session	2nd session
Oak	763	586
Park	314	179
River	256	63

24. Strategy Focus At River Pool, late enrollments added 29 swimmers to the 2nd session. The total number of swimmers enrolled in the 2nd session is how many fewer than in the 1st?

What addition sentence can help?

25. Write a Problem Write a problem using the information in the table. Include too much information in your problem.

26. The world's largest basket is the building in the photo. It is 186 feet tall from the base to the top of the handles. What is the height of the handles?

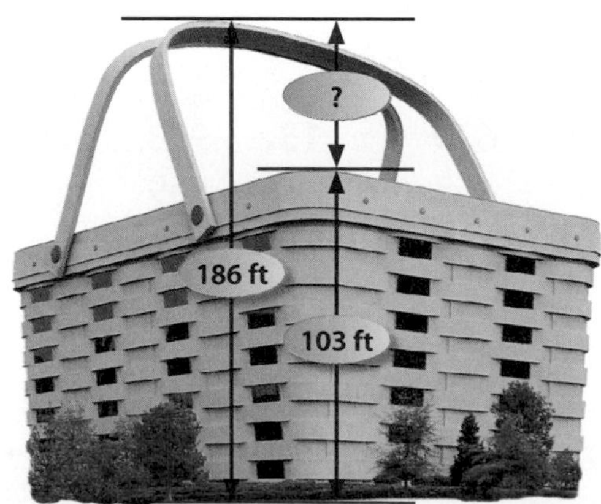

27. Ana made 14 hats. After giving some hats to Ty's family and some to Liv's family, she had 3 hats left. If she gave Ty's family 6 hats, which of these shows one way to find how many hats Ana gave to Liv's family?

A 14 + 3 − 6 = ▢

B 14 − 3 − 6 = ▢

C 14 − 3 + 6 = ▢

D 14 + 3 + 6 = ▢

Algebra Connections

Using Properties to Complete Number Sentences

The properties of addition can help you find missing numbers.

Commutative (Order) Property You can add numbers in any order and the sum will be the same. Example: $4 + 3 = 3 + 4$

Identity (Zero) Property The sum of any number and zero is that same number. Example: $9 + 0 = 9$

Associative (Grouping) Property You can group addends in any way and the sum will be the same. Example: $(5 + 2) + 3 = 5 + (2 + 3)$

Example: $26 + \square = 26$

Think: 26 plus what number is equal to 26?

You can use the Identity Property.

$26 + 0 = 26$

Example:

$36 + (14 + 12) = (36 + \square) + 12$

Think: What number makes the two sides equal?

Use the Associative Property.

$36 + (14 + 12) = (36 + 14) + 12$

Copy and complete. Write the missing number.

1. $19 + \square = 19$

2. $15 + 32 = 32 + \square$

3. $28 + (17 + 32) = (28 + \square) + 32$

4. $\square + 27 = 27$

5. $\square + 8 = 8 + 49$

6. $(16 + 14) + \square = 16 + (14 + 53)$

7. $(\square + 9) + 72 = 96 + (9 + 72)$

8. $\square + 473 = 473$

For **9** and **10**, copy and complete the number sentence. Use it to help solve the problem.

9. Vin walked 9 blocks from home to the library. Then he walked 5 blocks farther to the store. Later he walked the same path back to the library. How many more blocks would he need to walk to his home?

$9 + 5 = 5 + \square$

$\square$ blocks

10. Bo scored 7 points in each of two tosses in a game. Then he made one more toss. He had the same total score as Ed. Ed scored 8 points in one toss and 7 points in each of two tosses. How many points did Bo score on his last toss?

$7 + 7 + \square = 8 + 7 + 7$

$\square$ points

Lesson

4-8

NS 2.1 Find the sum or difference of two whole numbers between 0 and 10,000.

Subtracting Greater Numbers

How can you subtract greater numbers?

The corner store had 2,325 sunglasses at the beginning of last month. How many sunglasses were not sold?

Estimate: 2,000 − 1,000 = 1,000

2,325 sunglasses in all

?	1,227

1,227 sunglasses sold last month

Guided Practice*

Do you know HOW?

Estimate. Then subtract.

1. 5,485 − 1,327

2. 8,256 − 277

3. 8,476 − 6,274

4. 9,432 − 305

Do you UNDERSTAND?

5. **Reasonableness** How can you tell that the answer in the example above is reasonable?

6. The music store had 3,255 CDs. It sold 1,265 of them. How many CDs does the store still have?

Independent Practice

Estimate. Then subtract.

7. 2,554 − 1,372

8. 8,438 − 3,425

9. 9,431 − 3,440

10. 5,396 − 695

11. 4,444 − 2,503

12. 6,538 − 4,050

13. 3,997 − 899

14. 3,555 − 2,546

15. 7,495 − 536

16. 5,932 − 4,933

17. 9,226 − 342

18. 5,783 − 641

19. 2,186 − 1,374

20. 7,435 − 5,568

21. 7,613 − 6,948

22. 9,070 − 483

*For another example, see Set D on page 97.

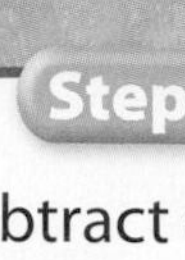

Step 1

Subtract ones. Regroup.

15 − 7 = 8

```
      1 15
  2, 3 2̸ 5̸
− 1, 2 2 7
----------
         8
```

Step 2

Subtract tens. Regroup.

11 − 2 = 9

```
       11
     2 1̸ 15
  2, 3̸ 2̸ 5̸
− 1, 2 2 7
----------
       9 8
```

Step 3

Subtract hundreds.

2 − 2 = 0

```
       11
     2 1̸ 15
  2, 3̸ 2̸ 5̸
− 1, 2 2 7
----------
     0 9 8
```

Step 4

Subtract thousands.

2 − 1 = 1

```
       11
     2 1̸ 15
  2, 3̸ 2̸ 5̸
− 1, 2 2 7
----------
  1, 0 9 8
```

1,098 sunglasses were not sold.

Problem Solving

Use the table at the right for **23–25**.

23. How many more pieces are needed to make a space ship than a truck?

Space Ship 8,965	
Truck 6,385	?

24. How many pieces are needed to make a robot and a car?

? Pieces in all

4,753	5,257

Model Toy Kits

Toy	Number of Pieces
Robot	4,753
Space Ship	8,965
Truck	6,385
Car	5,257

25. Which toy has more pieces, a car or a truck? How many more?

Truck 6,385	
Car 5,257	?

26. Writing to Explain Hector subtracted 1,954 from 8,254 and got 7,700. Is his answer reasonable? Why or why not?

27. Sandy played three video games. Her score for Game 1 was 1,856. Her score for Game 2 was 3,470. Her score for Game 3 was 4,674. How many more points did she score in Game 3 than in Game 1?

A 1,204 **B** 2,818 **C** 6,530 **D** 10,000

Lesson

4-9

NS 2.1 Find the sum or difference of two whole numbers between 0 and 10,000.

Subtracting Across Zero

How do you subtract from a number with one or more zeros?

How much more does the club need?

Find: 305 − 178

305:

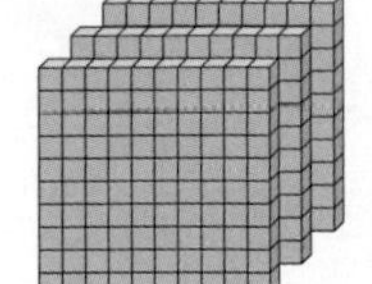

Another Example **How do you subtract from a number with two zeros?**

Find 600 − 164.

Subtract the ones.
0 ones < 4 ones
So, regroup.

$$\begin{array}{r} \overset{5}{\not6}\;\overset{10}{\not0}\;0 \\ -\;1\;6\;4 \\ \hline \end{array}$$

You can't regroup 0 tens.
So, regroup 1 hundred.
6 hundreds 0 tens =
5 hundreds 10 tens

$$\begin{array}{r} \overset{5}{\not6}\;\overset{\overset{9}{\not{10}}}{\not0}\;\overset{10}{\not0} \\ -\;1\;6\;4 \\ \hline \end{array}$$

Now regroup tens.
10 tens 0 ones = 9 tens 10 ones
Subtract the ones, the tens, and then the hundreds.

$$\begin{array}{r} \overset{5}{\not6}\;\overset{\overset{9}{\not{10}}}{\not0}\;\overset{10}{\not0} \\ -\;1\;6\;4 \\ \hline 4\;3\;6 \end{array}$$

Guided Practice*

Do you know HOW?

In **1–6**, find each difference.

1. 402 − 139

2. 300 − 157

3. 607 − 439

4. 820 − 167

5. 200 − 74

6. 501 −186

Do you UNDERSTAND?

7. In the examples above, why do you write 10 above the 0 in the tens place?

8. Lia says that she needs to regroup every time she subtracts from a number with a zero. Do you agree? Explain.

*For another example, see Set E on page 97.

Regroup to subtract the ones. There are no tens in 305 to regroup. Regroup 1 hundred.

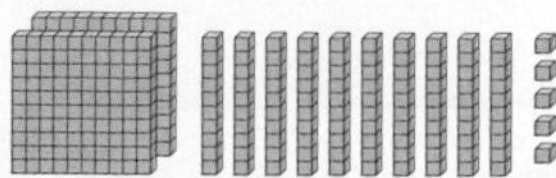

305 is the same as 2 hundreds 10 tens 5 ones.

```
  2 10
  3̸ 0̸ 5
- 1 7 8
```

Regroup the tens.

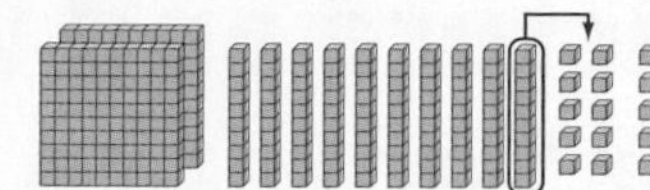

305 is the same as 2 hundreds 9 tens 15 ones.

```
     9
  2 1̸0̸ 15
  3̸ 0̸ 5̸
- 1 7 8
```

Subtract the ones, the tens, and then the hundreds.

```
     9
  2 1̸0̸ 15
  3̸ 0̸ 5̸
- 1 7 8
  1 2 7
```

The club needs $127.

Independent Practice

In **9–18**, find each difference.

9. $\begin{array}{r} 203 \\ -\ 157 \\ \hline \end{array}$ **10.** $\begin{array}{r} 400 \\ -\ 371 \\ \hline \end{array}$ **11.** $\begin{array}{r} 304 \\ -\ 95 \\ \hline \end{array}$ **12.** $\begin{array}{r} 401 \\ -\ 282 \\ \hline \end{array}$ **13.** $\begin{array}{r} 500 \\ -\ 64 \\ \hline \end{array}$

14. $\begin{array}{r} 600 \\ -\ 439 \\ \hline \end{array}$ **15.** $\begin{array}{r} 306 \\ -\ 248 \\ \hline \end{array}$ **16.** $\begin{array}{r} 705 \\ -\ 123 \\ \hline \end{array}$ **17.** $\begin{array}{r} 800 \\ -\ 74 \\ \hline \end{array}$ **18.** $\begin{array}{r} 900 \\ -\ 506 \\ \hline \end{array}$

Problem Solving

19. The average person eats about 126 pounds of fresh fruit in a year. Write a number sentence to help you find how many pounds of processed fruit you eat. Then solve.

20. Writing to Explain The Art Club needs 605 beads. A large bag of beads has 285 beads. A small bag of beads has 130 beads. Will one large bag and one small bag be enough beads? Explain.

21. Dina counted 204 items on the library cart. There were 91 fiction books, 75 nonfiction books, and some magazines. Which number sentence shows one way to find the number of magazines?

A 204 − 91 − 75 = ▢ **C** 204 − 91 + 75 = ▢

B 204 + 91 + 75 = ▢ **D** 204 + 91 − 75 = ▢

Lesson

4-10

MR 2.3 Use a variety of methods, such as words, numbers, symbols, charts, graphs, tables, diagrams, and models, to explain mathematical reasoning. Also **NS 2.0** Calculate and solve problems involving addition, subtraction, multiplication, and division.

Problem Solving

Draw a Picture and Write a Number Sentence

There are two lunch periods at Central School. If 221 students eat during the first lunch period, how many students eat during the second lunch period?

Central School
Grades K-6
458 Students

Another Example Are there other types of subtraction situations?

There are 85 students in Grade 2 at Central School. That is 17 more students than in Grade 3. How many students are in Grade 3?

Plan and Solve

Use a diagram to show what you know.

Gr. 2	85	
Gr. 3	?	17

You know there are 17 more students in Grade 2 than in Grade 3. So you can subtract to find the number of students in Grade 3.

Answer

$$\begin{array}{r} \overset{7}{\cancel{8}}\overset{15}{\cancel{5}} \\ -\ 1\ 7 \\ \hline 6\ 8 \end{array}$$

There are 68 students in Grade 3.

Check

Make sure the answer is reasonable.

85 − 17 is about 90 − 20, or 70.

68 is close to 70, so 68 is reasonable.

The number 68 is reasonable, and the question in the problem was answered.

Explain It

1. Harry wrote 17 + ☐ = 85 for the diagram above. Is his number sentence correct? Why or why not?
2. **Number Sense** Why can't we use the same type of diagram for this problem as we used for the problem at the top of the page?

Plan and Solve

Draw a diagram to show what you know.

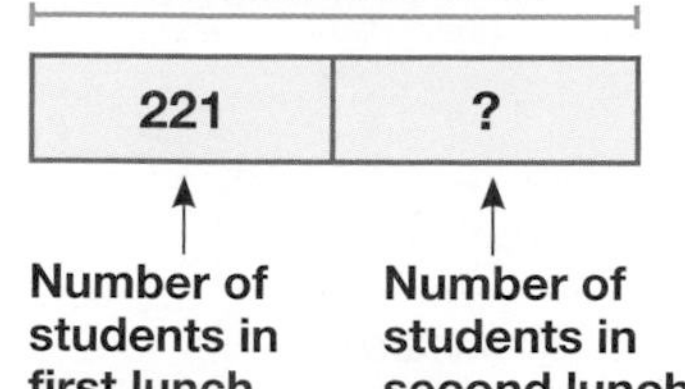

You know the total and one part so you can subtract to find the other part.

Answer

$$\begin{array}{r} 458 \\ -\ 221 \\ \hline 237 \end{array}$$

There are 237 students who eat during the second lunch period.

Check

Make sure the answer is reasonable.

458 − 221 is about 460 − 220, or 240.

237 is close to 240, so 237 is reasonable.

The number 237 is reasonable and the right question was answered.

Guided Practice*

Do you know HOW?

1. A total of 254 people entered a bicycle race. So far 135 people have finished the race. How many people are still racing?

254 people in all

135	?

Do you UNDERSTAND?

2. **Writing to Explain** How do you know what operation to use to solve Problem 1?

3. **Write a Problem** Write a problem that can be solved by adding or subtracting. Then give your problem to a classmate to solve.

Independent Practice

4. The height of Yosemite Falls is 2,425 feet. The height of Staircase Falls is 1,300 feet. How much taller is Yosemite Falls than Staircase Falls?

Yosemite Falls	2,425	
Staircase Falls	1,300	?

Stuck? Try this....

- What do I know?
- What am I asked to find?
- What diagram can I use to help understand the problem?
- Can I use addition, subtraction, multiplication, or division?
- Is all of my work correct?
- Did I answer the right question?
- Is my answer reasonable?

For another example, see Set F on page 97.

Independent Practice

In the United States House of Representatives, the number of representatives each state has depends upon the number of people who live in the state.

Use the table at the right for **5–7**.

U.S. Representatives

State	Number
California	53
Florida	25
Michigan	15
Texas	32

5. Copy and complete the diagram below. New York has 14 more representatives than Michigan. How many representatives does New York have?

? representatives in New York

15	14

6. Draw a diagram to find how many more representatives California has than Florida.

7. How many representatives are there all together from the four states listed in the chart?

8. When the House of Representatives started in 1789, there were 65 members. Now there are 435 members. How many more members are there now?

9. There are 50 states in the United States. Each state has 2 senators. Write a number sentence to find the total number of senators.

Think About the Process

10. Max exercised 38 minutes on Monday and 25 minutes on Tuesday. Which number sentence shows how long he exercised on the two days?

A 40 + 30 = ☐

B 40 − 30 = ☐

C 38 − 25 = ☐

D 38 + 25 = ☐

11. Nancy had $375 in the bank. She took $200 out to buy a scooter that cost $185. Which number sentence shows how much money is left in the bank?

A $375 + $185 = ☐

B $375 − $185 = ☐

C $375 − $200 = ☐

D $375 + $185 + $200 = ☐

Write each number in word form.

1. 3,914

2. 260,782

Order the numbers from greatest to least.

3. 608 643 640

4. 8,137 7,985 8,132

Round to the nearest thousand.

5. 1,298

6. 2,517

7. 4,036

8. 7,854

9. 9,625

Estimate and then find each sum or difference. Check that your answer is reasonable.

10. $\begin{array}{r} 96 \\ +\ 48 \\ \hline \end{array}$

11. $\begin{array}{r} 521 \\ -\ 73 \\ \hline \end{array}$

12. $\begin{array}{r} 657 \\ +\ 896 \\ \hline \end{array}$

13. $\begin{array}{r} 2{,}834 \\ +\ 759 \\ \hline \end{array}$

14. $\begin{array}{r} 4{,}103 \\ -\ 2{,}624 \\ \hline \end{array}$

Error Search Find each sum or difference that is not correct. Write it correctly and explain the error.

15. $\begin{array}{r} 69 \\ +\ 35 \\ \hline 94 \end{array}$

16. $\begin{array}{r} 338 \\ +\ 976 \\ \hline 1{,}214 \end{array}$

17. $\begin{array}{r} 502 \\ -\ 142 \\ \hline 360 \end{array}$

18. $\begin{array}{r} 7{,}149 \\ +\ 2{,}805 \\ \hline 9{,}954 \end{array}$

19. $\begin{array}{r} 9{,}473 \\ -\ 6{,}598 \\ \hline 2{,}975 \end{array}$

Number Sense

Estimating and Reasoning Write true or false for each statement. If it is false, explain why.

20. The sum of 68 and 35 is less than 100.

21. The difference 225 − 157 is greater than 100.

22. The sum of 1,647 and 1,712 is greater than 3,000.

23. The difference 1,306 − 417 is less than 1,000.

24. The sum of 258 and 409 is less than 700.

25. The difference 519 − 398 is less than 100.

Test Prep

1. Which number sentence is shown? (4-1)

A $3 + 7 = 10$

B $17 - 7 = 10$

C $10 - 3 = 7$

D $10 - 7 = 3$

2. To find $67 - 19$ on a hundred chart, Casie started at 67 and then went up 2 rows. What should she do next? (4-2)

31	32	33	34	35	36	37	38	39	40
41	42	43	44	45	46	47	48	49	50
51	52	53	54	55	56	57	58	59	60
61	62	63	64	65	66	67	68	69	70

A Move right 1 square.

B Move left 1 square.

C Move right 9 squares.

D Move left 9 squares.

3. To subtract $62 - 17$ mentally, Talia subtracted $62 - 20 = 42$ first. What should she do next? (4-3)

A Add $42 + 2$.

B Add $42 + 3$.

C Subtract $42 - 2$.

D Subtract $42 - 3$.

4. What regrouping is shown? (4-6)

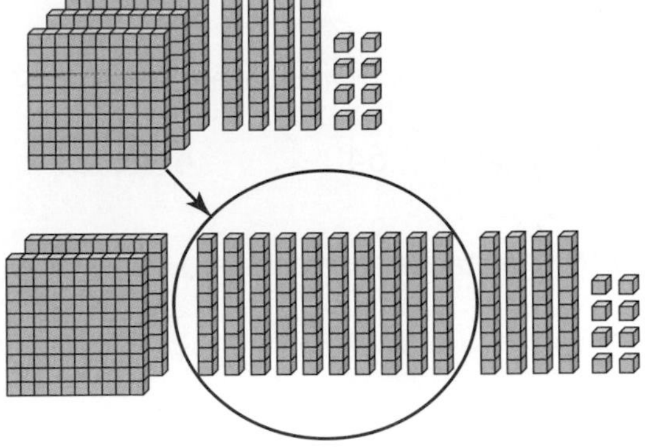

A 3 hundreds 4 tens 8 ones as 2 hundreds 3 tens 18 ones

B 3 hundreds 4 tens 8 ones as 2 hundreds 14 tens 8 ones

C 2 hundreds 4 tens 8 ones as 1 hundreds 14 tens 8 ones

D 2 hundreds 4 tens 8 ones as 2 hundreds 3 tens 18 ones

5. Gus scored 485 points on a video game. Olivia scored 196 points. How many more points did Gus score than Olivia? (4-7)

A 681

B 389

C 299

D 289

6. Of the 263 students at summer camp, 114 are boys. Which is the best estimate for the number of girls? (4-4)

A 250

B 150

C 120

D 100

Test Prep

7. Will had $205. He spent $67 on a bike. How much did he have left? (4-9)

A $162

B $148

C $138

D $38

8. Tropical Fish Warehouse received 98 goldfish on Monday. By Friday, they had sold 76 goldfish. How many goldfish had not been sold? (4-5)

A 22

B 32

C 38

D 174

9. What is 5,436 − 3,529? (4-8)

A 2,113

B 2,107

C 1,911

D 1,907

10. The zoo has 31 kinds of snakes and 22 kinds of lizards. Which number sentence shows the best way to estimate how many more kinds of snakes than lizards are in the zoo? (4-4)

A $30 - 20 = 10$

B $30 + 20 = 50$

C $40 - 20 = 20$

D $40 - 30 = 10$

11. Kim has 3,681 points. How many more points does she need to reach the gold level? (4-9)

Data

Level	Points Needed
Gold	5,000
Silver	4,000
Bronze	3,000

A 2,681

B 1,329

C 1,319

D 1,219

12. Nessie saw 23 deer and 17 squirrels at the park. Which picture can be used to find how many more deer than squirrels she saw? (4-10)

A

?	
23	17

B

17	
23	?

C

23	
17	?

D

23
17

Reteaching

Set A, pages 66–67

Write a number sentence. Solve.

Anthony has 10 flags. He gives 7 flags to his friends to wave during a parade on July 4th. How many flags does Anthony have left?

10 flags in all

7	?

Anthony has 3 flags left.

$10 - 7 = 3$

Remember that you can subtract to find a missing addend.

Write a number sentence. Solve.

1. The ceiling in a room is 12 feet high. A ladder is 8 feet tall. How much higher is the ceiling than the top of the ladder?

Set B, pages 68–70

Use a hundred chart to find 76 − 18.

51	52	53	54	55	56	57	58	59	60
61	62	63	64	65	66	67	68	69	70
71	72	73	74	75	76	77	78	79	80

Start at 76. Count up 2 rows to subtract 20. Move right 2 spaces because you only need to subtract 18.

$76 - 18 = 58$

Remember to first subtract the tens. Then move to the right or left if necessary to adjust the ones.

Use a hundred chart to subtract.

1. 88 − 20
2. 53 − 30
3. 52 − 14
4. 36 − 19
5. 66 − 43
6. 72 − 16

Set C, pages 72–76

Estimate 486 − 177.

One Way

$$\begin{array}{r} 486 \\ -\ 177 \\ \hline \end{array} \rightarrow \begin{array}{r} 500 \\ -\ 200 \\ \hline 300 \end{array}$$

Round each number to the nearest hundred.

Another Way

$$\begin{array}{r} 486 \\ -\ 177 \\ \hline \end{array} \rightarrow \begin{array}{r} 500 \\ -\ 175 \\ \hline 325 \end{array}$$

Use compatible numbers.

Remember to change each number in the same way when using mental math.

Use mental math to subtract.

1. 56 − 14
2. 97 − 34

Estimate. Round to the nearest ten.

3. 367 − 319
4. 872 − 112

Estimate. Use compatible numbers.

5. 472 − 228
6. 911 − 347

Set D, pages 78–84, 86–87

Find 236 − 127.

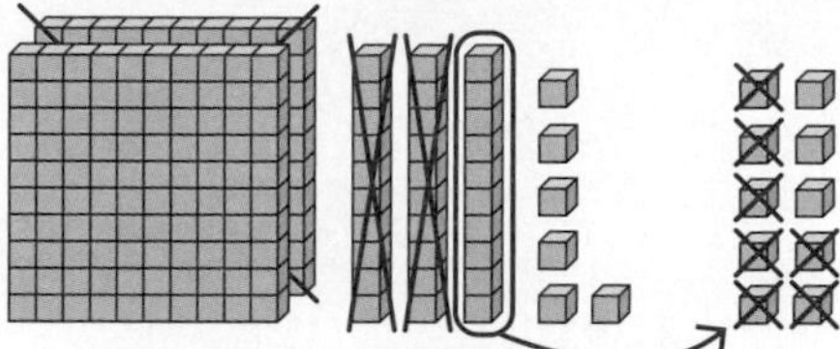

Estimate: 200 − 100 = 100

```
  2 16            2 16
 2 3̸ 6̸  Regroup  2 3̸ 6̸
-1 2 7   tens.   -1 2 7
     9            1 0 9
```

109 is close to 100, so the answer is reasonable.

Remember to subtract ones, then tens, and then hundreds.

Find each difference.

1. 53 − 29
2. 397 − 138
3. 1,516 − 753
4. 4,735 − 1,376

Set E, pages 88–89

Find 306 − 129.

Estimate: 300 − 100 = 200

```
                              9
 2 10                      2 1̸0̸ 16
 3̸ 0̸ 6   There are        3̸  0̸  6̸   Regroup
-1 2 9   no tens.        -1  2  9    tens.
         Regroup          1  7  7
         hundreds.
```

177 is close to 200, so the answer is reasonable.

Remember to regroup hundreds first when you have 0 tens.

Find each difference.

1. 308 − 125
2. 105 − 47
3. 200 − 136
4. 602 − 384

Set F, pages 90–92

There were 234 students who ordered hot lunches. Of those students, 136 students ordered ravioli. The other students ordered lasagna. How many students ordered lasagna?

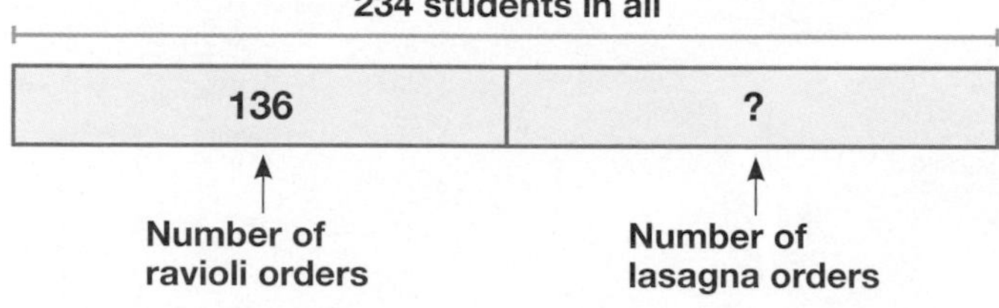

You know the total and one part, so you can subtract to find the other part: 234 − 136 = ▢.

234 − 136 = 98

98 students ordered lasagna.

Remember to draw a picture to help you write a number sentence.

Draw a picture. Write a number sentence and solve.

1. A total of 293 people entered a running race. So far, 127 people have finished the race. How many people are still racing?

Topic 5

Solids and Shapes

1 This sculpture in Madrid, Spain, is made from 6 tons of bananas! Which solid figure best describes the shape of this sculpture? You will find out in Lesson 5-1.

2 Which geometric term describes the wings of a biplane? You will find out in Lesson 5-4.

3 Which polygons did famous architect Frank Lloyd Wright use when he designed this home in Stanford, CA? You will find out in Lesson 5-5.

4 What is the first thing you notice about this bicycle? You will find out what is unusual in Lesson 5-7.

Review What You Know!

Vocabulary

Choose the best term from the box.

- circle
- cube
- square
- triangle

1. A shape that has 4 sides all the same length is called a __?__.
2. A solid that has six square faces is called a __?__.
3. A shape with 3 sides is called a __?__.

Name Solids and Shapes

Write the name of each figure.

4. 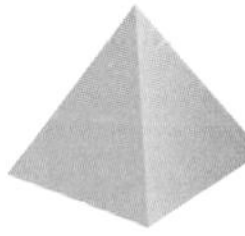

5. 

6. 

7. 

Shapes

Write the number of sides each figure has.

8. 

9. 

10. 

11. 

12. **Writing to Explain** Which solid rolls, a cone or a cube? Explain why it rolls.

Lesson
5-1

MG 2.5 Identify, describe, and classify common three-dimensional geometric objects (e.g., cube, rectangular solid, sphere, prism, pyramid, cone, cylinder). Also MG 2.6

Solid Figures

What is a solid figure?

A solid figure is a geometric figure that has length, width, and height.

Some common solid figures and their names are shown at the right.

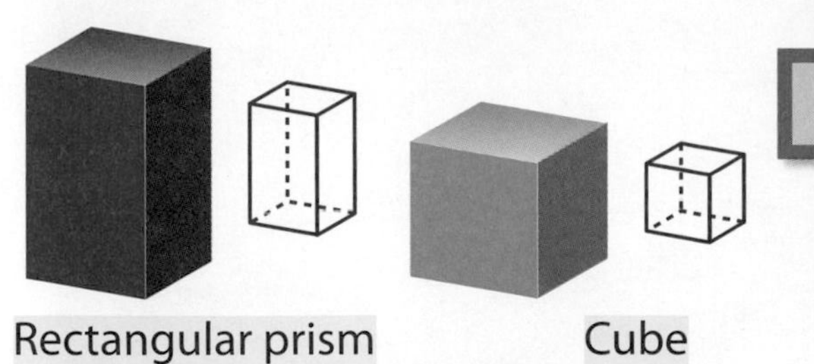

Rectangular prism   Cube

Another Example How do solid figures help you describe objects in the world around you?

Many things in the real world are shaped like the solid figures shown above. Name the solid figure each object looks like.

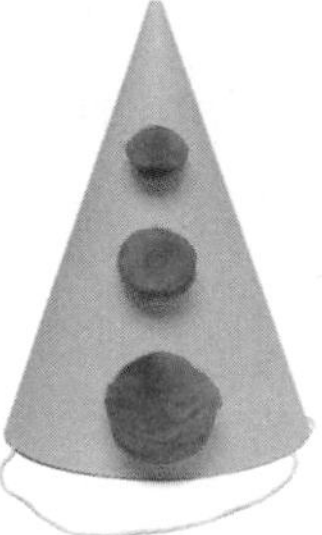

The clown's hat looks like a cone.

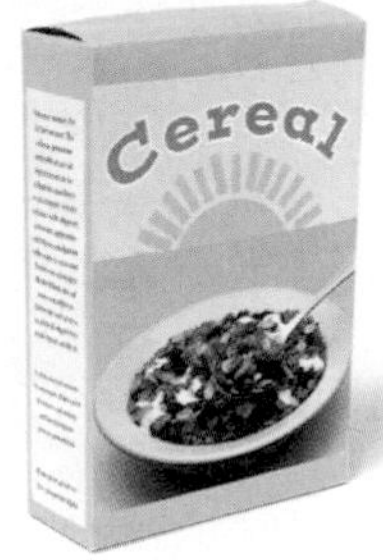

The cereal box looks like a rectangular prism.

The tennis ball looks like a sphere.

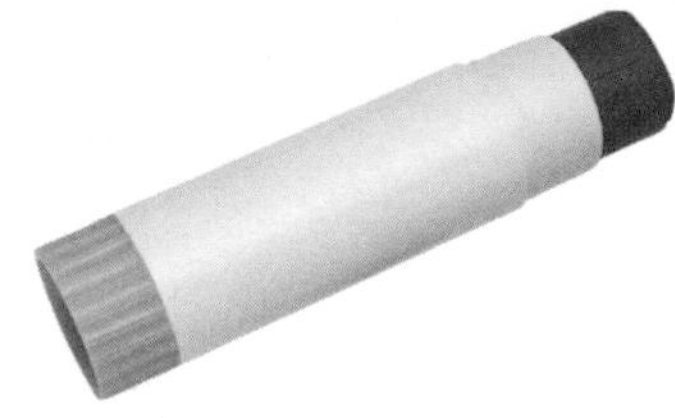

The glue stick looks like a cylinder.

Explain It

1. Explain why the clown's hat looks like a cone.
2. Why is it wrong to say that the cereal box looks like a cube?
3. Which of the 4 objects pictured can roll? Explain.

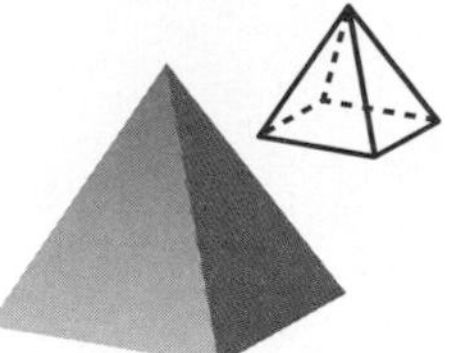

Pyramid

Cylinder

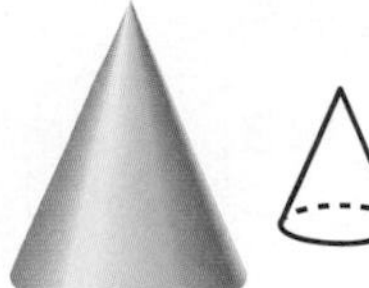

Cone

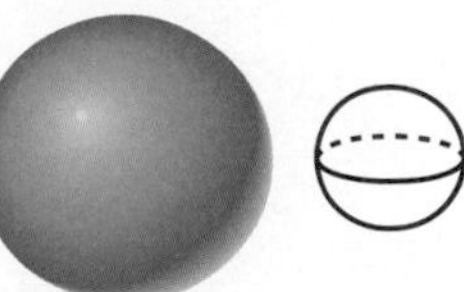

Sphere

Guided Practice*

Do you know HOW?

Name the solid figure.

1. 

2. 

Name the solid figure that each object looks like.

3. 

4. 

5. 

6. 

Do you UNDERSTAND?

For **7–10**, look at the solid figures above.

7. Which solid figure has no flat surfaces?

8. Which solid figures can roll? Which cannot roll?

9. How are the cone and the cylinder alike? How are they different?

10. How are the cone and the pyramid alike? How are they different?

11. **Writing to Explain** Look at the pictures below. Does the name of a solid figure change if the figure is turned on its side? Explain.

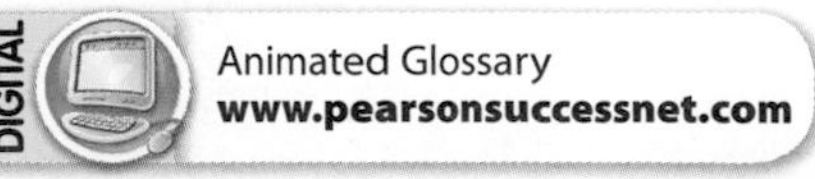

**For another example, see Set A on page 124.*

Independent Practice

In **12–17**, name the solid figure.

12. 

13. 

14. 

15. 

16. 

17. 

In **18–26**, name the solid figure that each object looks like.

18. 

19. 

20. 

21. 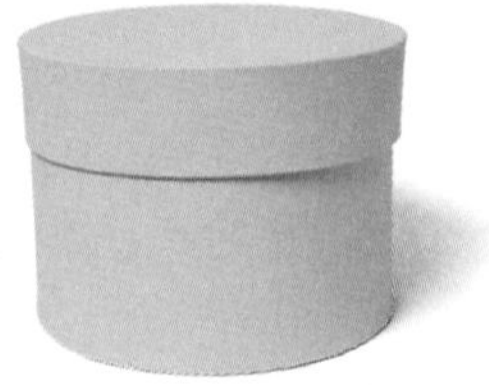

22. 

23. 

24. 

25. 

26. 

In **27–32**, name an object in your classroom or at home that is shaped like each solid figure.

27. Sphere

28. Cube

29. Cylinder

30. Rectangular prism

31. Pyramid

32. Cone

Problem Solving

Kayla used blocks to make the figures shown in **33** and **34**. Give the solid figure name for each type of block. Tell how many blocks of each type Kayla used in each figure.

33.

34.

35. Three pizzas were cut into 8 slices each. Six friends ate all of the pizza, and each person ate the same number of slices. How many slices did each person eat?

36. **Writing to Explain** Spheres and cylinders are both solid figures that can roll. Why are so many sports played with objects shaped like spheres rather than objects shaped like cylinders?

37. What solid figure would you make if you stacked two rectangular prisms of the same size?

38. What solid figures can be stacked to make a round tower with a flat top?

39. Which solid figure name best describes the shape of the banana sculpture shown at the right?

A Cylinder

B Pyramid

C Rectangular prism

D Sphere

40. **Number Sense** There are 10 girls and 9 boys in Catherine's class. Which number sentence can be used to find how many children are in the class?

A $10 \times 9 = \square$ **C** $10 - 9 = \square$

B $10 \div 9 = \square$ **D** $10 + 9 = \square$

Lesson

5-2

MG 2.0 Describe and compare the attributes of plane and solid geometric figures and use their understanding to show relationships and solve problems.

Relating Solids and Shapes

How can you describe parts of solid figures?

Some solid figures have faces, vertices, and edges.

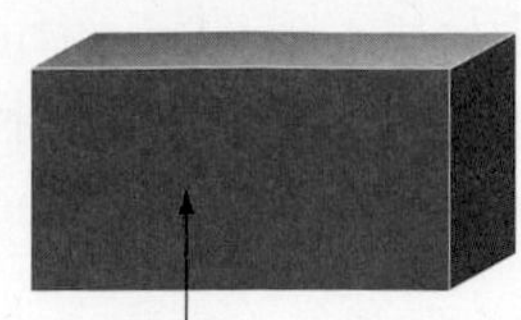

Each flat surface is a face.

A rectangular prism has 6 faces.
The shape of each face is a rectangle.

Another Example **Do all solid figures have faces, edges, and vertices?**

Flat surfaces of solid figures that can roll are not called faces.

A cylinder has two flat surfaces.

But a cylinder can roll.

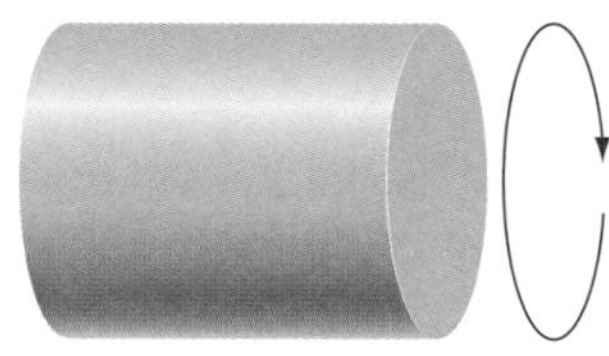

So, the flat surfaces of a cylinder are not faces.

Remember, an edge is where 2 faces meet. So, a cylinder does not have edges or vertices.

A cone does not have faces or edges. A cone has one vertex.

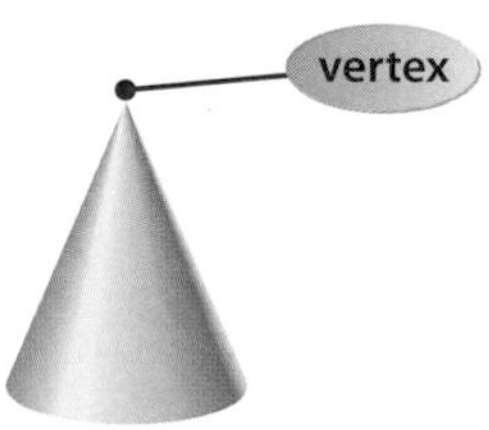

Explain It

1. Explain why the flat surface of a cone is not called a face.
2. Do you think that the flat surfaces of a pyramid are called faces? Explain.

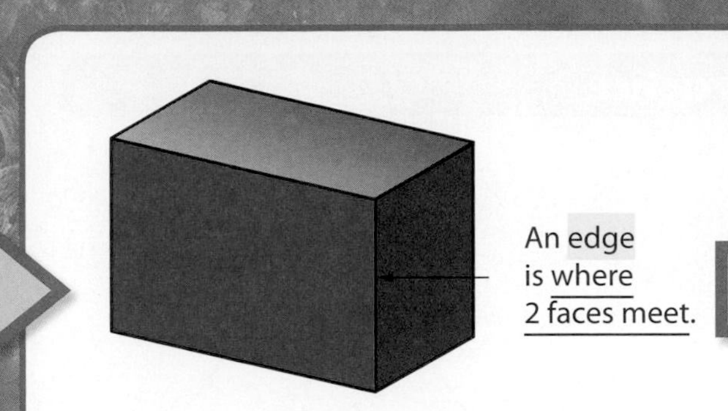

A rectangular prism has 12 edges.

A rectangular prism has 8 vertices.

Guided Practice*

Do you know HOW?

For **1–6**, use the cube and cone pictured below.

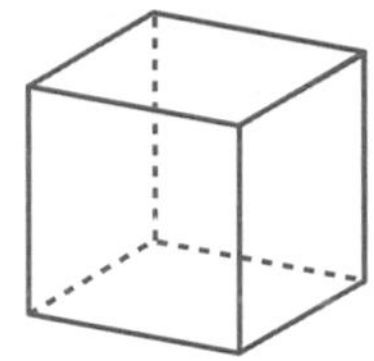

1. How many faces does the cube have in all?
2. What is the shape of each face of the cube?
3. How many edges does the cube have?
4. How many vertices does the cube have?
5. How many edges does the cone have?
6. How many vertices does the cone have?

Do you UNDERSTAND?

For **7–10**, use the solids pictured below.

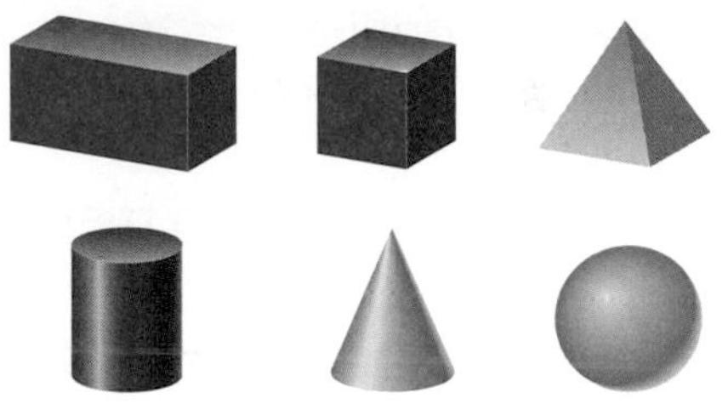

7. Which solid has faces that are all the same size and shape? What is the name of this shape?
8. Which two solids have the same number of edges?
9. Which of these solid figures do not have faces?
10. Besides the rectangular prism, which solid has 6 faces, 12 edges, and 8 vertices?

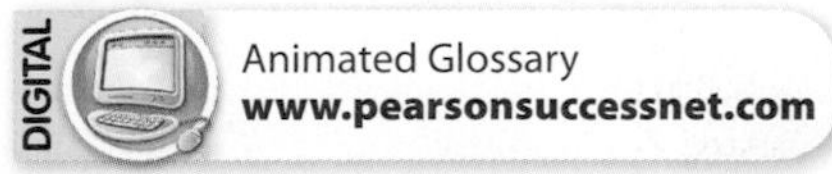

For another example, see Set A on page 124.

Independent Practice

For **11–14**, use the pyramid pictured at the right.

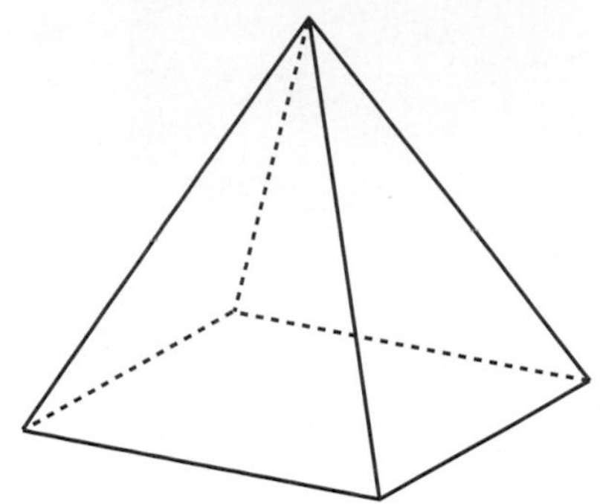

11. How many edges does this pyramid have?

12. How many vertices does this pyramid have?

13. How many faces does this pyramid have?

14. What are the shapes of the faces? How many faces of each shape are there?

Problem Solving

15. **Writing to Explain** Why does a cube have the same number of faces, edges, and vertices as a rectangular prism?

This wedge of cheese looks like a solid figure called a *triangular prism*. Use the photo for **16–19**.

16. How many faces does a triangular prism have?

17. What are the shapes of the faces?

18. How many vertices does a triangular prism have?

19. How many edges does a triangular prism have?

20. Tran bought a bag of 24 stickers. He plans to put one sticker on each face of this cube. How many stickers will be left over?

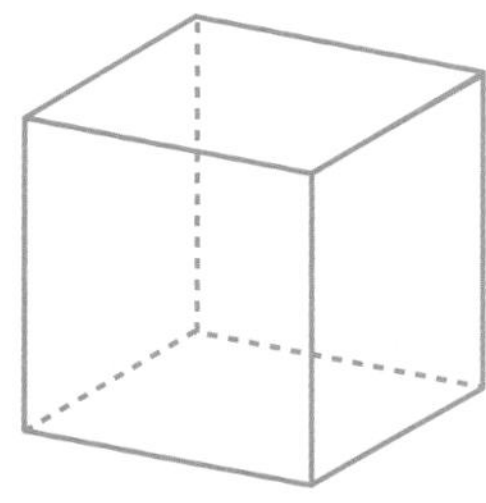

A 12 **C** 18

B 16 **D** 21

21. What is the total value of the 8 coins shown below?

A 36¢ **C** 56¢

B 46¢ **D** 71¢

Mixed Problem Solving

Different musical instruments make different sounds. The shape of an instrument can affect how it sounds. Use the table at the right to answer **1–5**.

1. Which instrument is made up of a long, narrow rectangular prism and a short cylinder?

2. Which of the percussion instruments has a cylinder shape?

3. Which instrument has the shape of a 3-sided figure?

4. What solid figure does the recorder look like?

5. The instrument that makes the sound with the greatest number of decibels is the loudest. Which instrument in the table below can make the loudest sound?

Musical Instruments

Name of Instrument	Group of Instruments
Banjo	String
Drum	Percussion
Recorder	Woodwind
Triangle	Percussion

Data

Instrument	Maximum Loudness (in decibels)
Trumpet	95
Cymbal	110
Bass drum	115
Piano	100

6. **Strategy Focus** Solve. Use the strategy Try, Check, and Revise.

   Elian plays three instruments. The drum weighs 5 pounds more than the guitar. The trumpet weighs 5 pounds less than the guitar. The trumpet weighs 3 pounds. How many pounds does the drum weigh?

Lesson
5-3

MG 2.6 Identify common solid objects that are the components needed to make a more complex solid object.
Also MG 2.5

Breaking Apart Solids

What solid figures can you make by breaking apart other solid figures?

You can cut a rectangular prism into 2 smaller rectangular prisms.

2 rectangular prisms

Guided Practice*

Do you know HOW?

In **1** and **2**, name the solid figures you would get if you cut the solid figure as shown.

1.

2. 

Do you UNDERSTAND?

3. What is an example of a rectangular prism that might be cut like the figure above?

4. Suppose you put two cubes together side-by-side. Draw the figure you would make. Then name the figure.

Independent Practice

In **5–10**, describe the solid figures you would get if you cut the solid figure as shown.

5. 

6. 

7. 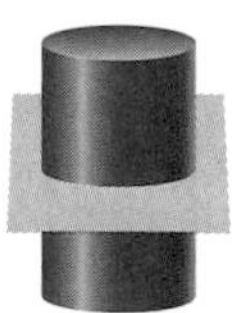

8. 

9. 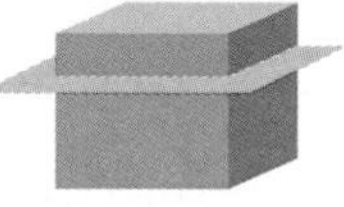

10. 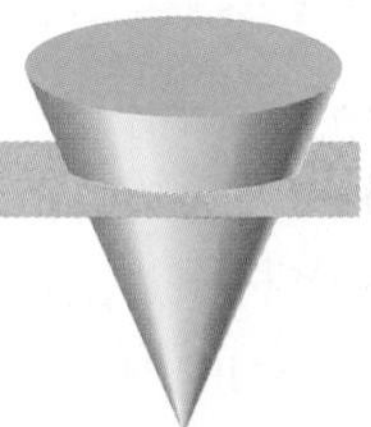

*For another example, see Set B on page 124.

Sphere

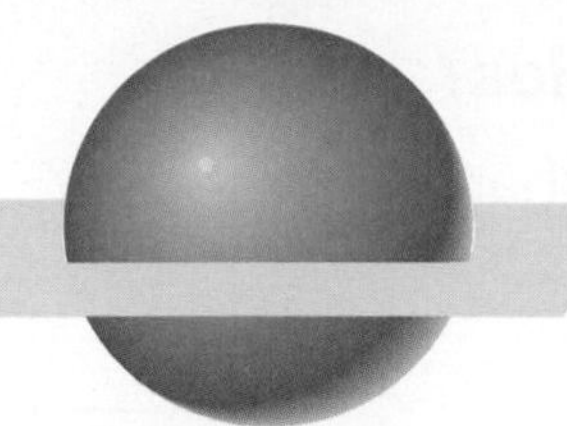

You can cut a sphere into 2 parts that each have 1 flat surface.

Cone

You can cut a cone into 1 smaller cone and 1 other solid figure.

Problem Solving

11. Jackson has an 18 inch wooden block. He cuts 2 inches off the block. If he makes 3 more cuts of the same length, how long is the piece of block he has left?

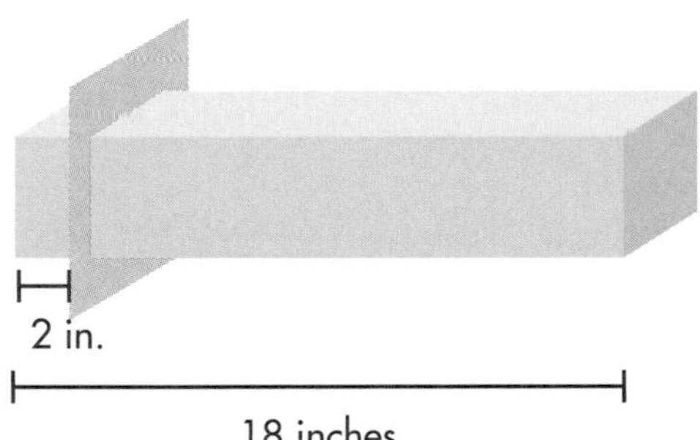

12. **Estimation** Ernesto has two library books. The book about bridges has 218 pages. The book about buildings has 54 pages. About how many more pages does the book about bridges have than the book about buildings? Round each number to the nearest ten to estimate.

13. Heather made a model of a house. What solid figures would she get if she cut the figure as shown?

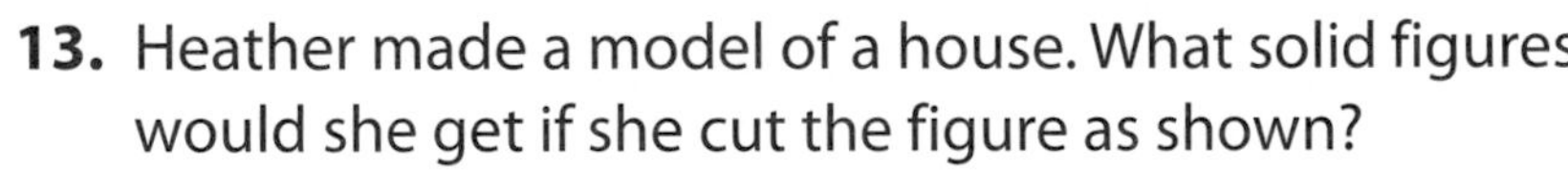

14. Mr. Louie walked along the front of the building. Then he walked along the side of the building. The front of the building was 138 feet long. The side of the building was 79 feet long. How many feet did Mr. Louie walk?

15. Which solid figure name best describes the shape of the juice can?

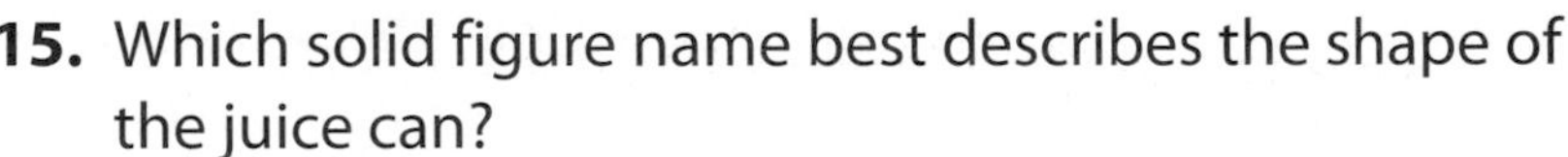

A Cube **C** Pyramid

B Cylinder **D** Sphere

Lesson

5-4

MG 2.0 Describe and compare the attributes of plane and solid geometric figures and use their understanding to show relationships and solve problems.
Also **MG 2.4**.

Lines, Segments, and Angles

How do you describe lines and angles?

Lines and parts of lines are used to make shapes and solid figures.

A point is an exact position.

A line is a set of points that is endless in two directions.

A line segment is a part of a line with two endpoints.

Another Example **You can describe an angle by the size of its opening.**

A ray is a part of a line with one endpoint.

An angle is formed by two rays with the same endpoint. That endpoint is the vertex of the angle.

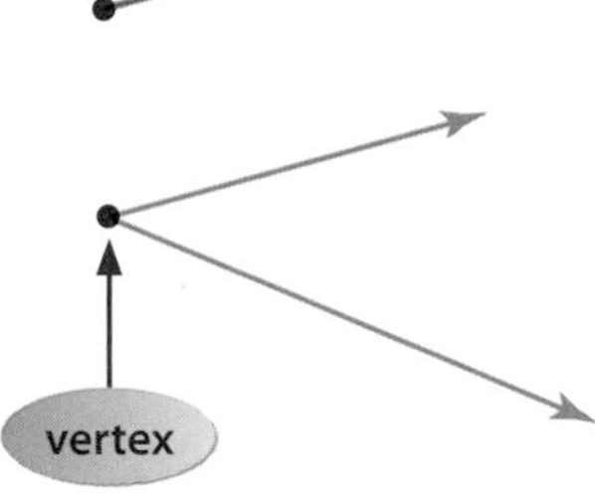

A right angle makes a square corner.

An acute angle is an angle that is less than a right angle.

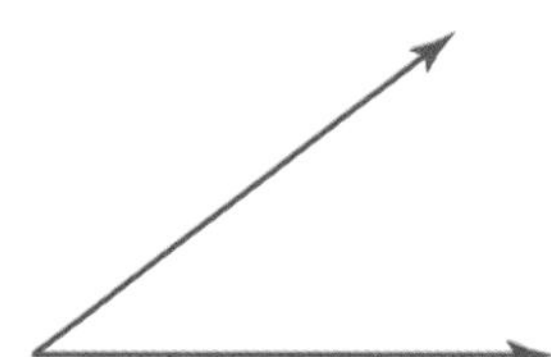

An obtuse angle is an angle that is greater than a right angle.

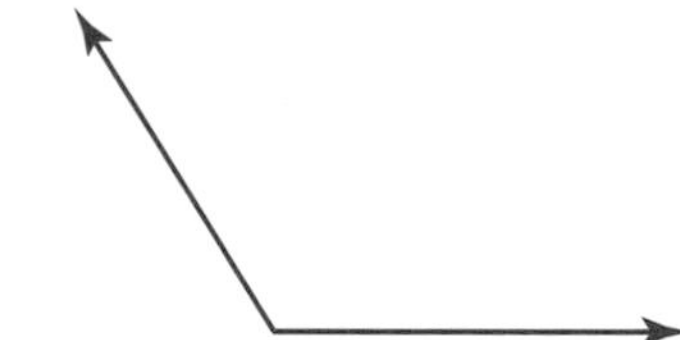

The two lines, line segments, or rays that make a right angle are perpendicular.

Explain It

1. How can you use the corner of a note card to decide if an angle is acute, right, or obtuse?
2. Explain why the two rays shown do not form an angle.

Intersecting lines cross at one point.

Parallel lines never cross.

Guided Practice*

Do you know HOW?

In **1** and **2**, write the name for each.

1.

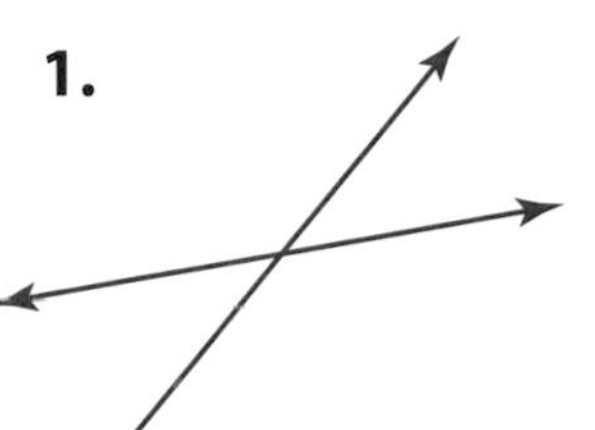

2.

In **3** and **4**, tell if each angle is right, acute, or obtuse.

3. **4.**

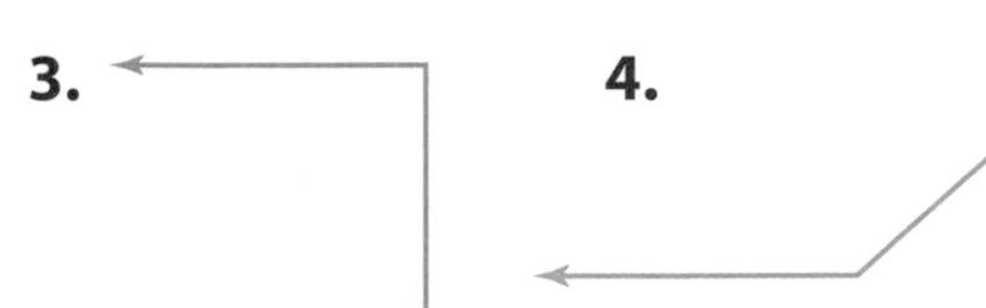

Do you UNDERSTAND?

5. What type of lines do the railroad tracks look like?

6. Describe something in your classroom that reminds you of perpendicular line segments.

Independent Practice

In **7–10**, write the name for each.

7. **8.** • **9.** **10.**

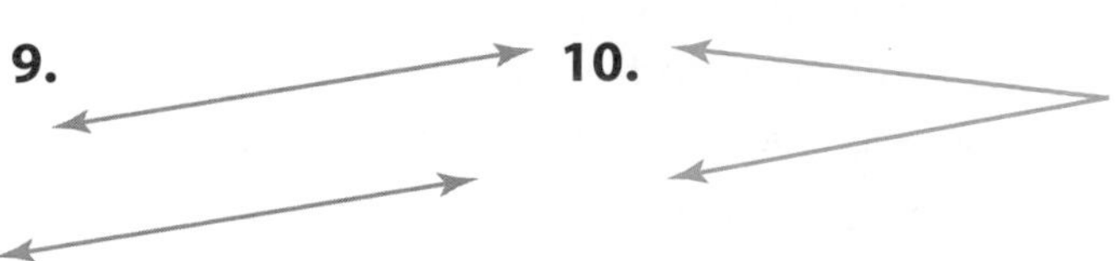

DIGITAL Animated Glossary **www.pearsonsuccessnet.com**

For another example, see Set C on page 124.

Independent Practice

In **11–18**, draw and label a picture of each.

11. Line segment **12.** Line **13.** Parallel lines **14.** Intersecting lines

15. Obtuse angle **16.** Right angle **17.** Ray **18.** Acute angle

Problem Solving

For **19–21**, use the map at the right. Tell if the two streets named look like intersecting lines or parallel lines.

19. Oak Street and Birch Street

20. Birch Street and Elm Street

21. If the streets continue, what kind of lines would Elm Street and Oak Street look like? Explain.

22. Look at the wings on the plane. What geometric term can you use to describe them?

23. Which best describes the place where these two lines intersect?

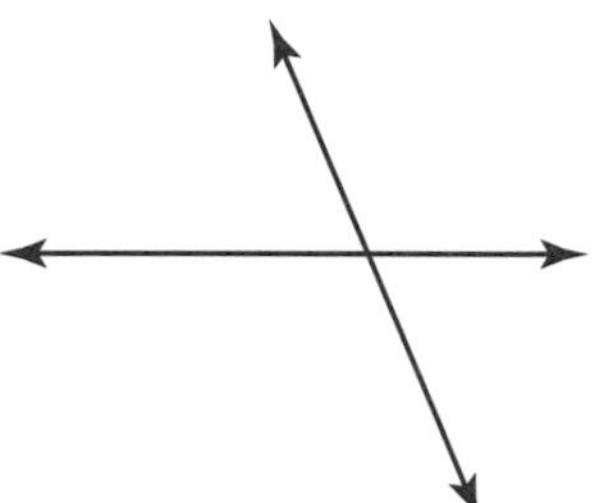

A Line **C** Line segment

B Point **D** Parallel lines

24. **Writing to Explain** Rosie rode her bicycle for 26 blocks. Luis rode his bicycle for 41 blocks. How many more blocks did Luis ride than Rosie? Explain how you found your answer.

25. Jessi is making a list of the states she has visited. So far, she has written the names of 7 states. If there are 50 states in all, how many states are not on Jessi's list?

50 states in all

7	?

In **26–28**, tell what type of angle is formed by the hands of the clock.

26.

27.

28.

29. **Writing to Explain** Are all obtuse angles the same size? Draw a picture to explain your answer.

For **30** and **31**, write the number that makes each number sentence true.

30. 3,000 + ▢ + 10 + 7 = 3,517

31. 50,000 + ▢ + 70 = 50,670

32. **Reasonableness** Marion says that the difference between 2,649 and 1,358 is about 2,300. Is her estimate reasonable? Explain your answer.

33. Which picture shows two perpendicular line segments?

A

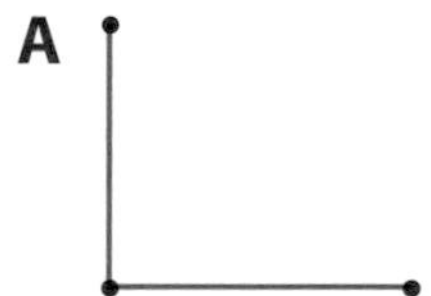

B

C

D

34. Megan has a chunk of cheese that is shaped like a rectangular prism. She cuts the chunk into 2 pieces.

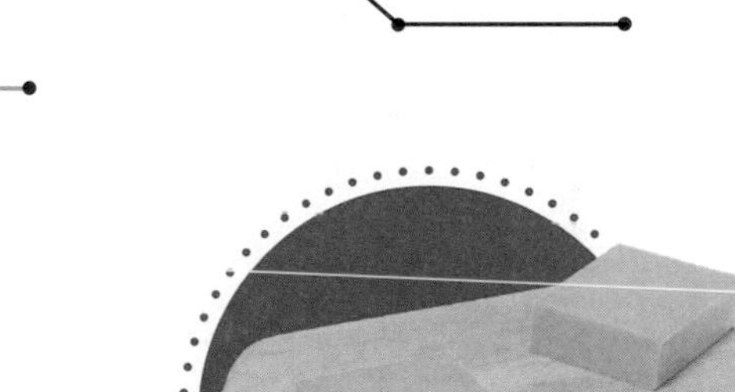

a Describe what each piece looks like.

b How many vertices, faces, and edges does each piece have?

35. In order to survive, a squirrel needs to gather about 825 acorns throughout the year. If a squirrel finds 167 acorns during the fall, about how many more acorns does it need to find during the rest of the year?

825 acorns in all

167	?

Lesson

5-5

MG 2.1 Identify, describe, and classify polygons (including pentagons, hexagons, and octagons). Also **MG 2.0**

Polygons

What is a polygon?

A polygon is a closed figure made up of line segments. Each line segment is a side of the polygon. The point where two sides meet is a vertex of the polygon.

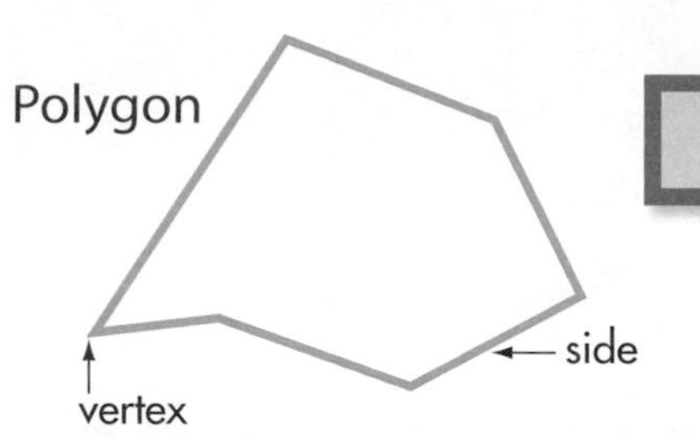

Guided Practice*

Do you know HOW?

Name the polygon.

1. 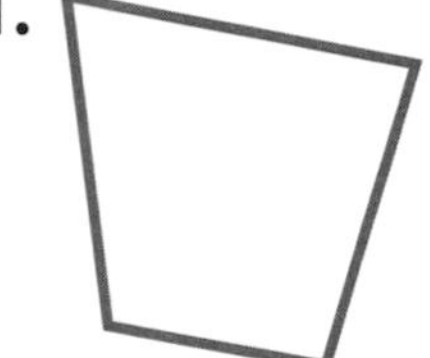

2. 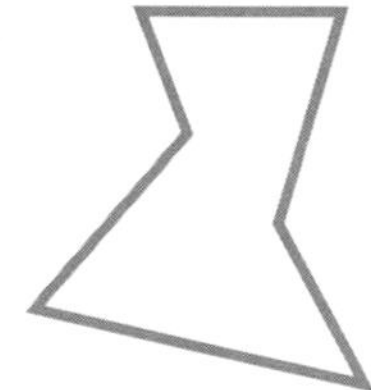

Is each figure a polygon? If it is not, explain why.

3. 

4. 

Do you UNDERSTAND?

Draw a polygon with 3 sides. Use the polygon for Exercises **5–7**.

5. How many vertices are there?

6. How many angles are there?

7. What is the name of the polygon?

8. Suppose that a polygon has 10 sides. How many angles does it have?

9. Describe an everyday object that is a model of a polygon. What is the name of the polygon?

Independent Practice

Name the polygon.

10. 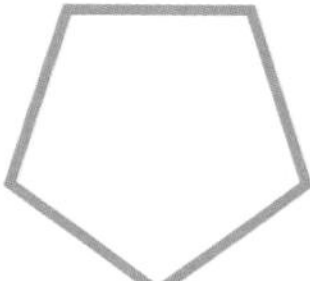

11. 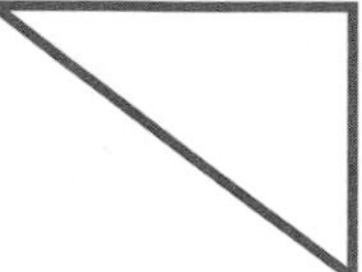

12. 

13. 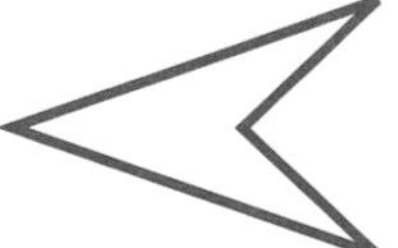

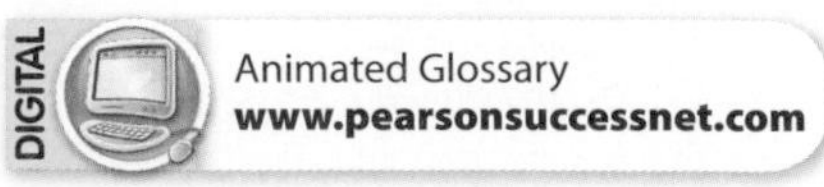

*For another example, see Set D on page 125.

Polygons are named by the number of sides they have. The sides form an angle at each vertex.

Data

Polygon	Number of Sides	Number of Vertices
Triangle	3	3
Quadrilateral	4	4
Pentagon	5	5
Hexagon	6	6
Octagon	8	8

Is each figure a polygon? If not, explain why.

14. 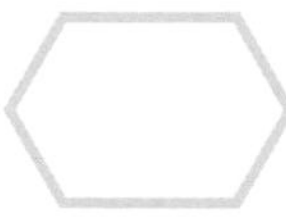

15. 

16. 

17. 

Problem Solving

In **18–21**, name the polygon that each traffic sign looks most like.

18. 

19. 

20. 

21. 

22. Reasoning Which polygon comes next in the pattern? Explain your answer.

23. What polygons were used to design this house?

24. Which polygon best represents the top of the box?

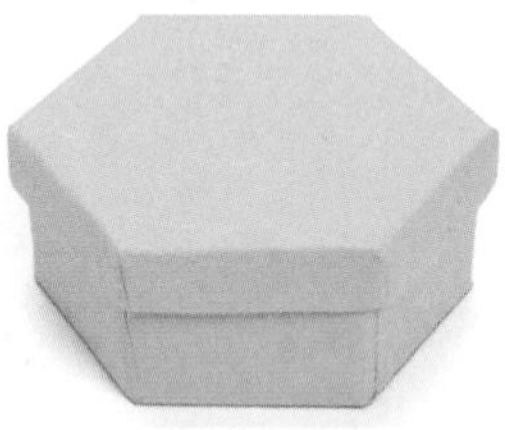

A Quadrilateral **C** Pentagon

B Octagon **D** Hexagon

Lesson
5-6

MG 2.2 Identify attributes of triangles (e.g., two equal sides for the isosceles triangle, three sides for the equilateral triangle, right angle for the right triangle).
Also MG 2.0, 2.4

Triangles

How can you describe triangles?

Triangles can be described by their sides.

Equilateral triangle

All three sides are the same length.

Isosceles triangle

At least two sides are the same length.

Scalene triangle

No sides are the same length.

Guided Practice*

Do you know HOW?

Tell if each triangle is equilateral, isosceles, or scalene.

1. 

2. 

Tell if each triangle is right, acute, or obtuse.

3. 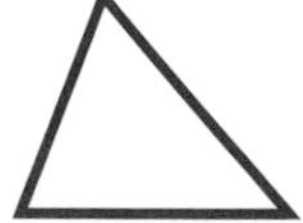

4. 

Do you UNDERSTAND?

5. How many acute angles are in an acute triangle?

6. How many obtuse angles are in an obtuse triangle?

7. Can a right triangle also be

a an isosceles triangle? Explain.

b an equilateral triangle? Explain.

8. Can an isosceles triangle also be equilateral? Explain.

Independent Practice

In **9–12**, tell if each triangle is equilateral, isosceles, or scalene. If a triangle has two names, give the name that best describes it.

9. 

10. 

11. 

12. 

DIGITAL Animated Glossary
www.pearsonsuccessnet.com

*For another example, see Set E on page 125.

Triangles can be described by their angles.

Right triangle

One angle is a right angle.

Acute triangle

All three angles are acute angles.

Obtuse triangle

One angle is an obtuse angle.

In **13–16**, tell if each triangle is right, acute, or obtuse.

13. 

14. 

15. 

16. 

Problem Solving

For **17** and **18**, use the picture of the musical triangle.

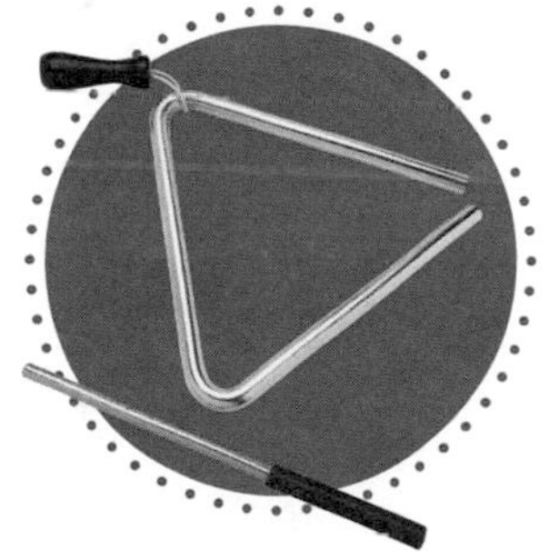

17. Does the musical triangle look most like an equilateral triangle, an isosceles triangle, or a scalene triangle?

18. Reasoning The shape of the musical triangle is not a geometric triangle. Explain why not.

19. Look at the sentence below. Write the word that will make it true.

An obtuse triangle has one obtuse angle and two __?__ angles.

20. Draw a picture to show how you could make one straight cut in a rectangle to form two right triangles.

21. Which pair of triangle names best describes this pennant?

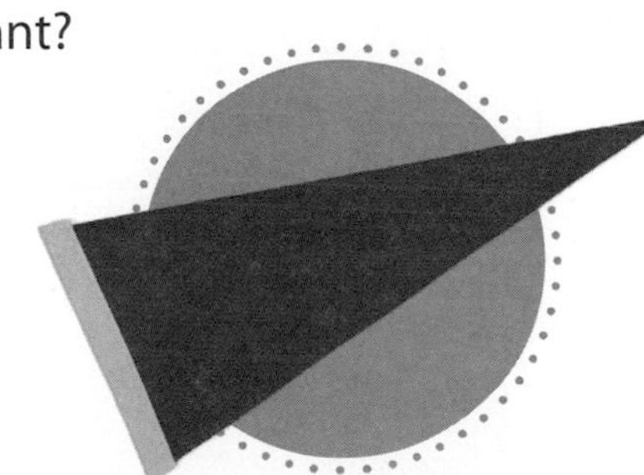

A Equilateral triangle, acute triangle

B Equilateral triangle, right triangle

C Isosceles triangle, acute triangle

D Isosceles triangle, obtuse triangle

22. Writing to Explain Why is it impossible for a triangle to have two right angles?

Lesson
5-7

MG 2.3 Identify attributes of quadrilaterals (e.g., parallel sides for the parallelogram, right angles for the rectangle, equal sides and right angles for the square). Also **MG 2.0, 2.4**

Quadrilaterals

What are some special names for quadrilaterals?

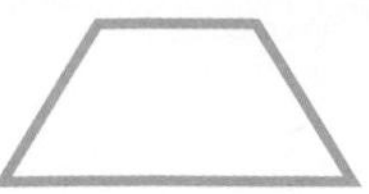

Trapezoid

Exactly one pair of parallel sides

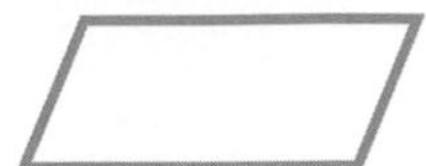

Parallelogram

Two pairs of parallel sides

Opposite sides are the same length.
Opposite angles are the same size.

Guided Practice*

Do you know HOW?

In **1–4**, write as many special names as possible for each quadrilateral.

1. **2.**

3. **4.**

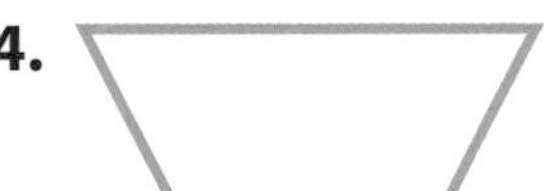

Do you UNDERSTAND?

5. This figure is a rectangle, but it is not a square. Why?

6. Draw a parallelogram with all four sides the same length. What is its special name?

7. Why is a square a parallelogram?

Independent Practice

In **8–12**, write as many special names as possible for each quadrilateral.

8. 

9. 

10. 

11. 

12. 

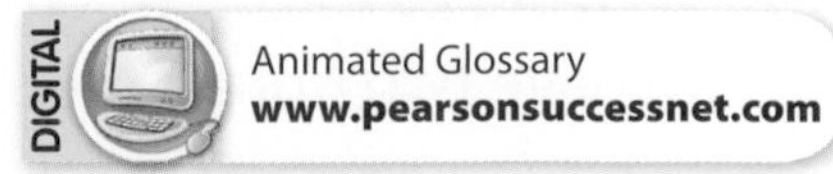

*For another example, see Set E on page 125.

Some quadrilaterals have more than one special name.

Rectangle	Rhombus	Square
Four right angles	All sides the same length	Four right angles and all sides the same length
A *rectangle* is a special *parallelogram*.	A *rhombus* is a special *parallelogram*.	A *square* is a special *parallelogram*. It is a combination of a *rectangle* and a *rhombus*.

In **13–16**, write the name that best describes the quadrilateral. Draw a picture to help.

13. A rectangle with all sides the same length

14. A quadrilateral with only one pair of parallel sides

15. A parallelogram with four right angles

16. A rhombus with four right angles

Problem Solving

17. The bike in the photo was designed with square wheels instead of round ones. How is a square different from a circle?

18. Reasoning I am a special quadrilateral with opposite sides the same length. What special quadrilateral could I be? (*Hint:* There is more than one correct answer.)

19. Writing to Explain How are a rectangle and a rhombus alike? How are they different?

20. Which picture shows more than $\frac{5}{8}$ of the square shaded?

A 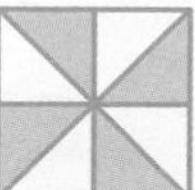

B 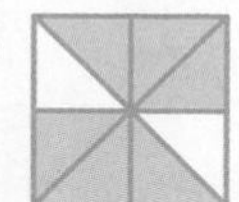

C 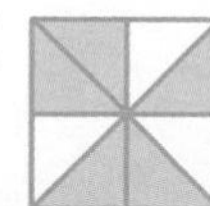

D 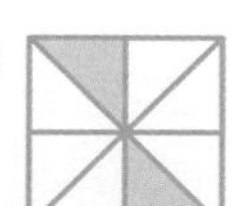

Lesson
5-8

MR 3.3 Develop generalizations of the results obtained and apply them in other circumstances.
Also **MG 2.0** Describe and compare the attributes of plane and solid geometric figures and use their understanding to show relationships and solve problems.

Problem Solving

Make and Test Generalizations

What is the same in all these polygons?

Guided Practice*

Do you know HOW?

Make and test a generalization for each set of polygons.

1. 

2.    

Do you UNDERSTAND?

3. Look at the polygons above. All of the sides of the second and third polygons **are** the same length. So why is the friend's generalization incorrect?

4. Draw a set of polygons that you can make a generalization about. Include a picture.

Independent Practice

In **5–7**, make a generalization for each set of polygons.

5. 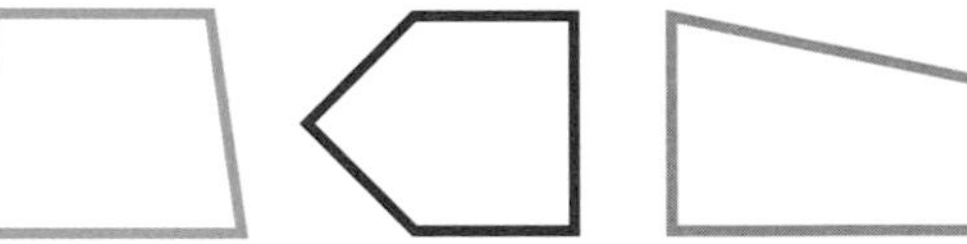

6.   

7.   

- What do I know?
- What am I asked to find?
- What diagram can I use to help understand the problem?
- Can I use addition, subtraction, multiplication, or division?
- Is all of my work correct?
- Did I answer the right question?
- Is my answer reasonable?

*For another example, see Set F on page 125.

Make a Generalization

Your friend says *I think the sides are all the same length.*

You say *I think they all have 4 sides.*

Test the Generalization

Your friend says *Wait! The top and bottom of this polygon are not the same length. My generalization is not correct!*

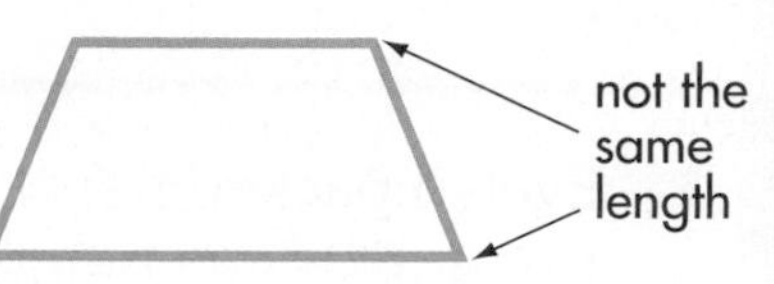

You say *The first polygon has 4 sides. The second has 4 sides. So does the third. My generalization is correct!*

8. Mr. Redbird makes tables that have 3 legs and tables that have 4 legs. The tables that he made this month have 18 legs in all. How many tables of each kind did he make?

9. Anna earns $4 for each hour that she babysits. She babysat for 2 hours last week and 5 hours this week. How much did she earn in all?

10. How are the four numbers 18, 24, 16, and 40 alike?

11. Compare each sum to its addends in these number sentences:

$34 + 65 = 99$ $8 + 87 = 95$ $435 + 0 = 435$

Make a generalization about addends and sums for whole numbers.

12. **Writing to Explain** Is this generalization true? If not, draw a picture to show why not.

If a shape is made up of line segments, then it is a polygon.

13. Ari gave his friends these clues about a secret number.

- The number has three digits.
- The hundreds digit is less than 3.
- The tens digit is twice the ones digit.
- The number is odd.

What are all the possible secret numbers?

14. What is the same in all these polygons?

A All have a pair of parallel sides.

B All have two right angles.

C All have one acute angle.

D All have four sides.

Test Prep

1. Evelyn packed her stuffed animals in the box shown below. Which solid best describes the box? (5-1)

A Cylinder

B Cube

C Pyramid

D Cone

2. A right angle is shown. Which clock face below shows the hands in an angle that is less than a right angle? (5-4)

A

B

C

D

3. What solids combine to form the barn? (5-3)

A Pyramid and a cone

B Rectangular prism and a cylinder

C Rectangular prism and a pyramid

D Rectangular prism and a cone

4. Which best describes the triangles? (5-8)

A They are all acute triangles.

B They are all isosceles triangles.

C They are all obtuse triangles.

D They are all scalene triangles.

5. Which of the following statements is true? (5-6)

A An equilateral triangle has no sides that are the same length.

B An equilateral triangle has 2 sides that are the same length.

C An equilateral triangle has 3 sides that are the same length.

D An equilateral triangle has 4 sides that are the same length.

6. Which figure is a pentagon? (5-5)

A

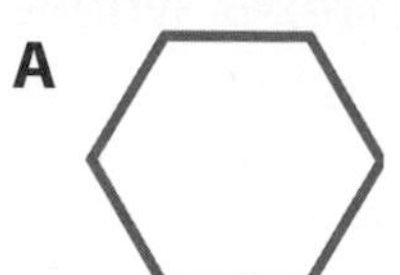

B

C

D

7. Below is part of a nature trail map. Which two trails represent parallel lines? (5-4)

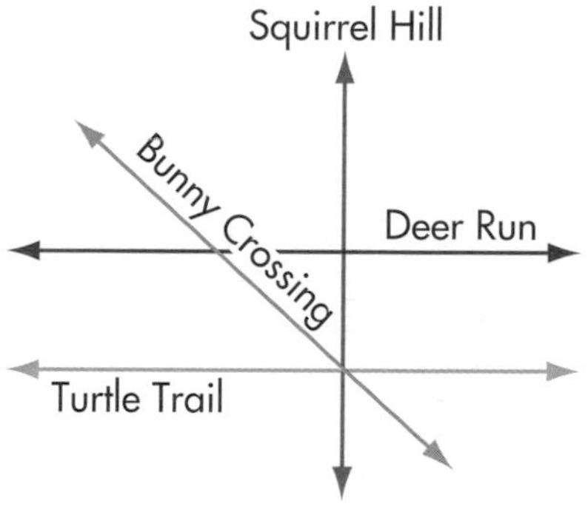

A Deer Run and Turtle Trail

B Deer Run and Squirrel Hill

C Bunny Crossing and Squirrel Hill

D Bunny Crossing and Turtle Trail

8. The students ran a course from the flag to the tree, to the trash can, and then back to the flag. What type of triangle did the course form? (5-6)

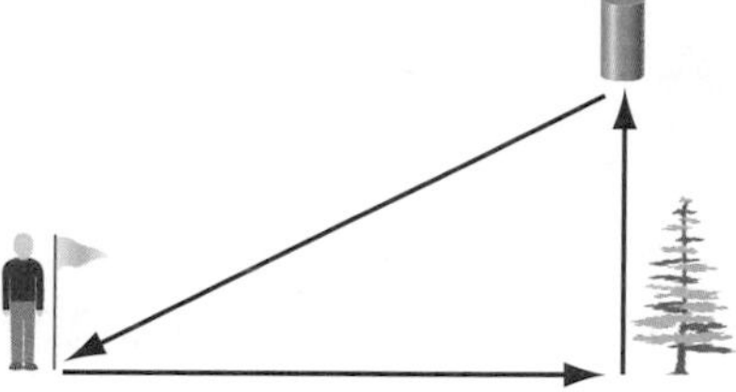

A Right triangle

B Isosceles triangle

C Equilateral triangle

D Acute triangle

9. One side of a parallelogram is 5 inches long. Another side is 8 inches long. What are the lengths of the other 2 sides of the parallelogram? (5-7)

A 5 inches and 5 inches

B 8 inches and 8 inches

C 5 inches and 8 inches

D They could be any length.

10. Claire made a fancy pillow in the shape of a rectangular prism. If she sews a bow at each vertex, how many bows will she need? (5-2)

A 3

B 6

C 7

D 8

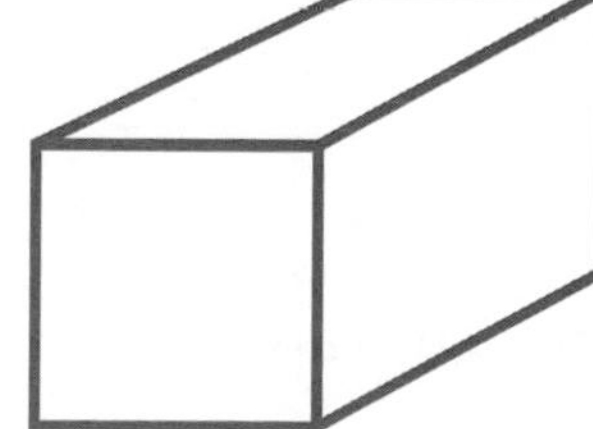

Reteaching

Set A, pages 100–106

Name this solid figure.

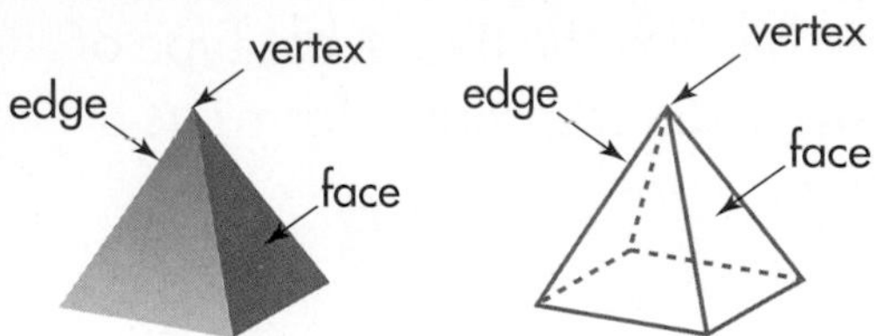

The figure has 5 faces, 8 edges, and 5 vertices. The figure has flat surfaces and a point at the top. The figure is a pyramid.

Remember that a vertex is where three or more edges meet.

Use the solid figure below.

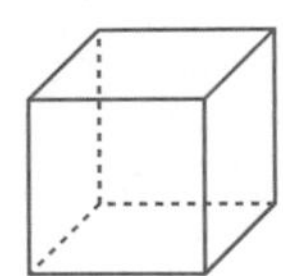

1. How many faces, edges, and vertices does this figure have?
2. Name this solid figure.

Set B, pages 108–109

What solid figures can you make by breaking apart the cube, as shown?

You can make 2 rectangular prisms.

Remember to look at the shape of the faces to help name a solid figure.

Name the solid figures you would get if you cut the figure as shown.

1. 
2. 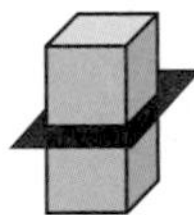

Set C, pages 110–113

Write the name for the following.

The lines cross at one point.

They are intersecting lines.

Is the angle right, acute, or obtuse?

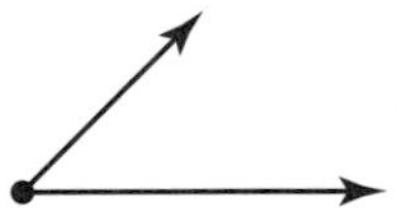

The angle is less than a right angle.

It is an acute angle.

Remember that parallel lines will never cross.

Write the name for each.

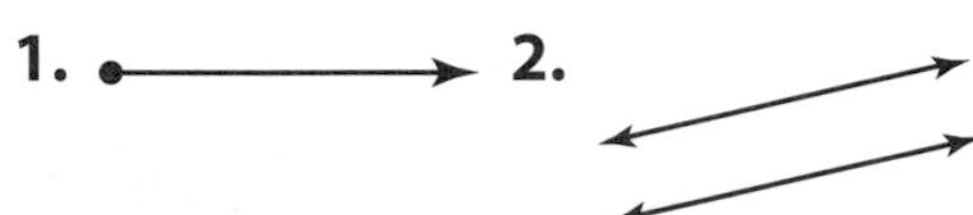

1.
2.

Tell if each angle is right, acute, or obtuse.

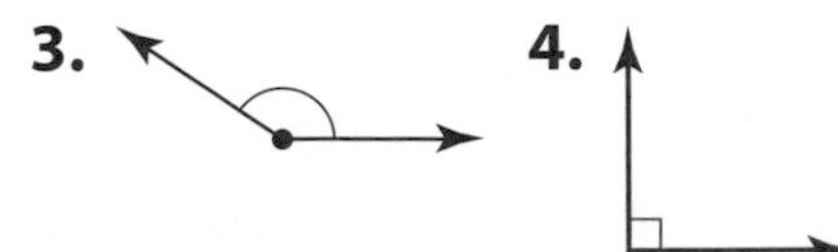

3.
4.

Set D, pages 114–115

Is the figure a polygon? If it is a polygon, give its name. If not, explain why.

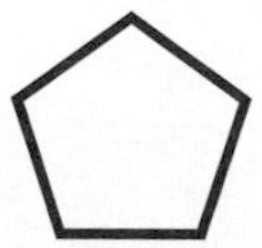

The figure is closed and is made up of straight line segments. It is a polygon.

The figure has 5 sides and 5 vertices. It is a pentagon.

Remember that a polygon is a closed figure made up of line segments.

Is each figure a polygon? If it is a polygon, give its name. If not, explain why.

1. 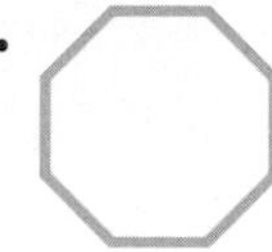

2.

Set E, pages 116–119

Is the triangle equilateral, isosceles, or scalene? Is the triangle right, acute, or obtuse?

None of the sides are the same length. One angle is an obtuse angle.

The triangle is a scalene triangle. The triangle is an obtuse triangle.

Name the following quadrilateral.

Opposite sides are parallel and have the same length.

The figure is a parallelogram.

Remember that the sides of an equilateral triangle are all the same length.

Describe each triangle by its sides and its angles.

1. 

2. 

Write as many special names as possible for each quadrilateral.

3. 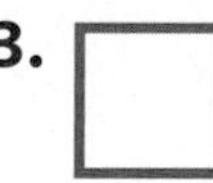

4. 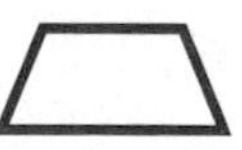

Set F, pages 120–121

Make and test a generalization for the set of polygons.

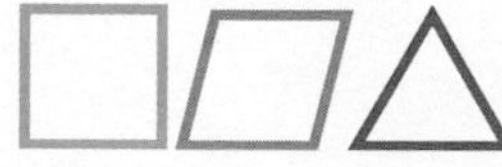

Step 1

Make a generalization.
In each polygon, all sides are the same length.

Step 2

Test the generalization.
In a square, rhombus, and equilateral triangle, all sides are the same length.

Remember that a generalization must apply to all of the polygons in the set.

Make and test a generalization for the set of polygons.

1. 

Topic 6 Multiplication Concepts

1 An armadillo needs more sleep than a horse. How many more hours of sleep does an armadillo need? You will find out in Lesson 6-3.

2 Dogface butterflies are known for their bright yellow wings. How many wings does a dogface butterfly have? You will find out in Lesson 6-4.

3 In 1999, the United States Mint began circulating new state quarters. How many states have new quarters every year? You will find out in Lesson 6-1.

Review What You Know!

Vocabulary

Choose the best term from the box.

- add
- equal groups
- skip count
- subtract

1. If you combine groups to find how many in all, you __?__.
2. __?__ have the same number of items.
3. When you say the numbers 2, 4, 6, 8, you __?__.

Equal Groups

Are the groups equal? Write *yes* or *no*.

4. 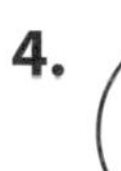  

5.   

Adding

Find each sum.

6. 5 + 5 + 5
7. 7 + 7
8. 3 + 3 + 3
9. 2 + 2 + 2 + 2
10. 6 + 6 + 6
11. 9 + 9 + 9

Repeated Addition

12. **Writing to Explain** Draw a picture to show how to solve 8 + 8 + 8 = ▢. Then copy and complete the number sentence.

Lesson

6-1

NS 3.1 Grade 2 Use repeated addition, arrays, and counting by multiples to do multiplication.
Also **AF 1.2, AF 1.3**

Multiplication as Repeated Addition

How can you find the total number of objects in equal groups?

Jessie used 3 bags to bring home the goldfish she won at a Fun Fair. She put the same number of goldfish in each bag. How many goldfish did she win?

Guided Practice*

Do you know HOW?

Copy and complete. Use counters.

1.

2 groups of ▢
4 + 4 = ▢
2 × ▢ = ▢

2. 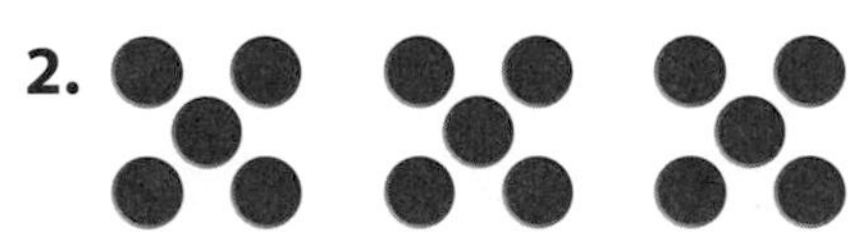

▢ groups of 5
5 + ▢ + ▢ = ▢
3 × ▢ = ▢

Do you UNDERSTAND?

3. Can you write 3 + 3 + 3 + 3 as a multiplication sentence? Explain.

4. Can you write 3 + 5 + 6 = 14 as a multiplication sentence? Explain.

5. Write an addition sentence and a multiplication sentence to solve this problem:

Jessie bought 4 packages of colorful stones to put in the fish bowl. There were 6 stones in each package. How many stones did Jessie buy?

Independent Practice

Copy and complete. Use counters or draw a picture to help.

6.

2 groups of ▢
6 + ▢ = ▢
2 × ▢ = ▢

7.

3 groups of ▢
7 + ▢ + ▢ = ▢
3 × ▢ = ▢

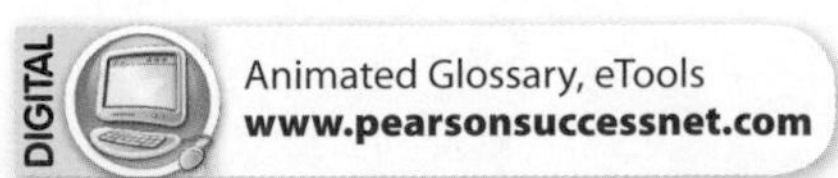

*For another example, see Set A on page 144.

The counters show 3 groups of 8 goldfish.

You can use addition to join equal groups.

$8 + 8 + 8 = 24$

Multiplication is an operation that gives the total number when you join equal groups.

What You Say 3 times 8 equals 24

What You Write $3 \times 8 = 24$

factor factor product

Factors are the numbers that are being multiplied. The product is the answer to a multiplication problem.

Addition sentence:

$8 + 8 + 8 = 24$

Multiplication sentence:

$3 \times 8 = 24$

So, $8 + 8 + 8 = 3 \times 8$.

Jessie won 24 goldfish.

Copy and complete each number sentence. Use counters or draw a picture to help.

8. $2 + 2 + 2 + 2 = 4 \times$ ☐

9. ☐ + ☐ + ☐ $= 3 \times 7$

10. $9 +$ ☐ + ☐ = ☐ $\times 9$

11. $6 + 6 + 6 + 6 + 6 =$ ☐ × ☐

Algebra Write +, −, or × for each ☐.

12. 4 ☐ 3 = 12

13. 3 ☐ 6 = 9

14. 4 ☐ 4 = 0

15. 6 ☐ 4 = 10

16. 5 ☐ 3 = 2

17. 2 ☐ 4 = 8

Problem Solving

18. What number sentence shows how to find the total number of erasers?

A $5 + 5 =$ ☐

B $15 - 5 =$ ☐

C $15 + 5 =$ ☐

D $3 \times 5 =$ ☐

19. Write an addition sentence and a multiplication sentence to solve this problem:

In 1999, the United States Mint began circulating state quarters. Every year, 5 new state quarters are released. After 10 years, how many state quarters will be released?

20. Writing to Explain Luka says that you can add or multiply to join groups. Is he correct? Explain.

21. Which picture shows 3 groups of 2?

A 

B 

C 

D 

Lesson

6-2

AF 1.5 Recognize and use the commutative and associative properties of multiplication (e.g., if 5 × 7 = 35, then what is 7 × 5? and if 5 × 7 × 3 = 105, then what is 7 × 3 × 5?). Also NS 3.1 Grade 2

Arrays and Multiplication

Hands-On
counters

How does an array show multiplication?

Dana keeps her entire CD collection in a holder on the wall. The holder has 4 rows. Each row holds 5 CDs. How many CDs are in Dana's collection?

The CDs are in an array. An array shows objects in equal rows.

Another Example Does order matter when you multiply?

Libby and Sydney both say their poster has more stickers. Who is correct?

$4 + 4 + 4 = 12$
$3 \times 4 = 12$

Libby's poster has 12 stickers.

$3 + 3 + 3 + 3 = 12$
$4 \times 3 = 12$

Sydney's poster has 12 stickers.

Both poster boards have the same number of stickers.

3 × 4 = 12 and **4 × 3 = 12**

The Commutative (Order) Property of Multiplication says you can multiply numbers in any order and the product is the same. So, $3 \times 4 = 4 \times 3$.

Explain It

1. Miguel has 5 rows of stickers. There are 3 stickers in each row. Write an addition sentence and a multiplication sentence to show how many stickers he has.
2. Show the Commutative Property of Multiplication by drawing two arrays. Each array should have at least 2 rows and show a product of 6.

The counters show 4 rows of 5 CDs.

Each row is a group. You can use addition to find the total.

5 + 5 + 5 + 5 = 20

Multiplication can also be used to find the total in an array.

What You Say 4 times 5 equals 20

What You Write $4 \times 5 = 20$

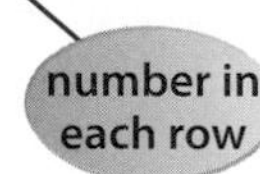

number of rows; number in each row

There are 20 CDs in Dana's collection.

Guided Practice*

Do you know HOW?

In **1** and **2**, write a multiplication sentence for each array.

1. 

2.  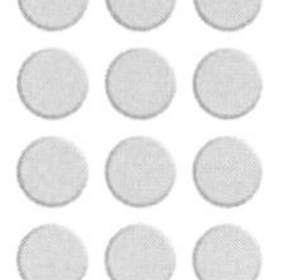

In **3** and **4**, draw an array to show each multiplication fact. Write the product.

3. 3×6

4. 5×4

In **5** and **6**, copy and complete each multiplication sentence. Use counters or draw an array to help.

5. $5 \times \square = 10$
$2 \times \square = 10$

6. $4 \times 3 = \square$
$3 \times \square = 12$

Do you UNDERSTAND?

7. Look at the example above. What does the first factor in the multiplication sentence tell you about the array?

8. **Writing to Explain** Why is the Commutative Property of Multiplication sometimes called the *order property*?

9. Scott puts some sports stickers in rows. He makes 6 rows with 5 stickers in each row. If he put the same stickers in 5 equal rows, how many would be in each row?

Independent Practice

In **10–12**, write a multiplication sentence for each array.

10. 

11. 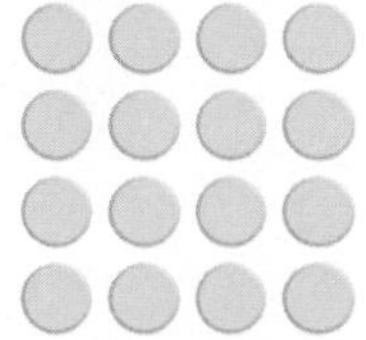

12.  

*For another example, see Set B on page 144.

Independent Practice

In **13–17**, draw an array to show each multiplication fact. Write the product.

13. 3×3 **14.** 5×6 **15.** 1×8 **16.** 4×3 **17.** 2×9

In **18–23**, copy and complete each multiplication sentence. Use counters or draw an array to help.

18. $4 \times \square = 8$
$2 \times \square = 8$

19. $6 \times 4 = \square$
$4 \times \square = 24$

20. $5 \times \square = 40$
$\square \times 5 = 40$

21. $3 \times 9 = 27$
$9 \times 3 = \square$

22. $7 \times 6 = 42$
$6 \times 7 = \square$

23. $9 \times 8 = 72$
$8 \times 9 = \square$

Problem Solving

24. Writing to Explain How do the arrays at the right show the Commutative Property of Multiplication?

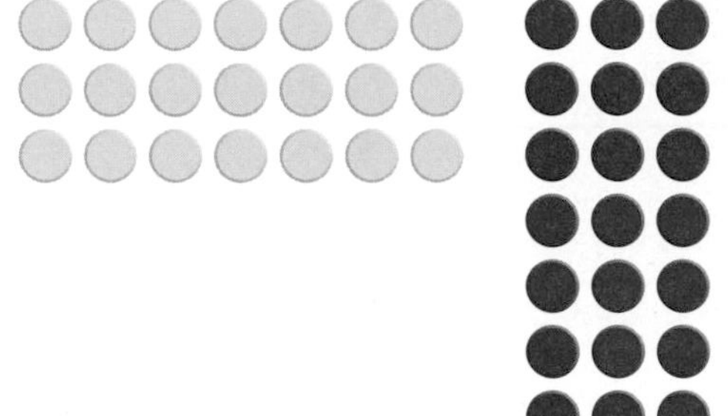

25. Number Sense How does an array show equal groups?

26. Taylor says that the product for 7×2 is the same as the product for 2×7. Is he correct? Explain.

27. Reasoning Margo has 23 pictures. Can she use all of the pictures to make an array with exactly two equal rows? Why or why not?

28. Dan bought the stamps shown at right. Which number sentence shows one way to find how many stamps Dan bought?

A $4 + 5 = \square$

B $5 \times 4 = \square$

C $5 + 4 = \square$

D $5 - 4 = \square$

Mixed Problem Solving

Josie made the artwork on the right using stars and circles. Answer the questions about her artwork.

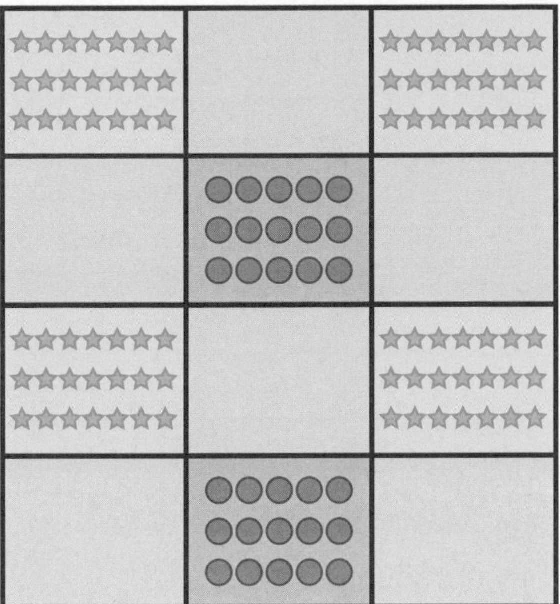

1. Explain the pattern shown in the artwork.

2. How many rows are in each array of stars?

3. Look at one array of circles. How many circles are in each row of the array?

4. Look at one array of stars. Write a number sentence for the array.

5. How many circles did Josie use in her artwork?

6. How many more stars than circles did Josie make?

7. Josie used the table below to plan how many of each shape she would need for different numbers of rows.

   Copy and complete the table.

Shapes Needed to Make Artwork

Data

Total Number of Rows	Total Number of Stars	Total Number of Circles
2	42	15
4	84	30
6	126	45
8		

8. Mark made 56 stars. He made 18 circles. How many shapes did he make in all?

9. **Strategy Focus** Solve. Use the strategy Write a Number Sentence.

   Maggie made a pattern using a total of 92 shapes. Of the 92 shapes Maggie used, 44 were circles and the rest were stars. How many stars did Maggie use?

Lesson
6-3

NS 2.0 Calculate and solve problems involving addition, subtraction, multiplication and division.
Also NS 3.1 Grade 2

Using Multiplication to Compare

Hands-On

counters

How can you use multiplication to compare?

Mike has 5 state quarters. Carl has two times as many, or twice as many as Mike. How many state quarters does Carl have?

Choose an Operation Multiply to find twice as many: $2 \times 5 = \square$

Mike's quarters

Guided Practice*

Do you know HOW?

Find each amount. You may use drawings or counters to help.

1. 3 times as many as 3
2. 2 times as many as 6
3. Twice as many as 3

Do you UNDERSTAND?

4. **Number Sense** Barry says you can add 5 + 5 to find how many state quarters Carl has. Is he correct? Why or why not?
5. Carl has 4 silver dollars. Mike has twice as many as Carl. How many silver dollars does Mike have?

Independent Practice

In **6–11**, find each amount. You may use drawings or counters to help.

6. 2 times as many as 7
7. 3 times as many as 8
8. Twice as many as 6
9. 4 times as many as 5
10. Twice as many as 9
11. 5 times as many as 4

In **12–15**, which coin or bill matches each value?

12. 2 times as much as 1 nickel
13. 10 times as much as 1 dime
14. 5 times as much as 1 nickel
15. 10 times as much as 1 nickel

dime

quarter

half dollar

one dollar

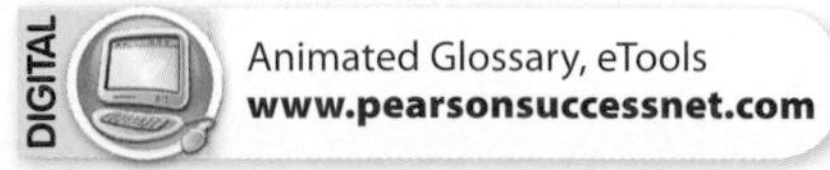

*For another example, see Set C on page 144.

What You Think

Mike has 5 state quarters.

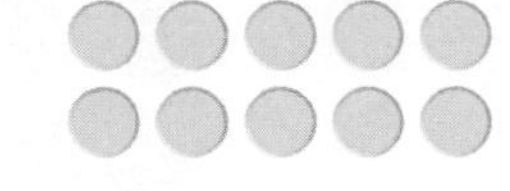

Carl has 2 times as many.

2 times as many is 10.

What You Write

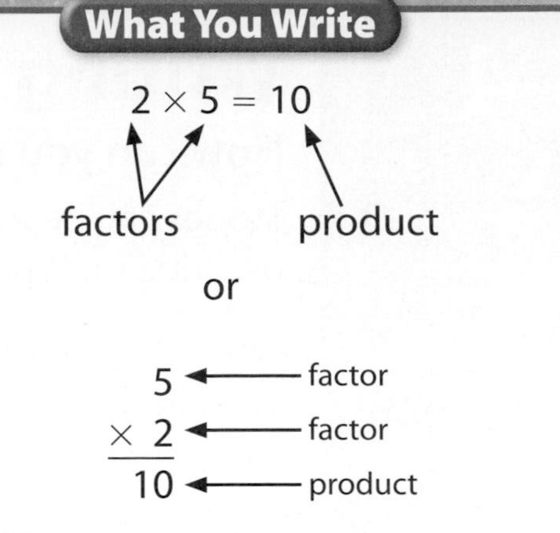

Carl has 10 state quarters.

Problem Solving

Number Sense For **16–17**, copy and complete.

16. 6 is twice as many as ▢.

17. 8 is eight times as many as ▢.

18. Reasoning Carol has 4 dolls. Her sister has twice as many. How many dolls do they have in all?

19. Writing to Explain How could this picture help you solve **Exercise 18**?

Carol's sister	4	4	twice as many
Carol	4		

20. A horse needs about 3 hours of sleep each day. An armadillo needs 6 times as much sleep as a horse. About how many hours of sleep does an armadillo need each day?

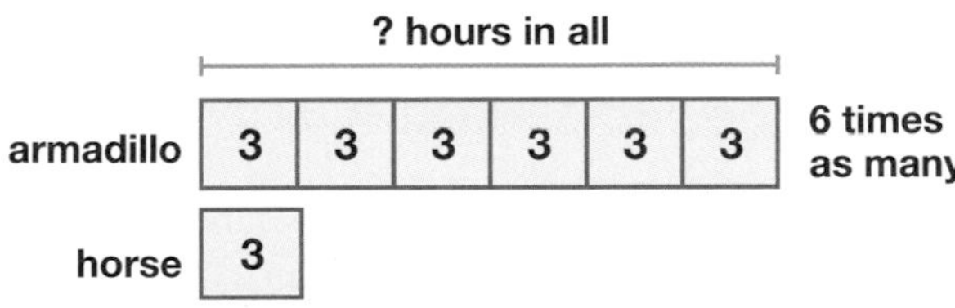

21. Two of the U. S. coins that are worth one dollar are shown below. The Susan B. Anthony coin was first issued in 1979. The Sacagawea coin was issued 21 years later. When was the Sacagawea coin issued?

22. What number sentence shows how to find twice as many marbles?

A $8 + 8 + 8 = $ ▢ **B** $1 \times 8 = $ ▢ **C** $2 \times 8 = $ ▢ **D** $3 \times 8 = $ ▢

Lesson
6-4

AF 2.0 Represent simple functional relationships. Also NS 3.1 Grade 2 Use repeated addition, arrays, and counting by multiples to do multiplication.

Writing Multiplication Stories

How can you describe a multiplication fact?

Stories can be written to describe multiplication facts.

Write a multiplication story for $3 \times 6 = \square$.

Guided Practice*

Do you know HOW?

In **1–4**, write a multiplication story for each problem. Then draw a picture and find each product.

1. 2×6

2. 3×5

3. 4×2

4. 3×8

Do you UNDERSTAND?

5. How would the story about Randy change if the multiplication sentence was $2 \times 6 = \square$?

6. How would the story about Eliza change if the multiplication sentence was $3 \times 5 = \square$?

7. **Number Sense** Could the story about carrots also be an addition story? Explain.

Independent Practice

Write a multiplication story for each problem. Then, draw a picture to find each product.

8. 7×3 **9.** 2×9 **10.** 4×5

Write a multiplication story for each picture. Use the picture to find the product.

11.

12.

*For another example, see Set D on page 145.

Equal Groups

Randy has 3 packs of 6 buttons. How many buttons does he have?

$3 \times 6 = 18$

Randy has 18 buttons.

An Array

Eliza planted 6 lilies in each of 3 rows. How many lilies did she plant?

$3 \times 6 = 18$

Eliza planted 18 lilies.

"Times as Many"

Kanisha has 6 carrots. Jack has 3 times as many. How many carrots does Jack have?

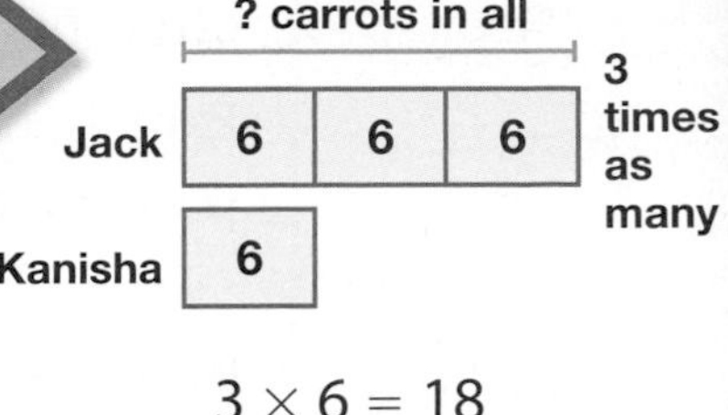

$3 \times 6 = 18$

Jack has 18 carrots.

Problem Solving

Number Sense For **13–15**, describe each story as an addition story, a subtraction story, or a multiplication story.

13. Kay has 6 pencils. She gave 4 of them to her friend. How many pencils does Kay have left?

14. Kay has 6 pencils. She bought 4 more pencils at the school store. How many pencils does Kay have now?

15. Kay has 6 bags of pencils. There are 2 pencils in each bag. How many pencils does Kay have?

16. A soccer team traveled to a soccer game in 4 vans. All four vans were full. Each van held 7 players. How many players went to the game?

A 47 **C** 24

B 28 **D** 11

17. Algebra Steve has some packages of balloons. There are 8 balloons in each package. He has 24 balloons in all. Draw a picture to find how many packages Steve has.

18. A group of 12 dogface butterflies is getting ready to migrate. How many wings will be moving when the group flies away?

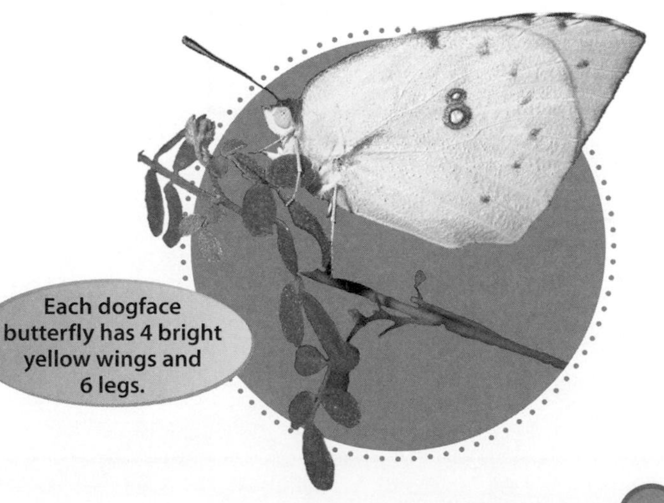

Each dogface butterfly has 4 bright yellow wings and 6 legs.

Lesson
6-5

MR 2.4 Express the solution clearly and logically by using the appropriate mathematical notation and terms and clear language; support solutions with evidence in both verbal and symbolic work.
Also **AF 2.1**.

Problem Solving

Writing to Explain

Gina's dad gave her 2 pennies on Monday. He promised to double that number of pennies every day after that for one week.

Explain how you can use the pattern to complete the table.

Data

Day	Number of pennies
Monday	2
Tuesday	4
Wednesday	8
Thursday	16
Friday	32
Saturday	
Sunday	

Another Example

How can you use *words, pictures, numbers,* or *symbols* to write a math explanation?

Jackie got on an elevator on the first floor. She went up 5 floors. Then she went down 2 floors. Then she went up 4 floors and got off the elevator. What floor is Jackie on?

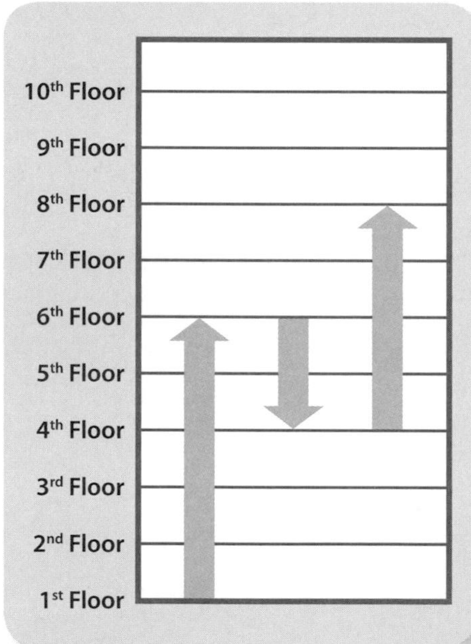

Jackie started on the first floor. Then she went up 5 floors.

$1 + 5 = 6$

Then she went down 2 floors.

$6 - 2 = 4$

Then she went up 4 floors and got off the elevator.

$4 + 4 = 8$

Jackie is on the eighth floor.

Explain It

1. Why is drawing a picture a good way to explain this problem?
2. How do the number sentences explain the problem?

Complete the table. Use *words, numbers,* or *symbols* to explain your work.

The number of pennies doubles each day. That means that Gina will get 2 times as many pennies as she got the day before.

First, I need to double 32.
32 + 32 = 64 pennies
Gina will get 64 pennies on Saturday.

Then, I need to double 64.
64 + 64 = 128 pennies
Gina will get 128 pennies on Sunday.

Data

Day	Number of Pennies
Monday	2
Tuesday	4
Wednesday	8
Thursday	16
Friday	32
Saturday	64
Sunday	128

Guided Practice*

Do you know HOW?

1. Brian bought 3 packs of baseball cards. There are 4 cards in each pack. How many baseball cards did he buy? Explain how you can solve this problem.

Do you UNDERSTAND?

2. If the pattern in the table above continued, how many pennies would Gina get next Monday?

3. **Write a Problem** Write a real-world problem. Explain how to solve it using words, pictures, numbers, or symbols.

Independent Practice

4. Pam is setting up tables and chairs. She puts 4 chairs at each table.

   a Explain how the number of chairs changes as the number of tables changes.

   b Copy and complete the table.

Number of Tables	1	2	3	4	5
Number of Chairs	4	8	12		

5. Aaron cut a log into 5 pieces. How many cuts did he make? Explain how you found the answer.

- What do I know?
- What am I asked to find?
- What diagram can I use to help understand the problem?
- Can I use addition, subtraction, multiplication, or division?
- Is all of my work correct?
- Did I answer the right question?
- Is my answer reasonable?

*For another example, see Set E on page 145.

Independent Practice

6. Copy and complete the table below. Then describe how the table helps you explain the pattern.

Cost of School Play Tickets

Number of Tickets	Cost
1	$5
2	$10
3	$15
4	
5	

7. Copy and complete the table below. If Margo continues the pattern, what is the first day she will exercise for 1 hour? Explain.

Margo's Exercise Schedule

Day	Minutes
Monday	20 minutes
Tuesday	30 minutes
Wednesday	40 minutes
Thursday	minutes
Friday	minutes

8. Hank earns $4 for raking lawns and $6 for mowing lawns. How much will Hank earn if he mows and rakes 2 lawns?

9. **a** Describe the pattern below.

   81, 82, 84, 87, 91

   b Write the next two numbers in the pattern and explain how you found them.

10. Jake is planting trees in a row that is 20 feet long. He plants a tree at the beginning of the row. Then he plants a tree every 5 feet. How many trees does he plant? Draw a picture to explain.

Think About the Process

11. Alexandra bought 5 bags of oranges. There were 6 oranges in each bag. Then she gave 4 oranges away. Which number sentence shows how many oranges Alexandra bought?

    A $5 + 6 = \square$

    B $5 \times 6 = \square$

    C $(5 \times 6) - 4 = \square$

    D $(5 + 6) - 4 = \square$

12. Tara ran 5 miles on Monday and 4 miles on Tuesday. Teresa ran 3 miles on Monday and 6 miles on Tuesday. Which number sentence shows how far Tara ran in all?

    A $3 + 6 = \square$

    B $5 + 4 = \square$

    C $5 - 4 = \square$

    D $5 + 4 + 3 + 6 = \square$

Write each number in expanded form.

1. 508

2. 6,914

3. 317,002

Order the numbers from greatest to least.

4. 739 196 942

5. 398 309 391

6. 4,588 8,213 2,798

7. 5,674 6,172 6,179

Name the figure.

8.  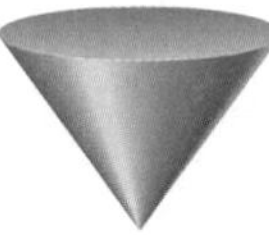

9. 

10. 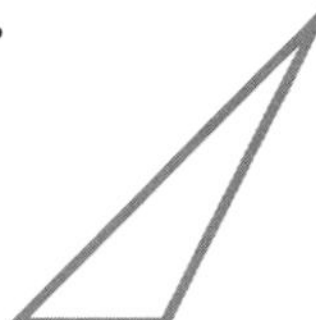

11. 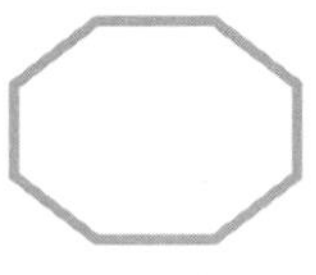

12. 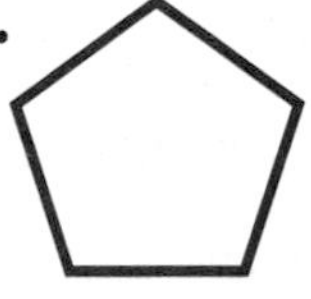

Find each sum or difference that is not correct. Write it correctly and explain the error.

13. $\begin{array}{r} 85 \\ +\ 97 \\ \hline 182 \end{array}$

14. $\begin{array}{r} 349 \\ +\ 763 \\ \hline 1{,}002 \end{array}$

15. $\begin{array}{r} 402 \\ -\ 158 \\ \hline 356 \end{array}$

16. $\begin{array}{r} 7{,}163 \\ +\ 942 \\ \hline 8{,}005 \end{array}$

17. $\begin{array}{r} 6{,}501 \\ -\ 3{,}286 \\ \hline 3{,}215 \end{array}$

Number Sense

Estimating and Reasoning Write true or false for each statement. If it is false, explain why.

18. The difference 832 − 264 is greater than 500.

19. The sum of 47 and 38 is greater than 100.

20. The sum of 578 and 316 is less than 1,000.

21. The difference 983 − 895 is less than 100.

22. The sum of 2,982 and 6,359 is greater than 10,000.

23. The difference 2,401 − 918 is less than 1,000.

Test Prep

1. Which has the same value as 5×2? (6-1)

A $5 + 2$

B $2 + 2 + 2 + 2$

C $2 + 2 + 2 + 5$

D $2 + 2 + 2 + 2 + 2$

2. Mrs. Salinas planted her flowers in the pattern shown below. What number sentence best shows how she planted them? (6-2)

A $3 \times 7 = \square$

B $3 \times 6 = \square$

C $3 + 7 = \square$

D $7 + 3 = \square$

3. Which story could be solved with 7×8? (6-4)

A Ken bought 7 bags of buns for the cookout. Each bag had 8 buns. How many buns did Ken buy?

B Rob has 7 red fish and 8 orange fish. How many fish does Rob have?

C Ted had 8 math problems for homework. He has finished 7. How many does he have left?

D Max has 7 pages in his album. He has 8 pictures. How many can he put on each page?

4. Maddie mailed 3 postcards during her vacation. Her sister mailed twice as many. How many postcards did Maddie's sister mail? (6-3)

A 9

B 6

C 5

D 2

5. Trent read the books shown below. Which number sentence shows how to find four times as many books as Trent read? (6-3)

A $4 + 8 = 12$

B $4 \times 8 = 32$

C $4 \times 9 = 36$

D $5 \times 8 = 40$

6. Tiffany bought the canisters of tennis balls shown below. How many tennis balls did she buy in all? (6-1)

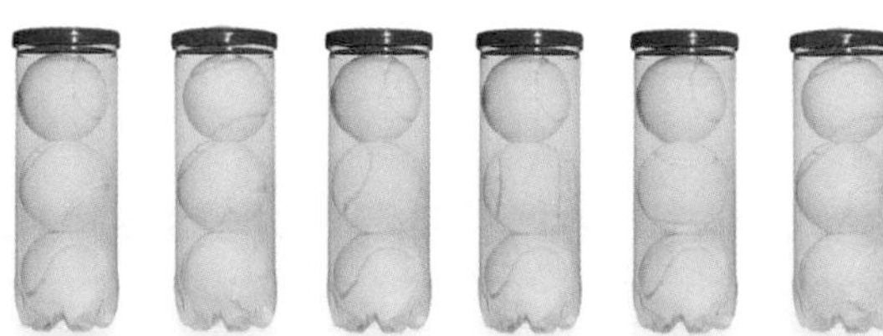

A 6

B 9

C 12

D 18

Test Prep

7. What number makes the number sentence true? (6-2)

$9 \times 7 = 63$

$7 \times \square = 63$

A 63

B 56

C 9

D 7

8. Ryan's pumpkin bread recipe calls for 2 cups of flour and 4 eggs for 1 loaf. He wants to make 3 loaves. Which can be used to find how many eggs Ryan needs? (6-1)

A 2×4

B 3×2

C 3×4

D 3×6

9. Which array shows 2×3? (6-2)

A 

B 

C 

D 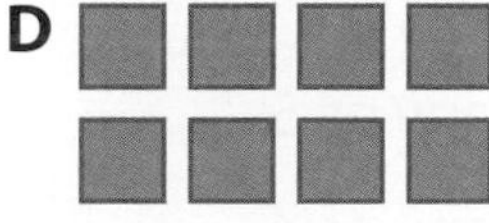

10. Which is **NOT** a correct explanation of how to solve the problem? (6-5)

Erin bought 3 packages of muffins. There were 2 muffins in each package. How many muffins did Erin buy?

A Add 2, three times: $2 + 2 + 2 = 6$

B Multiply 3 by 2: $3 \times 2 = 6$

C Add 3 and 2: $3 + 2 = 5$

D Draw a picture showing 3 packages of 2 muffins and then count the muffins.

11. For the Fourth of July, Reggie put 4 rows of flags in his yard. Each row had 5 flags. How many flags did Reggie have in all? (6-2)

A 15

B 20

C 24

D 25

12. If you know that $6 \times 90 = 540$, then what is 90×6? (6-2)

A 54

B 60

C 90

D 540

Reteaching

Set A, pages 128–129

Find the total number of counters.

●● ●● ●●

There are 3 groups of 2 counters.

You can use addition to join groups.

$2 + 2 + 2 = 6$

You can also multiply to join equal groups.

$3 \times 2 = 6$

So, $2 + 2 + 2 = 3 \times 2$.

Remember that multiplication is a quick way of joining equal groups.

Copy and complete.

1. 2 groups of ☐
   5 + ☐ = ☐
   2 × ☐ = ☐

2. 3 groups of ☐
   6 + ☐ + ☐ = ☐
   3 × ☐ = ☐

Set B, pages 130–132

Draw an array to show 2×3.
Then write the product.

This array shows 2 rows of 3.

■■■ 2 rows
■■■ 3 in each row

$3 + 3 = 6$ or $2 \times 3 = 6$.

Draw an array to show 3×2.

This array shows 3 rows of 2.

■■ 3 rows
■■ 2 in each row
■■

$2 + 2 + 2 = 6$ or $3 \times 2 = 6$.

Remember to use the Commutative (order) Property of Multiplication.

Draw an array to show each fact. Write the product.

1. 2×4
2. 3×5
3. 4×4

Copy and complete each multiplication sentence.

4. 5 × ☐ = 10
   2 × ☐ = 10
5. 3 × ☐ = 21
   7 × ☐ = 21

Set C, pages 134–135

Find 2 times as many as 6.

$2 \times 6 = 12$ or

$$\begin{array}{r} 6 \\ \times\ 2 \\ \hline 12 \end{array}$$

Remember that you multiply by 2 to find *twice as many*.

Find each amount. You may use drawings or counters to help.

1. 3 times as many as 5
2. 5 times as many as 4
3. Twice as many as 7

Reteaching

Set D, pages 136–137

Write a multiplication story for 3×5.

Draw a picture to find the product.

Jessica is putting pretzels into 3 bags. She will put 5 pretzels in each bag. How many pretzels does Jessica have in all?

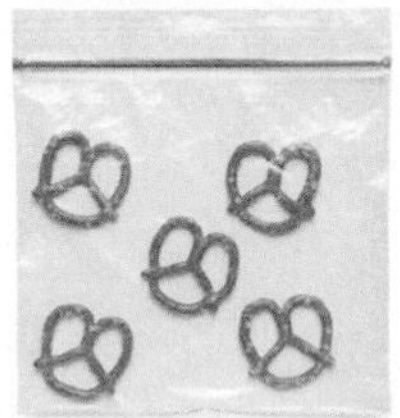

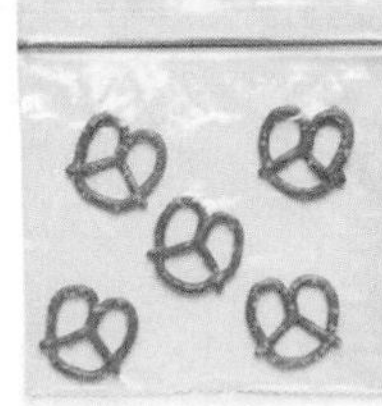

Jessica has 15 pretzels.

Remember that your multiplication story should always end with a question.

Write a multiplication story for each. Draw a picture to find each product.

1. 3×9 **2.** 5×6 **3.** 7×2

Write a multiplication story for each picture. Use the picture to find the product.

4. 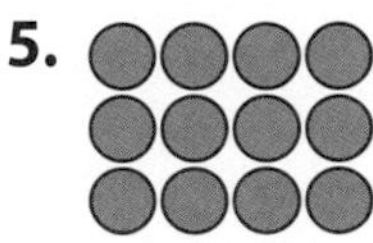

5.

Set E, pages 138–140

You can use words, pictures, numbers, or symbols to explain an answer. When you explain your answer to a problem, be sure that you:

- clearly show your explanation using words, pictures, numbers, or symbols.
- tell what the numbers mean in your explanation.
- tell why you took certain steps.

Remember that another person should be able to follow your explanation.

Solve. Explain how you found each answer.

1. Gina earns $3 for making dinner and $5 for changing the sheets on her bed. How much will Gina earn in one week if she makes dinner 3 times and changes the sheets one time?
2. Jack is setting up tables for a party. Each table has 6 chairs. How many chairs does he need for 10 tables?

Topic 7

Multiplication Facts: Use Patterns

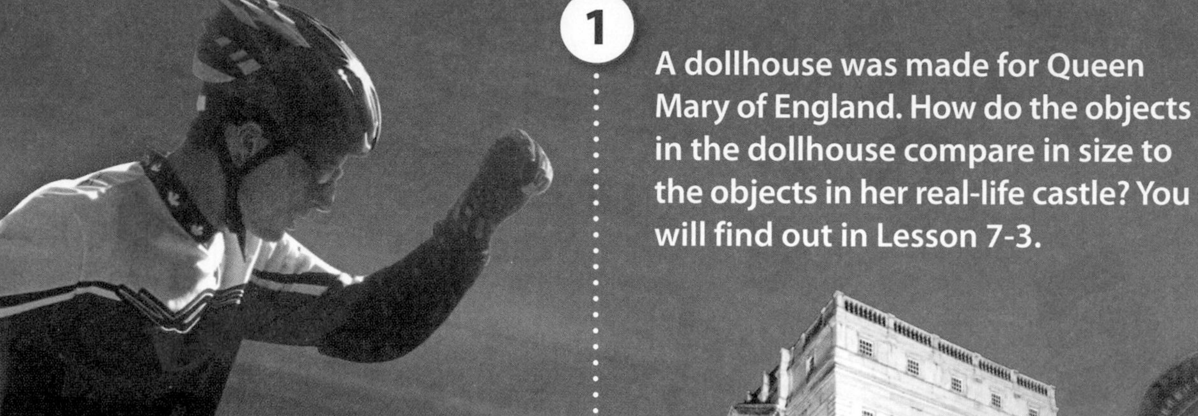

1 A dollhouse was made for Queen Mary of England. How do the objects in the dollhouse compare in size to the objects in her real-life castle? You will find out in Lesson 7-3.

2 How many wheels are on the bikes of a unicycle relay team? You will find out in Lesson 7-3.

3

How many hearts does an earthworm have? You will find out in Lesson 7-1.

4

How much did miners during the California Gold Rush pay for a glass of water? You will find out in Lesson 7-4.

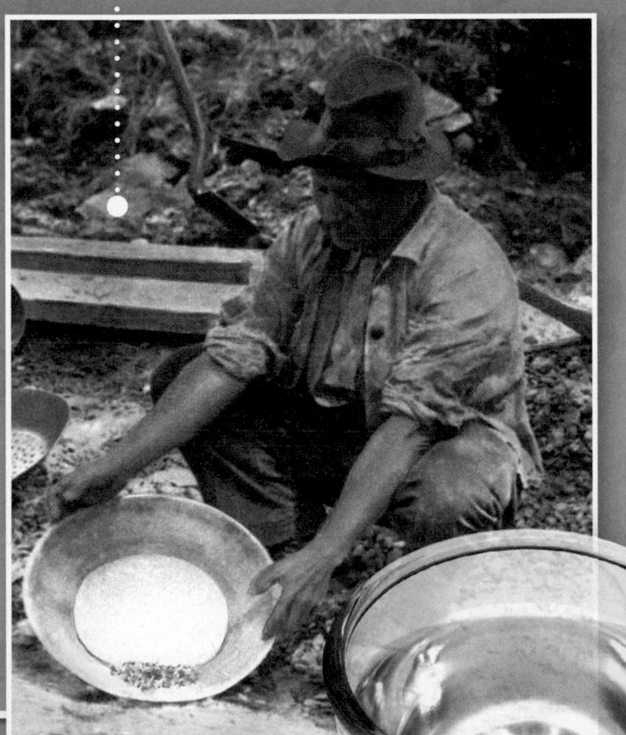

Review What You Know!

Vocabulary

Choose the best term from the box.

- addends
- product
- factors
- sum

1. The numbers you multiply are ___?___.
2. The answer in an addition problem is the ___?___.
3. The answer in a multiplication problem is the ___?___.

Skip Counting

Write the missing numbers.

4. 10, 20, ▢, 40, 50, ▢
5. 10, 15, 20, ▢, ▢, 35

Repeated Addition

Find each sum.

6. 1 + 1 + 1 + 1 + 1 + 1 + 1
7. 2 + 2 + 2 + 2 + 2 + 2

Adding

Find each sum.

8. 80 + 16
9. 90 + 18
10. 70 + 14
11. 110 + 22
12. 110 + 11
13. 120 + 12

Multiplication

14. **Writing to Explain** Explain how to find how many items are in 3 groups if there are 4 items in each group. Draw a picture to help.

Lesson

7-1

NS 2.2 Memorize to automaticity the multiplication table for numbers between 1 and 10.

2 and 5 as Factors

How can you use patterns to multiply by 2 and 5?

How many socks are in 7 pairs of socks? Find 7×2.

1 pair	2 pairs	3 pairs	4 pairs	5 pairs	6 pairs	7 pairs
1×2	2×2	3×2	4×2	5×2	6×2	7×2
2	4	6	8	10	12	14

There are 14 socks in 7 pairs.

Other Examples

What are the patterns in multiples of 2 and 5?

The products for the 2s facts are multiples of 2.
The products for the 5s facts are multiples of 5.
Multiples are the products of a number and other whole numbers.

Data

2s Facts	
$0 \times 2 = 0$	$5 \times 2 = 10$
$1 \times 2 = 2$	$6 \times 2 = 12$
$2 \times 2 = 4$	$7 \times 2 = 14$
$3 \times 2 = 6$	$8 \times 2 = 16$
$4 \times 2 = 8$	$9 \times 2 = 18$

Data

5s Facts	
$0 \times 5 = 0$	$5 \times 5 = 25$
$1 \times 5 = 5$	$6 \times 5 = 30$
$2 \times 5 = 10$	$7 \times 5 = 35$
$3 \times 5 = 15$	$8 \times 5 = 40$
$4 \times 5 = 20$	$9 \times 5 = 45$

Patterns for 2s Facts

- Multiples of 2 are even numbers. Multiples of 2 end in 0, 2, 4, 6, or 8.
- Each multiple of 2 is 2 more than the one before it.

Patterns for 5s Facts

- Each multiple of 5 ends in 0 or 5.
- Each multiple of 5 is 5 more than the one before it.

Explain It

1. Is 83 a multiple of 2 or a multiple of 5? How do you know?
2. **Reasoning** How can patterns help you find 10×2?

How many fingers are on 7 gloves?

Choose an Operation Find 7×5.

$1 \times 5 = 5$
$2 \times 5 = 10$
$3 \times 5 = 15$
$4 \times 5 = 20$
$5 \times 5 = 25$
$6 \times 5 = 30$
$7 \times 5 = 35$

There are 35 fingers on 7 gloves.

Guided Practice*

Do you know HOW?

Find each product.

1. 2×6 **2.** 2×3 **3.** 7×2

4. 5×3 **5.** 5×5 **6.** 6×5

7. 4×2 **8.** 5×2 **9.** 8×5

Do you UNDERSTAND?

10. How can you skip count to find the number of socks in 9 pairs? in 10 pairs?

11. How can you skip count to find how many fingers are on 9 gloves? on 10 gloves?

12. **Number Sense** Bert says that 2×8 is 15. How can you use patterns to know that his answer is wrong?

Independent Practice

For **13–26**, find each product.

13. 2×2 **14.** 5×2 **15.** 3×5 **16.** 8×2 **17.** 9×5

18. 3×5 **19.** 2×4 **20.** 4×5 **21.** 9×2 **22.** 5×7

23. Find 5 times 6.

24. Multiply 2 by 5.

25. Find the product of 7 and 5.

26. Find 6×2.

DIGITAL Animated Glossary **www.pearsonsuccessnet.com**

For another example, see Set A on page 162.

Independent Practice

Algebra Compare. Use $<$, $>$, or $=$.

27. $2 \times 5 \bigcirc 5 \times 2$ **28.** $4 \times 5 \bigcirc 4 \times 6$ **29.** $2 \times 5 \bigcirc 2 \times 4$

30. $6 \times 5 \bigcirc 5 \times 5$ **31.** $9 \times 5 \bigcirc 5 \times 9$ **32.** $7 \times 2 \bigcirc 2 \times 9$

Problem Solving

For **33–35**, use the table at the right.

33. How much does it cost to bowl three games without renting shoes?

34. Maru rented some bowling shoes. She also bowled two games. How much money did she spend?

Data

Bowling	
Cost per game	$5
Daily shoe rental	$2

35. Wendy paid for 2 games with a twenty-dollar bill. How much change did she get back?

36. **Writing to Explain** Eric has some nickels. He says they are worth exactly 34 cents. Can you tell if he is correct or not? Why or why not?

38. Use the picture below. How many hearts do 3 earthworms have?

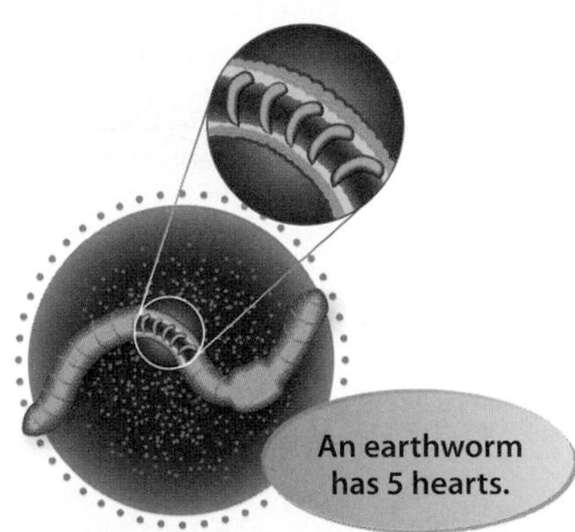

37. April has the coins shown below.

If April counted the value of these coins, which list shows numbers she could have named?

A 5, 10, 16, 20, 25

B 5, 10, 15, 22, 25

C 10, 15, 20, 25, 30

D 10, 15, 22, 25, 30

39. **Algebra** What two 1-digit factors could you multiply to get a product of 30?

40. Jake went bowling. On his first turn, he knocked down 2 pins. On his second turn, he knocked down twice that many. So far, how many pins in all has he knocked down?

Mixed Problem Solving

Animals get special features, called inherited traits, from their parents. Use the table on the right to answer the questions.

Some Traits of Animals	
Kind of Animal	**Inherited Trait**
Birds	2 eyes, 2 legs, 2 wings
Fish	2 eyes
Insects	2 antennas, 6 legs, 3 body parts
Apes	2 hands, 5 fingers on each hand, 2 legs, 5 toes on each foot, 2 eyes

1. A mother and her two babies are on a tree branch. They have six wings in all. Which kind of animal from the table could these be?

2. Two adult apes and two baby apes are near the water. How many fingers do the apes have in all?

3. One of these animals is on a tree branch. It has six legs in all. Which kind of animal from the table could this be?

4. Which has more legs—two birds or one insect? How many more?

5. Look at the table below.

Kind of Animal	Number of Body Parts	Number of Legs
Insect	3	6
Spider	2	8

Danny saw three of the same kind of animal on the sidewalk. He counted six body parts in all. Did Danny see 3 spiders or 3 insects?

6. **Strategy Focus** Solve. Use the strategy Draw a Picture.

Trini had 31 baby fish and 5 adult fish in a fish tank. She put 18 of the baby fish in another tank, and all of the adult fish in a third tank. How many baby fish are left in the first tank? Check if your answer is reasonable.

Lesson
7-2

NS 2.2 Memorize to automaticity the multiplication table for numbers between 1 and 10.
Also **AF 1.3, MR 1.1**

9 as a Factor

How can patterns be used to find 9s facts?

The owner of a flower shop puts 9 roses in each package. How many roses are in 8 packages?

Use patterns to find 8 × 9.

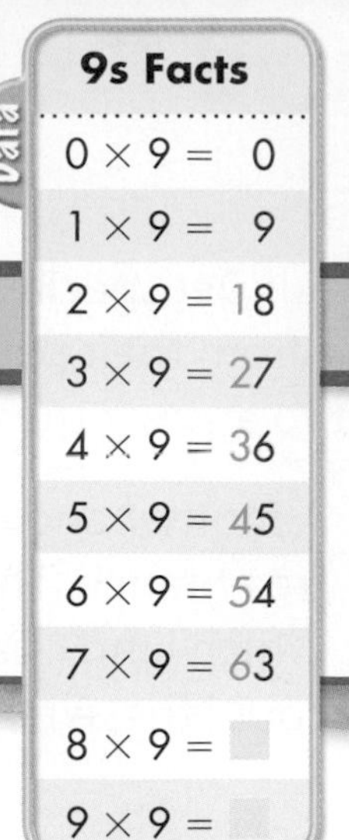

Data

9s Facts
0 × 9 = 0
1 × 9 = 9
2 × 9 = 18
3 × 9 = 27
4 × 9 = 36
5 × 9 = 45
6 × 9 = 54
7 × 9 = 63
8 × 9 =
9 × 9 =

Guided Practice*

Do you know HOW?

Find each product.

1. 9 × 2 **2.** 5 × 9 **3.** 7 × 9

4. 4 × 9 **5.** 2 × 8 **6.** 6 × 9

7. 3 × 9 **8.** 5 × 5 **9.** 8 × 9

Do you UNDERSTAND?

10. Writing to Explain Use the patterns above to find 9 × 9. Then explain how you found the product.

11. Number Sense Paul thinks that 3 × 9 is 24. Use a 9s pattern to show that he is wrong.

Independent Practice

Find each product.

12. 9 × 0 **13.** 5 × 8 **14.** 9 × 4 **15.** 8 × 9 **16.** 9 × 9

17. 1 × 9 **18.** 5 × 9 **19.** 9 × 2 **20.** 7 × 9 **21.** 5 × 2

22. 6 × 5 **23.** 9 × 1 **24.** 6 × 9 **25.** 9 × 5 **26.** 9 × 7

27. 9 × 2 **28.** 7 × 9 **29.** 8 × 2 **30.** 0 × 9 **31.** 2 × 3

*For another example, see Set B on page 162.

One Way

Use these patterns.

- The ones digit decreases by 1 each time. So the next ones digit is 2.
- The tens digit increases by 1 each time. So the next tens digit is 7.

$8 \times 9 = 72$

There are 72 roses in 8 packages.

Another Way

Use these patterns to find the product.

- The tens digit is 1 less than the factor being multiplied by 9.
- The digits of the product have a sum of 9.

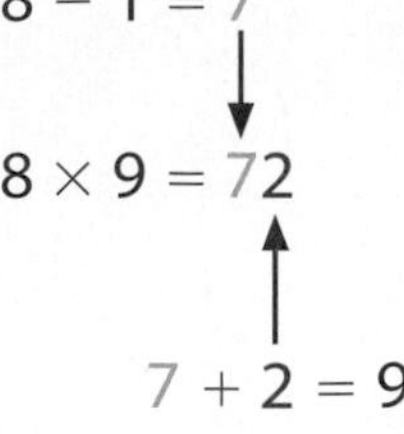

$8 \times 9 = 72$

There are 72 roses in 8 packages.

Algebra Copy and complete. Use +, −, or ×.

32. $2 \times 6 = 10 \square 2$ **33.** $5 \times 7 = 45 \square 10$ **34.** $9 \times 9 = 80 \square 1$

35. $20 - 2 = 2 \square 9$ **36.** $9 \square 3 = 30 - 3$ **37.** $9 \square 1 = 2 \square 5$

Problem Solving

The library is having a used book sale. For **38–41**, use the table at the right.

38. How much do 4 hardcover books cost?

Library Book Sale (Data)

Item	Price
Paperback Books	$2
Hardcover Books	$5
Books on CDs	$9

39. How much more would Chico spend if he bought 3 books on CDs rather than 3 hardcover books?

40. Maggie bought only paperback books. The clerk told her she owed $15. How does Maggie know that the clerk made a mistake?

41. **Writing to Explain** Mr. Lee bought 2 books on CDs and 9 paperback books. Did he spend more on CDs or paperbacks? Tell how you know.

42. The owner of a flower shop counted the flowers in groups of 9. Which list shows the numbers he named?

9 sunflowers in each vase.

A 9, 19, 29, 39, 49, 59 **C** 18, 27, 36, 45, 56, 65

B 6, 12, 18, 24, 36, 42 **D** 9, 18, 27, 36, 45, 54

Lesson
7-3

NS 2.6 Understand the special properties of 0 and 1 in multiplication and division.
Also **AF 1.0** Select appropriate symbols, operations and properties to represent, describe, simplify, and solve simple number relationships.

Multiplying with 0 and 1

What are the patterns in multiples of 1 and 0?

Kira has 8 plates with 1 orange on each plate.
How many oranges does Kira have?

Find 8×1.

Guided Practice*

Do you know HOW?

Find each product.

1. 1×7 **2.** 5×0 **3.** 5×1

4. 0×0 **5.** 1×1 **6.** 8×1

7. 7×0 **8.** 1×9 **9.** 0×6

Do you UNDERSTAND?

10. Writing to Explain How can you use the properties above to find 375×1 and 0×754?

11. Draw an array to show that $1 \times 8 = 8$.

12. Chad has 6 plates. There is 1 apple and 0 grapes on each plate. How many apples are there? How many grapes are there?

Independent Practice

Find each product.

13. 0×4 **14.** 1×6 **15.** 1×3 **16.** 3×0 **17.** 4×1

18. 0×9 **19.** 1×3 **20.** 1×7 **21.** 0×7 **22.** 8×0

23. 8×1 **24.** 0×2 **25.** 1×2 **26.** 9×0 **27.** 0×1

DIGITAL Animated Glossary **www.pearsonsuccessnet.com**

*For another example, see Set C on page 162.

8 groups with 1 in each group equals 8 in all.

$8 \times 1 = 8$

Kira has 8 oranges.

1 plate with 8 oranges also equals 8 oranges.

$1 \times 8 = 8$

The Identity (One) Property of Multiplication: when you multiply a number and 1, the product is that number.

If Kira has 4 plates with 0 oranges on each plate, she has 0 oranges.

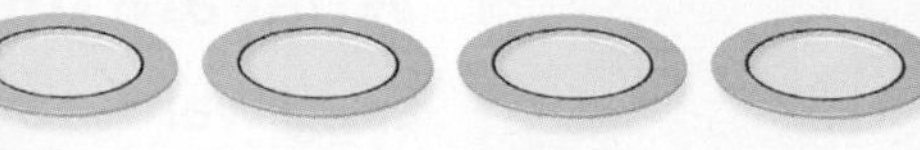

$4 \times 0 = 0$

If $4 \times 0 = 0$ then $0 \times 4 = 0$.

The Zero Property of Multiplication: when you multiply a number and 0, the product is 0.

Algebra Copy and complete. Write <, >, or = for each ◯.

28. 1×6 ◯ 8×0

29. 8×1 ◯ 1×9

30. 1×4 ◯ 4×1

31. 0×654 ◯ 346×0

32. 2×9 ◯ 9×1

33. 0×754 ◯ 5×1

Algebra Copy and complete. Write $\times$, $+$, or $-$ for each □.

34. 4 □ 1 = 4
4 □ 1 = 5
4 □ 1 = 3

35. 4 □ 0 = 4
4 □ 0 = 0

36. 6 □ 1 = 5
6 □ 1 = 6
6 □ 1 = 7

Problem Solving

37. What is the missing factor?
$548 \times \square = 548$

A 0 **B** 1 **C** 2 **D** 4

38. Writing to Explain The product of two factors is 0. One of the factors is 0. Can you tell what the other factor is? Explain your answer.

39. A unicycle relay team has 4 riders. Each rider has one unicycle. If each unicycle has 1 wheel, how many wheels does the team have?

40. Reasoning Why do you think the Identity Property of Multiplication is sometimes called the One Property of Multiplication?

41. Objects in Windsor Castle are 12 times the size of the miniature versions in Queen Mary's dollhouse. How tall is a real-life painting if it is 1 inch tall in the dollhouse?

Lesson

7-4

NS 2.2 Memorize to automaticity the multiplication table for numbers between 1 and 10.

10 as a Factor

What are the patterns in multiples of 10?

Greg wants to train for a race that is 10 weeks away. The chart shows his training schedule. How many miles will Greg run to train for the race?

Choose the Operation
Find 10×10.

Data

Weekly Schedule	
Activity	**Miles**
Swimming	4 miles
Running	10 miles
Biking	9 miles

Guided Practice*

Do you know HOW?

Find each product.

1. 2×10 **2.** 6×10

3. 10×1 **4.** 10×3 **5.** 10×7

Do you UNDERSTAND?

6. Writing to Explain Is 91 a multiple of 10? Explain.

7. How many miles will Greg bike in 10 weeks?

Independent Practice

Find each product.

8. 4×10 **9.** 9×10 **10.** 10×6 **11.** 5×5 **12.** 10×10

13. 5×10 **14.** 8×2 **15.** 10×7 **16.** 9×9 **17.** 6×10

18. 10×10 **19.** 2×10 **20.** 5×9 **21.** 3×10 **22.** 10×8

23. 6×5 **24.** 10×1 **25.** 1×9 **26.** 10×9 **27.** 10×5

28. 10×2 **29.** 7×2 **30.** 10×4 **31.** 10×8 **32.** 0×6

33. 5×8 **34.** 10×0 **35.** 10×3 **36.** 9×7 **37.** 10×7

*For another example, see Set D on page 163.

10s Facts	
0 × 10 = 0	5 × 10 = 50
1 × 10 = 10	6 × 10 = 60
2 × 10 = 20	7 × 10 = 70
3 × 10 = 30	8 × 10 = 80
4 × 10 = 40	9 × 10 = 90
	10 × 10 =

Use patterns to find the product.

- Write the factor you are multiplying by 10.
- Write a zero to the right of that factor. A multiple of 10 will always have a zero in the ones place.

$$10 \times 10 = 100$$

Greg will run 100 miles.

Problem Solving

Use the table at the right for **38** and **39**. It shows the food that was bought for 70 third graders for a school picnic.

Food Item	Number of Packages	Number in Each Package
Hot dogs	8	10
Rolls	10	9
Juice boxes	9	9

38. Find the total number of each item bought.

a Hot dogs

b Rolls

c Juice boxes

39. How many extra juice boxes were bought?

40. Writing to Explain Look at the table at the top of page 156. Greg multiplied 5 × 10 to find how many more miles he biked than swam in the 10 weeks. Does that make sense? Why or why not?

41. Strategy Focus Solve. Use the strategy Draw a Picture.

Mai had 3 packs of pens. Each pack had 10 pens. She gave 5 pens to Ervin. How many pens did she have left?

42. Number Sense Raul has only dimes in his pocket. Could he have exactly 45 cents? Explain.

43. During the California Gold Rush, miners sometimes paid $10 for a glass of water. What was the total cost if 7 miners each bought a glass of water?

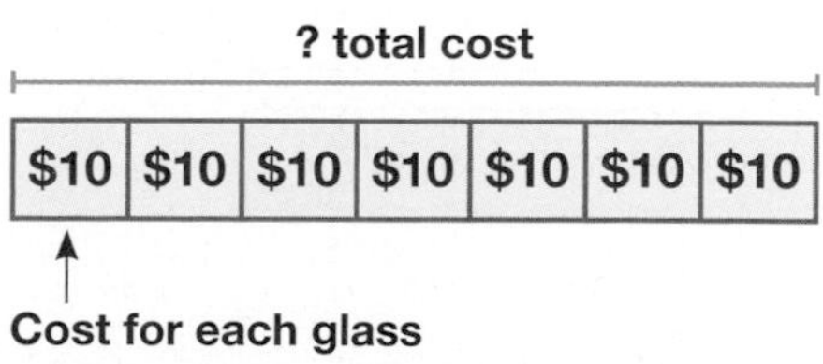

44. Which sign makes the number sentence true?

8 ☐ 5 = 40

A +

B −

C ×

D ÷

Lesson

7-5

MR 2.0 Use strategies, skills, and concepts in finding solutions. Also **NS 2.8**.

Problem Solving

Two-Question Problems

Sometimes you must use the answer to one problem to solve another problem.

Problem 1: Four girls and five boys went to the movies. How many children went to the movies?

Problem 2: Children's movie tickets cost $5 each. What was the total cost of the tickets for these children?

Movie Plex
Admit One
Child
$5

Guided Practice*

Do you know HOW?

1a. A movie ticket for an adult costs $9. How much do 3 adult tickets cost?

? Total cost

$9	$9	$9

b. Mr. Jones paid for 3 adult tickets with $40. How much change will he get?

$40

$27	?

Do you UNDERSTAND?

2. What operations were used to solve Problems 1a and 1b? Tell why.

3. Writing to Explain Why do you need the answer to Problem 1a to solve 1b?

4. Write a Problem Write 2 problems that use the answer from the first problem to solve the second one.

Independent Practice

5a. Jared bought a baseball cap for $12 and a T-shirt for $19. How much did the items cost all together?

?

$12	$19

b. Suppose Jared paid with a $50 bill. How much change should he get?

$50

$31	?

- What do I know?
- What am I asked to find?
- What diagram can I use to help understand the problem?
- Can I use addition, subtraction, multiplication, or division?
- Is all of my work correct?
- Did I answer the right question?
- Is my answer reasonable?

*For another example, see Set E on page 163.

Solve

Problem 1

Four girls and five boys went to the movies. How many children went to the movies?

? Children in all

4 girls	5 boys

$4 + 5 = 9$

Nine children went to the movies.

Solve

Problem 2

Children's movie tickets cost $5 each. What was the total cost of the tickets for these children?

? Total cost

$5	$5	$5	$5	$5	$5	$5	$5	$5

9 × $5 = $45

The total cost of the tickets was $45.

Cara and some friends bought gifts in a museum shop. The gifts were from Hawaii. In **6–8**, use the answer from the first problem to solve the second problem.

6a Cara bought a poster and a shirt. How much did her gifts cost?

b Cara gave the clerk $30. How much change should she get?

7a Dan bought 3 cups. How much did Dan spend on cups?

b Dan also bought a CD. How much did Dan spend in all?

8a Teri bought the most expensive and the least expensive gift. How much did she spend?

b Teri's sister bought a CD. How much did the two girls spend in all?

9. On Monday, Roberta swam 10 laps. On Tuesday, she swam twice as many laps as on Monday. Which pair of number sentences can be used to find:

a how many laps Roberta swam on Tuesday?
b how many laps Roberta swam in all?

A $2 \times 10 = 20$
$20 + 10 = 30$

B $2 \times 10 = 20$
$20 - 10 = 10$

C $10 + 2 = 12$
$12 + 10 = 22$

D $10 + 2 = 12$
$12 - 10 = 2$

Test Prep

1. Which symbol makes the number sentence true? (7-3)

$5 \times 0 \bigcirc 2 \times 1$

A >

B <

C =

D ×

2. Salvador's family used 3 canoes at Bass Lake. Each canoe had 2 people. How many people went canoeing? (7-1)

A 5

B 6

C 8

D 9

3. Using the *sum of the digits* pattern, which number is a multiple of 9? (7-2)

A 55

B 43

C 36

D 26

4. The 3rd graders at Willow Elementary were put in 9 groups of 10. How many 3rd graders were there? (7-4)

A 19

B 90

C 99

D 900

5. Sally bought 2 packages of balloons. Each package had 8 balloons. How many balloons did Sally buy? She gave 4 balloons to her brother. How many did she have left? (7-5)

A Sally bought 18 balloons and had 14 left.

B Sally bought 10 balloons and had 6 left.

C Sally bought 16 balloons and had 10 left.

D Sally bought 16 balloons and had 12 left.

6. What is 10×10? (7-4)

A 100

B 110

C 1,000

D 1,010

7. Each starfish has 5 arms.

If Shelly counted the arms in groups of 5, which list shows numbers she could have named? (7-1)

A 5, 6, 7, 8

B 10, 24, 30, 40

C 10, 15, 20, 25

D 18, 24, 30, 36

Test Prep

8. Todd has 7 aquariums. Each aquarium has 9 fish and 3 plants. What is the total number of fish? (7-2)

A 63

B 62

C 27

D 21

9. Which of these best describes all the snake lengths? (7-1)

Data

Snake	Length in Feet
Black Mamba	14
King Cobra	16
Taipan	10

A They are all greater than 12.

B They are all less than 15.

C They are all multiples of 5.

D They are all multiples of 2.

10. A pet store had 7 hamster cages. Each cage had 0 hamsters. How many hamsters did the pet store have? (7-3)

A 0

B 1

C 7

D 10

11. Which number makes the number sentence true? (7-3)

$\square \times 8 = 8$

A 8

B 2

C 1

D 0

12. Len has 3 rolls of quarters. Ryan has 8 rolls. How many more rolls does Ryan have than Len? Each roll has $10 worth of quarters. How much more money does Ryan have than Len? (7-5)

A Ryan has 11 more rolls, so he has $110 more than Len.

B Ryan has 5 more rolls, so he has $55 more than Len.

C Ryan has 5 more rolls, so he has $50 more than Len.

D Ryan has 6 more rolls, so he has $60 more than Len.

13. Rosa bought the ribbon shown below. How many yards of ribbon did Rosa buy? (7-1)

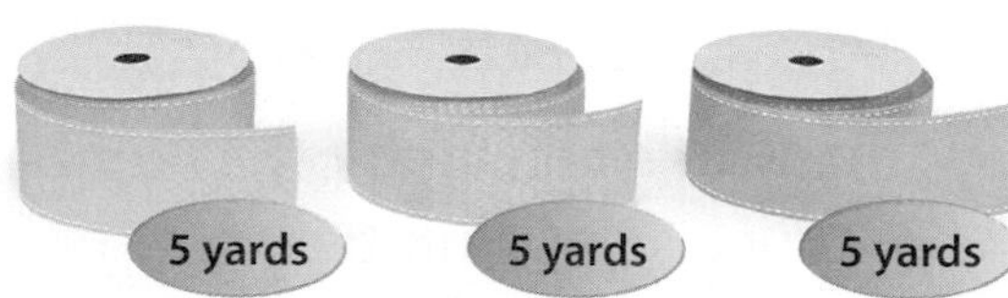

A 8

B 12

C 15

D 18

Reteaching

Set A, pages 148–150

Find 8×5.

You can use a pattern to multiply by 5s.

- You can skip count to multiply by 5: 5, 10, 15, 20, and so on.
- Each multiple of 5 ends with a 0 or a 5.
- Each multiple of 5 is 5 more than the one before it.

$8 \times 5 = 40$

Remember that making a table and using a pattern can help you to multiply by 2 or 5.

Find each product.

1. 2×4 **2.** 2×7 **3.** 3×2

4. 5×4 **5.** 5×9 **6.** 3×5

7. 6×2 **8.** 5×5 **9.** 8×5

Set B, pages 152–153

Find 7×9. Use a pattern.

The tens digit is 1 less than the factor being multiplied by 9.

Think $7 - 1 = 6$ so $7 \times 9 = 6$

The digits of the product have a sum of 9.

Think $9 - 6 = 3$ so $7 \times 9 = 63$

$7 \times 9 = 63$

Remember you can use patterns and known facts to find products for facts involving 9s.

Write each product.

1. 9×5 **2.** 7×9 **3.** 10×9

4. 9×4 **5.** 5×9 **6.** 3×9

7. 9×1 **8.** 8×9 **9.** 9×9

Set C, pages 154–155

The **Identity Property of Multiplication** says that when you multiply a number and 1, the product is that number.

$1 \times 6 = 6$ $12 \times 1 = 12$

The **Zero Property of Multiplication** says when you multiply a number and 0, the product is 0.

$0 \times 6 = 0$ $12 \times 0 = 0$

Remember that you can think about an array with 1 row when you multiply by 1.

Find each product.

1. 7×0 **2.** 1×10 **3.** 0×9

4. 3×1 **5.** 7×0 **6.** 1×5

Reteaching

Set D, pages 156–157

Find 7×10.

To find the product:

- Write the factor you are multiplying by 10.
- To the right of that factor, write a zero in the ones place.

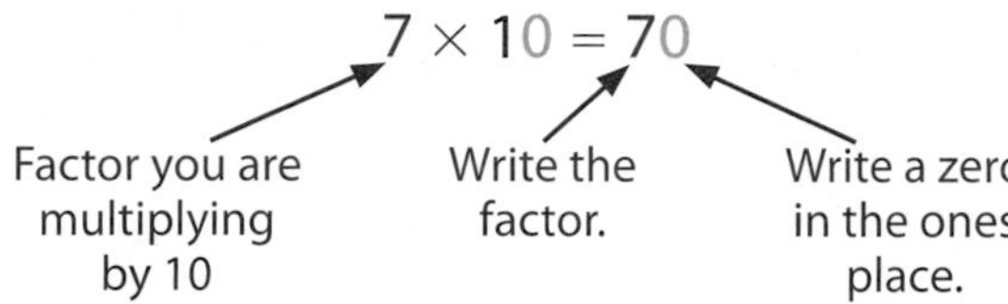

Remember that a multiple of 10 will always have a zero in the ones place.

Find each product.

1. 3×10 **2.** 5×10

3. 10×2 **4.** 10×6

5. $\begin{array}{r} 10 \\ \times \; 4 \\ \hline \end{array}$ **6.** $\begin{array}{r} 10 \\ \times \; 8 \\ \hline \end{array}$ **7.** $\begin{array}{r} 10 \\ \times \; 9 \\ \hline \end{array}$

Set E, pages 158–159

In two-question problems, you must solve one problem before you can solve the other.

Problem 1: A family of two adults and three children went to an air show. How many people in the family went to the air show?
$2 + 3 = 5$

Problem 2: Each pass to the air show cost \$10. How much did the family spend on passes for the air show?
$5 \times \$10 = \$50$

The family spent a total of \$50 on passes for the air show.

Remember to solve the first problem before you try to solve the second problem.

1. a For lunch, Julia bought a sandwich for \$8 and a glass of juice for \$3. How much did her lunch cost?

b Julia gave the clerk a \$20 bill. How much change should she get?

2. a A group of three girls and five boys went to the zoo. How many children are in the group?

b Each ticket to the zoo cost \$5. What was the total cost of tickets for these children?

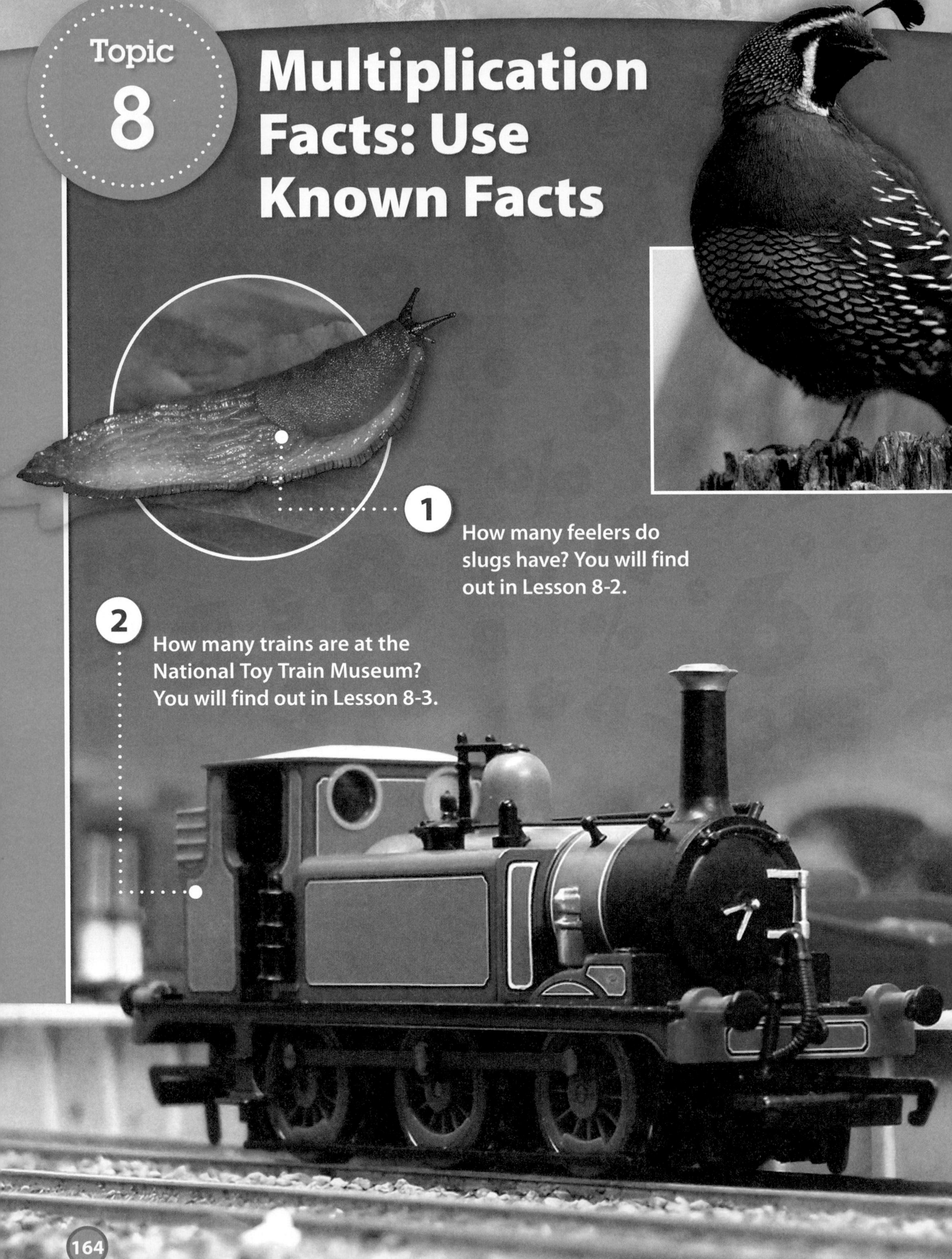

Topic 8

Multiplication Facts: Use Known Facts

1 How many feelers do slugs have? You will find out in Lesson 8-2.

2 How many trains are at the National Toy Train Museum? You will find out in Lesson 8-3.

3

The valley quail is the state bird of California. Will you always find more than 6 eggs in their nests? You will find out in Lesson 8-5.

4

How long does Comet Encke take to orbit the Sun? You will find out in Lesson 8-1.

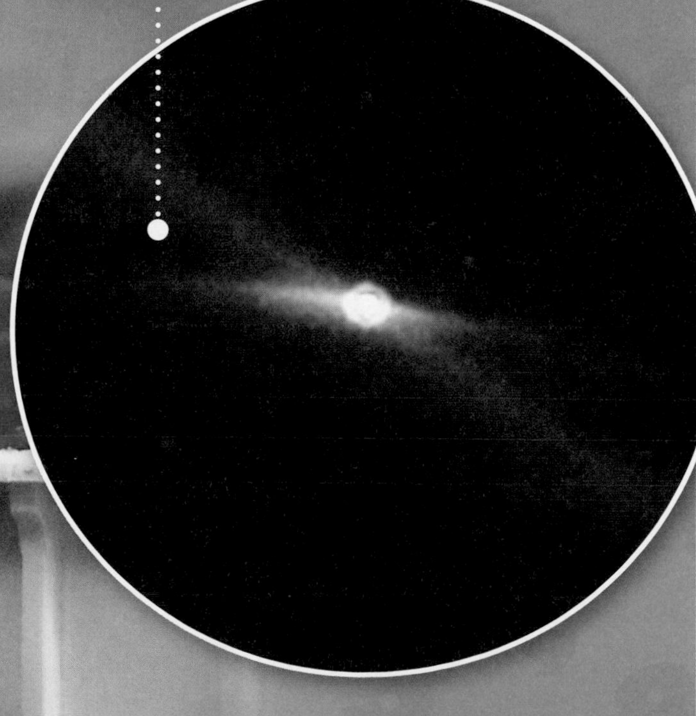

Review What You Know!

Vocabulary

Choose the best term from the box.

- addend
- array
- factor
- multiply

1. When you put together equal groups to get the total number, you ___?___.
2. When numbers are multiplied, each number is called a(n) ___?___.
3. When you display objects in rows and columns, you make a(n) ___?___.

Multiplication

Find each product.

4. 3×2
5. 4×5
6. 7×2
7. 6×1
8. 8×0
9. 5×9

Arrays

Draw an array for each multiplication fact.

10. 6×2
11. 4×9
12. Write a multiplication number sentence for the array shown at the right. Explain why you used the numbers you did.

13. **Writing to Explain** Is an array for 2×9 the same as or different from an array for 9×2? Draw a picture and explain your answer.

Lesson

8-1

NS 2.2 Memorize to automaticity the multiplication table for numbers between 1 and 10.

3 as a Factor

counters

How can you break apart arrays to multiply with 3?

The canoes are stored in 3 rows. There are 6 canoes in each row. What is the total number of canoes stored?

Find 3×6.

Choose an Operation Multiply to find the total for an array.

Guided Practice*

Do you know HOW?

In **1–6**, multiply. You may use counters or draw pictures to help.

1. 3×4

2. 3×11

3. 3×5

4. 3×9

5. 12×3

6. 3×6

Do you UNDERSTAND?

7. How can you use $2 \times 8 = 16$ to find 3×8?

8. Selena arranged plants in 3 rows at the community garden. She put 6 plants in each row. How many plants in all did Selena arrange into the rows?

Independent Practice

In **9–28**, find the product. You may draw pictures to help.

9. 3×2 **10.** 4×9 **11.** 3×10 **12.** 2×9 **13.** 4×3

14. 8×3 **15.** 1×7 **16.** 5×3 **17.** 0×3 **18.** 3×8

19. 7×3 **20.** 9×8 **21.** 3×3 **22.** 5×4 **23.** 3×9

24. 1×3 **25.** 6×3 **26.** 9×5 **27.** 3×4 **28.** 3×7

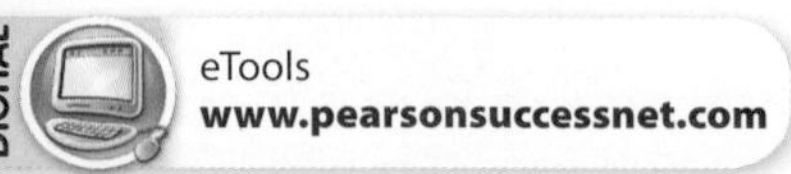

DIGITAL eTools **www.pearsonsuccessnet.com**

*For another example, see Set A on page 184.

What You Show

Find 3×6.

Use 1s facts and 2s facts to help multiply with 3.

Make an array for each multiplication sentence.

$2 \times 6 = 12$

$1 \times 6 = 6$

$12 + 6 = 18$

What You Think

3×6 is 3 rows of 6.
That is 2 sixes plus 6 more.

2 sixes are 12.
1 six is 6.

$12 + 6 = 18$

$3 \times 6 = 18$

There are 18 canoes in all.

Problem Solving

For **29** and **30**, use the table at the right.

29. What is the total number of stamps in a package of car stamps and a package of outer space stamps?

30. Cara bought 1 package of reptile stamps. What is the total number of reptile stamps she bought? Draw an array.

Data

Number of Stamps in Different Packages

Kind of Stamp	Number of Rows	Number in Each Row
Dinosaurs	3	7
Cars	3	9
Outer Space	3	8
Reptiles	5	6

31. Number Sense Suppose you need to find 3×9.

a What two multiplication facts can help you find 3×9?

b How could you use 3×9 to help you find 9×3?

32. It takes about 3 years for Comet Encke to orbit the Sun. About how many years will it take Comet Encke to orbit the Sun 5 times?

A About 5 years

B About 10 years

C About 15 years

D About 20 years

33. Mr. Torres had packages of tomatoes on the counter. Each package had 3 tomatoes in it.

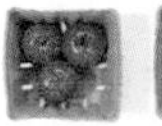   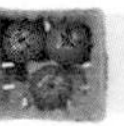  

If Mr. Torres counted the tomatoes in groups of 3, which list shows numbers he could have named?

A 6, 12, 16, 19

B 6, 9, 12, 15

C 3, 6, 10, 13

D 3, 7, 11, 15

Lesson
8-2

NS 2.2 Memorize to automaticity the multiplication table for numbers between 1 and 10.

4 as a Factor

counters

How can you use doubles to multiply with 4?

Anna painted piggy banks to sell at the student art show. She painted a bank on each of the 7 days of the week for 4 weeks. How many piggy banks did she paint in all?

Find 4×7.

Choose an Operation Multiply to find the total for an array.

Guided Practice*

Do you know HOW?

In **1–6**, multiply. You may use counters or draw pictures to help.

1. 4×6

2. 5×4

3. 4×9

4. 1×4

5. $\begin{array}{r} 1 \\ \times\ 4 \\ \hline \end{array}$

6. $\begin{array}{r} 10 \\ \times\ \ 4 \\ \hline \end{array}$

Do you UNDERSTAND?

7. Besides the way shown above, what is another way to break apart 4×7 using facts you know?

8. If you know $2 \times 8 = 16$, how can you find 4×8?

9. Nolan made lamps to sell at the school art show. He made 9 lamps each week for 4 weeks. How many lamps did Nolan make in all?

Independent Practice

In **10–29**, find the product. You may draw pictures to help.

10. 4×8 **11.** 3×8 **12.** 4×3 **13.** 6×4 **14.** 9×6

15. 4×4 **16.** 5×9 **17.** 10×4 **18.** 0×4 **19.** 2×9

20. 3×4 **21.** 2×8 **22.** 4×5 **23.** 7×4 **24.** 6×4

25. $\begin{array}{r} 2 \\ \times\ 4 \\ \hline \end{array}$ **26.** $\begin{array}{r} 7 \\ \times\ 4 \\ \hline \end{array}$ **27.** $\begin{array}{r} 9 \\ \times\ 4 \\ \hline \end{array}$ **28.** $\begin{array}{r} 10 \\ \times\ \ 7 \\ \hline \end{array}$ **29.** $\begin{array}{r} 4 \\ \times\ 8 \\ \hline \end{array}$

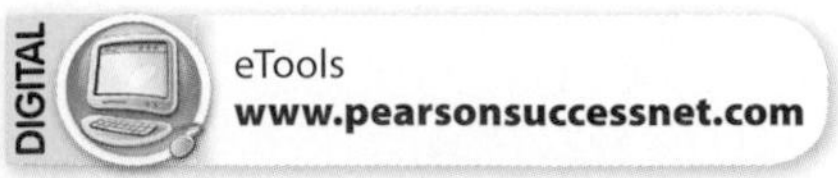

*For another example, see Set B on page 184.

What You Show

Find 4×7.

To multiply by 4, you can think of a 2s fact, then double it.

You can make arrays.

$2 \times 7 = 14$

$2 \times 7 = 14$

$14 + 14 = 28$

What You Think

4×7 is 4 rows of 7. That is 2 sevens plus 2 sevens.

2 sevens are 14.

$14 + 14 = 28$

So, $4 \times 7 = 28$.

Anna painted 28 piggy banks in all.

Problem Solving

For **30** and **31**, use the table at the right for the supplies James needs to buy for the Trail Walk trip.

Trail Walk Trip Supplies

Item	Number of Packages Needed	Number of Items in Each Package
Apples	2	8
Cereal Bars	4	6
Juice Drinks	4	3

30. What is the total number of cereal bars he needs to buy?

31. How many more apples than juice drinks does James need?

32. Martin studied slugs in science class. He learned that each slug has 4 feelers. That evening, he saw 8 slugs. How many feelers did the slugs have in all?

33. **Writing to Explain** Lila had 9 weeks of rock climbing lessons. She had 4 lessons each week. Explain why Lila can use 4×9 to find the product of 9×4.

34. Which of these best describes all the numbers on the shirts?

A They are all even numbers.

B They are all multiples of 3.

C They are all greater than 10.

D They are all 2-digit numbers.

35. Bess had boxes of candles on the table. Each box had 4 candles in it.

If Bess counted the candles in groups of 4, which list shows numbers she could have named?

A 8, 12, 16, 20

B 8, 12, 14, 18

C 4, 6, 12, 14

D 4, 8, 10, 14

Lesson

8-3

NS 2.2 Memorize to automaticity the multiplication table for numbers between 1 and 10.

6 and 7 as Factors

counters

How can you break apart arrays to multiply?

The musicians in the band march in 6 equal rows. There are 8 musicians in each row. How many musicians are in the band?

Find 6×8.

Choose an Operation Multiply to find the total for an array.

Another Example How can you break apart arrays to multiply by 7?

The singers in the chorus are standing in equal rows. There are 8 singers in each row. There are 7 rows. How many singers are in the chorus?

What You Show

Find 7×8.

Use 5s facts and 2s facts to help multiply with 7. Make an array for each multiplication sentence.

$5 \times 8 = 40$

$2 \times 8 = 16$

What You Think

7×8 is 7 rows of 8.

That is 5 eights plus 2 eights.

5 eights are 40.
2 eights are 16.

$40 + 16 = 56$

So, $7 \times 8 = 56$.

The chorus has 56 singers.

Explain It

1. What other multiplication facts might help to find 7×8?
2. How could you use 5×7 and 2×7 to find 7×7?

What You Show

Find 6×8.

Use 5s facts and 1s facts.

Make an array for each multiplication sentence.

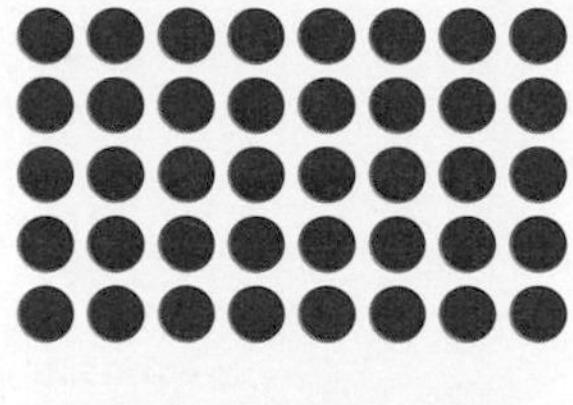

$5 \times 8 = 40$

$1 \times 8 = 8$

What You Think

6×8 is 6 rows of 8. That is 5 eights plus 1 more eight.

5 eights are 40.
8 more is 48.
$40 + 8 = 48$

So, $6 \times 8 = 48$.

The band has 48 musicians.

Guided Practice*

Do you know HOW?

In **1–6**, multiply. You may draw pictures or use counters to help.

1. 6×10

2. 7×6

3. 8×6

4. 2×7

5. Find 4 times 7.

6. Multiply 6 and 5.

Do you UNDERSTAND?

7. Writing to Explain Draw a picture of two arrays that show that 6×9 is equal to 5×9 plus 1×9. Explain your drawing.

8. The students who are graduating are standing in 7 equal rows. There are 9 students in each row. How many students are graduating?

Independent Practice

In **9–23**, find the product. You may draw pictures to help.

9. 6×7 **10.** 7×9 **11.** 9×6 **12.** 5×7 **13.** 6×4

14. 6×6 **15.** 10×7 **16.** 8×6 **17.** 7×7 **18.** 7×3

19. 5×7 **20.** 3×6 **21.** 4×7 **22.** 7×8 **23.** 10×6

DIGITAL eTools
www.pearsonsuccessnet.com

For another example, see Set C on page 184.

Problem Solving

24. The National Toy Train Museum has 5 large layouts for trains. One day, each layout had the same number of trains. How many trains were on display at the museum that day? Use the picture at the right.

6 trains in each layout

25. **Number Sense** Marge says that 1×0 is equal to $1 + 0$. Is she correct? Why or why not?

26. Miguel had baskets of oranges. Each held 6 oranges.

If Miguel counted the oranges in groups of 6, which list shows numbers he could have named?

A 6, 12, 21, 26

B 6, 11, 16, 21

C 12, 16, 20, 24

D 12, 18, 24, 30

27. **Writing to Explain** Nan made the arrays shown to find 6×3. Explain how to change the arrays to find 7×3. Use objects and draw a picture.

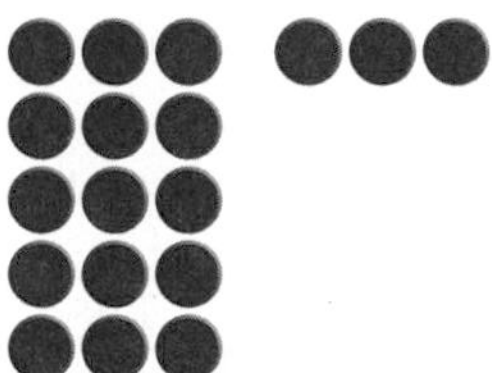

For **28** and **29**, use the drawings of the trains below.

28. A group of tourists needs 7 rows of seats in Car 5 of the Réseau train. How many seats are left for other passengers?

29. **Estimation** Use rounding to the nearest ten to find about how many seats in all are on the Atlantique and the Sud-Est trains.

Atlantique
485 total seats
3 seats each row | 3 seats each row | 3 seats each row | 4 seats each row | 4 seats each row

Réseau
377 total seats
3 seats each row | 3 seats each row | 3 seats each row | 4 seats each row | 4 seats each row

Sud-Est
345 total seats
3 seats each row | 3 seats each row | 3 seats each row | 4 seats each row | 4 seats each row

Algebra Connections

Number Sentences with More Than One Operation

Some number sentences have more than one operation. Rules called the *order of operations* tell the order in which you do the operations.

Rules for Order of Operations

- First, do operations inside the parentheses ( ).
- Next, do multiplications in order from left to right.
- Then do additions and subtractions in order from left to right.

Example: $(8 - 2) \times 7 = \square$

Think: Which operations are used? Are parentheses used?

Do operations inside the parentheses.

$$(8 - 2) \times 7$$
$$6 \times 7$$

Next, do the multiplication.

$$6 \times 7 = 42$$

Example: $5 + 3 \times 6 = \square$

Do the multiplication. $5 + 3 \times 6$

$5 + 18$

Then do the addition. $5 + 18 = 23$

Copy and complete each number sentence using the order of operations.

1. $(5 + 3) \times 6 = \square$ **2.** $7 + 3 \times 2 = \square$ **3.** $(7 + 3) \times 2 = \square$

4. $(8 + 4) \times 2 = \square$ **5.** $3 + 2 \times 9 = \square$ **6.** $(7 - 1) \times 4 = \square$

7. $8 + 0 \times 6 = \square$ **8.** $(2 + 2) \times 7 = \square$ **9.** $(6 - 3) \times 4 = \square$

10. $16 - 4 \times 3 = \square$ **11.** $13 + 9 \times 0 = \square$ **12.** $45 - 3 \times 2 = \square$

For **13** and **14**, copy and complete the number sentence below each problem. Use it to help solve the problem.

13. Nat had 2 train sets that each had 7 cars. He took 3 cars away from each set. How many cars in all are in the train sets now?
$(7 - \square) \times 2 = \square$

14. Joan had 5 pencils. Then she bought 4 packs of pencils. Each pack had 6 pencils. What is the total number of pencils Joan has now?
$5 + 4 \times \square = \square$

15. Write a Problem Write a problem that could be solved using the number sentence $3 + (6 \times 2) = \square$.

Lesson

8-4

NS 2.2 Memorize to automaticity the multiplication table for numbers between 1 and 10.

8 as a Factor

How can you use doubles to multiply with 8?

At the school fun fair, students try to toss a table tennis ball into a bowl. There are 8 rows of bowls. There are 8 bowls in each row. How many bowls are there in all?

Choose an Operation Multiply to find the total for an array. Find 8×8.

Guided Practice*

Do you know HOW?

In **1–6**, multiply.

1. 8×7

2. 8×9

3. 6×8

4. 10×8

5. $\begin{array}{r} 5 \\ \times\ 8 \\ \hline \end{array}$

6. $\begin{array}{r} 8 \\ \times\ 3 \\ \hline \end{array}$

Do you UNDERSTAND?

7. How could the fact $5 \times 8 = 40$ help you find 8×8?

8. How can you use 4×7 to find 8×7?

9. Mrs. Reyes needs to order bricks for her garden. She needs 8 rows of bricks. Each row will have 7 bricks. How many bricks in all should Mrs. Reyes order?

Independent Practice

In **10–27**, find the product.

10. 8×4 **11.** 7×8 **12.** 2×9 **13.** 5×7 **14.** 8×2

15. 8×6 **16.** 5×9 **17.** 8×5 **18.** 0×8 **19.** 4×9

20. $\begin{array}{r} 10 \\ \times\ 8 \\ \hline \end{array}$ **21.** $\begin{array}{r} 3 \\ \times\ 7 \\ \hline \end{array}$ **22.** $\begin{array}{r} 8 \\ \times\ 8 \\ \hline \end{array}$ **23.** $\begin{array}{r} 9 \\ \times\ 4 \\ \hline \end{array}$ **24.** $\begin{array}{r} 8 \\ \times\ 9 \\ \hline \end{array}$

25. Find 6 times 9. **26.** Multiply 8 and 1. **27.** Find 9 times 8.

*For another example, see Set D on page 185.

One Way

Use 2s facts to find 8×8.

8×8 is 4 groups of 2 eights.

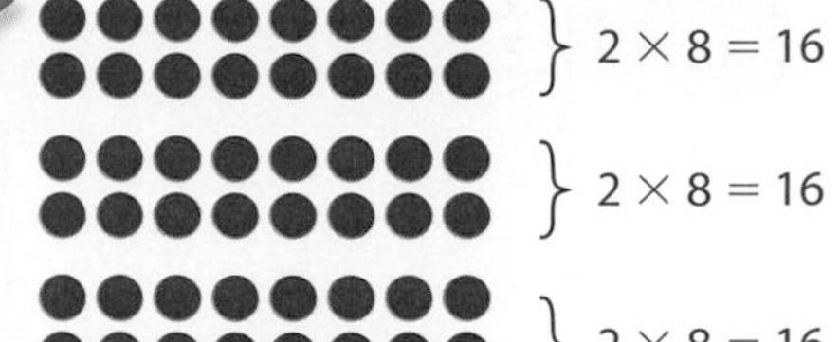

Another Way

Double a 4s fact to find 8×8.

8×8 is 4 eights plus 4 eights.

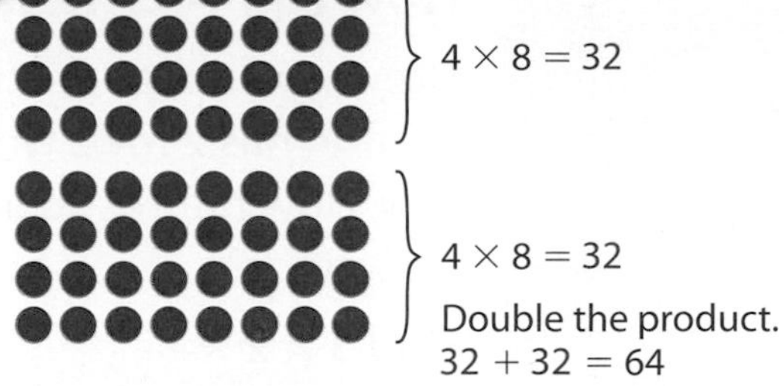

So, $8 \times 8 = 64$.

There are 64 bowls in all.

Problem Solving

For **28–30**, find the total number of tiles.

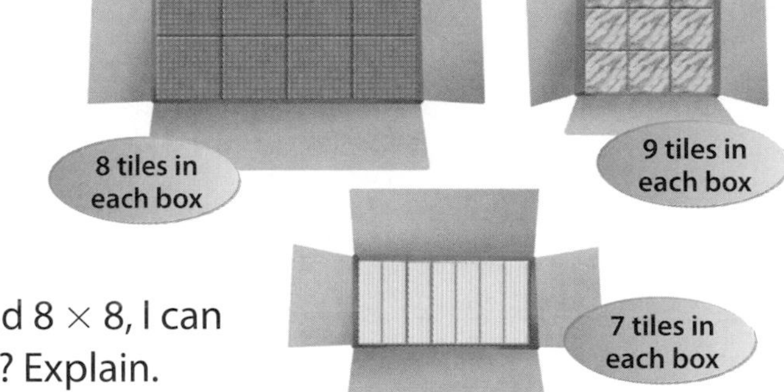

28. Mischa bought 8 boxes of orange tiles.

29. Aaron bought 6 boxes of yellow tiles.

30. Liz bought 7 boxes of green tiles.

31. **Writing to Explain** Sophi says, "To find 8×8, I can find 2×8 and double it." Do you agree? Explain.

For **32** and **33**, use the table at the right.

32. **Algebra** The total amount of money Nate spent at the clothing sale is $(2 \times \$9) + \$42$. What did he buy?

33. Willa bought a shirt and a sweater. She had $14 left. How much money did she start with?

Clothing Sale	
Shirt	$23
Belt	$9
Sweater	$38
Pair of Jeans	$42

34. Ms. Vero had boxes of crayons in a closet. Each box had 8 crayons in it.

   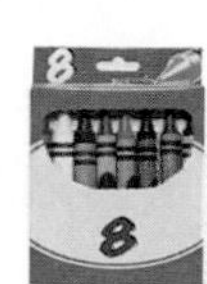  

If Ms. Vero counted the crayons in groups of 8, which list shows numbers she could have named?

A 8, 16, 28, 32 **C** 16, 20, 24, 28

B 8, 14, 18, 24 **D** 16, 24, 32, 40

Lesson
8-5

AF 1.5 Recognize and use the commutative and associative properties of multiplication (e.g., if $5 \times 7 = 35$, then what is 7×5? and if $5 \times 7 \times 3 = 105$, then what is $7 \times 3 \times 5$?)

Multiplying with 3 Factors

How can you multiply 3 numbers?

Drew is joining 3 sections of a quilt. Each section has 2 rows with 4 squares in each row. How many squares in all are in these 3 sections?

Find $3 \times 2 \times 4$.

Guided Practice*

Do you know HOW?

In **1–6**, multiply. You may use objects or draw a picture to help.

1. $2 \times 4 \times 2$ **2.** $3 \times 4 \times 3$

3. $2 \times 2 \times 3$ **4.** $2 \times 5 \times 2$

5. $3 \times 2 \times 4$ **6.** $2 \times 6 \times 2$

Do you UNDERSTAND?

7. In the example above, if you find 3×4 first, do you get the same product? Explain.

8. Sara has 4 quilt pieces. Each piece has 3 rows with 3 squares in each row. How many squares are in Sara's quilt pieces?

Independent Practice

In **9–16**, find the product. You may draw a picture to help.

9. $2 \times 3 \times 2$ **10.** $5 \times 2 \times 2$ **11.** $3 \times 6 \times 1$ **12.** $3 \times 3 \times 2$

13. $2 \times 2 \times 2$ **14.** $2 \times 3 \times 4$ **15.** $3 \times 3 \times 3$ **16.** $6 \times 2 \times 2$

In **17–22**, write the missing number.

17. $3 \times (2 \times 5) = 30$, so $(3 \times 2) \times 5 = \square$ **18.** $5 \times (7 \times 2) = (7 \times 2) \times \square$

19. $4 \times (2 \times 2) = 16$, so $(4 \times 2) \times 2 = \square$ **20.** $8 \times (3 \times 6) = (8 \times 3) \times \square$

21. $(7 \times 3) \times 4 = \square \times (3 \times 4)$ **22.** $5 \times (2 \times 9) = (5 \times \square) \times 9$

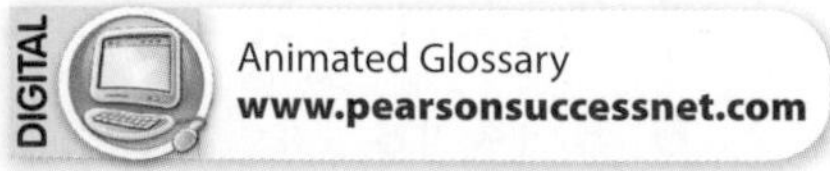

*For another example, see Set E on page 185.

One Way

Find 3×2 first.

$(3 \times 2) \times 4$

$6 \times 4 = 24$

6 rows, 4 squares in each row

There are 24 squares in all.

Another Way

Find 2×4 first.

$3 \times (2 \times 4)$

$3 \times 8 = 24$ 3 pieces, 8 squares in each piece

There are 24 squares in Drew's quilt pieces.

The Associative (Grouping) Property of Multiplication says that you can change the grouping of the factors and the product will be the same.

Problem Solving

For **23–25**, find the total number of eggs.

23. There are 5 valley quail nests in the woods. Each nest has 6 eggs.

24. In another area, there are 3 valley quail nests with 6 eggs in each nest, and 2 more nests with 8 eggs in each.

25. **Estimation** About how many eggs would you find in 10 valley quail nests?

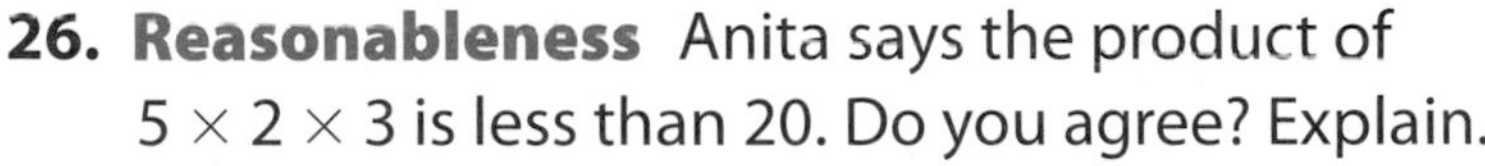

26. **Reasonableness** Anita says the product of $5 \times 2 \times 3$ is less than 20. Do you agree? Explain.

For **27** and **28**, use the table at the right.

Sports Card Sale (Data)

Kind of Cards	Number of Cards in Each Pack
Baseball	8
Basketball	5
Football	7
Hockey	6

27. Ellis bought 3 packs of baseball cards and 2 packs of basketball cards. How many cards did he buy in all?

28. Mandy bought 1 pack of each of the four kinds of cards. What is the total number of cards she bought?

29. Which number makes this number sentence true?

$4 \times (3 \times 2) = (4 \times \square) \times 2$

A 12 **B** 7 **C** 3 **D** 2

Lesson

8-6

MR 1.2 Determine when and how to break a problem into simpler parts.
Also **NS 2.1**, **NS 2.2**, **NS 2.8**.

Problem Solving

Multiple-Step Problems

Some word problems have hidden questions that need to be answered before you can solve the problem.

Keisha bought 2 yards of felt to make some puppets. Tanya bought 6 yards of felt. The felt cost \$3 a yard. How much did the two girls spend on felt?

Another Example

Keisha plans to make 3 puppets. Tanya will make 3 times as many puppets as Keisha. Each puppet needs 2 buttons for its eyes. How many buttons will Tanya need?

Find and solve the hidden question.

How many puppets will Tanya make?

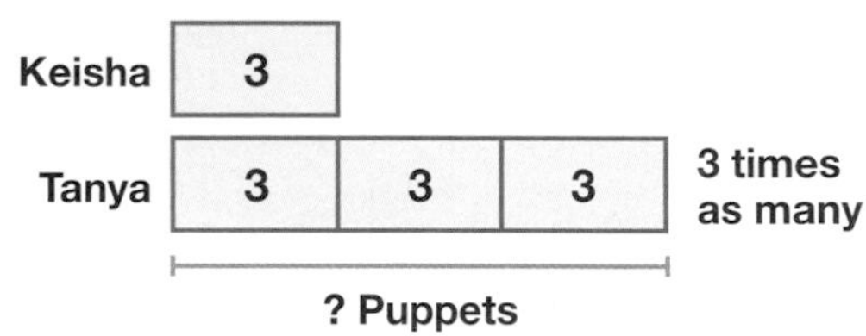

3×3 puppets $=$ 9 puppets

Tanya will make 9 puppets.

Use the answer to the hidden question to solve the problem.

How many buttons will Tanya need?

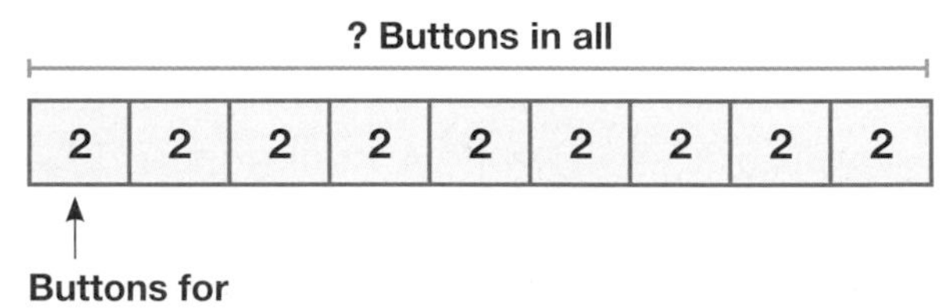

9×2 buttons $=$ 18 buttons

Tanya will need 18 buttons.

Explain It

1. Philip wrote $3 + 3 + 3 = \square$ instead of $3 \times 3 = \square$ for the diagram for the hidden question. Is his number sentence correct? Why or why not?
2. **Number Sense** What number sentences could you write to find how many buttons both girls need? Explain your thinking.

Find and solve the hidden question.

How much felt did the girls buy in all?

2 yards + 6 yards = 8 yards

The girls bought 8 yards of felt.

Use the answer to the hidden question to solve the problem.

How much did the girls spend in all?

$8 \times \$3 = \$24$

The two girls spent $24 on felt.

Guided Practice*

Do you know HOW?

1. Keisha bought glue for $3, sequins for $6, and lace for $4 to decorate her puppets. She paid for these items with a $20 bill. How much change should she get?

The hidden question is "What is the total cost of the three items?"

Do you UNDERSTAND?

2. Describe another way to solve the problem above about buying felt.

3. **Write a Problem** Write a problem that has a hidden question. Then solve your problem.

Independent Practice

4. The library has 4 videos and some books about dinosaurs. There are 5 times as many books as videos. How many dinosaur books does the library have?

Stuck? Try this....

- What do I know?
- What am I asked to find?
- What diagram can I use to help understand the problem?
- Can I use addition, subtraction, multiplication, or division?
- Is all of my work correct?
- Did I answer the right question?
- Is my answer reasonable?

For another example, see Set F on page 185.

Independent Practice

Use the pictures for **5–9**.

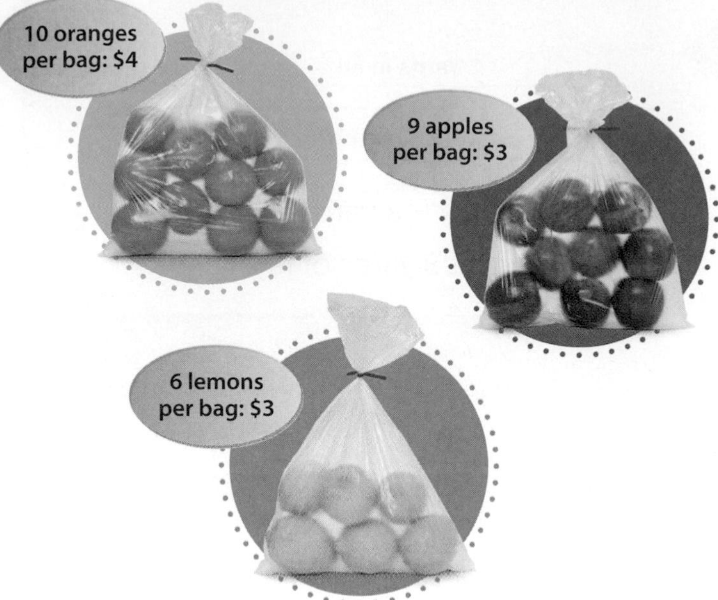

5. Craig bought 2 bags of oranges. After he ate 3 of the oranges, how many oranges were left?

 *First find how many oranges Craig bought.*

? Oranges in all

10	10

20

3	?

6. Delia bought 2 bags of lemons and 3 bags of apples. How much did she spend on fruit?

7. Mrs. Evans bought 2 bags of oranges and 2 bags of lemons. How many pieces of fruit did she buy?

8. Mr. Day bought one bag each of apples, oranges, and lemons. He paid with a $20 bill. What change should he get?

9. **Writing to Explain** Which costs more, 30 oranges or 30 lemons? How much more? Explain how you found your answer.

Think About the Process

10. Al had $38. He spent $4 on an action figure and $10 on a board game. Which number sentence shows how much money Al has left?

A $38 + $4 + $10 = ▢

B $38 − ($4 + $10) = ▢

C $38 − $4 = ▢

D 38 + $10 = ▢

11. Jose has 4 action figures. His brother has 3 times as many action figures. Which number sentence shows how many figures the boys have in all?

A $4 + 3 = ▢$

B $4 \times 3 = ▢$

C $4 - 3 = ▢$

D $4 + (3 \times 4) = ▢$

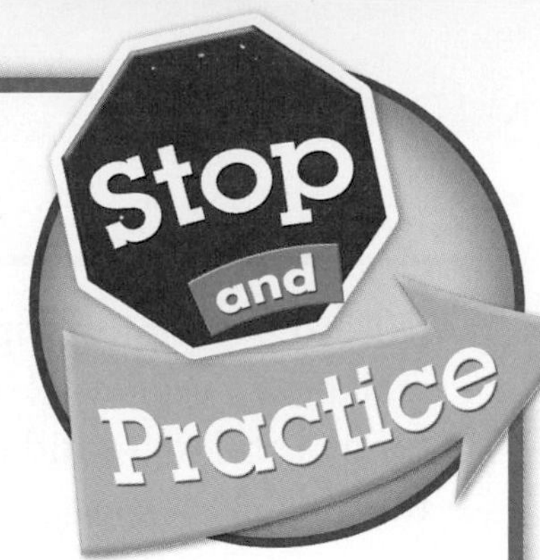

Write each number in standard form.

1. nine thousand, four hundred eight
2. fifty thousand, six hundred twelve

Round to the nearest hundred.

3. 643 **4.** 972 **5.** 2,559 **6.** 7,028

Write if each angle is right, acute, or obtuse.

7. 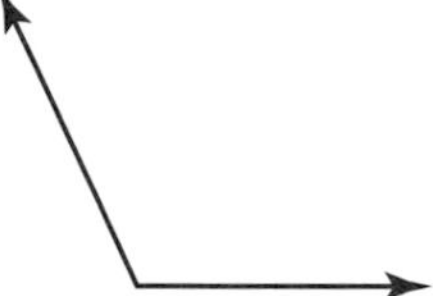 **8.** 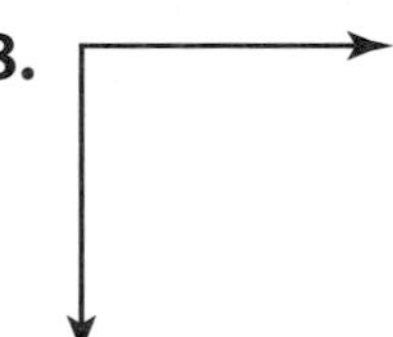 **9.**  **10.** 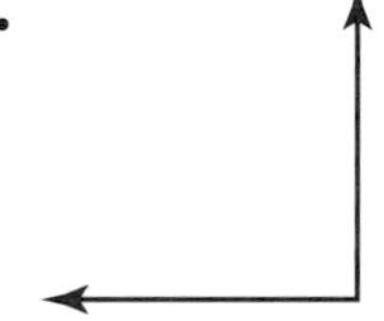

Find each product.

11. 2×9 **12.** 5×7 **13.** 10×8 **14.** 4×6 **15.** 3×0

Error Search Find each sum or difference that is not correct. Write it correctly and explain the error.

16. $175 + 49 = 124$ **17.** $568 + 932 = 1{,}500$ **18.** $314 - 228 = 96$ **19.** $8{,}297 + 2{,}516 = 10{,}813$ **20.** $7{,}342 - 5{,}837 = 1{,}605$

Number Sense

Estimating and Reasoning Write true or false for each statement. If it is false, explain why.

21. The product of 7 and 6 is greater than 76.
22. The difference 809 − 742 is less than 100.
23. The product $3 \times 2 \times 2$ is greater than 100.
24. The difference 4,135 − 1,968 is greater than 1,000.
25. The product of 0 and 10 is less than the product of 1 and 10.

Test Prep

1. During a camping trip, Martin walked a 7-mile trail 4 times. How many total miles did he walk on the trail? (8-3)

A 28

B 24

C 21

D 11

2. There are 3 periods in a hockey game. How many periods are there in 5 hockey games? (8-1)

A 8

B 12

C 15

D 18

3. Which shows a way to find 4×6? (8-2)

A $4 + 6$

B $12 + 12$

C $6 + 6 + 6$

D $12 + 2$

4. Jon bought 3 packages of invitations. Each package had 8 invitations. He sent out 20 invitations. Which of these shows one way to find the number of invitations Jon had left? (8-6)

A Multiply 3 by 8 and then subtract 20.

B Multiply 3 by 20 and then subtract 8.

C Multiply 5 by 8 and then add 20.

D Multiply 3 by 8 and then add 20.

5. Which is a way to find 7×6? (8-3)

A $35 + 14$

B $30 + 12$

C $35 + 6$

D $30 + 14$

6. Sven feeds his fish 2 pellets of food 3 times a day. How many pellets of food does he feed his fish in 7 days? (8-5)

A 13

B 14

C 21

D 42

7. Mrs. Chavez put new light switch covers in her house. She put in 8 double light switch covers and 7 single light switch covers. The double covers use 4 screws and the single covers use 2 screws. How many screws did she use? (8-6)

A 32

B 39

C 44

D 46

8. Mr. Hernandez bought 8 bags of limes. Each bag had 4 limes. How many limes did he buy? (8-2)

A 32

B 28

C 24

D 12

9. Each box has 6 muffins.

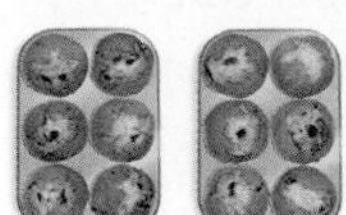  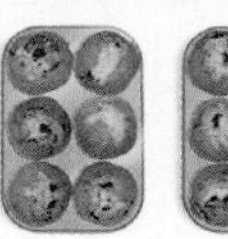 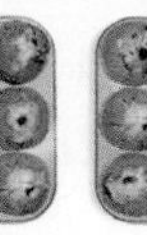 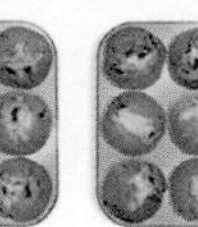

If the baker counted the muffins in groups of 6, which list shows numbers she could have named? (8-3)

A 6, 12, 16, 24

B 6, 12, 16, 22

C 12, 18, 24, 32

D 12, 18, 24, 30

10. Which shows a way to find 8×6? (8-4)

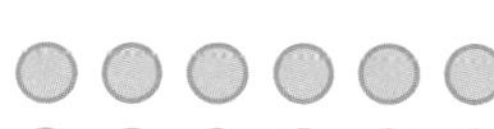

A $8 + 6$

B $24 + 24 + 24$

C $12 + 12 + 12 + 12$

D $16 + 16 + 16 + 16$

11. What number makes the number sentence true? (8-5)

$6 \times (9 \times 2) = (6 \times 9) \times \square$

A 2

B 6

C 9

D 54

12. The Cougars basketball team has 8 players. The coach ordered 3 pairs of socks for each player. How many pairs did he order? (8-4)

A 16

B 24

C 32

D 48

13. Tony measured the distance between his house and some of his favorite places to go. Which of these best describes all the distances in the table? (8-1)

Data

Place	Miles Away
School	9
Movie theater	15
Favorite restaurant	24
Grandparent's house	30

A They are all greater than 18.

B They are all multiples of 5.

C They are all multiples of 3.

D They are all less than 30.

14. Mala saw 6 boats launched into the water at each of 9 boat ramps. How many boats did Mala see launched? (8-3)

A 45

B 48

C 54

D 56

Reteaching

Set A, pages 166–167

Find 3×7.

You can break an array into facts you know.

$3 \times 7 = 3$ groups of 7
That is 2 sevens plus 1 more seven.

$2 \times 7 = 14$
$1 \times 7 = 7$
$14 + 7 = 21$

So, $3 \times 7 = 21$.

Remember that you can use facts you already know to help you multiply.

Find the product.

1. 3×8
2. 6×3
3. 4×3
4. 2×3
5. 9×3
6. 1×3
7. 3×3
8. 3×5
9. 10×3

Set B, pages 168–169

Find 4×7.

Think of a 2s fact, then double the product.

$4 \times 7 = 4$ groups of 7.

$2 \times 7 = 14$
$2 \times 7 = 14$
$14 + 14 = 28$

So, $4 \times 7 = 28$.

Remember that you can draw arrays to solve multiplication facts.

Find the product.

1. 4×10
2. 3×4
3. 6×4
4. 4×5
5. 4×4
6. 9×4
7. 8×4
8. 4×2
9. 11×4

Set C, pages 170–172

Find 7×6.

Use 5s facts and 2s facts to multiply with 7.

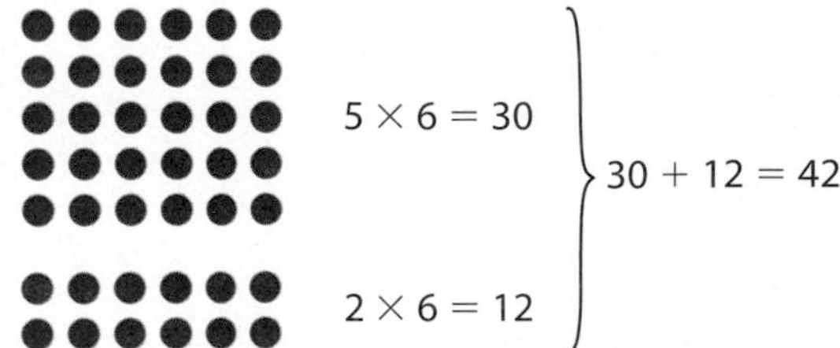

So, $7 \times 6 = 42$.

Remember that you can use known facts to multiply with 6 and 7.

Find the product.

1. 7×9
2. 8×7
3. 6×9
4. 3×6
5. 7×4
6. 6×8
7. 7×7
8. 6×2
9. 12×7

Set D, pages 174–175

Find 8×6. You can double a 4s fact.

Find 4×6. Then double the product.

$4 \times 6 = 24$

$4 \times 6 = 24$

$24 + 24 = 48$

So, $8 \times 6 = 48$.

Remember to check that your picture accurately shows the arrays for the numbers that are multiplied.

Find the product.

1. 7×8
2. 8×8
3. 1×8
4. 8×9
5. 10×8
6. 5×8
7. $\begin{array}{r} 2 \\ \times\ 8 \\ \hline \end{array}$
8. $\begin{array}{r} 3 \\ \times\ 8 \\ \hline \end{array}$
9. $\begin{array}{r} 11 \\ \times\ 8 \\ \hline \end{array}$

Set E, pages 176–177

Find $4 \times 5 \times 2$.

The Associative Property of Multiplication says that you can change the grouping of the factors, and the product will be the same.

One Way

$(4 \times 5) \times 2$

$20 \quad \times 2 = 40$

Another Way

$4 \times (5 \times 2)$

$4 \times \quad 10 = 40$

So, $4 \times 5 \times 2 = 40$.

Remember you may draw a picture to help you multiply 3 factors.

Find the product.

1. $3 \times 2 \times 5$
2. $5 \times 3 \times 4$
3. $1 \times 9 \times 8$
4. $7 \times 2 \times 5$
5. $6 \times 3 \times 4$
6. $4 \times 3 \times 2$

Set F, pages 178–180

Some problems have hidden questions.

Jeff charged \$10 to wash a car and \$7 to walk a dog. How much money did Jeff earn for washing 6 cars and walking 1 dog?

Find and solve the hidden question.
How much money did Jeff earn washing 6 cars?
$6 \times \$10 = \$60$
Then solve the problem.
How much money did Jeff earn in all?
$\$60 + \$7 = \$67$
Jeff earned \$67.

Remember to carefully read the order in which things happen.

1. At the fair, Bonnie wants to get 2 rings and 1 pen. Each ring costs 8 tickets, and each pen costs 6 tickets. How many tickets does she need in all?
2. Mrs. Green bought 2 bags of apples. Each bag had 10 apples. She used 4 apples. How many apples did she have left?

Topic 9

Division Concepts

1 Skateboarding became popular in California in the 1950s. How many skateboards can be made with 36 wheels? You will find out in Lesson 9-1.

2 The same number of astronauts traveled on Apollo 11 and Apollo 12. How many astronauts traveled to the Moon on each space mission? You will find out in Lesson 9-3.

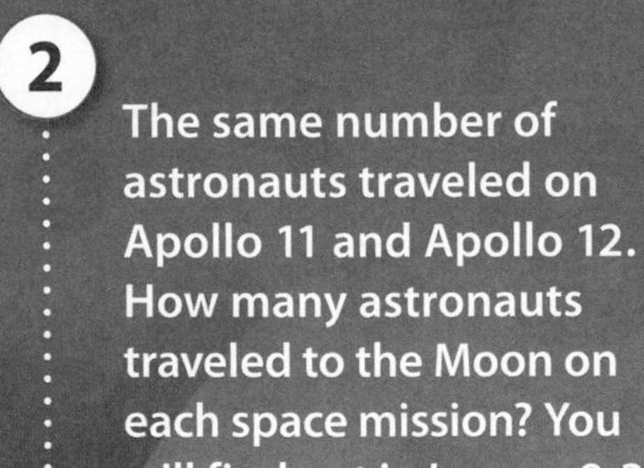

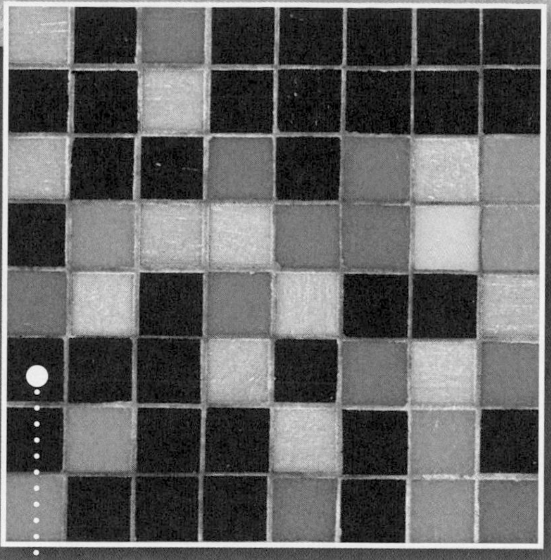

3 A mosaic is a type of art made with tiles. How many tiles are in this mosaic? You will find out in Lesson 9-4.

4 Each paddleboat can seat two people. Each person on shore has two friends. How many paddleboats will the entire group need? You will find out in Lesson 9-2.

Review What You Know!

Vocabulary

Choose the best term from the box.

- factor
- product
- sentence
- subtract

1. When you take some away and find how many are left, you __?__.
2. A number __?__ is made up of numbers and symbols.
3. A number that is being multiplied is called a __?__.

Subtraction

Find each difference.

4. 15 − 3 **5.** 10 − 2 **6.** 16 − 4

7. 30 − 5 **8.** 18 − 3 **9.** 20 − 4

Multiplication

Find each product.

10. 3×5 **11.** 7×9 **12.** 8×6

13. 4×7 **14.** 9×8 **15.** 10×2

Multiplication Stories

16. **Writing to Explain** Write a multiplication story for $3 \times 7 = \square$. Draw a picture to find the product. Tell how your story shows multiplication.

Lesson
9-1

NS 3.2, Grade 2 Use repeated subtraction, equal sharing, and forming equal groups with remainders to do division.

Division as Sharing

How many are in each group?

Three friends have 12 toys to share equally. How many toys will each person get?

Think of putting 12 toys into 3 equal groups.

Division is an operation that is used to find how many equal groups or how many are in each group.

Guided Practice*

Do you know HOW?

Use counters or draw a picture to solve.

1. 15 bananas, 3 boxes
How many bananas in each box?

2. 16 plants, 4 pots
How many plants in each pot?

Do you UNDERSTAND?

3. Copy and complete.

●●●●●●
●●●●●●
●●●●●●

$18 \div 3 = \square$

4. Can 12 grapes be shared equally among 5 children? Explain.

Independent Practice

Use counters or draw a picture to solve.

5. 18 marbles, 6 sacks
How many marbles in each sack?

6. 36 stickers, 4 people
How many stickers for each person?

7. 16 crayons, 2 people
How many crayons for each person?

8. 12 pictures, 4 pages
How many pictures on each page?

9. 24 bottles, 4 cases
How many bottles in each case?

10. 27 CDs, 9 packages
How many CDs in each package?

*For another example, see Set A on page 200.

What You Think

Put one at a time in each group.

When all the toys are grouped, there will be 4 in each group.

What You Write

You can write a division sentence to find the number in each group.

12	÷	3	=	4
Total		Number of equal groups		Number in each group

Each person will get 4 toys.

Complete each division sentence.

11. 12

?	?

$12 \div 2 =$ ▢

12. 16

?	?	?	?	?	?	?	?

$16 \div 8 =$ ▢

Problem Solving

13. Writing to Explain James is putting 18 pens into equal groups. He says that there will be more pens in each of 2 equal groups than in each of 3 equal groups. Is he correct? Explain.

14. Most skateboards have 4 wheels. How many skateboards can be made with 36 wheels? Draw a picture to help.

15. Joy had 12 shells. She gave 2 to her mother and shared the rest equally with Rob. How many shells did Joy and Rob each get?

16. Max has the stickers shown. He wants to put an equal number of stickers on each of 2 posters. Which number sentence shows how many stickers Max should put on each poster?

A $7 + 2 = 9$

B $7 \times 2 = 14$

C $14 \div 7 = 2$

D $14 \div 2 = 7$

Lesson
9-2

NS 3.2, Grade 2 Use repeated subtraction, equal sharing, and forming equal groups with remainders to do division.

Division as Repeated Subtraction

Hands-On
counters

How many equal groups?

June has 10 strawberries to serve to her guests. If each guest eats 2 strawberries, how many guests can June serve?

Guided Practice*

Do you know HOW?

Use counters or draw a picture to solve.

1. 16 gloves
   2 gloves in each pair
   How many pairs?

2. 15 tennis balls
   3 balls in each can
   How many cans?

Do you UNDERSTAND?

3. Suppose June had 12 strawberries and each guest ate 2 strawberries. How many guests could she serve? Use counters or draw a picture to solve.

4. **Number Sense** Show how you can use repeated subtraction to find how many groups of 4 there are in 20. Then write the division sentence for the problem.

Independent Practice

Use counters or draw a picture to solve.

5. 12 wheels
   4 wheels on each wagon
   How many wagons?

6. 30 markers
   5 markers in each package
   How many packages?

7. 8 apples
   4 apples in each bag
   How many bags?

8. 18 pencils
   2 pencils on each desk
   How many desks?

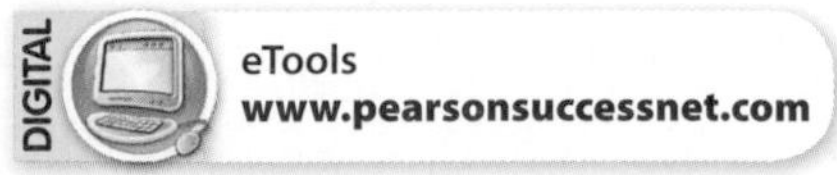

*For another example, see Set B on page 200.

One Way

You can use repeated subtraction to find how many groups of 2 are in 10.

$10 - 2 = 8$
$8 - 2 = 6$
$6 - 2 = 4$
$4 - 2 = 2$
$2 - 2 = 0$

You can subtract 2, five times. There are five groups of 2 in 10.

There are no strawberries left.

June can serve 5 guests.

Another Way

You can write a division sentence to find the number of groups.

Write: $10 \div 2 = 5$

Read: Ten divided by 2 equals 5.

June can serve 5 guests.

Problem Solving

9. **Number Sense** Raymond has 16 model planes that he wants to display. Will he need more shelves if he puts 8 on a shelf or 4 on a shelf? Explain.

For **10–12**, match each problem to a picture or a repeated subtraction. Then write the division sentence to solve.

10. 24 books
6 in a box
How many boxes?

11. 24 books
3 in a box
How many boxes?

12. 24 books
8 in a box
How many boxes?

a

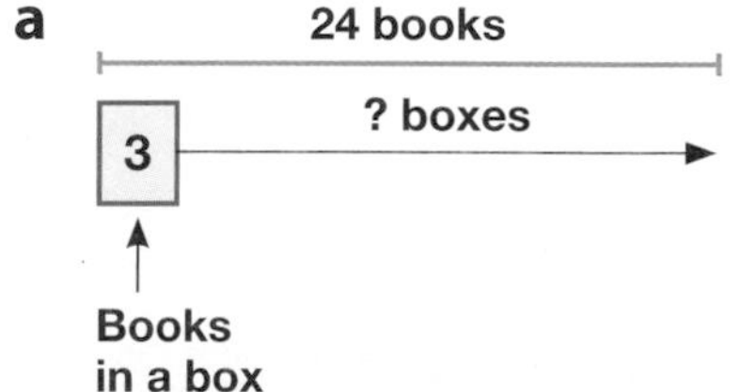

b $24 - 8 = 16$
$16 - 8 = 8$
$8 - 8 = 0$

c

24 books
? boxes
6
Books
in a box

13. How many paddle boats are needed for 18 people if each paddle boat is full?

14. Toni has 6 tulips and 6 daisies. She wants to put 4 flowers in each vase. Which number sentence shows how many vases she needs?

A $12 + 4 = 16$

B $12 - 4 = 8$

C $6 \times 4 = 24$

D $12 \div 4 = 3$

Lesson

9-3

NS 3.0, Grade 2 Model and solve simple problems involving multiplication and division.

Writing Division Stories

Hands-On
counters

What is the main idea of a division story?

Mrs. White asked her students to write a division story for the number sentence $15 \div 3 = \square$.

Mike and Kia decided to write stories about putting roses in vases.

Guided Practice*

Do you know HOW?

Write a division story for each number sentence. Then use counters or draw a picture to solve.

1. $8 \div 4 = \square$

2. $10 \div 2 = \square$

3. $20 \div 5 = \square$

4. $14 \div 7 = \square$

Do you UNDERSTAND?

5. How are Mike's and Kia's stories alike? How are they different?

6. **Number Sense** When you write a division story, what information do you need to include?

Independent Practice

Write a division story for each number sentence. Then use counters or draw a picture to solve.

7. $18 \div 3 = \square$ 8. $25 \div 5 = \square$ 9. $16 \div 4 = \square$ 10. $30 \div 6 = \square$

11. **Number Sense** Choose two of the stories you wrote for the exercises above. For each, tell whether you found the number in each group or the number of equal groups.

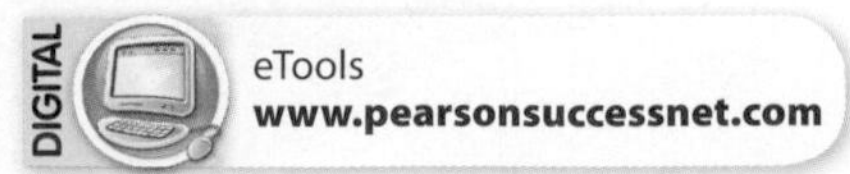

*For another example, see Set C on page 201.

Mike's Story

I have 15 roses. I want an equal number of roses in each of 3 vases. How many roses should I put in each vase?

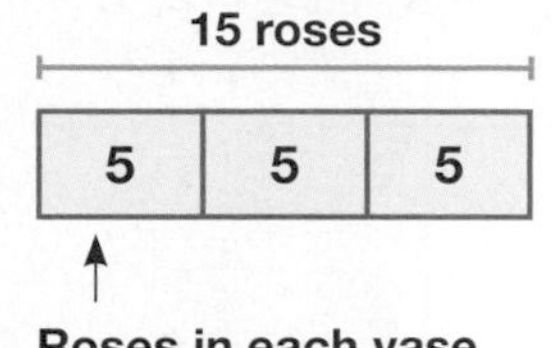

$15 \div 3 = 5$

I should put 5 roses in each vase.

Kia's Story

I have 15 roses to put into vases. I want to put 3 roses into each vase. How many vases will I need?

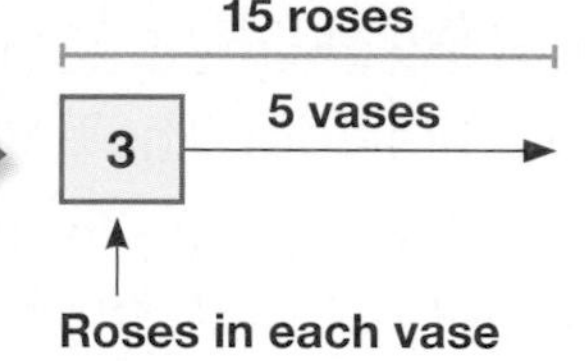

$15 \div 3 = 5$

I will need 5 vases.

Problem Solving

The table shows the number of players needed for each kind of sports team. Use the table for **12–14**.

There are 36 third graders at sports camp who want to play on different teams.

Data

Sports Team	Number
Baseball	9 players
Basketball	5 players
Tennis	2 players

12. If everyone wants to play baseball, how many teams will there be?

13. **Writing to Explain** Could everyone play basketball at the same time? Why or why not?

14. Twenty of the third graders went swimming. The rest of them played tennis. How many tennis teams were there?

15. In all, six astronauts traveled in space on Apollo 11 and Apollo 12. How many astronauts were on each mission?

16. Carmen rides her bike to school from 3 to 5 times a week. Which is a reasonable number of times Carmen will ride her bike in 4 weeks?

A More than 28

B From 12 to 20

C From 14 to 28

D Fewer than 12

Lesson

9-4

MR 2.3 Use a variety of methods, such as words, numbers, symbols, charts, graphs, tables, diagrams, and models, to explain mathematical reasoning. Also **MG 2.0, MR 1.1**

Problem Solving

Act It Out and Draw a Picture

Hands-On
square tiles
grid paper

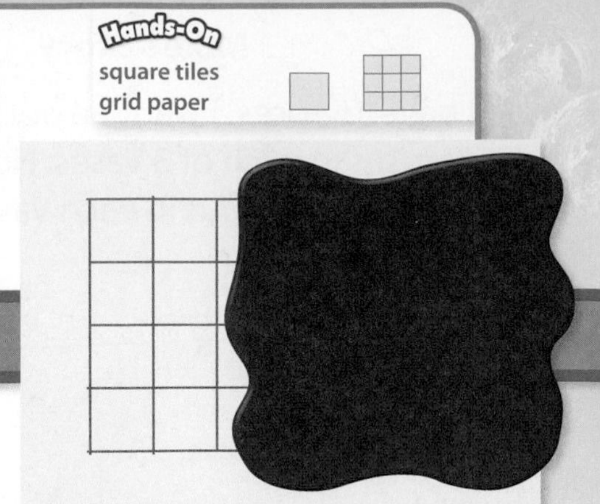

Naomi spilled some ink on her paper. The ink covered up part of her picture of a tile floor. The entire floor was shaped like a rectangle covered by 24 square tiles. How many tiles were in each row?

Another Example How can drawing a picture help you solve a problem?

Some ink spilled and covered up part of a picture of a tile floor. The tile floor was shaped like a rectangle. There were 21 square tiles in the whole floor. How many tiles were in each row?

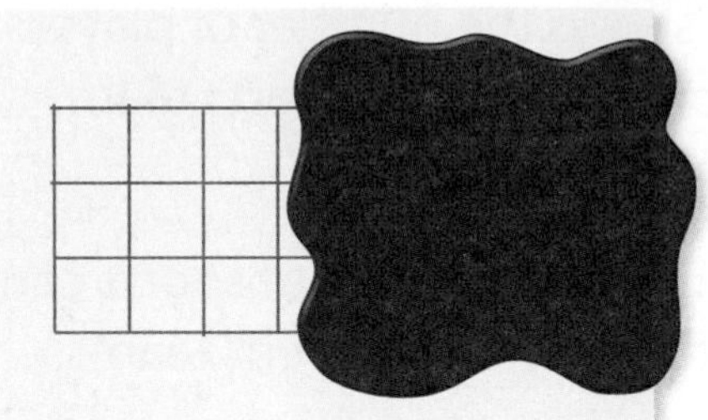

Plan

What strategy can I use?

I can draw a picture to show what I know.

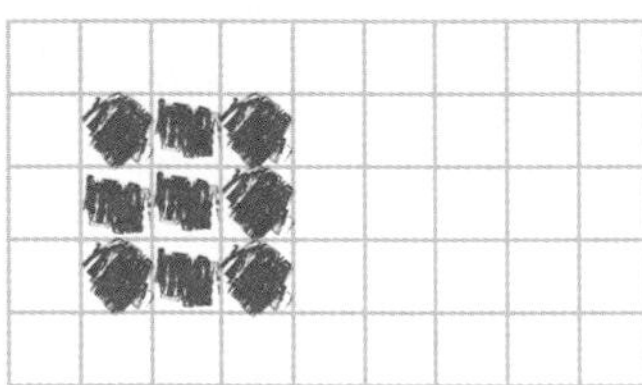

Solve

I can finish the picture to solve the problem.

There should be 21 squares in all.

$7 + 7 + 7 = 21$

There were 7 tiles in each row.

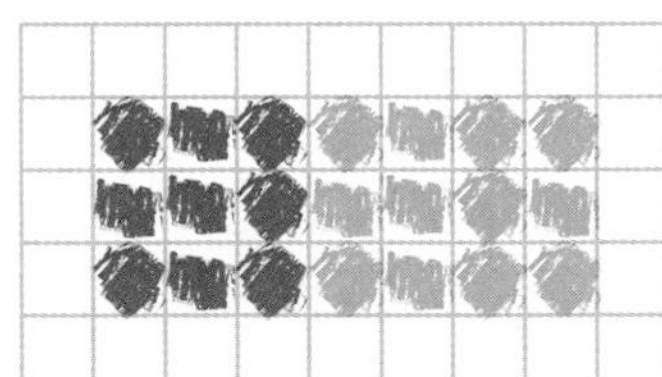

Explain It

1. How do you know how many tiles to draw to finish the picture in the problem above?
2. Explain how to check the solution to this problem.

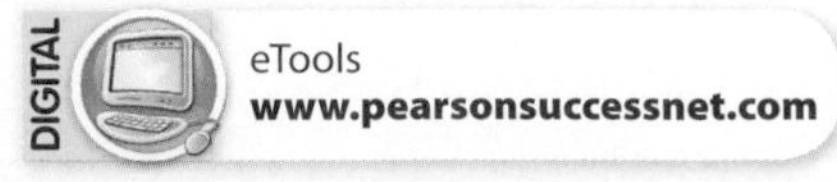

Understand and Plan

What strategy can I use?

I can act it out by using objects to show what I know.

Solve

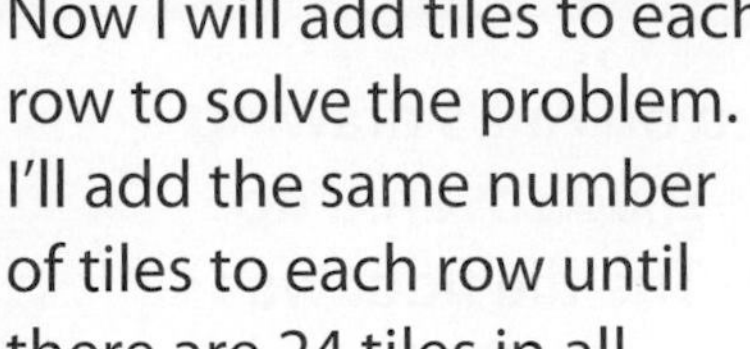

Now I will add tiles to each row to solve the problem. I'll add the same number of tiles to each row until there are 24 tiles in all.

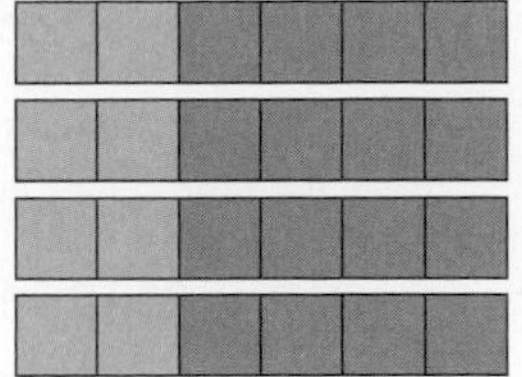

$6 + 6 + 6 + 6 = 24$

There were 6 tiles in each row.

Guided Practice*

Do you know HOW?

Solve. Use objects or draw a picture.

1. Paint covered part of a tile floor. The square floor had 16 tiles. How many tiles had paint on them?

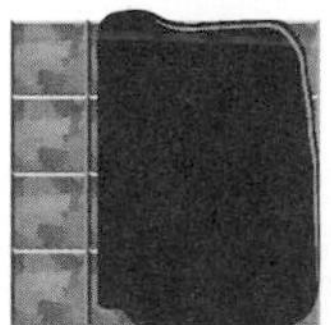

Do you UNDERSTAND?

2. What strategy did you use to find the number of tiles covered by paint in Exercise 1?

3. **Write a Problem** Write and solve a problem that you can solve by using objects or drawing a picture.

Independent Practice

Solve. Use objects or draw a picture.

4. Kim painted part of a tiled section of a wall. The whole section of tiles was shaped like a rectangle. There were 27 square tiles. How many tiles were in each row?

Stuck? Try this....

- What do I know?
- What am I asked to find?
- What diagram can I use to help understand the problem?
- Can I use addition, subtraction, multiplication, or division?
- Is all of my work correct?
- Did I answer the right question?
- Is my answer reasonable?

For another example, see Set D on page 201.

Independent Practice

5. Some glue spilled on Ana's drawing of a tile floor. The glue covered up some of the tiles. The tile floor was shaped like a rectangle. There were 20 square tiles in the whole floor. How many of the tiles had glue on them?

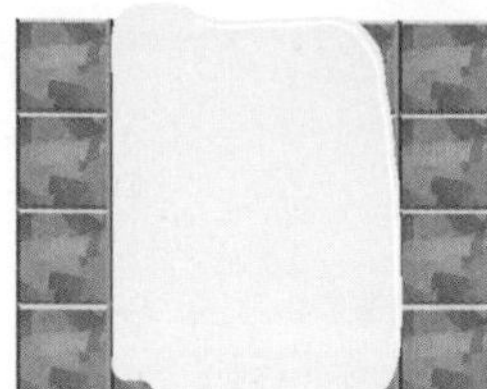

6. Joyce wants to make a design using all 64 square tiles in the mosaic shown below. She wants to use the mosaic four times. How many yellow tiles does she need?

7. Jeff's family took a car trip for a summer vacation. The family drove 362 miles to a national park. Then the family drove 174 miles to hike in the mountains. How many miles did the family drive all together?

? miles in all

362 miles	174 miles

8. Mari needs to make 215 programs in all for the class play. So far, she has made 89 programs. How many more programs does she still need to make?

215 programs in all

89 made	?

Think About the Process

9. Which of the following can be used to find how many days there are in 8 weeks?

A 8×7

B $8 \div 2$

C $8 + 7$

D $8 - 2$

10. Mrs. Clay bought 28 picture frames packed equally into 4 boxes. Which number sentence shows how to find the number of frames in each box?

A $28 - 4 = \square$

B $28 + 4 = \square$

C $28 \times 4 = \square$

D $28 \div 4 = \square$

Write each number in expanded form.

1. 7,409 **2.** 38,617 **3.** 926,054

Order the numbers from least to greatest.

4. 918 909 1,062 **5.** 934 1,121 1,119

6. 5,609 5,600 5,610 **7.** 8,736 8,832 8,734

Estimate and then find each sum. Check that your answer is reasonable.

8. $\begin{array}{r} 73 \\ +\ 59 \\ \hline \end{array}$ **9.** $\begin{array}{r} 386 \\ +\ 94 \\ \hline \end{array}$ **10.** $\begin{array}{r} 869 \\ +\ 253 \\ \hline \end{array}$ **11.** $\begin{array}{r} 1{,}925 \\ +\ 678 \\ \hline \end{array}$ **12.** $\begin{array}{r} 2{,}017 \\ +\ 4{,}697 \\ \hline \end{array}$

Estimate and then find each difference. Check that your answer is reasonable.

13. $\begin{array}{r} 64 \\ -\ 39 \\ \hline \end{array}$ **14.** $\begin{array}{r} 213 \\ -\ 95 \\ \hline \end{array}$ **15.** $\begin{array}{r} 502 \\ -\ 317 \\ \hline \end{array}$ **16.** $\begin{array}{r} 1{,}756 \\ -\ 849 \\ \hline \end{array}$ **17.** $\begin{array}{r} 3{,}048 \\ -\ 1{,}629 \\ \hline \end{array}$

Find each product.

18. 6×8 **19.** 10×1 **20.** $2 \times 2 \times 2$ **21.** 4×7 **22.** 9×0

Error Search Find each sum or difference that is not correct. Write it correctly and explain the error.

23. $\begin{array}{r} 95 \\ +\ 18 \\ \hline 103 \end{array}$ **24.** $\begin{array}{r} 207 \\ +\ 536 \\ \hline 743 \end{array}$ **25.** $\begin{array}{r} 630 \\ -\ 472 \\ \hline 228 \end{array}$ **26.** $\begin{array}{r} 8{,}492 \\ +\ 2{,}053 \\ \hline 10{,}445 \end{array}$ **27.** $\begin{array}{r} 5{,}134 \\ -\ 4{,}127 \\ \hline 1{,}007 \end{array}$

Number Sense

Estimating and Reasoning Write true or false for each statement. If it is false, explain why.

28. $67 + 45 < 100$ **29.** $8 \times 10 > 18$

30. $218 - 53 < 100$ **31.** $1{,}069 - 937 > 100$

32. $3{,}429 + 5{,}198 < 10{,}000$ **33.** $0 \times 9 > 1 \times 9$

Test Prep

1. Mason has 12 pinecones. His birdfeeder design uses 3 pinecones. Which number sentence shows how many birdfeeders he can make? (9-2)

A $12 + 3 = 15$

B $12 \div 3 = 4$

C $12 - 3 = 9$

D $12 \times 3 = 36$

2. Which story could be solved with $20 \div 4$? (9-3)

A Harold caught 20 fish. All but 4 of them were catfish. How many of the fish were something other than catfish?

B Becky bought 20 bags of crystal beads. Each bag had 4 crystal beads. How many crystal beads did she buy?

C Batina has made 20 doll dresses. If she makes 4 more, how many doll dresses will she have made?

D Coach Sid has 20 baseballs. Each group needs 4 balls for the practice drill. How many groups can he form?

3. Five friends have 15 pencils to share equally. Which number sentence shows how many pencils each friend will get? (9-1)

A $15 \div 5 = 3$

B $15 + 5 = 20$

C $15 \times 5 = 75$

D $15 - 5 = 10$

4. Mrs. Vincent bought 16 kiwis for her 4 children to share equally. How many kiwis will each child get? (9-1)

A 3

B 4

C 5

D 12

5. There are 8 drum sticks. Two drum sticks make a set. How many sets of drum sticks are there? (9-2)

A 16

B 6

C 4

D 2

6. Which division sentence is shown by the repeated subtraction? (9-2)

$15 - 3 = 12$
$12 - 3 = 9$
$9 - 3 = 6$
$6 - 3 = 3$
$3 - 3 = 0$

A $15 \div 3 = 5$

B $18 \div 3 = 3$

C $18 \div 3 = 6$

D $18 \div 6 = 3$

7. The pet store had 24 parakeets to put equally in 8 cages. How many birds should be put in each cage? (9-1)

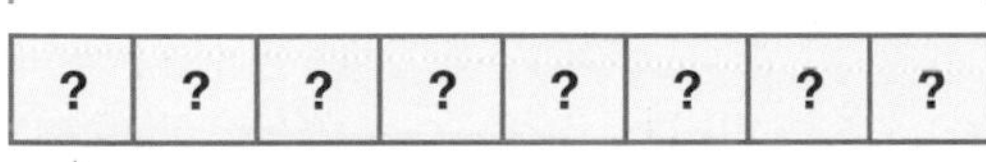

Birds in each cage

A 6

B 4

C 3

D 2

8. Which symbol makes the number sentence true? (9-2)

16 ◯ 8 = 2

A +

B −

C ×

D ÷

9. Which story could be solved with $36 \div 6$? (9-3)

A Chauncy used 36 sea shells to make 6 necklaces. Each necklace had the same number of shells. How many shells were on each necklace?

B Patrick planted 36 trees on Arbor Day. If he plants 6 more, how many trees will he have planted?

C The zoo's gift shop ordered 36 bags with 6 plastic animals in each. How many plastic animals did the gift shop order?

D Ray counted 36 coins in his bank. All but 6 of them were quarters. How many of the coins were something other than quarters?

10. The pictures below are examples of the small triangle tangram piece rotated to several different positions.

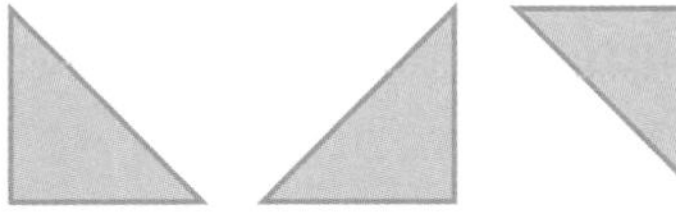

Which of the following shapes can **NOT** be made by joining two of the triangles? (9-4)

A A square

B A parallelogram

C A triangle

D A trapezoid

Reteaching

Set A, pages 188–189

Kim has 18 stickers. She wants to divide them equally among 3 of her friends. How many stickers can she give to each friend?

Put 1 at a time into each group.

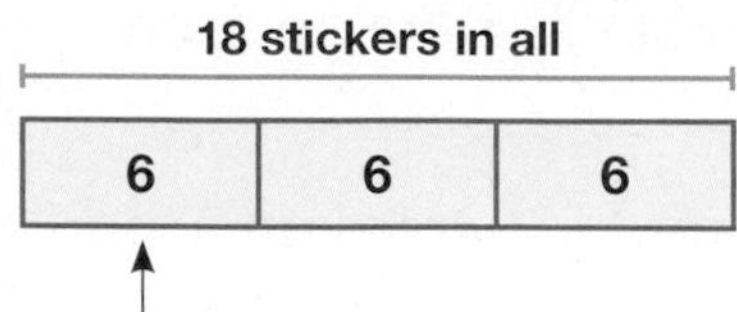

You can also divide to find the number in each group.

$18 \div 3 = 6$

Kim can give 6 stickers to each of her 3 friends.

Remember that you can think of division as sharing equally.

Use counters or draw a picture to solve. Make equal groups.

1. 15 apples
3 bowls
How many in each bowl?

2. 10 students
2 groups
How many students in each group?

3. 20 cans of soup
5 boxes
How many cans in each box?

Set B, pages 190–191

Barbara uses 4 eggs to make a cake. If she has 12 eggs, how many cakes can she make?

$12 - 4 = 8$	Use repeated subtraction to
$8 - 4 = 4$	find how many groups.
$4 - 4 = 0$	You can subtract 4 three times.

Barbara can make 3 cakes.

Remember that you can think of division as sharing equally or as repeated subtraction.

Use counters or draw a picture to solve each problem.

1. 6 books
3 books on each shelf
How many shelves?

2. 18 students
6 students on each team
How many teams?

Set C, pages 192–193

Write a division story for 20 ÷ 5.

If 20 children form 5 equal teams, how many children are on each team?

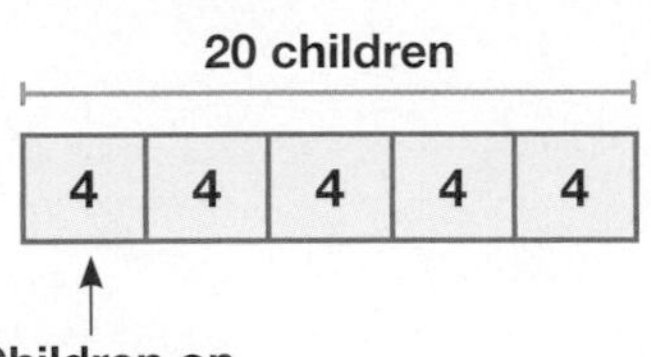

20 ÷ 5 = 4

There are 4 children on each team.

Remember that division stories can ask for the number in each group or the number of equal groups.

Write a division story for each number sentence. Draw a picture to help.

1. 15 ÷ 3 = ▢
2. 21 ÷ 7 = ▢
3. 24 ÷ 6 = ▢
4. 30 ÷ 5 = ▢

Set D, pages 194–196

Some blue paint spilled on a tile floor. The tile floor was in the shape of a square. There were 9 tiles in the whole floor. How many of the tiles had blue paint on them?

Draw a picture to show what you know.

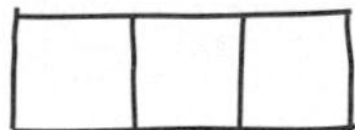

Finish the picture to solve. Show 9 tiles in all.

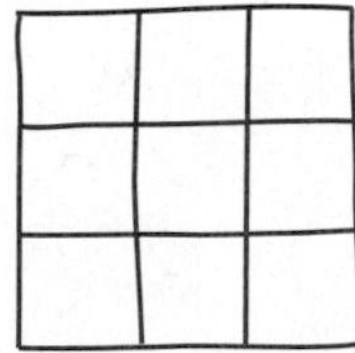

Six tiles had blue paint on them.

Remember to check that your picture matches the information in the problem.

1. Carmela painted over a part of some tiles. The whole group of tiles was in the shape of a rectangle. There were 28 tiles in the whole group. How many tiles did Carmela paint over?

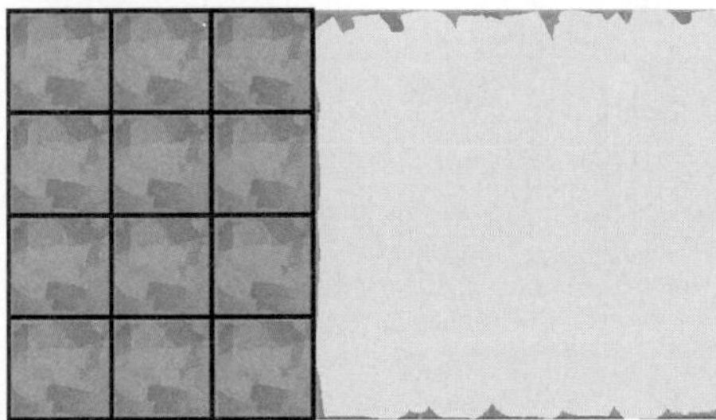

Topic 10

Division Facts

1 Tejano music uses twelve-string guitars. Are 40 strings enough to make 4 of these guitars? You will find out in Lesson 10-1.

2 The public subway in London is called the Underground, or the tube. How long is the East London tube line? You will find out in Lesson 10-6.

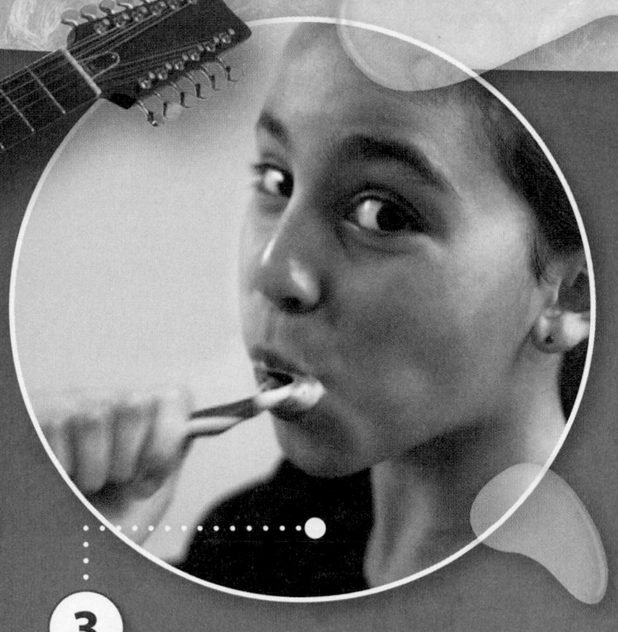

3 How much water might you use when you brush your teeth? You will find out in Lesson 10-2.

4 The golden poppy is the state flower of California. Do all golden poppies have the same number of petals? You will find out in Lesson 10-4.

Review What You Know!

Vocabulary

Choose the best term from the box.

- array
- difference
- factor
- product

1. The answer in multiplication is the __?__.
2. In $3 \times 5 = 15$, 5 is a(n) __?__.
3. Objects placed in equal rows form a(n) __?__.

Subtraction

Subtract.

4. 21 − 7	**5.** 15 − 5	**6.** 27 − 9
14 − 7	10 − 5	18 − 9
7 − 7	5 − 5	9 − 9

Multiplication Facts

7. 5×4	**8.** 7×3	**9.** 3×8
10. 9×2	**11.** 6×5	**12.** 4×7
13. 6×7	**14.** 8×4	**15.** 5×9

Equal Groups

16. Writing to Explain Describe why this picture of 12 counters doesn't show equal groups. Then change the drawing so it does show equal groups.

Lesson
10-1

NS 2.3 Use the inverse relationship of multiplication and division to compute and check results.

Relating Multiplication and Division

Hands-On
counters

How can multiplication facts help you divide?

This array can show multiplication and division.

Multiplication	Division
5 rows of 6 drums	30 drums in 5 equal rows
$5 \times 6 = 30$	$30 \div 5 = 6$
30 drums	6 drums in each row

Guided Practice*

Do you know HOW?

Copy and complete. Use counters or draw a picture to help.

1. $4 \times \square = 12$
   $12 \div 4 = \square$
2. $6 \times \square = 36$
   $36 \div 6 = \square$
3. $2 \times \square = 18$
   $18 \div 2 = \square$
4. $8 \times \square = 32$
   $32 \div 8 = \square$

Do you UNDERSTAND?

5. **Number Sense** What multiplication fact can help you find $54 \div 6$?
6. Look at the fact family for 5, 6, and 30. What do you notice about the products and the dividends?
7. **Writing to Explain** Is $4 \times 6 = 24$ part of the fact family for 3, 8, and 24? Explain.

Independent Practice

Copy and complete. Use counters or draw a picture to help.

8. $8 \times \square = 16$
   $16 \div 8 = \square$
9. $5 \times \square = 35$
   $35 \div 5 = \square$
10. $6 \times \square = 48$
    $48 \div 6 = \square$
11. $9 \times \square = 36$
    $36 \div 9 = \square$
12. $3 \times \square = 27$
    $27 \div 3 = \square$
13. $8 \times \square = 56$
    $56 \div 8 = \square$
14. Write the fact family for 5, 8, and 40.

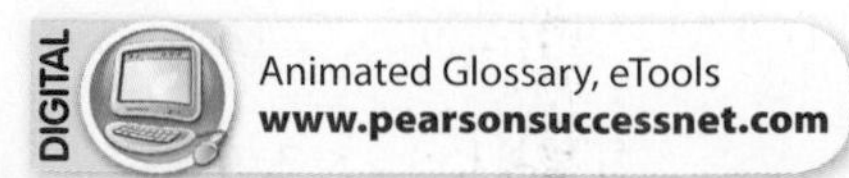

*For another example, see Set A on page 222.

A fact family shows how multiplication and division are related.

Fact family for 5, 6, and 30:

$5 \times 6 = 30$	$30 \div 5 = 6$
$6 \times 5 = 30$	$30 \div 6 = 5$

dividend (30), divisor (6), quotient (5)

The dividend is the number of objects to be divided.

The divisor is the number by which another number is divided.

The quotient is the answer to a division problem.

Problem Solving

15. Writing to Explain Why does the fact family for $2 \times 2 = 4$ have only two facts?

For **16** and **17**, write the rest of the fact family for each array.

16.

$3 \times 4 = 12$
$12 \div 3 = 4$

17.

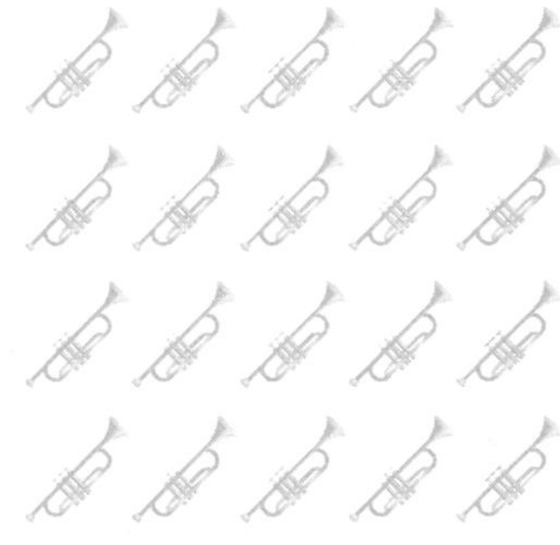

$4 \times 5 = 20$
$20 \div 4 = 5$

18. There are 28 cheerleaders in a parade. They form lines with 4 cheerleaders in each line. How many lines are there?

19. How many strings in all are used to make 4 guitars for Tejano music?

20. What number makes this number sentence true?

$\square \div 3 = 9$

A 3 **B** 12 **C** 18 **D** 27

Lesson
10-2

NS 2.3 Use the inverse relationship of multiplication and division to compute and check results.

Fact Families with 2, 3, 4, and 5

What multiplication fact can you use?

Dee has 14 noisemakers. She puts the same number on each of 2 tables. How many will be on each table?

What You Think	What You Write
2 times what number is 14? $2 \times 7 = 14$	$14 \div 2 = 7$ There will be 7 noisemakers on each table.

Another Example What is another way to write a division problem?

Dee is making balloon animals for her party. She has 24 balloons. It takes 4 balloons to make each animal. How many balloon animals can she make?

4 times what number is 24?
$4 \times 6 = 24$

There are two ways to write a division problem.

$24 \div 4 = 6$

24 ← dividend, 4 ← divisor, 6 ← quotient

$4\overline{)24}$ with 6 above: divisor → 4, dividend → 24, quotient → 6

Dee can make 6 balloon animals.

Explain It

1. Copy and complete the fact family:

   $4 \times 6 = 24$
   $24 \div 4 = 6$

2. How do you know what multiplication fact to use to find $24 \div 4$?

3. **Number Sense** Dee says she could make more than 10 balloon animals if she was able to make an animal using only 3 balloons. Do you agree? Why or why not?

Dee has 40 stickers. She puts 5 stickers on each bag. How many bags can she decorate?

What You Think	What You Write
5 times what number is 40? $5 \times 8 = 40$	$40 \div 5 = 8$ Dee can decorate 8 bags.

Dee wants to put 15 cups in 3 rows on the table. How many cups will she put in each row?

What You Think	What You Write
3 times what number is 15? $3 \times 5 = 15$	$15 \div 3 = 5$ Dee will put 5 cups in each row.

Guided Practice*

Do you know HOW?

In **1–3**, copy and complete each fact family.

1. $2 \times 7 = 14$
$14 \div 2 = 7$

2. $5 \times 8 = 40$
$40 \div 5 = 8$

3. $3 \times 5 = 15$
$15 \div 3 = 5$

In **4–9**, find each quotient.

4. $27 \div 3$ **5.** $16 \div 4$ **6.** $40 \div 4$

7. $2\overline{)18}$ **8.** $4\overline{)28}$ **9.** $5\overline{)30}$

Do you UNDERSTAND?

10. Identify the dividend, divisor and quotient in Exercise 9.

11. **Number Sense** How can you tell without dividing that $15 \div 3$ will be greater than $15 \div 5$?

12. How can you use multiplication to help you find 36 divided by 4?

Independent Practice

Find each quotient.

13. $10 \div 2$ **14.** $25 \div 5$ **15.** $21 \div 3$ **16.** $18 \div 3$

17. $2\overline{)16}$ **18.** $5\overline{)50}$ **19.** $3\overline{)24}$ **20.** $4\overline{)36}$

*For another example, see Set B on page 222.

Independent Practice

Find each quotient.

21. $12 \div 4$ **22.** $45 \div 5$ **23.** $4\overline{)16}$ **24.** $5\overline{)40}$

25. Find 12 divided by 2. **26.** Divide 20 by 5. **27.** Find 32 divided by 4.

Algebra Find each missing number.

28. $2 \times \square = 8$ **29.** $15 \div 3 = \square$ **30.** $\square \div 3 = 2$

31. $7 \times 4 = \square$ **32.** $\square \times 5 = 40$ **33.** $32 \div \square = 8$

Number Sense Write $<$ or $>$ to compare.

34. $4 \times 2 \bigcirc 4 \div 2$ **35.** $2 \times 3 \bigcirc 6 \div 2$ **36.** $5 + 8 \bigcirc 5 \times 8$

Problem Solving

37. **Writing to Explain** Joey says, "I can't solve $8 \div 2$ by using the fact $2 \times 8 = 16$." Do you agree or disagree? Explain.

38. Anna wants to make one array with 2 rows of 8 tiles and another array with 3 rows of 5 tiles. How many tiles does she need all together?

39. You might use 2 gallons of water when you brush your teeth. There are 16 cups in 1 gallon. About how many cups of water might you use when brushing your teeth?

40. Bob has 15 pennies and 3 dimes. Miko has the same amount of money, but she has only nickels. How many nickels does Miko have?

41. Which number sentence is in the same fact family as $3 \times 6 = 18$?

A $3 \times 3 = 9$

B $2 \times 9 = 18$

C $6 \div 3 = 2$

D $18 \div 6 = 3$

42. Mike bought 3 bags of marbles with 5 marbles in each bag. He gave 4 marbles to Marsha. How many marbles did Mike have left?

A 11 **C** 19

B 15 **D** 21

43. Sammy wants to buy a remote control car for $49 and three small cars for $5 each. What is the total amount he will spend?

Algebra Connections

Division and Number Sentences

Remember that the two sides of a number sentence can be equal or unequal. A symbol >, <, or = tells how the sides compare. Estimation or reasoning can help you tell if one side is greater without doing any computations.

> means *is greater than*
< means *is less than*
= means *is equal to*

Example: 10 ÷ 2 ◯ 8 ÷ 2

Each whole is being divided into 2 equal groups. The greater whole will have a greater number of items in each group.

Since 10 is greater than 8, the quotient on the left side is greater. Write the symbol >.

10 ÷ 2 (>) 8 ÷ 2

Copy and complete by writing >, <, or =.

1. 20 ÷ 5 ◯ 25 ÷ 5 **2.** 12 ÷ 3 ◯ 12 ÷ 4 **3.** 3 × 18 ◯ 3 × 21

4. 24 ÷ 2 ◯ 8 **5.** 19 + 19 ◯ 2 × 19 **6.** 100 ◯ 5 × 30

7. 1 × 53 ◯ 1 × 43 **8.** 9 ◯ 36 ÷ 4 **9.** 9 ÷ 3 ◯ 18 ÷ 3

10. 16 ÷ 2 ◯ 1 + 9 **11.** 35 ÷ 5 ◯ 2 + 3 **12.** 24 ÷ 4 ◯ 24 ÷ 2

In **13** and **14**, copy and complete the number sentence below each problem. Use it to help explain your answer.

13. Mara and Bobby each have 40 pages to read. Mara will read 4 pages each day. Bobby will read 5 pages each day. Who needs more days to read 40 pages?

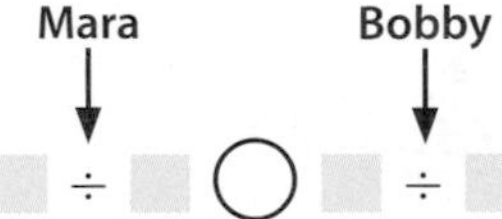

14. Tim had a board that was 12 feet long. He cut the board into 3 equal pieces. Ellen had a board that was 18 feet long. She cut the board into 3 equal pieces. Who had the longer pieces?

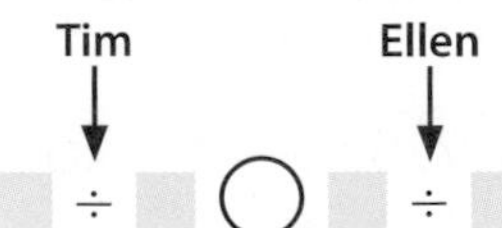

15. Write a Problem Write a problem described by 16 ÷ 2 > 14 ÷ 2.

Lesson

10-3

NS 2.3 🔑 Use the inverse relationship of multiplication and division to compute and check results.

Fact Families with 6 and 7

How do you divide with 6 and 7?

There are 48 dogs entered in a dog show. The judge wants 6 dogs in each group. How many groups will there be?

Choose an Operation Divide to find how many groups.

Guided Practice*

Do you know HOW?

1. Copy and complete the fact family.

$8 \times 6 = 48$
$48 \div 6 = 8$

In **2–10**, find each quotient.

2. $12 \div 6$ **3.** $30 \div 6$ **4.** $42 \div 6$

5. $14 \div 7$ **6.** $42 \div 7$ **7.** $63 \div 7$

8. $6\overline{)24}$ **9.** $6\overline{)54}$ **10.** $6\overline{)60}$

Do you UNDERSTAND?

11. **Number Sense** How can you tell without dividing that $42 \div 6$ will be greater than $42 \div 7$?

12. Write the fact family for 7, 8, and 56.

13. There are 54 children in 6 ballet classes. Each class is the same size. How many children are in each class?

Independent Practice

Find each quotient.

14. $18 \div 6$ **15.** $36 \div 4$ **16.** $21 \div 7$ **17.** $36 \div 6$ **18.** $27 \div 3$

19. $6\overline{)48}$ **20.** $2\overline{)20}$ **21.** $7\overline{)56}$ **22.** $5\overline{)35}$ **23.** $6\overline{)36}$

24. $6\overline{)30}$ **25.** $7\overline{)63}$ **26.** $6\overline{)12}$ **27.** $7\overline{)7}$ **28.** $7\overline{)70}$

29. Find 49 divided by 7. **30.** Divide 28 by 7. **31.** Find 56 divided by 7.

32. Find 60 divided by 6. **33.** Divide 21 by 7. **34.** Find 48 divided by 6.

*For another example, see Set C on page 222.

Find 48 ÷ 6.

What You Think	What You Write
What number times 6 is 48? $8 \times 6 = 48$	$48 \div 6 = 8$ There will be 8 groups.

Another dog was entered. There will now be 7 dogs in each group. How many groups will there be now?

Find 49 ÷ 7.

What You Think	What You Write
What number times 7 is 49? $7 \times 7 = 49$	$49 \div 7 = 7$ There will be 7 groups.

Problem Solving

Use the pictures below for **35–38**.

35. Rita needs 15 gold beads for an art project.

a How many packages of beads does she need?

b How much do the beads cost?

36. Eve bought 2 packages of red beads and 2 packages of blue beads.

a How many beads did she buy?

b How much did she spend?

37. **Writing to Explain** Guy bought 28 red beads and 18 blue beads. How many packages did he buy? Explain how you solved the problem.

38. **Number Sense** Andy bought exactly 35 beads. Which color beads could he have bought? Explain your thinking.

39. There are 6 rafts on the river. Each raft holds 8 people. Which number sentence is in the fact family for these numbers?

A $48 - 6 = 42$

B $48 \div 6 = 8$

C $48 + 6 = 54$

D $48 - 8 = 40$

40. The school auditorium has 182 seats. People are sitting in 56 of the seats. Which is the best estimate of the number of seats that do **NOT** have people sitting in them?

A 20 **B** 120 **C** 240 **D** 250

Lesson

10-4

NS 2.3 Use the inverse relationship of multiplication and division to compute and check results.

Fact Families with 8 and 9

What multiplication fact can you use?

John has 56 straws. How many spiders can he make?

Find $56 \div 8$.

What number times 8 is 56?

$7 \times 8 = 56$

John can make 7 spiders.

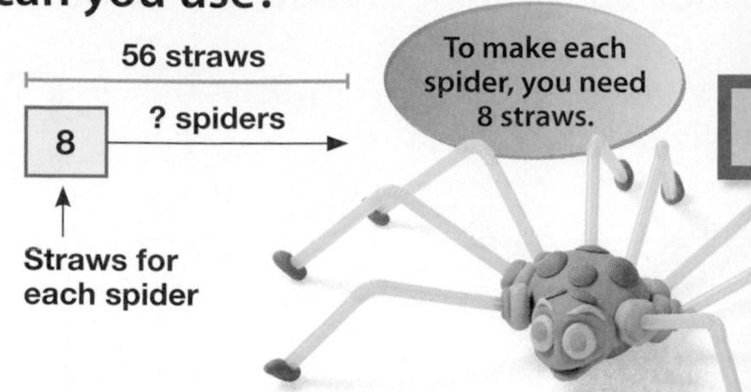

Guided Practice*

Do you know HOW?

Find each quotient.

1. $16 \div 8$ **2.** $64 \div 8$ **3.** $36 \div 9$

4. $27 \div 9$ **5.** $45 \div 9$ **6.** $63 \div 9$

7. $8\overline{)24}$ **8.** $8\overline{)72}$ **9.** $8\overline{)80}$

Do you UNDERSTAND?

10. What multiplication fact could you use to find $18 \div 9$?

11. **Number Sense** Carla and Jeff each use 72 straws. Carla makes animals with 9 legs. Jeff makes animals with 8 legs. Who makes more animals? Explain.

Independent Practice

Find each quotient.

12. $32 \div 8$ **13.** $28 \div 7$ **14.** $18 \div 9$ **15.** $48 \div 8$ **16.** $81 \div 9$

17. $5\overline{)45}$ **18.** $9\overline{)54}$ **19.** $7\overline{)56}$ **20.** $4\overline{)28}$ **21.** $8\overline{)56}$

22. $9\overline{)27}$ **23.** $9\overline{)90}$ **24.** $8\overline{)16}$ **25.** $8\overline{)64}$ **26.** $8\overline{)48}$

27. Find 72 divided by 9. **28.** Divide 40 by 8. **29.** Find 56 divided by 8.

30. Find 81 divided by 9. **31.** Divide 45 by 9. **32.** Find 64 divided by 8.

33. Write fact families for the numbers in **30** and **31**. How are the fact families different?

*For another example, see Set D on page 223.

Luz made 9 animals. She used 54 straws. She used the same number of straws for each animal. How many straws did Luz use for each animal?

Find 54 ÷ 9.

54 straws

?	?	?	?	?	?	?	?	?

Number of straws for each animal

What You Think	What You Write
9 times what number is 54?	$54 \div 9 = 6$
$9 \times 6 = 54$	Luz used 6 straws for each animal.

Problem Solving

Algebra Write < or > to compare.

34. $36 \div 9 \bigcirc 9$ **35.** $65 \bigcirc 8 \times 8$ **36.** $63 \div 9 \bigcirc 8$

37. Which number sentence is **NOT** in the same fact family as the others?

A $8 \times 4 = 32$ **B** $32 \div 8 = 4$ **C** $2 \times 4 = 8$ **D** $4 \times 8 = 32$

Use the ticket prices at the right for **38–41**.

38. The clerk at the playhouse sold \$64 of youth tickets. How many youth tickets did the clerk sell?

39. Melinda bought 2 children's tickets and 2 adult tickets. How much did she spend?

Data

Playhouse Ticket Prices

Type of Ticket	Price of Ticket
Child	\$4
Youth	\$8
Adult	\$9

40. Writing to Explain Mr. Stern bought 4 children's tickets and 2 adult tickets. How much more did he spend for the adult tickets than the children's tickets? Explain.

41. Reasoning The clerk at the playhouse sold \$72 worth of adult tickets. Ten people bought adult tickets online. Did more people buy tickets at the playhouse or online? Tell how you know.

42. Greta has 8 golden poppies in a vase. Each poppy has the same number of petals. How many petals are on each poppy?

Lesson

10-5

NS 2.6 Understand the special properties of 0 and 1 in multiplication and division.

Dividing with 0 and 1

How do you divide with 1 or 0?

Dividing by 1

Find $3 \div 1$

What number times 1 is 3?

$3 \times 1 = 3$

So, $3 \div 1 = 3$.

Rule: Any number divided by 1 is itself.

Guided Practice*

Do you know HOW?

Find each quotient.

1. $8 \div 8$ **2.** $2 \div 1$ **3.** $0 \div 5$

4. $1\overline{)8}$ **5.** $6\overline{)6}$ **6.** $10\overline{)0}$

Do you UNDERSTAND?

7. How can you tell without dividing that $375 \div 375 = 1$?

8. Writing to Explain Describe how you can find $0 \div 267$, without dividing.

Independent Practice

Find each quotient.

9. $7 \div 7$ **10.** $0 \div 4$ **11.** $10 \div 1$ **12.** $0 \div 6$ **13.** $10 \div 10$

14. $1\overline{)4}$ **15.** $1\overline{)7}$ **16.** $8\overline{)0}$ **17.** $5\overline{)5}$ **18.** $1\overline{)5}$

19. $2\overline{)14}$ **20.** $5\overline{)25}$ **21.** $7\overline{)56}$ **22.** $4\overline{)24}$ **23.** $9\overline{)81}$

24. $6\overline{)36}$ **25.** $7\overline{)49}$ **26.** $8\overline{)64}$ **27.** $9\overline{)90}$ **28.** $5\overline{)20}$

29. $7\overline{)56}$ **30.** $8\overline{)48}$ **31.** $7\overline{)42}$ **32.** $7\overline{)70}$ **33.** $4\overline{)32}$

34. Divide 0 by 9. **35.** Find 9 divided by 9. **36.** Find 6 divided by 1.

37. Divide 3 by 3. **38.** Find 0 divided by 8. **39.** Find 7 divided by 1.

*For another example, see Set E on page 223.

1 as a Quotient

Find 3 ÷ 3.

Think 3 times what number equals 3?

$3 \times 1 = 3$

So, 3 ÷ 3 = 1.

Rule: Any number (except 0) divided by itself is 1.

Dividing 0 by a Number

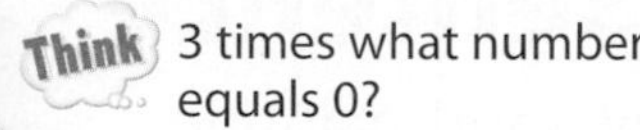

Find 0 ÷ 3.

Think 3 times what number equals 0?

$3 \times 0 = 0$

So, 0 ÷ 3 = 0.

Rule: 0 divided by any number (except 0) is 0.

Dividing by 0

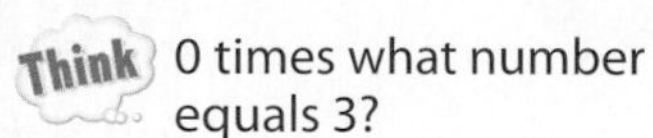

Find 3 ÷ 0.

Think 0 times what number equals 3?

There is no such number.

So, 3 ÷ 0 can't be done.

Rule: You cannot divide by 0.

Problem Solving

Algebra In **40–43**, copy and complete.

40. 3 ÷ 3 ◯ 3 × 0

41. 17 ÷ 17 ◯ 1 ÷ 1

42. 0 ÷ 6 ◯ 0 ÷ 1

43. 6 × 1 ◯ 6 ÷ 1

Use the sign at the right for **44–47**.

44. Paul hiked one trail 3 times for a total distance of 12 miles. Which trail did he hike?

45. Reasoning Addie hiked 3 different trails for a total distance of 11 miles. Which trails did she hike?

46. Yoko hiked the blue trail once and the green trail twice. How many miles did she hike on the green trail?

47. Writing to Explain Marty hiked one trail 4 times. He hiked more than 10 miles but less than 16 miles. Which trail did he hike? Explain.

48. Which number makes the number sentence below true?

54 ÷ ▢ = 9

A 5

B 6

C 7

D 8

49. Which number makes the number sentence below true?

▢ × 6 = 42

A 48

B 36

C 6

D 7

Lesson

10-6

MR 2.0 Use strategies, skills, and concepts in finding solutions. Also **NS 2.3**, **AF 1.1**

Problem Solving

Draw a Picture and Write a Number Sentence

Jeff is setting up the sand-painting booth at the school carnival. He put the sand from one bag of sand into 5 buckets. If each bucket has the same amount of sand, how much sand is in each bucket?

45 pounds of sand

Another Example Are there other types of division situations?

Alison is setting up the prize booth. She has 48 prizes. She will put 8 prizes in each row. How many rows can she make?

Plan and Solve

Use a diagram to show what you know.

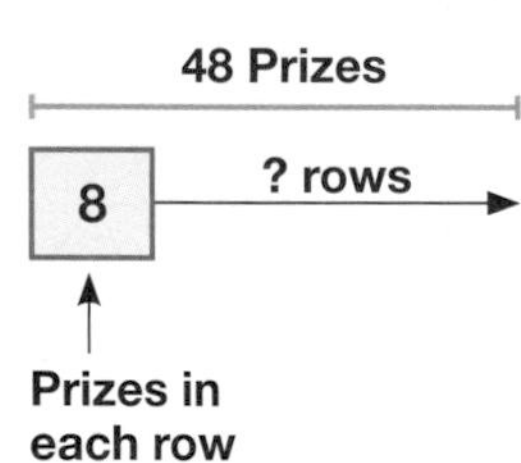

Answer

Write a number sentence

$48 \div 8 = 6$

Alison can make 6 rows.

Check

Make sure the answer is reasonable.

Use multiplication or repeated addition to check.

$6 \times 8 = 48$

or

$8 + 8 + 8 + 8 + 8 + 8 = 48$

Explain It

1. Explain how you can check the quotient in division by using either multiplication or addition.
2. **Number Sense** If Alison wants fewer than 6 rows of prizes, should she put more or fewer prizes in each row? Explain your thinking.

Plan and Solve

Use a diagram to show what you know.

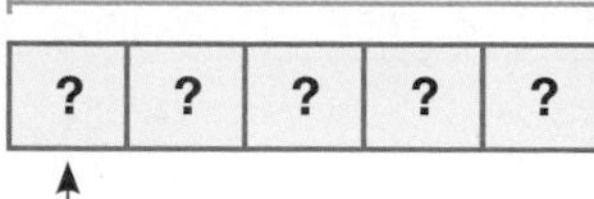

You know the total amount of sand and that there are 5 buckets. Divide to find how much sand is in each bucket.

Answer

Write a number sentence.

$45 \div 5 = 9$

There are 9 pounds of sand in each bucket.

Check

Make sure the answer is reasonable.

Use multiplication or repeated addition to check.

$5 \times 9 = 45$

or

$9 + 9 + 9 + 9 + 9 = 45$

Guided Practice*

Do you know HOW?

1. Larry and Pat made 18 posters. Each made the same number. How many did each make? Write a number sentence and solve.

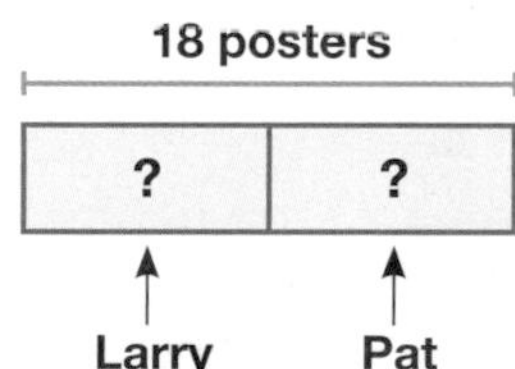

Do you UNDERSTAND?

2. What operation did you use for Problem 1? Tell why.

3. **Write a Problem** Write a problem that you can solve by subtracting. Draw a diagram. Write a number sentence and solve.

Independent Practice

For **4** and **5**, draw a diagram to show what you know. Then write a number sentence and solve.

4. There are 8 cars on a Ferris wheel. Each car holds 3 people. How many people can ride the Ferris wheel at the same time?

5. There were 24 children in a relay race. There were 6 teams in all. How many children are on each team?

- What do I know?
- What am I asked to find?
- What diagram can I use to help understand the problem?
- Can I use addition, subtraction, multiplication, or division?
- Is all of my work correct?
- Did I answer the right question?
- Is my answer reasonable?

*For another example, see Set F on page 223.

Independent Practice

6. The London Underground has twelve lines. The District line is 8 times as long as the East London line. Use the diagram to write a number sentence to find the length of the East London line.

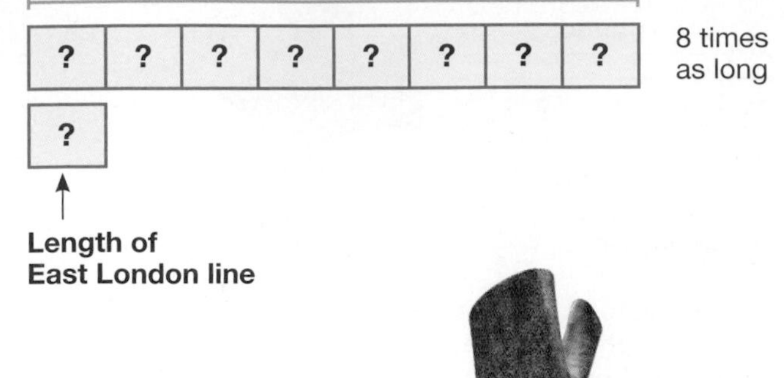

For **7** and **8**, use the animal pictures at the right. Write a number sentence and solve.

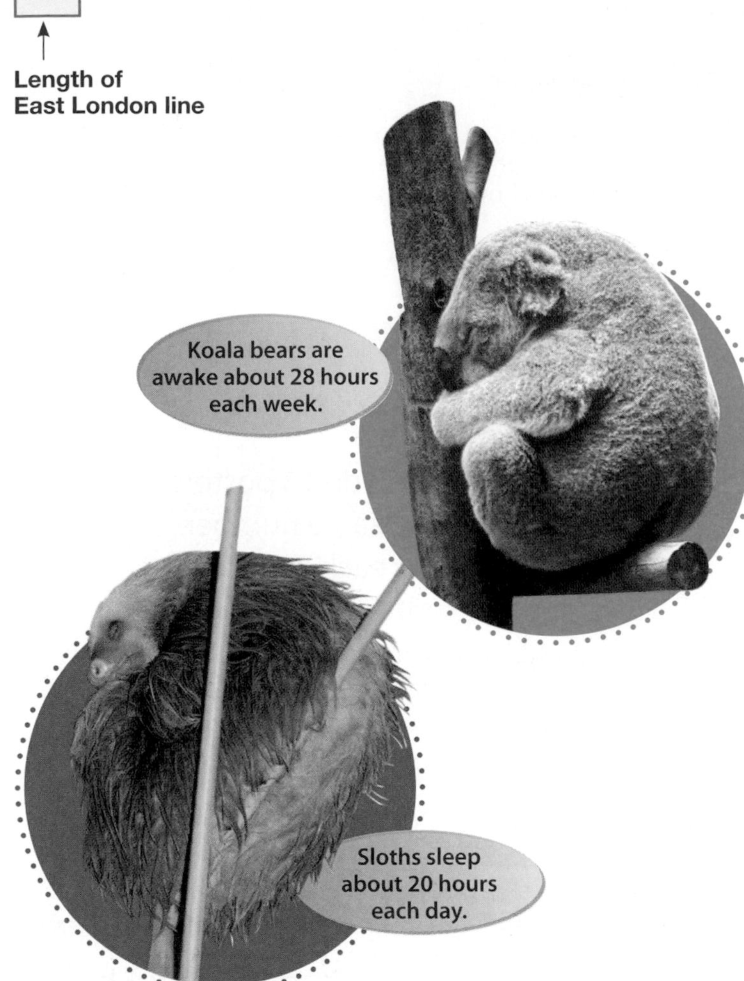

7. About how many hours is a sloth awake each day?

   Tip *There are 24 hours in a day.*

8. About how many hours is a koala bear awake each day?

   Tip *There are 7 days in a week.*

Think About the Process

9. Alma bought 2 bracelets for \$6 at the craft fair. Each bracelet cost the same amount. Which number sentence shows how much each bracelet cost?

   A $2 \times \$6 = \square$

   B $2 + \$6 = \square$

   C $\$6 - 2 = \square$

   D $\$6 \div 2 = \square$

10. Tomas bought a book for \$4, crayons for \$2, and a pen for \$1. He gave the clerk \$10. Which number sentence shows how to find his change?

    A $\$4 + \$2 + \$1 = \square$

    B $\$4 \times \$2 \times \$1 = \square$

    C $\$10 - \$6 = \square$

    D $\$10 - (\$4 + \$2 + \$1) = \square$

Stop and Practice

Compare the numbers. Use <, >, or =.

1. 948 ◯ 998 **2.** 1,017 ◯ 879 **3.** 6,392 ◯ 6,401

Name the solid figure.

4. 

5. 

6. 

Find each product.

7. 3×6 **8.** 7×9 **9.** 4×10 **10.** 9×5 **11.** 8×1

Copy and complete. Use counters or draw a picture to help.

12. $3 \times \square = 27$
$27 \div 3 = \square$

13. $6 \times \square = 24$
$24 \div 6 = \square$

14. $4 \times \square = 32$
$32 \div 4 = \square$

Error Search Find each sum or difference that is not correct. Write it correctly and explain the error.

15. 954 + 138 = 1,192

16. 489 + 527 = 1,016

17. 503 − 76 = 417

18. 3,627 + 7,490 = 10,117

19. 8,051 − 4,156 = 3,895

Number Sense

Estimating and Reasoning Write true or false for each statement. If it is false, explain why.

20. The product of 8 and 8 is greater than 80.

21. The quotient $72 \div 8$ is greater than 10.

22. The product $3 \times 2 \times 4$ is less than 50.

23. The quotient $54 \div 9$ is greater than the quotient $63 \div 9$.

24. The difference 9,314 − 9,296 is less than 100.

25. The product of 5 and 10 is greater than the product of 2 and 5.

Test Prep

1. Which number makes both number sentences true? (10-1)

   $9 \times \square = 54$
   $54 \div 9 = \square$

   A 8
   B 7
   C 6
   D 5

2. Which number sentence is true? (10-5)

   A $6 \div 6 = 0$
   B $5 \div 1 = 1$
   C $0 \div 4 = 4$
   D $7 \div 1 = 7$

3. Nancy has 4 CDs. Each CD has 8 songs. Which number sentence is in this fact family? (10-2)

   A $32 \div 4 = 8$
   B $32 - 8 = 24$
   C $8 - 4 = 4$
   D $2 \times 4 = 8$

4. Gavin has 7 pages of his picture album filled. Each page has 6 pictures, for a total of 42 pictures. Which number sentence is **NOT** in the same fact family as the others? (10-3)

   A $7 \times 6 = 42$
   B $6 \times 7 = 42$
   C $42 \div 7 = 6$
   D $5 \times 7 = 35$

5. Mrs. Hendrix bought 45 pounds of modeling clay. She wants to divide it evenly among her 5 art classes. How many pounds of modeling clay will each class get? (10-2)

   A 40
   B 9
   C 8
   D 7

6. Beth bought a box of dog treats. The box had 48 treats. If Beth gives her dog 6 treats a day, how many days will the box of treats last? (10-3)

   A 6
   B 7
   C 8
   D 9

7. What number makes this number sentence true? (10-4)

   $\square \div 9 = 8$

   A 81
   B 72
   C 17
   D 8

8. Peg put 18 rocks into 2 equal piles. How many rocks were in each pile? (10-2)

   A 6
   B 8
   C 9
   D 36

9. Neil has 30 nails and 6 boards. Which number sentence shows how many nails he can put in each board if he puts the same number in each? (10-6)

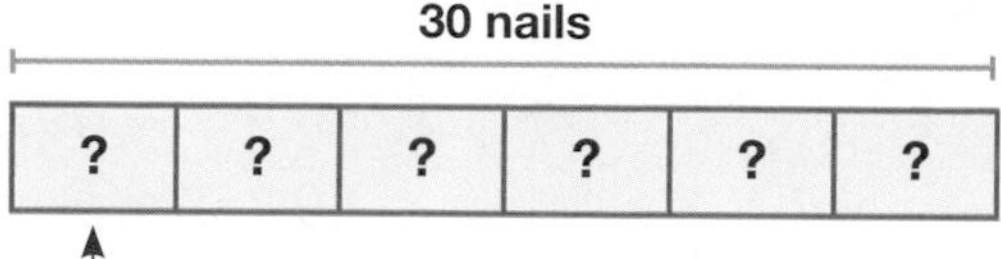

A $30 + 6 = 36$

B $30 - 6 = 24$

C $30 \div 6 = 5$

D $6 \times 30 = 180$

10. The drawing below shows how Janet planted 18 daisies in her flowerbed.

$6 \times 3 = 18$

Which division sentence can be found using the drawing of Janet's daisies? (10-1)

A $6 \div 3 = 2$

B $18 \div 9 = 2$

C $24 \div 3 = 8$

D $18 \div 6 = 3$

11. Mrs. Manchez bought 3 boxes of tissue. How many rooms will get a box of tissue if she puts 1 box in each room? (10-5)

A 9

B 3

C 1

D 0

12. A league has 7 basketball teams. Each team has 8 players, for a total of 56 players. Which number sentence is **NOT** in the same fact family as the others? (10-4)

A $9 \times 7 = 63$

B $8 \times 7 = 56$

C $56 \div 8 = 7$

D $7 \times 8 = 56$

13. Mr. Yarbrough bought 20 pounds of sand. Each bag contained 5 pounds of sand. Which number sentence shows how to find the number of bags of sand Mr. Yarbrough bought? (10-6)

A $20 \div 5 = 4$

B $5 \times 20 = 100$

C $20 - 5 = 15$

D $20 + 5 = 25$

14. What is $24 \div 8$? (10-4)

A 16

B 6

C 4

D 3

Reteaching

Set A, pages 204–205

Use the array to help you find the fact family for 4, 7, and 28.

Multiplication	**Division**
$4 \times 7 = 28$	$28 \div 4 = 7$
$7 \times 4 = 28$	$28 \div 7 = 4$

Remember that a fact family shows how multiplication and division are related.

Copy and complete.

1. $3 \times \square = 27$
$27 \div 3 = \square$

2. $\square \times 7 = 49$
$49 \div 7 = \square$

3. $7 \times \square = 56$
$56 \div 7 = \square$

4. $5 \times \square = 25$
$25 \div 5 = \square$

Set B, pages 206–208

Hanna read 21 pages of a book in 3 days. If Hanna read the same number of pages each day, how many pages did she read each day?

Find $21 \div 3$.

What number times 3 equals 21?

$7 \times 3 = 21$

Write: $21 \div 3 = 7$

Hanna read 7 pages each day.

Remember to think of a related multiplication fact to solve a division problem.

Find each quotient.

1. $27 \div 3$ **2.** $12 \div 2$

3. $32 \div 8$ **4.** $35 \div 5$

5. $50 \div 5$ **6.** $8 \div 2$

7. $20 \div 4$ **8.** $18 \div 3$

Set C, pages 210–211

Joseph has 24 spelling words to practice in the next 6 days. How many words does he need to practice each day?

Find $24 \div 6$.

What number times 6 equals 24?

$4 \times 6 = 24$

Write: $24 \div 6 = 4$

Joseph has 4 words to practice each day.

Remember that division problems can be written in two ways.

Find the quotient.

1. $63 \div 7$ **2.** $36 \div 6$

3. $42 \div 6$ **4.** $60 \div 6$

5. $7\overline{)14}$ **6.** $6\overline{)30}$

7. $6\overline{)48}$ **8.** $7\overline{)42}$

Set D, pages 212–213

There are 36 students who want to play baseball. Each team needs 9 players. How many teams will there be?

Find $36 \div 9$.

What number times 9 equals 36?

$4 \times 9 = 36$

Write: $36 \div 9 = 4$

There will be 4 teams.

Remember that you divide to find how many groups.

Find the quotient.

1. $64 \div 8$ **2.** $18 \div 9$

3. $9\overline{)54}$ **4.** $8\overline{)32}$

5. Divide 24 by 8.

6. Find 45 divided by 9.

Set E, pages 214–215

Find $8 \div 1$, $8 \div 8$, and $0 \div 8$.

When any number is divided by 1, the quotient is that number. $\mathbf{8 \div 1 = 8}$

When any number (except 0) is divided by itself, the quotient is 1. $\mathbf{8 \div 8 = 1}$

When zero is divided by any number (except 0), the quotient is 0. $\mathbf{0 \div 8 = 0}$

Remember that you cannot divide any number by 0.

Find each quotient.

1. $4 \div 1$ **2.** $7 \div 7$ **3.** $0 \div 5$

4. $1\overline{)5}$ **5.** $3\overline{)0}$ **6.** $9\overline{)9}$

7. $6\overline{)6}$ **8.** $1\overline{)7}$ **9.** $4\overline{)0}$

Set F, pages 216–218

Carl has 48 balloons to tie in 6 equal groups. How many balloons will be in each group?

48 balloons

?	?	?	?	?	?

Balloons in each group

Draw a diagram to show what you know.

Write a number sentence.
$48 \div 6 = 8$
There will be 8 balloons in each group.

Remember to read carefully.

Draw a diagram and write a number sentence to solve.

1. A roller coaster has 10 cars that each hold 6 people. How many people can ride the roller coaster at one time?

2. There were 36 children on a field trip. The children formed 6 equal groups. How many children were in each group?

Topic 11

Patterns and Relationships

1 How many years will it take an animal symbol to repeat in the Chinese calendar? You will find out in Lesson 11-2.

2 How fast can a penguin swim? You will find out in Lesson 11-3.

3 Are the rocks of Stonehenge arranged in a pattern? You will find out in Lesson 11-6.

4

How many eggs can an ostrich hen lay in a year? You will find out in Lesson 11-4.

Review What You Know!

Vocabulary

Choose the best term from the box.

- compare
- divide
- multiply
- regroup

1. To put together equal groups to find the total number, you __?__.

2. To decide if 4 has more ones or fewer ones than 8, __?__ the numbers.

3. To separate into equal groups, you __?__.

Number Patterns

Write the missing number in each pattern.

4. 3, 6, 9, 12, ▢, 18

5. 4, 8, 12, ▢, 20, 24

6. 8, 7, 6, ▢, 4, 3

7. 30, 25, 20, 15, ▢, 5

Multiplication Facts

Find each product.

8. 4×3 **9.** 3×5 **10.** 7×2

11. 5×6 **12.** 2×4 **13.** 3×7

Division Facts

Find each quotient.

14. $20 \div 4$ **15.** $10 \div 5$ **16.** $18 \div 6$

17. $28 \div 4$ **18.** $24 \div 6$ **19.** $56 \div 8$

20. **Writing to Explain** Janelle bought 4 cans of tennis balls. There are 3 balls in each can. How many tennis balls did she buy? Explain how you solved the problem.

Lesson
11-1

AF 2.2 Extend and recognize a linear pattern by its rules (e.g., the number of legs on a given number of horses may be calculated by counting by 4s or by multiplying the number of horses by 4). Also **MR 1.1**

Repeating Patterns

How can you continue a repeating pattern?

Rashad is making patterns with shapes. What three shapes should come next in this pattern?

A repeating pattern is made up of shapes or numbers that form a part that repeats.

Guided Practice*

Do you know HOW?

1. Draw the next three shapes to continue the pattern.

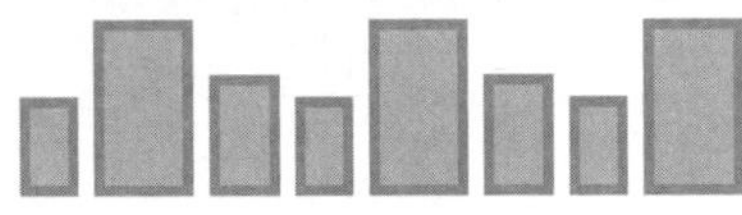

2. Write the next three numbers to continue the pattern.
9, 2, 7, 6, 9, 2, 7, 6, 9

Do you UNDERSTAND?

3. In the example above, describe the pattern using words.

4. What is the 10th shape in the pattern below? How do you know?

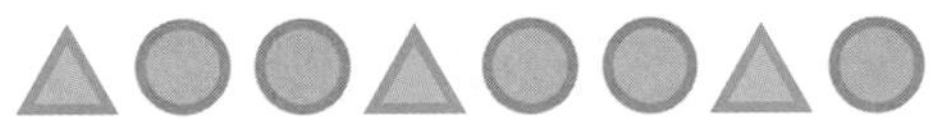

Independent Practice

In **5–8**, draw the next three shapes to continue the pattern.

5.

6.

7.

8.

In **9–12**, write the next three numbers to continue the pattern.

9. 1, 1, 2, 1, 1, 2, 1, 1, 2

10. 5, 7, 4, 8, 5, 7, 4, 8, 5, 7, 4

11. 2, 8, 2, 9, 2, 8, 2, 9, 2, 8, 2, 9

12. 4, 0, 3, 3, 4, 0, 3, 3, 4, 0, 3

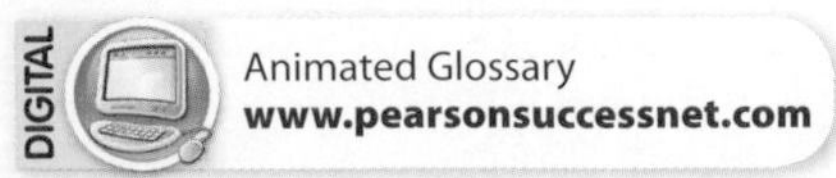

*For another example, see Set A on page 244.

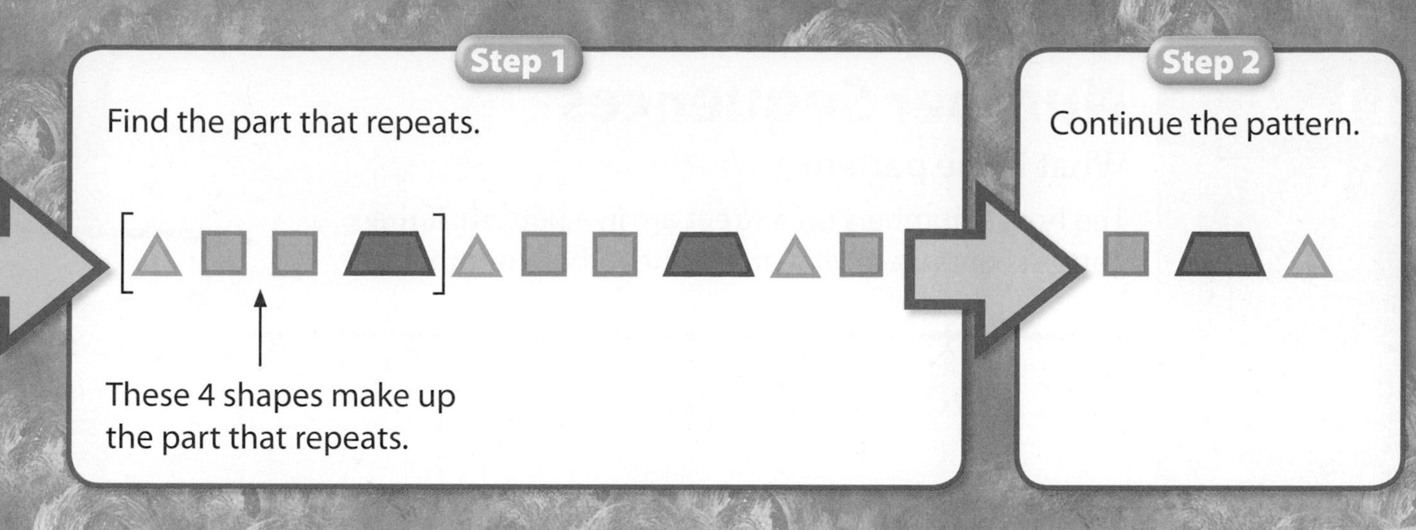

Problem Solving

13. Hilda is making a pattern with the shapes below. If she continues the pattern, what will the 11th shape in the pattern be? Draw a picture to show the shape.

14. Marcus is using shapes to make the pattern below. He wants the completed pattern to show the part that repeats 5 times. How many circles will be in Marcus' finished pattern?

15. Louisa put beads on a string to make a bracelet. She used a blue bead, then three green beads, then a blue bead, then three green beads, and so on, until she used 18 green beads. How many beads did she use in all?

16. Estimation A box of toy blocks has 108 blocks. Jiang used 72 of the blocks to make a building. About how many blocks are left in the box? Explain how you estimated.

17. The table shows the number of students in each grade at a school.

Which grade has more than 145 but fewer than 149 students?

A First **C** Second

B Third **D** Fourth

Data

Grade	Number of Students
First	142
Second	158
Third	146
Fourth	139

18. Writing to Explain Balloons are sold in bags of 30. There are 4 giant balloons in each bag. How many giant balloons will you get if you buy 120 balloons? Explain.

Lesson
11-2

AF 2.2 Extend and recognize a linear pattern by its rules (e.g.; the number of legs on a given number of horses may be calculated by counting by 4s or by multiplying the number of horses by 4).

Number Sequences

What is the pattern?

The house numbers on a street are in a pattern. If the pattern continues, what are the next three numbers?

Guided Practice*

Do you know HOW?

In **1** and **2**, find a rule for the pattern. Use your rule to continue each pattern.

1.

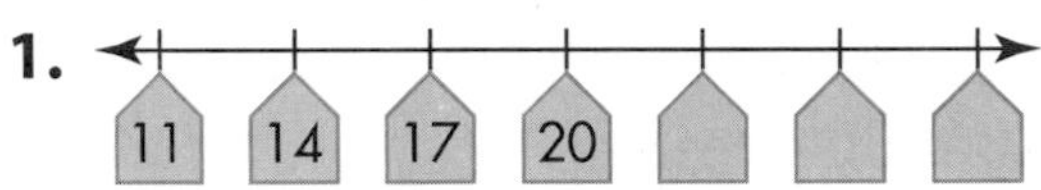

2. 48, 42, 36, 30, 24, ▢, ▢, ▢

Do you UNDERSTAND?

3. In the example above, if 16 is the 1st number in the pattern, what is the 10th number?

4. Rudy is using "add 2" as his rule to make a pattern. He started with 4 and wrote the numbers below for his pattern. Which number does not belong in this pattern? Explain.

4, 6, 8, 9, 10, 12

Independent Practice

In **5–16**, find a rule for the pattern. Use your rule to continue each pattern.

5. 21, 18, 15, ▢, ▢

6. 4, 11, 18, ▢, ▢

7. 5, 10, 15, ▢, ▢

8. 5, 7, 9, ▢, ▢, 15

9. 250, 300, 350, ▢, ▢

10. 92, 80, 68, ▢, ▢

11. 790, 780, 770, ▢, ▢

12. 16, 27, 38, ▢, ▢

13. 96, 101, 106, ▢, 116, ▢

14. 43, 47, 51, ▢, ▢, 63

15. 120, 105, 90, ▢, ▢, 45

16. 99, 90, 81, 72, ▢, ▢

*For another example, see Set B on page 244.

Step 1

Find the pattern.

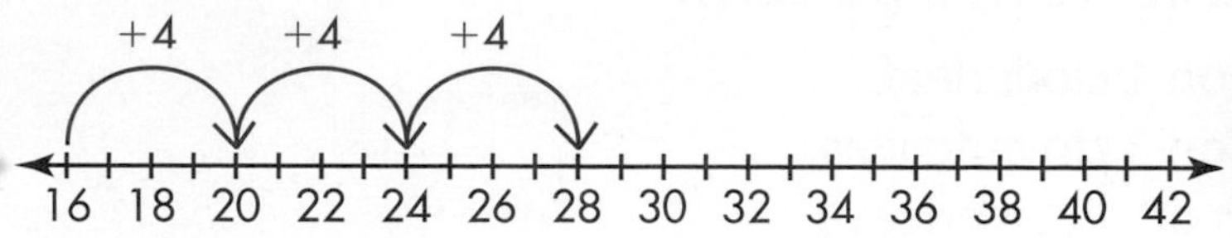

Each number is 4 more than the number before it.

Step 2

Use this rule to continue the pattern.

Rule: Add 4

$28 + 4 = 32$

$32 + 4 = 36$

$36 + 4 = 40$

The next numbers in the pattern are 32, 36, and 40.

Problem Solving

17. Orlando delivers mail. He sees that one mailbox does not have a number. If the numbers are in a pattern, what is the missing number?

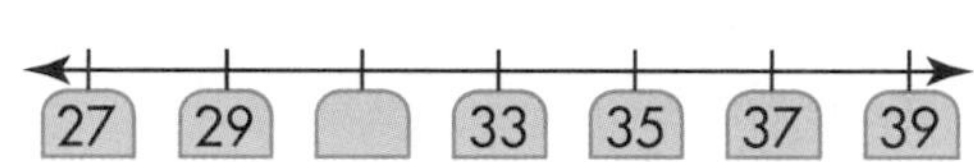

18. In the Chinese calendar, each year has an animal as a symbol. There are 12 animals. It was the year of the snake in 2001 and will be again in 2013. The year 2005 was the year of the rooster. When is the next year of the rooster?

19. Suppose you were born in the year of the horse. How old will you be the next time the year of the horse is celebrated?

The pattern of animals repeats every 12 years.

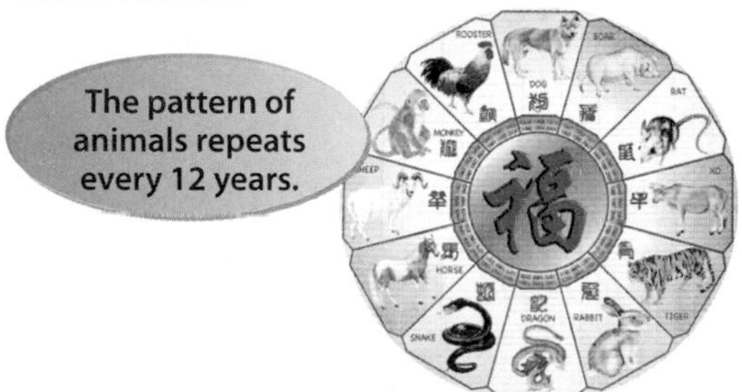

20. **Reasoning** The numbers below are in a pattern.

24, 27, 30, 33

Which number would be part of the pattern?

A 34 **C** 39

B 38 **D** 44

21. Mia counted the pencils in a box.

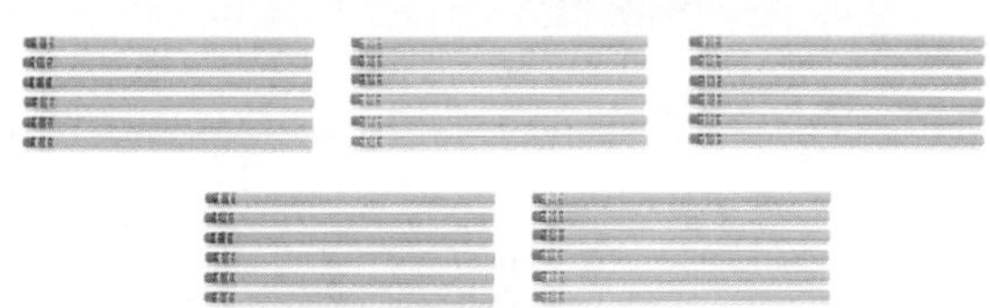

If she counted the pencils in groups of 6, which list shows numbers Mia could have named?

A 24, 36, 48, 52 **C** 6, 12, 24, 32

B 6, 24, 48, 56 **D** 12, 18, 24, 30

Lesson
11-3

AF 2.2 Extend and recognize a linear pattern by its rules (e.g., the number of legs on a given number of horses may be calculated by counting by 4s or by multiplying the number of horses by 4). Also **AF 2.1**

Extending Tables

What pairs of numbers fit a pattern?

There are 3 leaflets on 1 cloverleaf.
There are 9 leaflets on 3 cloverleaves.
There are 12 leaflets on 4 cloverleaves.
How many leaflets are there on 2 cloverleaves? on 5 cloverleaves?

Guided Practice*

Do you know HOW?

In **1** and **2**, copy and complete each table.

1.

Number of Boxes	*Total Number of Hats*
2	6
5	15
7	21
▢	27

2.

Number of Cars	2	3	5	9
Total Number of Wheels	8	12	20	▢

Do you UNDERSTAND?

3. In the example above, 4 and 12 are a pair of numbers that fit the pattern. Does the pair 6 and 16 fit the pattern? Explain.

4. Reasonableness A rule for this table is "add 5 to my age."

My Age	*Joe's Age*
5	10
8	13
9	15

Which number does not belong?

Independent Practice

In **5–7**, copy and complete each table.

5.

Number of Spiders	*Number of Legs*
1	8
2	▢
3	24
4	32
▢	56

6.

Regular Price	*Sale Price*
$29	$22
$25	$18
▢	$16
$22	▢
$19	$12

7.

Weight of Book in Ounces	9	11	12	16
Total Weight of Carton in Ounces	18	20	21	▢

8. For each table in 5–7, write another pair of numbers that belongs to the table.

*For another example, see Set C on page 244.

One Way

Draw pictures and count the leaflets.

2 cloverleaves have 6 leaflets.

5 cloverleaves have 15 leaflets.

Another Way

Fill in a table by using a rule.

Rule: Multiply by 3

Number of Cloverleaves	*Number of Leaflets*
1	3
2	6
3	9
4	12
5	15

Problem Solving

For **9** and **10**, the table at the right shows the number of batteries needed for different numbers of one kind of flashlight.

Batteries for Flashlights

Number of Flashlights	Number of Batteries
1	3
4	12
7	21

9. How many batteries do 8 flashlights need? 10 flashlights?

10. Writing to Explain How many more batteries do 6 flashlights need than 4 flashlights? Explain how you found your answer.

11. Number Sense What is the greatest number you can make using each of the digits 1, 7, 0, and 6 once?

12. A penguin can swim 11 miles per hour. At this speed, how far can it swim in 3 hours? Use a table to help.

13. Alan has 35 fewer coins than Suzy has. Which of these shows the number of coins that Alan and Suzy could have?

A Alan 65, Suzy 105

B Alan 105, Suzy 70

C Alan 105, Suzy 65

D Alan 70, Suzy 105

14. If the pattern at the right continues, how long will each side of the next square be?

A 8 feet

B 9 feet

C 10 feet

D 11 feet

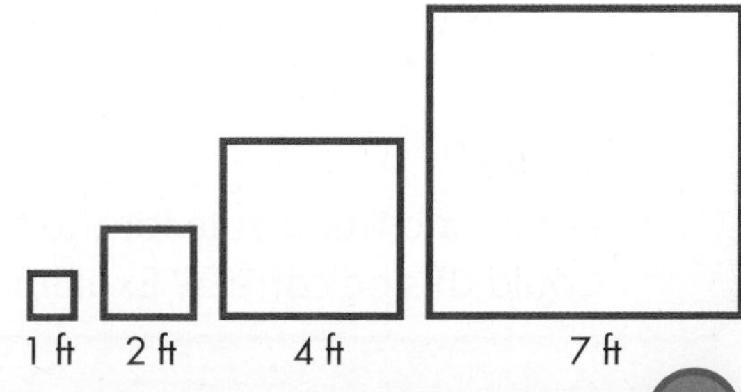

Lesson

11-4

AF 2.1 Solve simple problems involving a functional relationship between two quantities (e.g., find the total cost of multiple items given the cost per unit).
Also **AF 1.3**, **AF 2.2**.

Writing Rules for Situations

What is a math rule for the situation?

Alex and his older brother Andy have the same birthday. If you know Alex's age, how can you find Andy's age? Look for a pattern in the table and find a rule.

Alex's age	2	4	6	7	9
Andy's age	8	10	12	13	15

Another Example What other rules are there for pairs of numbers?

Nell saves some of the money she earns. The table shows how much she earned and how much she saved for five days. What is a rule for the table? What are the missing numbers?

Earned	65¢	45¢	50¢	30¢	▢
Saved	50¢	30¢	▢	15¢	25¢

Step 1

Find a rule for the table.

Look for a pattern.

Earned	65¢	45¢	50¢	30¢	▢
Saved	50¢	30¢	▢	15¢	25¢

Each time, the amount saved is 15¢ less than the amount earned.

One rule is "subtract 15¢ from the amount earned."

Step 2

Check that your rule works for all pairs.

Rule: Subtract 15¢ from the amount earned.

65¢ − 15¢ = 50¢
45¢ − 15¢ = 30¢
30¢ − 15¢ = 15¢

The rule works for each pair.

What amount is 15¢ less than 50¢?
50¢ − 15¢ = 35¢

25¢ is 15¢ less than what amount?
25¢ = ▢ − 15¢   15¢ + 25¢ = 40¢

The missing amounts are 35¢ and 40¢.

Explain It

1. David said that a rule for the table above is "Add 15¢." Could this be correct? Explain.

Step 1

Find a rule for the table.

Compare each pair of numbers. Look for a pattern.

Alex's age	2	4	6	7	9
Andy's age	8	10	12	13	15

In each pair, Andy's age is 6 more than Alex's age.
Rule: Add 6

Step 2

Check that your rule works for all pairs.

$2 + 6 = 8$
$4 + 6 = 10$
$6 + 6 = 12$
$7 + 6 = 13$
$9 + 6 = 15$

This rule works for each pair.

Guided Practice*

Do you know HOW?

In **1** and **2**, use the table below.

Hours Worked	4	8	7	2	6
Amount Earned	$24	$48		$12	

1. Write a rule for the table.

2. Write the missing numbers.

Do you UNDERSTAND?

3. In the example above, what does the rule "add 6" mean in the problem?

4. Marty uses the rule "subtract 9" for his table. If the first number is 11, what is the second number in the number pair?

Independent Practice

In **5–9**, find a rule for the table. Use your rule to complete the table.

5.

Earned	$15	$12	$17	$9	$11
Spent	$7		$9		$3

6.

Earned	$14	$18	$12	$16	$8
Saved	$7	$9			$4

7.

Price	$36	$28	$33	$40	$25
Discount	$24	$16		$28	

8.

Number of Chairs	*Number of Legs*
3	12
2	8
5	20
7	
	36

9.

Number of Teams	*Number of Players*
4	20
3	15
5	
6	30
8	

**For another example, see Set C on page 244.*

Problem Solving

For **10** and **11**, use the table at the right.

10. The table shows the ages of a Velvet mesquite tree and a Saguaro cactus plant at a garden. When the Velvet mesquite tree was 48 years old, how old was the Saguaro cactus?

11. Reasonableness Phil says the Saguaro cactus is about 100 years older than the Velvet mesquite tree. Is his estimate reasonable? Explain.

Data

Plant's Age in Years	
Velvet Mesquite Tree	**Saguaro Cactus**
1 year	36
15	50
67	102
48	■

12. Use the table below. How many eggs can 4 ostrich hens lay in a year? 5 ostrich hens?

Number of Ostrich Hens	1	2	3	4	5
Number of Eggs	50	100	150	■	■

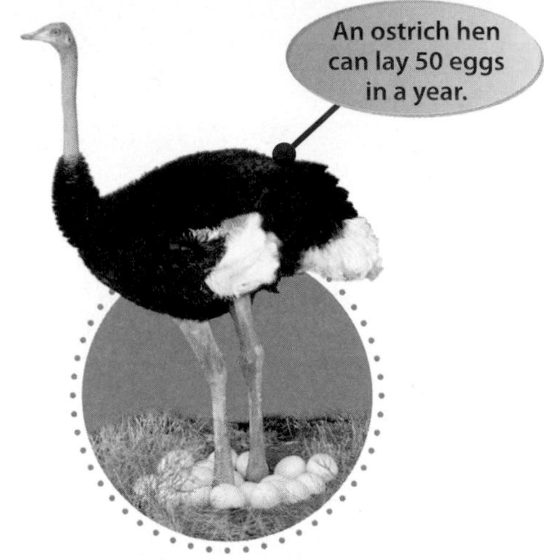

For **13** and **14**, the table shows the number of baskets that Betty needs for different numbers of apples. She needs to put an equal number of apples into each basket.

Data

Betty's Apple Baskets					
Number of Apples	28	56	7	21	14
Number of Baskets	4	■	1	3	2

13. How many baskets does Betty need for 56 apples?

A 8 **B** 7 **C** 6 **D** 5

14. What is a rule for the table?

A Subtract 24 **C** Divide by 7

B Subtract 6 **D** Add 12

15. An art museum has 47 paintings in one room and 24 paintings in another room. Which is the best estimate of the total number of paintings?

A 50 **C** 80

B 70 **D** 100

16. Esther is 8 years older than Manuel. Which of these shows the ages that Esther and Manuel each could be?

A Esther 15, Manuel 23

B Esther 16, Manuel 15

C Esther 15, Manuel 7

D Esther 7, Manuel 15

Mixed Problem Solving

In the 1700s, many people helped Americans gain freedom from rule by Britain. The time line shows the years of some of these events.

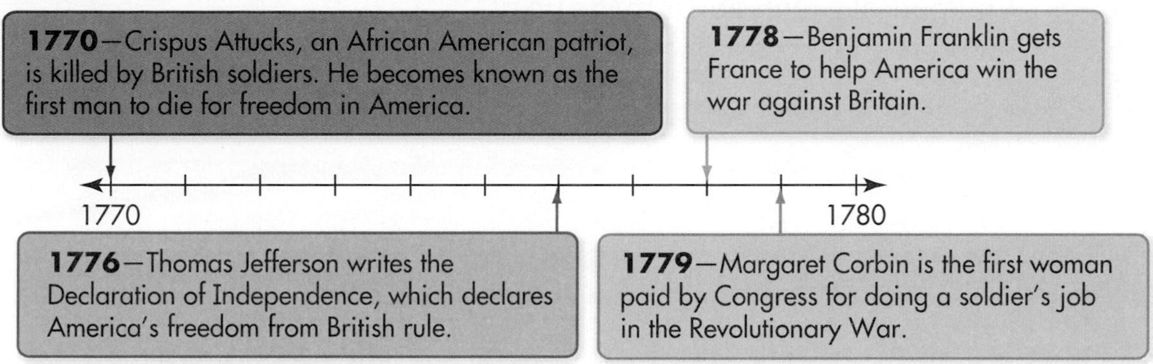

1. Which event happened before 1778, but after 1770?

2. Which event happened about 10 years after Crispus Attucks died?

3. How many years after the Declaration of Independence was written did France begin to help America?

4. How many years have passed since the Declaration of Independence was written?

Use the table at the right for **5–7**.

5. What event happened more than 100 years after the Declaration of Independence was written?

6. How many years after the first Women's Rights Convention were women given the right to vote?

Data

Year	Event
1776	Declaration of Independence
1787	Constitution is signed
1848	First Women's Rights Convention
1920	Women are given the right to vote.

7. **Strategy Focus** Solve. Use the strategy Write a Number Sentence.

   Benjamin Franklin was born in 1706. How old was he when the Constitution of the United States was signed?

Lesson

11-5

AF 1.1 Represent relationships of quantities in the form of mathematical expressions, equations, or inequalities. Also **AF 1.0**

Translating Words to Expressions

How can you translate words to numerical expressions?

In a reading contest, Kara read 5 more books than Jon. What numerical expression shows how many books Kara read?

A numerical expression is made up of numbers and at least one operation symbol.

Jon read 8 books.

Other Examples

Teri read 3 fewer books than Jon read.

Word phrase
"3 fewer books than the 8 books Jon read"

Numerical expression
8 − 3

Dina read twice as many books as Jon read.

Word phrase
"twice as many as the 8 books Jon read"

Numerical expression
2 × 8

For 4 weeks, Jon read the same number of books each week.

Word phrase
"the 8 books Jon read, put into 4 equal groups"

Numerical expression
8 ÷ 4

Guided Practice*

Do you know HOW?

Write a numerical expression for each.

1. 18 less than 25
2. half of 14

"Half" means 2 equal groups.

3. the total of 24, 16, and 32

Do you UNDERSTAND?

4. In the example above, Jon read 7 fewer books than Eduardo. Write a numerical expression to show how many books Eduardo read.
5. **Reasoning** Does the word "fewer" always tell you to subtract? Explain.

Independent Practice

In **6–9**, write a numerical expression for each word phrase.

6. 7 times as many as 8
7. the product of 9 and 8
8. the difference of 56 and 48
9. the sum of 15, 24, and 18

*For another example, see Set D on page 245.

What You Think

Word phrase:

"5 more books than the 8 books Jon read"

To find 5 more than a number, use addition.

What You Write

To show the number of books Kara read, write "the sum of 8 and 5" as a numerical expression.

Numerical expression:

$8 + 5$

Problem Solving

In **10–17,** write a numerical expression for each word phrase.

10. 8 points taken away from 16 points

11. 28 players separated into 4 equal teams

12. \$15 less than \$35

13. 4 times as long as 9 inches

14. twice as old as 7 years old

15. 24 grapes shared equally by 4 people

16. the total of 18 children and 13 adults

17. 45 yards shorter than 120 yards

There are 10 cars in a parking lot. For **18–21,** write a numerical expression for the number of cars described in each word phrase.

18. 7 fewer cars

19. half the number of cars

20. 5 times as many cars

21. 12 more cars

22. **Geometry** Juana has a wooden block. The block is a rectangular prism that is 12 inches long. Juana cut the block into 6 cubes that are all the same size. How long is each side of a cube?

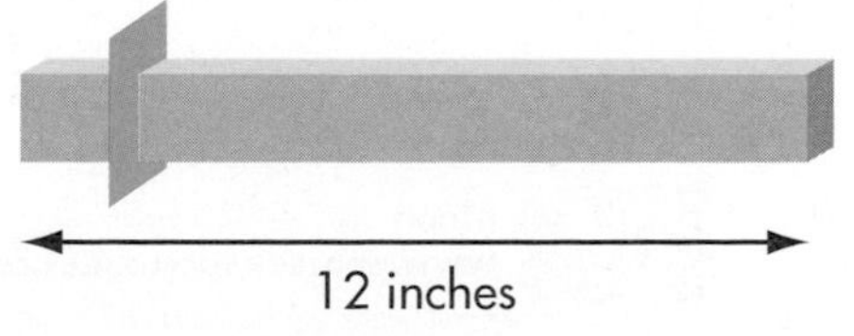

23. Walt bought 16 muffins packed equally into 4 boxes. Which numerical expression shows how to find the number of muffins in each box?

A $16 \div 4$

B 16×4

C $16 - 4$

D $16 + 4$

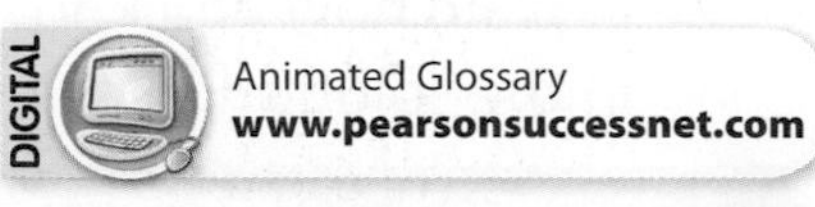

Lesson

11-6

MR 2.0 Use strategies, skills, and concepts in finding solutions. Also **NS 2.0, MR 2.3.**

Problem Solving

Act It Out and Use Reasoning

Hands-On

counter

Juana collected old pennies, nickels, and dimes. Her collection has at least one of each kind of coin.

How many of each kind of coin does Juana have?

Juana's Collection

2 pennies

2 fewer nickels than dimes

10 coins in all

nickel

penny

dime

Another Example What are other kinds of relationships?

Ken's Collection of Dimes, Nickels, and Pennies

3 nickels

4 more dimes than nickels

15 coins in all

How many of each coin are in his collection?

Read and Understand

What do I know? There are 15 coins in all, and 3 of the coins are nickels.

There are 4 more dimes than nickels.

Use objects to show what you know.

Plan and Solve

Use reasoning to make conclusions.

Since there are 3 nickels, there are 12 pennies and dimes together.

Try 3 nickels, 7 dimes, and 5 pennies. Since $3 + 7 + 5 = 15$, this is correct.

There are 5 pennies, 3 nickels, and 7 dimes in the collection.

Explain It

1. Which number of coins in Ken's collection is given to you? Which information do you need to find?
2. Explain how you know 7 is the number of dimes in the solution above.

Read and Understand

What do I know? Juana has 10 coins in all, and 2 of the coins are pennies.

There are 2 fewer nickels than dimes.

Use objects to show what you know.

Plan and Solve

Use reasoning to make conclusions.

She has 2 pennies, so there are 8 nickels and dimes together.

Try 2 nickels and 4 dimes. But $2 + 2 + 4$ is not equal to 10.

Try 3 nickels and 5 dimes. Since $2 + 3 + 5 = 10$, this is correct.

There are 2 pennies, 3 nickels, and 5 dimes in Juana's collection.

Guided Practice*

Do you know HOW?

Find the number of each kind of stamp in the collection. Use counters.

1. Ricardo has 9 stamps in all. He has 2 nation stamps and 3 more inventor stamps than flower stamps.

   Nation Stamps = ▢
   Inventor Stamps = ▢
   Flower Stamps = ▢

Do you UNDERSTAND?

2. What did you do to find the number of inventor stamps in Ricardo's collection?

3. **Write a Problem** Write a problem about coin collections that you can solve by using reasoning.

Independent Practice

Find the number of each kind of object in Anya's collection. Use counters or draw pictures to help.

4. **Anya's Collection of Minerals, Gemstones and Rocks**
   6 minerals
   3 fewer gemstones than rocks.
   15 objects in all.

   Minerals = ▢
   Gemstones = ▢
   Rocks = ▢

Stuck? Try this....

- What do I know?
- What am I asked to find?
- What diagram can I use to help understand the problem?
- Can I use addition, subtraction, multiplication, or division?
- Is all of my work correct?
- Did I answer the right question?
- Is my answer reasonable?

For another example, see Set E on page 245.

5. There are 10 fish in all in Percy's fish tank. Four of the fish are angel fish. There are 4 more mollie fish than tetra fish. How many of each kind of fish are in the tank?

6. Norah's dog weighs 9 pounds more than her cat. Her dog weighs 6 pounds less than Jeff's dog. Norah's cat weighs 7 pounds. How much does Jeff's dog weigh?

7. The students in Mr. Cole's class voted on which kind of collection they should start as a class. The graph shows the results. How many more votes did the collection with the greatest number of votes get than the collection with the least number of votes?

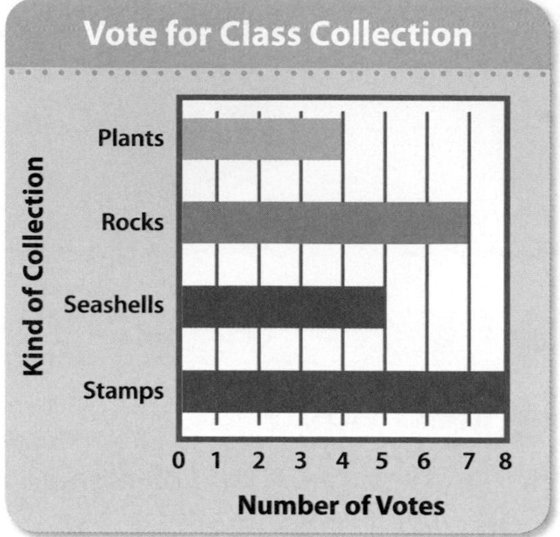

8. Isadora has 15 seashells in her collection. The seashells are oyster shells, clam shells, and conch shells. There are 6 clam shells. There are 2 fewer clam shells than oyster shells. How many conch shells are in the collection?

9. Lyn, Kurt, and Steve wrote a riddle about their ages. Lyn is 7 years older than Steve. Steve is 5 years old. The sum of their ages is 25 years. How old is Kurt?

10. Stonehenge is an ancient monument in England made up of a pattern of rocks that looks like this:

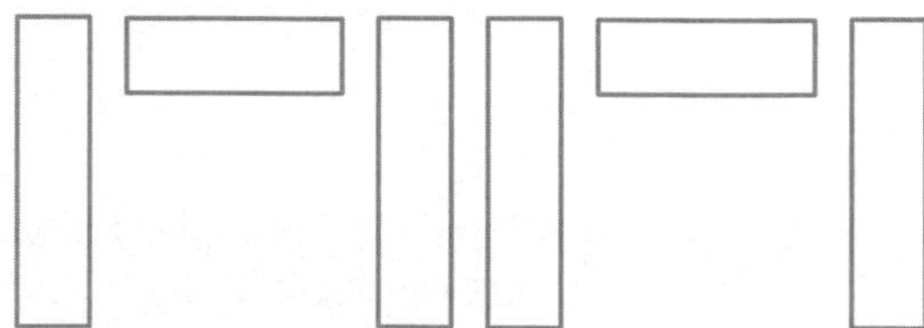

Draw the shape that comes next in this pattern.

11. Think About the Process At the town pet show, Dina saw 48 pets. There were 6 birds and 7 cats. The remaining pets were dogs. Which number sentence shows one way to find the number of pets that were dogs?

A $48 - 6 - 7 = \square$

B $48 + 6 \div 7 = \square$

C $48 - 6 \times 7 = \square$

D $6 \times 7 \times 48 = \square$

Write the place of the underlined digit. Then write its value.

1. 31<u>2</u>,937
2. <u>6</u>4,285
3. <u>2</u>70,591

Name the solid figures you would get if you cut the solid figure as shown.

4. 

5. 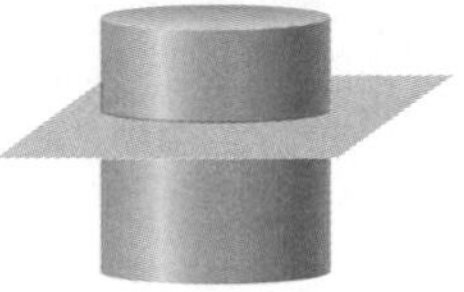

6. 

Find the missing numbers in each pattern. Write a rule for the pattern.

7. 40, 35, 30, ▭, ▭
8. 7, 11, 15, ▭, ▭
9. 28, 25, 22, ▭, ▭

Copy and complete. Use counters or draw a picture to help.

10. $2 \times \square = 14$
$14 \div 2 = \square$

11. $8 \times \square = 40$
$40 \div 8 = \square$

12. $9 \times \square = 54$
$54 \div 9 = \square$

Error Search Find each product or quotient that is not correct. Write it correctly and explain the error.

13. $3 \times 6 = 9$
14. $7 \times 5 = 75$
15. $72 \div 9 = 8$
16. $36 \div 4 = 8$
17. $21 \div 3 = 7$

Number Sense

Estimating and Reasoning Write true or false for each statement. If it is false, explain why.

18. The product of 1 and 6 is greater than 6.

19. The difference 8,423 − 7,591 is less than 1,000.

20. The product of 7 and 8 is greater than the product of 6 and 8.

21. The quotient $42 \div 6$ is less than 5.

22. The quotient $27 \div 9$ is greater than the quotient $18 \div 9$.

Test Prep

1. What is the rule for the pattern? (11-2)

29, 24, 19, 14, 9

A Subtract 4

B Subtract 5

C Divide by 4

D Divide by 5

2. Fran has 3 grapes. Ivan has 6 times as many grapes as Fran. Which numerical expression shows how to find the number of grapes Ivan has? (11-5)

A $6 + 3$

B $6 - 3$

C 6×3

D $6 \div 3$

3. What rule can be used to find the number of legs on 7 grasshoppers? (11-4)

Number of Grasshoppers	3	5	7	9
Number of Legs	18	30	▢	54

A Add 15

B Divide by 6

C Multiply by 5

D Multiply by 6

4. Hank and some friends had a party at the zoo. Below is a guide to find the total price of admission for groups of different sizes.

Total Number of Children	*Total Admission Price*
3	$21
5	$35
7	▢
9	$63

What is the cost for 7 children? (11-3)

A $37

B $48

C $49

D $56

5. Coach Kizer needs to form equal sized teams. The table shows the number of teams formed for different numbers of players.

Number of Players	24	32	40	72
Number of Teams	3	4	▢	9

What rule can be used to find how many teams are formed if there are 40 players? (11-4)

A Divide by 8

B Divide by 6

C Multiply by 8

D Multiply by 6

6. Jasmine has a wallpaper border in her room. Which shows the next 3 objects in the pattern? (11-1)

A 

B 

C 

D 

7. Football players came out of the tunnel in the pattern shown below.

What number belongs on the blank jersey? (11-2)

A 26

B 25

C 24

D 22

8. What is a rule for the pattern? (11-2)

11, 20, 29, 38, 47

A Add 10

B Multiply by 9

C Multiply by 10

D Add 9

9. Joe has 18 pets. Ten of his pets are fish. The rest are birds and hamsters. He has 2 fewer birds than hamsters. How many birds does he have? (11-6)

A 2

B 3

C 4

D 5

10. The table shows the number of eggs Mrs. Inez needs for banana bread. Each loaf gets the same number of eggs. How many eggs does she need for 5 loaves? (11-3)

Number of Loaves	*Number of Eggs*
1	2
2	4
3	6

A 8

B 10

C 12

D 14

11. Which numerical expression shows 2 feet shorter than 18 feet? (11-5)

A $2 - 18$

B $18 \div 2$

C $18 + 2$

D $18 - 2$

Topic 11

Reteaching

Set A, pages 226–227

Draw the next three shapes to continue the pattern.

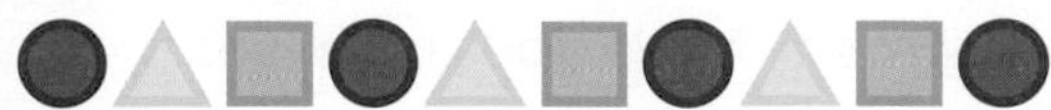

Find the part of the pattern that repeats.

Then continue the pattern.

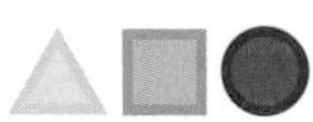

Remember to first find the part of the pattern that repeats.

Draw the next three shapes or numbers to continue the pattern.

1.

2. 3, 5, 7, 9, 3, 5, 7, 9, 3, 5, 7

Set B, pages 228–229

Find a rule for the pattern. Use your rule to continue the pattern.

24, 21, 18, 15, 12, ___, ___, ___,

−3 −3 −3 −3 −3 −3 −3

Rule: Subtract 3

$12 - 3 = 9 \quad 9 - 3 = 6 \quad 6 - 3 = 3$

The next numbers in the pattern are 9, 6, and 3.

Remember to check that your rule works with all of the given numbers for the pattern.

Find a rule for each pattern. Use your rule to continue the pattern.

1. 5, 7, 9, ___, ___, ___

2. 22, 18, 14, ___, ___, ___

Set C, pages 230–234

Find a rule and fill in the table.

Number of Ants	1	2	3	4	5
Number of Legs	6		18	24	

One rule is "multiply the number of ants by 6."

Number of Ants	1	2	3	4	5
Number of Legs	6	12	18	24	30

The missing numbers are 12 and 30.

Remember to use the number pairs in a table to find a rule.

Find the missing numbers. Write a rule.

1.

Number of Cars	1	2	3	4
Number of Wheels	4	8		

2.

Saved	\$8	\$12	\$15	\$6	\$10
Earned	\$16	\$24			\$20

Set D, pages 236–237

Some friends made posters for a music night. Kelli made 3 times as many posters as Rob. Suppose ▢ stands for the number of posters Rob made. Write a numerical expression to show how many posters Kelli made.

Word phrase
"3 times as many posters as Rob made"

Write:
Numerical expression
$3 \times$ ▢

Remember that ▢ stands for a value in the problem.

1. Some friends each brought food for a picnic. Nan brought 4 times as many bread slices as the number of friends. Suppose ▢ stands for the number of friends. Write a numerical expression to show how many bread slices Nan brought.
2. The same friends will share 16 peaches equally. Write a numerical expression to show how many peaches each friend should get.

Set E, pages 238–240

When you solve a problem by acting it out, follow these steps.

Step 1
Choose objects to act out the problem.

Step 2
Show what you know using the objects.

Step 3
Act out the problem.

Step 4
Use reasoning to find the answer.

Remember to decide what the objects represent before you act out the problem.

Solve. Find the number of each kind of object in the collection.

1. **Ben's Sticker Collection**
   - 17 stickers in all
   - 6 star stickers
   - 3 fewer smiley face stickers than planet stickers

   Star Stickers = ▢
   Smiley Face Stickers = ▢
   Planet Stickers = ▢

Topic 12

Fraction Concepts

1 The Honey Run Covered Bridge near Chico, California is the only covered bridge in the United States with 3 roof levels. What fraction of the length of the entire roof is each level? Find out in Lesson 12-4.

2 What fraction of Earth's land surface is desert? You will find out in Lesson 12-6.

3

What fraction of the bones in your body are in your feet? You will find out in Lesson 12-3.

4

Is the flag of Nigeria made up of equal parts? You will find out in Lesson 12-1.

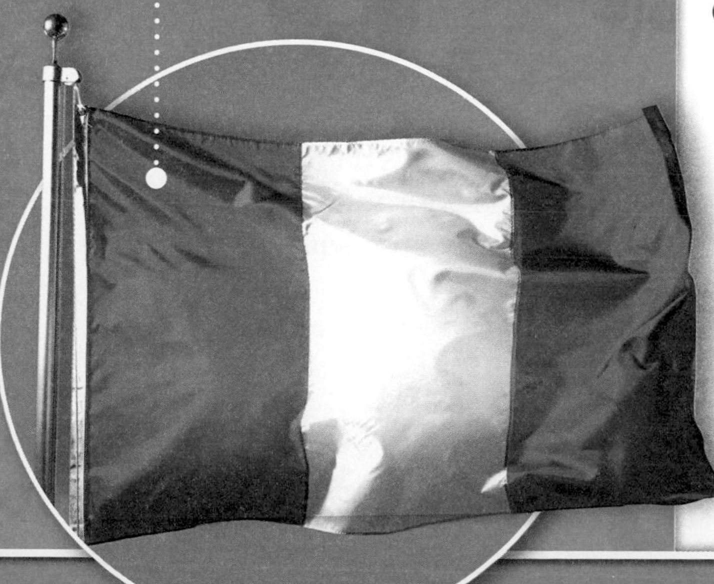

Review What You Know!

Vocabulary

Choose the best term from the box.

- compare
- greater
- less
- multiply

1. The number 219 is __?__ than the number 392.
2. The number 38 is __?__ than the number 19.
3. When you decide if 15 has more tens or fewer tens than 24, you __?__ the numbers.

Arrays

Find the product for each array.

4. ● ● ●
● ● ●

5. ● ● ● ●
● ● ● ●
● ● ● ●

Compare Numbers

Compare. Write >, <, or =.

6. 427 ◯ 583
7. 910 ◯ 906
8. 139 ◯ 136
9. 4,500 ◯ 4,500
10. 693 ◯ 734
11. 1,050 ◯ 1,005
12. **Writing to Explain** Which number is greater, 595 or 565? Explain which digits you used to decide.

Lesson

12-1

NS 3.0 Understand the relationship between whole numbers, simple fractions, and decimals.

Dividing Regions into Equal Parts

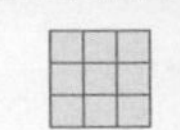

grid paper

How can you divide a whole into equal parts?

Show two ways to divide the grid paper into equal parts.

When a region is divided into two equal parts, the parts are called halves.

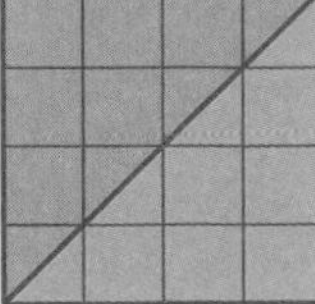

The parts do not need to be the same shape, but they must be equal in area.

6 equal parts
sixths

6 equal parts
sixths

10 equal parts
tenths

10 equal parts
tenths

Guided Practice*

Do you know HOW?

In **1–4**, tell if each shows equal or unequal parts. If the parts are equal, name them.

1. 

2. 

3. 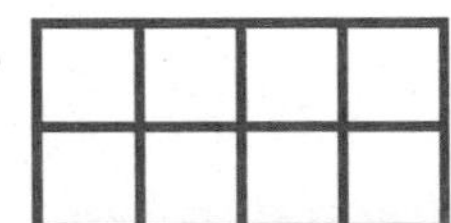

4. 

Do you UNDERSTAND?

5. In the examples on grid paper above, explain how you know the two parts are equal.

6. Use grid paper. Draw a picture to show sixths.

7. Amar divided his garden into equal areas, as shown below. What is the name of the equal parts of the whole?

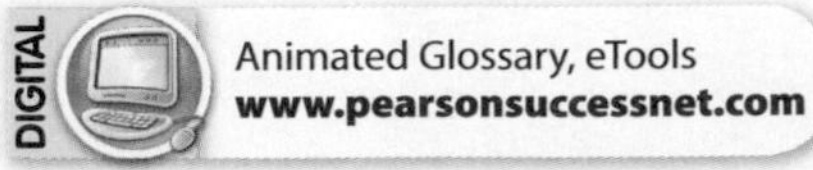

DIGITAL Animated Glossary, eTools **www.pearsonsuccessnet.com**

For another example, see Set A on page 270.

Here are some names of equal parts of a whole.

2 equal parts
halves

3 equal parts
thirds

4 equal parts
fourths

5 equal parts
fifths

6 equal parts
sixths

8 equal parts
eighths

10 equal parts
tenths

12 equal parts
twelfths

Independent Practice

In **8–11**, tell if each shows equal or unequal parts. If the parts are equal, name them.

8. 

9. 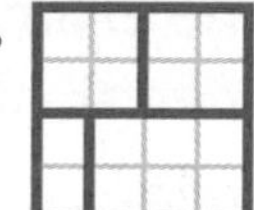

10. 

11. 

In **12–15**, use grid paper. Draw a region showing the equal parts named.

12. fourths **13.** halves **14.** tenths **15.** eighths

Problem Solving

In **16–18**, use the table of flags.

Flags of Different Nations

Nation	Flag
Mauritius	
Nigeria	
Poland	
Seychelles	

16. **Reasoning** The flag of this nation has more than three parts. The parts are equal. Which nation is this?

17. The flag of Nigeria is made up of equal parts. What is the name of the parts of this flag?

18. Which flag does **NOT** have equal parts?

19. Which shape is **NOT** divided into equal parts?

A 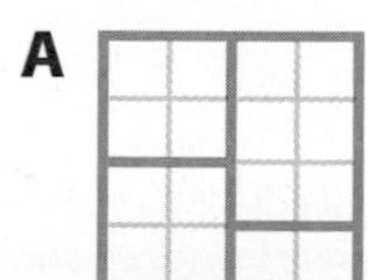

B 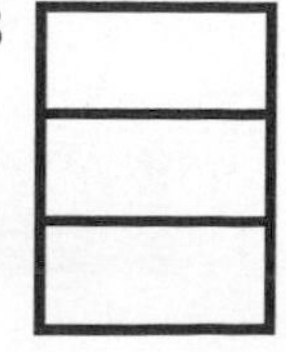

C 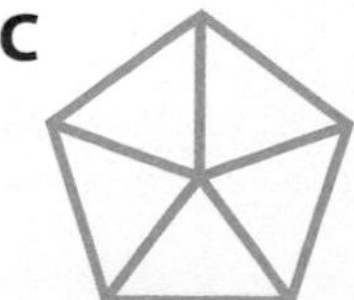

D 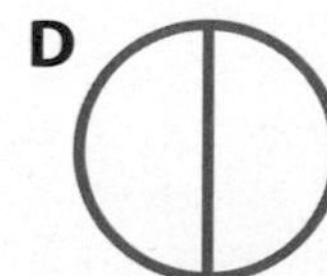

Lesson
12-2

NS 3.0 Understand the relationship between whole numbers, simple fractions, and decimals.

Fractions and Regions

How can you show and name part of a region?

Mr. Kim made a pan of fruit bars. He served part of the pan of bars to friends. What part of the whole pan was served? What part was left?

A fraction is a symbol, such as $\frac{1}{2}$ or $\frac{2}{3}$, that names equal parts of a whole.

Guided Practice*

Do you know HOW?

In **1** and **2**, write the fraction of each figure that is orange.

1.

2. 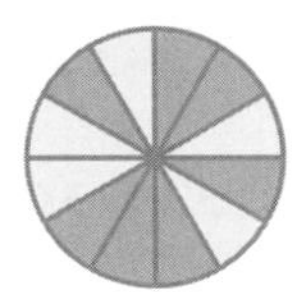

In **3** and **4**, draw a picture to show each fraction.

3. $\frac{3}{4}$ **4.** $\frac{4}{7}$

Do you UNDERSTAND?

5. In the example above, what fraction names all of the parts in the pan of bars?

6. Mrs. Gupta bought a pizza. She ate part of it. What fraction of the pizza did she eat? What fraction of the pizza was left?

Independent Practice

In **7–10**, write the fraction of each figure that is green.

7. 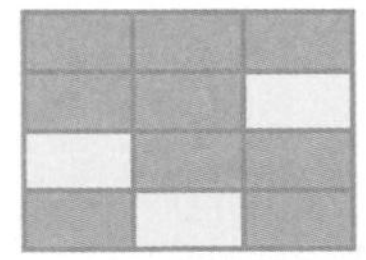

8. 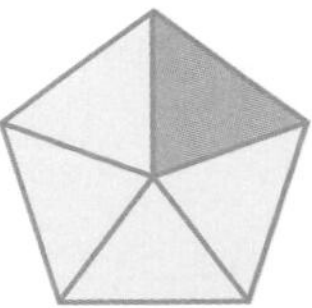

9. 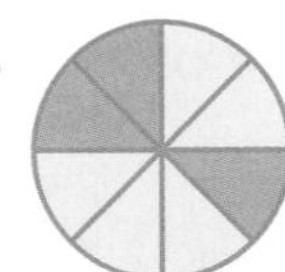

10. 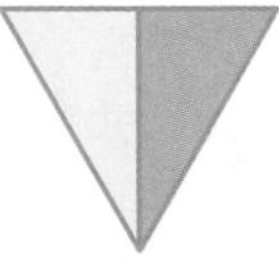

In **11–15**, draw a picture to show each fraction.

11. $\frac{1}{3}$ **12.** $\frac{2}{4}$ **13.** $\frac{1}{6}$ **14.** $\frac{7}{10}$ **15.** $\frac{2}{2}$

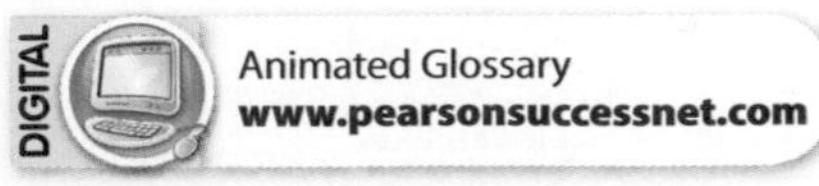

*For another example, see Set B on page 270.

What You Write

Numerator → $\frac{4}{9}$ ← 4 equal parts served
Denominator → ← 9 equal parts **in all**

Numerator → $\frac{5}{9}$ ← 5 equal parts left
Denominator → ← 9 equal parts **in all**

The numerator tells how many equal parts are described. It is the number above the fraction bar.

The denominator tells the total number of equal parts. It is the number below the bar.

What You Say

Four ninths of the pan of fruit bars was served.

Five ninths of the pan of fruit bars was left.

Problem Solving

For **16–19**, use the sign at the right.

Size of Pizza	Price
Small	$7
Medium	$9
Large	$11

16. Ben and his friends ordered a medium pizza. Ben ate 1 slice of the pizza. What fraction of the pizza did Ben eat?

17. Aida's family bought a large pizza. The family ate 4 slices of the pizza. What fraction of the pizza was left?

18. Tami's family bought 3 small pizzas. Leo's family bought 2 medium pizzas. How much more did Tami's family spend than Leo's family?

19. Which costs more, 6 small pizzas or 4 large pizzas? How much more?

20. Reasonableness A pan of macaroni and cheese is divided into 12 unequal parts. Alana serves 3 of the parts. Is it reasonable to say she has served $\frac{3}{12}$ of the macaroni and cheese? Explain.

21. Look at the picture of the quilt. What fraction of the quilt is white?

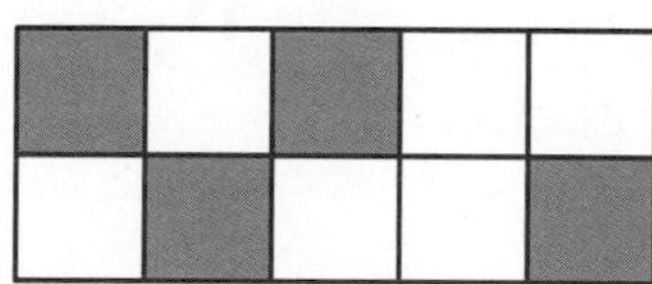

A $\frac{4}{6}$ 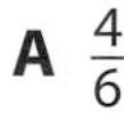

C $\frac{6}{10}$

B $\frac{6}{6}$

D $\frac{2}{5}$

Lesson

12-3

NS 3.0 Understand the relationship between whole numbers, simple fractions, and decimals.

Fractions and Sets

Hands-On
counters

How can a fraction name part of a group?

A group of 12 people is in line for movie tickets. What fraction of the group of people are wearing red? What fraction of the people are not wearing red?

A fraction can name equal parts of a set or group of objects.

8 of the people are wearing red.

Guided Practice*

Do you know HOW?

In **1** and **2**, write the fraction of the counters that are red.

1.

2.

In **3** and **4**, draw counters to show the fraction given.

3. $\frac{4}{5}$

4. $\frac{3}{8}$

Do you UNDERSTAND?

5. In the example above, why is the denominator the same for the part of the group wearing red and for the part of the group not wearing red?

6. A group of 9 students is waiting for a bus. Six of them are wearing jackets. What fraction of the students in the group are wearing jackets? What fraction of the students are not wearing jackets?

Independent Practice

In **7–9**, write the fraction of the counters that are yellow.

7.

8. 

9. 

In **10–12**, draw a picture of the set described.

10. 5 shapes, $\frac{3}{5}$ of the shapes are circles

11. 8 shapes, $\frac{5}{8}$ of the shapes are triangles

12. 2 shapes, $\frac{1}{2}$ of the shapes are squares

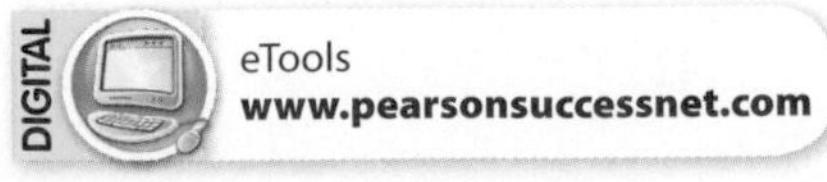

*For another example, see Set B on page 270.

What You Write

$\frac{8}{12}$ ← Number of people wearing red
← Total number of people

$\frac{4}{12}$ ← Number of people **not** wearing red
← Total number of people

What You Say

Eight twelfths of the people are wearing red.

Four twelfths of the people are not wearing red.

Problem Solving

For **13–15**, write the fraction of the group of buttons described.

13. Pink buttons

14. Blue buttons

15. Buttons with only two holes

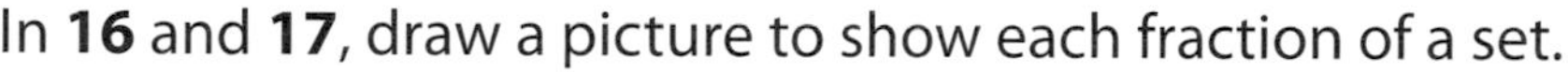

In **16** and **17**, draw a picture to show each fraction of a set.

16. Flowers: $\frac{3}{4}$ are yellow

17. Apples: $\frac{1}{2}$ are green

18. What fraction of your body's bones are **NOT** in your feet?

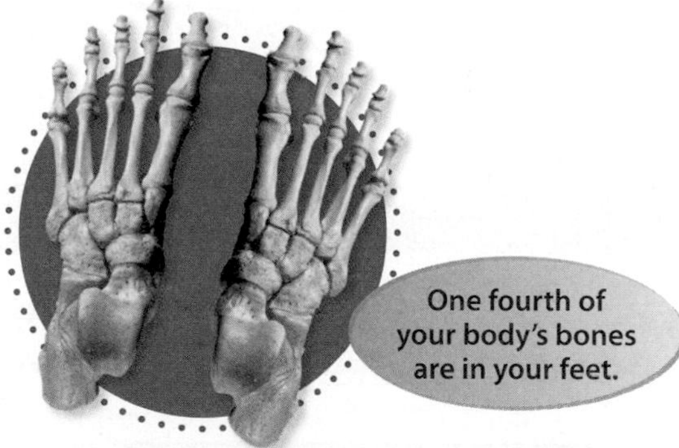

19. Number Sense A family of 5 is buying concert tickets. If $\frac{2}{5}$ of the tickets they buy are for adults, how many adult tickets does the family need?

20. What fraction of the flower petals have fallen off the flower?

A $\frac{3}{5}$ **C** $\frac{8}{10}$

B $\frac{2}{8}$ **D** $\frac{2}{10}$

Lesson

12-4

NS 3.0 Understand the relationship between whole numbers, simple fractions, and decimals. Also **MR 2.3**.

Fractions and Length

Hands-On
fraction strips

How can a fraction name part of a length?

What fraction of this necklace length is blue? What fraction is not blue?

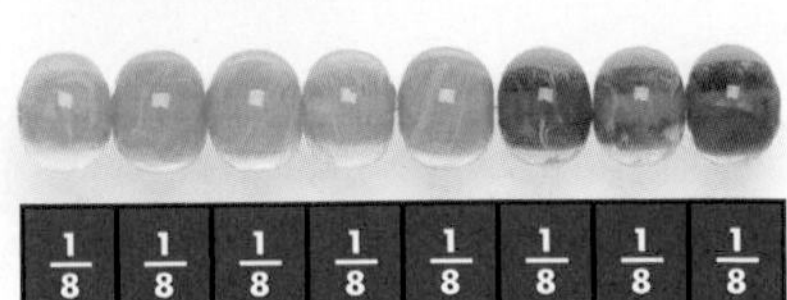

A fraction can name part of a length.

Guided Practice*

Do you know HOW?

In **1** and **2**, what fraction of the length of the 1 strip do the other strips show? Use fraction strips to help.

1.

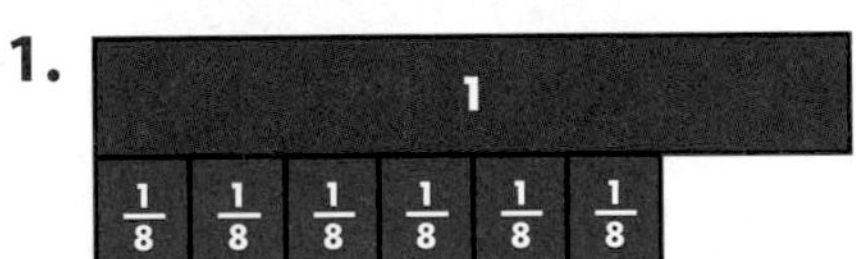

2.

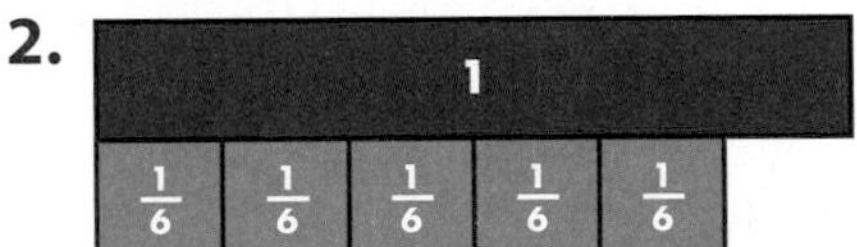

Do you UNDERSTAND?

3. In the example above, how do the fraction strips help you solve the problem?

4. What fraction of the ribbon length below is green? What fraction of the ribbon length is not green?

Independent Practice

In **5–8**, what fraction of the length of the 1 strip do the other strips show? Use fraction strips to help.

5.

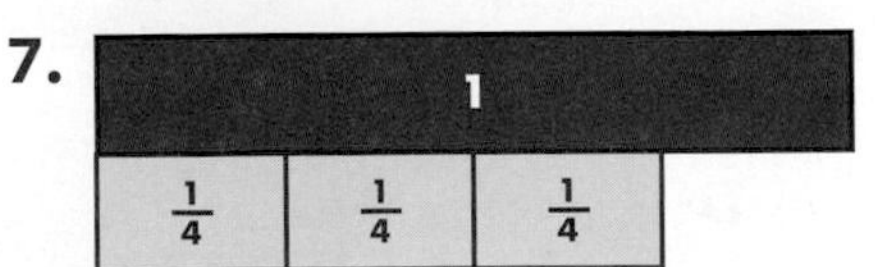

6.

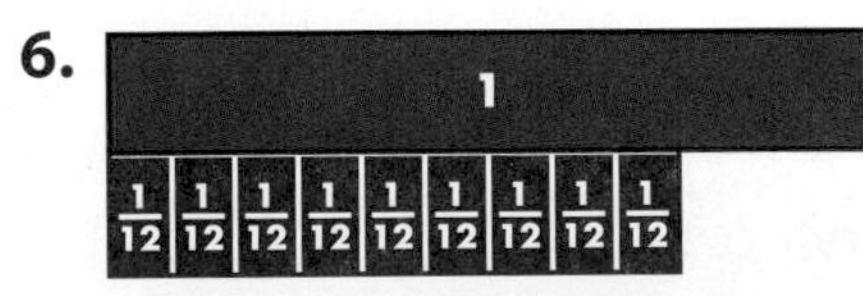

7.

8.

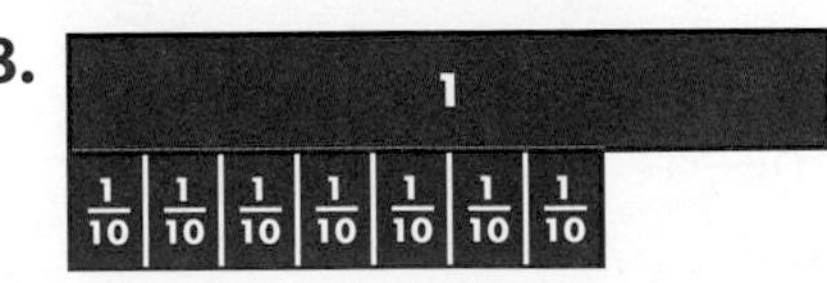

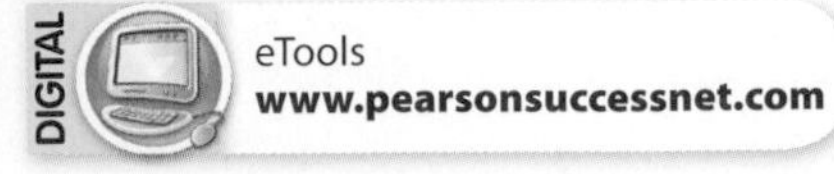

*For another example, see Set C on page 270.

What You Write

$\frac{5}{8}$ ← Number of parts of the length that are blue
← Total number of parts in the necklace length

$\frac{3}{8}$ ← Number of parts of the length that are **not** blue
← Total number of parts in the necklace length

What You Say

Five eighths of the necklace length is blue.

Three eighths of the necklace length is not blue.

Problem Solving

For **9** and **10**, what fraction of each length of yarn is green?

9. 

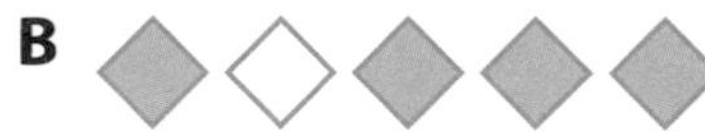

10. 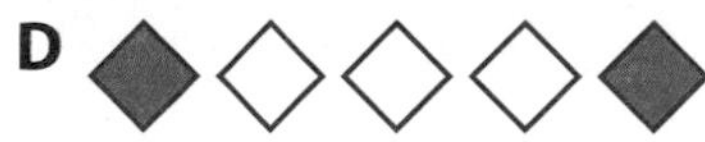

11. Estimation Nick wants to buy two items. He estimated that the total cost of the items is $100. One item costs $58. What is one reasonable price of the other item?

12. For her part in the school play, Carmen must memorize 10 lines. Each line has about 10 words. About how many words does Carmen need to memorize?

13. Which group shows fewer than $\frac{3}{5}$ of the shapes shaded?

A ◆ ◇ ◆ ◇ ◆

B ◆ ◇ ◆ ◆ ◆

C ◆ ◆ ◆ ◆ ◆

D ◆ ◇ ◇ ◇ ◆

14. The Honey Run Covered Bridge is near Chico, California. The longest roof covers more than $\frac{1}{2}$ of the bridge. The other two roofs cover $\frac{1}{3}$ and $\frac{1}{8}$ of the bridge. Which fraction of the bridge does the 30-foot roof cover, $\frac{1}{3}$ or $\frac{1}{8}$? Explain.

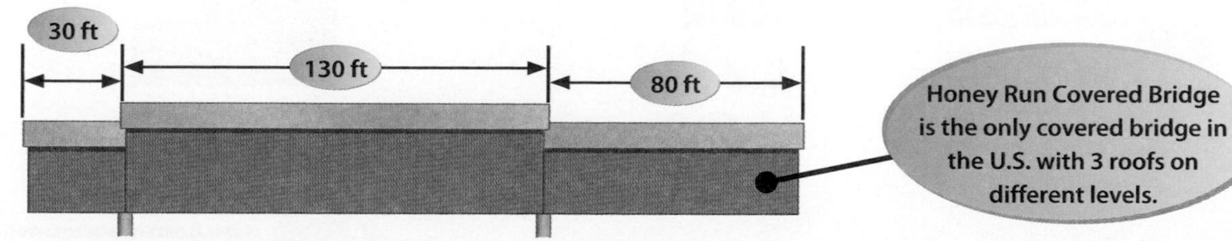

Lesson
12-5

NS 3.1 Compare fractions represented by drawings or concrete materials to show equivalency and to add and subtract simple fractions in context (e.g., $\frac{1}{2}$ of a pizza is the same amount as $\frac{2}{4}$ of another pizza that is the same size; show that $\frac{3}{8}$ is larger than $\frac{1}{4}$).

Using Models to Compare Fractions

Hands-On
fraction strips

How can you compare fractions?

Nola and Edwin are painting two boards that are the same size and the same shape. Who painted a greater amount—Nola or Edwin?

Compare $\frac{1}{2}$ and $\frac{2}{5}$.

Nola painted $\frac{1}{2}$ of one board.

Edwin painted $\frac{2}{5}$ of the other board.

Guided Practice*

Do you know HOW?

In **1** and **2**, compare. Write >, <, or =. Use fraction strips to help.

1. 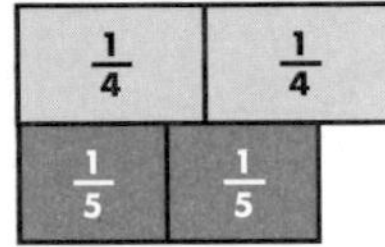

$\frac{2}{4} \bigcirc \frac{2}{5}$

2. 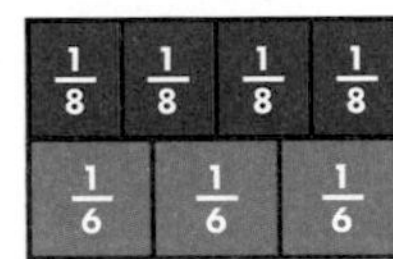

$\frac{4}{8} \bigcirc \frac{3}{6}$

Do you UNDERSTAND?

3. In the problem above about Zoe and Nat, can you tell who painted a greater area of board? Explain.

4. Bob and Irene are painting two walls that are the same size and shape. Irene painted $\frac{2}{3}$ of one wall. Bob painted $\frac{3}{4}$ of the other wall. Who painted a greater amount?

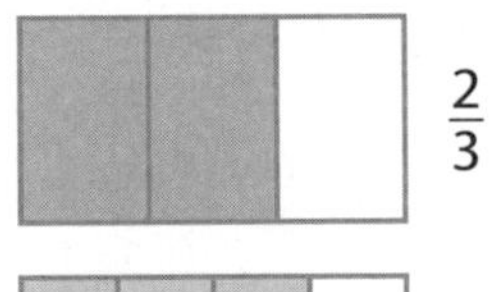

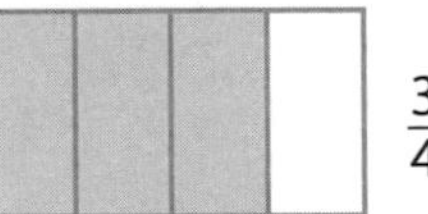

Independent Practice

In **5–7**, compare. Write >, <, or =. Use fraction strips to help.

5. 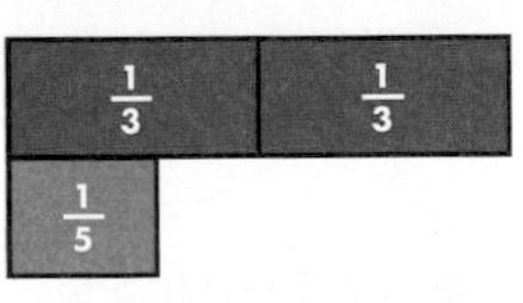

$\frac{2}{3} \bigcirc \frac{1}{5}$

6. 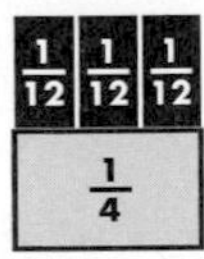

$\frac{3}{12} \bigcirc \frac{1}{4}$

7. 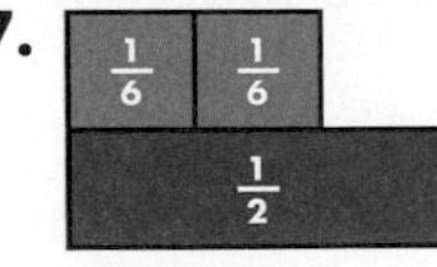

$\frac{2}{6} \bigcirc \frac{1}{2}$

*For another example, see Set D on page 271.

You can use fraction strips.

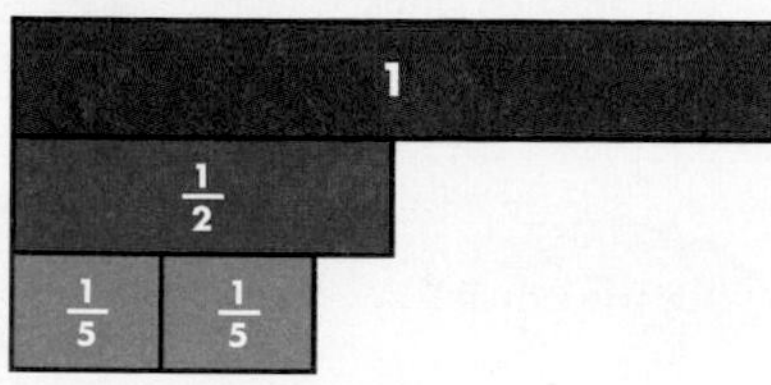

Compare the fraction strips.

$\frac{1}{2}$ is greater than $\frac{2}{5}$.

$\frac{1}{2} > \frac{2}{5}$

Nola painted a greater amount.

Zoe painted $\frac{1}{2}$ of one board. Nat painted $\frac{1}{2}$ of a board with a different area. Is the half Zoe painted equal to the half Nat painted?

Draw a picture.

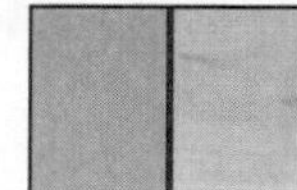

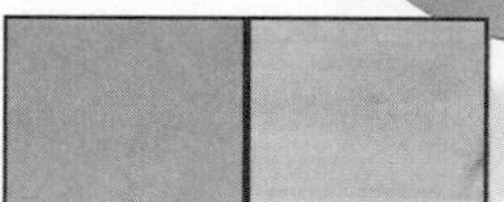

The boards have different areas. Zoe's half is not equal to Nat's half.

Problem Solving

The fraction strips below the 1-strip at the right represent three loaves of bread that Mrs. Rai sliced for a meal. The strips show how much of each loaf was left after the meal.

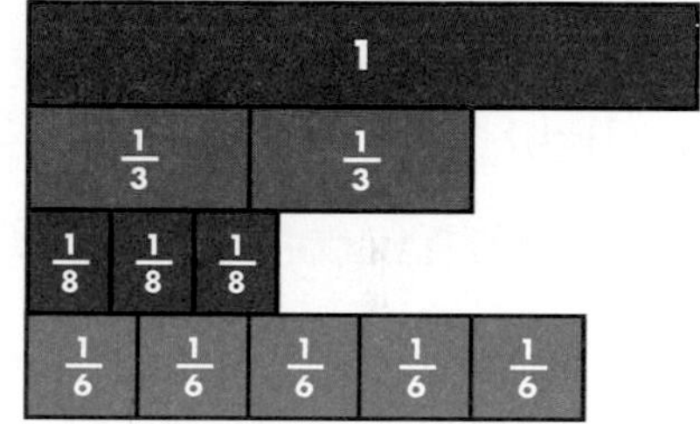

For **8** and **9**, copy and complete each number sentence to find the loaf with the greater amount left after the meal.

8. The loaf cut in sixths or the loaf cut in thirds
$\frac{5}{6} \bigcirc \frac{2}{3}$

9. The loaf cut in eighths or the loaf cut in thirds
$\frac{3}{8} \bigcirc \frac{2}{3}$

10. Writing to Explain Lupe ate $\frac{1}{3}$ of a sandwich. Jed ate $\frac{1}{3}$ of a different sandwich. Jed ate more than Lupe. How is that possible?

11. Kobe fed his hamster and his rabbit. He gave the rabbit 3 carrot pieces for each 2 carrot pieces he gave the hamster. If the hamster got 8 carrot pieces, how many carrot pieces did the rabbit get?

12. Which group shows more than $\frac{5}{7}$ of the shapes shaded?

A 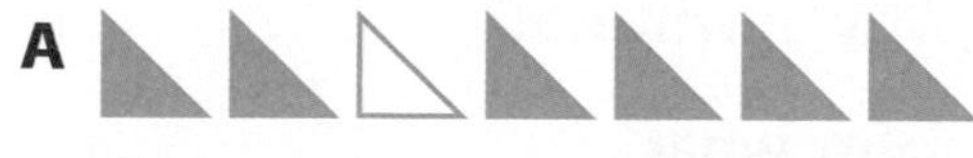

C 

B 

D 

Lesson

12-6

NS 3.1 Compare fractions represented by drawings or concrete materials to show equivalency and to add and subtract simple fractions in context (e.g., $\frac{1}{2}$ of a pizza is the same amount as $\frac{2}{4}$ of another pizza that is the same size; show that $\frac{3}{8}$ is larger than $\frac{1}{4}$).

Finding Equivalent Fractions

Hands-On
fraction strips

How can different fractions name the same part of a whole?

Sonya has decorated $\frac{1}{2}$ of the border. What are two other ways to name $\frac{1}{2}$?

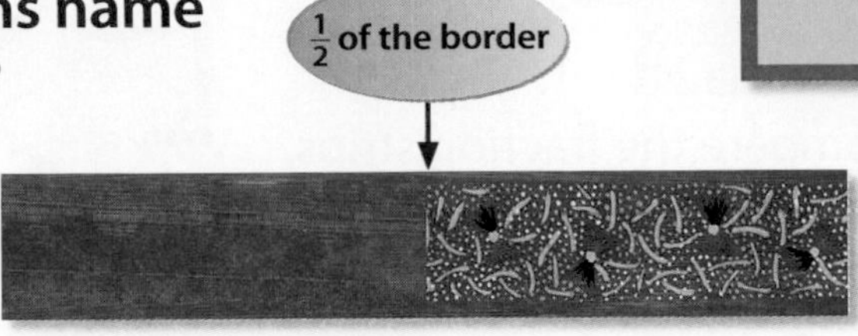

Different fractions can name the same part of a whole.

Another Example How can you write a fraction in simplest form?

In Lessons 10-1 through 10-5, you learned division facts that will help you find equivalent fractions.

Mario has colored $\frac{4}{6}$ of a border. What is the simplest form of $\frac{4}{6}$?

The simplest form of a fraction is a fraction with a numerator and denominator that cannot be divided by the same divisor, except 1.

$\frac{4}{6}$ of the length of the border

One Way

Use models.

1			
$\frac{1}{6}$	$\frac{1}{6}$	$\frac{1}{6}$	$\frac{1}{6}$
$\frac{1}{3}$		$\frac{1}{3}$	

$\frac{4}{6} = \frac{2}{3}$

The simplest form of $\frac{4}{6}$ is $\frac{2}{3}$.

Another Way

Divide the numerator and denominator by the same number.

Find a divisor that both the numerator and denominator can be divided by evenly.

Both 4 and 6 can be evenly divided by 2.

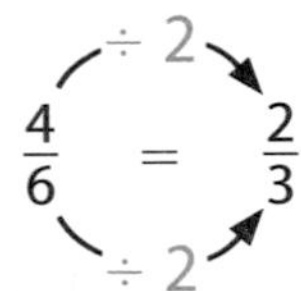

$$\frac{4}{6} = \frac{2}{3} \quad (\div 2 \text{ numerator and denominator})$$

The numerator and denominator of $\frac{2}{3}$ cannot be divided evenly by the same divisor except 1. The simplest form of $\frac{4}{6}$ is $\frac{2}{3}$.

Explain It

1. **Number Sense** Is $\frac{1}{3}$ the simplest form of $\frac{2}{6}$? Why or why not?
2. Wendi has colored $\frac{2}{4}$ of a banner. In simplest form, what fraction of the banner did Wendi color?

$\frac{1}{2} = \frac{\square}{8}$ You can use fraction strips. The denominators of the fractions tell which fraction strips to use.

Find how many $\frac{1}{8}$s are equal to $\frac{1}{2}$.

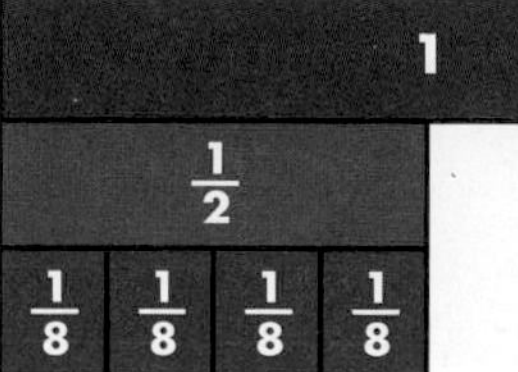

Four $\frac{1}{8}$ strips are equal to $\frac{1}{2}$, so $\frac{1}{2} = \frac{4}{8}$.
Another name for $\frac{1}{2}$ is $\frac{4}{8}$.

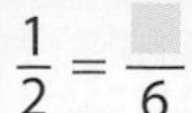

$\frac{1}{2} = \frac{\square}{6}$ You can use fraction strips. The denominator is 6 so use $\frac{1}{6}$ strips.

Find how many $\frac{1}{6}$s are equal to $\frac{1}{2}$.

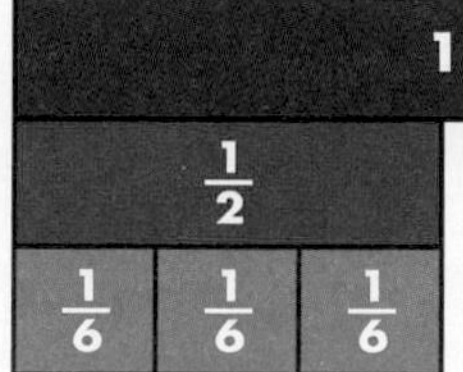

Three $\frac{1}{6}$ strips are equal to $\frac{1}{2}$, so $\frac{1}{2} = \frac{3}{6}$.
Another name for $\frac{1}{2}$ is $\frac{3}{6}$.

Guided Practice*

Do you know HOW?

1. Copy and complete the number sentence. Use fraction strips or make drawings on grid paper.

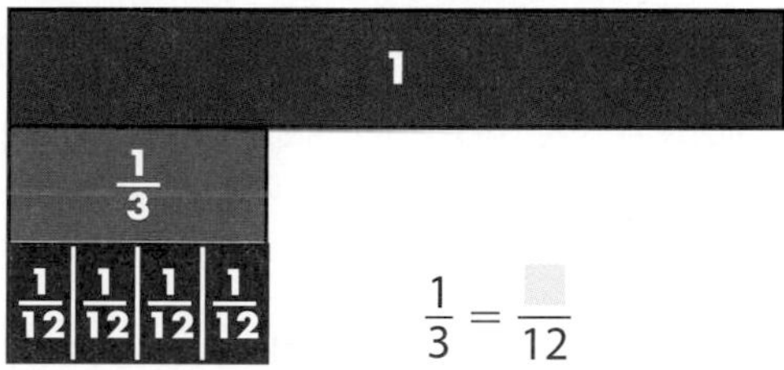

$\frac{1}{3} = \frac{\square}{12}$

Find the simplest form of each fraction.

2. $\frac{5}{10}$ 3. $\frac{6}{9}$ 4. $\frac{2}{4}$

Do you UNDERSTAND?

5. In the example above, what pattern do you see in the numerator and denominator of fractions that name $\frac{1}{2}$?

6. Vijay folded a rope into fourths. Then he showed $\frac{1}{4}$ of the length. Write $\frac{1}{4}$ one other way.

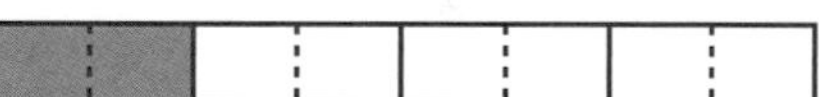

Independent Practice

In **7–9**, copy and complete each number sentence. Use fraction strips or make drawings on grid paper to help.

7. 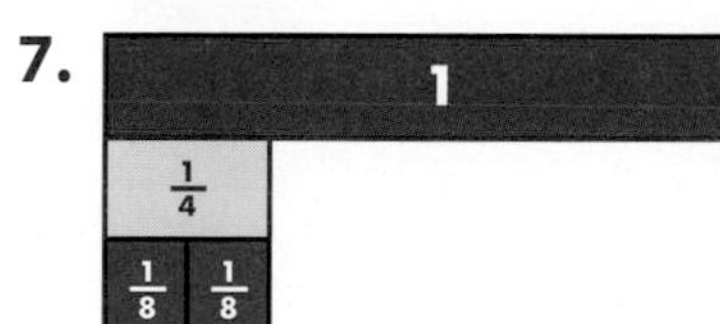

$\frac{1}{4} = \frac{\square}{8}$

8. 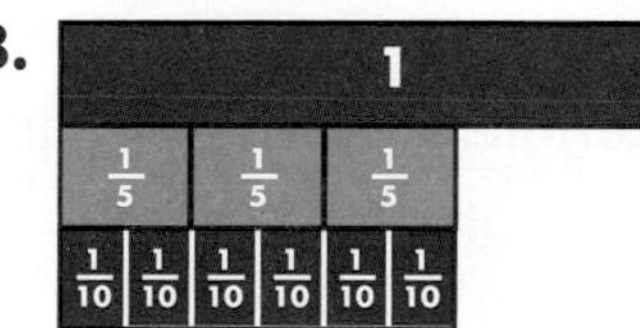

$\frac{3}{5} = \frac{\square}{10}$

9. 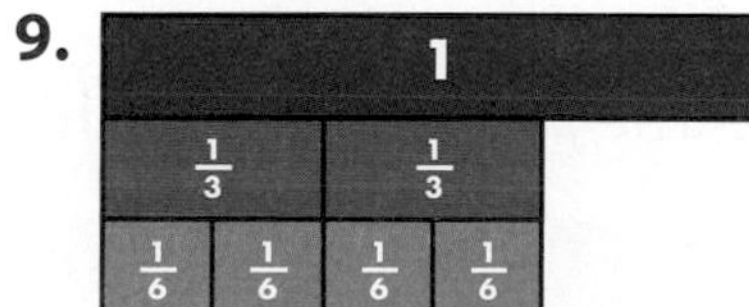

$\frac{2}{3} = \frac{\square}{6}$

Animated Glossary, eTools
www.pearsonsuccessnet.com

For another example, see Set E on page 271.

Independent Practice

For **10–12**, copy and complete each number sentence. Use fraction strips or make drawings on grid paper to help.

10. 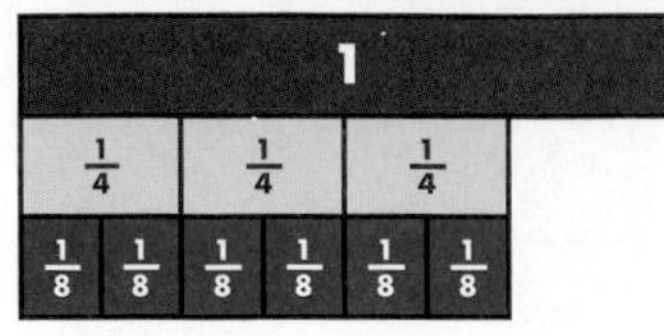

$\frac{6}{8} = \frac{\square}{4}$

11. 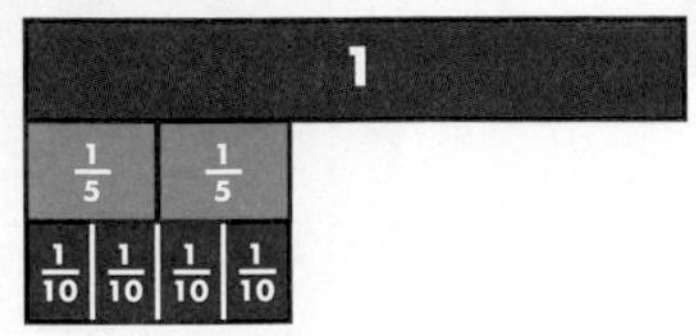

$\frac{2}{5} = \frac{\square}{10}$

12. 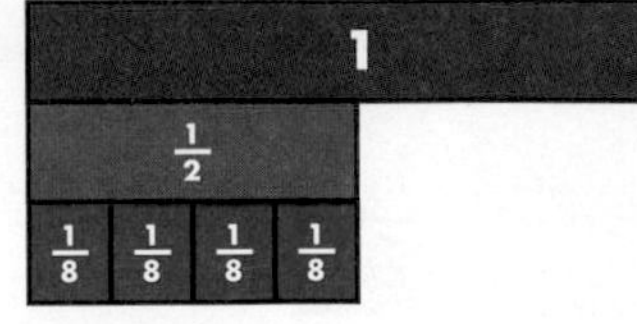

$\frac{1}{2} = \frac{\square}{8}$

For **13–20**, write each fraction in simplest form.

13. $\frac{3}{6}$ **14.** $\frac{9}{12}$ **15.** $\frac{8}{12}$ **16.** $\frac{5}{15}$

17. $\frac{2}{10}$ **18.** $\frac{7}{8}$ **19.** $\frac{8}{10}$ **20.** $\frac{6}{12}$

Problem Solving

21. Evie painted $\frac{1}{6}$ of a board. What is one other way to name $\frac{1}{6}$?

22. **Number Sense** Carlos said that $\frac{3}{4}$ must be less than $\frac{3}{8}$ because 4 is less than 8. Do you agree? Explain.

23. **Writing to Explain** How do you know that $\frac{2}{3}$ is in simplest form?

24. Two eighths of a necklace is red. What part of the necklace is not red?

25. **Reasonableness** Jan reads 4 to 6 books every month. What is a reasonable number of books Jan would read in 7 months? Explain your answer.

26. About $\frac{2}{6}$ of Earth's land surface is desert. Write a fraction equivalent to $\frac{2}{6}$.

27. The shaded part of which rectangle is a fraction equal to $\frac{1}{4}$?

A 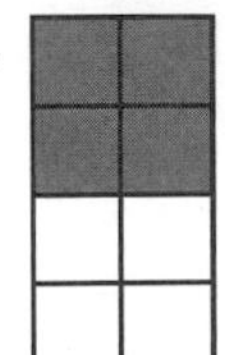

B 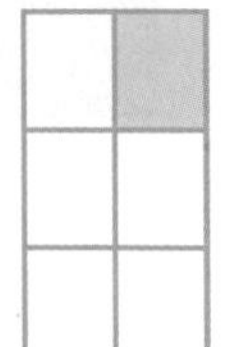

C 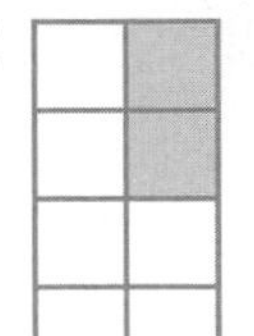

D 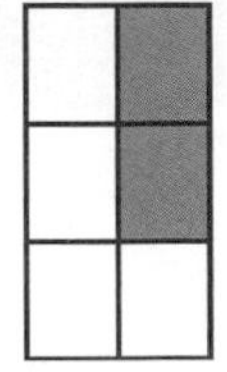

Mixed Problem Solving

Light travels in waves. You see a sweater and it looks red. The sweater absorbs the wavelengths of all colors except red. The red wavelengths bounce off, or reflect off, the sweater and you see the red color.

The diagram below shows colors and their wavelengths measured in units called nanometers. A nanometer is a very small part of a meter. The shortest wavelengths are at the left. The longest are at the right.

violet	blue	green	yellow	orange	red
400	470	525	575	610	700

Use the diagram to answer the questions.

1. Which color has the longest wavelength?

2. What is the wavelength of the color that has the shortest wavelength?

3. About how many more nanometers long is the wavelength of the color green than the wavelength of the color blue?

4. Misha has a yellow shirt. What might be the wavelength of the waves that are reflected off the shirt?

5. Look at the table below.

Data

Kind of Wave	Length of Wave (in centimeters)
Light	less than 1
Microwave	1
Radio	100

Which kind of wave listed is the longest?

6. **Strategy Focus** Solve the problem. Use the strategy Draw a Picture.

A scientist measured the wavelength of light waves that reflected off a block. Green paint covered $\frac{3}{6}$ of the block, and blue paint covered $\frac{2}{6}$ of the block. Name the fraction of the block that was not painted blue or green.

Lesson

12-7

NS 3.1 Compare fractions represented by drawings or concrete materials to show equivalency and to add and subtract simple fractions in context (e.g., $\frac{1}{2}$ of a pizza is the same amount as $\frac{2}{4}$ of another pizza that is the same size; show that $\frac{3}{8}$ is larger than $\frac{1}{4}$).

Using Equivalent Fractions

How can you use equivalent fractions to compare fractions?

Cory and Mel are painting stripes of the same size. Cory painted $\frac{2}{3}$ of one stripe. Mel painted $\frac{1}{2}$ of the other stripe. Who painted a greater amount—Cory or Mel? Compare $\frac{2}{3}$ and $\frac{1}{2}$.

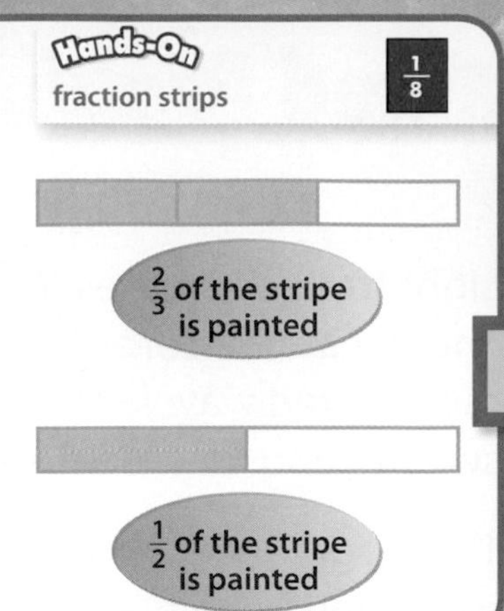

Another Example How can you use equivalent fractions to order fractions?

Chet, Kim, and Lara are each painting stripes. Each stripe is the same size. Chet has painted $\frac{1}{4}$ of a stripe, Kim has painted $\frac{6}{8}$ of a stripe, and Lara has painted $\frac{1}{2}$ of a stripe. Who has painted the least amount?

One Way

Show each fraction with models.

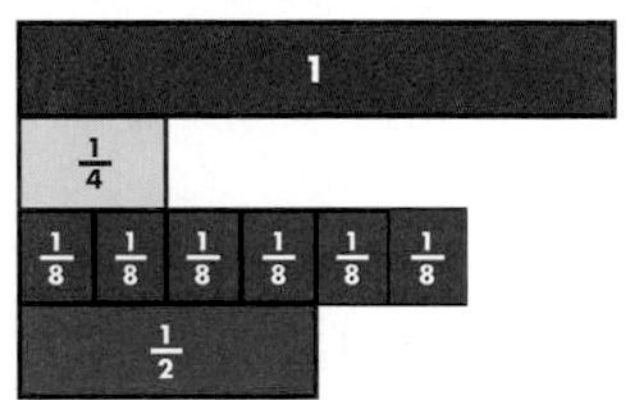

The fraction strip models show that $\frac{1}{2}$ and $\frac{6}{8}$ are greater than $\frac{1}{4}$.

Chet has painted the least amount.

Another Way

Find equivalent fractions.

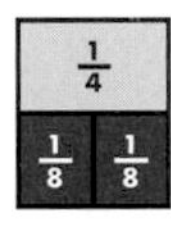

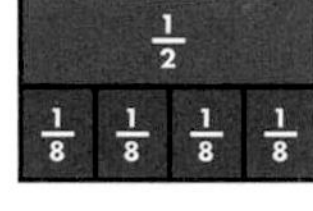

$\frac{1}{4} = \frac{2}{8}$ $\qquad$ $\frac{1}{2} = \frac{4}{8}$

Compare the equivalent fractions. Use what you found to compare the original fractions.

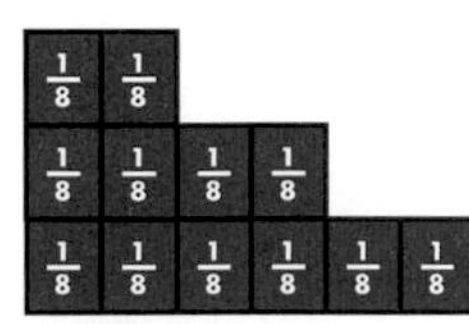

$\frac{2}{8} < \frac{4}{8} < \frac{6}{8}$

$\downarrow \quad \downarrow \quad \downarrow$

So, $\frac{1}{4} < \frac{1}{2} < \frac{6}{8}$

Explain It

1. Why were both $\frac{1}{4}$ and $\frac{1}{2}$ changed to eighths?

One Way

Show each fraction with models.

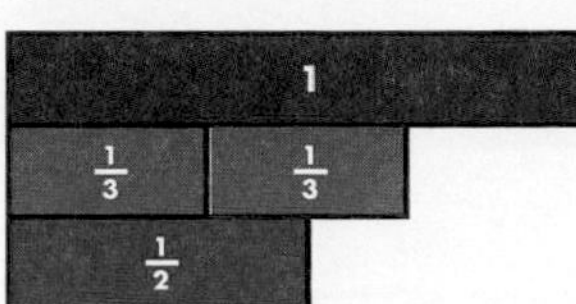

The fraction strips show that $\frac{2}{3} > \frac{1}{2}$.

Another Way

Find equivalent fractions.

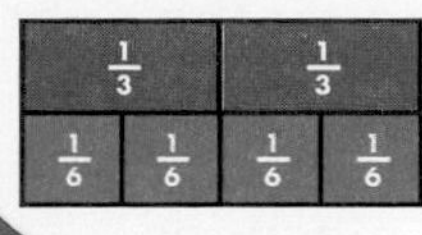

$\frac{2}{3} = \frac{4}{6}$

$\frac{1}{2} = \frac{3}{6}$

Compare the equivalent fractions. Use your answer to compare the original fractions.

$\frac{4}{6} > \frac{3}{6}$

↓ ↓

$\frac{2}{3} > \frac{1}{2}$

Cory painted a greater amount than Mel.

Guided Practice*

Do you know HOW?

In **1** and **2**, compare. Write >, <, or =.

1. $\frac{3}{4} \bigcirc \frac{1}{2}$

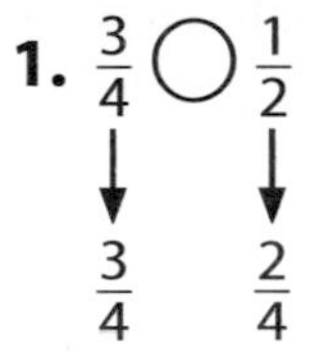

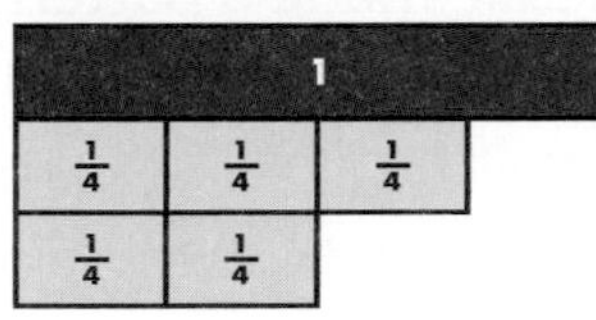

2. $\frac{1}{4} \bigcirc \frac{3}{8}$

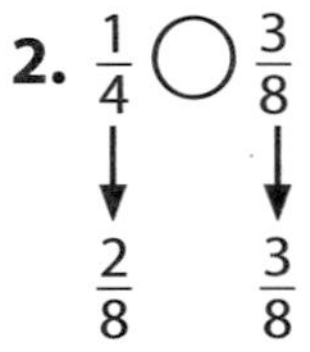

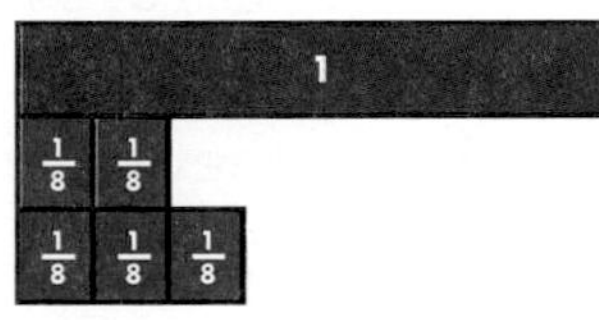

Do you UNDERSTAND?

3. In the problem above, how many more sixths should Mel paint to equal the amount that Cory painted?

4. Sky painted $\frac{2}{3}$ of a stripe. Dan painted $\frac{3}{4}$ of a stripe of the same size. Who painted a greater amount—Sky or Dan?

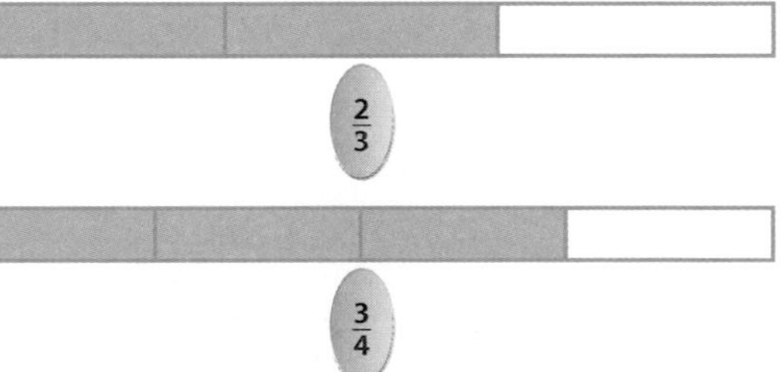

Independent Practice

In **5–7**, compare. Write >, <, or =. You may use fraction strips or drawings.

5. $\frac{2}{3} \bigcirc \frac{1}{4}$

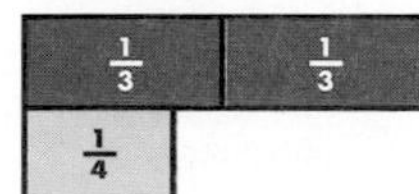

6. $\frac{3}{12} \bigcirc \frac{1}{4}$

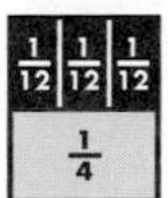

7. $\frac{2}{6} \bigcirc \frac{1}{2}$

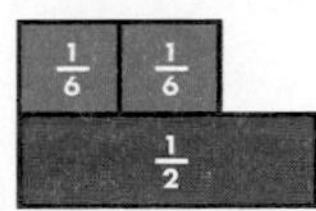

*For another example, see Set E on page 271.

For **8** and **9**, use the drawings at the right.

Three strips of fabric are each the same size. Ben cut the strips into pieces as shown. The shaded parts show how much of each strip was left after Ben used some of the pieces. Copy and complete each number sentence to show the strip with the greater amount left.

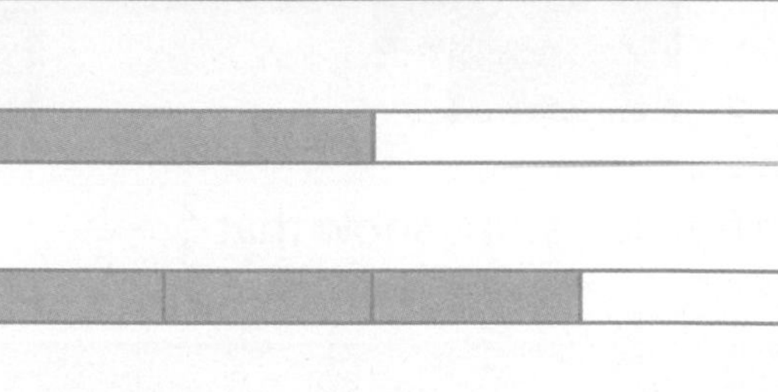

8. The strip cut in eighths or the strip cut in fourths? $\frac{5}{8} \bigcirc \frac{3}{4}$

9. The strip cut in halves or the strip cut in fourths? $\frac{1}{2} \bigcirc \frac{3}{4}$

10. **Writing to Explain** Kimo painted $\frac{1}{3}$ of a fence rail. Raul painted $\frac{1}{3}$ of a different fence rail. Kimo painted a greater amount than Raul. How is that possible?

11. **Strategy Focus** Solve. Use the strategy Use Objects and Draw a Picture.

Bessie made a pattern of tiles on the wall. She used 2 red tiles for every 3 yellow tiles. If she used 9 yellow tiles, how many red tiles did she use?

12. Which lists the fractions in order from least to greatest?

A $\frac{1}{2}, \frac{1}{3}, \frac{1}{4}$

B $\frac{2}{5}, \frac{3}{10}, \frac{4}{12}$

C $\frac{2}{4}, \frac{3}{6}, \frac{4}{8}$

D $\frac{1}{4}, \frac{1}{3}, \frac{7}{12}$

13. Sue has 3 packs of 5 marbles. Bob has 4 packs of 7 marbles. How many marbles do they have in all?

A 23 marbles

B 33 marbles

C 43 marbles

D 53 marbles

14. Which group shows fewer than $\frac{4}{6}$ of the shapes shaded?

A ● ○ ○ ● ● ●

B ● ● ● ● ● ●

C ● ● ● ○ ● ●

D ○ ● ○ ● ○ ●

15. What fraction of the figure is blue?

A $\frac{1}{6}$

B $\frac{1}{4}$

C $\frac{1}{3}$

D $\frac{3}{6}$

Compare the numbers. Use <, >, or =.

1. 1,102 ◯ 853 **2.** 3,687 ◯ 3,698 **3.** 7,092 ◯ 5,940

Estimate and then find each sum or difference.
Check that your answer is reasonable.

4. $\begin{array}{r} 96 \\ +\ 47 \\ \hline \end{array}$ **5.** $\begin{array}{r} 435 \\ -\ 68 \\ \hline \end{array}$ **6.** $\begin{array}{r} 716 \\ -\ 624 \\ \hline \end{array}$ **7.** $\begin{array}{r} 2{,}084 \\ +\ 3{,}759 \\ \hline \end{array}$

Find each product.

8. 8×7 **9.** 10×9 **10.** $3 \times 2 \times 2$ **11.** 6×0 **12.** 7×4

Find each quotient.

13. $56 \div 7$ **14.** $9 \div 1$ **15.** $24 \div 4$ **16.** $40 \div 8$

Copy and complete each number sentence.

17. $\frac{1}{2} = \frac{4}{\blacksquare}$ **18.** $\frac{1}{3} = \frac{\blacksquare}{6}$ **19.** $\frac{2}{3} = \frac{\blacksquare}{12}$ **20.** $\frac{3}{5} = \frac{\blacksquare}{10}$

Error Search Find each sum or difference that is not correct.
Write it correctly and explain the error.

21. $\begin{array}{r} 13 \\ +\ 17 \\ \hline 30 \end{array}$ **22.** $\begin{array}{r} 238 \\ +\ 149 \\ \hline 377 \end{array}$ **23.** $\begin{array}{r} 461 \\ -\ 345 \\ \hline 16 \end{array}$ **24.** $\begin{array}{r} 6{,}570 \\ +\ 2{,}891 \\ \hline 9{,}461 \end{array}$ **25.** $\begin{array}{r} 1{,}842 \\ -\ 1{,}536 \\ \hline 316 \end{array}$

Number Sense

Estimating and Reasoning Write true or false for each statement.
If it is false, explain why.

26. The product 7×10 is greater than 710.

27. The difference $1{,}258 - 1{,}108$ is greater than 100.

28. The sum $178 + 129$ is less than 300.

29. The difference $309 - 164$ is less than 100.

30. The quotient $49 \div 7$ is less than 10.

Lesson

12-8

AF 2.0 Represent simple functional relationships. Also MR 3.0 Move beyond a particular problem by generalizing to other situations.

Problem Solving

Make a Table and Look for a Pattern

A video game company tested 20 games. Three of the games did not work. If 120 games are tested, how many of them might not work?

Guided Practice*

Do you know HOW?

Copy and complete the table to solve.

1. Ms. Simms is buying bags of blocks. Out of the 50 blocks in each bag, 3 are cubes. If Ms. Simms buys 250 blocks, how many will be cubes?

Cubes	3				
Total Blocks	50				

Do you UNDERSTAND?

2. Look at the example above. If the video game store bought 50 games, about how many games might not work? Explain.

3. **Write a Problem** Write a problem that can be solved by making a table and using a pattern. Then solve the problem.

Independent Practice

Copy and complete the table to solve.

4. Erasers are sold in packages of 6. In each package, 2 of the erasers are pink. How many pink erasers will you get if you buy 30 erasers?

Pink Erasers	2				
Total Erasers	6				

Stuck? Try this....

- What do I know?
- What am I asked to find?
- What diagram can I use to help understand the problem?
- Can I use addition, subtraction, multiplication, or division?
- Is all of my work correct?
- Did I answer the right question?
- Is my answer reasonable?

*For another example, see Set F on page 271.

Plan

Make a table.

Then, write in the information you know.

Might Not Work	3					
Total Games	20					

Solve

Extend the table. Look for a pattern to help. Then find the answer in the table.

Might Not Work	3	6	9	12	15	18
Total Games	20	40	60	80	100	120

If 120 games are tested, 18 might not work.

In **5** and **6**, copy and complete each table to solve.

5. Sue planted 8 daffodil bulbs. Two of the bulbs didn't grow. Suppose that pattern continues and Sue plants 32 bulbs. How many bulbs most likely won't grow?

Didn't Grow	2			
Total Bulbs	8			

6. Sue planted 12 tulip bulbs of mixed colors. When the bulbs grew, there were 4 red tulips. Suppose that pattern continues and Sue plants 48 bulbs. How many of the tulips will likely be red?

Red Tulips	4			
Total Tulips	12			

7. Reasoning Tad planted 15 tulips in a row. He followed the pattern shown below. What is the color of the last tulip in the row?

8. Reasoning Look back at Problem 5. Suppose Sue decided to plant 20 daffodil bulbs.

a How many bulbs would most likely not grow?

b How many bulbs would most likely grow?

9. Which equivalent fraction completes the pattern below?

$\frac{1}{4}$ $\frac{2}{8}$ $\frac{3}{12}$ $\frac{\square}{\square}$

A $\frac{3}{14}$

B $\frac{4}{14}$

C $\frac{3}{16}$

D $\frac{4}{16}$

10. Number Sense Suppose Sue wants 10 red tulips. How many tulip bulbs should she plant? See Problem 6.

11. Look back at Problem 6. If Sue planted 48 tulip bulbs, how many of the tulips will **NOT** be red?

Test Prep

1. What is the name of the equal parts of the whole pizza? (12-1)

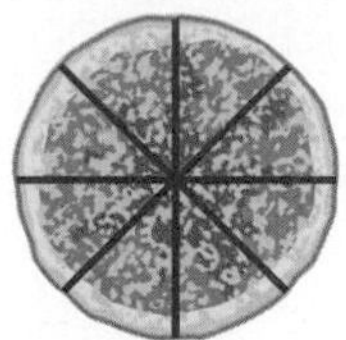

A sixths

B sevenths

C eighths

D ninths

2. The stage was divided into equal parts. What fractional part of the stage was used for flute players? (12-2)

Trombones	Drums	Trombones
Clarinets	Trombones	Clarinets
Flutes	Triangles	Flutes

A $\frac{1}{9}$

B $\frac{2}{9}$

C $\frac{2}{7}$

D $\frac{3}{9}$

3. Blair bought the fruit shown below. What fraction of the pieces of fruit are oranges? (12-3)

A $\frac{5}{7}$

B $\frac{6}{12}$

C $\frac{5}{12}$

D $\frac{1}{5}$

4. Allison is buying packages of sliced meat for the picnic. Each package has 20 slices of meat. Out of the 20 slices, 5 are turkey. If Allison buys 80 slices, how many are turkey? (12-8)

Turkey Slices	5	10	■	■
Total Slices	20	40	60	80

A 11

B 15

C 16

D 20

5. Which lists the fractions in order from least to greatest? (12-7)

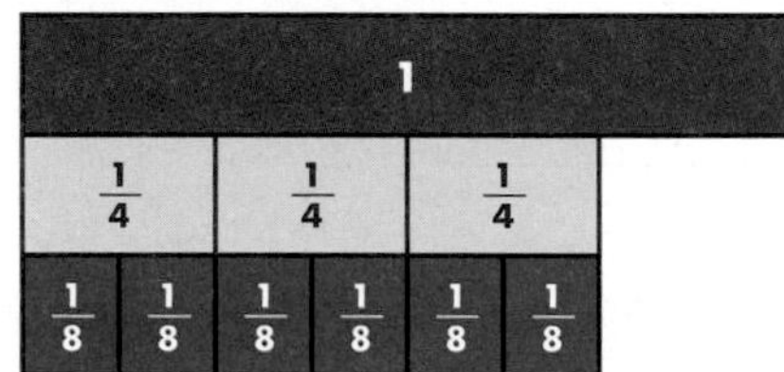

A $\frac{3}{4}, \frac{3}{8}, \frac{5}{8}$

B $\frac{3}{8}, \frac{5}{8}, \frac{3}{4}$

C $\frac{5}{8}, \frac{3}{4}, \frac{3}{8}$

D $\frac{3}{8}, \frac{3}{4}, \frac{5}{8}$

6. Which fraction is in simplest form? (12-6)

A $\frac{2}{3}$

B $\frac{6}{8}$

C $\frac{2}{4}$

D $\frac{9}{12}$

7. What number makes the statement true? (12-6)

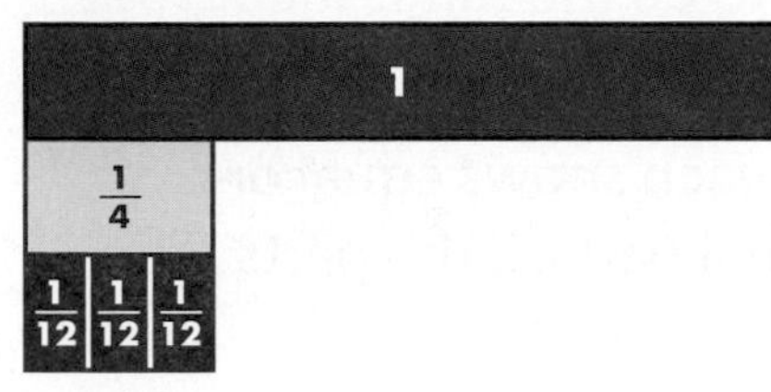

$\frac{1}{4} = \frac{\square}{12}$

A 3

B 4

C 6

D 9

8. During the time allowed, Deja swam $\frac{3}{4}$ of the length of the pool. Loren swam $\frac{4}{5}$ of it. Use the models to find which symbol makes the comparison true. (12-5)

$\frac{3}{4} \bigcirc \frac{4}{5}$

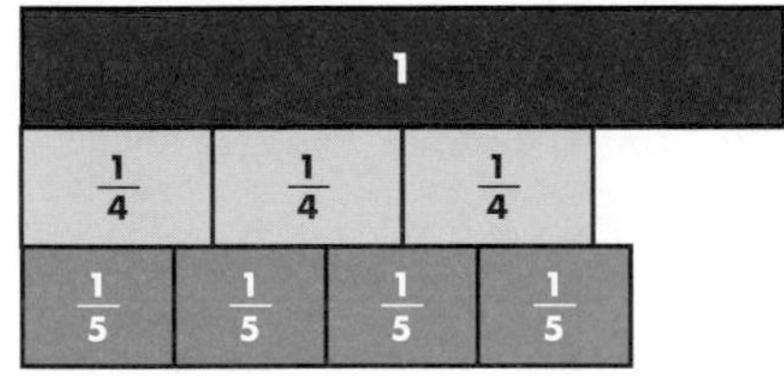

A $=$

B $\times$

C $>$

D $<$

9. Ty is gluing a wire along the bottom of a board. What part of the board has he finished wiring? (12-4)

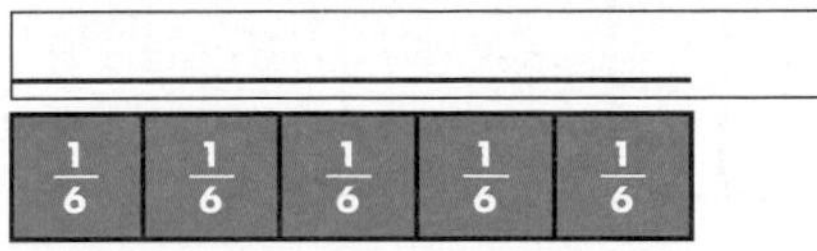

A $\frac{6}{6}$

B $\frac{4}{5}$

C $\frac{5}{6}$

D $\frac{1}{6}$

10. The rectangle shows $\frac{1}{3}$ shaded.

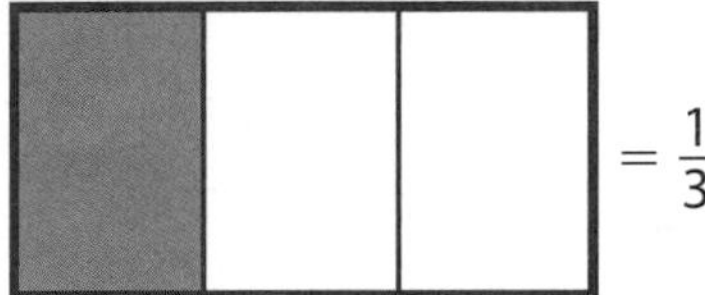

$= \frac{1}{3}$

The shaded part of which rectangle below is equal to $\frac{1}{3}$? (12-7)

A

$= \frac{6}{12}$

B

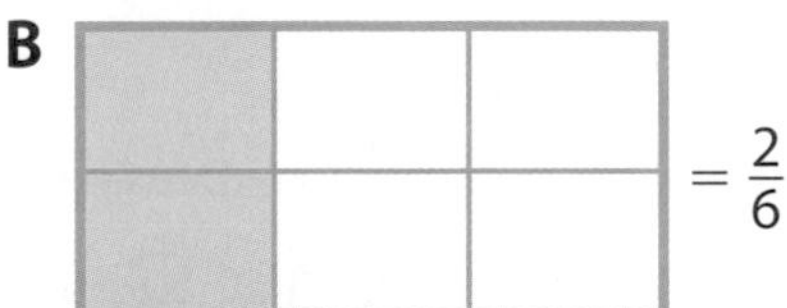

$= \frac{2}{6}$

C

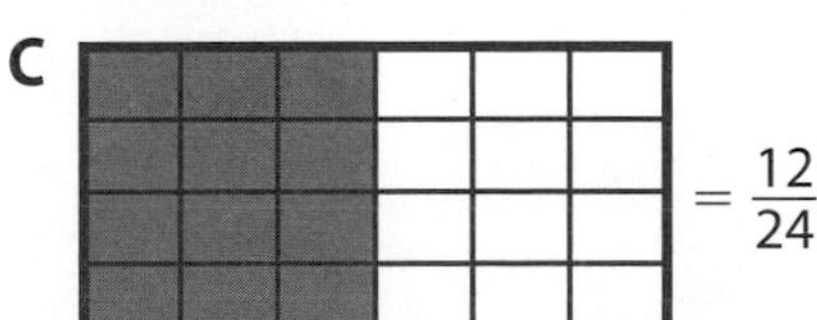

$= \frac{12}{24}$

D

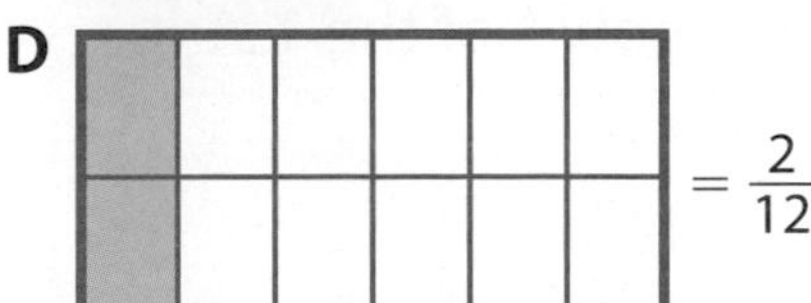

$= \frac{2}{12}$

Reteaching

Set A, pages 248–249

Tell if the shape is divided into equal parts of a whole and name them.

There are 8 equal parts.

The equal parts are called eighths.

Remember that equal parts do not need to be the same shape, but they must be equal in area.

Tell if each shows equal or unequal parts. If the parts are equal, name them.

1. 

2. 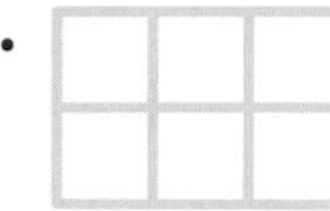

Set B, pages 250–253

What fraction of the triangles are pink?

$\frac{\text{numerator}}{\text{denominator}} = \frac{\text{number of pink triangles}}{\text{total number of triangles}} = \frac{5}{8}$

$\frac{5}{8}$ of the triangles are pink.

Remember that fractions can name regions or sets.

Write the fraction of the figure that is red.

1.

Write the fraction of the counters that are red.

2.

Set C, pages 254–255

What fraction of the length of the 1 strip do the other strips show?

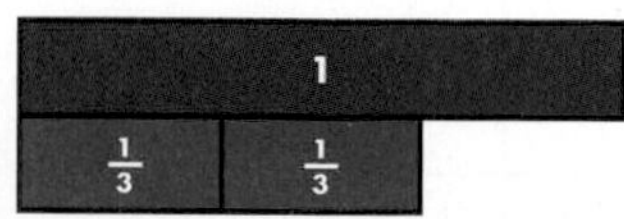

Two $\frac{1}{3}$ strips show $\frac{2}{3}$ of the 1 strip.

Remember that fraction strips divide the whole strip into equal parts.

What fraction of the length of the 1 strip do the other strips show?

1. 

2. 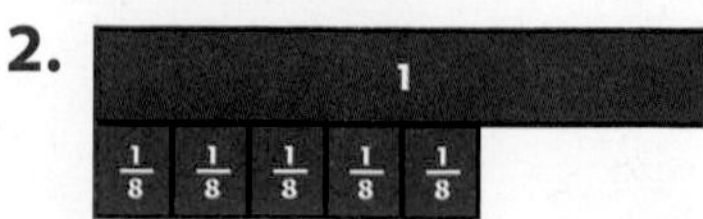

Set D, pages 256–257

Compare $\frac{3}{8}$ and $\frac{1}{2}$.

$\frac{3}{8} \bigcirc \frac{1}{2}$

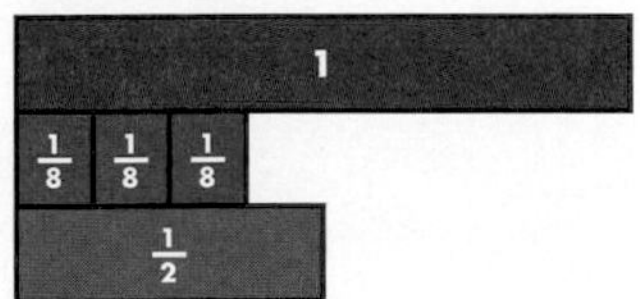

$\frac{3}{8} < \frac{1}{2}$

Remember that if two fractions have the same denominator, the fraction with the greater numerator is the greater fraction.

Compare. Write <, >, or =.

1. 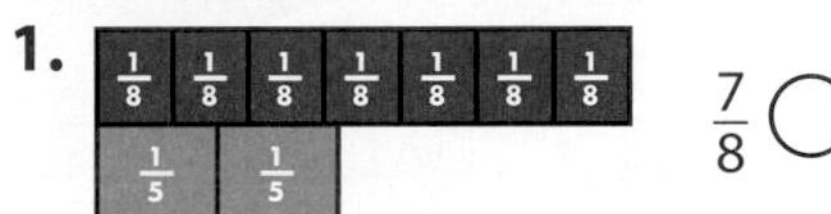

$\frac{7}{8} \bigcirc \frac{2}{5}$

Set E, pages 258–260, 262–264

Pilar and Jeff are painting two lines that are the same length. Pilar painted $\frac{1}{2}$ of one line. Jeff painted $\frac{1}{3}$ of the other line. Who painted a greater amount—Pilar or Jeff?

Find equivalent fractions.

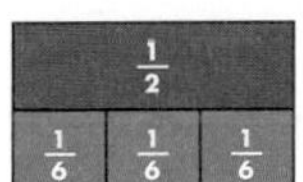

$\frac{1}{2} = \frac{3}{6}$

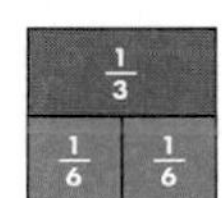

$\frac{1}{3} = \frac{2}{6}$

Compare the equivalent fractions. $\frac{3}{6} > \frac{2}{6}$

So, $\frac{1}{2} > \frac{1}{3}$. Pilar painted more.

Remember that you can use equivalent fractions to help compare.

Compare. Write >, <, or =.

1. $\frac{1}{4} \bigcirc \frac{1}{2}$
$\downarrow \quad \downarrow$
$\frac{2}{8} \quad \frac{4}{8}$

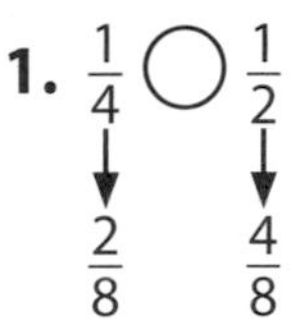

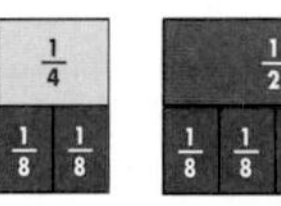

2. $\frac{2}{5} \bigcirc \frac{3}{10}$
$\downarrow \quad \downarrow$
$\frac{4}{10} \quad \frac{3}{10}$

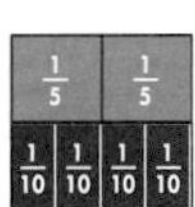

Set F, pages 266–267

Make a table to solve the problem.

Bags of marbles have 20 marbles in each bag. Out of the 20 marbles, 4 are green. If you buy 80 marbles, how many are green?

Make a table showing what you know. Look for a pattern and continue it.

Green Marbles	4	8	12	16
Total Marbles	20	40	60	80

16 marbles will be green.

Remember it can help to make a table when the amounts change according to a pattern.

1. Pens are sold in packages of 8. In each package there are 2 red pens. How many red pens will you get if you buy 40 pens?

Red Pens	2				
Total Pens	8				

Topic 13

Adding and Subtracting Fractions

1 What fraction of paper used in the United States is recycled? You will find out in Lesson 13-2.

2 What fraction of the energy used in the United States comes from natural gas? You will find out in Lesson 13-4.

3 The tiger beetle and the caterpillar hunter beetle are helpful insects that live in California. Which type of beetle is longer? You will find out in Lesson 13-3.

4 How much does the shoreline of Iceland grow each year? You will find out in Lesson 13-1.

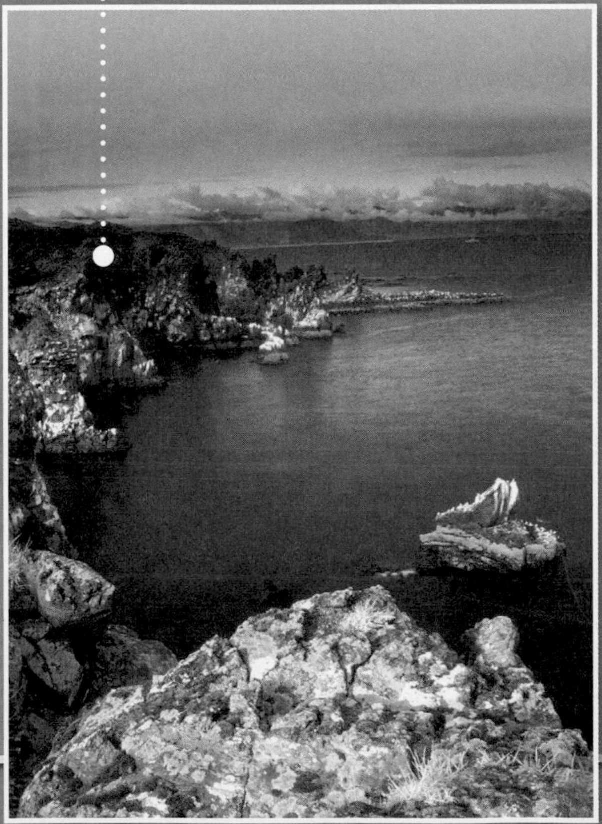

Review What You Know!

Vocabulary

Choose the best term from the box.

- denominator
- fraction
- fourths
- numerator

1. When a region is divided into four equal parts, the parts are called __?__.
2. A __?__ is a symbol used to name equal parts of a whole or a set.
3. A __?__ is the number below the fraction bar that tells the total number of equal parts.

Fractions and Regions

Name the parts of the whole.

4. 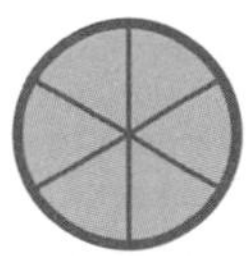

5. 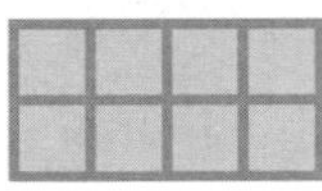

Fractions and Sets

Write the fraction of the counters that are red.

6. ● ● ● ○ ○ ○ ○ ○ ○

7. ● ● ● ● ● ● ● ● ○ ○ ○ ○

Equivalent Fractions

Copy and complete each number sentence.

8. $\frac{1}{4} = \frac{2}{\square}$

9. $\frac{2}{5} = \frac{\square}{10}$

10. **Writing to Explain** Explain how to find two other ways to name $\frac{1}{2}$.

Lesson
13-1

NS 3.1 Compare fractions represented by drawings or concrete materials to show equivalency and to add and subtract simple fractions in context (e.g., $\frac{1}{2}$ of a pizza is the same amount as $\frac{2}{4}$ of another pizza that is the same size; show that $\frac{2}{8}$ is larger than $\frac{1}{4}$).

Using Models to Add Fractions

Hands-On
fraction strips

How can you add fractions?

Mia used $\frac{3}{8}$ of the block of clay to make the frog. She used $\frac{1}{8}$ of the block to make the lily pad. What fraction of the block did she use in all?

Find $\frac{3}{8} + \frac{1}{8}$.

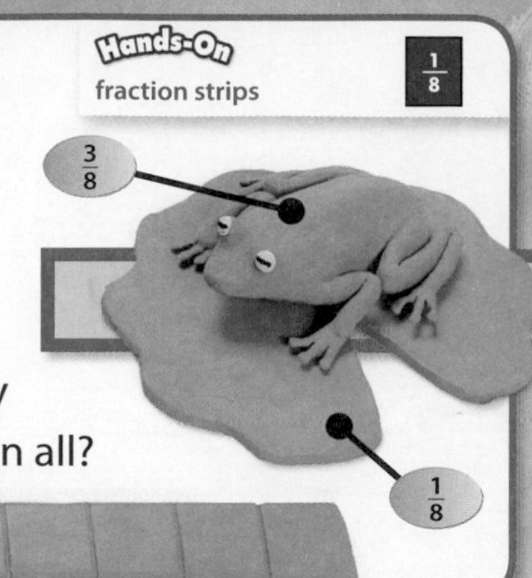

Guided Practice*

Do you know HOW?

In **1** and **2**, add. Write the sum in simplest form. You may use fraction strips or draw a picture to help.

1. $\frac{2}{5} + \frac{1}{5}$

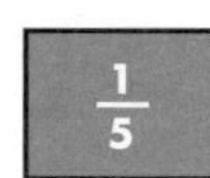

2. $\frac{2}{12} + \frac{4}{12}$

Do you UNDERSTAND?

3. Suppose you add two fractions with the same denominator. What can you say about the sum before you write it in simplest form?

4. Alonso used $\frac{2}{6}$ of a loaf of bread to make peanut butter sandwiches. He used $\frac{2}{6}$ of the loaf to make tuna sandwiches. What fraction of the bread loaf did he use in all?

Independent Practice

Leveled Practice In **5–14**, add. Write the sum in simplest form. You may draw a picture to help.

5. $\frac{3}{6} + \frac{2}{6}$ $\frac{1}{6}$ $\frac{1}{6}$ $\frac{1}{6}$ $\frac{1}{6}$ $\frac{1}{6}$

6. $\frac{2}{8} + \frac{4}{8}$

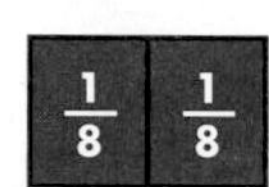

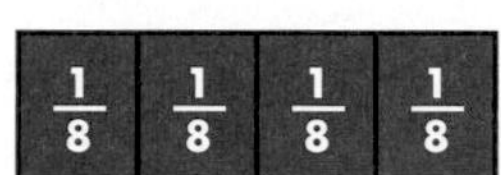

7. $\frac{1}{4} + \frac{2}{4}$

8. $\frac{1}{3} + \frac{1}{3}$

9. $\frac{3}{10} + \frac{5}{10}$

10. $\frac{2}{5} + \frac{1}{5}$

11. $\frac{3}{12} + \frac{5}{12}$

12. $\frac{1}{6} + \frac{2}{6}$

13. $\frac{5}{8} + \frac{2}{8}$

14. $\frac{4}{10} + \frac{3}{10}$

*For another example, see Set A on page 290.

Step 1

Add.

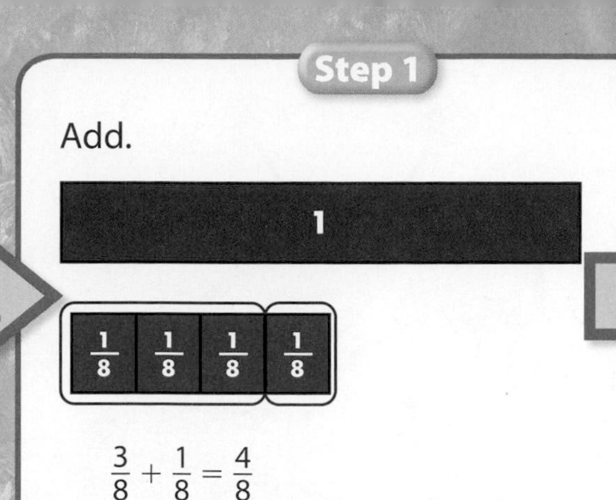

$\frac{3}{8} + \frac{1}{8} = \frac{4}{8}$

Step 2

Write the sum in simplest form.

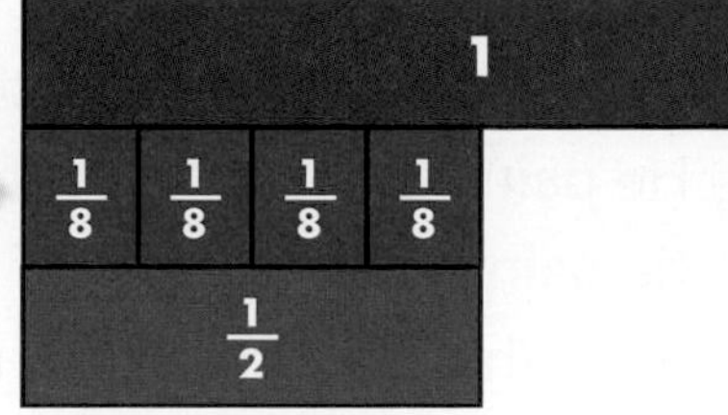

$\frac{4}{8} = \frac{1}{2}$

So, in simplest form, $\frac{3}{8} + \frac{1}{8} = \frac{4}{8}$, or $\frac{1}{2}$.

All together, Mia used $\frac{1}{2}$ of the block of clay.

Problem Solving

15. Ken ate $\frac{2}{4}$ of a large sandwich and Janet ate $\frac{1}{4}$ of it. Write an addition sentence that shows the fraction of the sandwich they ate all together.

16. Chad found 12 seashells. Four of them were bubble shells. The rest were jingle shells. In simplest form, what fraction of the shells were jingle shells?

17. Rashad colored $\frac{3}{5}$ of a flag red and $\frac{1}{5}$ of the same flag green. What fraction of the flag did he color in all?

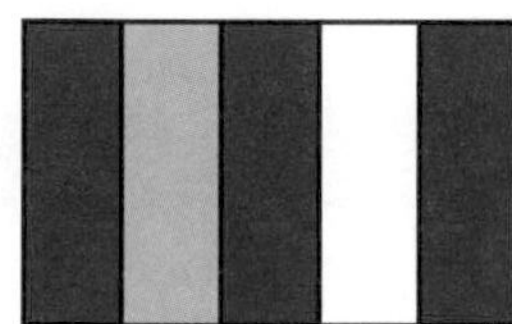

18. Nia painted $\frac{4}{8}$ of a fence rail and Tracy painted $\frac{2}{8}$ of it. In simplest form, what fraction of the rail did they paint in all?

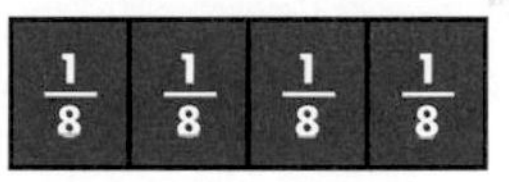

A $\frac{6}{4}$ **B** $\frac{3}{4}$ **C** $\frac{1}{2}$ **D** $\frac{2}{8}$

19. The shore of Iceland grows each year. If it grew $\frac{2}{5}$ inch one year and $\frac{3}{5}$ inch the next year, how much did it grow in the two years?

20. Writing to Explain Cassie drank $\frac{5}{8}$ of a glass of juice. Julie drank $\frac{3}{4}$ of the same size glass of juice. Who drank more juice? Explain.

21. Which fraction comes next in the pattern?

$\frac{1}{2}, \frac{2}{4}, \frac{3}{6}, \frac{4}{8},$ ▢

A $\frac{5}{15}$ **B** $\frac{3}{7}$ **C** $\frac{5}{10}$ **D** $\frac{5}{9}$

22. Estela cut a rectangle into sixths. Draw a picture of a rectangle divided into sixths. Use grid paper to help.

Lesson
13-2

NS 3.2 Add and subtract simple fractions (e.g., determine that $\frac{1}{8} + \frac{3}{8}$ is the same as $\frac{1}{2}$).

Adding Fractions

How can you add fractions?

Jorge was painting a birdhouse roof. He painted $\frac{6}{12}$ of the roof green. Then he painted another $\frac{2}{12}$ of the roof red. What fraction of the roof did he paint in all?

Find $\frac{6}{12} + \frac{2}{12}$.

Guided Practice*

Do you know HOW?

In **1–4**, add. Write each sum in simplest form.

1. $\frac{5}{8} + \frac{1}{8}$

2. $\frac{4}{10} + \frac{4}{10}$

3. $\frac{2}{5} + \frac{3}{5}$

4. $\frac{2}{9} + \frac{1}{9}$

Do you UNDERSTAND?

5. In the example above, how do you know if the sum is in simplest form?

6. Kate was painting a banner. She painted $\frac{1}{6}$ of it blue. Then she painted $\frac{2}{6}$ more of the banner red. What fraction of the banner did she paint in all?

Independent Practice

In **7–24**, add. Write each sum in simplest form.

7. $\frac{1}{2} + \frac{1}{2}$

8. $\frac{2}{7} + \frac{4}{7}$

9. $\frac{1}{9} + \frac{5}{9}$

10. $\frac{1}{4} + \frac{1}{4}$

11. $\frac{3}{11} + \frac{7}{11}$

12. $\frac{4}{10} + \frac{2}{10}$

13. $\frac{1}{5} + \frac{2}{5}$

14. $\frac{1}{8} + \frac{1}{8}$

15. $\frac{3}{6} + \frac{2}{6}$

16. $\frac{3}{7} + \frac{1}{7}$

17. $\frac{8}{12} + \frac{2}{12}$

18. $\frac{2}{4} + \frac{1}{4}$

19. $\frac{4}{9} + \frac{3}{9}$

20. $\frac{2}{10} + \frac{7}{10}$

21. $\frac{2}{5} + \frac{2}{5}$

22. $\frac{4}{8} + \frac{4}{8}$

23. $\frac{1}{6} + \frac{3}{6}$

24. $\frac{4}{11} + \frac{5}{11}$

For another example, see Set B on page 290.

Step 1

Find $\frac{6}{12} + \frac{2}{12}$.

To add fractions with the same denominator:

$\frac{6}{12} + \frac{2}{12} = \frac{8}{12}$ ← Add the numerators. ← Use the same denominator.

Step 2

Write the sum in simplest form.

Divide the numerator and denominator by the same number.

$\frac{8}{12} = \frac{2}{3}$ (÷ 4 numerator, ÷ 4 denominator)

8 is evenly divided by 4.

12 is evenly divided by 4.

$\frac{6}{12} + \frac{2}{12} = \frac{8}{12}$

In simplest form, $\frac{8}{12} = \frac{2}{3}$.

Jorge painted $\frac{2}{3}$ of the roof in all.

Problem Solving

25. Gail's family was on a summer car trip. They drove $\frac{5}{10}$ of the total distance on Monday. On Tuesday they drove $\frac{2}{10}$ of the total distance. What fraction of the total distance did they drive all together in those two days?

26. Writing to Explain Mrs. Dena put peanuts on top of $\frac{1}{8}$ of a pie. She put walnuts on top of $\frac{3}{8}$ of the pie. What fraction of the pie has nuts on top? Write your answer in simplest form. Explain how you found your answer.

27. Phil compared the distances between Oakland and other cities. How many more miles are between Oakland and Cleveland than between Oakland and Chicago?

A 4,609 **C** 628

B 953 **D** 325

Data

Distance Between Oakland and Other Cities

City	Number of Miles
Boston	3,095
Chicago	2,142
Cleveland	2,467

28. Katie walked her dog for 12 minutes on Monday. The next day, she walked her dog 3 times as long as on Monday. For how many minutes did Katie walk her dog on Tuesday?

? minutes in all

Tuesday	12	12	12	3 times as long
Monday	12			

29. In 1990, people in the United States were recycling $\frac{2}{6}$ of the paper used. Now we recycle more paper. If we recycle $\frac{1}{6}$ more than in 1990, what fraction of the paper used do we recycle now?

Lesson

13-3

NS 3.1 Compare fractions represented by drawings or concrete materials to show equivalency and to add and subtract simple fractions in context (e.g., $\frac{1}{2}$ of a pizza is the same amount as $\frac{2}{4}$ of another pizza that is the same size; show that $\frac{3}{8}$ is larger than $\frac{1}{4}$).

Using Models to Subtract Fractions

Hands-On fraction strips

How can you subtract fractions?

Helen had $\frac{5}{8}$ of a yard of cloth. She cut $\frac{1}{8}$ of a yard for a scarf. What fraction of a yard of cloth was left?

Choose an Operation $\frac{5}{8} - \frac{1}{8} = \square$

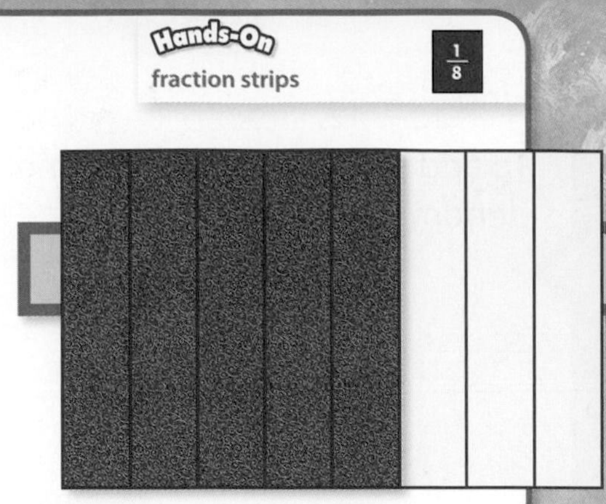

Guided Practice*

Do you know HOW?

In **1** and **2**, subtract. Write the difference in simplest form. You may use fraction strips or draw a picture to help.

1. $\frac{6}{8} - \frac{4}{8}$

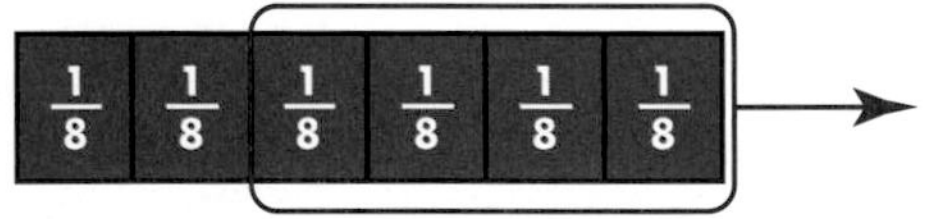

2. $\frac{3}{4} - \frac{1}{4}$

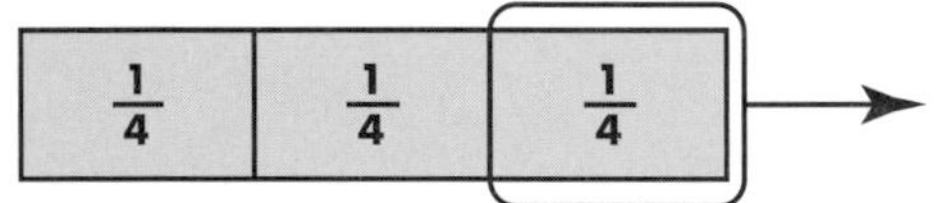

Do you UNDERSTAND?

3. Suppose you subtract two fractions with the same denominator. What can you say about the difference before you write it in simplest form?

4. Ethan lives $\frac{9}{10}$ of a mile from school. His friend Luis lives $\frac{3}{10}$ of a mile from school. How much farther from school does Ethan live than Luis? Write the answer in simplest form.

Independent Practice

Leveled Practice In **5–10**, subtract. Write the difference in simplest form. You may draw a picture to help.

5. $\frac{2}{3} - \frac{1}{3}$ 1/3 1/3

6. $\frac{4}{6} - \frac{2}{6}$

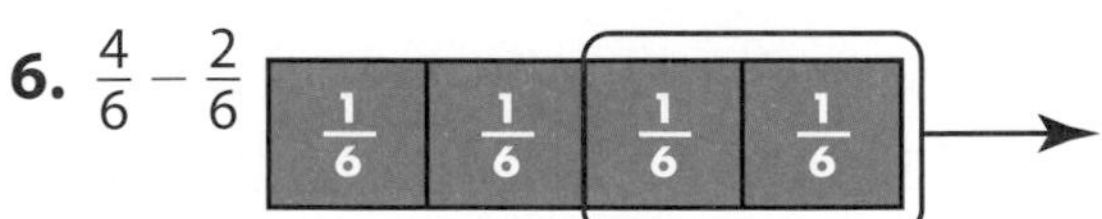

7. $\frac{4}{5} - \frac{2}{5}$ **8.** $\frac{7}{9} - \frac{4}{9}$ **9.** $\frac{10}{12} - \frac{4}{12}$ **10.** $\frac{3}{4} - \frac{2}{4}$

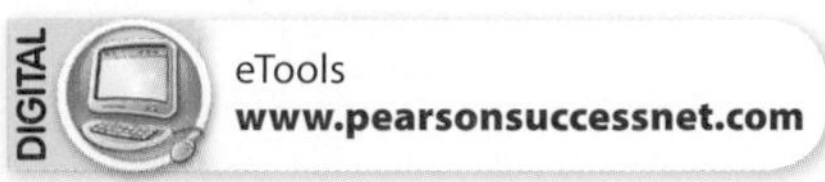

*For another example, see Set C on page 291.

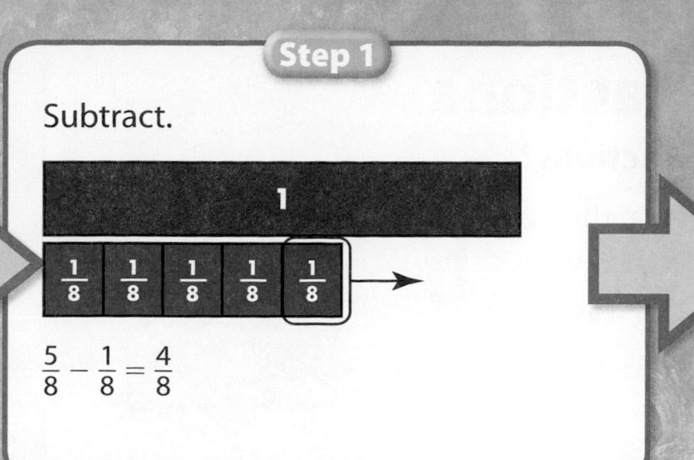

$\frac{5}{8} - \frac{1}{8} = \frac{4}{8}$

Step 2

Write the difference in simplest form.

$\frac{4}{8} = \frac{1}{2}$

So, $\frac{5}{8} - \frac{1}{8} = \frac{4}{8}$, or $\frac{1}{2}$.

One half yard of cloth was left.

Problem Solving

11. Selena had $\frac{3}{4}$ of a whole sheet of grid paper. She cut off $\frac{2}{4}$ of the whole sheet. Write a subtraction sentence that shows the fraction of the whole sheet that was left.

12. **Number Sense** There are 56 crayons. The crayons are placed onto 8 tables so that the same number of crayons is on each table. How many crayons in all would be on 3 tables?

13. Ted saw that there was $\frac{5}{8}$ of a pizza in the refrigerator. He ate $\frac{1}{8}$ of the pizza. What fraction of the pizza was left? Write the fraction in simplest form.

14. A diner had $\frac{8}{12}$ of a supreme pizza on the shelf. Then Marion served $\frac{4}{12}$ of the pizza to a table of customers. In simplest form, what fraction of the pizza was left?

A $\frac{4}{4}$

B $\frac{1}{3}$

C $\frac{1}{4}$

D $\frac{2}{12}$

15. Use the pictures of beetles at the right. How much longer is the caterpillar hunter beetle than the tiger beetle?

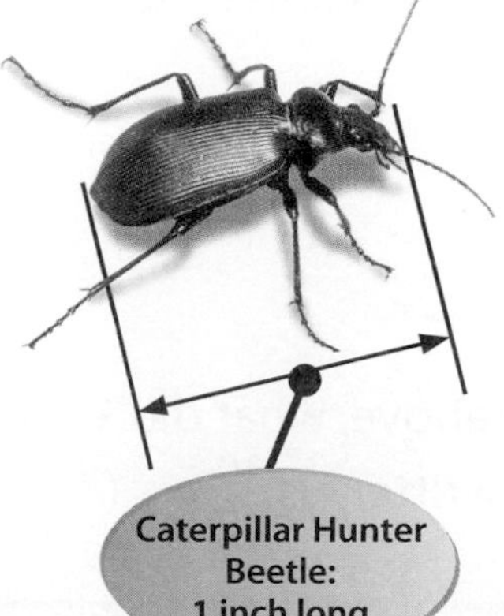

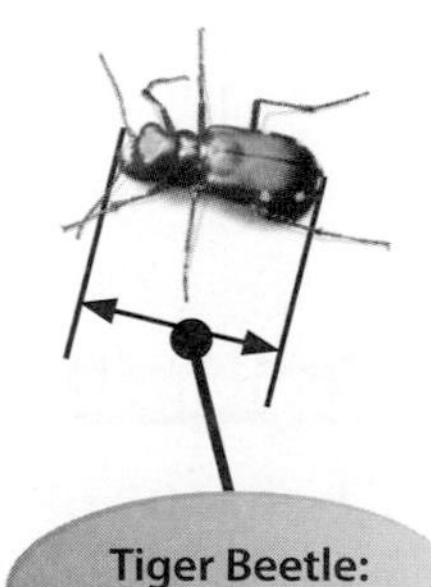

Lesson

13-4

NS 3.2 Add and subtract simple fractions (e.g., determine that $\frac{1}{8} + \frac{3}{8}$ is the same as $\frac{1}{2}$).

Subtracting Fractions

How can you subtract fractions?

Susanna had $\frac{3}{4}$ of a sandwich in the refrigerator. She ate $\frac{1}{4}$ of the sandwich. What fraction of the sandwich was left?

Choose an Operation $\frac{3}{4} - \frac{1}{4} = \square$

Another Example **How can you subtract from 1?**

Lea baked a pan of pasta. She divided the pan of pasta into tenths. Lea's family ate $\frac{3}{10}$ of the pan of pasta at lunch. The family ate another $\frac{4}{10}$ of the pan of pasta at dinner. How much of the pan of pasta was left?

Step 1

Find the part of the pan of pasta that was eaten.

$\frac{1}{10}$ $\frac{1}{10}$ $\frac{1}{10}$ $\frac{1}{10}$ $\frac{1}{10}$ $\frac{1}{10}$ $\frac{1}{10}$

$\frac{4}{10} + \frac{3}{10}$

$\frac{4}{10} + \frac{3}{10} = \frac{7}{10}$ ← Add the numerators. ← Use the same denominator.

Step 2

Subtract the part that was eaten from the whole pan of pasta.

$1 - \frac{7}{10}$

↓ Write 1 as a fraction with denominator 10.

$1 = \frac{10}{10}$

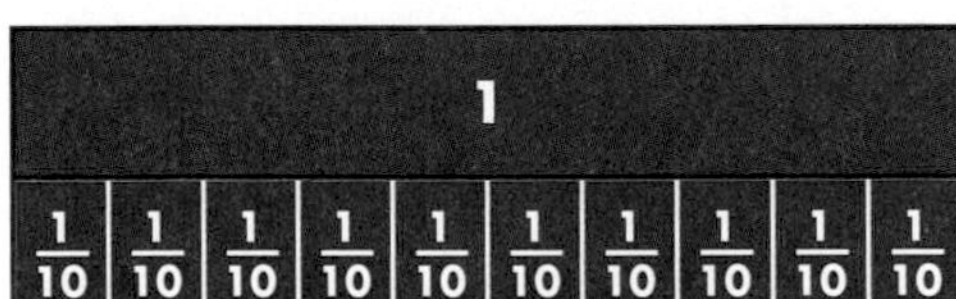

$\frac{10}{10} - \frac{7}{10} = \frac{3}{10}$ ← Subtract the numerators. ← Use the same denominator.

The answer, $\frac{3}{10}$, is in simplest form.

$\frac{3}{10}$ of the pan of pasta was left.

Explain It

1. In the example above, what did 1 represent in $1 - \frac{7}{10}$? Why was the 1 written as $\frac{10}{10}$?

Step 1

Find $\frac{3}{4} - \frac{1}{4}$.

To subtract fractions with the same denominator:

$\frac{3}{4} - \frac{1}{4} = \frac{2}{4}$ ← Subtract the numerators. ← Keep the same denominator.

Step 2

Write the difference in simplest form.

Divide the numerator and denominator by the same number.

$\frac{2}{4} = \frac{1}{2}$ (÷ 2, ÷ 2) Divide the numerator and denominator by 2.

So, $\frac{3}{4} - \frac{1}{4} = \frac{2}{4}$, and in simplest form, $\frac{2}{4} = \frac{1}{2}$.

Susanna left $\frac{1}{2}$ of the sandwich.

Guided Practice*

Do you know HOW?

In **1–4**, subtract. Write each difference in simplest form.

1. $\frac{6}{9} - \frac{3}{9}$

2. $1 - \frac{7}{12}$

3. $\frac{5}{6} - \frac{4}{6}$

4. $\frac{9}{10} - \frac{3}{10}$

Do you UNDERSTAND?

5. In the example above, how can you check that the difference is correct?

6. David saw $\frac{3}{8}$ of a pie in the refrigerator. He ate $\frac{1}{8}$ of the pie. What fraction of the pie was left?

Independent Practice

In **7–27**, subtract. Write each difference in simplest form.

7. $\frac{3}{4} - \frac{2}{4}$

8. $1 - \frac{4}{7}$

9. $1 - \frac{1}{3}$

10. $\frac{4}{5} - \frac{2}{5}$

11. $1 - \frac{3}{9}$

12. $\frac{11}{12} - \frac{7}{12}$

13. $\frac{5}{6} - \frac{2}{6}$

14. $\frac{6}{8} - \frac{4}{8}$

15. $\frac{8}{10} - \frac{7}{10}$

16. $\frac{5}{8} - \frac{3}{8}$

17. $1 - \frac{1}{2}$

18. $\frac{10}{11} - \frac{3}{11}$

19. $\frac{6}{7} - \frac{3}{7}$

20. $1 - \frac{4}{9}$

21. $1 - \frac{2}{3}$

22. $1 - \frac{3}{4}$

23. $\frac{4}{5} - \frac{1}{5}$

24. $\frac{8}{12} - \frac{4}{12}$

25. $\frac{9}{10} - \frac{6}{10}$

26. $\frac{9}{12} - \frac{5}{12}$

27. $\frac{7}{8} - \frac{3}{8}$

For another example, see Set D on page 291.

28. Hector baked a loaf of bread. He cut the loaf into twelfths. He gave $\frac{4}{12}$ of the loaf to Alicia and $\frac{3}{12}$ to Ed. What fraction of the loaf of bread was left?

29. **Writing to Explain** Stuart had $\frac{7}{8}$ of a pizza in the refrigerator. He ate $\frac{1}{8}$ of the pizza. What fraction of the pizza was left? Write your answer in simplest form. Explain how you found your answer.

Use the table at the right for **30** and **31**.

Data

Juice Boxes for Camping Trip	
Number of Campers	**Number of Juice Boxes**
1	4
2	8
3	12

30. The table shows the number of juice boxes Rita needs to buy for different numbers of campers. If each camper gets the same number of juice boxes, how many are needed for 8 campers?

31. **Writing to Explain** How many more juice boxes does Rita need to buy for 5 campers than for 3 campers? Explain how you found your answer.

32. **Number Sense** Petey, Arun, and their father were sharing a sandwich. Petey ate $\frac{1}{4}$ of the sandwich. Arun ate $\frac{1}{4}$, and their father ate $\frac{1}{2}$ of the sandwich. How much of the sandwich was left?

33. About $\frac{1}{4}$ of the energy used in the United States comes from natural gas. What fraction of the energy used does not come from natural gas?

34. Jill spent \$3 on milk, \$4 on bread, and \$5 on cereal. If she got \$8 in change, how much money did Jill pay?

A \$5 **B** \$10 **C** \$20 **D** \$50

35. A restaurant has 15 tables. Ten of the tables can seat 2 people. The rest of the tables can seat 4 people. How many people can the restaurant seat at one time?

36. Jay baked a pan of cornbread. He divided the pan of cornbread into eighths. Jay's family ate $\frac{2}{8}$ of the pan of cornbread at lunch. They ate $\frac{3}{8}$ of the pan of cornbread at dinner. How much of the pan of cornbread was left?

Algebra Connections

Greater, Less, or Equal

You know that the two sides of a number sentence can be equal or unequal. Estimation or reasoning can help you decide which symbol (>, <, or =) shows how the sides compare.

> means is greater than
< means is less than
= means is equal to

Example: $\frac{3}{8} + \frac{1}{8} \bigcirc 1$

Think If you add $\frac{1}{8}$ to $\frac{3}{8}$, is the sum greater than 1?

Since $1 = \frac{8}{8}$, the sum of the fractions is less than 1. Write "<".

$\frac{3}{8} + \frac{1}{8} < 1$

Copy and complete. Replace the circle with <, >, or =. Check your answers.

1. $\frac{1}{3} + \frac{1}{3} \bigcirc 1$
2. $23 + 10 \bigcirc 30$
3. $50 - 30 \bigcirc 60 - 30$
4. $6 \times 5 \bigcirc 6 \times 9$
5. $12 \div 2 \bigcirc 18 \div 2$
6. $\frac{7}{9} + \frac{2}{9} \bigcirc 1$
7. $\frac{2}{10} + \frac{1}{10} \bigcirc \frac{1}{10}$
8. $59 - 14 \bigcirc 69 - 24$
9. $\frac{5}{6} - \frac{3}{6} \bigcirc \frac{1}{6}$
10. $\frac{4}{5} - \frac{1}{5} \bigcirc 1$
11. $42 + 17 \bigcirc 50 + 17$
12. $\frac{3}{4} - \frac{1}{4} \bigcirc \frac{1}{2}$

For **13** and **14**, copy and complete the number sentence below each problem. Use it to help find your answer.

13. Andy ate $\frac{1}{4}$ of a fruit bar in the morning. He ate $\frac{2}{4}$ of the fruit bar in the afternoon. Reg ate 1 whole fruit bar at lunch. Who ate a greater amount of fruit bar?

    ______ + ______ ◯ ______

14. Look at the number of pieces of fruit in the two boxes below. Mori bought 3 boxes of oranges. Kendra bought 3 boxes of pears. Who bought more pieces of fruit?

15. **Write a Problem** Write a problem using this number sentence: $\frac{4}{8} + \frac{1}{8} > \frac{3}{8} + \frac{1}{8}$.

Lesson

13-5

MR 2.3 Use a variety of methods, such as words, numbers, symbols, charts, graphs, tables, diagrams, and models, to explain mathematical reasoning. Also **NS 3.2** Add and subtract simple fractions (e.g., determine that $\frac{1}{8}+\frac{3}{8}$ is the same as $\frac{1}{2}$).

Problem Solving

Draw a Picture and Write a Number Sentence

Mrs. Vega had $\frac{3}{4}$ of a whole veggie wrap. She gave $\frac{2}{4}$ of the whole wrap to Trina. She gave the rest of it to Alex. What fraction of the whole wrap did she give to Alex?

Another Example In what other kinds of situations can you draw pictures to solve?

Roberto and Kim each had a sandwich of the same size. They each ate some of their own sandwich. Roberto had $\frac{1}{4}$ of a sandwich left. Kim had $\frac{2}{4}$ of a sandwich left. How much more of a sandwich did Kim have left than Roberto?

Read and Understand

Use a diagram to show what you know.

$\frac{2}{4}$		← Kim
?	$\frac{1}{4}$	← Roberto

Since you are comparing amounts, you can subtract. $\frac{2}{4}-\frac{1}{4}=?$

Plan and Solve

Subtract to solve the problem.

$\frac{2}{4}-\frac{1}{4}=\frac{1}{4}$

Kim had $\frac{1}{4}$ of a sandwich more than Roberto.

Explain It

1. Suppose Tammy wrote $\frac{1}{4}+?=\frac{2}{4}$ for the diagram above. Is this number sentence correct? Explain.
2. Jen and Tracy each had a fruit bar of the same size. They each ate some of their own fruit bar. Jen ate $\frac{1}{3}$ of her fruit bar. Tracy ate $\frac{2}{3}$ of her fruit bar. How much more of a fruit bar did Tracy eat than Jen?

Plan and Solve

Use a diagram to show what you know.

$\frac{3}{4}$ of a wrap in all

$\frac{2}{4}$	?

You know the total and one part. Subtract to find the other part.

$\frac{3}{4} - \frac{2}{4} = \square$

Solve and Answer

Subtract to solve the problem.

$$\frac{3}{4} - \frac{2}{4} = \frac{1}{4}$$

Mrs. Vega gave $\frac{1}{4}$ of the veggie wrap to Alex.

Guided Practice*

Do you know HOW?

Draw a picture and write a number sentence to solve.

1. Miyoko had a piece of ribbon that was $\frac{7}{8}$ yard long. She cut off $\frac{2}{8}$ yard to make a bow. She used the rest of the ribbon to make a tail for her kite. How much ribbon did she use for the kite?

Do you UNDERSTAND?

2. What did you do to find the fraction of the ribbon that Miyoko used for the kite?

3. **Write a Problem** Write a problem with fractions that you can solve by drawing a picture and writing a number sentence.

Independent Practice

Draw a picture and write a number sentence to solve.

4. Bev and Gus each had a fruit bar of the same size. They each ate some of their own fruit bar. Bev had $\frac{3}{4}$ of a fruit bar left. Gus had $\frac{1}{4}$ of a fruit bar left. How much more of a fruit bar did Bev have left than Gus?

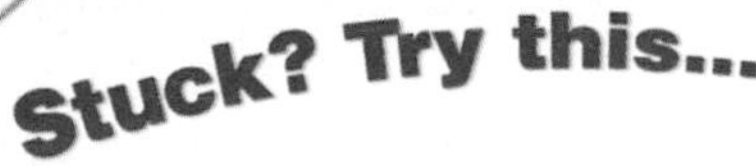

- What do I know?
- What am I asked to find?
- What diagram can I use to help understand the problem?
- Can I use addition, subtraction, multiplication, or division?
- Is all of my work correct?
- Did I answer the right question?
- Is my answer reasonable?

*For another example, see Set E on page 291.

Independent Practice

5. Leo colored $\frac{3}{5}$ of a flag blue. Then he colored another $\frac{1}{5}$ of the same flag yellow. What fraction of the flag did he color in all?

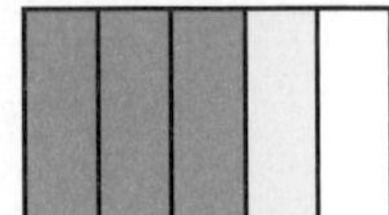

6. Josh wants to buy some art supplies. How much money does Josh need to buy a paint brush and 4 jars of paint?

Data

Art Supplies	
Jar of paint	$4
Marker	$3
Paint brush	$6

In **7** and **8**, use the pictograph.

7. Mrs. Riley's class voted on which kind of activity they should do during gym time. The pictograph shows the results. Which activity received the most votes?

8. Writing to Explain How do you know that two activities did not receive the same number of votes?

Votes for Gym Time Activity	
Basketball	☺☺☺☺☺☺☺
Races	☺☺☺☺☺☺
Skip Rope	☺☺☺☺☺
Volleyball	☺☺☺☺☺☺☺☺

Each ☺ = 1 vote.

9. Gloria and Louisa both walk to school. Gloria lives $\frac{9}{10}$ mile from school. Louisa lives $\frac{6}{10}$ mile from school. How much farther does Gloria have to walk than Louisa? Copy and complete the picture at the right. Solve the problem.

Gloria	?	
Louisa	$\frac{6}{10}$	?

Think About the Process

10. Each week has 7 days. Which of the following is used to find out how many days are in 2 weeks?

A 7 − 2 **C** 7 ÷ 2

B 2 + 7 **D** 2 × 7

11. Mr. Wilson's class has 27 students. Mrs. Pak's class has 32 students. Which number sentence shows how many more students are in Mrs. Pak's class than are in Mr. Wilson's class?

A 32 − 27 = ▢ **C** 32 ÷ 27 = ▢

B 32 + 27 = ▢ **D** 32 × 27 = ▢

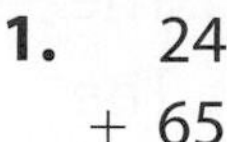

Estimate and then find each sum. Check that your answer is reasonable.

1. $\begin{array}{r} 24 \\ +\ 65 \\ \hline \end{array}$ **2.** $\begin{array}{r} 39 \\ +\ 76 \\ \hline \end{array}$ **3.** $\begin{array}{r} 638 \\ +\ 823 \\ \hline \end{array}$ **4.** $\begin{array}{r} 4{,}207 \\ +\ 1{,}985 \\ \hline \end{array}$

Estimate. Then find each difference. Check that your answer is reasonable.

5. $\begin{array}{r} 83 \\ -\ 27 \\ \hline \end{array}$ **6.** $\begin{array}{r} 285 \\ -\ 89 \\ \hline \end{array}$ **7.** $\begin{array}{r} 602 \\ -\ 234 \\ \hline \end{array}$ **8.** $\begin{array}{r} 5{,}413 \\ -\ 2{,}278 \\ \hline \end{array}$

Find each product.

9. 4×7 **10.** 7×9 **11.** 0×8 **12.** 10×6 **13.** 8×5

14. 7×8 **15.** 5×9 **16.** 4×3 **17.** 3×9 **18.** 2×10

Find each quotient.

19. $54 \div 6$ **20.** $40 \div 8$ **21.** $18 \div 3$ **22.** $45 \div 5$ **23.** $72 \div 9$

24. $36 \div 9$ **25.** $63 \div 7$ **26.** $42 \div 6$ **27.** $21 \div 7$ **28.** $18 \div 9$

Error Search Find each sum or difference that is not correct. Write it correctly and explain the error.

29. $\begin{array}{r} 183 \\ +\ 127 \\ \hline 310 \end{array}$ **30.** $\begin{array}{r} 685 \\ -\ 289 \\ \hline 404 \end{array}$ **31.** $\frac{2}{5} + \frac{1}{5} = \frac{1}{5}$ **32.** $\frac{7}{8} - \frac{3}{8} = \frac{1}{4}$

Number Sense

Estimating and Reasoning Write true or false for each statement. If it is false, explain why.

33. $3 \times 10 > 300$

34. $27 \div 3 > 10$

35. $90 + 8 < 100$

36. $\frac{1}{4} + \frac{2}{4} > 1$

37. $\frac{3}{6} + \frac{2}{6} < 1$

38. $\frac{6}{8} - \frac{3}{8} > 1$

Test Prep

1. Stacy rode her bike $\frac{1}{5}$ mile to her grandmother's house. Then she rode $\frac{3}{5}$ mile to her aunt's house. How far did Stacy ride? (13-1)

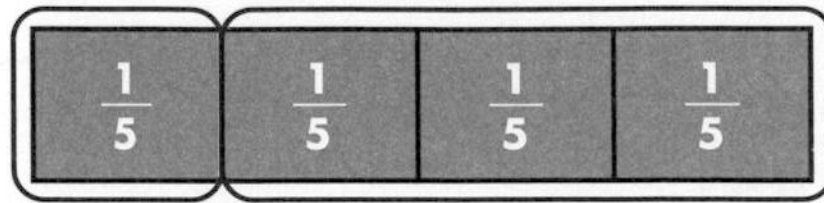

A $\frac{5}{4}$ miles

B $\frac{4}{5}$ mile

C $\frac{2}{5}$ mile

D $\frac{4}{10}$ mile

2. Bethany bought $\frac{7}{8}$ yard of ribbon. She used $\frac{5}{8}$ yard to decorate a costume. In simplest form, how much ribbon does she have left? (13-3)

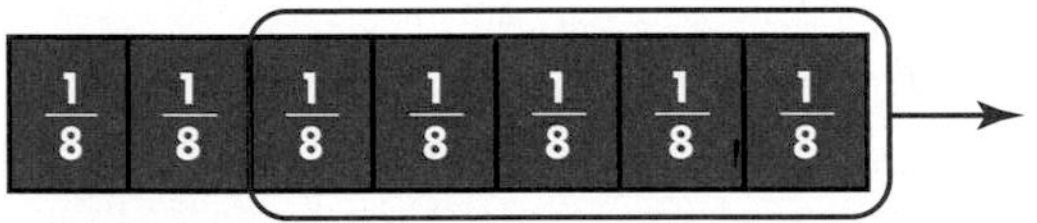

A $\frac{1}{4}$ yard

B $\frac{1}{3}$ yard

C $\frac{3}{4}$ yard

D $\frac{4}{3}$ yards

3. What is $\frac{7}{10} - \frac{4}{10}$? (13-4)

A $\frac{1}{5}$

B $\frac{3}{10}$

C $\frac{2}{5}$

D $\frac{1}{2}$

4. Anna Lucia is knitting a scarf. The first week she finished $\frac{2}{9}$ of it. The second week, she finished $\frac{4}{9}$ of it. In simplest form, what part did she finish the first two weeks? (13-2)

A $\frac{6}{18}$

B $\frac{5}{9}$

C $\frac{2}{9}$

D $\frac{2}{3}$

5. Mrs. Blanca bought $\frac{3}{4}$ pound of sausage and $\frac{1}{4}$ pound of bacon. In simplest form, how much more sausage than bacon did Mrs. Blanca buy? (13-4)

A 1 pound

B $\frac{5}{8}$ pound

C $\frac{1}{2}$ pound

D $\frac{3}{8}$ pound

6. Mason ate $\frac{5}{12}$ of a pizza. Corbin ate $\frac{1}{12}$ of the same pizza. In simplest form, how much of the pizza did they eat in all? (13-2)

A $\frac{1}{3}$

B $\frac{6}{24}$

C $\frac{1}{4}$

D $\frac{1}{2}$

Test Prep

7. What is $\frac{3}{10} + \frac{3}{10}$, in simplest form? (13-1)

A $\frac{6}{20}$

B $\frac{6}{10}$

C $\frac{3}{5}$

D $\frac{4}{5}$

8. What is $\frac{1}{7} + \frac{3}{7}$? (13-2)

A $\frac{4}{7}$

B $\frac{2}{7}$

C $\frac{4}{14}$

D $\frac{2}{14}$

9. A weather reporter said that it rained $\frac{3}{4}$ of an inch on Tuesday and $\frac{1}{4}$ of an inch on Wednesday. Which number sentence could be used to find how much more it rained on Tuesday than on Wednesday? (13-5)

A $\frac{3}{4} + \frac{1}{4} = \frac{4}{4}$

B $\frac{1}{4} + \frac{3}{4} = \frac{4}{8}$ or $\frac{1}{2}$

C $\frac{3}{4} - \frac{1}{4} = \frac{2}{4}$ or $\frac{1}{2}$

D $\frac{3}{4} - \frac{1}{4} = \frac{2}{0}$

10. A package of modeling clay was divided into eighths. Estelle got $\frac{1}{8}$ of the clay. David got $\frac{4}{8}$ of the clay. Eugene got $\frac{2}{8}$ of the clay. How much of the clay was left? (13-4)

A $\frac{7}{8}$

B $\frac{3}{8}$

C $\frac{1}{4}$

D $\frac{1}{8}$

11. Chelle bought $\frac{3}{8}$ pound of ham and $\frac{1}{8}$ pound of salami. Which picture models how much lunch meat Chelle bought? (13-5)

A

$\frac{3}{8}$

$\frac{1}{8}$	$\frac{1}{8}$	$\frac{1}{8}$

B

?

$\frac{3}{8}$	$\frac{1}{8}$

C

$\frac{1}{8}$

$\frac{3}{8}$	?

D

$\frac{3}{8}$

$\frac{1}{8}$	?

Set A, pages 274–275

Find $\frac{1}{6} + \frac{3}{6}$.

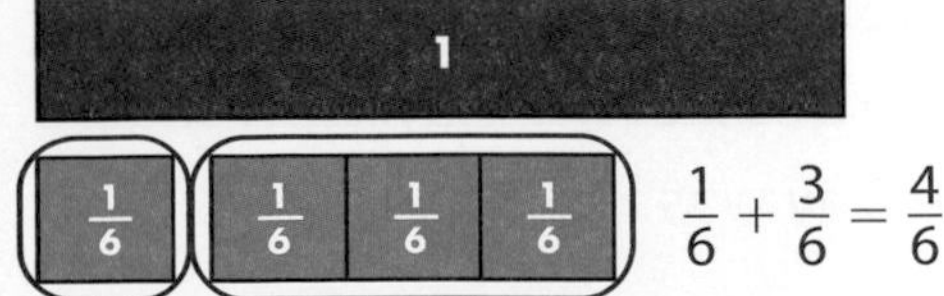

$\frac{1}{6} + \frac{3}{6} = \frac{4}{6}$

Write the sum in simplest form.

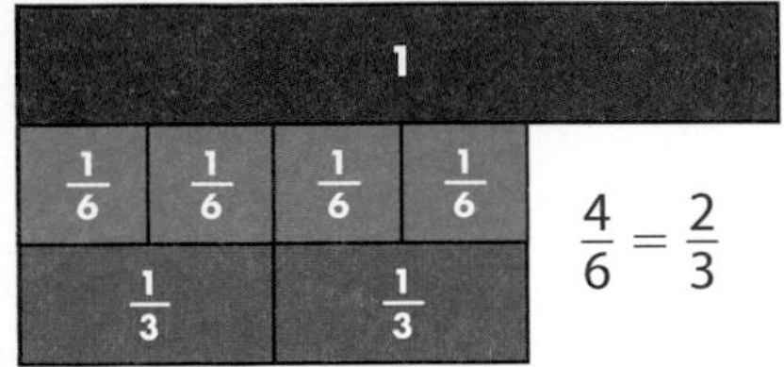

$\frac{4}{6} = \frac{2}{3}$

So, $\frac{1}{6} + \frac{3}{6} = \frac{4}{6}$, or $\frac{2}{3}$.

Remember to write the sum in simplest form.

Add. You may use fraction strips or draw a picture to help. Write the sum in simplest form.

1. $\frac{3}{10} + \frac{2}{10}$

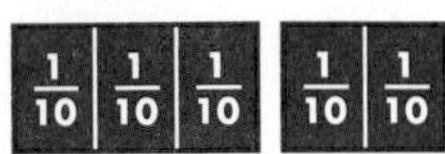

2. $\frac{1}{4} + \frac{1}{4}$

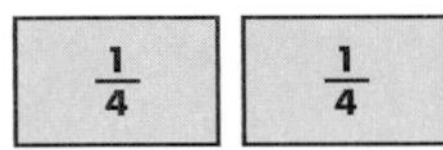

3. $\frac{5}{8} + \frac{2}{8}$

Set B, pages 276–277

Find $\frac{2}{9} + \frac{4}{9}$.

These fractions have the same denominator.

$\frac{2}{9} + \frac{4}{9} = \frac{6}{9}$ ← Add the numerators. ← Use the same denominator.

Write the sum in simplest form.

$\frac{6 \div 3}{9 \div 3} = \frac{2}{3}$ Divide the numerator and denominator by the same number.

$\frac{6}{9} = \frac{2}{3}$

So, $\frac{2}{9} + \frac{4}{9} = \frac{6}{9}$, or $\frac{2}{3}$.

Remember to use the same denominator.

Add. Write the sum in simplest form.

1. $\frac{1}{6} + \frac{1}{6}$ **2.** $\frac{2}{8} + \frac{4}{8}$

3. $\frac{1}{3} + \frac{1}{3}$ **4.** $\frac{4}{16} + \frac{6}{16}$

5. $\frac{2}{7} + \frac{1}{7}$ **6.** $\frac{5}{12} + \frac{4}{12}$

7. $\frac{2}{5} + \frac{2}{5}$ **8.** $\frac{1}{4} + \frac{2}{4}$

9. $\frac{5}{10} + \frac{3}{10}$ **10.** $\frac{8}{13} + \frac{4}{13}$

11. $\frac{4}{9} + \frac{3}{9}$ **12.** $\frac{5}{11} + \frac{4}{11}$

Set C, pages 278–279

Find $\frac{6}{8} - \frac{2}{8}$.

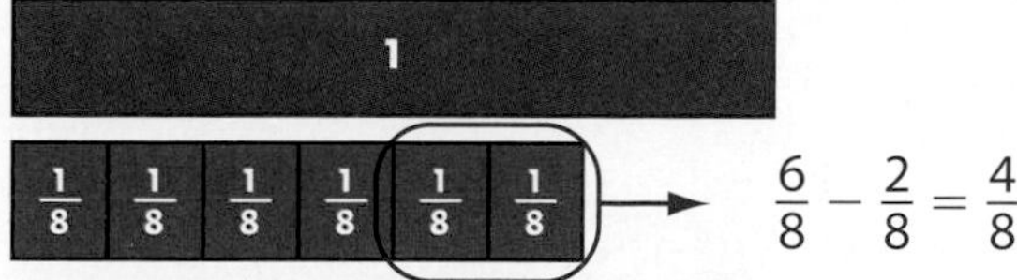

$\frac{6}{8} - \frac{2}{8} = \frac{4}{8}$

Write the difference in simplest form.

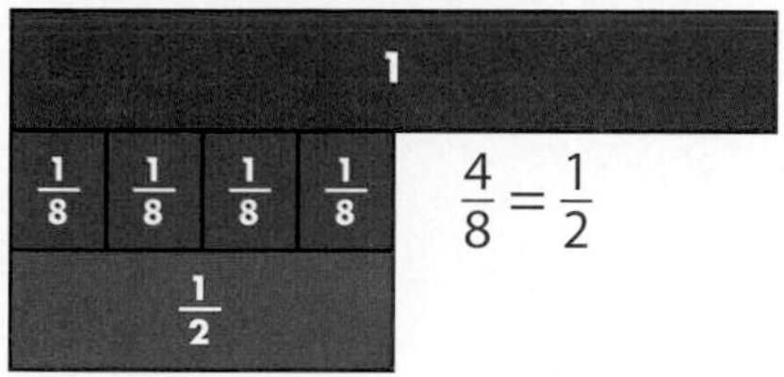

$\frac{4}{8} = \frac{1}{2}$

So, $\frac{6}{8} - \frac{2}{8} = \frac{4}{8}$, or $\frac{1}{2}$.

Remember to write the difference in simplest form.

Subtract. You may use fraction strips or draw a picture to help. Write the difference in simplest form.

1. $\frac{5}{6} - \frac{3}{6}$

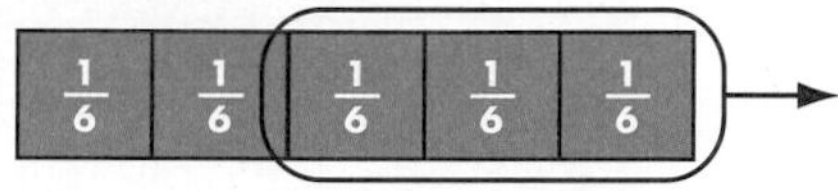

2. $\frac{8}{10} - \frac{2}{10}$

Set D, pages 280–282

Find $\frac{9}{10} - \frac{5}{10}$.

These fractions have the same denominator.

$\frac{9}{10} - \frac{5}{10} = \frac{4}{10}$ ← Subtract the numerators. ← Use the same denominator.

$\frac{4 \div 2}{10 \div 2} = \frac{2}{5}$ Write the difference in simplest form.

So, $\frac{9}{10} - \frac{5}{10} = \frac{4}{10}$, or $\frac{2}{5}$.

Remember to subtract the numerators only.

Subtract. Write the difference in simplest form.

1. $\frac{3}{4} - \frac{1}{4}$
2. $\frac{4}{5} - \frac{2}{5}$
3. $\frac{7}{8} - \frac{5}{8}$
4. $\frac{11}{12} - \frac{3}{12}$

Set E, pages 284–286

Ed has $\frac{1}{3}$ of a granola bar left. Al has $\frac{2}{3}$ of the same size bar left. How much more does Al have left than Ed?

Use a diagram to show what you know. You are comparing amounts, so subtract.

$\frac{1}{3}$ ← Ed

$\frac{2}{3}$ ← Al

$\frac{2}{3} - \frac{1}{3} = \frac{1}{3}$

Al has $\frac{1}{3}$ of a bar more than Ed.

Remember to draw a picture.

Solve. Draw a picture and write a number sentence.

1. Ira had $\frac{3}{4}$ of a sandwich. He gave $\frac{1}{4}$ of the sandwich to Tom. He gave the rest to June. What fraction of the sandwich did he give to June?

Topic 14

Multiplying Greater Numbers

1 How many passengers can be seated in a cable car? You will find out in Lesson 14-5.

2 About how much does a manatee weigh compared to a golden eagle? You will find out in Lesson 14-1.

3 How far can a jerboa jump? You will find out in Lesson 14-6.

4 About how many baseballs are used during one inning of a major league game? You will find out in Lesson 14-3.

Review What You Know!

Vocabulary

Choose the best term from the box.

- addends
- factors
- product
- sum

1. When you add to combine numbers, another name for the total is the __?__.
2. The Commutative Property of Multiplication says that the __?__ can be multiplied in any order and the answer will be the same.
3. In the number sentence $9 \times 6 = 54$, the number 54 is called the __?__.

Multiplication

Multiply.

4. 5×9 **5.** 8×7 **6.** 6×6

7. 4×7 **8.** 7×5 **9.** 4×2

10. 7×10 **11.** 8×9 **12.** 6×8

Arrays

Draw an array of dots for each multiplication.

13. 3×9 **14.** 4×8

15. **Write a Problem** Write a problem for the number sentence $7 \times 6 = \square$.

Lesson

14-1

NS 2.4 Solve simple problems involving multiplication of multidigit numbers by one-digit numbers (3,671 × 3 = __).

Using Mental Math to Multiply

Hands-On
place-value blocks

How can you multiply by multiples of 10, 100, and 1,000?

Use place-value blocks to find each product.

6 × 100 is 6 groups of 1 hundred or 600.

5 × 1,000 is 5 groups of 1 thousand or 5,000.

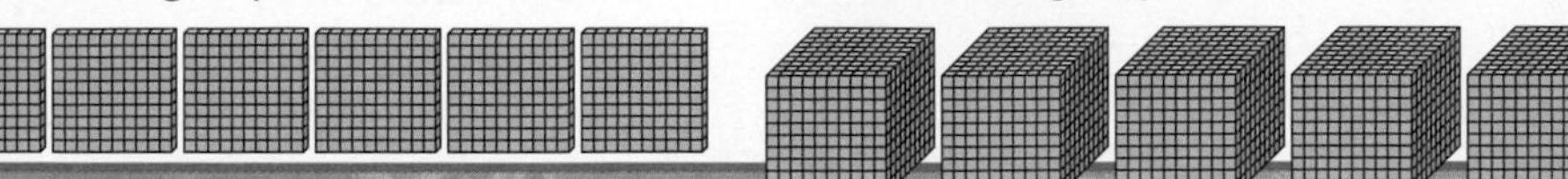

Guided Practice*

Do you know HOW?

In **1–8**, use place-value blocks or patterns to find each product.

1. 8 × 100

2. 7 × 1,000

3. 6 × 1,000

4. 9 × 100

5. 6 × 40

6. 3 × 700

7. 9 × 50

8. 5 × 3,000

Do you UNDERSTAND?

9. In Lesson 7-4, you used patterns to multiply by 10. What pattern do you see when you multiply by 100? by 1,000?

10. The memory card for Jay's digital camera holds 70 pictures. How many pictures can 4 memory cards hold?

11. Your friend says, "The product 6 × 5 is 30, so 6 × 500 is 300." Is he correct? Explain.

Independent Practice

In **12–27**, use mental math to find the product.

12. 4 × 10

13. 9 × 100

14. 2 × 1,000

15. 3 × 60

16. 8 × 80

17. 6 × 50

18. 40 × 7

19. 900 × 4

20. 500 × 9

21. 70 × 5

22. 100 × 8

23. 2 × 6,000

24. 200 × 8

25. 300 × 6

26. 4 × 500

27. 3 × 400

*For another example, see Set A on page 318.

Find 3×70.

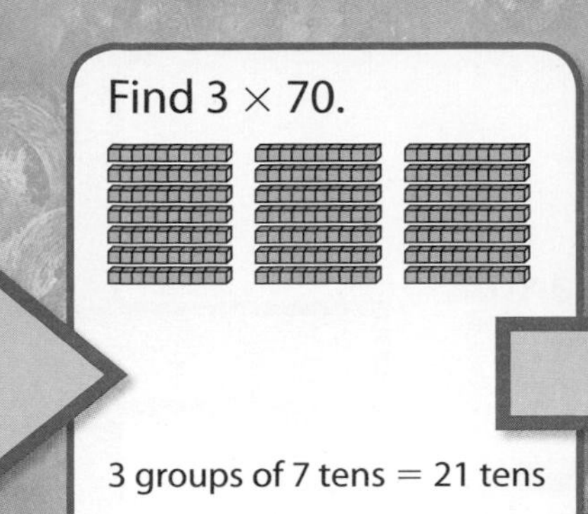

3 groups of 7 tens = 21 tens

$3 \times 70 = 210$

Find 4×300.

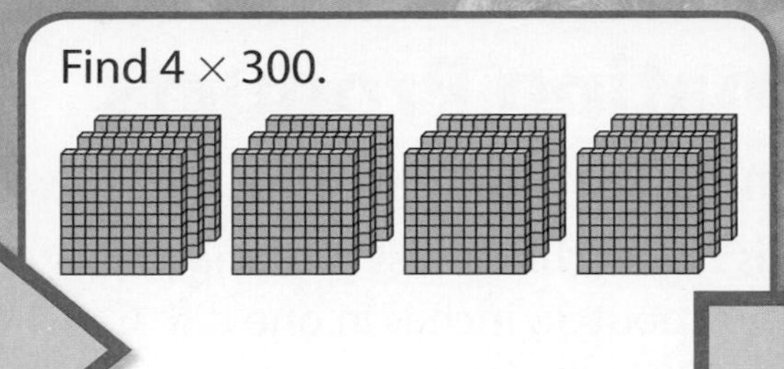

4 groups of 3 hundreds = 12 hundreds

$4 \times 300 = 1{,}200$

Find $2 \times 4{,}000$.

Use a pattern.

$2 \times 4 = 8$
$2 \times 40 = 80$
$2 \times 400 = 800$
$2 \times 4{,}000 = 8{,}000$

Problem Solving

For **28** and **29**, use the table at the right.

28. If you use a washing machine for 3 loads, how many gallons of water would you use? Draw pictures of place-value blocks to show the problem.

29. Writing to Explain How much water would you save if you took a 10-minute shower instead of a bath each day for 5 days? Explain how you solved the problem.

Data

Use of Water

Use	Estimated Number of Gallons
Bath	50
Dishwasher (1 load)	10
Shower (10 minutes)	20
Toilet (1 flush)	5
Washing Machine (1 load)	50

30. Each person in the United States uses about 200 gallons of water each day. About 125 gallons are used in the bathroom. How many gallons of water are used in other ways?

31. A golden eagle weighs about 11 pounds. A manatee can weigh 100 times as much as a golden eagle. How much can a manatee weigh?

32. An African elephant drinks about 50 gallons of water each day. How many gallons of water does the elephant drink in 7 days?

33. There are 6 floors in a building. Each floor has 20 windows. Some windows have 2 curtains. How many windows in all does the building have?

A 240
B 122
C 120
D 28

Lesson
14-2

NS 2.4 Solve simple problems involving multiplication of multidigit numbers by one-digit numbers (3,671 × 3 = __).

Estimating Products

How can you estimate products?

Bamboo is one of the fastest growing plants on Earth. It can grow about 36 inches in one day. Can it grow more than 200 inches in one week?

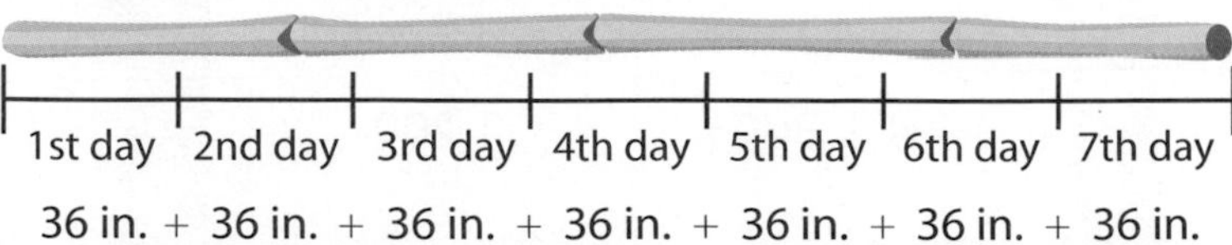

Other Examples

A bamboo plant can grow about 252 inches in 1 week. Does it grow more than 2,500 inches in 7 weeks?

Estimate 7 × 252.

Round 252 to the nearest hundred.

7 × 252
↓ 252 rounds to 300.
7 × 300 = 2,100

7 × 252 is about 2,100.

2,100 < 2,500
So, the bamboo plant does not grow more than 2,500 inches in 7 weeks.

Each stem on a bamboo plant can grow about 1,080 inches in 1 year. If a bamboo plant has 6 stems, does the plant produce more than 5,000 inches of stems in 1 year?

Estimate 6 × 1,080.

Round 1,080 to the nearest thousand.

6 × 1,080
↓ 1,080 rounds to 1,000.
6 × 1,000 = 6,000

6 × 1,080 is about 6,000.

6,000 > 5,000
The bamboo plant can produce more than 5,000 inches of stems in 1 year.

Guided Practice*

Do you know HOW?

In **1–4**, estimate each product.

1. 6 × 18

2. 3 × 52

3. 5 × 749

4. 4 × 1,965

Do you UNDERSTAND?

5. In the example about how much stems grow in 1 year, is the exact answer more than or less than the estimate of 6,000? How do you know?

*For another example, see Set B on page 318.

Step 1

Estimate 7×36.

Round 36 to the nearest ten.

7×36
↓ 36 rounds to 40.
$7 \times 40 = 280$

7×36 is about 280.

Step 2

Compare the estimate to 200 inches.

$280 > 200$

So, a bamboo plant can grow more than 200 inches in 1 week.

Independent Practice

In **6–15**, estimate each product.

6. 9×47 **7.** 2×613 **8.** 4×751 **9.** $7 \times 1{,}164$ **10.** $4 \times 2{,}789$

11. 2×46 **12.** 8×315 **13.** 5×890 **14.** $3 \times 6{,}483$ **15.** 4×709

Problem Solving

For **16–18**, use the graph at the right.

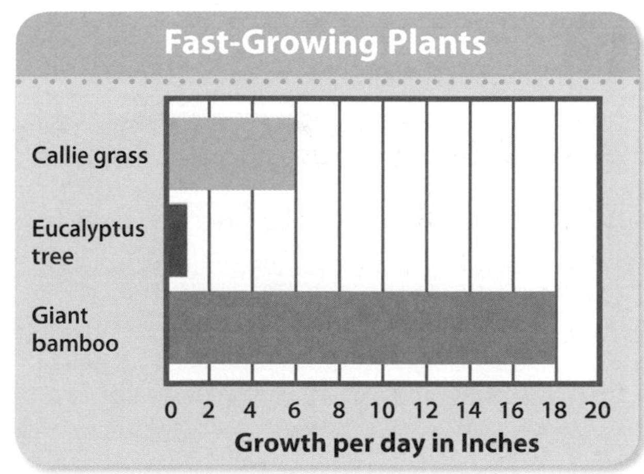

16. Writing to Explain Does a giant bamboo plant grow more than 100 inches in 6 days? Explain how to round to estimate the answer.

17. Reasonableness Jim says a eucalyptus tree grows more in 8 days than Callie grass grows in 2 days. Is his statement reasonable? Explain.

18. How much more does giant bamboo grow in one day than Callie grass?

19. Think About the Process Mr. James is buying 5 trees. Each tree costs \$199. Which number sentence shows the best way to estimate the total cost of the trees?

A $5 \times \$100 = \$500$

B $5 + \$200 = \$205$

C $5 \times \$200 = \$1{,}000$

D $10 + \$200 = \$2{,}000$

Lesson
14-3

MR 2.3 Use a variety of methods, such as words, numbers, symbols, charts, graphs, tables, diagrams, and models, to explain mathematical reasoning. Also **NS 3.1, Gr. 2** Use repeated addition, arrays, and counting by multiples to do multiplication.

Multiplication and Arrays

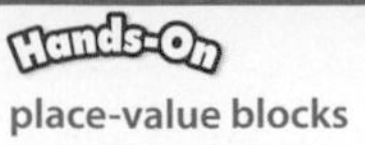

place-value blocks

How can you use arrays to show how to multiply with greater numbers?

Lava lamps in a store are arranged in 4 equal rows. What is the total number of lava lamps?

Choose an Operation Multiply to find the total for an array.

Guided Practice*

Do you know HOW?

In **1–4**, use place-value blocks or draw an array to find each product.

1. 5×14 **2.** 3×21

3. 2×38 **4.** 4×29

Do you UNDERSTAND?

5. In the example above, what multiplication fact could you use to find the total number of ones?

6. Light bulbs are arranged in 3 equal rows on a shelf in the store. There are 17 bulbs in each row. What is the total number of bulbs on the shelf?

Independent Practice

In **7–11**, draw an array to find the product.

You can draw lines to show tens, and Xs to show ones. This picture shows 23.

———— ———— × × ×

7. 3×26 **8.** 5×15 **9.** 2×18 **10.** 4×16 **11.** 7×21

In **12–21**, find each product. You may use place-value blocks or draw a picture to help.

12. 2×47 **13.** 6×28 **14.** 5×31 **15.** 3×45 **16.** 4×32

17. 8×15 **18.** 3×29 **19.** 5×22 **20.** 2×38 **21.** 4×19

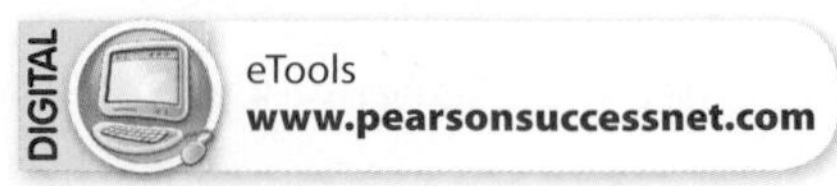

*For another example, see Set C on page 318.

Step 1

Use an array to show 4×13.

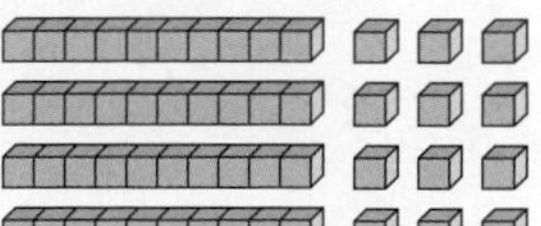

4 rows with 1 ten and 3 ones in each row.

Step 2

Find how many in all.

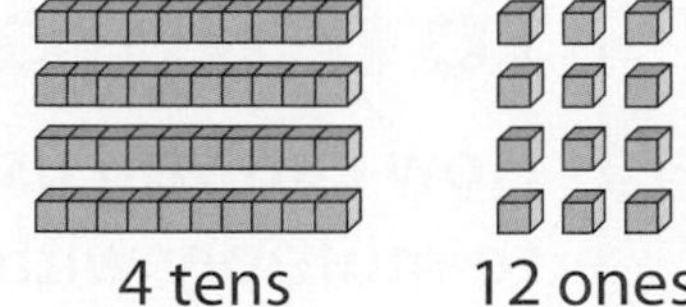

4 tens 12 ones

Count by tens and then count on with the ones to find the total.

10, 20, 30, 40
41, 42, 43, 44, 45, 46, 47, 48, 49, 50, 51, 52

There are 52 lava lamps.

Problem Solving

For **22** and **23**, use the table.

22. Jake walked for 1 minute. How many times did Jake's heart beat?

23. **Strategy Focus** Solve. Use the strategy Try, Check, and Revise.

While doing one of the activities, Jake counted his heartbeats. He found that his heart rate in one minute was greater than 120, but less than 130. Which activity was he doing? Explain how you solved the problem.

Data

Jake's Heart Rate

Activity	**Number of Heartbeats in 10 Seconds**
Bicycling	21
Resting	13
Running	22
Walking	18

The number of heartbeats in 1 minute is 6 times as many as in 10 seconds.

24. The soup cans in a store display were arranged in rows. There were 27 cans in each row. There were 3 rows. Which number sentence describes the array of soup cans?

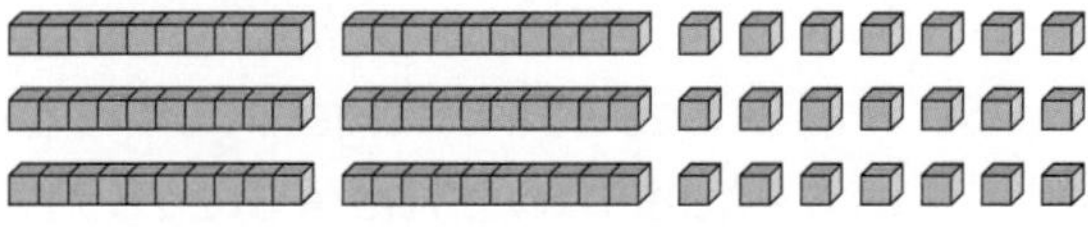

A $3 \times 27 = 81$

B $6 \times 21 = 126$

C $6 + 21 = 27$

D $2 \times 27 = 54$

25. What multiplication sentence could you write for this array?

××××
××××

_____ _____ _____

_____ _____ _____

26. In one inning, each baseball was used for 7 pitches. Write a number sentence that shows the total number of pitches thrown that inning.

4 baseballs are used each inning.

Lesson

14-4

NS 2.4 Solve simple problems involving multiplication of multidigit numbers by one-digit numbers (3,671 × 3 = __).
Also **MR 1.2** Determine when and how to break a problem into simpler parts.

Breaking Apart to Multiply

How can you use breaking apart to multiply with greater numbers?

A parking lot has the same number of spaces in each row. How many spaces are in the lot?

Choose an Operation Multiply to find the total for an array.

Other Examples

You can break apart to multiply with four-digit numbers.

A ball park has 2 parking lots. There are 1,345 spaces in each lot. What is the total number of parking spaces in the lots?

What You Show

Use an array to show 2 × 1,345.

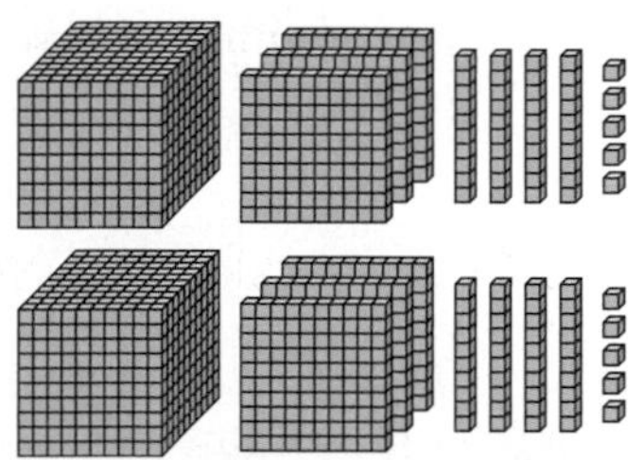

What You Write

2 × 1,000 = 2 thousands or 2,000
2 × 300 = 6 hundreds or 600
2 × 40 = 8 tens or 80
2 × 5 = 10 ones or 10
2,000 + 600 + 80 + 10 = 2,690

There are 2,690 parking spaces in the lots.

Guided Practice*

Do you know HOW?

Copy and complete.

1. 4 × 136
4 × 1 hundred = ▢ hundreds or 400
4 × 3 tens = ▢ tens or 120
4 × 6 ones = 24 ones or ▢
▢ + ▢ + ▢ = ▢

In **2** and **3**, find each product. You may use place-value blocks or drawings to help.

2. 3 × 28

3. 2 × 1,427

Do you UNDERSTAND?

4. In the example at the top of the page, what three groups is the array broken into?

5. The buses at a bus garage are parked in 4 equal rows. There are 239 buses in each row. What is the total number of buses parked at the garage?

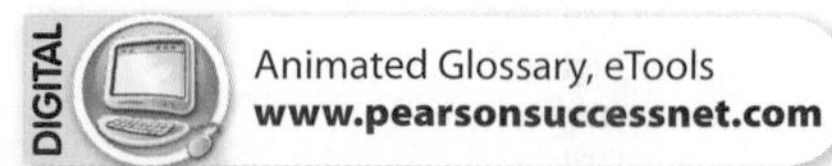

*For another example, see Set D on page 319.

Step 1

Use an array to show 3 × 126.

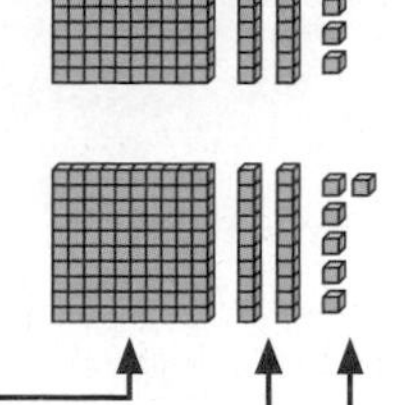

3 × 100 = 300
3 × 20 = 60
3 × 6 = 18

Step 2

Add each part to get the product.

3 rows of 1 hundred = 3 hundreds or 300
3 rows of 2 tens = 6 tens or 60
3 rows of 6 ones = 18 ones or 18
300 + 60 + 18 = 378

300, 60, and 18 are called partial products because they are parts of the product.

3 × 126 = 378

There are 378 parking spaces in the lot.

Independent Practice

In **6–10**, find each product. You may use place-value blocks or drawings to help.

6. 2 × 49 **7.** 3 × 168 **8.** 6 × 327 **9.** 2 × 3,751 **10.** 4 × 2,365

Problem Solving

For **11–13**, find the total number of miles traveled in the number of weeks given.

Data

Kind of Job	Distance Traveled in 1 Week
Nurse	Walks 18 miles
Bicycle messenger	Rides 192 miles
Truck driver	Drives 2,564 miles

11. Bicycle messenger: 6 weeks

12. Nurse: 7 weeks

13. Truck driver: 3 weeks

14. Raoul is counting the chairs in 8 rows. Each row has 108 chairs. Which number sentence shows the best way to estimate the total number of chairs in the rows?

A 8 + 140 = 148 **C** 8 × 100 = 800

B 10 + 140 = 150 **D** 8 × 200 = 1,600

15. Nilda bought a bookcase and a desk. What was the total cost of the items?

16. Estimation Walt has $80. Does he have enough money to buy a chair and a desk? Explain how to round to estimate.

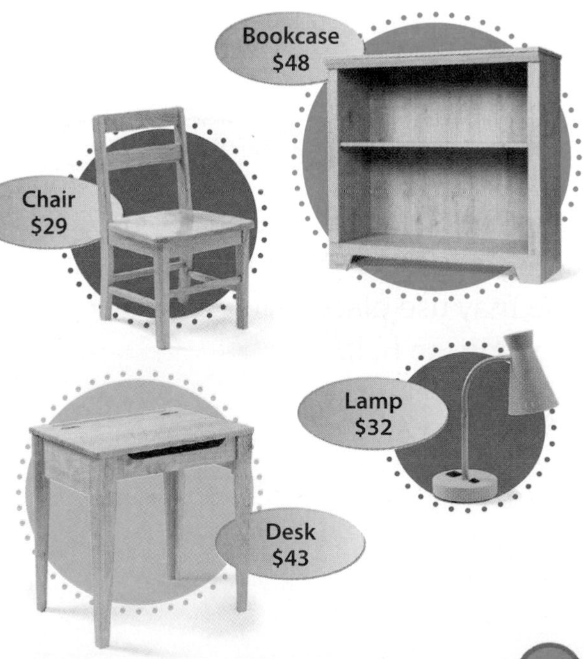

Lesson
14-5

NS 2.4 Solve simple problems involving multiplication of multidigit numbers by one-digit numbers (3,671 × 3 = __).

Using an Expanded Algorithm

Hands-On
place-value blocks

How can you use place value to multiply?

How many calories are in 3 peaches?

Find 3 × 46.

Estimate: 3 × 50 = 150

Data

Calories

Fruit	Number of calories
Peach	46
Orange	35
Pear	40

Guided Practice*

Do you know HOW?

In **1** and **2**, copy and complete. Use place-value blocks or draw pictures to help.

1. 16 × 3
18
▢▢
▢▢

2. 34 × 5
20
▢▢▢
▢▢▢

In **3** and **4**, find each product. You may use place-value blocks or drawings to help.

3. 67 × 2

4. 54 × 7

Do you UNDERSTAND?

For **5–7**, use the example above.

5. What factors give the partial product 18? What factors give the partial product 120?

6. What is the next step after you find the partial products?

7. How many calories are in 2 oranges?

Independent Practice

Leveled Practice In **8** and **9**, copy and complete. In **10–12**, find each product. You may use place-value blocks or drawings to help.

You can draw lines to show tens, and Xs to show ones. This picture shows 27.

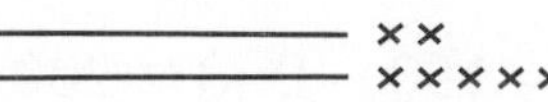

8. 36 × 2
12
▢▢
▢▢

9. 53 × 4
12
▢▢▢
▢▢▢

10. 18 × 7

11. 42 × 6

12. 3 × 65

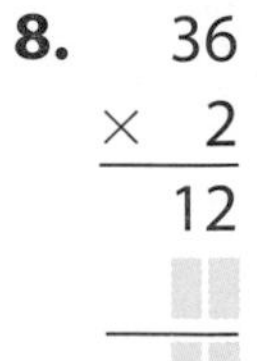

*For another example, see Set E on page 319.

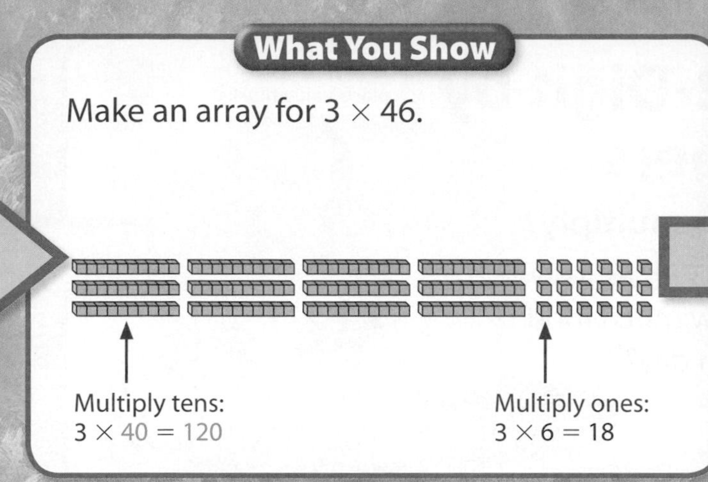

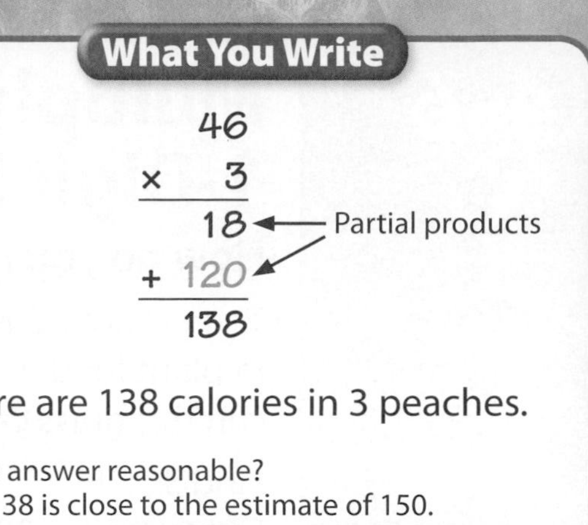

There are 138 calories in 3 peaches.

Is the answer reasonable?
Yes. 138 is close to the estimate of 150.

Problem Solving

13. Sam's family is planning a vacation. The table shows the cost of each one-way plane ticket from his town to three cities.

a How much more is a one-way ticket to Atlanta than a one-way ticket to Chicago?

b How much would Sam's family spend for 3 round-trip tickets to Kansas City?

A round-trip ticket costs twice as much as a one-way ticket.

Data

Airfare

City	Cost of One-Way Ticket
Atlanta	$87
Chicago	$59
Kansas City	$49

14. Reasoning How can knowing that $5 \times 14 = 70$ help you find 5×16? Explain your strategy.

15. Algebra The product of this whole number and 25 is greater than 50 but less than 100. What's the number?

16. How many passengers in all can be seated in 4 cable cars?

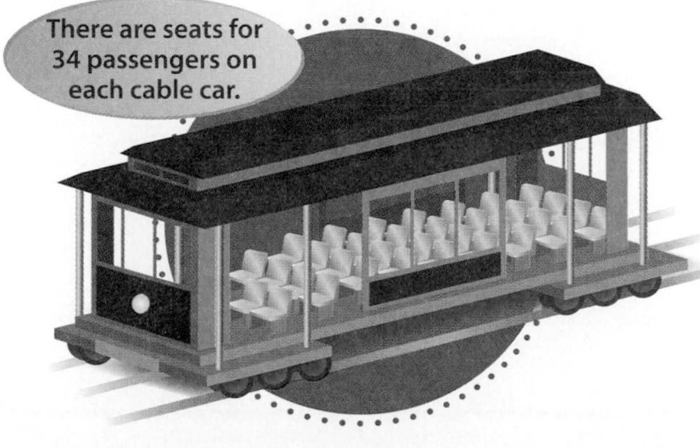

17. Writing to Explain To find 24×7, Joel adds the partial products 28 and 14. Is he correct? Explain.

18. Mr. Cruz weighed 8 cartons. Each carton weighed 17 pounds. How many pounds was this in all?

A 25 pounds
B 136 pounds
C 856 pounds
D 8,056 pounds

Lesson 14-6

NS 2.4 Solve simple problems involving multiplication of multidigit numbers by one-digit numbers (3,671 × 3 = __).

Multiplying 2-Digit by 1-Digit Numbers

Hands-On
place-value blocks

How do you regroup to multiply?

The grass carp fish can eat 3 times its weight in plant food each day. How much food can this grass carp eat each day?

Find 3 × 26.

Estimate: 3 × 30 = 90

This grass carp weighs 26 pounds.

Another Example How do you regroup to multiply without using place-value blocks?

A bluefin tuna can swim 67 feet in 1 second. How many feet can it swim in 4 seconds?

Find 4 × 67.

Estimate: 4 × 70 = 280

? feet in all

67	67	67	67

Number of feet the tuna swims each second

Step 1

Multiply the ones.
Regroup, if needed.

4 × 7 = 28 ones
Regroup 28 ones as 2 tens 8 ones.

$$\begin{array}{r} {}^{2} \\ 67 \\ \times\ 4 \\ \hline 8 \end{array}$$

Step 2

Multiply the tens.
Add regrouped tens.

4 × 6 tens = 24 tens
24 tens + 2 tens = 26 tens

$$\begin{array}{r} {}^{2} \\ 67 \\ \times\ 4 \\ \hline 268 \end{array}$$

The tuna can swim 268 feet.

Is the answer reasonable?
Yes, 268 is close to the estimate of 280.

Explain It

1. Why is a small 2 written above the 6? Why do you add the 2 instead of multiply with it?
2. A dolphin can swim 44 feet in 1 second. How many feet can it swim in 5 seconds?

Step 1

Multiply the ones. Regroup, if needed.

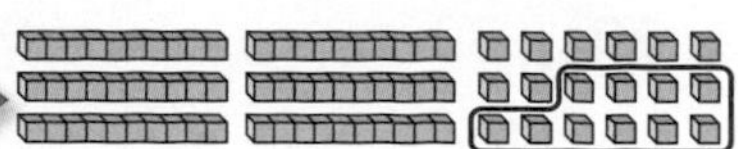

$$\begin{array}{r} {}^{1}\\ 26 \\ \times\ 3 \\ \hline 8 \end{array}$$

3 × 6 = 18 ones
Regroup 18 ones as 1 ten 8 ones.

Step 2

Multiply the tens. Add regrouped tens.

3 × 2 tens = 6 tens
6 tens + 1 ten = 7 tens

$$\begin{array}{r} {}^{1}\\ 26 \\ \times\ 3 \\ \hline 78 \end{array}$$

The fish would eat 78 pounds of food.

Guided Practice*

Do you know HOW?

In **1** and **2**, copy and complete. You may use drawings to help.

1. $\begin{array}{r} \square\\ 13 \\ \times\ 6 \\ \hline \square 8 \end{array}$

2. $\begin{array}{r} \square\\ 24 \\ \times\ 7 \\ \hline \square\square 8 \end{array}$

In **3** and **4**, find each product. You may use place-value blocks or drawings to help.

3. $\begin{array}{r} 78 \\ \times\ 4 \\ \hline \end{array}$

4. $\begin{array}{r} 35 \\ \times\ 8 \\ \hline \end{array}$

Do you UNDERSTAND?

5. In the example above, why is the estimate greater than the exact answer?

6. In the example above, how much food could this grass carp eat in 4 days?

7. A blue shark can swim 36 feet in 1 second. How many feet can it swim in 3 seconds?

Independent Practice

In **8–15**, estimate and then find each product. You may use place-value blocks or drawings to help.

8. $\begin{array}{r} 49 \\ \times\ 2 \\ \hline \end{array}$

9. $\begin{array}{r} 37 \\ \times\ 3 \\ \hline \end{array}$

10. $\begin{array}{r} 64 \\ \times\ 5 \\ \hline \end{array}$

11. $\begin{array}{r} 52 \\ \times\ 9 \\ \hline \end{array}$

12. 6 × 53

13. 7 × 38

14. 4 × 44

15. 5 × 42

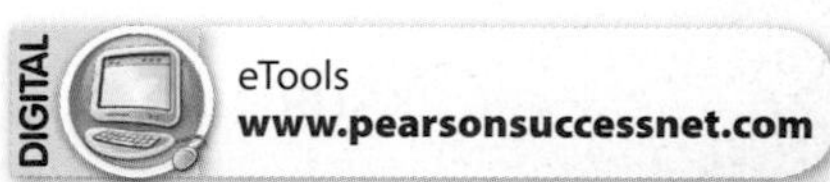

*For another example, see Set E on page 319.

Independent Practice

In **16–24**, find each product.

16. $\begin{array}{r} 46 \\ \times\ 7 \\ \hline \end{array}$ **17.** $\begin{array}{r} 23 \\ \times\ 9 \\ \hline \end{array}$ **18.** $\begin{array}{r} 85 \\ \times\ 4 \\ \hline \end{array}$ **19.** $\begin{array}{r} 19 \\ \times\ 6 \\ \hline \end{array}$ **20.** $\begin{array}{r} 89 \\ \times\ 2 \\ \hline \end{array}$

21. 2×48 **22.** 91×3 **23.** 86×5 **24.** 6×47

Problem Solving

25. The ostrich is the fastest bird on land. An ostrich can run 66 feet in 1 second. The cheetah is the fastest mammal on land. A cheetah can run 94 feet in 1 second. How many fewer feet can an ostrich run in 1 second than a cheetah?

26. The length of the body of this jerboa is shown in the picture. How far can this jerboa jump?

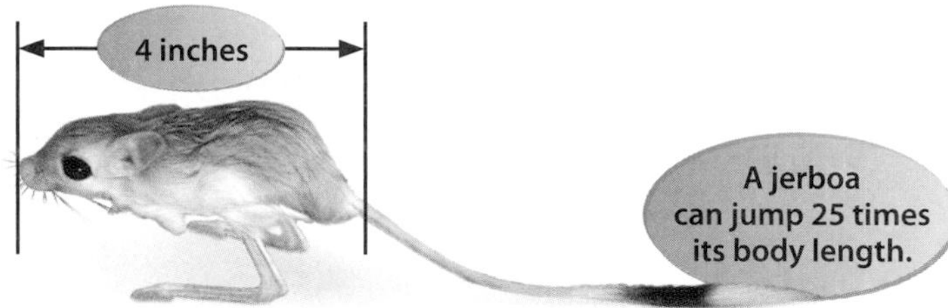

27. **Estimation** Dionne used rounding to estimate the product of 58 and another number. Her estimate of the product was 300. Which number is the best choice for the other factor?

A 3 **B** 5 **C** 8 **D** 10

28. At a museum, the visitors formed 8 tour groups to go on tours. Each group had 32 visitors. How many visitors were going on tours?

A 40 **C** 256

B 246 **D** 2,416

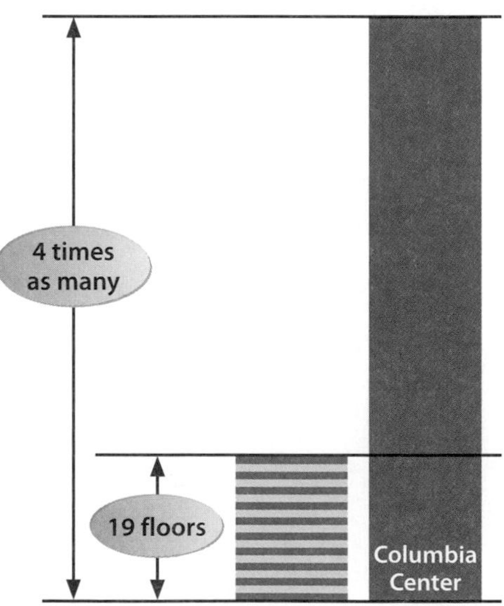

29. The Columbia Center building has 4 times as many floors as a 19-floor building. How many more floors does the Columbia Center building have than the 19-floor building?

Algebra For **30–32**, copy and complete. Use $<$, $>$, or $=$.

30. $53 \times 6 \bigcirc 308$ **31.** $19 \times 5 \bigcirc 145$ **32.** $24 \times 4 \bigcirc 12 \times 8$

Algebra Connections

Using Multiplication Properties

Remember to use the properties of multiplication to help you complete number sentences.

Commutative (Order) Property You can multiply factors in any order and the product is the same. $5 \times 9 = 9 \times 5$

Identity (One) Property When you multiply a number and 1, the product is that number. $1 \times 8 = 8$

Zero Property When you multiply a number and 0, the product is 0. $0 \times 7 = 0$

Associative (Grouping) Property You can change the grouping of the factors, and the product is the same. $(3 \times 2) \times 4 = 3 \times (2 \times 4)$

Example: $\square \times 8 = 0$

Think What number multiplied by 8 is equal to 0?

You can use the Zero Property.

$\underline{0} \times 8 = 0$

Example:

$6 \times (9 \times 7) = (6 \times \square) \times 7$

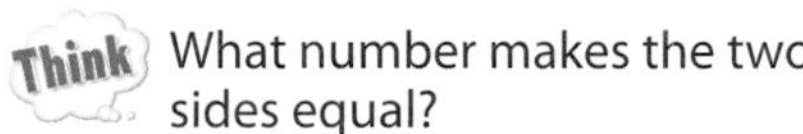

Use the Associative Property.

$6 \times (9 \times 7) = (6 \times \underline{9}) \times 7$

Copy and complete with the number that makes the two sides equal.

1. $10 \times \square = 10$

2. $12 \times 8 = 8 \times \square$

3. $6 \times (2 \times 5) = (6 \times \square) \times 5$

4. $\square \times 5 = 0$

5. $\square \times 7 = 7 \times 11$

6. $(4 \times 3) \times \square = 4 \times (3 \times 8)$

7. $6 \times \square = 9 \times 6$

8. $\square \times 9 = 9$

9. $(\square \times 7) \times 2 = 5 \times (7 \times 2)$

In **10** and **11**, copy and complete the number sentence. Solve the problem.

10. Gemma made 8 rows of stickers on a sheet with 9 stickers in each row. Then she placed the same number of stickers in 9 rows on another sheet. How many stickers were in each of these rows?

$8 \times 9 = 9 \times \square$

How many stickers did she have in all?

11. Hal and Den each have copies of the same photos. Hal arranges 5 photos on each of 6 pages in 2 albums. Den needs 5 pages in 2 albums for the same photos. How many photos are on each page in Den's albums?

$(6 \times 5) \times 2 = (5 \times \square) \times 2$

How many photos does each boy have?

12. **Write a Problem** Write a problem to match the number sentence on the right.

$\square \times 12 = 12 \times 3$

Lesson
14-7

NS 2.4 Solve simple problems involving multiplication of multidigit numbers by one-digit numbers (3,671 × 3 = __). Also **MR 2.1** Use estimation to verify the reasonableness of calculated results.

Multiplying 3- and 4-Digit Numbers

How can you multiply greater numbers?

Mrs. Roth is designing a building that is shaped like a hexagon. What is the total distance around the building?

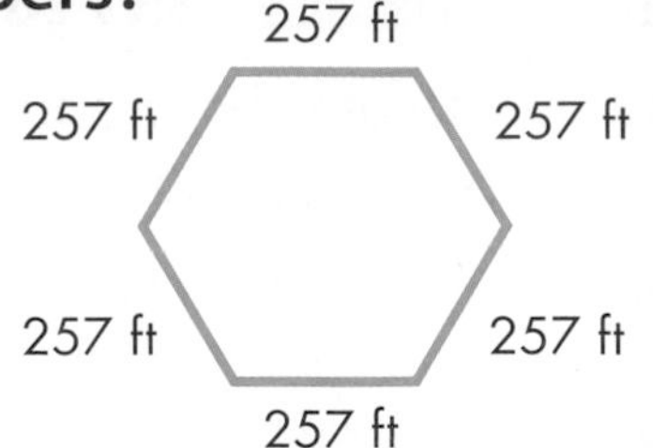

Choose an Operation Find 6 × 257.

Estimate: 6 × 300 = 1,800

Another Example How can you multiply thousands?

Mr. Kim is designing a factory that is shaped like a square. Each side of the factory is 1,728 feet long. What is the total distance around the factory?

Choose an Operation You have already learned that multiplication can be used to join equal groups. Since 4 equal groups of 1,728 are being joined, multiply. Find 4 × 1,728.

Estimate: 4 × 2,000 = 8,000

Step 1

Multiply the ones. Regroup if needed.

```
    3
 1,728
×    4
     2
```

Step 2

Multiply the tens. Add any regrouped tens. Regroup if needed.

```
   13
 1,728
×    4
    12
```

Step 3

Multiply the hundreds. Add any regrouped hundreds. Regroup if needed.

```
  213
 1,728
×    4
   912
```

Step 4

Multiply the thousands. Add any regrouped thousands.

```
 2 13
 1,728
×    4
 6,912
```

The total distance around the factory is 6,912 feet. The answer is reasonable.

Explain It

1. What does the small 3 mean in Step 1?
2. Mrs. Vega is designing a park that is shaped like an equilateral triangle. Each side of the park is 2,456 feet long. What is the total distance around the park?

Step 1

Multiply the ones. Regroup if needed.

$$\begin{array}{r} {}^{4} \\ 257 \\ \times \quad 6 \\ \hline 2 \end{array}$$

Step 2

Multiply the tens. Add any regrouped tens. Regroup if needed.

$$\begin{array}{r} {}^{3\,4} \\ 257 \\ \times \quad 6 \\ \hline 42 \end{array}$$

Step 3

Multiply the hundreds. Add any regrouped hundreds.

$$\begin{array}{r} {}^{3\,4} \\ 257 \\ \times \quad 6 \\ \hline 1{,}542 \end{array}$$

The total distance around the building is 1,542 feet.

Guided Practice*

Do you know HOW?

In **1–4**, copy and complete. Find the product.

1.
$$\begin{array}{r} {}^{\square\,2} \\ 249 \\ \times \quad 3 \\ \hline \square\square 7 \end{array}$$

2.
$$\begin{array}{r} {}^{\square\,\square} \\ 187 \\ \times \quad 5 \\ \hline \square\square 5 \end{array}$$

3.
$$\begin{array}{r} {}^{\square\,\square\,5} \\ 1{,}328 \\ \times \quad 7 \\ \hline \square{,}\square\square 6 \end{array}$$

4.
$$\begin{array}{r} {}^{\square\,\square\,\square} \\ 2{,}396 \\ \times \quad 4 \\ \hline \square{,}\square\square 4 \end{array}$$

Do you UNDERSTAND?

In **5–7**, use the example above.

5. After you multiply the tens, how many regrouped tens do you add?

6. **Writing to Explain** Is the answer 1,542 feet reasonable? Explain.

7. Suppose Mrs. Roth changes the shape of the building into an octagon with each side 257 feet long. What would the total distance around the building be?

Independent Practice

Leveled Practice In **8** and **9**, copy and complete. In **10–17**, find each product.

8.
$$\begin{array}{r} {}^{\square\,\square} \\ 318 \\ \times \quad 9 \\ \hline \square{,}\square\square 2 \end{array}$$

9.
$$\begin{array}{r} {}^{\square\,\square} \\ 4{,}057 \\ \times \quad 6 \\ \hline \square\square{,}\square\square 2 \end{array}$$

10. $\begin{array}{r} 609 \\ \times \quad 8 \\ \hline \end{array}$

11. $\begin{array}{r} 1{,}946 \\ \times \quad 2 \\ \hline \end{array}$

12. $\begin{array}{r} 5{,}172 \\ \times \quad 9 \\ \hline \end{array}$

13. $\begin{array}{r} 746 \\ \times \quad 3 \\ \hline \end{array}$

14. $\begin{array}{r} 2{,}803 \\ \times \quad 5 \\ \hline \end{array}$

15. $\begin{array}{r} 492 \\ \times \quad 7 \\ \hline \end{array}$

16. $\begin{array}{r} 3{,}748 \\ \times \quad 4 \\ \hline \end{array}$

17. $\begin{array}{r} 142 \\ \times \quad 8 \\ \hline \end{array}$

*For another example, see Set E on page 319.

Independent Practice

In **18–22**, find the product.

18. 518×4

19. $3{,}792 \times 7$

20. $6{,}240 \times 6$

21. 904×5

22. $1{,}637 \times 9$

Problem Solving

23. Marci enjoys visiting bridges. The table shows the lengths of bridges in different cities.

a How many feet would Marci walk if she walked across the Rainbow Bridge and then walked back across the bridge to where she started?

b Which bridge is almost 1,000 feet longer than the St. Johns Bridge?

Bridge Lengths

Name of Bridge	Length
Delaware Memorial	2,150 ft
Golden Gate	4,200 ft
Rainbow	950 ft
St. Johns	1,207 ft

c How many feet longer is the Golden Gate Bridge than the St. Johns Bridge?

24. Reasoning If you know that $5 \times 4{,}200 = 21{,}000$, how can you use this product to find $6 \times 4{,}200$? Explain your answer.

25. Algebra The product of 3 and this 3-digit number is greater than 600 but less than 606. What is the 3-digit number?

26. The Chrysler Building is 1,046 feet tall. The Sears Tower is 1,450 feet tall. How many feet taller is the Sears Tower than the Chrysler Building?

Sears Tower	1,450 feet tall	
Chrysler Building	1,046	?

27. On Sunday, 2,158 cars drove over a bridge. Four times as many cars drove over the bridge on Monday as on Sunday. How many cars drove over the bridge on Monday?

A 6,158 **C** 8,722

B 8,632 **D** 9,632

28. The Transamerica Pyramid, located in San Francisco, California, has 48 floors. The 48th floor is 2,025 square feet. Round 2,025 to the nearest hundred.

29. A hippopotamus can eat 130 pounds of vegetable matter a day. How many pounds of vegetable matter can a hippopotamus eat in a week?

A 91 **C** 910

B 137 **D** 1,040

Mixed Problem Solving

Read the article below. Then, answer the questions.

Not Just a Pretty Design

The garden spider is finally still after about an hour of work. It is sitting near the center of the web it has made. It is waiting for an insect to become trapped. The insect will be its food.

The web looks like a bicycle wheel with spokes. The silk threads that come out from the center point are called radial threads. Other silk threads go across the spokes to make circle shapes, or spirals. These spiral threads are sticky.

A garden spider's web can be as wide as 16 inches. The radial threads in the web are between 5 and 10 inches long. There are hundreds of spiral threads. Some of the spiral threads are less than 1 inch long. Others can be as long as 2 inches.

You can see that the garden spider's web is more than just a pretty design. It is a complex trap with many parts.

This garden spider's web has 30 radial threads.

1. In the last sentence of the article, what does the word complex mean?

2. What do you think will happen next?

3. If each radial thread is about 8 inches long, about how long in all are the radial threads of this web?

In **4** and **5**, use the table.

4. How much longer is a Tarantula than a Funnel-web spider?

5. **Strategy Focus** Use the strategy Draw a Picture and Write a Number Sentence to solve this problem.

   Which kind of spider is about 5 times as long as the Black Widow?

Data

Kind of Spider	Body Length (millimeters)
Black Widow	19 mm
Funnel-web	12 mm
Tarantula	100 mm
Wolf	25 mm

Lesson
14-8

MR 2.0 Use strategies, skills, and concepts in finding solutions.
NS 2.4 🔑 Solve simple problems involving multiplication of multidigit numbers by one-digit numbers (3,671 × 3 = __).
Also NS 2.0

Problem Solving

Draw a Picture and Write a Number Sentence

Oscar bought 5 cases of bottled water. How many bottles of water did Oscar buy?

24 bottles per case

Another Example

Melody wants to buy a case of juice boxes. There are 3 times as many boxes in a jumbo case as in a regular case. How many juice boxes are in a jumbo case?

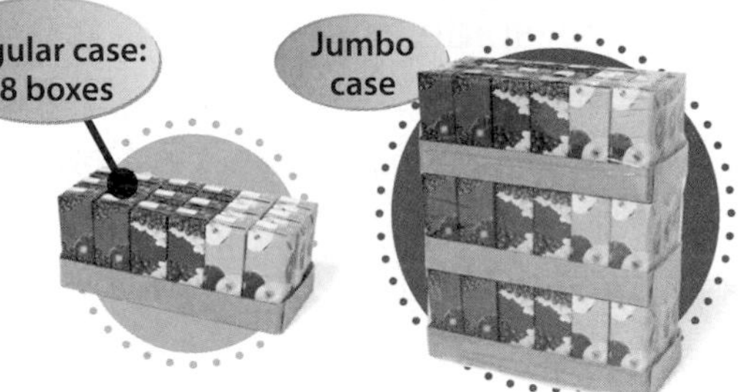

Plan

Use a picture or a diagram to show what you know.

Regular Case	18			
Jumbo Case	18	18	18	3 times as many

? juice boxes

Then write a number sentence to find the number that is 3 times as many as 18.

$3 \times 18 = \square$

Solve

Find 3×18.

$$\begin{array}{r} \scriptsize 2 \\ 18 \\ \times \ 3 \\ \hline 54 \end{array}$$

A jumbo case has 54 juice boxes.

Check

Make sure the answer is reasonable.

Estimate to check.

18 rounds to 20.

$20 \times 3 = 60$

54 is close to 60, so the answer is reasonable.

Explain It

1. **Number Sense** Why can't you use the same type of diagram for this problem as you used for the problem at the top of the page?
2. Describe another way that you could check that the answer to the problem above is correct.

Plan

Use a picture or a diagram to show what you know.

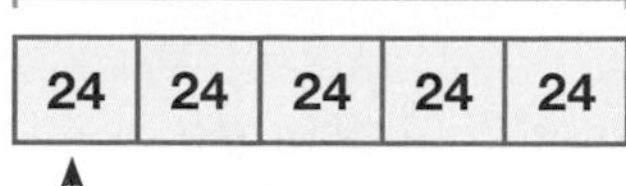

You know the number in each group and that the groups are equal. So you can multiply to find the total.

Solve

Find 5×24.

$$\begin{array}{r} 24 \\ \times \ \ 5 \\ \hline 120 \end{array}$$

Oscar bought 120 bottles of water.

Check

Make sure the answer is reasonable.

Estimate to check.

24 rounds to 20.

$20 \times 5 = 100$

The answer is reasonable because 120 is close to 100.

Guided Practice*

Do you know HOW?

1. A doll collection is displayed in 8 rows with 16 dolls in each row. How many dolls are in the collection?

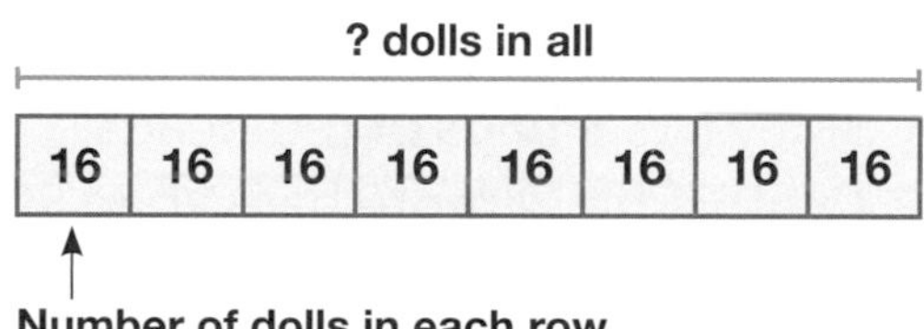

Do you UNDERSTAND?

2. **Writing to Explain** Why do you multiply to solve Problem 1?

3. **Write a Problem** Write a problem that can be solved by drawing a picture. Draw the picture. Solve.

Independent Practice

4. Eduardo has 36 football cards. He has 3 times as many baseball cards. How many baseball cards does he have?

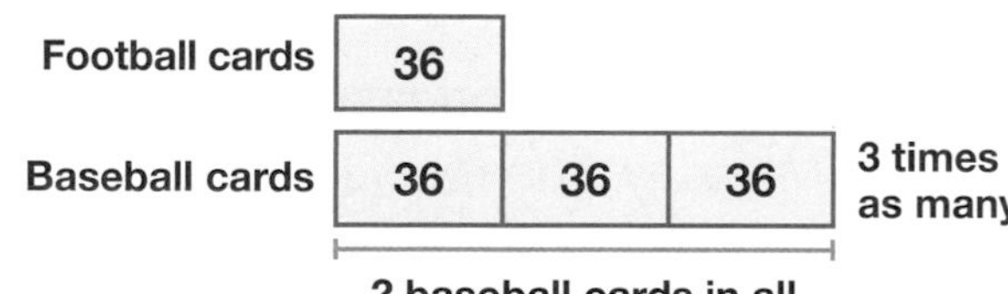

5. **Writing to Explain** Noah has 95 books to put on 4 shelves. If he puts 24 books on each shelf, will all the books fit on the shelves?

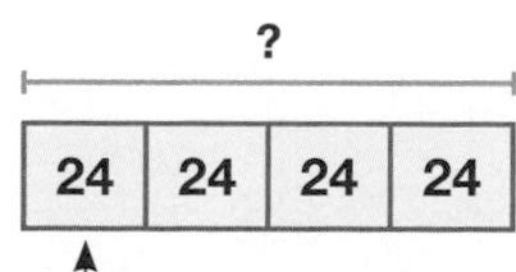

- What do I know?
- What am I asked to find?
- What diagram can I use to help understand the problem?
- Can I use addition, subtraction, multiplication, or division?
- Is all of my work correct?
- Did I answer the right question?
- Is my answer reasonable?

*For another example, see Set F on page 319.

Independent Practice

The table shows about how many calories a 100-pound person uses doing different activities. Use the table for **6–8**.

Calories Used in 1 Minute	
Activity	**Number of Calories**
Biking	5
Jogging	8
Rollerblading	4
Walking	4

6. Martha went jogging for 15 minutes. How many calories did she use?

? calories in all

8	8	8	8	8	8	8	8	8	8	8	8	8	8	8

Number of calories used each minute

7. Julio walked for 25 minutes. Then he went rollerblading for 20 minutes. How many calories did he use?

8. Cathy plans to ride her bike for 15 minutes every day. How many calories will she use in a week?

9. Frank rode his bike for an hour. Then he went rollerblading for 25 minutes. How many more minutes did he spend riding his bike than rollerblading?

10. **Estimation** The U.S. Department of Health reports that many children spend about 32 hours each week in front of a computer screen. About how many hours is that in a month?

1 month is about 4 weeks.

11. Stacy has 3 bags of red beads. Cynthia has 2 more bags than Stacy. There are 24 beads in each bag.

a How many beads does each girl have?

b How many beads do the girls have all together?

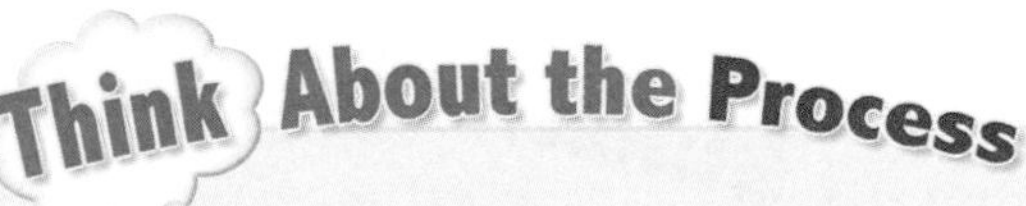

12. Mike earns \$4 an hour doing yard work. He worked 12 hours last week and 23 hours this week. Which number sentence shows how much he earned this week?

A \$23 + \$12 = ▢

B 12 × \$4 = ▢

C 23 × \$4 = ▢

D (23 × \$4) × 7 = ▢

13. Katy read 46 pages of a book on Monday. She read 25 pages on Tuesday. She still has 34 pages to read. Which number sentence shows how many pages are in the book?

A 46 + 25 = ▢

B 46 − 34 = ▢

C (46 + 25) − 34 = ▢

D 46 + 25 + 34 = ▢

Write the place of the underlined digit. Then write its value.

1. 439,702 **2.** 27,149 **3.** 813,658

Find each sum or difference. Estimate to check if the answer is reasonable.

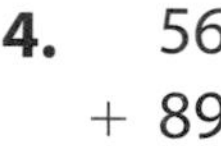

4. $\begin{array}{r} 56 \\ +\ 89 \\ \hline \end{array}$ **5.** $\begin{array}{r} 302 \\ -\ 74 \\ \hline \end{array}$ **6.** $\begin{array}{r} 641 \\ -\ 253 \\ \hline \end{array}$ **7.** $\begin{array}{r} 9{,}875 \\ +\ 4{,}136 \\ \hline \end{array}$

Estimate and then find each product.

8. $\begin{array}{r} 47 \\ \times\ 6 \\ \hline \end{array}$ **9.** 8×93 **10.** $\begin{array}{r} 726 \\ \times\ 4 \\ \hline \end{array}$ **11.** $\begin{array}{r} 1{,}946 \\ \times\ 3 \\ \hline \end{array}$ **12.** $\begin{array}{r} 8{,}504 \\ \times\ 7 \\ \hline \end{array}$

Find each quotient.

13. $36 \div 6 = \square$ **14.** $14 \div 2 = \square$ **15.** $0 \div 4 = \square$ **16.** $81 \div 9 = \square$

Add or subtract. Write each sum or difference in simplest form.

17. $\frac{1}{4} + \frac{1}{4}$ **18.** $\frac{3}{12} + \frac{1}{12}$ **19.** $\frac{6}{10} - \frac{2}{10}$ **20.** $\frac{7}{8} - \frac{3}{8}$

Error Search Find each product or quotient that is not correct. Write it correctly and explain the error.

21. $3 \times 16 = 38$ **22.** $5 \times 45 = 225$ **23.** $24 \div 3 = 7$ **24.** $42 \div 6 = 7$

Number Sense

Estimating and Reasoning Write true or false for each statement. If it is false, explain why.

25. The product of 9 and 0 is greater than 90.

26. The quotient $18 \div 2$ is less than 10.

27. The difference $8{,}116 - 8{,}001$ is greater than 100.

28. The product 7×19 is greater than 7×30.

29. The product $3 \times 3 \times 3$ is greater than 30.

Topic 14
Test Prep

1. Jillian bought 7 packages of paper. Each package had 500 sheets. How many sheets of paper did Jillian buy? (14-1)

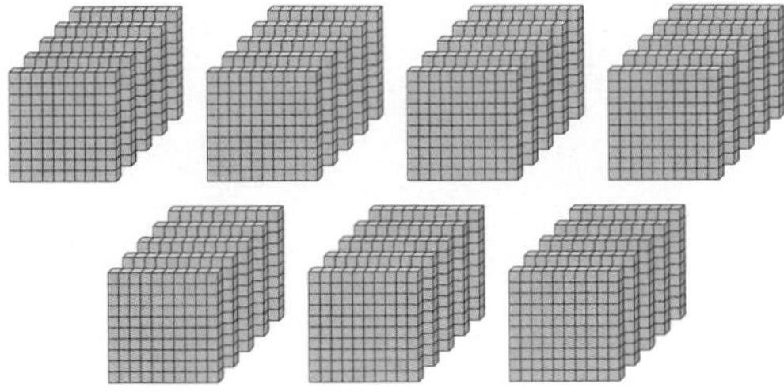

A 35,000

B 3,500

C 135

D 35

2. There are 128 fluid ounces in a gallon. If Stephanie made 5 gallons of punch, which number sentence shows the best way to estimate how many fluid ounces of punch she made? (14-2)

A $5 \times 100 = 500$

B $5 \times 200 = 1{,}000$

C $10 \times 100 = 1{,}000$

D $10 \times 200 = 2{,}000$

3. Mr. Gomez bought 26 packages of juice boxes for the school picnic. Each package had 8 juice boxes. How many juice boxes did he buy? (14-6)

A 214

B 208

C 202

D 168

4. Vella's bookcase has 6 shelves. Each shelf displays 3 dolls. Which number sentence shows how many dolls are displayed in the bookcase? (14-8)

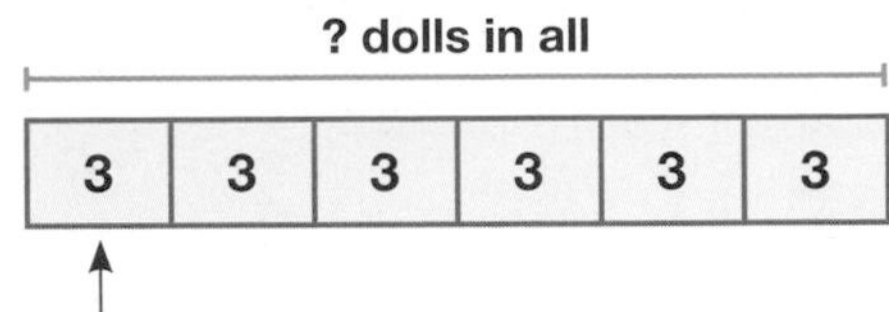

A $6 \times 3 = 18$

B $6 \div 3 = 2$

C $6 + 3 = 9$

D $6 - 3 = 3$

5. Henry bought 3 bags of oranges. Each bag had 16 oranges. How many oranges did he buy? Use the array to solve. (14-3)

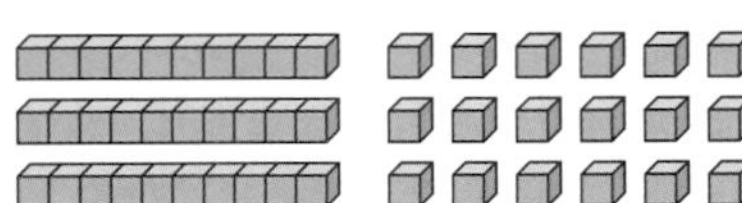

A 19

B 38

C 48

D 54

6. When you multiply 6×25, which pair of partial products do you find? (14-4)

A 300 and 12

B 30 and 12

C 30 and 120

D 300 and 120

7. What is 6×804? (14-7)

A 4,224

B 4,624

C 4,804

D 4,824

8. Which addition sentence shows how to use partial products to find 2×178? (14-4)

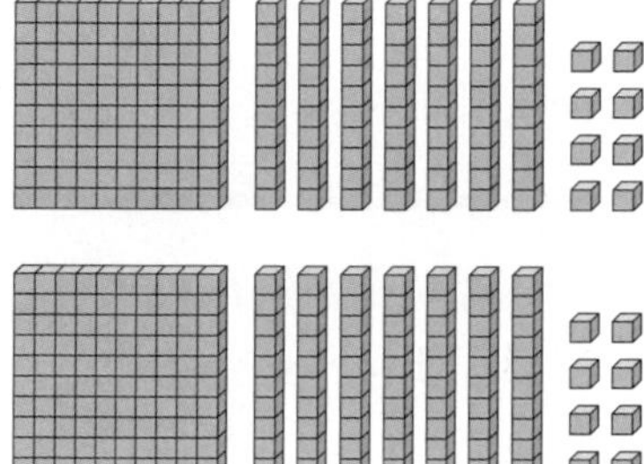

A $200 + 140 + 16 = 356$

B $200 + 140 + 14 = 354$

C $200 + 14 + 16 = 230$

D $2 + 14 + 8 = 24$

9. What is $4 \times 7{,}375$? (14-7)

A 28,280

B 29,200

C 29,480

D 29,500

10. Vi gets \$35 a day to babysit. How much does she get if she babysits 9 days? (14-6)

A \$2,745

B \$324

C \$315

D \$275

11. What is the product? (14-5)

$$\begin{array}{r} 37 \\ \times \quad 6 \\ \hline 42 \\ \square\square\square \\ \hline \square\square\square \end{array}$$

A 60

B 122

C 192

D 222

12. Which number sentence comes next in the pattern? (14-1)

$8 \times 6 = 48$
$8 \times 60 = 480$
$8 \times 600 = 4{,}800$

A $8 \times 600 = 48{,}000$

B $8 \times 6{,}000 = 48{,}000$

C $80 \times 60 = 4{,}800$

D $80 \times 600 = 48{,}000$

13. Fun and Learn Preschool bought 112 bags of sand. Each bag weighed 5 pounds. How many pounds of sand did they buy? (14-7)

A 117 pounds

B 550 pounds

C 560 pounds

D 5,510 pounds

Reteaching

Set A, pages 294–295

Find $7 \times 4{,}000$.

Use basic facts and patterns.

$7 \times 4 = 28$ ← basic fact
$7 \times 40 = 280$
$7 \times 400 = 2{,}800$
$7 \times 4{,}000 = 28{,}000$

$7 \times 4{,}000 = 28{,}000$

Remember that when the product of a basic fact contains a zero, that zero is not part of the pattern.

Use place-value blocks or patterns to find the product.

1. 7×300 **2.** $9 \times 6{,}000$

3. $4 \times 5{,}000$ **4.** 5×200

5. 8×900 **6.** $3 \times 3{,}000$

Set B, pages 296–297

Estimate 6×218.

Round 218 to the nearest hundred. Then multiply.

6×218
↓ 218 rounds to 200.
$6 \times 200 = 1{,}200$

6×200 is about 1,200.

Remember that you round up if the next digit to the right of the rounding place is 5 or greater and round down if that digit is 4 or less.

Estimate each product.

1. 5×39 **2.** 8×67

3. 3×472 **4.** 6×821

5. $4 \times 2{,}653$ **6.** $9 \times 1{,}379$

Set C, pages 298–299

Draw an array to find 4×23.

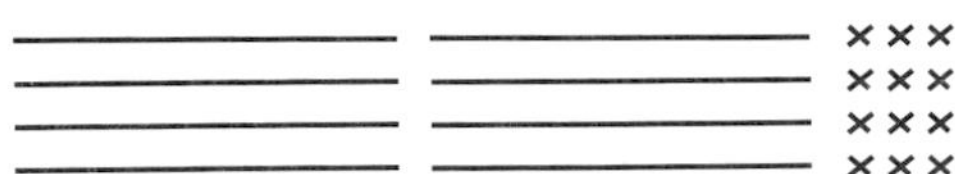

Count by tens.
10, 20, 30, 40, 50, 60, 70, 80

Then count by ones to find the total.
81, 82, 83, 84, 85, 86, 87, 88, 89, 90, 91, 92

$4 \times 23 = 92$

Remember to keep your drawings simple.

Find each product. Use place-value blocks or draw a picture to help.

1. 3×27 **2.** 4×18

3. 5×14 **4.** 3×32

5. 7×31 **6.** 4×42

Reteaching

Set D, pages 300–301

Break apart numbers to find 2×134.

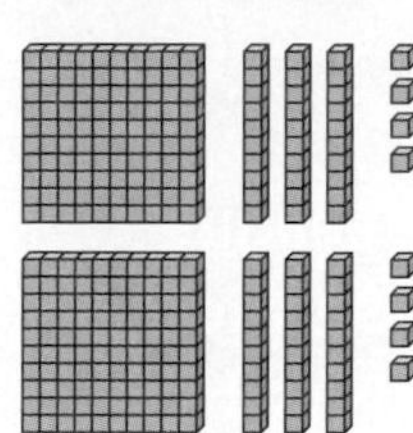

2 rows of 1 hundred = 2 hundreds or 200

2 rows of 3 tens = 6 tens or 60

2 rows of 4 ones = 8 ones or 8

200, 60, and 8 are partial products.

Add the partial products to find the product.
$200 + 60 + 8 = 268$

Remember to include a zero when you record the value of the tens.

Find each product. You may use place-value blocks or draw a picture to help.

1. 4×73
2. 2×59
3. 2×138
4. 3×264
5. $4 \times 1{,}826$
6. $5 \times 3{,}917$

Set E, pages 302–306, 308–310

Find 6×27.

$$\begin{array}{r} 27 \\ \times \quad 6 \\ \hline 42 \\ +\ 120 \\ \hline 162 \end{array}$$

42 and 120 are partial products

Find 4×359.

$$\begin{array}{r} {}^{2\,3} \\ 359 \\ \times \quad 4 \\ \hline 1{,}436 \end{array}$$

- Multiply the ones. Regroup.
- Multiply the tens. Add regrouped tens.
- Multiply the hundreds. Add regrouped hundreds.

Remember to check that your answer is reasonable.

Estimate and then find each product.

1. 29×6
2. 42×5
3. 378×7
4. 546×3
5. $1{,}695 \times 4$
6. $7{,}198 \times 9$

Set F, pages 312–314

Kendra has 24 planet stickers. She has 4 times as many flower stickers. How many flower stickers does she have?

? flower stickers in all

flower stickers	24	24	24	24	4 times as many
planet stickers	24				

$4 \times 24 = 96$ flower stickers

Remember that drawing a picture can help you.

Draw a picture. Write a number sentence and solve.

1. Melody buys 5 bags of marbles. Each bag has 15 marbles in it. How many marbles does she buy in all?

Topic 15

Dividing by 1-Digit Numbers

1 When Little League began in 1939, there were 30 players. How many teams did they form? You will find out out in Lesson 15-4.

2 How much can a coral reef grow in one year? You will find out in Lesson 15-5.

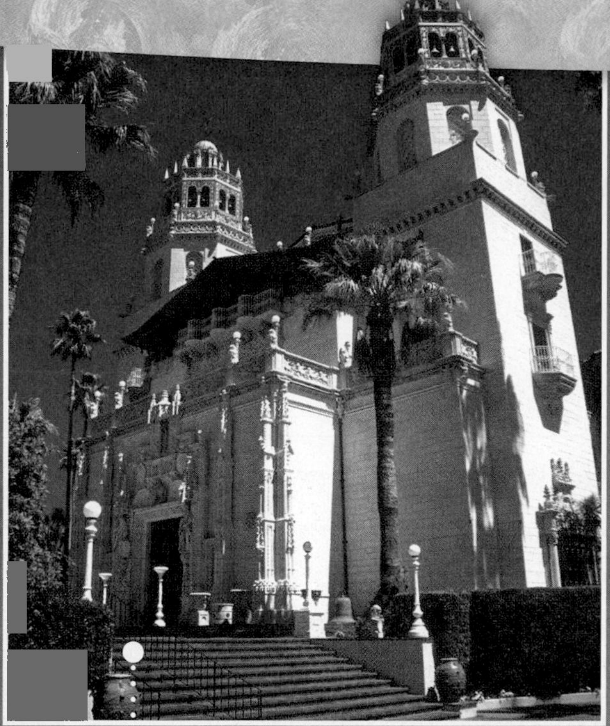

3 How many stairs will you climb during a tour of Hearst Castle in San Simeon, California? You will find out in Lesson 15-1.

4 How many gallons of air does a person breathe each day? Find out in Lesson 15-2.

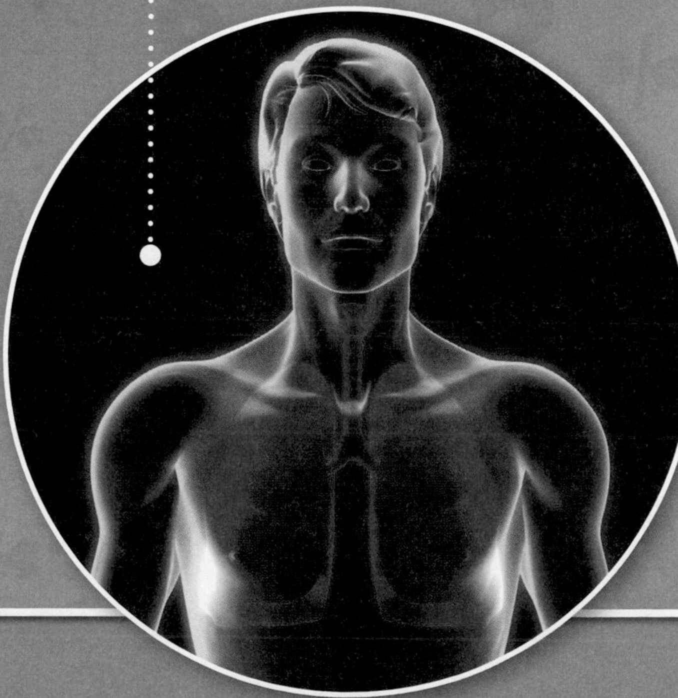

Review What You Know!

Vocabulary

Choose the best term from the box.

- division
- quotient
- fact
- regroup

1. The answer in division is called the ___?___.

2. A ___?___ family shows how multiplication and division are related.

3. When there are not enough ones to subtract, you can ___?___ tens for ones.

Division Facts

Divide.

4. $12 \div 3$ **5.** $18 \div 2$ **6.** $30 \div 6$

7. $54 \div 9$ **8.** $64 \div 8$ **9.** $63 \div 7$

Multiplication

Multiply.

10. 4×19 **11.** 7×14 **12.** 4×23

Subtraction

Subtract.

13. $72 - 60$ **14.** $346 - 200$

15. $1{,}308 - 1{,}200$ **16.** $4{,}275 - 3{,}000$

17. Writing to Explain Lea poured 40 ounces of paint into 5 jars. Each jar had the same amount of paint. How much paint was in each jar? Draw a picture and solve. Explain why your drawing helps.

Lesson

15-1

NS 2.5 Solve division problems in which a multidigit number is evenly divided by a one-digit number (135 ÷ 5 = __).

Mental Math

How can you divide multiples of 10, 100, and 1,000 using patterns?

You know that 12 ÷ 3 = 4.

120 ÷ 3 = 40

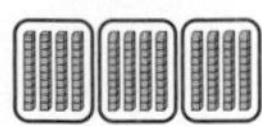

1,200 ÷ 3 = 400

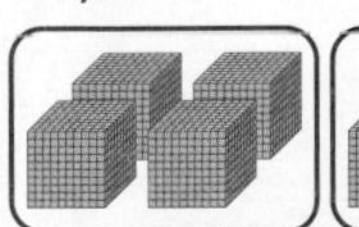

12,000 ÷ 3 = 4,000

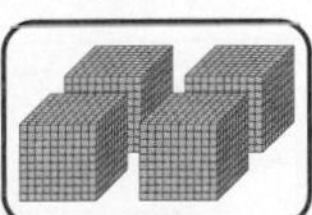

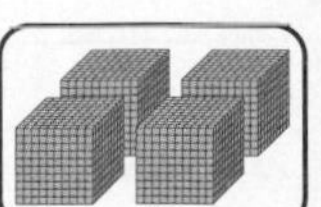

Guided Practice*

Do you know HOW?

In **1–4**, use patterns and mental math to find each quotient.

1. 36 ÷ 4
360 ÷ 4
3,600 ÷ 4

2. 40 ÷ 8
400 ÷ 8
4,000 ÷ 8

3. 180 ÷ 6

4. 1,400 ÷ 2

Do you UNDERSTAND?

5. Look at Another Way above. Why are 2 zeros written to the right of 4?

6. What basic fact can you use to find the quotient of 1,800 ÷ 3?

7. Jay says, "28 ÷ 4 is 7, so 2,800 ÷ 4 is 700." Do you agree? Explain.

Independent Practice

In **8–15**, use patterns to find each quotient.

8. 15 ÷ 3
150 ÷ 3
1,500 ÷ 3

9. 54 ÷ 9
540 ÷ 9
5,400 ÷ 9

10. 32 ÷ 4
320 ÷ 4
3,200 ÷ 4

11. 72 ÷ 8
720 ÷ 8
7,200 ÷ 8

12. 21 ÷ 7
210 ÷ 7
2,100 ÷ 7

13. 12 ÷ 6
120 ÷ 6
1,200 ÷ 6

14. 20 ÷ 5
200 ÷ 5
2,000 ÷ 5

15. 63 ÷ 9
630 ÷ 9
6,300 ÷ 9

In **16–25**, use mental math to find each quotient.

16. 160 ÷ 2 **17.** 4,900 ÷ 7 **18.** 60 ÷ 3 **19.** 350 ÷ 5 **20.** 5,600 ÷ 8

21. 3,200 ÷ 8 **22.** 120 ÷ 6 **23.** 80 ÷ 4 **24.** 360 ÷ 6 **25.** 8,100 ÷ 9

*For another example, see Set A on page 346.

One Way

Find 2,400 ÷ 6.

Use place value.

2,400 is the same as 24 × 100 or 24 hundreds.

24 ÷ 6 = 4
So, 24 hundreds ÷ 6 = 4 hundreds.

2,400 ÷ 6 = 400

Another Way

Find 2,400 ÷ 6.

Use a rule.

24 ÷ 6 = 4
So, 2,400 ÷ 6 is 4 followed by 2 zeros.

2,400 ÷ 6 = 400

Problem Solving

For **26–30**, use the table at the right.

26. How many times does a horse's heart beat in one minute?

27. How many times does a chicken's heart beat in one minute?

28. In 5 minutes, how many more times does a bat's heart beat than a chicken's heart?

Data

Animal Heart Rates

Animal	Number of Heartbeats in 5 Minutes
Bat	3,500
Chicken	1,500
Frog	150
Horse	200
Mouse	3,100

29. In 5 minutes, which animal's heart beats 10 times the number that a frog's heart beats?

30. Write the animals' names in order from fewest to most heartbeats in 5 minutes.

31. Kara leads tours in the Hearst Castle. During 2 tours she climbed a total of 800 stairs. If the tours were exactly the same, how many stairs did she climb during each tour?

Most tours of Hearst Castle include climbing 150 to 400 stairs.

32. The 1,400 people who attended a music concert were equally divided into 7 seating areas. How many people were in each seating area?

A 140 **C** 1,393

B 200 **D** 1,407

33. **Number Sense** How many $5 bills make $30? How many make $300?

Lesson

15-2

MR 2.1 Use estimation to verify the reasonableness of calculated results. Also **NS 2.5**

Estimating Quotients

How do you estimate with division?

The Mills family is planning a car trip that will be 1,764 miles long. The family wants to drive an equal number of miles on each of 6 days. About how many miles should the family drive each day?

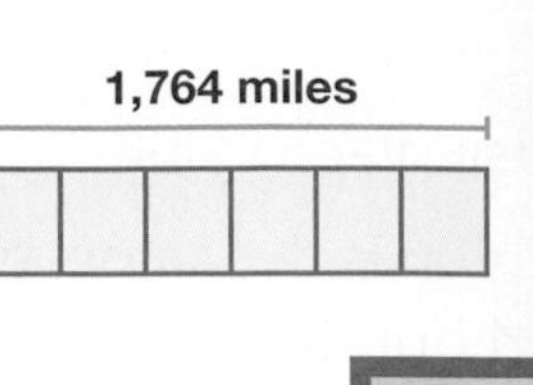

Estimate You need to know *about* how many miles, so an estimate is enough.

Guided Practice*

Do you know HOW?

In **1–8**, estimate each quotient.

1. 83 ÷ 4

2. 248 ÷ 5

3. 572 ÷ 7

4. 4,138 ÷ 6

5. 91 ÷ 9

6. 306 ÷ 5

7. 2,293 ÷ 8

8. 2,710 ÷ 4

Do you UNDERSTAND?

9. In the example above, why is 1,800 ÷ 6 equal to 300 and not 30?

10. What division could you use to estimate 317 ÷ 4?

11. Timmy wants to put 346 toy cars into 5 equal groups. About how many cars should he put in each group?

Independent Practice

In **12–35**, estimate each quotient.

12. 73 ÷ 7

13. 164 ÷ 2

14. 479 ÷ 8

15. 172 ÷ 3

16. 416 ÷ 5

17. 1,983 ÷ 4

18. 361 ÷ 9

19. 505 ÷ 7

20. 7,168 ÷ 9

21. 1,329 ÷ 6

22. 324 ÷ 8

23. 546 ÷ 9

24. 729 ÷ 8

25. 2,036 ÷ 5

26. 697 ÷ 7

27. 812 ÷ 9

28. 364 ÷ 4

29. 206 ÷ 4

30. 427 ÷ 7

31. 489 ÷ 6

32. 278 ÷ 7

33. 8,097 ÷ 9

34. 2,536 ÷ 5

35. 4,917 ÷ 7

For another example, see Set A on page 346.

Use a division fact.

There are 6 days. What numbers can be divided evenly by 6?

6, 12, 18, and so on.

1,764 miles is about 1,800 miles.

For division, 1,800 and 6 are numbers that are easy to work with.

Then use mental math.

Find 1,800 ÷ 6.

18 ÷ 6 = 3, so 1,800 ÷ 6 = 300.

The family should drive about 300 miles each day.

Problem Solving

For **36–38**, use the table at the right.

Ramos Family Vacation Ideas Car Trip Distances

Trip	Number of Miles
Blue Mountain	1,135
Camp Carlson	1,589
Forest Park	473
River Land	766
Sands Point Beach	2,740

36. The Ramos family wants to take 4 days to drive to River Land. The family wants to drive an equal number of miles each day. About how many miles should the family drive each day?

37. About how many more miles is the trip to Camp Carlson than to Forest Park?

38. **Reasonableness** The Ramos family wants to take 4 days to drive to Blue Mountain. They plan to drive about 300 miles each day. Is this reasonable? Explain.

39. Ashley has 87 insects in her nature collection. She has three times as many leaves as insects in her collection. How many leaves does Ashley have in her collection?

40. Mr. Lowell bought 8 baseball caps. All of the caps were the same price. The total cost was $72. What is the cost of each baseball cap?

A $576 **B** $80 **C** $64 **D** $9

41. **Algebra** What number makes the number sentence true?

179 × ☐ = 179

42. In 3 days, a person breathes about 9,100 gallons of air. About how many gallons of air does a person breathe in 1 day?

Lesson

15-3

NS 2.5 Solve division problems in which a multidigit number is evenly divided by a one-digit number (135 ÷ 5 = __) Also MR 2.3.

Connecting Models and Symbols

Hands-On
place-value blocks

How can you model division with greater numbers?

The third graders made 56 sandwiches for a picnic. They put an equal number of sandwiches on each of 4 plates. How many sandwiches are on each plate?

Another Example How can place value help you divide?

Helen has 54 baseball cards. She wants to put an equal number of cards in each of 3 albums. How many cards will go in each album?

Choose an Operation Division is used to find the size of equal groups. Helen needs to find 54 ÷ 3.

In Lesson 4-5, you learned how to use place value to help subtract. Now you will use place value to help divide.

Estimate Use numbers that are easy to divide. 60 is close to 54 and 60 ÷ 3 = 20. There should be about 20 cards in each album.

Draw place-value blocks to show 54.

$3\overline{)54}$

Divide the tens into 3 equal groups.

$$\begin{array}{r} 1 \\ 3\overline{)54} \\ -3 \end{array}$$

1 ten in each group
3 tens used

Regroup the extra tens as ones.

$$\begin{array}{r} 1 \\ 3\overline{)54} \\ -3 \\ \hline 2 \end{array}$$

2 tens are left

Divide the ones into 3 equal groups.

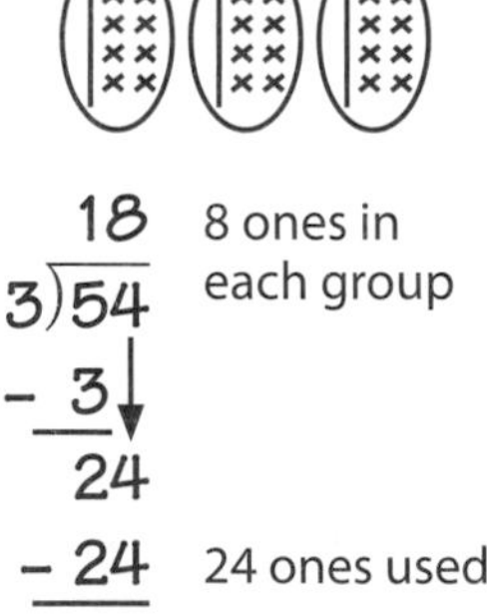

$$\begin{array}{r} 18 \\ 3\overline{)54} \\ -3\downarrow \\ \hline 24 \\ -24 \\ \hline 0 \end{array}$$

8 ones in each group
24 ones used
No ones left

There will be 18 cards in each album.

Explain It

1. Why do you trade the tens for ones?

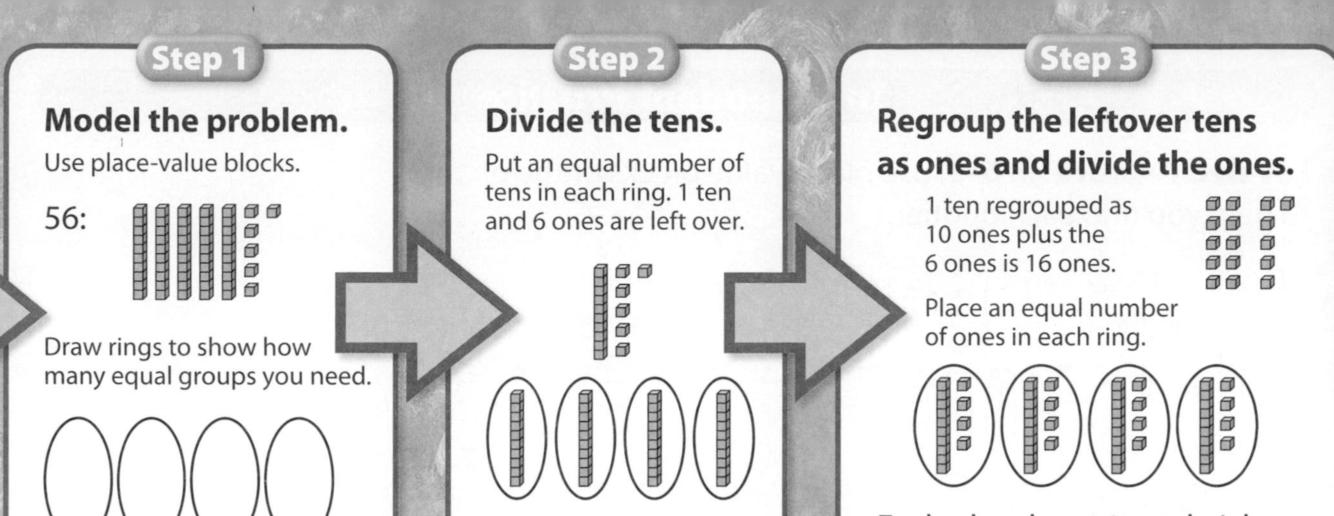

Guided Practice*

Do you know HOW?

Use place-value blocks or the pictures. Copy and complete to find the quotient.

1. 32 ÷ 2

a Draw place-value blocks to show 32.

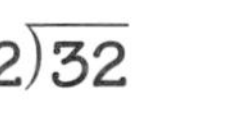

b Divide the tens into 2 equal groups.

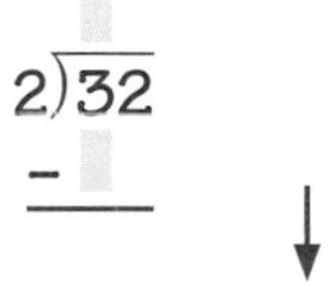

c Regroup the extra ten as ones.

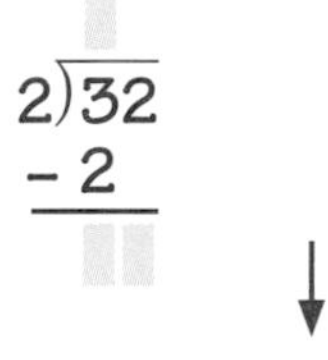

d Divide the ones.

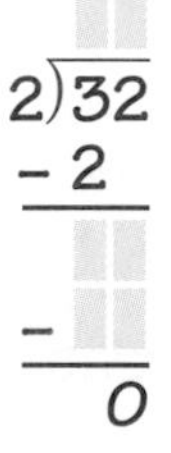

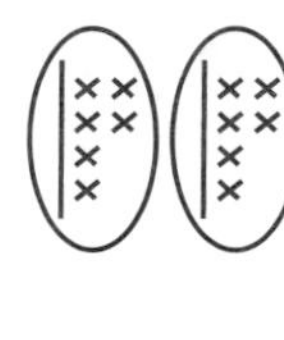

Do you UNDERSTAND?

2. In Exercise 1, how do the pictures help you divide?

3. In the example above, why do you draw four rings?

4. In the example above, suppose the 3rd graders made 68 sandwiches for the picnic. How many would they need to put on each plate?

5. The third graders have 42 straws for a picnic. They want to put an equal number of straws in each of three cups. How many straws should they put in each cup?

*For another example, see Set B on page 346.

Independent Practice

Leveled Practice In **6–9**, use place-value blocks or the pictures to help you find each quotient.

6. 48 ÷ 3

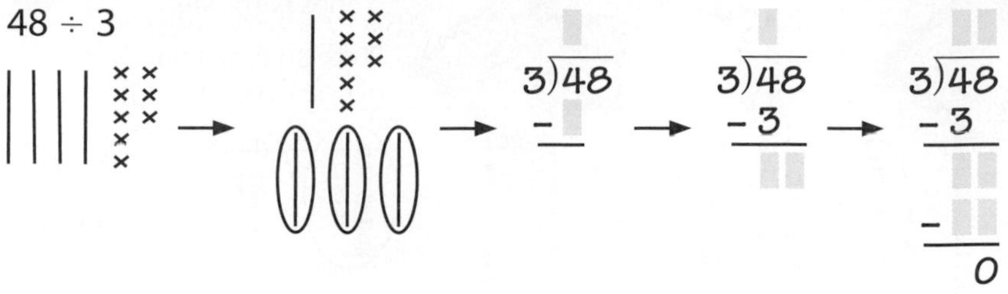

$3\overline{)48}$ → $3\overline{)48}$, -3 → $3\overline{)48}$, -3, $-$, 0

7. 34 ÷ 2

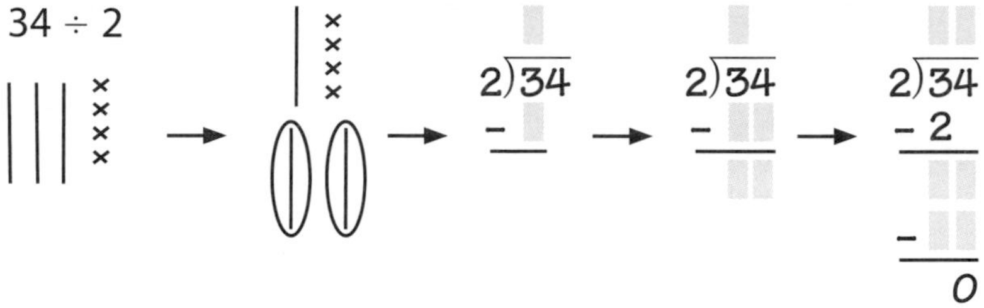

$2\overline{)34}$ → $2\overline{)34}$ → $2\overline{)34}$, -2, $-$, 0

8. 51 ÷ 3

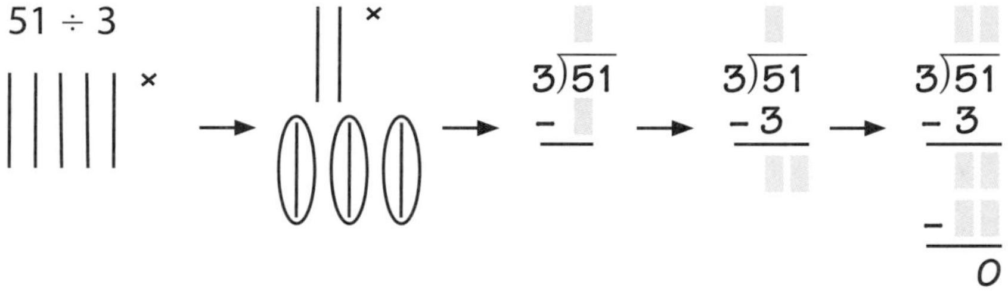

$3\overline{)51}$ → $3\overline{)51}$, -3 → $3\overline{)51}$, -3, $-$, 0

9. 72 ÷ 4

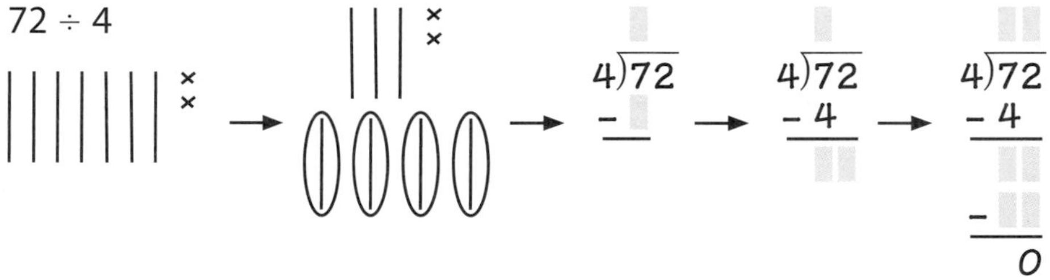

$4\overline{)72}$ → $4\overline{)72}$, -4 → $4\overline{)72}$, -4, $-$, 0

In **10–19**, draw pictures to help find each quotient.

10. 36 ÷ 2 **11.** 68 ÷ 4 **12.** 45 ÷ 3 **13.** 65 ÷ 5 **14.** 84 ÷ 6

15. 42 ÷ 3 **16.** 80 ÷ 5 **17.** 76 ÷ 4 **18.** 42 ÷ 2 **19.** 91 ÷ 7

Problem Solving

20. There are 64 children playing games. They want to make 4 equal teams. How many children should be on each team?

21. **Number Sense** How can you tell if the quotient 46 ÷ 2 is greater than 20 without dividing?

22. Mr. Wen has $42. He wants to give an equal amount to each of his three children. What amount should he give to each child?

23. Indira painted $\frac{1}{4}$ of the length of a board. What is one other way to name $\frac{1}{4}$?

$\frac{1}{4}$ painted

Use the table for **24–26**.

Number of Items in Package

Item	Small	Medium	Large
Paper Plates	36	52	90
Paper Cups	24	48	96

24. Marisol buys a medium package of paper plates. She wants to put an equal number of plates on each of four tables. How many plates should she put on each table?

25. Marisol buys a large package of paper cups. She wants to put an equal number of cups on each of six tables. How many cups should she put on each table?

26. Suppose Bruce buys a small package and a medium package of paper plates. How many fewer paper plates would he have than if he bought a large package of paper plates?

27. Leslie estimates that it will take 150 hours to paint her house. If Leslie paints for 8 hours each day, about how many days will it take her to paint the house?

A 10 **C** 20

B 15 **D** 60

28. Malik is displaying baseball cards in an album. He can fit 4 cards on a page. How many pages does he need to display 96 baseball cards?

A 20 **C** 24

B 22 **D** 25

29. For a cooking contest, 85 chefs were equally divided into 5 different teams. How many chefs were on each team?

A 17 **C** 80

B 18 **D** 90

30. Mr. Mason bought 3 folding chairs. All of the chairs were the same price. The total cost was $57. How much money did each chair cost?

A $60 **C** $19

B $54 **D** $18

Lesson

15-4

NS 2.5 Solve division problems in which a multidigit number is evenly divided by a one-digit number (135   5   __). Also **NS 2.3** Use the inverse relationship of multiplication and division to compute and check results.

Dividing 2-Digit Numbers

How do you divide with paper and pencil?

Dara and Toby are dividing each kind of fruit equally into four boxes. How many apples should they put in each box?

Choose an Operation Division is used to find the size of equal groups. Find 76 ÷ 4.

Estimate There are about 80 apples, and 80 ÷ 4 = 20. They should put about 20 apples in each box.

Data

Kind of Fruit	Number
Apples	76
Pears	56
Oranges	92

Guided Practice*

Do you know HOW?

In **1–4**, copy and complete. Find each quotient. Check your answers.

1. 3)48 — quotient 1□; − 3; 1□; − □□; 0

2. 6)84 — quotient 1□; − 6; 2□; − □□; 0

3. 2)38 — quotient 1□; − 2; □□; − □□; 0

4. 5)85 — quotient 1□; − 5; □□; − □□; 0

Do you UNDERSTAND?

5. In the example above, why is a 1 written above the 7?

6. **Number Sense** Charles says that 68 ÷ 4 = 18. Multiply to find out if he is correct.

7. Use the table above. Dara and Toby are dividing up the pears and the oranges equally into four boxes.

a How many pears should they put in each box?

b How many oranges?

Independent Practice

In **8–12**, copy and complete to find each quotient. Check your answers.

8. 2)76 — quotient 3□; − 6; □6; − □□; 0

9. 6)78 — quotient □□; − □; □8; − □□; □

10. 3)81 — quotient 2□; − 6; □1; − □□; 0

11. 4)92 — quotient □□; − □; □2; − □□; □

12. 5)95 — quotient 1□; − 5; □5; − □□; 0

*For another example, see Set B on page 346.

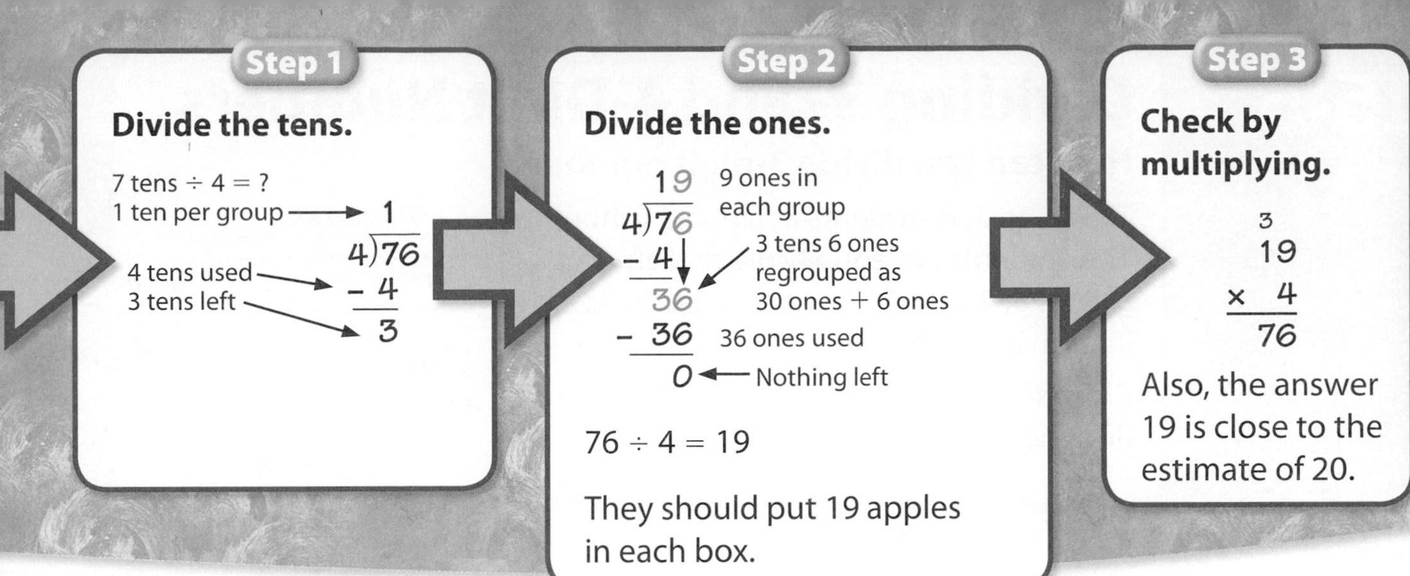

Problem Solving

For **13–15**, use the table at the right.

Fruits Picked (Data)

Kind of Fruit	Number
Lemons	84
Peaches	96
Pears	72
Oranges	79

13. Carla picked the peaches. She put an equal number of peaches into each of six crates. How many peaches did Carla put in each crate?

14. Justine picked the lemons and put an equal number of lemons into each of three crates. How many lemons did she put in each crate?

15. Estimation About how many pears and oranges were picked in all?

16. For the concert, the 64 band members were divided equally into 4 different groups. How many band members were in each group?

17. Little League baseball began in 1939 in Pennsylvania. There were 30 players equally divided among 3 teams. How many players were on each team?

18. Algebra Which of the following numbers makes this number sentence true?

$8 \times 9 > 4 \times \square$

A 17

B 18

C 19

D 21

19. Mrs. Adams bought 5 blankets. All of the blankets were the same price. The total cost was $95. How much did each blanket cost?

A $475

B $90

C $19

D $18

Lesson

15-5

NS 2.5 Solve division problems in which a multidigit number is evenly divided by a one-digit number (135 ÷ 5 = __).

Dividing 3- and 4-Digit Numbers

How can you divide 3-digit numbers?

There are 378 students at Lindale School. The students are equally divided among grades 3, 4, and 5. How many students are in each grade?

378 students

?	?	?

Students in each grade

Choose an Operation Division helps you find the size of equal groups. Find 378 ÷ 3.

Other Examples

Dividing Greater Numbers

Step 1

Divide the thousands.

There are only 2 thousands. Regroup them into 20 hundreds.

$$4\overline{)2{,}472}$$

Step 2

Divide the hundreds.

24 hundreds ÷ 4 = 6 hundreds per group

$$\begin{array}{r} 6 \\ 4\overline{)2{,}472} \\ -\,24 \end{array}$$

Step 3

Divide the tens.

7 tens ÷ 4 = 1 ten per group

$$\begin{array}{r} 61 \\ 4\overline{)2{,}472} \\ -\,24 \\ \hline 7 \\ -\,4 \\ \hline 3 \end{array}$$

Step 4

Divide the ones.

$$\begin{array}{r} 618 \\ 4\overline{)2{,}472} \\ -\,24 \\ \hline 7 \\ -\,4 \\ \hline 32 \\ -\,32 \\ \hline 0 \end{array}$$

Guided Practice*

Do you know HOW?

In **1** and **2**, copy and complete.

1.

$$\begin{array}{r} 1\square\square \\ 3\overline{)429} \\ -\,3 \\ \hline \square\square \\ -\,\square\square \\ \hline \square \\ -\,\square \\ \hline 0 \end{array}$$

2.

$$\begin{array}{r} 3\square\square \\ 5\overline{)1{,}635} \\ -\,1{,}5 \\ \hline \square\square \\ -\,\square\square \\ \hline \square\square \\ -\,\square\square \\ \hline 0 \end{array}$$

Do you UNDERSTAND?

3. In Step 1 of the example about students, why do you write 1 in the quotient?

4. The school received a shipment of 672 paperback books. The books were equally divided among 8 cartons. How many books were in each carton?

*For another example, see Set C on page 347.

Step 1

Divide the hundreds.

$$\begin{array}{r} 1 \\ 3\overline{)378} \\ -\ 3\downarrow \\ 7 \end{array}$$

Step 2

Divide the tens.

$$\begin{array}{r} 12 \\ 3\overline{)378} \\ -\ 3 \\ 7 \\ -\ 6\downarrow \\ 18 \end{array}$$

Step 3

Divide the ones.

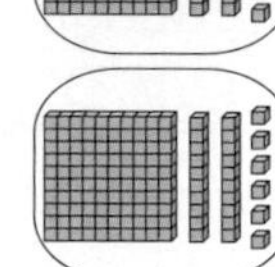

$$\begin{array}{r} 126 \\ 3\overline{)378} \\ -\ 3 \\ 7 \\ -\ 6 \\ 18 \\ -\ 18 \\ 0 \end{array}$$

$378 \div 3 = 126$

There are 126 students in each grade.

Independent Practice

In **5–8**, copy and complete. Find each quotient.

5.
$$\begin{array}{r} 7\square \\ 4\overline{)296} \\ -\ 28 \\ \square\square \\ -\ \square\square \\ \square \end{array}$$

6.
$$\begin{array}{r} 1\square\square \\ 2\overline{)356} \\ -\ 2 \\ \square\square \\ -\ 14 \\ \square\square \\ -\ \square\square \\ 0 \end{array}$$

7.
$$\begin{array}{r} 2\square\square \\ 6\overline{)1,284} \\ -\ 12 \\ \square \\ -\ \square \\ \square\square \\ -\ \square\square \\ 0 \end{array}$$

8.
$$\begin{array}{r} 1,\square\square\square \\ 3\overline{)3,693} \\ -\ 3 \\ \square \\ -\ 6 \\ \square \\ -\ \square \\ 3 \\ -\ \square \\ 0 \end{array}$$

Problem Solving

9. Green Hills School has 498 students. There is an equal number of students in each of three grades. How many students are in each grade?

10. Some coral reefs can grow 8 inches each year. At this rate, how many years would it take a coral reef to grow 120 inches?

11. **Reasonableness** Pine School has 875 students divided equally in five grades. Janie says there are more than 200 students in each grade. Is she correct? Explain.

12. The 1,268 seats in a stadium are divided into 4 equal sections. How many seats are in each section?

A 317 **B** 316 **C** 314 **D** 312

Lesson

15-6

NS 2.5 Solve division problems in which a multidigit number is evenly divided by a one-digit number (135 ÷ 5 = __). Also **NS 2.0, NS 2.3**

Zero in the Quotient

Do zeros matter?

Naja has 424 shells to put into 4 jars. She wants an equal number of shells in each jar. How many shells should she put in each jar?

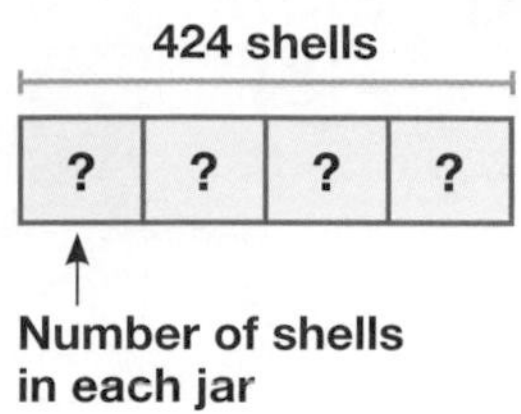

Estimate 424 is about 400 and 400 ÷ 4 = 100. There should be about 100 shells in each jar.

Another Example Do zeros matter when dividing greater numbers?

Reg has 3,246 shells to put into 3 jars. He wants to put an equal number of shells in each jar. How many shells should he put in each jar?

Divide the thousands.

$$\begin{array}{r} 1 \\ 3\overline{)3,246} \\ -3 \end{array}$$

Divide the hundreds.

$$\begin{array}{r} 1,0 \\ 3\overline{)3,246} \\ -3 \\ 2 \end{array}$$

There are not enough hundreds to put any in each group. Write 0 in the quotient to show zero hundreds.

Divide the tens.

$$\begin{array}{r} 1,08 \\ 3\overline{)3,246} \\ -3 \\ 24 \\ -24 \end{array}$$

Divide the ones.

$$\begin{array}{r} 1,082 \\ 3\overline{)3,246} \\ -3 \\ 24 \\ -24 \\ 6 \\ -6 \\ 0 \end{array}$$

Multiply to check.

$$\begin{array}{r} \scriptstyle 2 \\ 1,082 \\ \times3 \\ \hline 3,246 \end{array}$$

Reg should put 1,082 shells in each jar.

Explain It

1. **Number Sense** In the quotient above, why do you write zero in the hundreds place?
2. Frances has 5,235 buttons to put into 5 jars. She wants to put an equal number of buttons in each jar. How many buttons should she put in each jar?

Divide the hundreds.

```
   1
4)424
 -4
```

Divide the tens.

```
   10
4)424
 -4↓
   2
```

There are not enough tens to put any in each group. Write 0 in the quotient to show zero tens.

Divide the ones.

```
  106
4)424
 -4 ↓
   24
  -24
    0
```

The answer 106 is reasonable because it is close to the estimate of 100.

Naja should put 106 shells in each jar.

Guided Practice*

Do you know HOW?

In **1** and **2**, copy and complete.

1.
```
   3▯▯
2)612
 -6
   ▯▯
  -▯▯
    ▯
```

2.
```
   1▯▯
6)642
 -6
   ▯▯
  -▯▯
    ▯
```

In **3–6**, divide. Check your answer.

3. 3)3,174 **4.** 7)5,649

5. 4)2,684 **6.** 5)7,255

Do you UNDERSTAND?

7. In the example above, how can you tell, without dividing, that 16 is not a reasonable quotient for 424 ÷ 4?

8. When you divide 525 by 5, there will be a zero in the quotient. Is the zero in the tens place or the ones place?

9. Todd has 327 pebbles to put into 3 jars. He wants an equal number of pebbles in each jar. How many pebbles should he put in each jar?

Independent Practice

In **10–21**, divide. Check your answer.

10. 2)416 **11.** 9)936 **12.** 5)535 **13.** 2)8,612

14. 3)612 **15.** 6)6,438 **16.** 3)9,186 **17.** 8)9,632

18. 6)654 **19.** 4)9,624 **20.** 7)7,546 **21.** 9)945

For another example, see Set C on page 347.

Problem Solving

For **22–26**, use the table at the right.

22. The students want to put the rocks into 6 jars with an equal number of rocks in each jar. How many rocks should the students put into each jar?

Data

Mr. West's Class Collections	
Item	**Number of Items**
Acorns	964
Leaves	1,535
Rocks	648
Shells	1,192

23. Reasoning The class wants to collect about 200 more of a certain collection to match the number of shells they have collected. Which collection does the class want to increase by about 200?

24. The students want to store the acorns in 4 jars. They will put the same number of acorns into each of the jars. How many acorns should they put in each jar?

25. The students want to put the leaves into 5 boxes. They will put an equal number of leaves in each box. How many leaves should the class put in each box?

26. Writing to Explain The class also has a bean collection. The students have all of the beans stored in 3 jars. There are 716 beans in each jar. How many more beans than shells does the class have? Explain how you found your answer.

27. Algebra Copy and complete each number sentence by writing $>$, $<$, or $=$.

$372 \div 4 \bigcirc 412 \div 4$

$832 \div 8 \bigcirc 8{,}320 \div 80$

28. During Math Day, 1,435 students from schools around the city were equally divided into 7 different groups. How many students were in each group?

A 115

B 117

C 205

D 250

29. Kurt did this division problem.

$972 \div 9 = 108$

Which problem could he do to check his answer?

A $108 \times 9 = \square$

B $108 \div 9 = \square$

C $108 + 9 = \square$

D $108 - 9 = \square$

Algebra Connections

Using Number Sentences to Compare

You know that the two sides of a number sentence can be equal or unequal. Estimation or reasoning can help you decide which symbol (>, <, or =) shows how the sides compare.

> means *is greater than*
< means *is less than*
= means *is equal to*

Example: $42 \div 3 \bigcirc 51 \div 3$

When you divide 42 into 3 equal groups, is the number in each group more than when you divide 51 into 3 equal groups?

Since 42 is less than 51, the left side is less. Write "<."

$42 \div 3 \bigcirc 51 \div 3$

Copy and complete by writing <, >, or =.

1. $56 \div 4 \bigcirc 52 \div 4$ **2.** $5 \times 96 \bigcirc 5 \times 112$ **3.** $178 + 178 \bigcirc 2 \times 178$

4. $26 \div 2 \bigcirc 26 - 13$ **5.** $6 \times 47 \bigcirc 7 \times 47$ **6.** $248 \div 8 \bigcirc 416 \div 8$

7. $75 \times 0 \bigcirc 85 \times 0$ **8.** $40 \bigcirc 3 \times 20$ **9.** $92 \div 2 \bigcirc 92 \div 4$

10. $1 \times 99 \bigcirc 1 + 99$ **11.** $2 + 61 \bigcirc 2 \times 61$ **12.** $316 \div 4 \bigcirc 72 \div 4$

For **13** and **14**, copy and complete the number sentence below each problem. Use it to help explain your answer.

13. Lex wants to put 64 marbles into 4 equal groups. Bill wants to put 52 marbles into 4 equal groups. Who will have more marbles in each group?

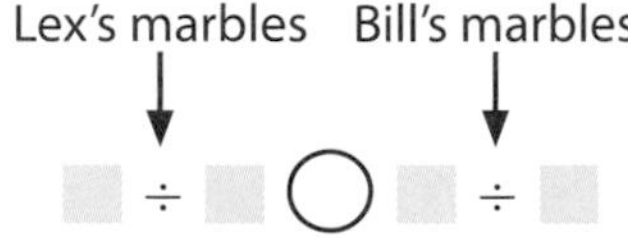

14. Kelli earned $30 last week doing yard work. This week, she earned $10 for each lawn she raked. She raked 4 lawns. In which week did she earn more?

Last week This week

$\square \bigcirc \square \times \square$

15. Write a Problem Write a problem that could be described by this number sentence: $39 \div 3 \bigcirc 57 \div 3$.

Lesson
15-7

NS 2.3 Use the inverse relationship of multiplication and division to compute and check results.
Also NS 2.0, MR 2.2

Dividing with Remainders

Hands-On
counters

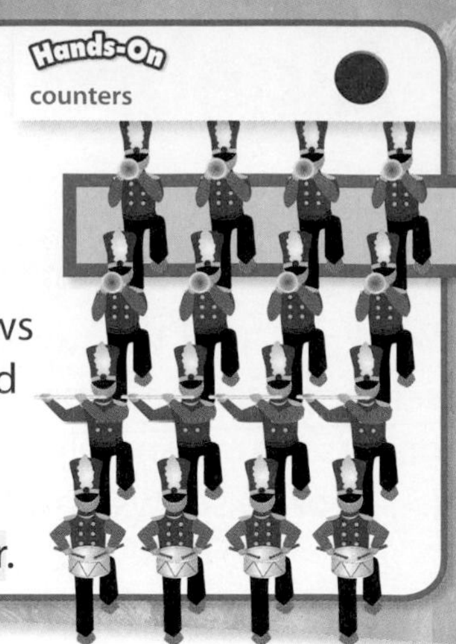

What happens when some are left?

If 23 members of a marching band march in rows of 4, how many rows are there? How many band members are left?

Division is used to find how many groups. The number left over after dividing is the remainder.

Guided Practice*

Do you know HOW?

In **1–6**, use counters or draw a picture to find each quotient and remainder.

1. 17 ÷ 3 **2.** 22 ÷ 6

3. 25 ÷ 4 **4.** 18 ÷ 5

5. 15 ÷ 2 **6.** 19 ÷ 7

Do you UNDERSTAND?

7. In the example above, what does the quotient 5 R3 mean?

8. There are 20 members in the marching band. Suppose they march in rows of 3. How many full rows of band members would there be? How many band members would be left?

Independent Practice

Leveled Practice In **9–12**, copy and complete. Check your answers.

9. $\begin{array}{r} \square \text{ R}\square \\ 3\overline{)14} \\ -\ \square\square \\ \hline \square \end{array}$ **10.** $\begin{array}{r} \square \text{ R}\square \\ 2\overline{)17} \\ -\ \square\square \\ \hline \square \end{array}$ **11.** $\begin{array}{r} \square \text{ R}\square \\ 7\overline{)27} \\ -\ \square\square \\ \hline \square \end{array}$ **12.** $\begin{array}{r} \square \text{ R}\square \\ 8\overline{)55} \\ -\ \square\square \\ \hline \square \end{array}$

In **13–20**, find each quotient and remainder. Check your answers.

13. $4\overline{)21}$ **14.** $6\overline{)46}$ **15.** $5\overline{)48}$ **16.** $9\overline{)41}$

17. $9\overline{)64}$ **18.** $8\overline{)58}$ **19.** $4\overline{)35}$ **20.** $6\overline{)39}$

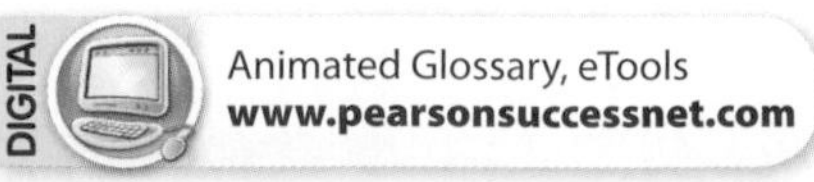
DIGITAL
Animated Glossary, eTools
www.pearsonsuccessnet.com

*For another example, see Set D on page 347.

What You Show

What You Think

If I put 23 counters in rows of 4, I get 5 full rows.

I used 5 × 4, or 20 counters. The 3 counters I have left are not enough for another group of 4, so the remainder is 3.

I can check by multiplying 5 × 4 and then adding 3.

What You Write

$$\begin{array}{r} 5 \text{ R3} \\ 4\overline{)23} \\ -\ 20 \\ \hline 3 \end{array}$$

Check:
5 × 4 = 20
20 + 3 = 23

There are 5 rows of band members with 3 band members left.

Problem Solving

For **21–23**, use the table at the right.

Data

Clayton School Marching Band Members

Instrument	Number of Band Members
Drum	23
Flute	14
Clarinet	18
Trumpet	12

21. Suppose the flute players march in rows of 3. How many rows of flute players would there be? How many flute players would be left over?

22. Suppose the drummers march in rows of 6. How many rows of drummers would there be? How many drummers would be left over?

23. How many band members are there in all?

24. A group of 68 people will be going rafting. Each raft can hold 8 people. The group will fill each raft before using the next one. How many rafts will be needed?

25. Writing to Explain Together, Nick and Leslie need to make 9 sandwiches. Nick thinks they will have enough if they each make 4 sandwiches. Do you agree? Explain.

26. Number Sense What is the greatest possible remainder you can have if you divide a number by 7? Explain.

27. Melanie has $20. She wants to buy as many cartons of juice as she can. Each carton costs $3. How many cartons of juice can she buy?

A 6 **C** 17

B 7 **D** 23

Lesson

15-8

MR **1.2** Determine when and how to break a problem into simpler parts.
Also **MR 2.2** Apply strategies and results from simpler problems to more complex problems.
Also **NS 2.8**.

Problem Solving

Multiple-Step Problems

In Lesson 8-6, you learned that some problems have hidden questions to be answered before you can solve the problem.

A museum collection of 36 dragonflies and 54 butterflies will be used in 2 new displays. There will be the same number of insects in both displays. How many insects will be in each display?

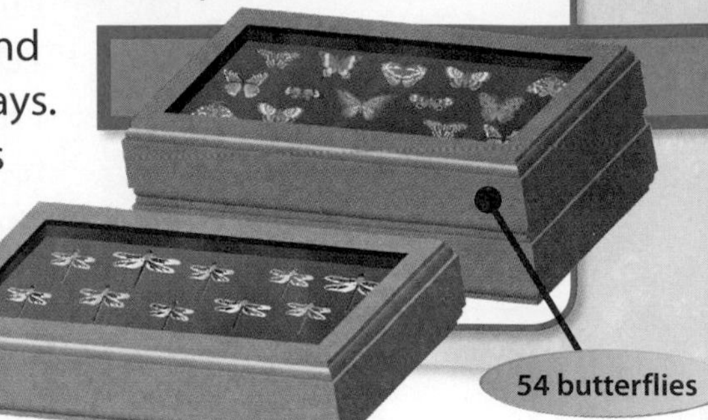

Another Example What is the hidden question?

A store has boxed sets of DVDs for sale. In each box, the DVDs are in 2 rows with 3 DVDs in each row. The total cost of a box is $72. Each DVD costs the same. What is the cost of one DVD?

Plan and Solve

What is the hidden question?

What is the total number of DVDs in each box?

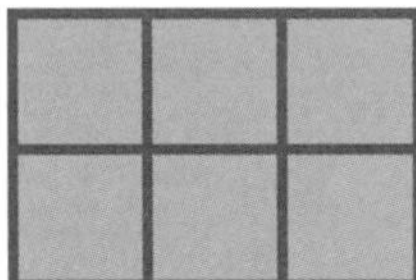

$2 \times 3 = 6$

There are 6 DVDs in each box.

Solve

Use the answer to the hidden question to solve the problem.

What is the cost of each DVD?

$$\begin{array}{r} 12 \\ 6\overline{)72} \\ -\ 6 \\ \hline 12 \\ -\ 12 \\ \hline 0 \end{array}$$

Each DVD costs $12.

Explain It

1. How do you know what the hidden question is in the problem above?
2. Explain how to check the solution to the problem above.

First, you need to find and solve the hidden question.

What is the total number of insects in the museum collection?

? insects in all

36 dragonflies	54 butterflies

$$\begin{array}{r} \scriptstyle 1 \\ 36 \\ +\ 54 \\ \hline 90 \end{array}$$

There are 90 insects in all.

Use the answer to the hidden question to solve the problem.

How many insects will be in each display?

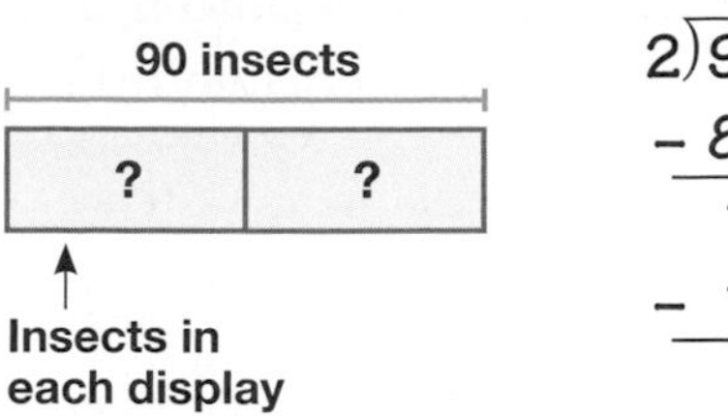

$$\begin{array}{r} 45 \\ 2\overline{)90} \\ -8 \\ \hline 10 \\ -\ 10 \\ \hline 0 \end{array}$$

There will be 45 insects in each display.

Guided Practice*

Do you know HOW?

Answer the hidden question. Then solve.

1. Twelve friends went camping. All except 4 of them went on a hike. The hikers carried 32 water bottles. Each hiker carried the same number of water bottles. How many water bottles did each hiker carry?

   HINT: Hidden Question—How many went on the hike?

Do you UNDERSTAND?

2. What operations did you use to solve Problem 1?

3. **Write a Problem** Write a problem that can be solved by finding and answering a hidden question.

Independent Practice

Leveled Practice Solve. Answer the hidden question first.

4. Mrs. Lum bought 12 rolls of pink ribbon and some rolls of yellow ribbon. The total cost of the rolls of ribbon is \$45. Each roll costs \$3. How many rolls of yellow ribbon did Mrs. Lum buy?

   HINT: Hidden Question—What is the total number of rolls of ribbon Mrs. Lum bought?

Stuck? Try this....

- What do I know?
- What am I asked to find?
- What diagram can I use to help understand the problem?
- Can I use addition, subtraction, multiplication, or division?
- Is all of my work correct?
- Did I answer the right question?
- Is my answer reasonable?

For another example, see Set D on page 347.

Independent Practice

5. **Writing to Explain** There were 24 students in a class. All of the students, except 2, went bowling. What is the total cost the students paid if each person who went bowling paid $5? Explain how you found your answer.

6. Vanya bought 5 medium packages of buttons and 3 small packages of beads. What was the total number of buttons she bought? Use the table at the right.

Number of Items in Package

Item	Small	Medium	Large
Beads	32	64	96
Buttons	18	38	56

7. Mr Alton wants to buy tickets for a show. The tickets are for seats in 3 rows with 3 seats in each row. The total cost of the tickets is $108. Each ticket costs the same. What is the cost of one ticket?

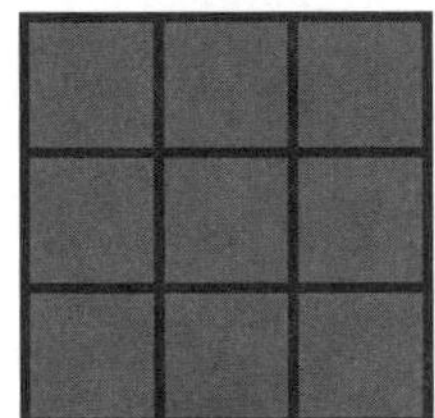

8. Mrs. Casey bought one adult admission ticket and one child admission ticket. Then she bought one adult ticket and one child ticket for a boat ride. What was the total amount Mrs. Casey spent?

County Fair

Kind of Ticket	Adult	Child
Admission	$8	$4
Boat Rides	$2	$1

9. **Think About the Process** Elio had $36 in his wallet. He used $9 to buy a book. Which number sentence shows how to find the amount of money he has left?

A $36 + 9$

B $36 - 9$

C 36×9

D $39 \div 9$

10. **Think About the Process** Martin raked 3 lawns yesterday and 4 lawns today. The total amount he earned was $42. He earned the same amount for each lawn. Which number sentence shows how to find how much he earned for each lawn he raked?

A $42 - 4 = \square$

B $42 + 4 = \square$

C $42 \times 3 = \square$

D $42 \div 7 = \square$

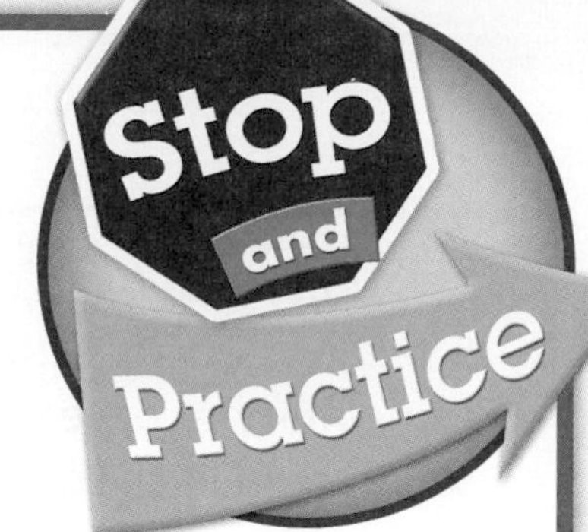

Add. Write the sum in simplest form.

1. $\frac{1}{8} + \frac{3}{8}$
2. $\frac{2}{10} + \frac{2}{10}$
3. $\frac{5}{11} + \frac{4}{11}$
4. $\frac{1}{4} + \frac{1}{4}$

Subtract. Write the difference in simplest form.

5. $\frac{3}{5} - \frac{2}{5}$
6. $\frac{8}{9} - \frac{2}{9}$
7. $\frac{8}{10} - \frac{3}{10}$
8. $1 - \frac{9}{12}$

Find each product.

9. 39×8
10. 56×7
11. 417×3
12. 286×5
13. $2{,}593 \times 4$

Find each quotient.

14. $3\overline{)78}$
15. $6\overline{)96}$
16. $2\overline{)562}$
17. $4\overline{)768}$

Error Search Find each product that is not correct. Write it correctly and explain the error.

18. $76 \times 4 = 300$
19. $39 \times 6 = 234$
20. $417 \times 2 = 816$
21. $286 \times 3 = 858$
22. $154 \times 9 = 13{,}860$

Number Sense

Estimating and Reasoning Write whether each statement is true or false. If the statement is false, explain why.

23. The sum of 128 and 292 is greater than 300.

24. The sum of 910 and 100 is less than 1,000.

25. The difference between 713 and 509 is less than 100.

26. The difference between 3,287 and 1,346 is less than 2,000.

27. The product of 4 and 29 is greater than 100.

28. The product of 5 and 862 is greater than 5,000.

29. The quotient of 82 ÷ 2 is greater than 40.

Test Prep

1. An auditorium has 2,000 seats in 5 sections. Each section has the same number of seats. How many seats are in each section? (15-1)

A 20

B 40

C 400

D 10,000

2. Mr. Ortiz earned \$6,496 by selling 8 paintings for the same price each. Which number sentence shows the best way to estimate the amount he earned for each painting? (15-2)

A $8 \times \$6{,}400 = \$51{,}200$

B $\$5{,}600 \div 8 = \$700$

C $\$6{,}400 \div 10 = \$640$

D $\$6{,}400 \div 8 = \$800$

3. What is $8{,}764 \div 7$? (15-5)

A 125

B 1,232

C 1,248

D 1,252

4. Don bought \$76 in plants. He spent \$24 on daisies and the rest on rose bushes. If Don bought 4 rose bushes that all had the same price, how much did each rose bush cost? (15-8)

A \$6

B \$13

C \$19

D \$52

5. Which number sentence does the diagram show? (15-3)

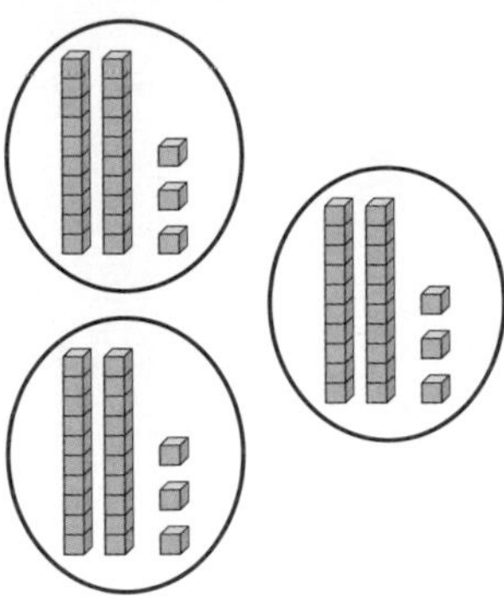

A $69 \div 3 = 22$

B $69 \div 3 = 23$

C $69 \div 3 = 20$

D $60 \div 3 = 20$

6. For the water balloon toss, 75 students were divided equally into 5 groups. How many students were in each group? (15-4)

A 375

B 25

C 15

D 14 groups with 5 left over

7. Four students stapled 824 school newsletters. How many newsletters did each student staple if they shared the stack evenly? (15-6)

A 3,296

B 208

C 206

D 28

Test Prep

8. The art teacher has one package of 240 cotton balls to use in her art classes. If she divides the cotton balls evenly among the 4 classes, how many cotton balls would each class have? (15-1)

A 6

B 60

C 80

D 960

9. What is the quotient? (15-4)

$$\begin{array}{r} \square\square \\ 3\overline{)78} \\ -\ \square \\ \hline \square\square \\ -\ \square\square \\ \hline 0 \end{array}$$

A 16

B 23

C 24

D 26

10. Juan practiced the tuba for a total of 225 minutes this week. If he practiced an equal amount of time on 5 different nights, how many minutes did he practice each night? (15-5)

A 45 minutes

B 50 minutes

C 55 minutes

D 1,125 minutes

11. What is 38 ÷ 9? (15-7)

A 4 R2

B 4 R3

C 4 R4

D 5 R3

12. To find 96 ÷ 4, Tim first divided the tens into 4 equal groups. What should Tim do next? (15-3)

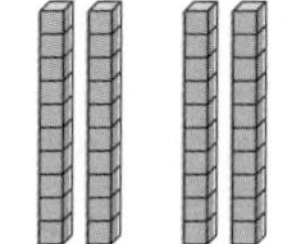

$$\begin{array}{r} 2 \\ 4\overline{)96} \\ 8 \\ \hline \end{array}$$

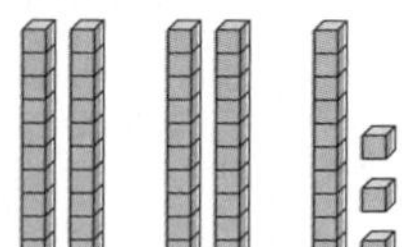

A Divide the ones.

B Subtract to find how many tens are left.

C Regroup the two extra tens as ones.

D Nothing, he is finished.

13. Montgomery uses 7 beads to make a keychain. If she bought a package with 300 beads, about how many key chains will she be able to make? (15-2)

A 60

B 50

C 40

D 4

14. What is 2,418 ÷ 2? (15-6)

A 1,209

B 1,206

C 1,029

D 129

Set A, pages 322–325

Estimate 1,326 ÷ 4.

Use numbers that are close to the numbers in the problem and easy to divide.

1,200 is close to 1,326. 1,200 can be evenly divided by 4.

Think 12 ÷ 4 = 3

Find 1,200 ÷ 4.

You can use patterns and mental math.

12 ÷ 4 = 3
120 ÷ 4 = 30
1,200 ÷ 4 = 300

Remember that you can use numbers that are close to the actual numbers and easy to divide.

Estimate each quotient.

1. 26 ÷ 3 **2.** 203 ÷ 2

3. 438 ÷ 6 **4.** 3,971 ÷ 5

5. 47 ÷ 8 **6.** 215 ÷ 4

7. 2,946 ÷ 7 **8.** 2,632 ÷ 9

Set B, pages 326–331

Find 57 ÷ 3.

Divide the tens.

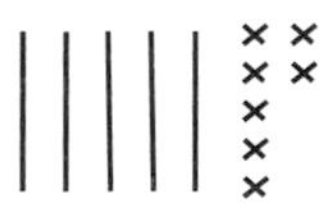

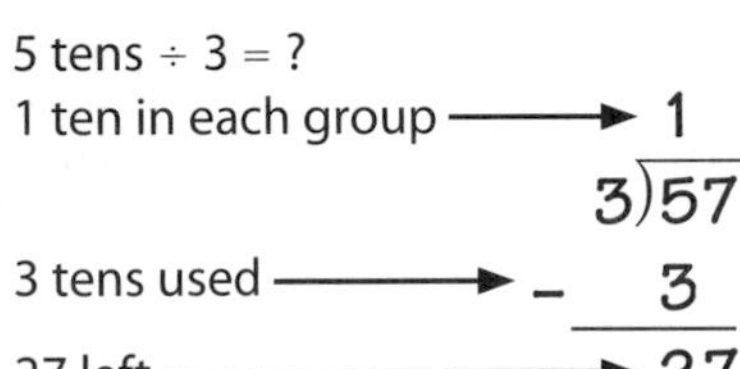

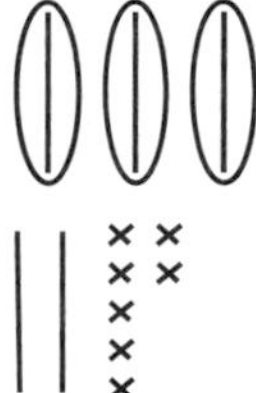

Divide the ones.

27 ones ÷ 3 = ?

19 ← 9 ones in each group
3)57
– 3
27
– 27 ← 27 ones used
0 ← Nothing left

57 ÷ 3 = 19

Remember to first divide the tens by the divisor. Then divide the ones by the divisor.

Copy and complete. You may use place-value blocks or pictures to help find each quotient. Check your answers.

1. 1▢
2)38
– 2
1▢
– ▢▢
0

2. 1▢
4)68
– 4
2▢
– ▢▢
0

3. 1▢
3)45
– 3
▢▢
– ▢▢
0

4. 1▢
7)91
– 7
▢▢
– ▢▢
0

Set C, pages 332–336

Find 2,472 ÷ 4.

Step 1

Divide the thousands.

There are only 2 thousands. Regroup them into 20 hundreds.

$$4\overline{)2{,}472}$$

Step 2

Divide the hundreds.

24 hundreds ÷ 4 = 6 hundreds per group

```
      6
 4)2,472
  - 24
```

Step 3

Divide the tens.

```
     61
 4)2,472
  - 24
      7
    - 4
```

Step 4

Divide the ones.

```
    618
 4)2,472
  - 24
      7
    - 4
     32
   - 32
      0
```

Remember that you might need to write a zero in the quotient.

Copy and complete. Find each quotient.

1.
```
   1▢▢
 6)792
 - 6
   ▢▢
 - ▢▢
    ▢▢
  - ▢▢
     0
```

2.
```
    7▢▢
 2)1,496
 - 14
     ▢
   - ▢
     ▢▢
   - ▢▢
      0
```

3. $4\overline{)816}$

4. $3\overline{)4{,}218}$

Set D, pages 338–342

There are 13 girls and 14 boys that will form teams to play volleyball. Each team needs 6 players. Extra players will be alternates. How many teams can be formed? How many players will be alternates?

Step 1

First find the total number of children.

13 + 14 = 27

Step 2

Use the answer to the hidden question to solve the problem.

Step 3

Solve.

```
   4 R3
 6)27
 - 24
    3
```

There will be 4 teams with 3 players left to be alternates.

Remember to answer the hidden question and use the answer to solve the problem.

Solve.

1. Three friends ordered 2 pizzas. Each pizza was cut into 8 slices. If each person ate the same number of slices, how many slices did each person eat? How many slices were left over?

Topic 16

Customary Measurement

1 How far must a frog jump to break the record in the Frog Jumping contest in Calaveras County? You will find out in Lesson 16-3.

2 This kind of hat is sometimes called a 10-gallon hat. Does it really hold ten gallons? You will find out in Lesson 16-4.

3

Mark Twain is a famous author. What does his name have to do with a unit of measure? You will find out in Lesson 16-1.

4

Owen, a baby hippo, and Mzee, a giant tortoise, met after a tsunami. When they first met, how much more did Mzee weigh than Owen? You will find out in Lesson 16-5.

Review What You Know!

Vocabulary

Choose the best term from the box.

- cubes
- feet
- miles
- pounds

1. You can measure weight in __?__.
2. You can measure the distance between cities in __?__.
3. You can measure the length of your classroom in __?__.

Compare Measurements

Choose the greater amount.

4. 3 inches or 3 feet
5. 20 quarts or 2 quarts
6. 6 pounds or 60 pounds
7. 2 minutes or 2 hours

Arrays

Writing to Explain Use the array for **8** and **9**. Write an answer for each question.

8. How can you find the number of dots in the array?

●●●
●●●
●●●
●●●

9. Suppose there were 6 dots in each row. How could you find the number of dots in the array?

MG 1.0 Choose and use appropriate units and measurement tools to quantify the properties of objects.
Also MG 1.1

Understanding Measurement

Hands-On
inch ruler

How can you describe the length of an object in different ways?

Measure the length of your desktop in pencil-lengths and in crayon-lengths.

Another Example How can you use inches to measure?

Find the length of the desktop in inches.

To use a ruler, line up the object with the 0 mark.

You may need to move the ruler to continue measuring. If so, make sure that you mark where the ruler ends before you move it.

When the ruler on the desk is moved, it will show about 6 more inches.

$12 + 6 = 18$

To the nearest inch, this desktop is 18 inches long.

Explain It

1. Estimate the length of your shoe in inches. Explain how you got your estimate.
2. Find the length of a pen to the nearest inch.
3. Explain why using a ruler is a better way to measure length than using a crayon.

Find the length.

More crayon-lengths than pencil-lengths equal the length of the desktop.

The desktop is 3 pencil-lengths or 6 crayon-lengths long.

Compare the units.

The crayon-length is a smaller unit than the pencil-length.

The smaller the unit used, the more units are needed to equal a given length.

Use a standard unit.

People use standard units to describe measurements.

A standard unit for measuring length is the inch (in.).

1 inch

Guided Practice*

Do you know HOW?

Estimate each length. Then measure to the nearest inch.

1. 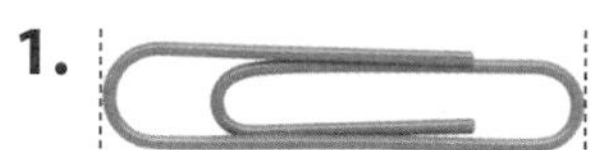

2. 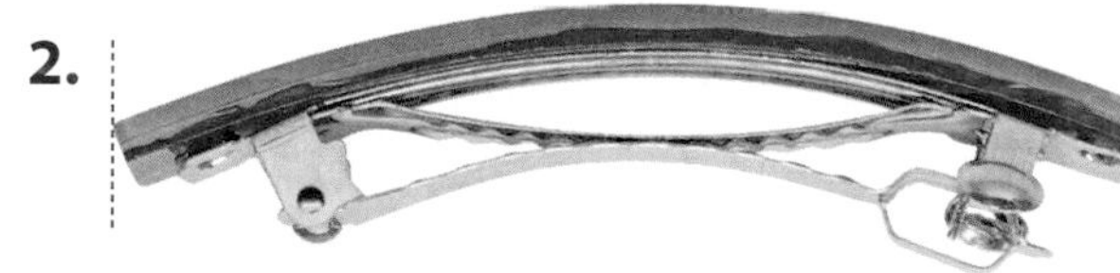

3. 

Do you UNDERSTAND?

4. In the example above, are more pencil-lengths or crayon-lengths equal to the length of the desktop?

5. Find the length of your desktop in paper clip-lengths. First estimate the length in paper clips.

6. What is the length of the candle to the nearest inch?

Independent Practice

In **7–10**, estimate each length. Then measure to the nearest inch.

7.

8.

9.

10. 

*For another example, see Set A on page 372.

Independent Practice

In **11–13**, estimate each length. Then measure to the nearest inch.

11. **12.**

13.

Problem Solving

14. A marker is 4 times as long as a piece of chalk. The piece of chalk is 2 inches long. How long is the marker?

marker ├──┼──┼──┼──┤
chalk ├──┤

15. Kevin's father is 72 inches tall. He is 26 inches taller than Kevin. How tall is Kevin?

Kevin's father	**72**	
Kevin	**?**	**26**

16. **Number Sense** Jeff's hand is 3 large paper clips long. Alan's hand is 8 small paper clips long. Could their hands be the same size? Explain. How would standard units help?

17. **Writing to Explain** You have a piece of string and a ruler. How can you decide how long this curve is?

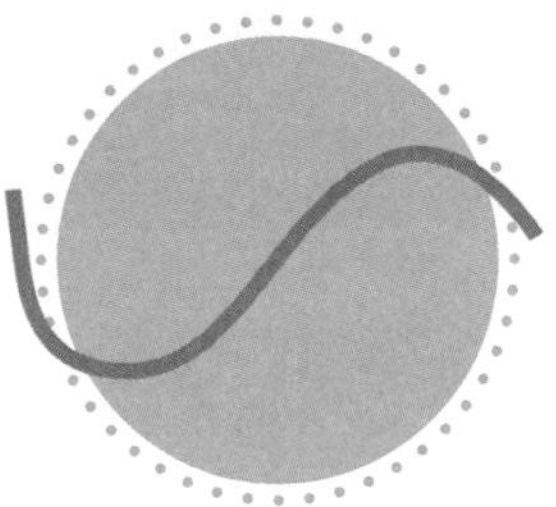

18. **Reasoning** The author Mark Twain's name is taken from riverboat slang. "Mark twain" meant "Mark two" for 2 fathoms. Two fathoms are equal to 12 feet. Which measurement unit is longer, a fathom or a foot?

Algebra In **19–24**, copy and complete each number sentence.

19. 35 + ☐ = 50 + 5 **20.** ☐ − 10 = 38 + 1 **21.** 40 − ☐ = 30 + 1

22. ☐ + 22 = 30 − 2 **23.** 50 − ☐ = 46 + 3 **24.** 32 − ☐ = 20 + 4

25. Without using a ruler, draw a line segment about 4 inches long. Then measure it to the nearest inch.

26. Al fed his friend's dog for 4 days. He used 2 cups of food 2 times each day. How many cups of food did Al use in all?

27. Juan has 15 pennies and 3 dimes. Olivia has the same amount of money, but she has only nickels. How many nickels does Olivia have?

28. Alberto had 104 peacock stickers. He put 68 of them in his old sticker book and gave 18 away. How many peacock stickers does Alberto have left to put in his new sticker book?

29. **Number Sense** Suppose two pizzas are the same size. One pizza is cut into eighths and the other pizza is cut into tenths. Which pizza has larger pieces?

30. **Reasoning** Ken has 8 quarters, 5 dimes, 5 nickels, and 5 pennies. This is all the money he has. Explain why the total value of all of Ken's coins could not be $2.81. Then find the correct amount he had.

31. Which of the pencil stickers below is 2 inches high? Use a ruler to measure.

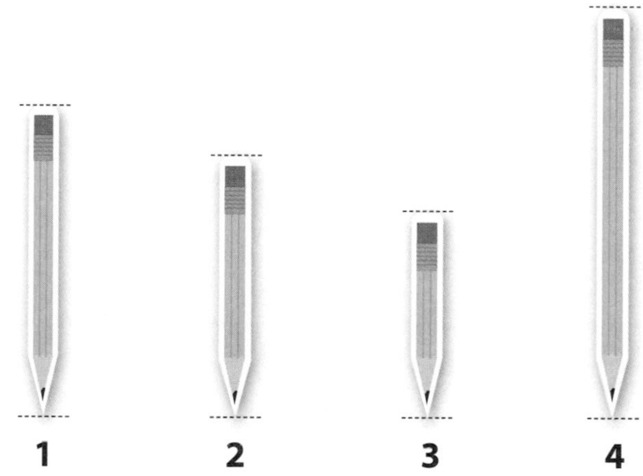

A Sticker 1 **C** Sticker 3

B Sticker 2 **D** Sticker 4

32. Ruth did 63 extra math problems in 7 days. She did the same number of problems each day. Which number sentence would you use to find the number of problems she did each day?

A $63 + 7 = \square$ **C** $63 \times 7 = \square$

B $63 - 7 = \square$ **D** $63 \div 7 = \square$

Lesson

16-2

MG 1.1 Choose the appropriate tools and units (metric and U.S.) and estimate and measure the length, liquid volume, and weight/mass of given objects.
Also **MG 1.0**

Fractions of an Inch

Hands-On
inch ruler

How do you measure to a fraction of an inch?

In the picture, what is the length of the red pepper to the nearest $\frac{1}{2}$ inch and to the nearest $\frac{1}{4}$ inch?

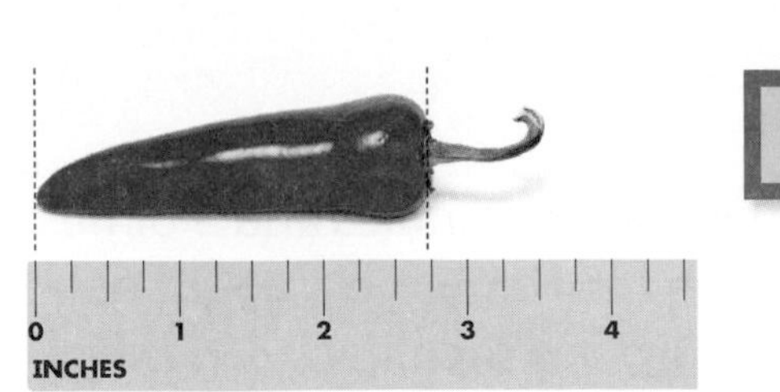

Other Examples

The nearest $\frac{1}{2}$ inch and $\frac{1}{4}$ inch can be the same.

In the picture, the length of the green bean is measured to the nearest $\frac{1}{2}$ inch and $\frac{1}{4}$ inch.

To the nearest $\frac{1}{2}$ inch:

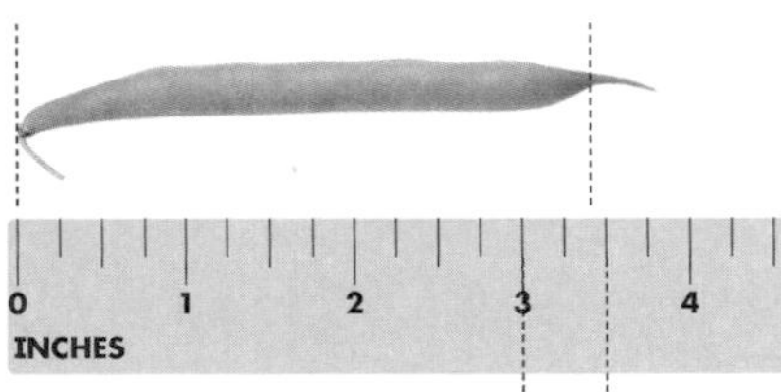

The red marks are the nearest $\frac{1}{2}$-inch marks.

To the nearest $\frac{1}{2}$ inch: $3\frac{1}{2}$ inches

To the nearest $\frac{1}{4}$ inch:

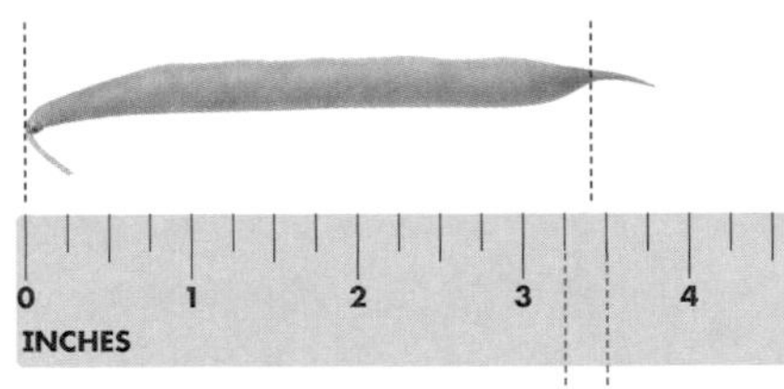

The blue marks are the nearest $\frac{1}{4}$-inch marks.

To the nearest $\frac{1}{4}$ inch: $3\frac{1}{2}$ inches

Guided Practice*

Do you know HOW?

Measure the length of each object to the nearest $\frac{1}{2}$ inch and $\frac{1}{4}$ inch.

1. 

2. 

Do you UNDERSTAND?

3. In measuring the red pepper above, between which two $\frac{1}{2}$-inch marks does the pepper end?

4. Is $2\frac{1}{2}$ inches or $2\frac{3}{4}$ inches closer to the actual length of the pepper? Explain.

*For another example, see Set A on page 372.

Measure to the nearest $\frac{1}{2}$ inch.

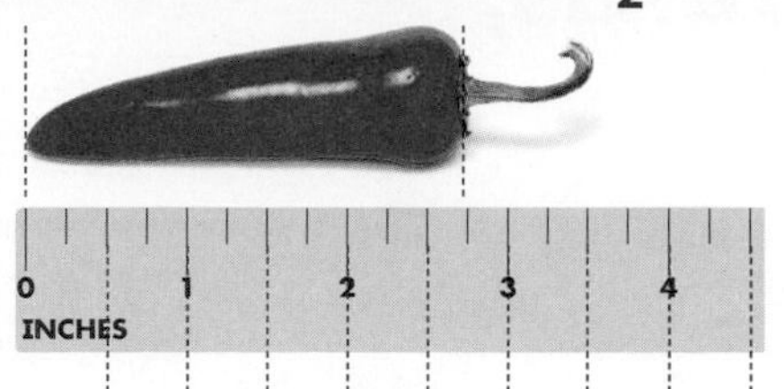

The red marks are all $\frac{1}{2}$-inch marks. The nearest $\frac{1}{2}$-inch marks are $2\frac{1}{2}$ inches and 3 inches.

To the nearest $\frac{1}{2}$ inch: $2\frac{1}{2}$ inches

Measure to the nearest $\frac{1}{4}$ inch.

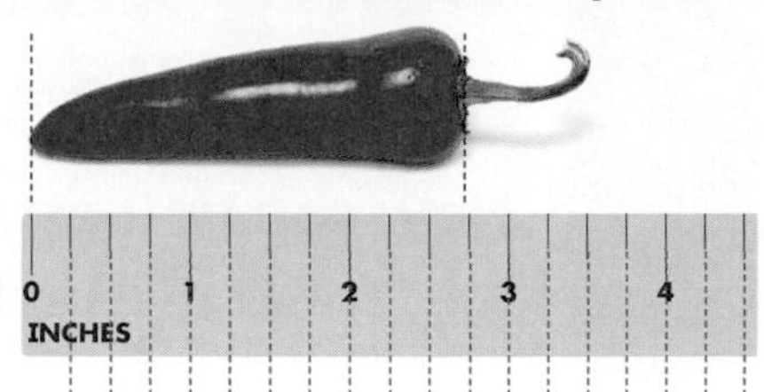

The blue marks are all $\frac{1}{4}$-inch marks. The nearest $\frac{1}{4}$-inch marks are $2\frac{1}{2}$ inches and $2\frac{3}{4}$ inches.

To the nearest $\frac{1}{4}$ inch: $2\frac{3}{4}$ inches

Independent Practice

Measure the length of each object to the nearest $\frac{1}{2}$ inch and $\frac{1}{4}$ inch.

5. 

6. 

7. 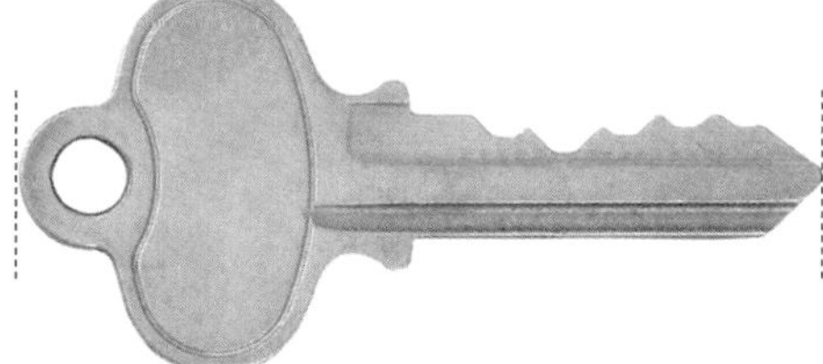

8. 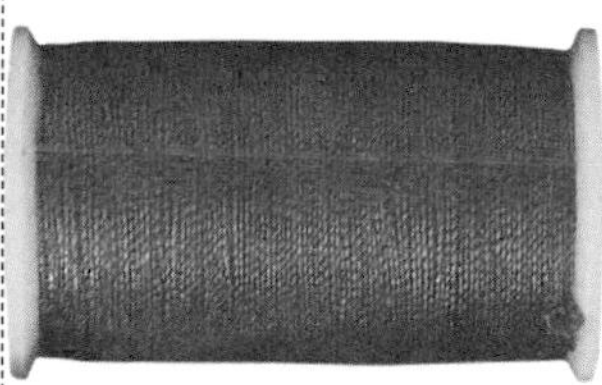

Problem Solving

9. Reasoning Can a piece of carrot be 3 inches long to the nearest inch, nearest $\frac{1}{2}$ inch, and nearest $\frac{1}{4}$ inch? Explain.

10. Karina has 3 rows of tomato plants in her garden. There are 9 plants in each row. How many tomato plants are in her garden?

11. What is the length of the asparagus to the nearest $\frac{1}{2}$ inch? Use a ruler to measure.

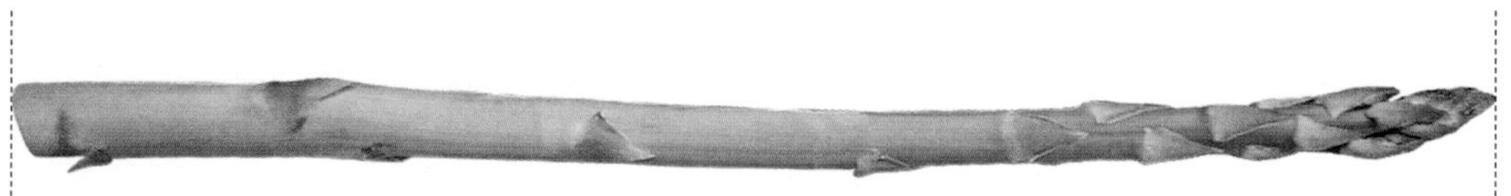

A 5 inches **B** $5\frac{1}{2}$ inches **C** 6 inches **D** $6\frac{1}{2}$ inches

Lesson

16-3

MG 1.1 Choose the appropriate tools and units (metric and U.S.) and estimate and measure the length, liquid volume, and weight/mass of given objects.

Using Inches, Feet, Yards, and Miles

How can you estimate and measure length?

Joe is writing about fire trucks. What units of length or distance might he use?

Guided Practice*

Do you know HOW?

In **1–3**, choose the better estimate.

1. The distance you travel on a train:
200 yards or 200 miles

2. A man's height:
6 feet or 6 yards

3. The length of a room:
3 feet or 30 feet

Do you UNDERSTAND?

4. In the example above, why would the width of the hose be measured in inches instead of feet?

5. What unit is the best to use when measuring the height of a bookcase? Why?

Independent Practice

In **6–13**, choose the better estimate.

6. The length of a pool:
20 inches or 20 yards

7. The length of a car:
3 feet or 16 feet

8. The distance you travel on an airplane:
800 feet or 800 miles

9. The height of a house:
15 yards or 15 miles

10. The length of a dollar bill:
6 inches or 6 yards

11. The length of a bicycle:
3 yards or 30 yards

12. The distance you might walk to the library:
2 miles or 20 miles

13. The length of a horse:
8 feet or 8 miles

*For another example, see Set B on page 372.

Besides the inch, some customary units of length are the foot (ft), yard (yd), and mile (mi).

A loaf of bread is about a foot long.

A baseball bat is about a yard long.

Most people can walk a mile in about 15 minutes.

The length of the ladder on the fire truck is best measured in feet.

The length of the fire hose is best measured in yards. The width of the fire hose is best measured in inches.

The distance a fire truck travels is best measured in miles.

Problem Solving

14. **Writing to Explain** Would you measure the length of a soccer field in yards or inches? Explain.

15. **Reasonableness** Choose the better estimate. The California red-legged frog is the largest frog that has always lived in the western United States. The record for the longest jump by this kind of frog was more than 20 feet. This jump was about 60 times the length of the frog. Is this frog about 4 inches long or about 4 feet long? Explain.

16. **Geometry** Which of the following shapes is a scalene triangle?

A 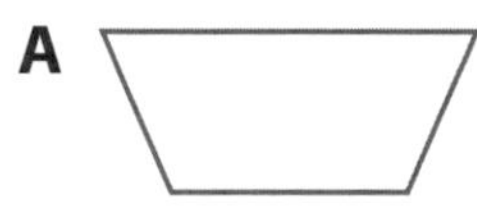

C 

B

D

17. Look at the poster below. What fraction of the squares on this poster show food?

A $\frac{1}{15}$

B $\frac{7}{15}$

C $\frac{8}{15}$

D $\frac{3}{5}$

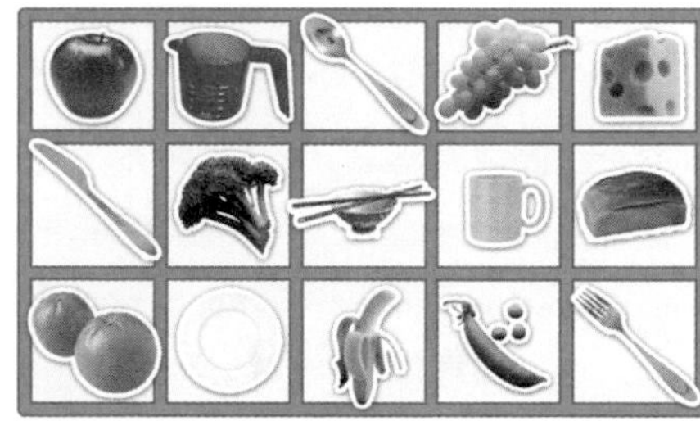

18. Which measurement best describes the length of a couch?

A 6 miles
B 6 yards
C 6 feet
D 6 inches

19. Which measurement best describes the height of a kitchen table?

A 1 foot
B 3 feet
C 6 feet
D 12 feet

Lesson
16-4

MG 1.1 Choose the appropriate tools and units (metric and U.S.) and estimate and measure the length, liquid volume, and weight/mass of given objects.
Also MG 1.0

Customary Units of Capacity

What customary units describe how much a container holds?

The capacity of a container is the volume of a container measured in liquid units. What is the capacity of this pail?

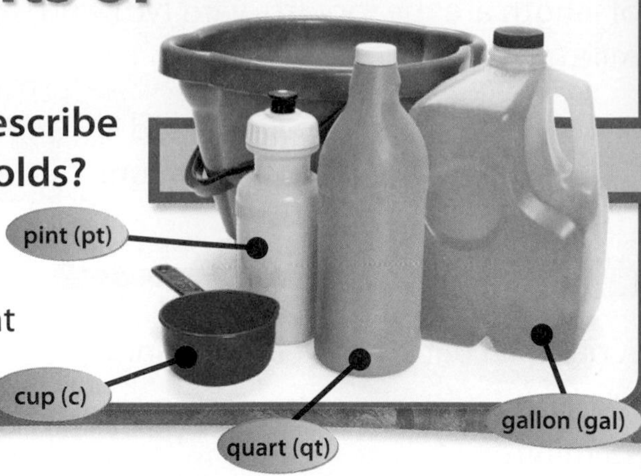

Guided Practice*

Do you know HOW?

For **1** and **2**, choose the better estimate for each.

1.

1 c or 1 qt

2.

3 pt or 3 gal

Do you UNDERSTAND?

3. **Number Sense** Why does it make sense to measure the pail above in gallons rather than in cups?

4. Find a container that you think holds about 1 gallon and another that holds about 1 cup. Then use measuring containers to see how well you estimated each capacity.

Independent Practice

For **5–12**, choose the better estimate for each.

5.

1 pt or 1 gal

6.

1 c or 1 pt

7.

1 c or 1 pt

8.

1 c or 1 qt

9. kitchen sink
22 c or 22 qt

10. water glass
1 c or 1 qt

11. baby bottle
1 qt or 1 c

12. tea kettle
3 qt or 3 c

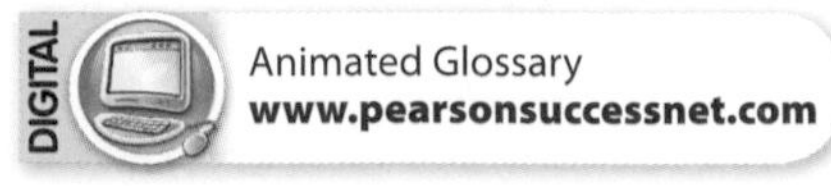

*For another example, see Set B on page 372.

Step 1

Cups, pints, quarts, and gallons are customary units of capacity.

Choose an appropriate unit and estimate.

The cup, pint, and quart are too small. So use gallons.

The pail looks like it will hold more than 1 gallon.

Units of Capacity
1 pint = 2 cups
1 quart = 2 pints
1 gallon = 4 quarts

Step 2

Measure the capacity of the pail.

Count how many times you can fill a gallon container and empty it into the pail.

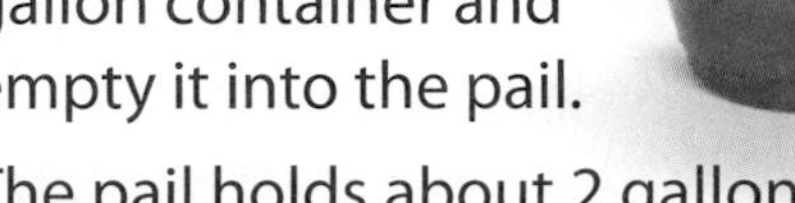

The pail holds about 2 gallons.

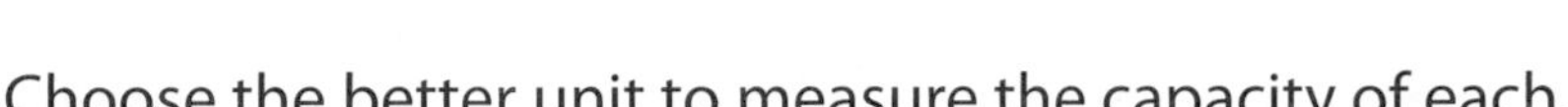

Choose the better unit to measure the capacity of each.

13. teacup
pt or c

14. swimming pool
pt or gal

15. water bottle
pt or gal

16. pitcher of juice
c or qt

Problem Solving

17. Writing to Explain Can containers with different shapes have the same capacity? Why or why not?

18. Look at the cowboy hat at the right. It is called a ten-gallon hat!

a Can this hat really hold 10 gallons? How do you know?

b Can this hat hold 1 gallon? How do you know?

19. Which measurement best describes the capacity of a bathtub?

A 50 cups
B 50 quarts
C 50 gallons
D 50 pints

20. Which of the objects below holds about 1 pint?

A Bowl of soup
B Punch bowl
C Gas tank
D Pool

21. Jeanne made 5 pitchers of lemonade. Each pitcher served 12 customers at her lemonade stand. If Jeanne had 1 pitcher of lemonade left, how many customers did Jeanne serve?

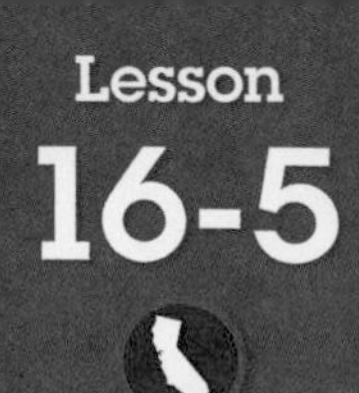

MG 1.1 Choose the appropriate tools and units (metric and U.S.) and estimate and measure the length, liquid volume, and weight/mass of given objects.
Also **MG 1.0**

Units of Weight

What customary units describe how heavy something is?

The weight of an object is a measure of how heavy the object is. What is the weight of this apple?

1 ounce (oz)

1 pound (lb)

about 1 ton (T)

Guided Practice*

Do you know HOW?

For **1** and **2**, choose the better estimate for each.

1.

1 oz or 1 lb

2.

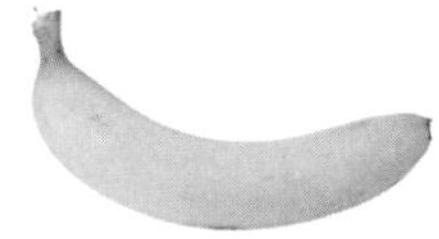

6 oz or 6 lb

Do you UNDERSTAND?

3. Number Sense If you buy a bag of 6 apples, what unit would you use for its weight? Explain.

4. Find an object that you think weighs about 1 pound and another that weighs about 1 ounce. Then weigh the objects to see how well you estimated.

Independent Practice

For **5–12**, choose the better estimate for each.

5.

10 oz or 10 lb

6.

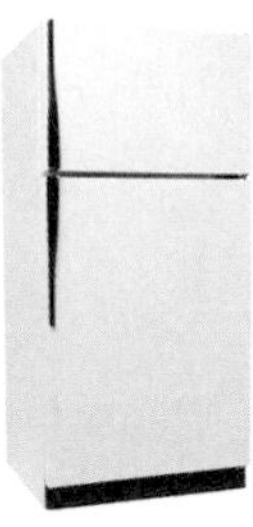

300 lb or 300 T

7.

200 lb or 2 T

8.

2 oz or 2 lb

9. cracker
1 oz or 1 lb

10. television set
30 oz or 30 lb

11. baseball hat
5 oz or 5 lb

12. elephant
60 lb or 6 T

*For another example, see Set B on page 372.

Step 1

Ounces, pounds, and tons are units of weight.

Choose a unit and estimate.

The units pound and ton are too big. Use ounces.

Units of Weight
16 ounces = 1 pound
2,000 pounds = 1 ton

The apple weighs less than 1 pound but more than 1 ounce.

Step 2

Weigh the apple.

Three stacks of three 1-ounce weights balance with the apple.

The apple weighs about 9 ounces.

For **13–16**, choose the better unit to measure the weight of each.

13. student desk
lb or T

14. lemon
oz or lb

15. bicycle
oz or lb

16. truck
oz or T

Problem Solving

17. How much does the orange weigh?

18. When would you use this scale instead of a pan balance?

19. **Number Sense** Which weighs more—a pound of rocks or a pound of feathers? Explain your thinking.

20. **Writing to Explain** Do small objects always weigh less than large objects? Use examples to explain your thinking.

21. When Owen and Mzee first met, Owen weighed 600 pounds. Mzee weighed 661 pounds. How much more did Mzee weigh than Owen when they first met?

Mzee
661 pounds

Owen
600 pounds

22. Which animal weighs about 1 ton?

A Squirrel
B Giraffe
C Wolf
D Monkey

Lesson

16-6

MG 1.4 Carry out simple unit conversions within a system of measurement (e.g., centimeters and meters, hours and minutes). Also NS 2.8, AF 1.4.

Converting Customary Units

How can you change units?

How many inches are in 3 feet? How many ounces are in 4 pounds?

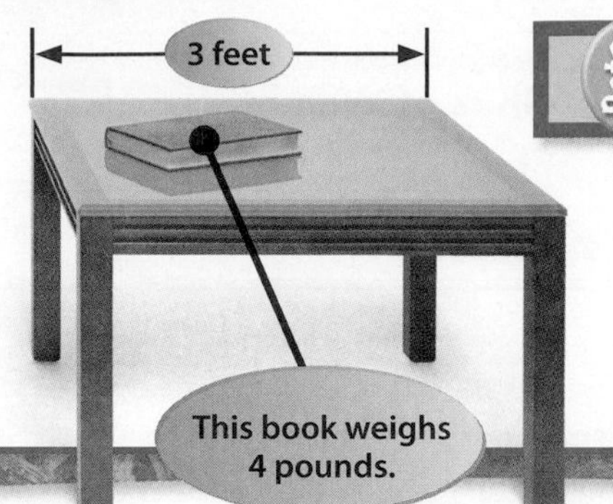

Data

Relating Customary Units
1 foot (ft) = 12 inches (in.)
1 yard (yd) = 3 feet
1 quart (qt) = 2 pints (pt)
1 gallon (gal) = 4 quarts (qt)
1 pound (lb) = 16 ounces (oz)

Guided Practice*

Do you know HOW?

For **1–3**, copy and complete to change the units.

1. 5 feet = ▢ inches
2. 3 gallons = ▢ quarts
3. 2 feet, 3 inches = ▢ inches

Do you UNDERSTAND?

4. **Reasoning** In the example above, how many yards long is the table? Explain.
5. Malena put 4 quarts of juice in a punch bowl. How many pints of juice did she put in the punch bowl?

Independent Practice

For **6–11**, copy and complete.

6. 6 yards = ▢ feet
7. 4 pounds = ▢ ounces
8. 7 quarts = ▢ pints
9. 8 yards = ▢ feet
10. 2 yards = ▢ inches
11. 8 gallons = ▢ quarts

For **12–15**, change the units.

12. How many quarts are in 4 gallons, 1 quart?
13. How many pints are in 2 quarts, 1 pint?
14. How many ounces are in 5 pounds, 13 ounces?
15. How many feet are in 12 yards, 2 feet?

*For another example, see Set C on page 373.

Since there are 12 inches in 1 foot, the number of inches in 3 feet is 3×12.

3×12 inches = ▢ inches

$$\begin{array}{r} 12 \\ \times \ 3 \\ \hline 36 \end{array}$$

There are 36 inches in 3 feet.

Since there are 16 ounces in 1 pound, the number of ounces in 4 pounds is 4×16.

4×16 ounces = ▢ ounces

$$\begin{array}{r} {}^{2} \\ 16 \\ \times \ 4 \\ \hline 64 \end{array}$$

There are 64 ounces in 4 pounds.

Problem Solving

16. Mr. Allen is 5 feet, 4 inches tall. How many inches tall is Mr. Allen?

17. The swim race is 200 yards long. How many feet long is the race?

For **18** and **19**, use the table at the right.

Sale on Trees

Item	Price
6 foot	\$21
12 foot	\$37
18 foot	\$58

18. **Estimation** About how much would one 18-foot tree and one 6-foot tree cost in all?

19. What is the total cost of four 12-foot trees?

20. **Number Sense** A tree was planted 32 years before 1980. How old was the tree in 2000?

For **21** and **22**, use the pictures at the right.

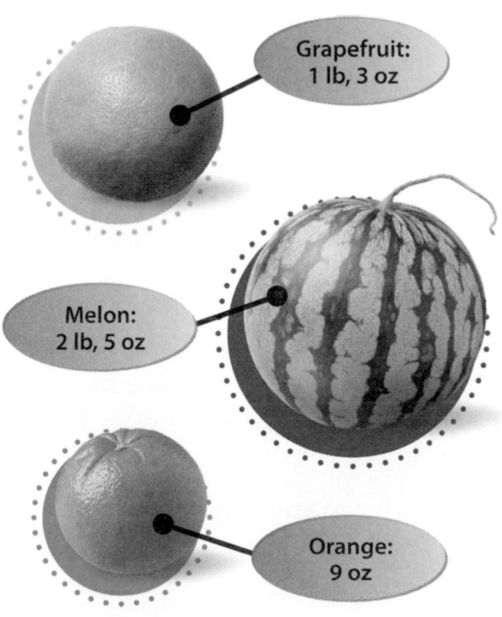

21. **Writing to Explain** Nelda bought a grapefruit, an orange, and a melon. Which weighed more, the grapefruit or the orange? Explain how you found your answer.

22. **a** How many oranges weigh about the same as 1 melon?

b How many grapefruits weigh about the same as 1 melon?

23. Which of the following is used to find how many quarts are in 3 gallons?

A 3×2 **B** 3×3 **C** 3×4 **D** 3×12

Lesson

16-7

MG 1.4 Carry out simple unit conversions within a system of measurement (e.g., centimeters and meters, hours and minutes). Also **AF 1.4** Express simple unit conversions in symbolic form (e.g., __ inches = __ feet × 12).

Units of Time

How can you change units of time?

The class is growing a plant from a seed. The project will last for 5 weeks. How many days are in 5 weeks? It might take 4 days for the seed to sprout. How many hours are in 4 days?

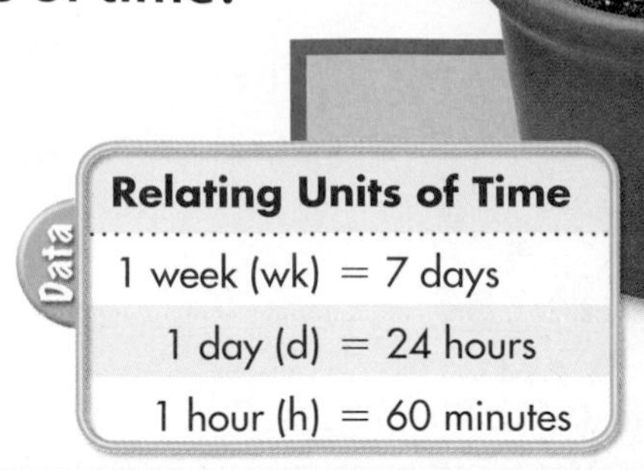

Data

Relating Units of Time		
1 week (wk)	=	7 days
1 day (d)	=	24 hours
1 hour (h)	=	60 minutes

Guided Practice*

Do you know HOW?

For **1–3**, copy and complete to change the units.

1. 8 weeks = ▢ days

2. 2 days = ▢ hours

3. How many days are in 2 weeks, 4 days?

Do you UNDERSTAND?

4. In the example above, why do you multiply the number of weeks by 7?

5. At the end of the first week, the class had worked on the science experiment for 6 hours. How many minutes did the class work on the experiment?

Independent Practice

For **6–15**, copy and complete to change the units.

6. 3 hours = ▢ minutes

7. 5 days = ▢ hours

8. 4 hours = ▢ minutes

9. 7 weeks = ▢ days

10. 3 weeks = ▢ days

11. 7 days = ▢ hours

12. How many hours are in 3 days, 5 hours?

13. How many minutes are in 5 hours, 10 minutes?

14. How many days are in 10 weeks?

15. How many hours are in 9 days?

*For another example, see Set C on page 373.

Since there are 7 days in 1 week, the number of days in 5 weeks is 5×7.

5×7 days = ▢ days

$$\begin{array}{r} 7 \\ \times\ 5 \\ \hline 35 \end{array}$$

There are 35 days in 5 weeks.

Since there are 24 hours in 1 day, the number of hours in 4 days is 4×24.

4×24 hours = ▢ hours

$$\begin{array}{r} {}^{1} \\ 24 \\ \times\ 4 \\ \hline 96 \end{array}$$

There are 96 hours in 4 days.

Problem Solving

16. In 30 more minutes, the International Space Station will complete an orbit. It has been in this orbit for 1 hour. How many minutes does it take the International Space Station to complete 1 orbit?

17. A group of high school students helped to prepare samples of materials to send to the International Space Station in 2001. The samples were returned to Earth from space after 4 years. In what year were the samples returned?

For **18** and **19**, use the table at the right.

18. Astronauts at the International Space Station took a spacewalk to do tasks outside the station. They finished their tasks in less time than was planned. How many minutes of actual time did the astronauts need?

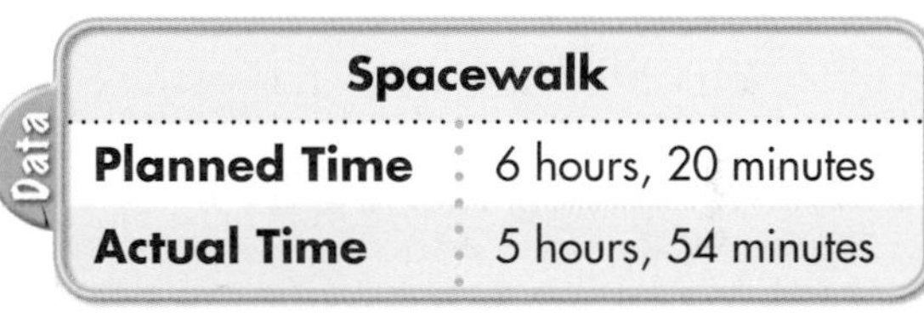

Spacewalk	
Planned Time	6 hours, 20 minutes
Actual Time	5 hours, 54 minutes

19. **Writing to Explain** How many fewer minutes than planned did the astronauts need? Explain how you found your answer.

20. The class plans to work in the community garden for 8 hours. How many minutes does the class plan to work in the garden?

21. How many days are in 6 weeks?

A 42 **C** 13

B 36 **D** 7

Lesson
16-8

MG 1.5, Grade 2 Determine the duration of intervals of time in hours (e.g., 11:00 A.M. to 4:00 P.M.).
Also MR 2.2 Apply strategies and results from simpler problems to more complex problems.

Elapsed Time

How can you find elapsed time?

Janey took part in a charity walk. The walk started at 7:00 A.M. It ended at 11:20 A.M. How long did the walk last?

Elapsed time is the total amount of time that passes from the starting time to the ending time.

Guided Practice*

Do you know HOW?

For **1–3**, find the elapsed time.

1. Start Time: 11:00 A.M.
   End Time: 5:00 P.M.

2. Start Time: 1:00 P.M.
   End Time: 4:45 P.M.

3. Start Time: 7:10 A.M.
   End Time: 8:00 A.M.

Do you UNDERSTAND?

4. In the example above, why do you count the minutes by 5s as the minute hand moves to each number on the clock?

5. During the charity walk, lunch was served from 12:00 P.M. until 2:10 P.M. How long was lunch served?

Independent Practice

For **6–14**, find the elapsed time.

6. Start Time: 6:30 P.M.
   End Time: 9:50 P.M.

7. Start Time: 11:00 A.M.
   End Time: 3:55 P.M.

8. Start Time: 5:40 P.M.
   End Time: 6:00 P.M.

9. Start Time: 8:10 A.M.
   End Time: 10:45 A.M.

10. Start Time: 9:15 A.M.
    End Time: 10:45 A.M.

11. Start Time: 10:00 A.M.
    End Time: 3:00 P.M.

12. Start Time: 3:20 P.M.
    End Time: 6:00 P.M.

13. Start Time: 7:30 A.M.
    End Time: 9:45 A.M.

14. Start Time: 12:45 P.M.
    End Time: 2:20 P.M.

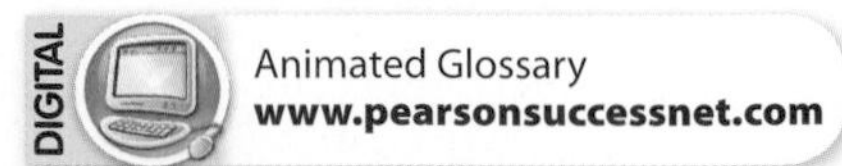

*For another example, see Set D on page 373.

Problem Solving

15. The picnic started at 12:10 P.M. and ended at 5:00 P.M. How long did the picnic last?

16. The baseball game started at 1:15 P.M. It lasted 2 hours, 45 minutes. What time did the game end?

17. The picnic started at 12:10 P.M. Kevin's family had arrived at the picnic 30 minutes earlier. What time did Kevin's family arrive at the picnic?

18. Mr. Parker had $\frac{5}{6}$ of a sandwich. He gave $\frac{2}{6}$ of the sandwich to Mikey. He gave the rest of the sandwich to Ben. What fraction of the sandwich did he give to Ben? Draw a picture.

Mrs. Flores keeps a list of the amount of time it takes for different items to bake. Use the table at the right for **19–20**.

19. Which items take less than $\frac{1}{2}$ hour to bake?

20. **Estimation** About how many more minutes does it take to bake the pasta dish than to bake the granola bars?

Item	Baking Time in Minutes
Bread	26
Granola Bars	21
Pasta Dish	48
Vegetables	24

21. The train leaves Carlton at 9:25 A.M. and arrives at Longview at 10:55 A.M. How long is the train ride?

A 1 hour, 20 minutes
B 1 hour, 25 minutes
C 1 hour, 30 minutes
D 1 hour, 35 minutes

Lesson

16-9

MR 1.1 Analyze problems by identifying relationships, distinguishing relevant from irrelevant information, sequencing and prioritizing information, and observing patterns. Also AF 1.0, MR 1.0

Problem Solving

Work Backward

Eric's family wants to arrive at the movie theater at 2:30 P.M. It takes them 30 minutes to travel to the theater, 15 minutes to get ready, and 30 minutes to eat lunch. What time should the family start eating lunch?

Arrive at Theater

Guided Practice*

Do you know HOW?

Solve the problem by drawing a picture and working backward.

1. The swim meet starts at 10:15 A.M. It takes Abby 15 minutes to walk to the pool. On her way, she needs 15 minutes to shop. It takes her 30 minutes to get ready. What time should Abby start getting ready?

Do you UNDERSTAND?

2. In the example above, why do the arrows in the last step move to the left?

3. **Write a Problem** Write a problem that you can solve by working backward.

Independent Practice

In **4** and **5**, solve the problem by drawing a picture and working backward.

4. Emilio read the thermometer one evening. The temperature was 56°F. This temperature was 9°F less than the temperature that afternoon. The afternoon temperature was 7°F greater than the temperature in the morning. What was the temperature in the morning?

5. Jana's dentist appointment is at 4:30 P.M. It takes Jana 20 minutes to walk to the dentist's office, 20 minutes to get ready, and 30 minutes to clean her room. What time should she start cleaning her room?

Stuck? Try this....

- What do I know?
- What am I asked to find?
- What diagram can I use to help understand the problem?
- Can I use addition, subtraction, multiplication, or division?
- Is all of my work correct?
- Did I answer the right question?
- Is my answer reasonable?

*For another example, see Set E on page 373.

Read and Understand

What do I know? Arrive 2:30 P.M., 30 minutes to travel, 15 minutes to get ready, 30 minutes to eat lunch

What am I being asked to find? The time the family should start eating lunch

Plan and Solve

Draw a picture to show each change.

Work backward from the end.

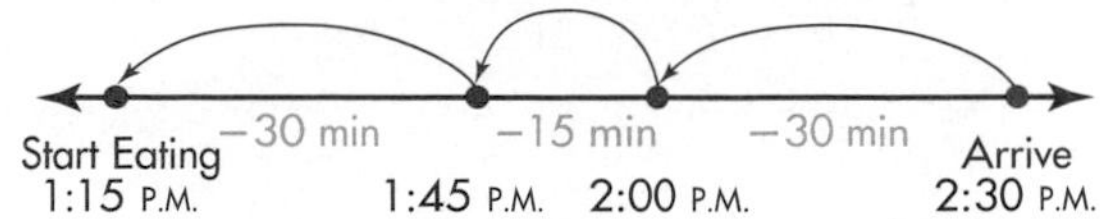

Eric's family should start eating lunch at 1:15 P.M.

6. Kent read the thermometer this evening. The temperature was 65°F. This temperature was 15°F less than the temperature in the afternoon. The afternoon temperature was 14°F greater than the temperature in the morning. What was the temperature in the morning?

7. Corinna read the thermometer at 7:00 P.M. The temperature was 16°C. This temperature was 9°C less than the temperature at 2:00 P.M. The temperature at 2:00 P.M. was 10°C higher than the temperature at 8:00 A.M. What was the temperature at 8:00 A.M.?

8. Wan-li drew these polygons. What is the same in all three polygons?

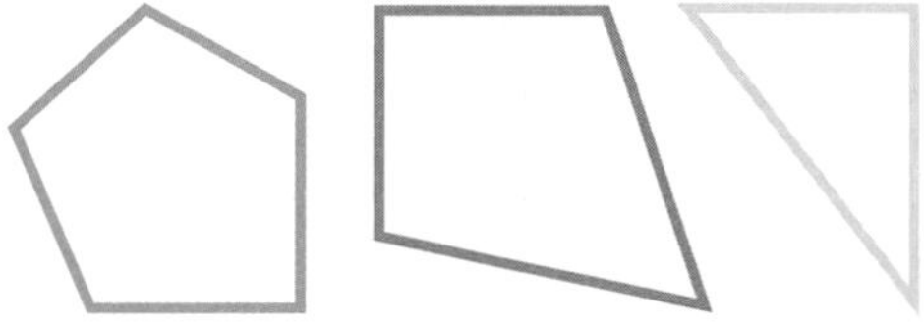

9. School starts at 8:15 A.M. It takes Shane 15 minutes to walk to school, 20 minutes to eat, 15 minutes to walk his dog, and 15 minutes to get ready. What time should he get up?

10. A scientist recorded the data shown in the table. About how long does it take a Venus flytrap to close after an insect or spider lands on it?

A Less than 1 second

B More than 1 second

C More than 1 minute

D More than 2 minutes

Data

Time Prey Landed	Time Flytrap Closed
2:07	$\frac{1}{2}$ second after 2:07
2:49	$\frac{3}{4}$ second after 2:49
2:53	$\frac{1}{2}$ second after 2:53

Test Prep

1. What is the length of the leaf to the nearest $\frac{1}{2}$ inch? (16-2)

A $3\frac{1}{2}$ inches

B 3 inches

C $2\frac{1}{2}$ inches

D 2 inches

2. Which of these units would be best to measure the capacity of a swimming pool? (16-4)

A Gallons

B Cups

C Pints

D Quarts

3. There are 4 quarts in a gallon. Which number sentence can be used to change 2 gallons to quarts? (16-6)

A 4 quarts $\times$ 4 = 16 quarts

B 4 quarts $\times$ 2 = 8 quarts

C 8 quarts $\times$ 4 = 32 quarts

D 4 quarts $\div$ 2 = 2 quarts

4. How many hours are in 4 days? (16-7)

A 52

B 84

C 96

D 100

5. The concert in the park started at 11:15 A.M. and ended at 2:50 P.M. How long did the concert last? (16-8)

A 2 hours, 35 minutes

B 3 hours, 25 minutes

C 3 hours, 30 minutes

D 3 hours, 35 minutes

6. Mira's goldfish is 2 inches long. Which could be Mira's goldfish? (16-1)

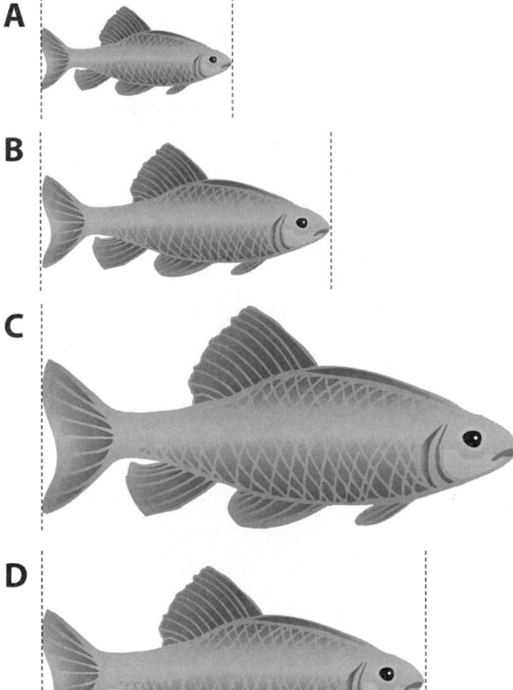

7. Which best describes the length of a large school bus? (16-3)

A 12 inches

B 12 feet

C 12 yards

D 12 miles

8. Avi got to school at 8:05 A.M. She was on the bus 15 minutes, stood at the bus stop for 10 minutes, and took 40 minutes to get ready, after she got up. What time did Avi get up? (16-9)

A 9:10 A.M.

B 7:05 A.M.

C 7:00 A.M.

D 6:55 A.M.

9. Which unit would best measure the weight of the world's heaviest land animal pictured below? (16-5)

A Inches

B Tons

C Pounds

D Ounces

10. Thomas hiked on a trail for 45 minutes without stopping. Which measurement best describes the length of the trail? (16-3)

A 3 miles

B 3 yards

C 3 feet

D 3 inches

11. Which of the following weighs closest to 1 pound? (16-5)

A

B

C

D

12. Emily is 2 feet, 8 inches tall. How many inches tall is Emily? There are 12 inches in a foot. (16-6)

A 28 inches

B 32 inches

C 36 inches

D 98 inches

13. Joni was playing in a soccer game. The game started at 11:10 A.M. and ended at 12:40 P.M. How long did the game last? (16-8)

A 30 minutes

B 1 hour, 10 minutes

C 1 hour, 30 minutes

D 2 hours, 30 minutes

Set A, pages 350–355

Measure to the nearest $\frac{1}{2}$ inch.

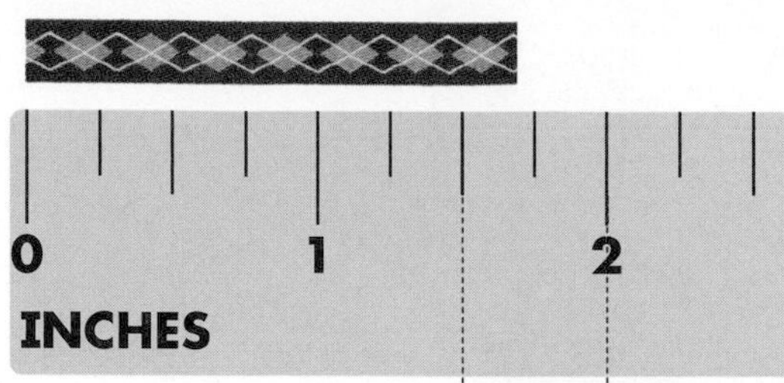

To the nearest $\frac{1}{2}$ inch: $1\frac{1}{2}$ inches

Measure to the nearest $\frac{1}{4}$ inch.

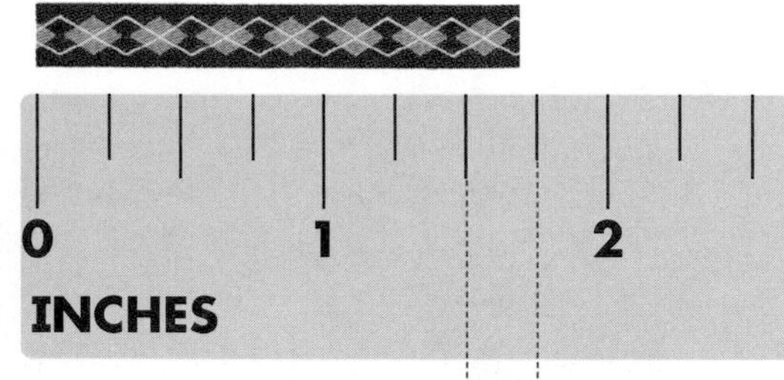

To the nearest $\frac{1}{4}$ inch: $1\frac{3}{4}$ inches

Remember that the nearest $\frac{1}{2}$ inch and $\frac{1}{4}$ inch measures for an object can be the same.

Measure the length of each object to the nearest inch, $\frac{1}{2}$ inch, and $\frac{1}{4}$ inch.

1.

2.

Set B, pages 356–361

Some customary units of length are the foot (ft), yard (yd), and mile (mi). An egg carton is about a foot long. A fence post is about a yard long. Distances between cities are measured in miles.

What is the capacity of this mug?

a gallon ← too much
a quart ← too much
a pint ← too much

Estimate using cups. The mug holds about 1 cup.

What is the weight of this eraser?

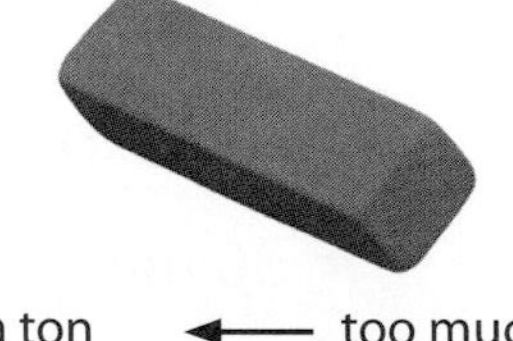

a ton ← too much
a pound ← too much

Estimate using ounces. The eraser weighs about 2 ounces.

Remember to use the examples to help estimate.

Choose the better estimate.

1. A dog's height:
3 feet or 13 feet

2. The distance you travel on a bus:
10 yards or 10 miles

3.

8 oz or 8 lb

4.

30 pt or 30 gal

Set C, pages 362–365

Change from feet to inches.

2 feet = ▢ inches

Change to inches.

You know that 1 foot equals 12 inches.

Multiply: 2 × 12 inches = 24 inches
2 feet = 24 inches

Remember to use the correct factors for the units you are changing.

Copy and complete.

1. 4 feet = ▢ inches
2. 6 quarts = ▢ pints
3. 5 weeks = ▢ days
4. 4 days = ▢ hours

Set D, pages 366–367

How long does the hockey game last?
Start Time: 11:00 A.M.
End Time: 2:35 P.M.

- Find the starting time: **11:00 A.M.**
- Count the hours: **12, 1, 2.**
- Count the minutes: **5, 10, 15, 20, 25, 30, 35.**

The game lasted 3 hours, 35 minutes.

Remember to count hours and then minutes.

Find the elapsed time.

1. Start Time: 9:00 A.M.
   End Time: 12:15 P.M.
2. Start Time: 5:00 P.M.
   End Time: 9:50 P.M.

Set E, pages 368–369

Jay needs to arrive at soccer practice at 10:00 A.M. It takes him 30 minutes to walk to the field. It takes him 10 minutes to walk his dog and 10 minutes to get ready. What time should Jay start getting ready?

Work backward from the end using the opposite of each change.

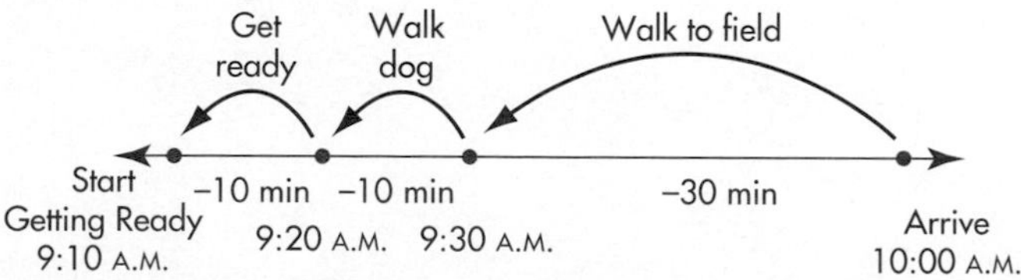

Jay should start getting ready at 9:10 A.M.

Remember to check your solution. Work forward to check.

Solve each problem by drawing a picture and working backward.

1. Hal needs to meet Lou at 1:00 P.M. It takes him 10 minutes to walk to Lou's house, 10 minutes to get ready, and 20 minutes to eat lunch. What time should he start eating lunch?

Topic 17

Metric Measurement

1 The sandgrouse soaks up water in its fluffy feathers and carries it many kilometers to its chicks. About how much water can a sandgrouse carry in its feathers? You will find out in Lesson 17-3.

2 What is the length in meters and centimeters of the footbridge on Tower Bridge in London, England? You will find out in Lesson 17-2.

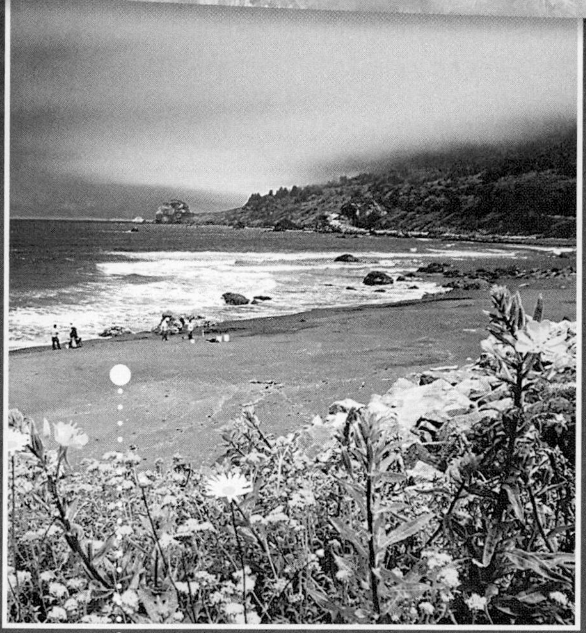

3

High Bluff beach is one of the most popular beaches in northern California. How many grains of sand are in 1 gram of sand? You will find out in Lesson 17-4.

4

What is the length of the world's smallest seahorse? You will find out in Lesson 17-1.

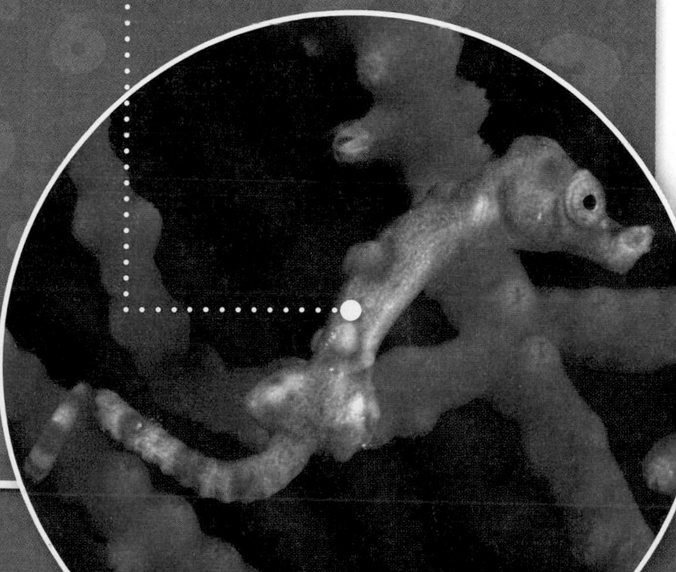

Review What You Know!

Vocabulary

Choose the best term from the box.

- estimate
- fraction
- tenth
- twelfth

1. If a whole is divided into equal parts, each part is a __?__ of the whole.
2. When you find a number that is about how many, you __?__.
3. When a region is divided into ten equal parts, each part is called a __?__.

Fractions and Length

Find what part of the length of the 1-strip the other strips show. Write the fraction.

4.

1					
$\frac{1}{10}$	$\frac{1}{10}$	$\frac{1}{10}$	$\frac{1}{10}$	$\frac{1}{10}$	$\frac{1}{10}$

5.

1		
$\frac{1}{10}$	$\frac{1}{10}$	$\frac{1}{10}$

Measurement

6. **Writing to Explain** Cal used a crayon to measure the length of a notebook. Then he used a paper clip to measure the same length. The crayon was longer than the paper clip. Did he use more crayons or paper clips to measure the notebook length? Explain.

Lesson
17-1

MG 1.1 Choose the appropriate tools and units (metric and U.S.) and estimate and measure the length, liquid volume, and weight/mass of given objects.

Using Centimeters and Decimeters

Hands-On
metric ruler

How can you estimate and measure in metric units?

What is the length of the grasshopper, to the nearest centimeter?

Other Examples

Some other metric units of length are the decimeter (dm) and the millimeter (mm).

10 centimeters = 1 decimeter
10 cm = 1 dm

This wrench is 1 dm long.

1 dm

10 millimeters = 1 centimeter
10 mm = 1 cm

A dime is about 1 mm thick.

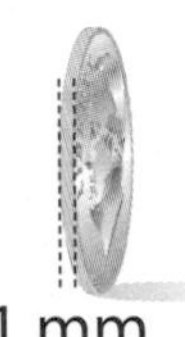

1 mm

Guided Practice*

Do you know HOW?

In **1** and **2**, estimate each length. Then measure to the nearest centimeter.

1. 

2. 

Do you UNDERSTAND?

3. A cricket is 1 cm shorter than the grasshopper above. Draw a line segment that is the same length as the cricket.

4. What is the length of the clamshell to the nearest centimeter?

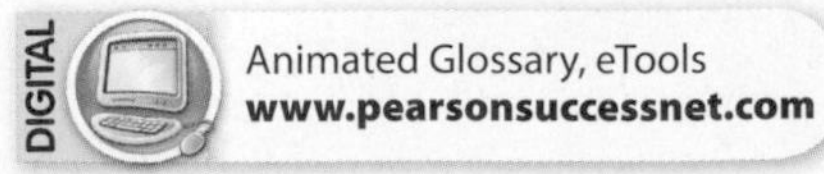

*For another example, see Set A on page 392.

A metric unit for measuring length is the centimeter (cm).

Your finger is about 1 cm wide. Use your finger width to help estimate lengths.

1 cm

Use the centimeter ruler to measure.

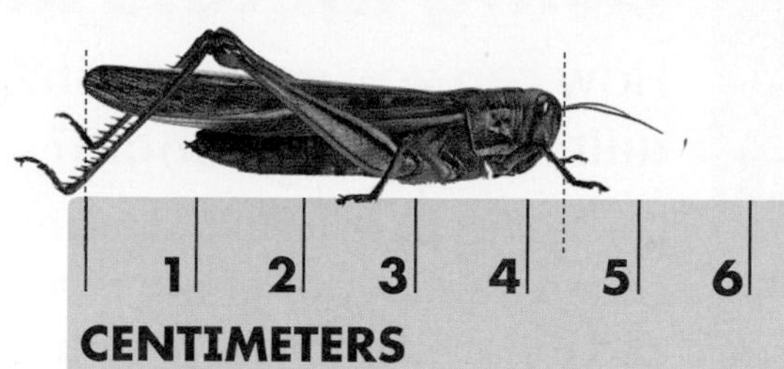

The grasshopper is 4 cm long, to the nearest centimeter.

Independent Practice

In **5–7**, estimate each length. Then measure to the nearest centimeter.

5. 

6. 

7. 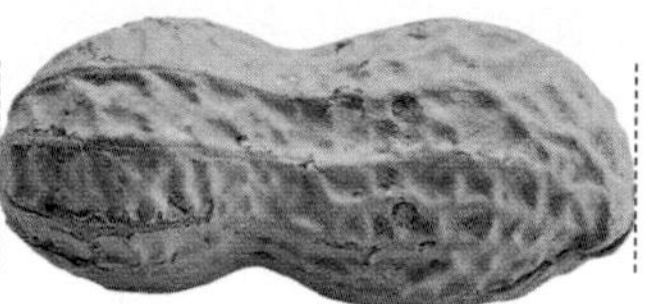

Problem Solving

8. What is the length of the flower to the nearest centimeter?

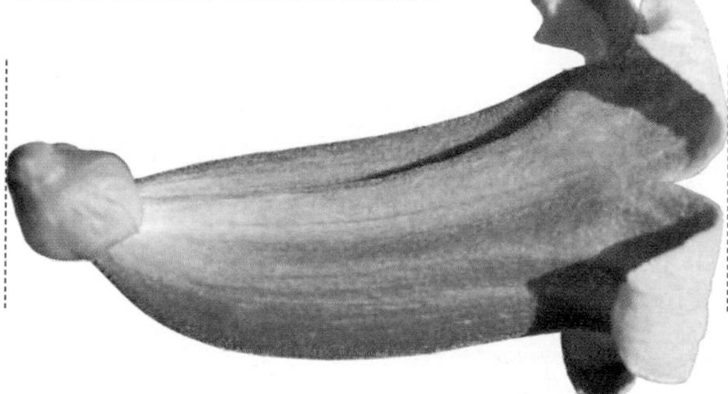

9. What is the length of the world's smallest seahorse to the nearest centimeter?

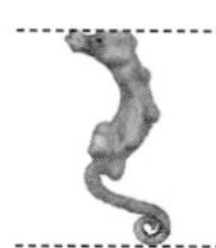

Algebra In **10–12**, copy and complete each number sentence.

10. $36 = 9 \times \square$

11. $7 \times \square = 56$

12. $60 = \square \times 10$

13. Which is the length of the crayon below? Use a centimeter ruler to measure.

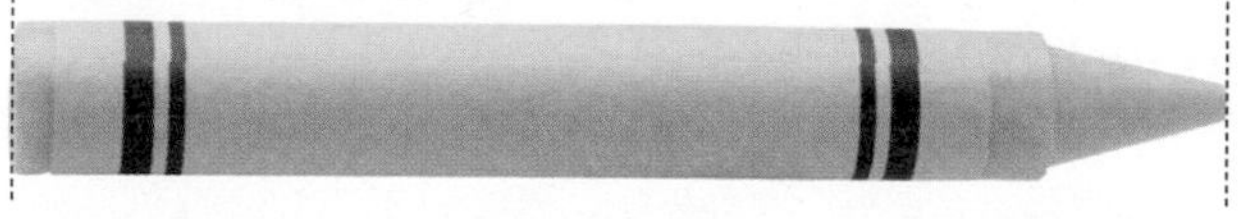

A 1 cm　**B** 4 cm　**C** 8 cm　**D** 1 dm

Lesson

17-2

MG 1.1 Choose the appropriate tools and units (metric and U.S.) and estimate and measure the length, liquid volume, and weight/mass of given objects.

Using Meters and Kilometers

How can you estimate and choose units to measure length?

Lou needs to tell a friend in another country about the length of a truck and the road it travels on. What units can Lou use?

Another Example How can you use <, >, or = to compare lengths?

Metric Units of Length
1 meter (m) = 100 centimeters (cm)
1 kilometer (km) = 1,000 meters (m)

Which is longer, 2 meters, 7 centimeters or 200 centimeters?

You can make a table that relates meters and centimeters.

Meters	1	2	3	4
Centimeters	100	200	300	400

2 meters, 7 centimeters is longer than 2 meters.
The table shows 2 meters is equal to 200 centimeters.
So 2 meters, 7 centimeters > 200 centimeters

Explain It

1. How could you make a table to compare 6 meters and 500 centimeters?
2. Which is the shorter length, 4 meters or 17 centimeters?

Metric units used for measuring longer lengths are the meter (m) and the kilometer (km).

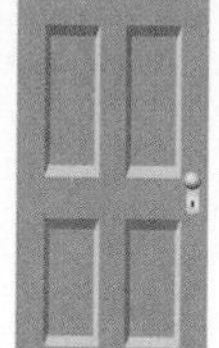

A doorknob is about 1 meter above the floor.

Most people can walk a kilometer in about 10 minutes.

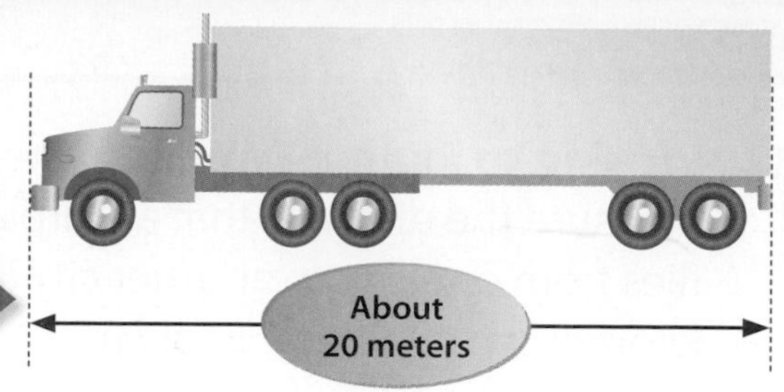

The length of a truck is best measured in meters.

The distance a truck travels on a road is best measured in kilometers.

Guided Practice*

Do you know HOW?

Which is the best unit to use? Choose meter or kilometer.

1. The length of a classroom
2. The length of a table in the lunchroom
3. The distance across your state

Do you UNDERSTAND?

4. In the example above, why is a kilometer the better unit to use to measure the length of the road?
5. **Writing to Explain** Which distance is greater, 850 meters or 1 kilometer? How do you know?

Independent Practice

In **6** and **7** tell if meter or kilometer is the better unit to use.

6. The height of a flagpole
7. The length of a bike trail

In **8** and **9**, use <, >, or = to compare the lengths. Copy and complete.

8. 8 centimeters ◯ 2 meters
9. 4 meters ◯ 400 centimeters

In **10** and **11**, choose the better estimate.

10. The height of an adult
    2 kilometers or 2 meters
11. The length of your foot
    20 centimeters or 20 meters

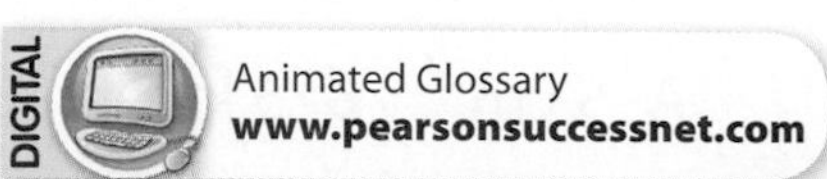

*For another example, see Set A on page 392.

Problem Solving

12. Writing to Explain Would you measure the distance that an airplane flies from one city to another city in kilometers or meters? Explain.

13. Number Sense A tree is 4 meters, 10 centimeters tall. Is this more than or less than 500 centimeters? Explain.

14. Use $<$, $>$, or $=$ to compare the lengths. Copy and complete the table to help.

Meters	1	2	3	4
Centimeters	100	200	■	■

3 meters, 15 centimeters ◯ 89 centimeters

4 meters, 63 centimeters ◯ 630 centimeters

In **15–17**, use the table at the right.

Data

Sale on Railings	
Length	**Price**
1 meter	$8
2 meters	$19
150 centimeters	$11

15. Estimation About how much would it cost to buy two 1-meter railings and two 2-meter railings?

16. How much more is the price of one 150-centimeter railing than the price of one 1-meter railing?

17. Mr. Casey needs a total of 3 meters of railing. The store is sold out of 1-m lengths. If he buys two 150-cm lengths of railing, will he have enough? Explain.

61 meters

18. The footbridge on Tower Bridge was built so workers could cross the River Thames in London, even when the main part of the bridge was open to let a boat pass. How many centimeters long is the footbridge?

19. Which measurement best describes the length of a car?

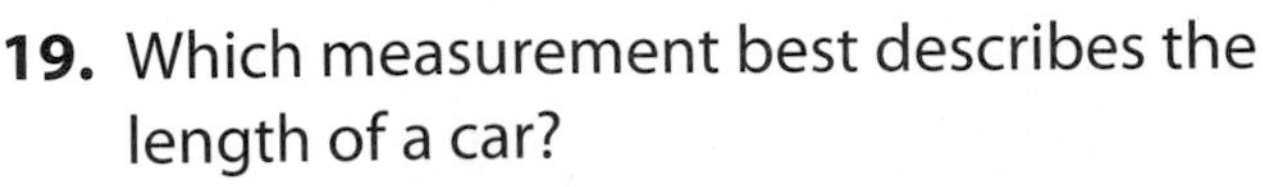

A 5 cm **B** 5 km **C** 5 m **D** 5 mm

Compare the numbers. Use <, >, or =.

1. 658 ◯ 658 2. 1,001 ◯ 992 3. 8,135 ◯ 8,140

Find each sum or difference. Estimate to check if the answer is reasonable.

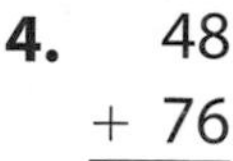

4. $\begin{array}{r} 48 \\ +\ 76 \\ \hline \end{array}$ 5. $\begin{array}{r} 513 \\ -\ 189 \\ \hline \end{array}$ 6. $\begin{array}{r} 126 \\ -\ 37 \\ \hline \end{array}$ 7. $\begin{array}{r} 8{,}705 \\ +\ 2{,}495 \\ \hline \end{array}$

Estimate and then find each product or quotient.

8. $\begin{array}{r} 64 \\ \times\ 3 \\ \hline \end{array}$ 9. 2×86 10. $\begin{array}{r} 793 \\ \times\ 5 \\ \hline \end{array}$ 11. $\begin{array}{r} 2{,}157 \\ \times\ 9 \\ \hline \end{array}$ 12. $\begin{array}{r} 3{,}098 \\ \times\ 8 \\ \hline \end{array}$

13. $6\overline{)96}$ 14. $4\overline{)628}$ 15. $2\overline{)2{,}682}$ 16. $5\overline{)1{,}745}$

Change the units. Copy and complete.

17. 3 feet = ▢ inches 18. 4 gallons = ▢ quarts

Error Search Find each sum or difference that is not correct. Write it correctly and explain the error.

19. $\frac{1}{4} + \frac{2}{4} = \frac{3}{4}$ 20. $\frac{2}{9} + \frac{4}{9} = \frac{1}{3}$ 21. $\frac{5}{7} - \frac{3}{7} = \frac{8}{7}$ 22. $\frac{4}{6} - \frac{1}{6} = \frac{1}{2}$

Number Sense

Estimating and Reasoning Write true or false for each statement. If it is false, explain why.

23. The product of 3 and 25 is greater than 50.

24. The difference 2,116 − 937 is greater than 1,000.

25. The quotient 183 ÷ 3 is less than 10.

26. The product 4 × 38 is less than 2 × 50.

27. The product of 3 and 305 is less than 1,000.

Lesson

17-3

MG 1.1 Choose the appropriate tools and units (metric and U.S.) and estimate and measure the length, liquid volume, and weight/mass of given objects.

Metric Units of Capacity

What metric units describe how much a container holds?

Two metric units of capacity are milliliters and liters. What is the capacity of this pail?

A milliliter is about 20 drops from this eyedropper.

Milliliter (mL)

This water bottle holds about 1 liter.

Liter (L)

Guided Practice*

Do you know HOW?

Choose the better estimate for each.

1. 

   250 mL or 2 L

2. 

   5 mL or 1 L

Do you UNDERSTAND?

3. **Writing to Explain** Suppose the capacity of the pail above is given in milliliters. Is this number greater or less than the number of liters? Explain.

4. Find a container that you predict will hold more than a liter and another that you predict will hold less than a liter. Then use a liter container to check your predictions.

Independent Practice

In **5–12**, choose the better estimate for each.

5. 

   40 mL or 40 L

6. 

   15 mL or 1 L

7. 

   14 mL or 14 L

8. 

   250 mL or 250 L

9. teacup
   15 L or 150 mL

10. bathtub
    115 mL or 115 L

11. bottle cap
    3 mL or 3 L

12. teapot
    1 L or 10 L

*For another example, see Set B on page 392.

Step 1

Choose an appropriate unit and estimate.

Units of Capacity
1,000 milliliters = 1 liter

A milliliter is too small. So use liters.

The pail will hold several liters.

Step 2

Measure the capacity.

Count how many times you can fill a liter container and empty it into the pail.

The pail holds about 8 liters.

In **13–16**, choose the unit you would use to measure the capacity of each.

13. soup can
mL or L

14. water pitcher
mL or L

15. swimming pool
ml or L

16. baby bottle
mL or L

Problem Solving

Estimation For **17–20**, is the capacity of each container more than a liter or less than a liter?

17. large pot

18. glass of juice

19. washing machine

20. mug

21. Reasoning Which cooler has a greater capacity? Explain your thinking.

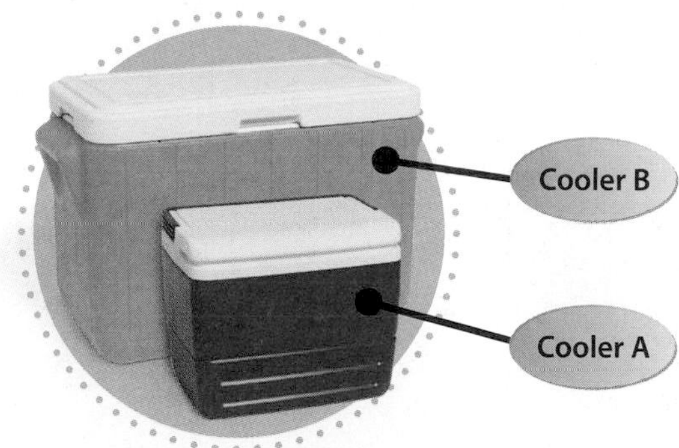

22. Which measurement best describes the capacity of a can of paint?

A 4 mL

B 4 L

C 40 L

D 40 mL

23. Number Sense A sandgrouse can soak up water in its fluffy feathers. It can carry the water many miles to its chicks. Does a sandgrouse carry 20 milliliters of water or 2 liters of water?

Lesson

17-4

MG 1.1 Choose the appropriate tools and units (metric and U.S.) and estimate and measure the length, liquid volume, and weight/mass of given objects.

Units of Mass

What metric units describe mass?

Mass is a measure of the amount of matter in an object. Grams and kilograms are two metric units of mass. What is the mass of this apple?

Guided Practice*

Do you know HOW?

Choose the better estimate for each.

1. 

5 g or 5 kg

2. 

40 g or 4 kg

Do you UNDERSTAND?

3. **Writing to Explain** There are 10 weights on the pan balance above. Why isn't the mass of the apple 10 grams?

4. Find an object that has a mass more than a kilogram and another that has a mass less than a kilogram. Then use a pan balance to see if you are correct.

Independent Practice

For **5–12**, choose the better estimate for each.

5. 

100 g or 10 kg

6. 

15 g or 15 kg

7. 

4 g or 400 g

8. 

400 g or 4 kg

9. bicycle

2 kg or 12 kg

10. feather

1 g or 1 kg

11. horse

5 kg or 550 kg

12. penny

3 g or 300 g

*For another example, see Set C on page 392.

Step 1

Choose a unit and estimate.

Units of Mass
1,000 grams = 1 kilogram

The unit kilogram is too big. Use grams.

The mass of the apple is less than 1 kilogram but more than 1 gram.

Step 2

Measure the mass of the apple.

Two 100-gram weights, six 10-gram weights, and two 1-gram weights balance with the apple.

The apple has a mass of 262 grams.

Problem Solving

For **13–17**, choose the best tool to measure each.

13. the capacity of a glass

14. the temperature of water

15. the length of a box

16. the weight of a pear

17. the length of time you sleep

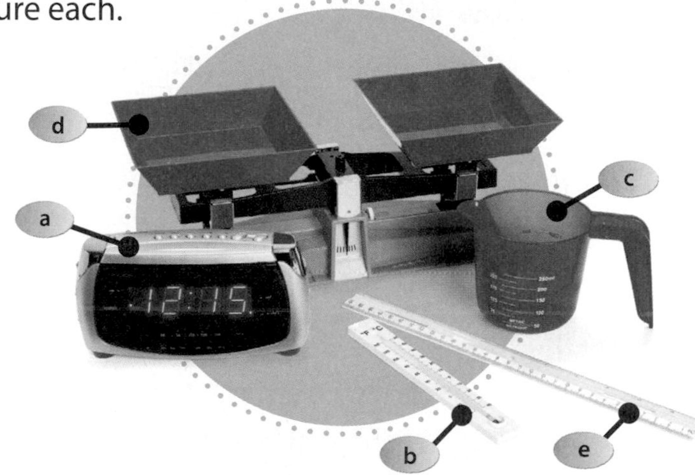

18. What is the mass of the orange?

Two 100-gram weights, four 10-gram weights, and two 1-gram weights balance with the orange.

19. Correct the mistakes in the shopping list below.

Shopping List
2 L of apples
3 kg of milk
5 cm of flour

20. A bag holds 500 grams of sand. About how many grains of sand are in the bag?

There are about 1,000 grains of sand in 1 gram.

21. Which measurement best describes the mass of a rabbit?

A 2 grams

B 2 kilograms

C 2 liters

D 2 meters

Lesson
17-5

MG 1.4 Carry out simple unit conversions within a system of measurement (e.g., centimeters and meters, hours and minutes). Also NS 2.8 and AF 1.4

Converting Units

How can you change units?

The Kim family is going on a trip in a motor home. The motor home is 9 meters long. How many centimeters are in 9 meters?

Data

Relating Metric Units
1 centimeter (cm) = 10 millimeters (mm)
1 meter (m) = 100 centimeters
1 kilometer (km) = 1,000 meters
1 liter (L) = 1,000 milliliters (mL)
1 kilogram (kg) = 1,000 grams (g)

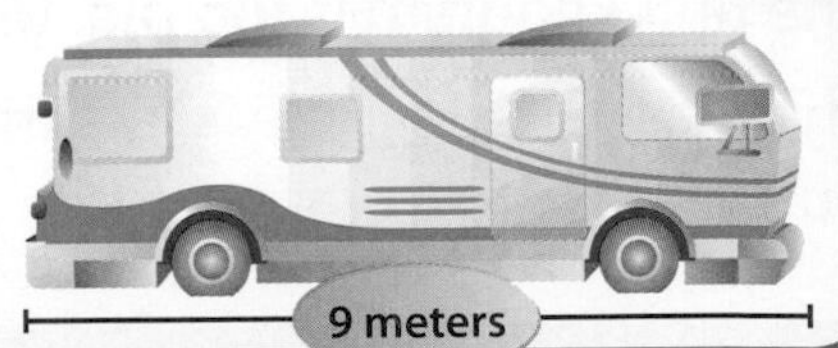

Guided Practice*

Do you know HOW?

In **1–3**, change the units. Copy and complete.

1. 4 meters = ▭ centimeters

2. 2 liters = ▭ milliliters

3. 7 kilometers = ▭ meters

Do you UNDERSTAND?

4. In the example above, why might you need to know how many centimeters long the motor home is?

5. Troy put 5 liters of water in a fish tank. How many milliliters of water did he put in the fish tank?

Independent Practice

In **6–15**, change the units. Copy and complete.

6. 8 liters = ▭ milliliters

7. 9 kilograms = ▭ grams

8. 4 centimeters = ▭ millimeters

9. 9 meters = ▭ centimeters

10. How many centimeters are in 5 meters, 2 centimeters?

11. How many meters are in 3 kilometers, 4 meters?

12. How many milliliters are in 6 liters, 25 milliliters?

13. How many grams are in 3 kilograms, 42 grams?

14. How many millimeters are in 1 meter, 6 centimeters, 2 millimeters?

15. How many milliliters are in 9 liters, 45 milliliters?

*For another example, see Set D on page 393.

▢ centimeters = ▢ meters × 100

▢ centimeters = 9 meters × 100

900 centimeters = 9 meters × 100

There are 900 centimeters in 9 meters.

The mass of a bowling ball is 5 kilograms. How many grams are in 5 kilograms?

▢ grams = ▢ kilograms × 1,000

▢ grams = 5 kilograms × 1,000

5,000 grams = 5 kilograms × 1,000

There are 5,000 grams in 5 kilograms.

Problem Solving

16. A crayon is 9 centimeters, 3 millimeters long. How many millimeters long is the crayon?

17. A walk to raise funds for charity is 5 kilometers long. There are 7,000 people who will walk. How many meters long is the walk?

18. A rock has a mass of 3000 grams. Write the mass of that rock in kilograms.

In **19** and **20**, use the table.

19. The Marin family wants to use an overnight campsite with electricity for five days. What is the total cost?

20. How much more is a five-day stay at an overnight campsite with electricity than without electricity?

Data

Blue Lake Camp

Item	Fee Each Day
Day Campsite	$7
Overnight Campsite	$15
Electricity	$9

21. Writing to Explain Justin received a box and an envelope in the mail. The mass of the box was 1 kilogram, 50 grams. The mass of the envelope was 1,200 grams. Which had a greater mass — the box or the envelope? Explain how you found your answer.

22. Which of the following is used to find out how many milliliters are in 3 liters?

A 3 × 1,000 **C** 3 × 12

B 1,000 ÷ 3 **D** 12 ÷ 3

23. There are 1,000 meters in 1 kilometer. How many meters are in 4 kilometers?

A 14 **B** 40 **C** 400 **D** 4,000

24. How many grams are in 9 kilograms?

Lesson

17-6

AF 2.1 Solve simple problems involving a functional relationship between two quantities (e.g., find the total cost of multiple items given the cost per unit).
Also **MR 2.3.**

Problem Solving

Make a Table and Look for a Pattern

Livia is training for a 25 km walk. She recorded how far she walked each day. If she continues the pattern, how far will Livia walk on Day 4? How far will she walk on Day 5?

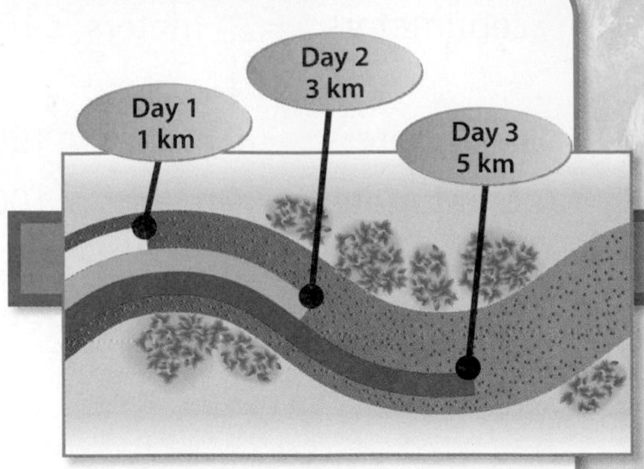

Guided Practice*

Do you know HOW?

Copy and complete the table. Write to explain the pattern. Solve.

1. Nat has a pole that is 1 meter long. He is cutting it into 20-centimeter long pieces. What length of pole is left after 3 cuts? after 4 cuts?

Cuts	0	1	2	3	4
Length (cm)	100	80	60		

Do you UNDERSTAND?

2. In the example above, how did the table help you to explain the pattern?

3. **Write a Problem** Write a problem that you can solve by writing an explanation of a pattern.

Independent Practice

In **4–7**, Copy and complete the table. Write to explain the pattern. Solve.

4. Nola is putting tiles in a row. Each tile is a square, and the length of its side is 4 centimeters. What is the length of 4 tiles together? 5 tiles?

Number of Tiles	1	2	3	4	5
Total Length (cm)	4	8	12		

Stuck? Try this....

- What do I know?
- What am I asked to find?
- What diagram can I use to help understand the problem?
- Can I use addition, subtraction, multiplication, or division?
- Is all of my work correct?
- Did I answer the right question?
- Is my answer reasonable?

*For another example, see Set E on page 393.

Plan

You can make a table to show what you know. Then look for a pattern.

Day	1	2	3	4	5
Distance walked (km)	1	3	5		

Explain the pattern.

Each day Livia increased the distance she walked by 2 km.

Solve

Use the pattern to complete the table and solve the problem.

Day 3: 5 km
Day 4: 5 km + 2 km = 7 km
Day 5: 7 km + 2 km = 9 km

Day	1	2	3	4	5
Distance walked (km)	1	3	5	7	9

Livia will walk 7 km on Day 4 and 9 km on Day 5.

5. Talia is cutting up a sheet of paper that is 24 centimeters long. She is cutting the sheet into pieces that are each 3 centimeters long. What is the length of the sheet that is left after Talia has made 3 cuts? 4 cuts?

Number of Cuts	0	1	2	3	4
Length Left (cm)	24	21	18		

6. Mr. Lum is putting fence rails together in a row. Each rail is 2 meters long. What is the length of 5 rails together? 6 rails?

Number of Rails	1	2	3	4	5	6
Total Length (m)	2	4	6	8		

7. Evan makes picture frames using wood. For each frame, he needs 60 cm of wood. What is the total length of wood he needs to make 4 frames? 5 frames?

Number of Frames	1	2	3	4	5
Total Length (cm)	60	120	180		

8. Nick earns money doing chores. How much would he earn if he washes windows, washes dishes, and does laundry?

Data

Item	Price
Clean yard	$8
Do laundry	$5
Vacuum floors	$3
Wash dishes	$2
Wash windows	$7

9. In the morning, Ray painted 12 windows. By the end of the day he had painted all 26 windows in the house. Which of these shows one way to find how many windows he painted in the afternoon?

A 26 + 12 **B** 26 − 12 **C** 26 × 12 **D** 26 ÷ 12

Test Prep

1. Which of the following is about 2 meters? (17-2)

A the length of a bumble bee

B the distance from first base to second base

C the height of a one-story house

D the height of a classroom door

2. What is the length of the apple core to the nearest centimeter? (17-1)

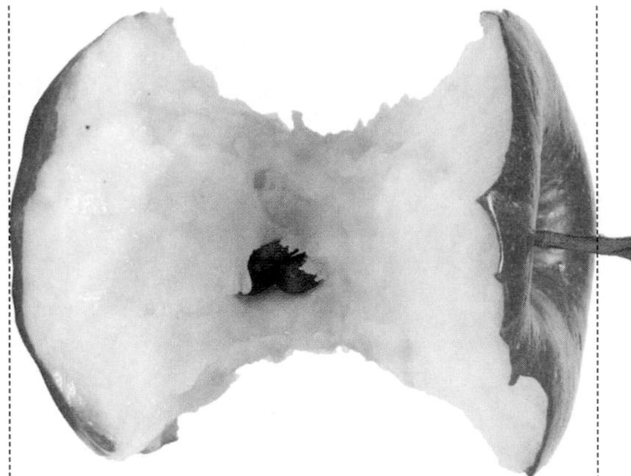

A 3 centimeters

B 6 centimeters

C 7 centimeters

D 8 centimeters

3. The black mamba snake at the zoo measures 3 meters, 9 centimeters long. How many centimeters is this? (17-5)

A 300 centimeters

B 309 centimeters

C 390 centimeters

D 903 centimeters

4. Which is the best estimate of the capacity of a bottle of syrup? (17-3)

A 709 pints

B 709 liters

C 709 cups

D 709 milliliters

5. There are 1,000 grams in a kilogram. Which can be used to change 4 kilograms to grams? (17-5)

A 4 kilograms $\div$ 1,000 = 4 grams

B 4 kilograms $\div$ 4 = 1,250 grams

C 4 kilograms $\times$ 1,000 = 4,000 grams

D 4 kilograms $\times$ 100 = 400 grams

6. Which best describes the length of a crayon? (17-2)

A 7 millimeters

B 7 centimeters

C 7 decimeters

D 7 kilometers

7. Which of the following can hold only about 2 liters of water? (17-3)

A Bathtub

B Swimming pool

C Coffee pot

D Medicine dropper

Test Prep

8. Pat bought a sub sandwich that was 36 centimeters long. She cut 4-centimeter slices. What was the length of the sandwich left after Pat cut off 5 slices? (17-6)

Slices Cut Off	0	1	2	3	4	5
Centimeters Left	36	32	28	24		

A 20 centimeters

B 18 centimeters

C 16 centimeters

D 12 centimeters

9. Which unit would be best to measure the mass of a mouse? (17-4)

A Grams

B Kilograms

C Liters

D Milliliters

10. Which could be about a decimeter long? (17-1)

A a lady bug

B a whale

C an ant

D a turtle

11. Which is the best estimate of the mass of a golf ball? (17-4)

A 450 kilograms

B 450 grams

C 45 kilograms

D 45 grams

12. There are 1,000 milliliters in 1 liter. How many milliliters are in 8 liters? (17-5)

A 8,000

B 4,000

C 800

D 80

13. Which would be the best to measure in kilometers? (17-2)

A the distance from California to Hawaii

B the length of a toothbrush

C the distance a snail can crawl in an hour

D the length of a soccer field

14. Trey is practicing for a swim meet. If he continues the pattern, how many laps will he swim on the 6th day? (17-6)

Day	1	2	3	4	5	6
Laps Swam	25	29	33	37		

A 46 laps

B 45 laps

C 44 laps

D 39 laps

Reteaching

Set A, pages 376–380

Estimate and measure the length of the bead to the nearest centimeter.

You can use your finger width as 1 centimeter to help estimate.

Estimate: about 3 centimeters long

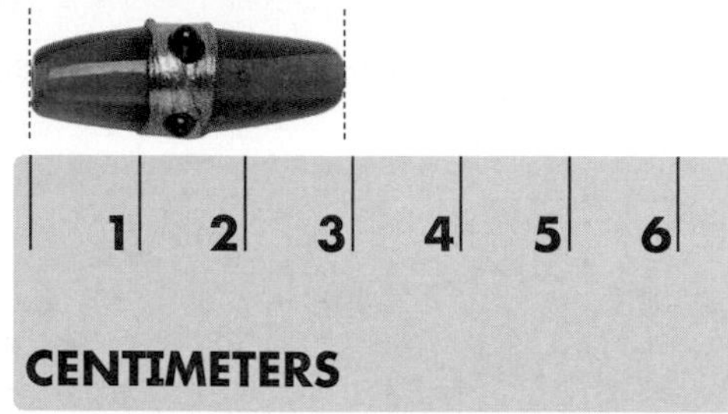

The bead is 3 centimeters long, to the nearest centimeter.

Remember to line up the object with the 0 mark on the ruler.

Estimate the length. Then measure to the nearest centimeter.

1. 

Choose the better estimate.

2. The length of a truck
10 meters or 10 kilometers

Use $<$, $>$, or $=$ to compare. Copy and complete.

3. 3 centimeters ◯ 3 meters

4. 5 kilometers ◯ 5 meters

Set B, pages 382–383

What is the capacity of this pitcher?

Choose an appropriate unit and estimate.

A milliliter is too small, so estimate using liters.

It looks like the pitcher will hold about 2 liters.

Remember that more than one unit can be used to measure the capacity of a container.

Choose the better estimate.

1. 150 mL or 150 L

2. 
5 mL or 5 L

Set C, pages 384–385

What is the mass of this bar of soap?

Choose a unit and estimate.

A kilogram is too much, so estimate using grams.

The bar of soap has about the same mass as 100 grapes, or about 100 grams.

Remember to use the examples of a gram and kilogram to help you estimate.

Choose the better estimate.

1. 
15 g or 15 kg

2.  

2 g or 2 kg

Set D, pages 386–387

Change from one unit to a different unit.

▢ centimeters = 3 meters

Change to centimeters.

You know that 1 meter = 100 centimeters.

Multiply: 3×100 centimeters = 300 cm

3 meters = 300 centimeters

Remember to use the correct numbers and operations when you are changing units.

Change the units. Copy and complete.

1. 5 meters = ▢ centimeters
2. 8 kilograms = ▢ grams
3. 4 liters = ▢ milliliters
4. 3 m 20 cm = ▢ cm
5. 3 m 2 cm = ▢ cm

Set E, pages 388–389

Vita makes bows using ribbon. What is the total length of ribbon she needs to make 4 bows? 5 bows?

Make a table and look for a pattern.

Explain the pattern.
Solve the problem.

Number of Bows	1	2	3	4	5
Total Length of Ribbon	30 cm	60 cm	90 cm	120 cm	150 cm

Vita needs 30 cm of ribbon for each bow she makes.

Vita needs 120 cm for 4 bows and 150 cm for 5 bows.

Remember to check your answers. Make sure all of your numbers fit the pattern.

1. Ned is training for a 40 km bike race. If he continues his pattern, how far will he ride on Day 4? On Day 5? Copy and complete the table. Write to explain the pattern.

Day	1	2	3	4	5
Distance Ned Rode	1 km	4 km	7 km	▢	▢

2. Roberto used Ned's table to estimate that on Day 9 Ned would ride more than 40 km. Do you agree? Explain.

Topic 18

Perimeter, Area, and Volume

1 How far would you need to walk to go around the outside of this maze in Williamsburg, Virginia? You will find out in Lesson 18-1.

2 How long is one side of this small chessboard? You will find out in Lesson 18-4.

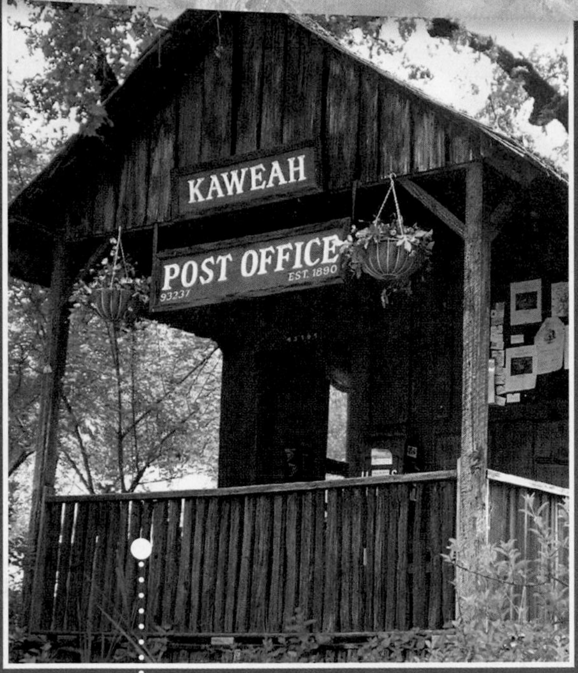

3 The post office in Kaweah, California is the smallest post office in the nation. How small is it? You will find out in Lesson 18-3.

4 What is the perimeter of the base of this glass house? You will find out in Lesson 18-2.

Review What You Know!

Vocabulary

Choose the best term from the box.

- equilateral
- rectangle
- polygon
- trapezoid

1. A(n) __?__ could have 5 sides.
2. A triangle with all three sides the same length is called a(n) __?__ triangle.
3. A __?__ is a special quadrilateral with 4 right angles.

Multiplication Facts

Find each product.

4. 3×8	**5.** 6×4	**6.** 5×7
7. 2×9	**8.** 7×3	**9.** 4×8

Geometry

Write the name that best describes each figure.

10. A quadrilateral with only one pair of parallel sides
11. A quadrilateral with four right angles and all sides the same length
12. A triangle with no sides the same length

Arrays

13. **Writing to Explain** Explain how to draw an array to show 3×6. Draw the array.

Lesson

18-1

MG 1.3 Find the perimeter of a polygon with integer sides.

Understanding Perimeter

How do you find perimeter?

Gus wants to make a playpen for his dog and put a fence around it. He made drawings of two different playpens. What is the perimeter of the playpen in each drawing?

The distance around a figure is its perimeter.

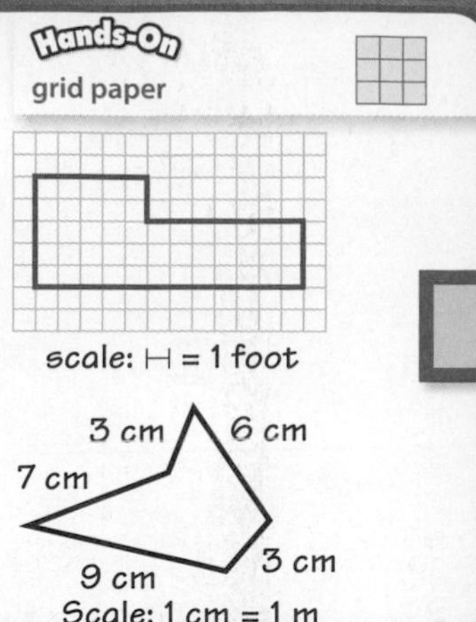

Guided Practice*

Do you know HOW?

In **1** and **2**, find the perimeter.

1.

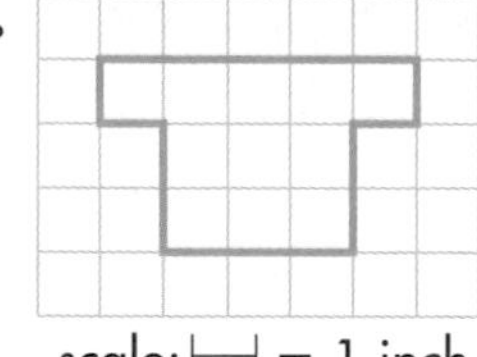

scale: ⊢⊣ = 1 inch

2.

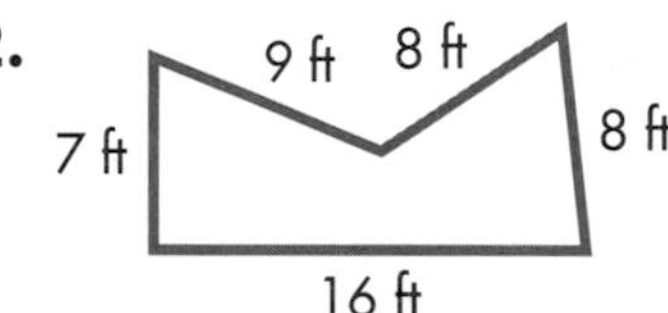

Do you UNDERSTAND?

3. In the example above, how do you know what unit Gus used for the first playpen?

4. What is the perimeter of the garden shown in the diagram below?

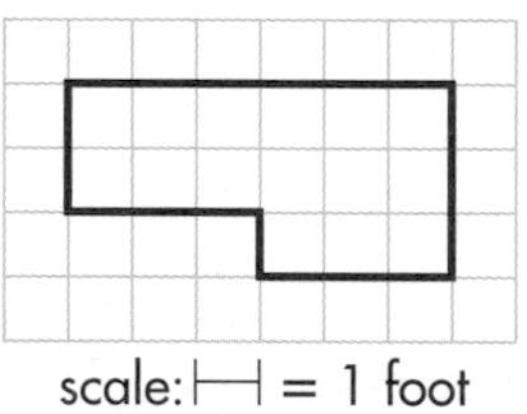

scale: ⊢⊣ = 1 foot

Independent Practice

In **5–7**, find the perimeter of each polygon.

5.

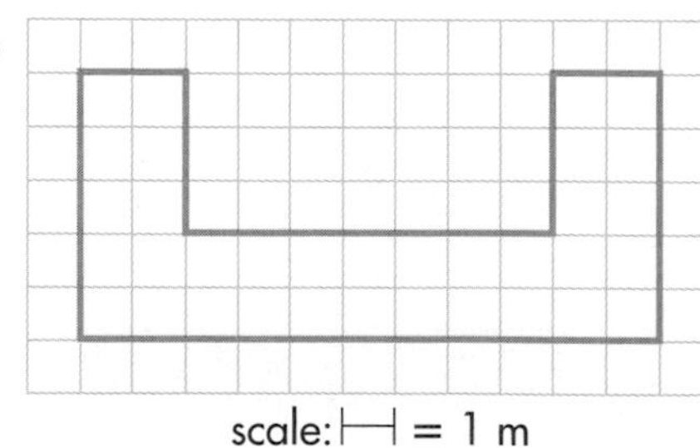

scale: ⊢⊣ = 1 m

6.

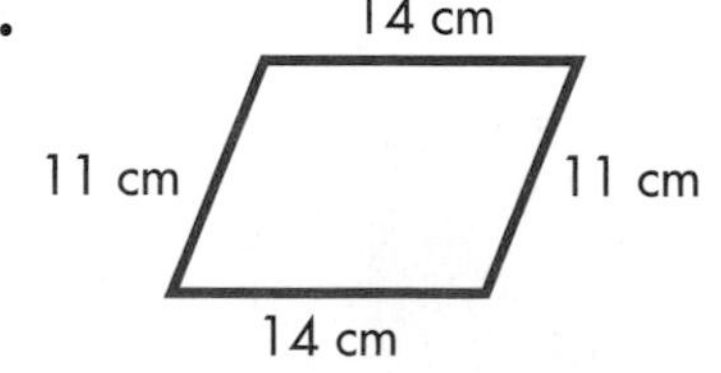

7.

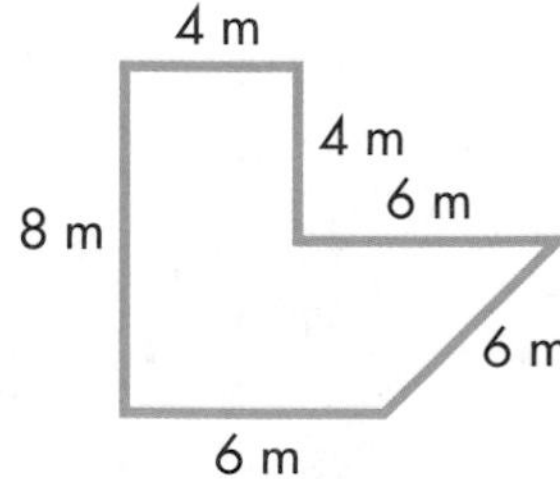

In **8–10**, draw a figure with the given perimeter. Use grid paper.

8. 14 units **9.** 8 units **10.** 20 units

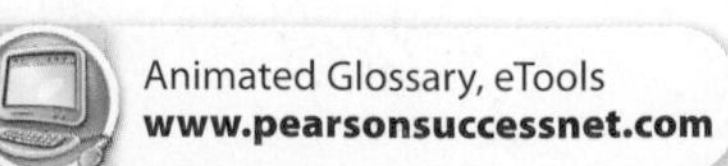

*For another example, see Set A on page 412.

One Way

You can find the perimeter by counting unit segments.

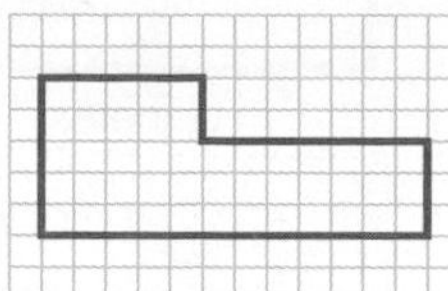

scale: ⊢⊣ = 1 foot

The perimeter of this playpen is 34 feet.

Another Way

Add the lengths of the sides to find the perimeter.

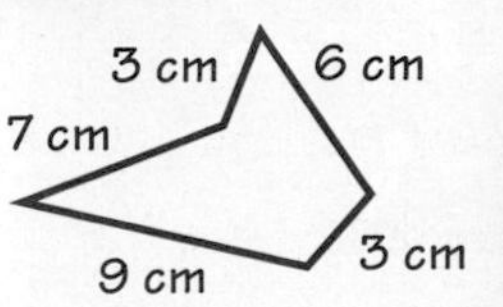

3 + 9 + 7 + 3 + 6 = 28

Each centimeter stands for 1 meter, so the perimeter is 28 meters.

Problem Solving

11. Mr. Karas needs to find the perimeter of the playground to build a fence around it. What is the perimeter of the playground?

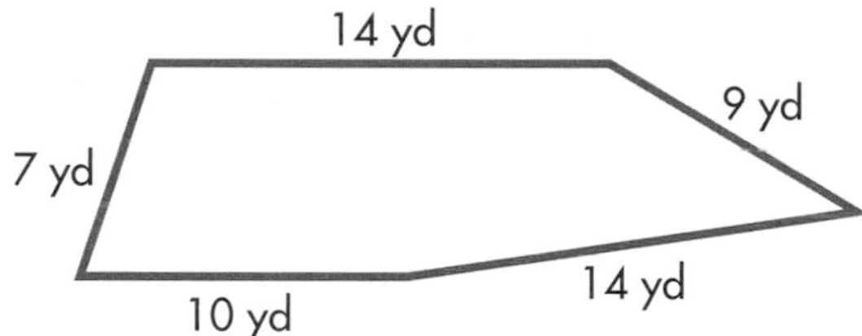

12. Mike needs to find the perimeter of the pool so he knows how many tiles to put around the edge. What is the perimeter of the pool?

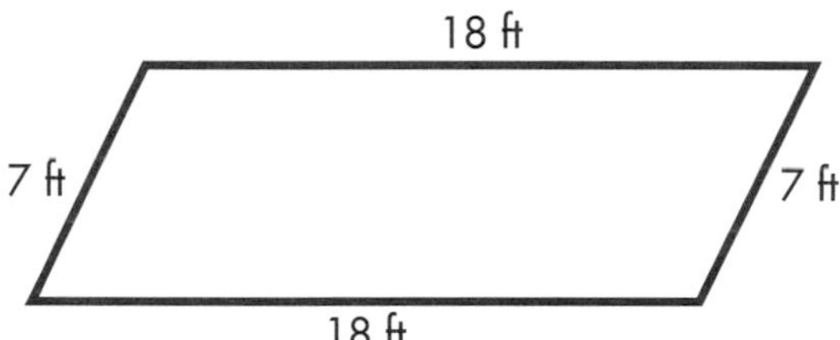

13. The distance around the outside of this maze in Williamsburg, Virginia, is the same as the perimeter of a rectangle. The picture shows the lengths of the sides of the rectangle. What is the perimeter of the maze?

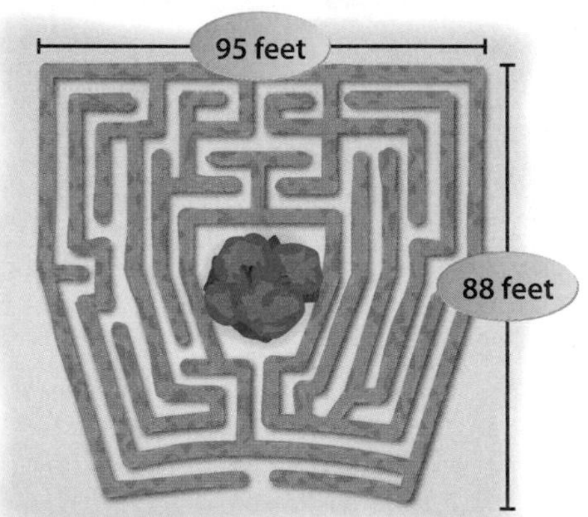

14. Jani has a magnet shown below.

What is the perimeter of Jani's magnet to the nearest inch? Use a ruler to measure.

A 2 in. **B** 4 in. **C** 5 in. **D** 6 in.

15. **Writing to Explain** Roberto has a magnet that is twice as long and twice as wide as Jani's magnet in Problem 14. Find the perimeter of Roberto's magnet. Explain your work.

Lesson

18-2

MG 1.3 Find the perimeter of a polygon with integer sides. Also **MG 2.3**.

Perimeter of Common Shapes

How can you find the perimeter of common shapes?

Mr. Coe needs to find the perimeter of two swimming pool designs. One pool shape is a rectangle. The other pool shape is a square. What is the perimeter of each pool?

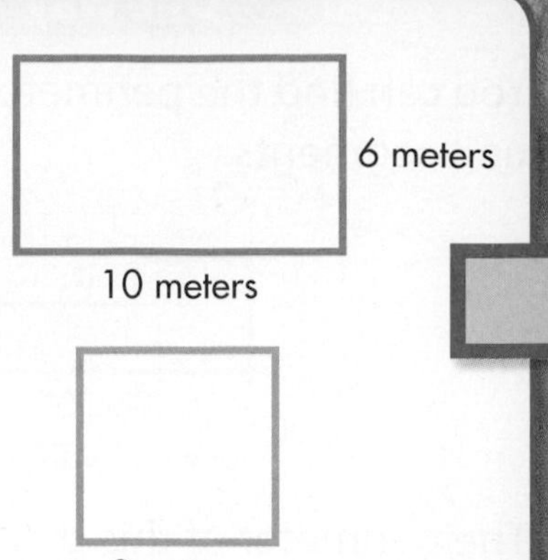

Guided Practice*

Do you know HOW?

For **1** and **2**, find the perimeter.

1. Rectangle

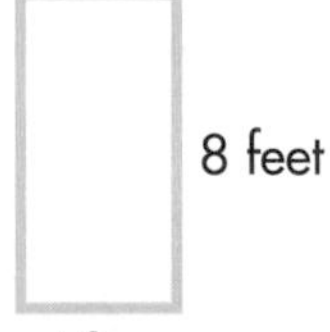

2. Square

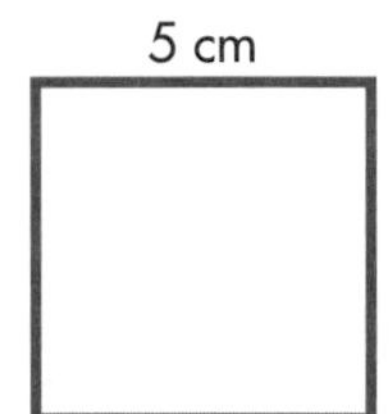

Do you UNDERSTAND?

3. In the examples above, explain how to find the missing lengths.

4. Darla drew an equilateral triangle. Each side was 9 inches long. What was the perimeter of the triangle?

Independent Practice

In **5** and **6**, use an inch ruler to measure the length of the sides of the polygon. Find the perimeter.

5. Square

6. Rectangle

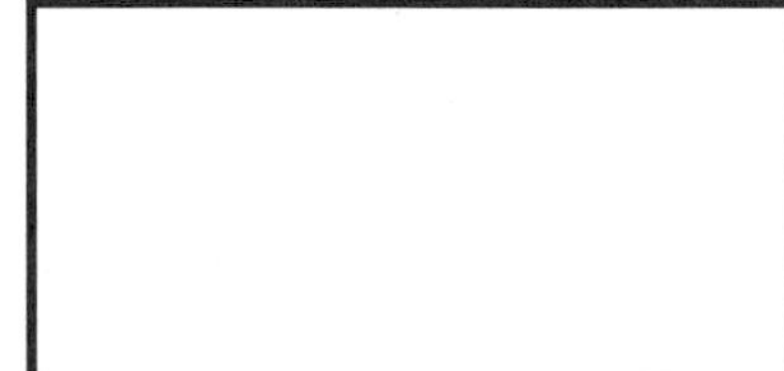

In **7** and **8**, find the perimeter of each polygon.

7. Rectangle

15 m

3 m

8. Equilateral triangle

4 yd

*For another example, see Set A on page 412.

Find the perimeter of the pool that has a rectangle shape.

Remember: Opposite sides of a rectangle are the same length.

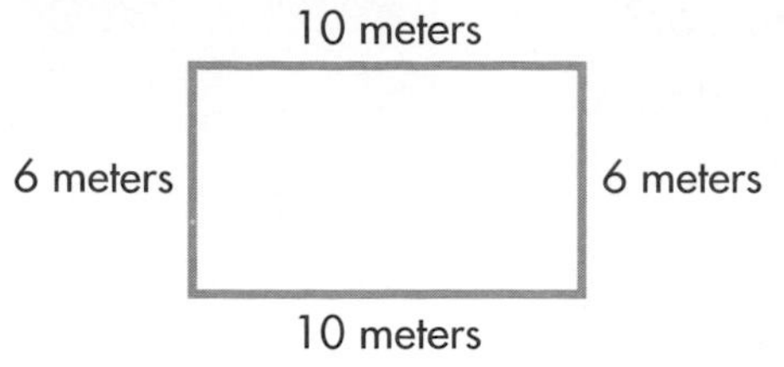

$10 + 6 + 10 + 6 = 32$

The perimeter of this pool is 32 meters.

Find the perimeter of the pool that has a square shape.

Remember: All four sides of a square are the same length.

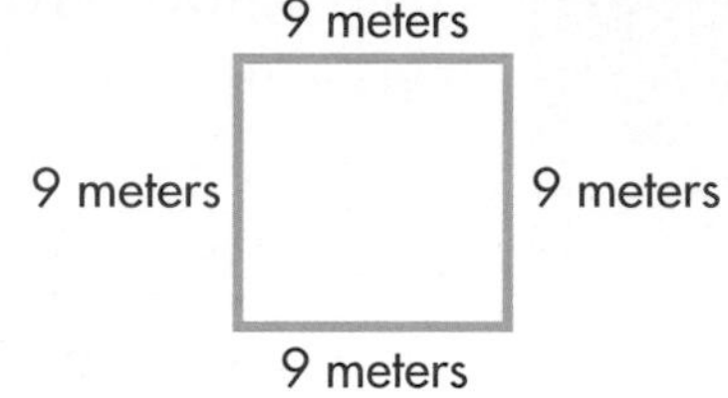

$9 + 9 + 9 + 9 = 36$

The perimeter of this pool is 36 meters.

Problem Solving

9. Writing to Explain Cora uses ribbons to make three different sizes of bows. How much more ribbon does it take to make 2 large bows than 2 small bows? Explain how you found your answer.

Data

Size of Bow	Length of Ribbon
Small	27 in.
Medium	36 in.
Large	49 in.

10. The base of Philip Johnson's Glass House in New Canaan, Connecticut, is a rectangle. What is the perimeter of the base of the Glass House?

11. What is the perimeter of the cloth patch outlined below?

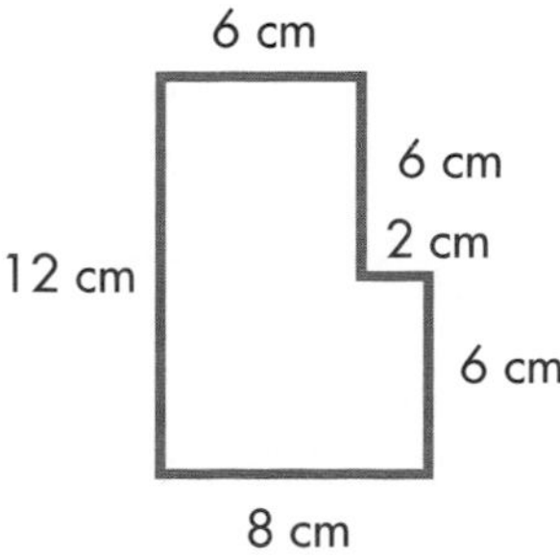

A 96 cm

B 40 cm

C 38 cm

D 32 cm

12. Ami's room is in the shape of a square. What is the perimeter of the room?

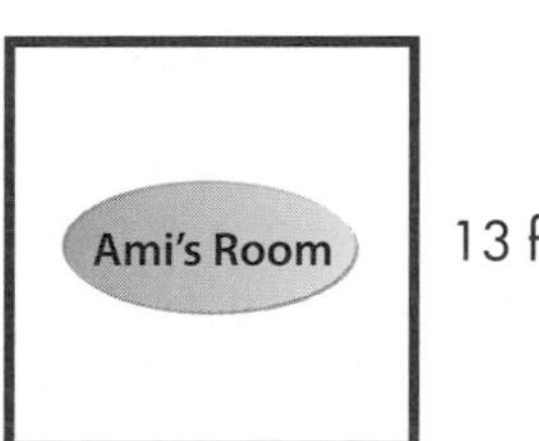

Lesson

18-3

MG 1.2 Estimate or determine the area and volume of solid figures by covering them with squares or by counting the number of cubes that would fill them.

Understanding Area

Hands-On: grid paper

How do you find area?

Raj needs to know how many tiles to buy to cover a floor. What is the area of the floor?

Area is the number of square units needed to cover the region inside a figure. A square unit is a square with sides that are each 1 unit long.

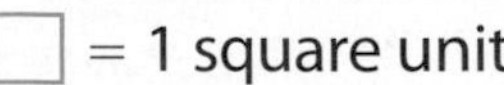

□ = 1 square unit

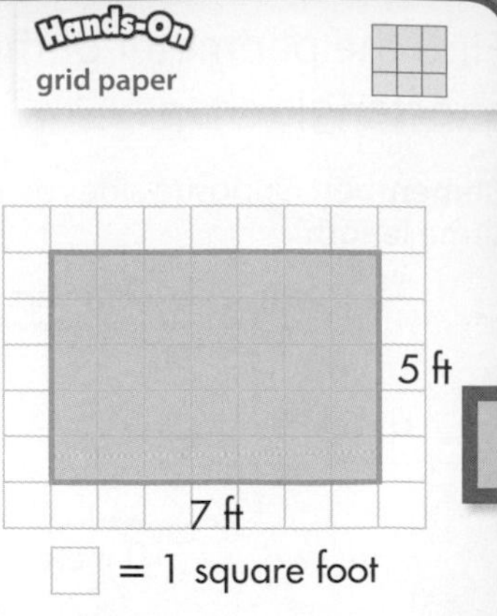

Guided Practice*

Do you know HOW?

In **1** and **2**, find the area of each figure.

1.

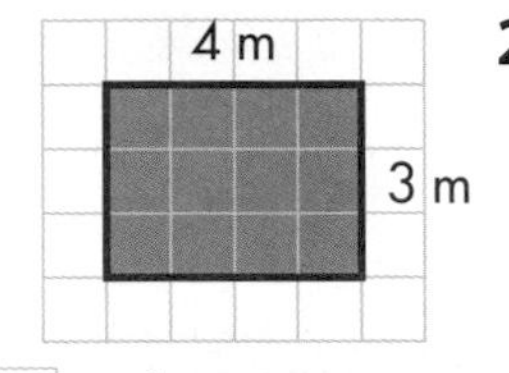

2.

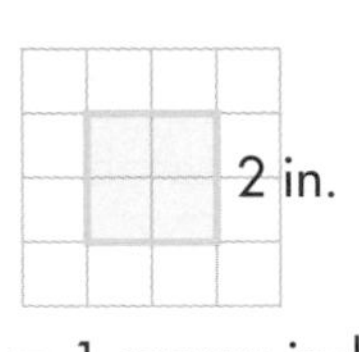

Do you UNDERSTAND?

3. Use the example above. Explain how finding the area is different from finding the perimeter of a figure.

4. The lid of Mella's jewelry box is a rectangle 3 inches wide. The area is 15 square inches. Use grid paper to draw a picture of the lid.

Independent Practice

In **5–10**, find the area of each figure.

5.

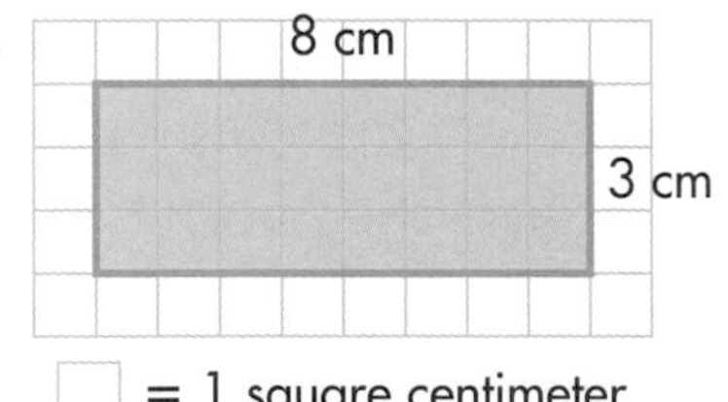

6.

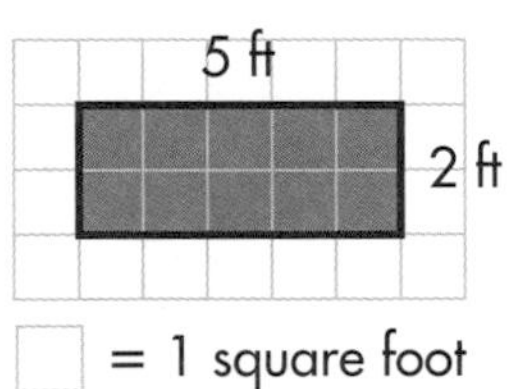

7.

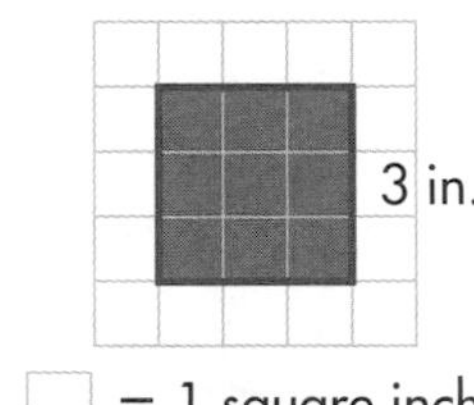

8.

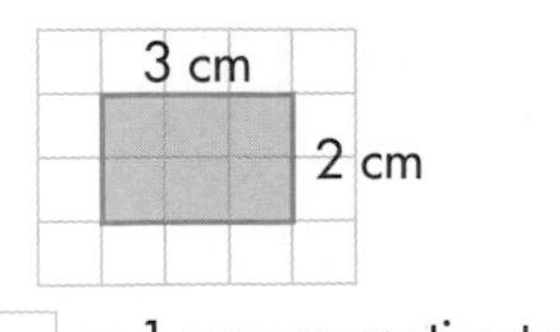

9.

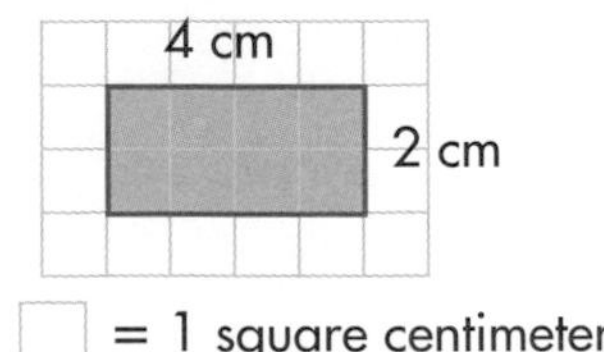

10.

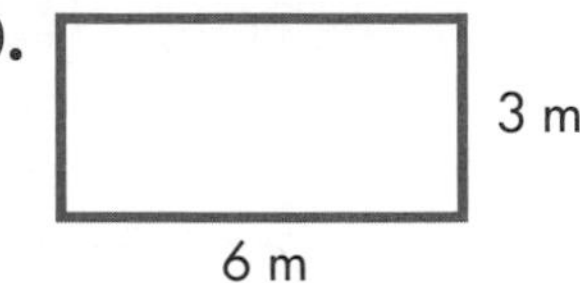

DIGITAL Animated Glossary, eTools **www.pearsonsuccessnet.com**

For another example, see Set B on page 412.

One Way

Count the square units.

There are 35 square units inside the figure.

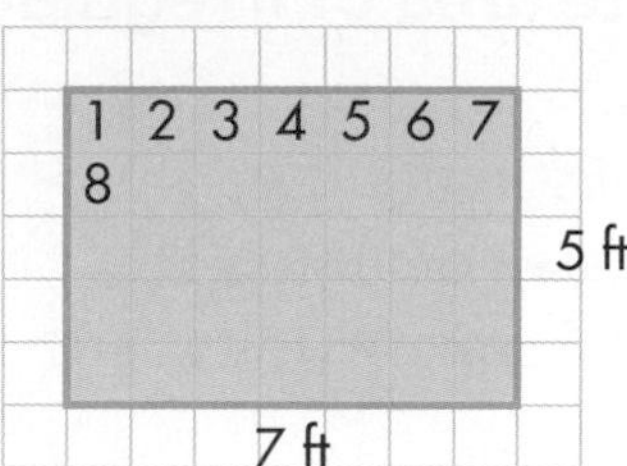

The lengths are given in feet. The area of the floor is 35 square feet.

Another Way

When you find the area of a rectangle or square, you can think of the grid squares as an array.

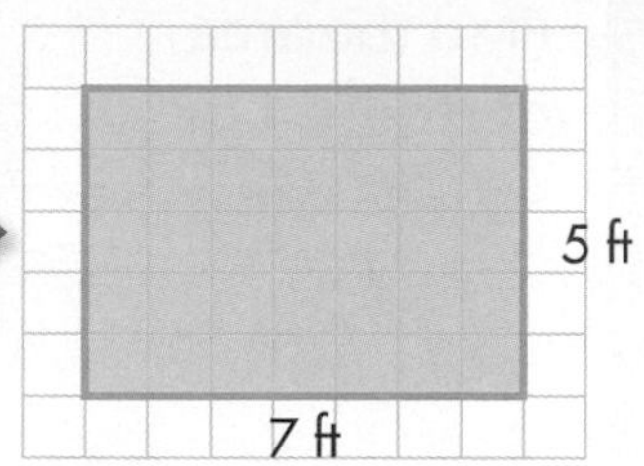

There are 5 rows with 7 squares in each row.

$5 \times 7 = 35$

The area of the floor is 35 square feet.

Problem Solving

11. The Kaweah, California Post Office was built in 1910. It is the nation's smallest post office. What is the area of the Kaweah Post Office?

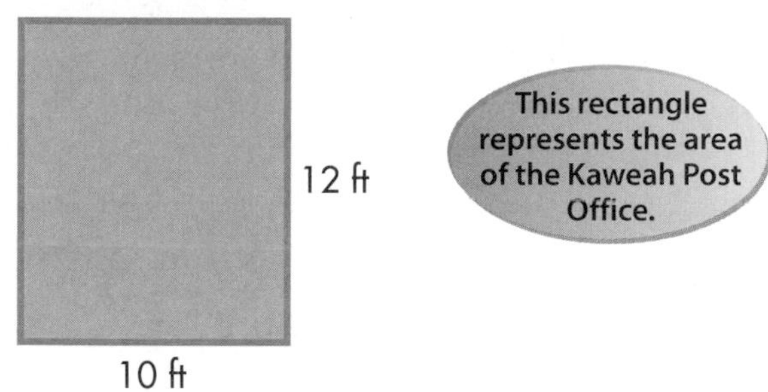

12. Use grid paper. Draw two different figures, each with an area of 24 square units. Find the perimeter of each figure.

13. **Writing to Explain** Tamiya cut a 12-inch piece of string into 3 equal parts. She also cut a 24-inch piece of ribbon into 8 equal parts. Which was longer, a piece of the string or a piece of the ribbon? Explain how you decided.

14. What is the area of the picture Abe made with square tiles?

A 20 square inches

B 21 square inches

C 24 square inches

D 30 square inches

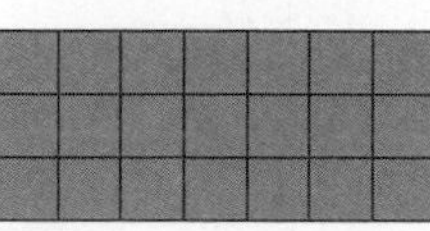

Lesson
18-4

MG 1.2 Estimate or determine the area and volume of solid figures by covering them with squares or by counting the number of cubes that would fill them.

Estimating and Measuring Area

How do you find and estimate area of irregular shapes?

Find the area of Figure 1 in square units.

Figure 1

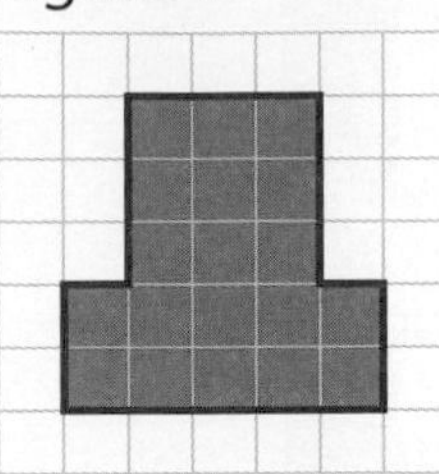

Estimate the area of Figure 2 in square units.

Figure 2

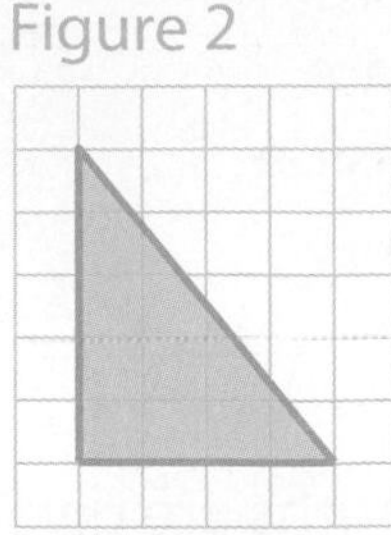

Guided Practice*

Do you know HOW?

1. Find the area in square units.

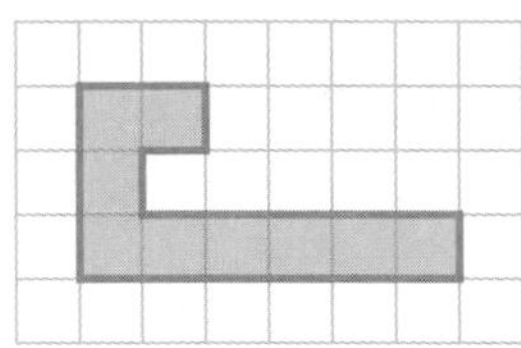

2. Estimate the area in square units.

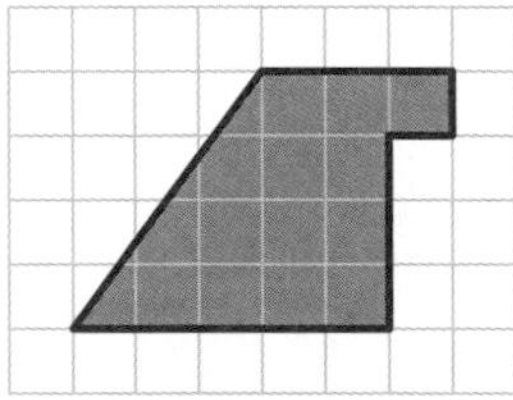

Do you UNDERSTAND?

3. Will partial squares always combine to form whole squares? Why or why not?

4. Kev needs to find the area of the floor so that he knows the number of tiles to buy to cover it. What is the area of the floor?

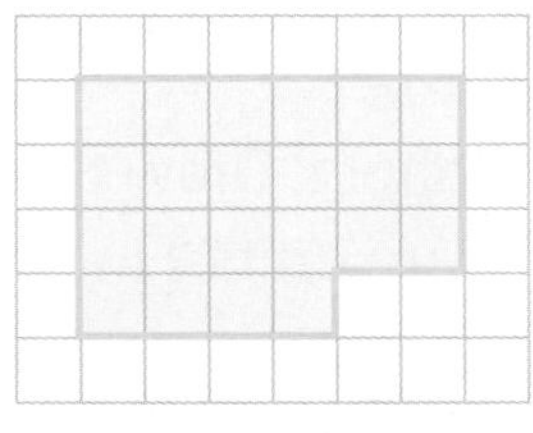

Independent Practice

In **5–7**, find each area in square units.

5.

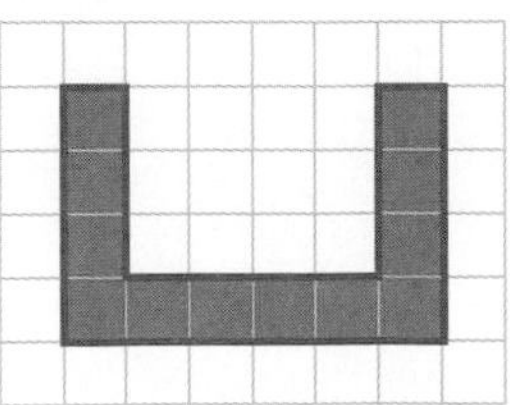

6.

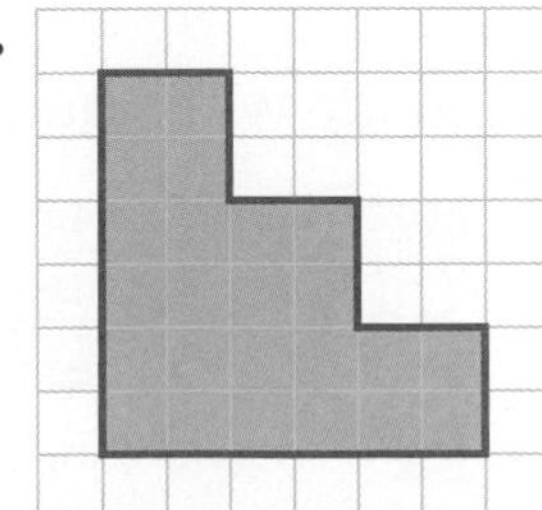

7.

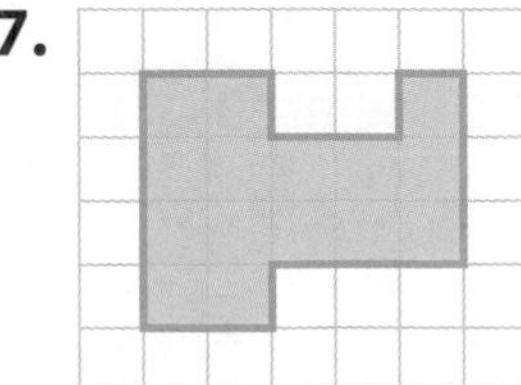

For another example, see Set C on page 413.

To find the area of Figure 1, count the squares.

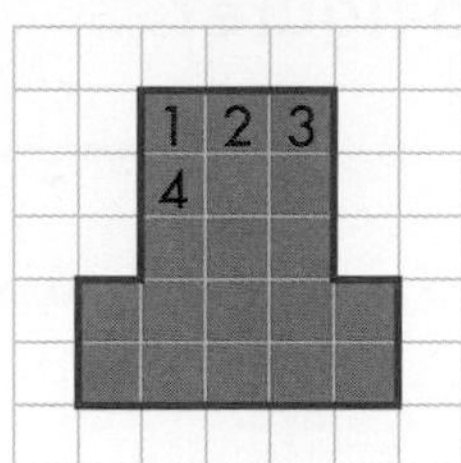

There are 19 square units inside Figure 1.

The area of Figure 1 is 19 square units.

To estimate the area of Figure 2, count whole squares first.

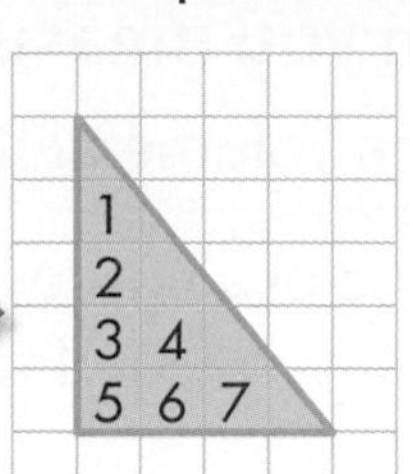

There are 7 whole squares.

Combine partial squares to make whole squares.

The partial squares make up about 3 whole squares.

$7 + 3 = 10$

The area of Figure 2 is about 10 square units.

In **8–10**, estimate each area in square units.

8. 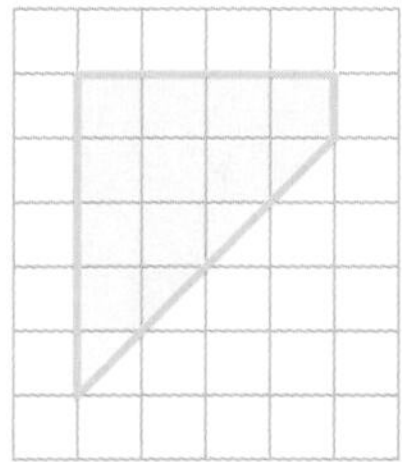

9. 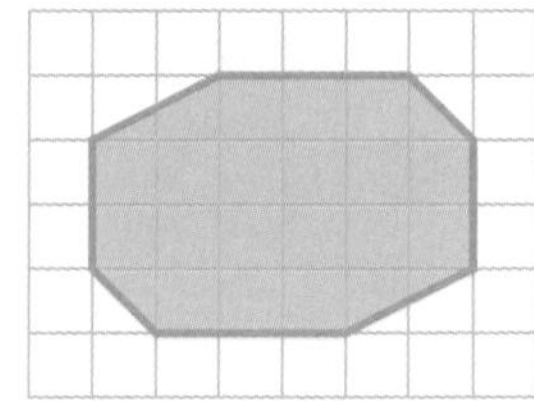

10. 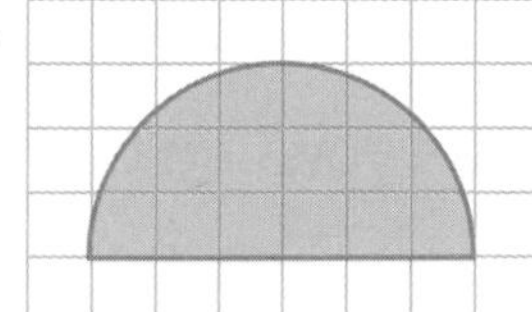

Problem Solving

11. Chen will use tiles to make a picture. He needs to estimate the area of the picture so that he buys enough tiles. Estimate the area of Chen's picture.

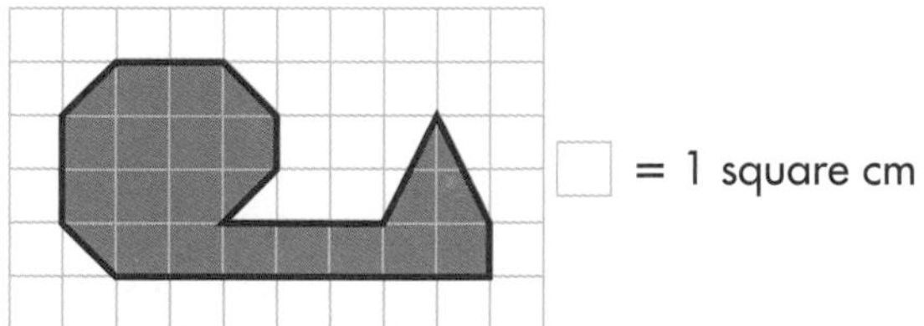

12. Suni put blue tiles on a wall. What is the area of the part of the wall with blue tiles?

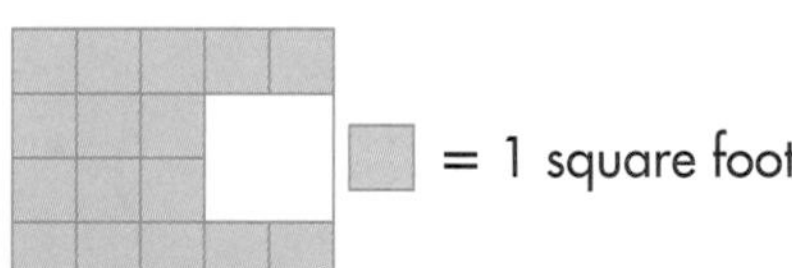

A 4 square feet
B 12 square feet
C 16 square feet
D 20 square feet

13. Writing to Explain Joe says the area of this chessboard is between 1 and 2 square inches. Do you agree? Explain.

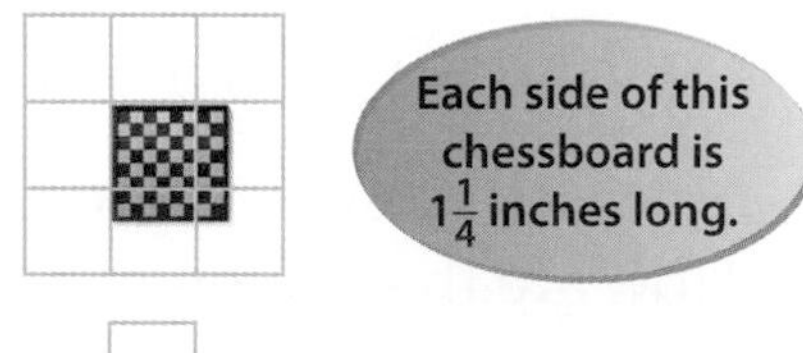

scale: = 1 sq in.

14. Reasonableness Bobby estimated that the sum of \$138 and \$241 is about \$480. Is his estimate reasonable? Explain.

Lesson
18-5

MG 1.2 Estimate or determine the area and volume of solid figures by covering them with squares or by counting the number of cubes that would fill them.

Volume

Hands-On
unit cubes

How can you measure the space inside a solid figure?

What is the volume of the box?

The volume of a figure is the number of cubic units needed to fill it.

A cubic unit is a cube with edges that are 1 unit long.

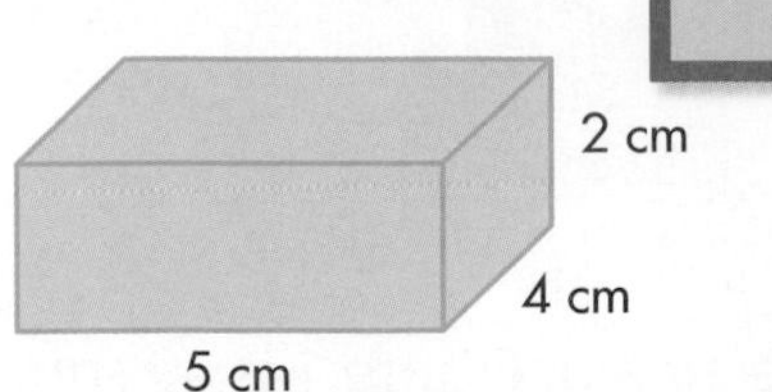

Another Example How can you measure the volume of other kinds of figures?

How can you find the volume of this figure?

Count all the cubes.

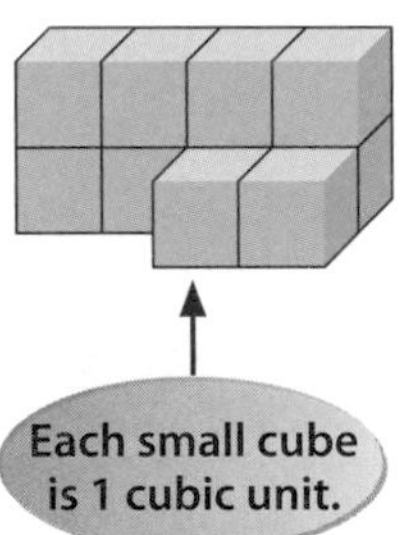

The figure has 2 rows of cubes.
There are 8 cubes in the back row.
There are 2 more cubes in the front row.
8 cubes + 2 cubes = 10 cubes

The volume of the figure is 10 cubic units.

Explain It

1. Describe how to find the volume of the figure below.

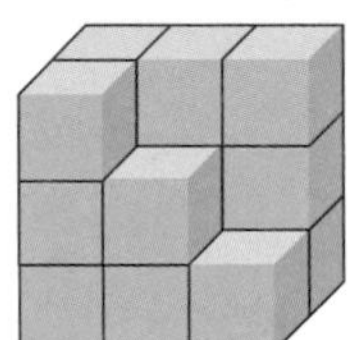

For **2** and **3**, use the figures at the right.

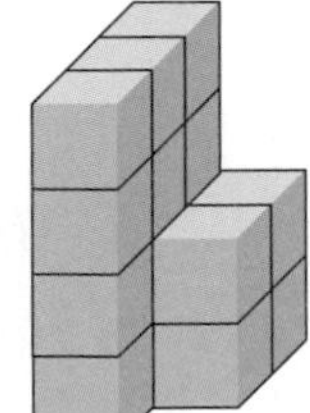

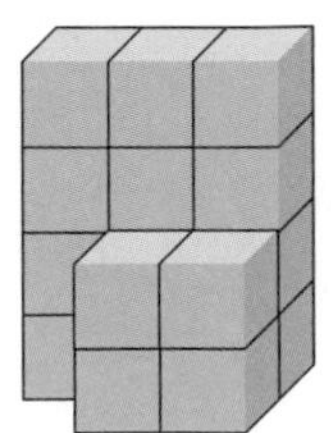

2. How are these two figures the same? How are they different?
3. Find the volume of each of the two figures.

Step 1

Make a model of the box using cubes.

The box is measured in centimeters.

The volume will be in cubic centimeters.

Step 2

Count all the cubes in 1 layer.

There are 20 cubes in each layer.
There are 2 layers.
20 cubes + 20 cubes = 40 cubes

Since there are 40 cubes, the volume is 40 cubic centimeters.

Guided Practice*

Do you know HOW?

Find the volume of each figure in cubic units.

1. 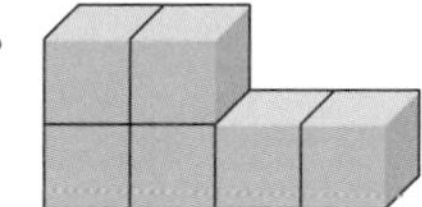

2. 

3. 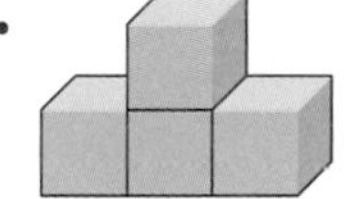

4. 

Do you UNDERSTAND?

5. How do you know the volume of the box above is 40 cubic centimeters and not 40 cubic meters?

6. Pedro has a box that is 4 inches long, 4 inches wide, and 2 inches tall. A model of the box is shown below. What is the volume of the box?

Tip *Each cube is one cubic inch.*

Independent Practice

For **7–9**, find the volume of each figure in cubic units.

7. 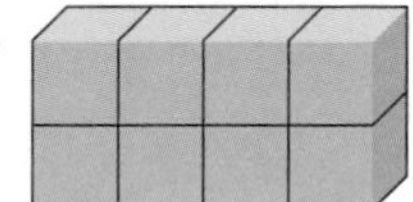

8. 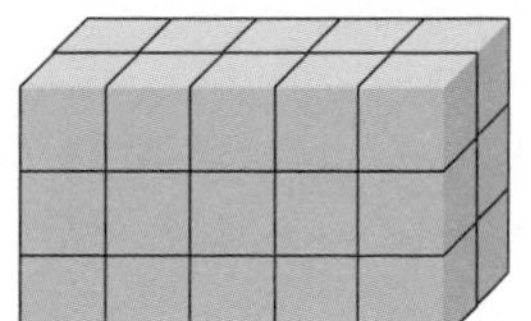

9. 

For another example, see Set D on page 413.

Independent Practice

For **10–12**, find the volume of each figure in cubic units.

10. 

11. 

12. 

Problem Solving

13. Estimation Use the cubes shown at the right to estimate the volume of the rectangular prism.

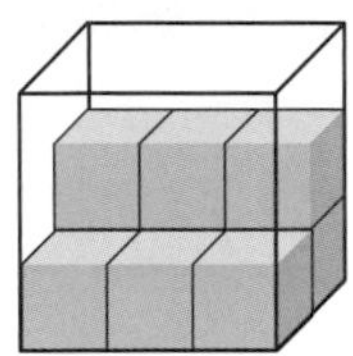

14. Derek made a rectangular prism with 4 layers of cubes. He put 5 cubes in each layer. What is the volume of the rectangular prism?

15. Draw or describe two different solid figures, each with a volume of 16 cubic units.

16. Reasoning One rectangular prism has 3 cubes in each of 7 layers. Another rectangular prism has 7 cubes in each of 3 layers. Which prism has the greater volume?

17. Dana has a jewelry box that looks like the model at the right. What is the volume of the jewelry box?

A 25 cubic inches

B 34 cubic inches

C 39 cubic inches

D 45 cubic inches

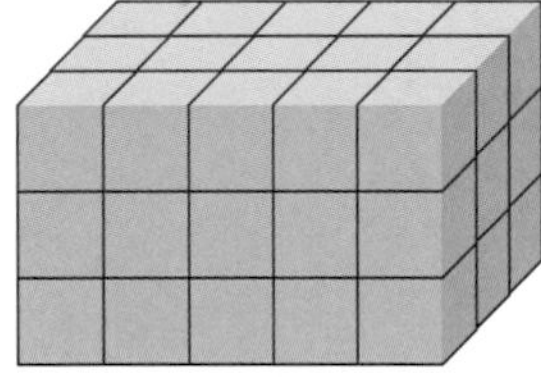

Each [cube] = 1 cubic inch.

18. Writing to Explain Carmen used cubes to build a figure. She said the volume of the figure was 15 square inches. Was she correct? Explain why or why not.

19. Tessa drinks 9 cups of water each day. In one week, how many cups of water does Tessa drink?

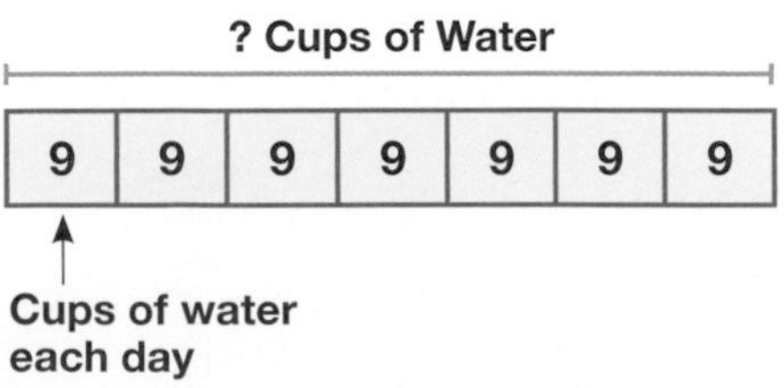

Stop and Practice

Write each number in word form.

1. 13,054
2. 719,620

Find each sum or difference. Estimate to check if the answer is reasonable.

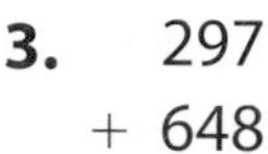

3. $\begin{array}{r} 297 \\ +\ 648 \\ \hline \end{array}$ **4.** $\begin{array}{r} 402 \\ -\ 136 \\ \hline \end{array}$ **5.** $\begin{array}{r} 3{,}061 \\ -\ 2{,}519 \\ \hline \end{array}$ **6.** $\begin{array}{r} 7{,}583 \\ +\ 5{,}042 \\ \hline \end{array}$

Estimate and then find each product or quotient.

7. $\begin{array}{r} 58 \\ \times\ 4 \\ \hline \end{array}$ **8.** 3×96 **9.** $\begin{array}{r} 425 \\ \times\ 7 \\ \hline \end{array}$ **10.** $\begin{array}{r} 5{,}713 \\ \times\ 6 \\ \hline \end{array}$ **11.** $\begin{array}{r} 7{,}984 \\ \times\ 9 \\ \hline \end{array}$

12. $3\overline{)57}$ **13.** $7\overline{)882}$ **14.** $4\overline{)3{,}456}$ **15.** $6\overline{)8{,}148}$

Change the units. Copy and complete.

16. 3 liters = ▢ milliliters **17.** 9 centimeters = ▢ millimeters

Error Search Find each sum or difference that is not correct. Write it correctly and explain the error.

18. $\frac{5}{8} + \frac{1}{8} = \frac{2}{4}$ **19.** $\frac{1}{3} + \frac{1}{3} = \frac{2}{3}$ **20.** $\frac{4}{5} - \frac{2}{5} = \frac{2}{5}$ **21.** $\frac{9}{12} - \frac{6}{12} = \frac{1}{3}$

Number Sense

Estimating and Reasoning Write true or false for each statement. If it is false, explain why.

22. The sum of $\frac{1}{4}$ and $\frac{1}{4}$ is greater than 1.

23. The difference 9,835 − 8,914 is greater than 1,000.

24. The product of 4 and 216 is less than 1,000.

25. The quotient 1,536 ÷ 3 is less than 500.

Lesson

18-6

MR 2.2 Apply strategies and results from simpler problems to more complex problems. Also MG 1.2 Estimate or determine the area and volume of solid figures by covering them with squares or by counting the number of cubes that would fill them.

Problem Solving

Solve a Simpler Problem

Janet wants to paint the door to her room. The shaded part of the figure shows the part of the door that needs paint.

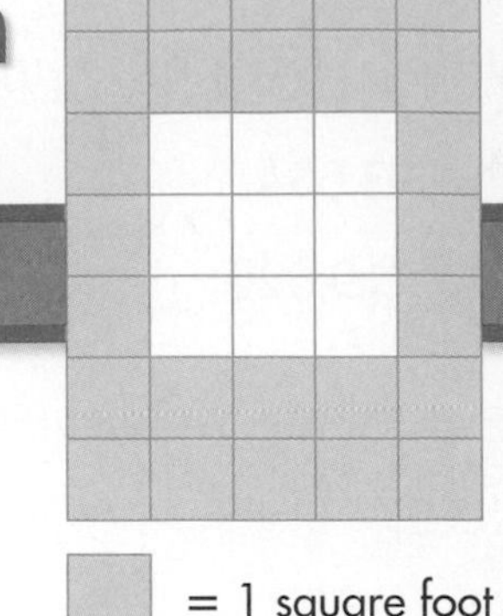

What is the area of the part of the door that needs paint?

= 1 square foot

Guided Practice*

Do you know HOW?

Solve. Use simpler problems.

1. Lil glued square beads on the shaded part of the frame. What is the area of the part she decorated?

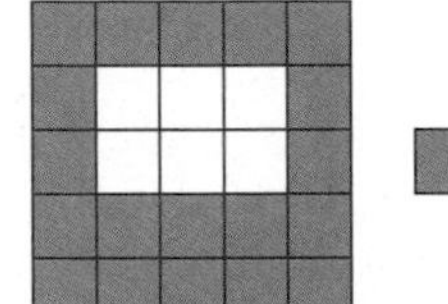

= 1 square inch

Do you UNDERSTAND?

2. What simpler problems did you use to solve Problem 1?

3. **Write a Problem** Write a problem that you can solve by solving simpler problems. You may draw a picture to help.

Independent Practice

For **4–8**, solve. Use simpler problems.

4. Reg wants to put tiles on a wall. The shaded part of the figure shows the part that needs tiles. What is the area of the shaded part?

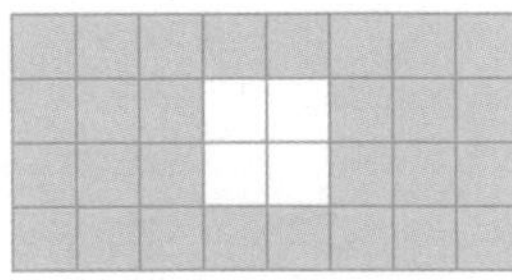

= 1 square foot

Stuck? Try this....

- What do I know?
- What am I asked to find?
- What diagram can I use to help understand the problem?
- Can I use addition, subtraction, multiplication, or division?
- Is all of my work correct?
- Did I answer the right question?
- Is my answer reasonable?

*For another example, see Set E on page 413.

Plan

I can solve simpler problems.

I can find the area of a rectangle and then the area of a square.

Then I can subtract to find the area of the shaded part.

Solve

<u>Area of the whole rectangle</u>
7 rows with 5 squares in each row
$7 \times 5 = 35$

<u>Area of the square</u>
3 rows with 3 squares in each row
$3 \times 3 = 9$

<u>Subtract</u>
$35 - 9 = 26$

The area of the part of the door that needs paint is 26 square feet.

5. Jim wants to tile the floor. The shaded part of the figure shows the part of the floor that needs tiles. What is the area of the shaded part?

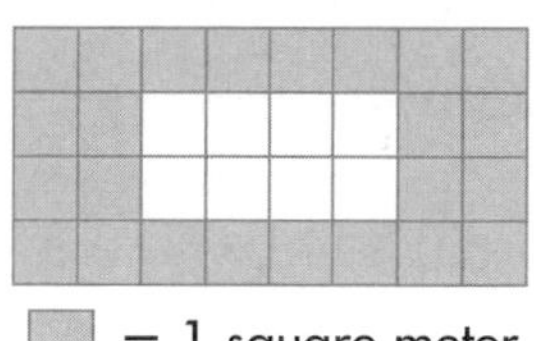

= 1 square meter

6. Dan wants to paint the floor of a pool. The shaded part of the figure shows the part of the floor that needs paint. What is the area of the shaded part?

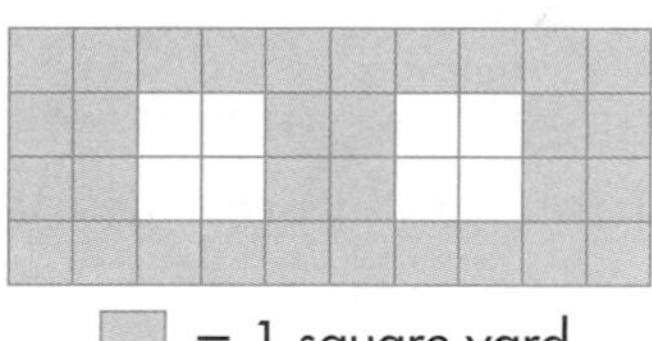

= 1 square yard

7. Macy drew two designs. How much greater is the area of the yellow figure than the area of the green figure?

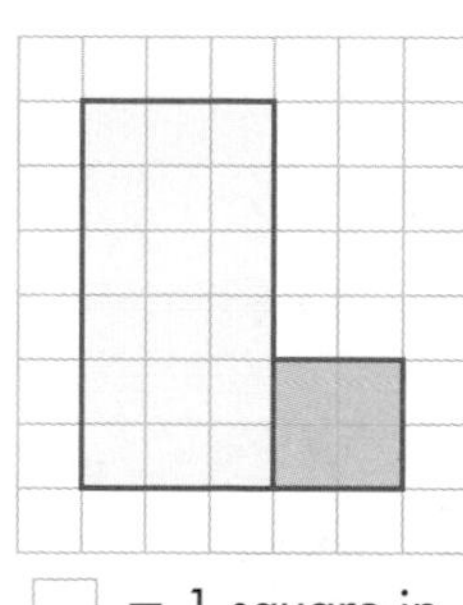

= 1 square in.

8. Mr. Eli grows vegetables in different patches on his farm. What is the total area of the corn and bean patches?

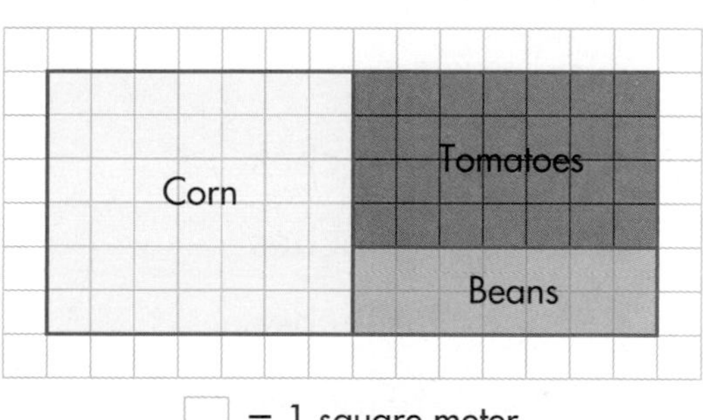

= 1 square meter

9. Neva built these figures using toothpicks. If she continues the pattern, how many toothpicks in all will she use for the 4th figure? the 5th figure?

1st figure

2nd figure

3rd figure

Test Prep

1. A drawing of the rose garden in the park is shown. What is the perimeter of the rose garden? (18-1)

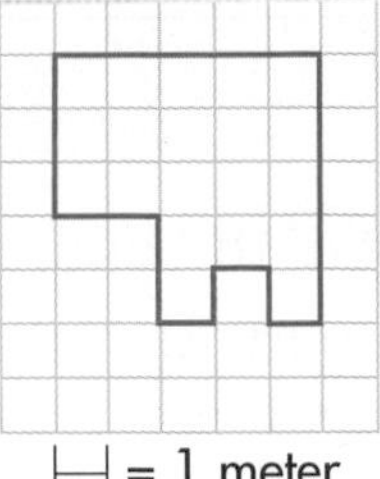

= 1 meter

A 23 meters

B 22 meters

C 21 meters

D 20 meters

2. Mrs. Utley made a quilt for her daughter's doll in the shape of a rectangle. What is the area of the doll's quilt? (18-3)

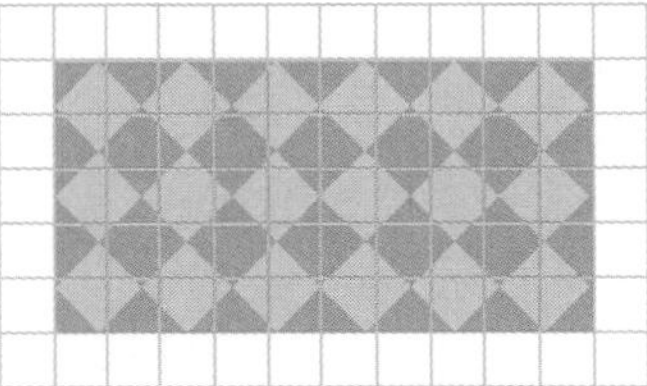

= 1 square inch

A 50 square inches

B 45 square inches

C 40 square inches

D 30 square inches

3. Which is the best estimate of the area of the shape shown below? (18-4)

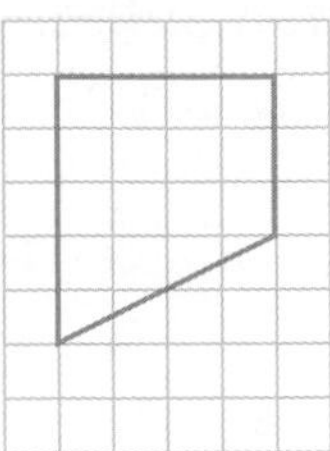

= 1 square inch

A 12 square inches

B 14 square inches

C 16 square inches

D 20 square inches

4. A model of the box that Mrs. Nitaksa's antique vase came in is shown below. What is the volume of the box? (18-5)

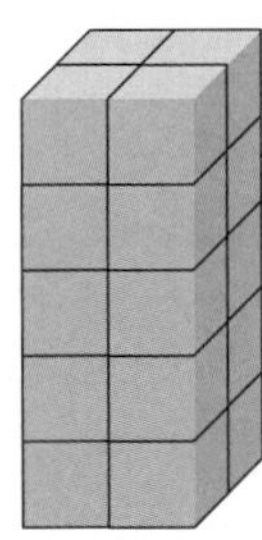

A 15 cubic units

B 16 cubic units

C 20 cubic units

D 24 cubic units

Test Prep

5. Janie wants to make a table skirt to go around the outside edge of the two tables she pushed together. A diagram of the tables is shown below. What is the perimeter of the tables? (18-1)

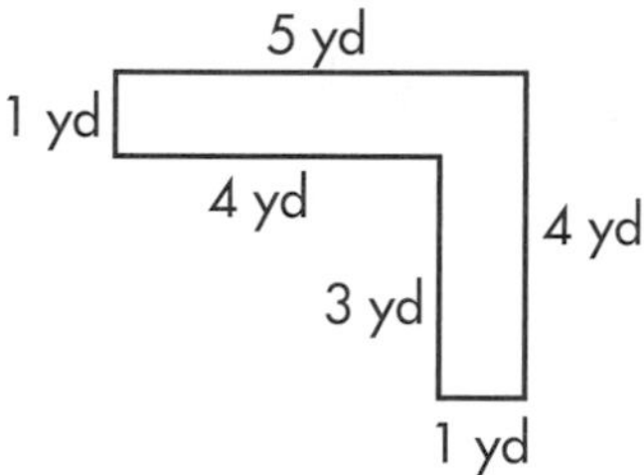

A 18 yards

B 15 yards

C 14 yards

D 12 yards

6. A hotel swimming pool is drawn below. How many square feet of green tile are around the pool? (18-6)

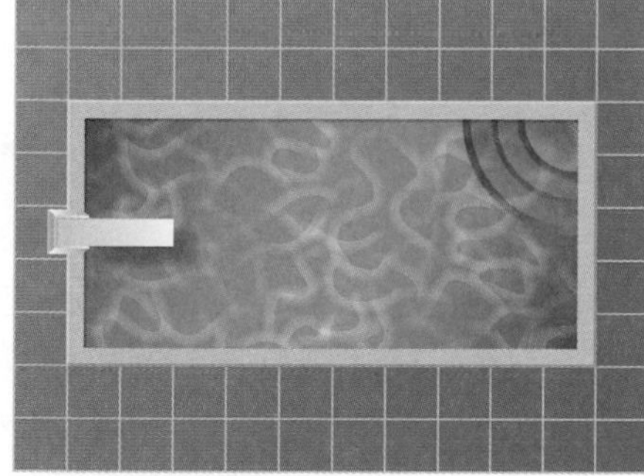

A 108 square feet

B 63 square feet

C 58 square feet

D 50 square feet

7. What is the area of the rectangle shown below? (18-3)

1 cm

4 cm

A 16 square centimeters

B 10 square centimeters

C 5 square centimeters

D 4 square centimeters

8. The patio in Pearl's backyard is in the shape of a square. What is the perimeter of the patio? (18-2)

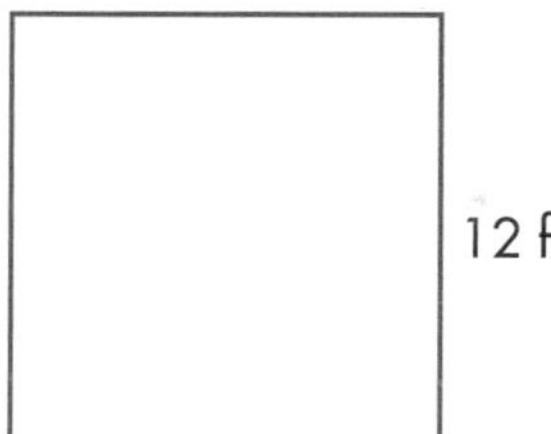

A 144 feet

B 48 feet

C 36 feet

D 24 feet

9. What is the area of this figure? (18-4)

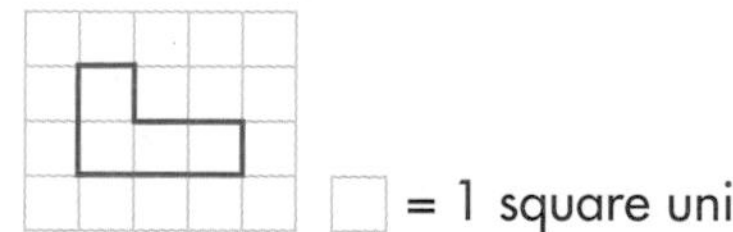

A 1 square unit

B 2 square units

C 3 square units

D 4 square units

Reteaching

Set A, pages 396–399

What is the perimeter of the figure below?

Add the lengths of the sides to find the perimeter.

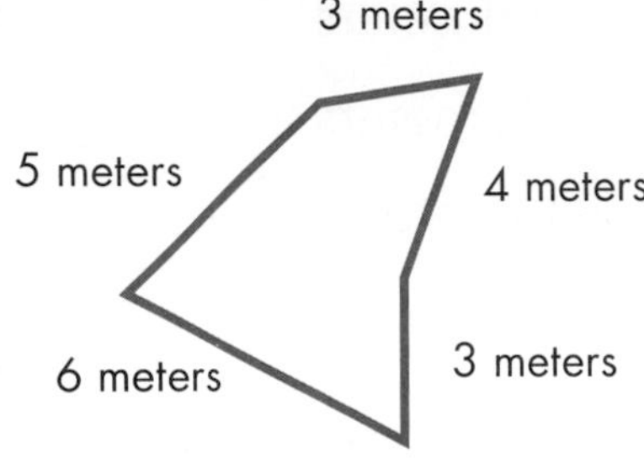

3 + 4 + 3 + 6 + 5 = 21 meters

The perimeter of the figure is 21 meters.

Remember the side on which you began adding so that you know where to stop.

Find the perimeter.

1.

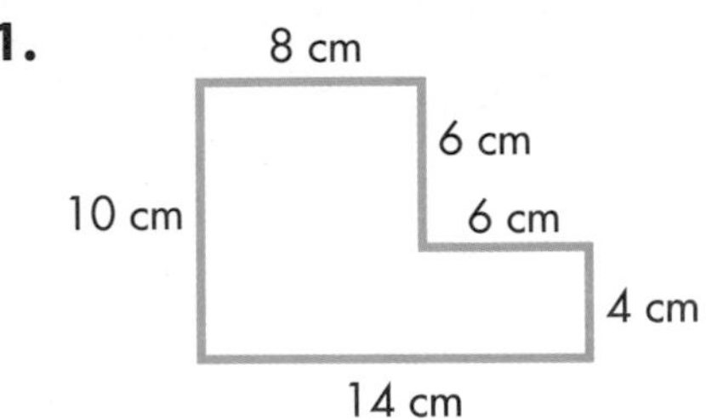

2.

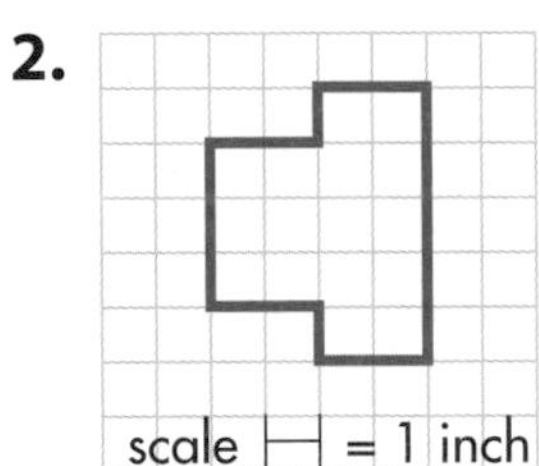

3.

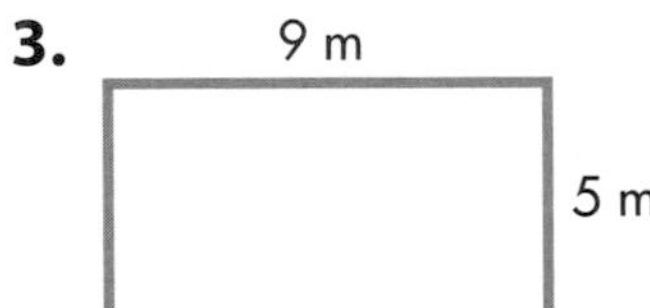

Set B, pages 400–401

What is the area of the rectangle?

For a rectangle or square, think of an array.

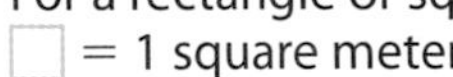
= 1 square meter

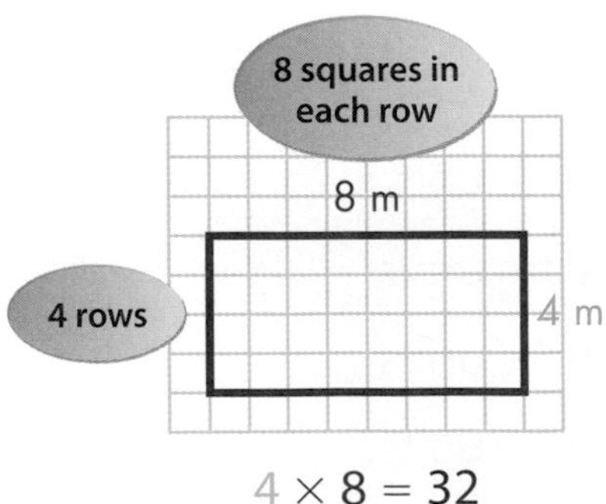

4 × 8 = 32

The area of the rectangle is 32 square meters.

Remember to give area measurements in square units.

Find the area of each figure.

1.

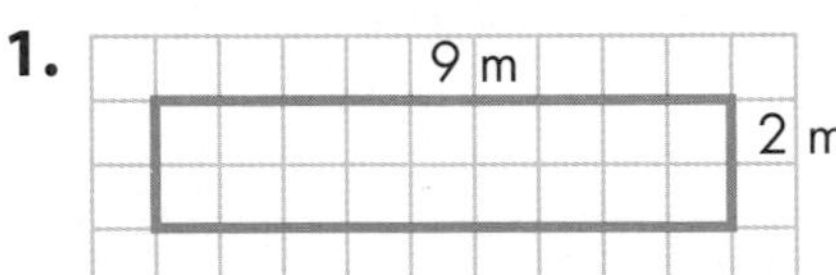

2.

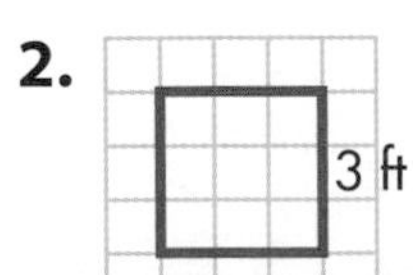

3.

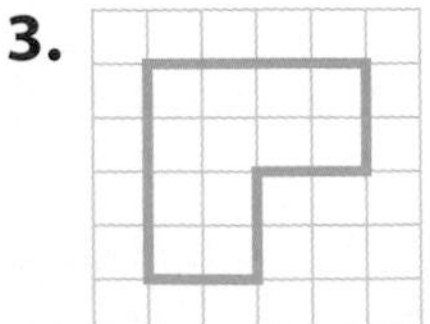

Set C, pages 402–403

Estimate the area of the irregular shape.

Count whole squares.

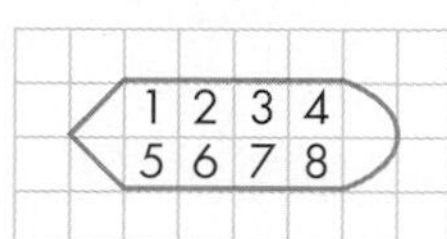

There are 8 whole squares.

Combine partial squares to make whole squares.

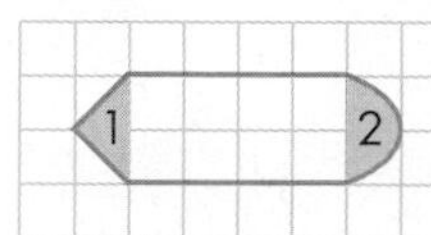

The partial squares make up about 2 whole squares.

$8 + 2 = 10$, so the area is about 10 sq units.

Remember to give area measurements in square units.

1. Estimate the area of this figure.

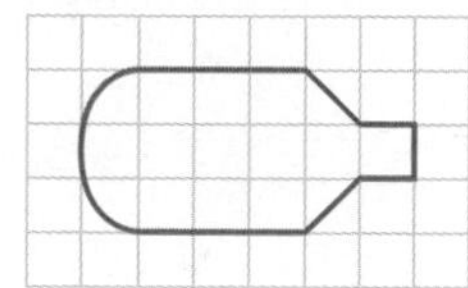

Set D, pages 404–406

What is the volume of the figure?

 Each small cube is 1 cubic unit.

Count the cubes.

So, the volume is 10 cubic units.

Remember to count all the cubes, even the ones you can't see.

Find the volume of each figure. Write your answers in cubic units.

1. 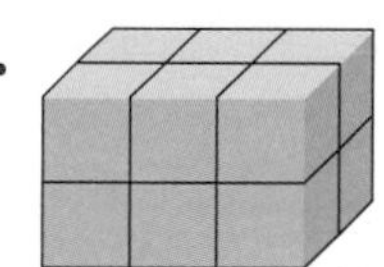

2. 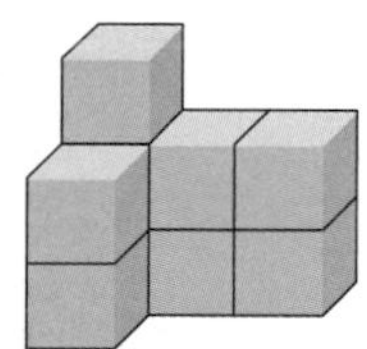

Set E, pages 408–409

What is the area of the shaded part of the rectangle?

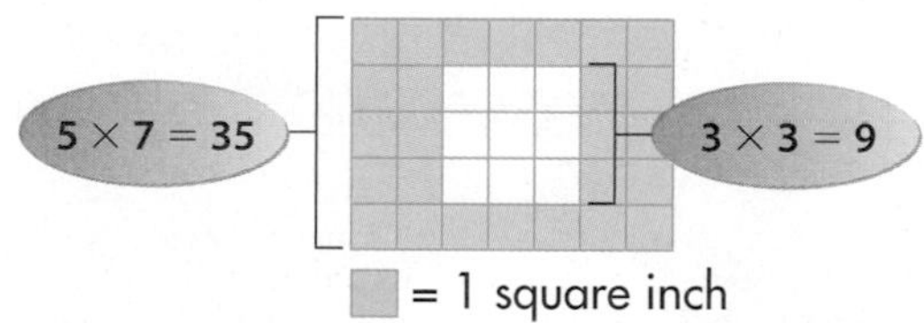

Use simpler problems.
Find the area of the whole rectangle.
Find the area of the square.
Subtract: $35 - 9 = 26$

The area of the shaded part of the rectangle is 26 square inches.

Remember to check your solution. Make sure your solution fits the information given in the problem.

1. Solve. Use simpler problems.

   Walt wants to put tiles on a wall. The shaded part of the figure is the part that needs tiles. What is the area of the shaded part?

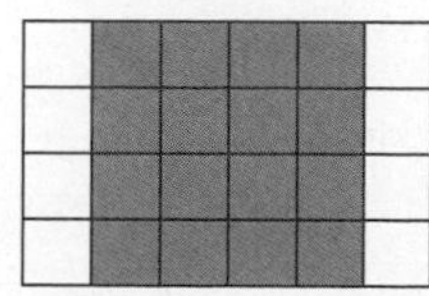

= 1 square foot

Topic 19

Decimal Operations and Money

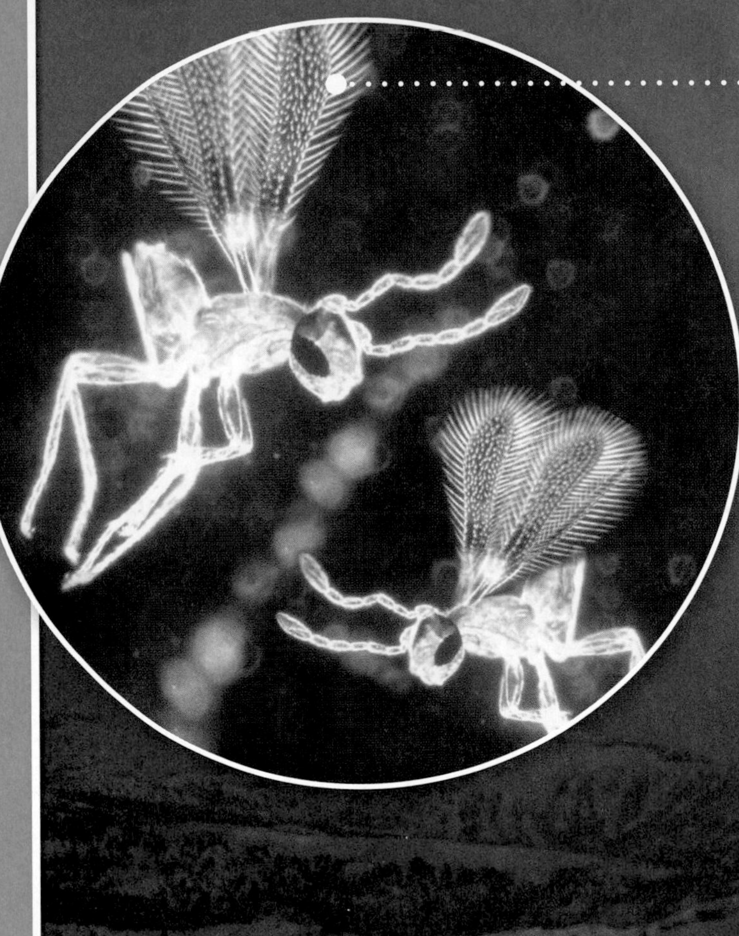

1 What is the length of the world's smallest insect? You will find out in Lesson 19-1.

2 How much will it cost to camp for 2 days at Castle Crags in California? You will find out in Lesson 19-3.

3 On March 1, 2002, the euro became the official money in several countries in Europe. What was the value of 1 American dollar in Euros? You will find out in Lesson 19-4.

4 How much does it cost the United States Mint to make a quarter? You will find out in Lesson 19-2.

Review What You Know!

Vocabulary

Choose the best term from the box.

- digits
- place
- one thousand
- tens

1. All of the numbers are made from ___?___.
2. The number 328 has a 3 in the hundreds ___?___.
3. Ten hundreds equal ___?___.

Fractions

Name the equal parts of the whole.

4.

5. 

Fractions and Regions

Write the fraction that is blue.

6. 

7. 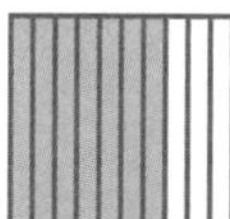

Place Value

Write each number in standard form.

8. 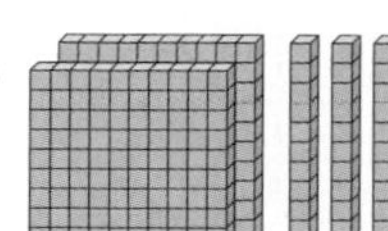

9. 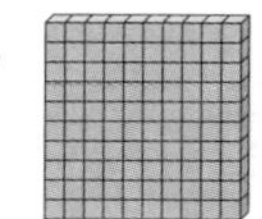

10. **Writing to Explain** Show the number 180 in a place-value chart. Explain how the chart helps show the value of a number.

Lesson

19-2

NS 3.4 Know and understand that fractions and decimals are two different representations of the same concept (e.g., 50 cents is $\frac{1}{2}$ of a dollar, 75 cents is $\frac{3}{4}$ of a dollar).

Using Money to Understand Decimals

money

How are decimals and fractions related to money?

How could Ben pay for the popcorn with only dollars, dimes, and pennies?

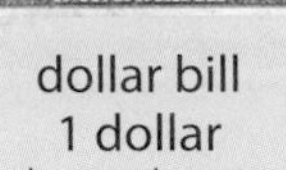

dollar bill	quarter	dime	nickel	penny
1 dollar	25 cents	10 cents	5 cents	1 cent
$1 or $1.00	25¢ or $0.25	10¢ or $0.10	5¢ or $0.05	1¢ or $0.01

Another Example What are other ways to write money amounts?

You can use what you have learned about place value in Lesson 1-1 to help you understand place value for money amounts.

Ten dimes are equal to one dollar.
A dime is one tenth of a dollar.
Each dime has a value of $0.10 or 10¢.

One hundred pennies are equal to one dollar.
A penny is one hundredth of a dollar.
Each penny has a value of $0.01 or 1¢.

The amount $4.95 can be made in different ways.

The decimal point is read by saying *and*. So $4.95 is read as *4 dollars and 95 cents*.

$4.95 = 4 dollars + 9 dimes + 5 pennies ← **Expanded Form**
= 4 ones + 9 tenths + 5 hundredths

$4.95 = 4 dollars + 95 pennies
= 4 ones + 95 hundredths

Explain It

1. How is a dime one tenth of a dollar?
2. How is a penny one hundredth of a dollar?
3. Write the cost of the yarn in expanded form.

One Way

Ben can use 1 dollar, 2 dimes, and 4 pennies.

$1.24

Another Way

Ben can use 1 dollar and 24 pennies.

$1.24

Other Examples

Four quarters make a dollar. So each quarter is $\frac{1}{4}$ of a dollar.

Write $\frac{1}{4}$ of a dollar as a decimal.

One quarter is $\frac{1}{4}$ of a dollar.

$\frac{1}{4} = \frac{25}{100}$

$\frac{1}{4}$ of a dollar = $0.25

Write $\frac{1}{2}$ of a dollar as a decimal.

Two quarters are $\frac{1}{2}$ of a dollar.

$\frac{1}{2} = \frac{50}{100}$

$\frac{1}{2}$ of a dollar = $0.50

Write $\frac{3}{4}$ of a dollar as a decimal.

Three quarters are $\frac{3}{4}$ of a dollar.

$\frac{3}{4} = \frac{75}{100}$

$\frac{3}{4}$ of a dollar = $0.75

Guided Practice*

Do you know HOW?

1. Copy and complete. $3.62 = ▯ dollars + ▯ dimes + ▯ pennies

3.62 = ▯ ones + ▯ tenths + ▯ hundredths

2. Write one and four hundredths as a decimal.

Do you UNDERSTAND?

3. In the example above, what are two other ways to show $1.24?

4. How could you show $4.17 with only dollars, dimes, and pennies?

For another example, see Set A on page 434.

Independent Practice

In **5–10**, copy and complete.

5. \$6.45 = ▮ dollars + ▮ dimes + ▮ pennies
6.45 = ▮ ones + ▮ tenths + ▮ hundredths

6. \$8.09 = ▮ dollars + ▮ dimes + ▮ pennies
8.09 = ▮ ones + ▮ tenths + ▮ hundredths

7. \$1.39 = ▮ dollars + ▮ dimes + ▮ pennies
1.39 = ▮ ones + ▮ tenths + ▮ hundredths

8. \$5.07 = ▮ dollars + ▮ dimes + ▮ pennies
5.07 = ▮ ones + ▮ tenths + ▮ hundredths

9. \$4.80 = ▮ dollars + ▮ dimes + ▮ pennies
4.80 = ▮ ones + ▮ tenths + ▮ hundredths

10. \$9.65 = ▮ dollars + ▮ dimes + ▮ pennies
9.65 = ▮ ones + ▮ tenths + ▮ hundredths

In **11–14**, write each number with a decimal point.

11. seven and fifty-two hundredths

12. eight and twelve hundredths

13. one and ninety-six hundredths

14. three and six hundredths

Problem Solving

In **15–16**, draw a picture of bills and coins that equal the amount of each price.

Draw rectangles for dollars and circles with letters for coins.

15.

16.

17. **Writing to Explain** Marnie has two dollars and fifteen pennies. Alfred has two dollars, one dime, and eight pennies. Who has a greater amount of money? Explain how you decided.

18. **Reasoning** Carl has two dollar bills, nine dimes, and 6 pennies. What coins does he need to make $3.00?

19. Tamiya has 23 pennies. How many hundredths of a dollar does she have?

20. Lars and Evelyn each have $1.38 in bills and coins. They have different coins. Show two ways to make $1.38. Draw a picture of each set of bills and coins.

21. Use a piece of centimeter grid paper. Make an outline of your hand with your fingers together. Estimate the area of the figure.

Use the table at the right for **22** and **23**.

22. Ms. Evans bought one quart of paint. She paid the exact price with six dollar bills and fourteen pennies. From which store did she buy the paint?

23. Mr. Park bought one quart of paint. He paid the exact price with dollars and coins. He used only one penny. From which store did he buy the paint?

Data

1 Quart of Paint

Store	**Price**
A-1 Supplies	$6.48
Crafts and More	$6.14
Paint Station	$6.04
Wagner's	$6.41

24. Draw another set of bills and coins to make the same amount as shown.

25. It costs the United States Mint about 4 hundredths of a dollar to make a quarter. Write 4 hundredths using a decimal point.

26. Which money amount represents $\frac{1}{4}$ of a dollar?

A $1.40 **C** $0.25

B $0.40 **D** $0.14

27. Which money amount represents 4 dollars, 7 dimes, and 3 pennies?

A $4.38 **C** $40.73

B $4.73 **D** $47.03

Lesson

19-3

NS 3.3 Solve problems involving addition, subtraction, multiplication, and division of money amounts in decimal notation and multiply and divide money amounts in decimal notation by using whole-number multipliers and divisors.

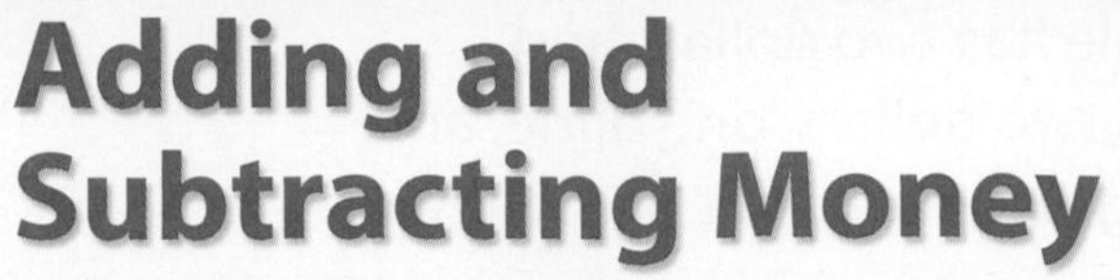

Adding and Subtracting Money

How can you add and subtract money?

Neta wants to buy a flower pot and a picture frame. What is the total cost of the two items?

? cost in all

$5.47	$6.89

Choose an Operation

$5.47 + $6.89 = ?

Another Example How can you subtract money?

The items Nancy bought cost a total of $12.36. She pays with $20. How much change should she get?

You can use what you have learned about subtracting across zero in Lesson 4-9 to help you understand subtracting money amounts.

$20

$12.36	?

Step 1

Write $20 as $20.00. Subtract as you would with whole numbers.

```
    1 9̶10 9̶10 10
  $2̶  0̶ .  0̶  0̶
-  1  2 .  3  6
      7    6  4
```

Step 2

Write the answer in dollars and cents.

```
    1 9̶10 9̶10 10
  $2̶  0̶ .  0̶  0̶
-  1  2 .  3  6
    $7 .  6  4
```

Write the dollar sign and the decimal point.

Nancy should get $7.64 in change.

Explain It

1. Suppose the total cost of the items Nancy bought was $19.36. Write the change she should get from $20 in two ways.

2. Use the prices at the top of the page. Maurice wants to buy a radio and a calculator. How much change should he get from $50?

Step 1

First, line up the decimal points. Add as you would with whole numbers.

```
   1 1
  $5.47
+  6.89
  12 36
```

Step 2

Write the answer in dollars and cents.

```
   1 1
  $5.47
+  6.89
 $12.36   Write the dollar sign
          and the decimal point.
```

The total cost of the flower pot and the picture frame is $12.36.

Guided Practice*

Do you know HOW?

In **1–4**, find the sum or difference.

1. $3.85 + 9.76

2. $10.07 − 1.68

3. $17.62 + 4.93

4. $20.00 − $3.64

Do you UNDERSTAND?

5. In the example above, Neta estimated that $13.00 would be enough to pay for the total cost of her items. Would $13.00 be enough? Explain.

6. Use the prices on page 422. Bo wants to buy a clock and a radio. What is the total cost of these items?

Independent Practice

In **7–20**, find each sum or difference.

7. $2.87 + 5.46

8. $6.24 + 9.97

9. $10.00 − 7.23

10. $25.00 − 14.39

11. $30.00 − 27.14

12. $13.06 + 9.56

13. $0.75 + 8.49

14. $10.50 − 3.62

15. $4.00 − $2.64

16. $20.00 − $6.81

17. $3.75 + $9.82

18. $1.00 − $0.36

19. $40.00 − $28.15

20. $9.09 + $2.83

**For another example, see Set B on page 434.*

Independent Practice

In **21–27**, find each sum or difference.

21. $20.00 − 15.37

22. $14.69 + 8.72

23. $0.58 + 6.73

24. $10.00 − 4.91

25. $5.00 − $3.74

26. $15.74 + $7.26

27. $40.20 − $23.10

Problem Solving

Norma and Devon compared the prices of four backpacks. The table to the right shows the prices. Use the table for **28–31**.

Cost of Backpacks

Brand	Cost
A	$24.19
B	$26.09
C	$22.99
D	$20.39

28. How much more does Brand B cost than Brand A?

29. Norma will buy Brand B and Brand D. She will pay with $50. How much change should she get?

30. Devon decided to buy Brand A. He paid with $40. How much change should he get?

31. What is the total cost of Brand C and Brand D?

? cost in all

$22.99	$20.39

32. Algebra Copy and complete. Write the number that completes each pattern.

25, 50, 75, 100, ▢, 150
75, 70, 65, 60, ▢, 50

33. A two-day camping pass for Castle Crags State Park costs $18. There is also a reservation fee of $7.50. What is the total cost for two days?

34. Lou has a $5 bill to buy a box of cereal that costs $4.62. How much change should he get back?

A $9.62 **B** $1.38 **C** 62¢ **D** 38¢

35. **Think About the Process** Deena bought a pair of socks that cost $3.72. She paid with $10.00. Which number sentence shows how to find how much change she should get back?

A $10.00 − $3.72 = ▢

B $10.00 + $3.72 = ▢

C $10.00 ÷ $3.72 = ▢

D $10.00 × $3.72 = ▢

Add. Write the sum in simplest form.

1. $\frac{1}{2} + \frac{1}{2}$
2. $\frac{3}{7} + \frac{2}{7}$
3. $\frac{6}{11} + \frac{4}{11}$
4. $\frac{4}{9} + \frac{2}{9}$

Subtract. Write the difference in simplest form.

5. $\frac{3}{4} - \frac{1}{4}$
6. $1 - \frac{3}{7}$
7. $1 - \frac{1}{3}$
8. $\frac{4}{5} - \frac{3}{5}$

Find each product.

9. $\begin{array}{r} 493 \\ \times \quad 5 \\ \hline \end{array}$
10. $\begin{array}{r} 812 \\ \times \quad 9 \\ \hline \end{array}$
11. 4×349
12. $\begin{array}{r} 2,567 \\ \times \quad 3 \\ \hline \end{array}$
13. $\begin{array}{r} 5,409 \\ \times \quad 6 \\ \hline \end{array}$

Find each quotient.

14. $4\overline{)68}$
15. $6\overline{)78}$
16. $7\overline{)455}$
17. $3\overline{)3,642}$

Write each number with a decimal point.

18. three and eighteen hundredths
19. one and forty-nine hundredths
20. six and seventy hundredths
21. nine and fifteen hundredths

Error Search Find each sum or difference that is not correct. Write it correctly and explain the error.

22. $\begin{array}{r} 52 \\ +\ 49 \\ \hline 91 \end{array}$
23. $\begin{array}{r} 738 \\ +\ 156 \\ \hline 894 \end{array}$
24. $\begin{array}{r} 613 \\ -\ 287 \\ \hline 336 \end{array}$
25. $\begin{array}{r} 4,329 \\ +\ 5,168 \\ \hline 9,487 \end{array}$
26. $\begin{array}{r} 2,057 \\ -\ 1,392 \\ \hline 665 \end{array}$

Number Sense

Estimating and Reasoning Write true or false for each statement. If it is false, explain why.

27. $4 \times 325 > 1,000$
28. $1,273 + 3,028 < 4,000$
29. $4,913 - 1,562 < 2,000$
30. $384 \div 3 < 100$
31. $2 \times 708 < 3 \times 906$
32. $1,253 - 1,108 > 100$

Lesson

19-4

NS 3.3 Solve problems involving addition, subtraction, multiplication, and division of money amounts in decimal notation and multiply and divide money amounts in decimal notation by using whole-number multipliers and divisors.

Multiplying with Money

How can you multiply money amounts?

Three friends are paying to visit the museum. How much will the friends need to pay for 3 children's tickets?

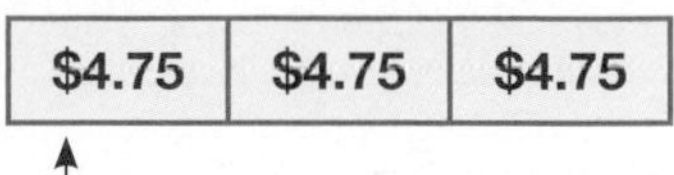

Museum Admission

Adults	$7.25
Students (12-18 years old)	$5.80
Children (under 12 years old)	$4.75

Guided Practice*

Do you know HOW?

In **1–4**, find the product.

1. $3.28 × 4

2. $1.07 × 9

3. $0.14 × 2

4. $6.34 × 7

Do you UNDERSTAND?

5. In the problem above, the friends estimated that $12.00 would be enough to pay for the total cost of 3 children's tickets. Is $12.00 enough? Explain.

6. Use the sign above. What is the total cost of 4 student tickets?

Independent Practice

In **7–22**, find each product.

7. $1.38 × 4

8. $0.02 × 3

9. $0.47 × 9

10. $6.19 × 5

11. $3.65 × 2

12. $2.30 × 6

13. $5.03 × 8

14. $4.98 × 7

15. 3 × $0.72

16. 8 × $1.86

17. 6 × $8.09

18. 9 × $7.60

19. 2 × $4.53

20. 4 × $0.70

21. 7 × $0.08

22. 5 × $9.31

*For another example, see Set C on page 435.

Step 1

Multiply the same way as with whole numbers.

$$\begin{array}{r} {}^{2\,1} \\ \$4.75 \\ \times \quad 3 \\ \hline 14\,25 \end{array}$$

Step 2

Write the answer in dollars and cents.

$$\begin{array}{r} {}^{2\,1} \\ \$4.75 \\ \times \quad 3 \\ \hline \$14.25 \end{array}$$

Write the dollar sign and the decimal point.

The friends will need to pay $14.25.

Problem Solving

For **23–25**, use the sign at the right.

23. Mrs. Larson wants to buy 3 jars of peanut butter for the bicycling club picnic. What would be the total cost of the 3 jars?

? cost in all

$3.09	$3.09	$3.09

Cost of each jar

Data

Shopwell Grocery One-Week Sale!

Item	Price
Bread, whole-wheat loaf	$2.79
Milk, quart	$0.89
Green pepper, pound	$1.49
Eggs, dozen	$1.99
Peanut butter, large jar	$3.09

24. Mr. Reed wants to buy 2 quarts of milk and 1 pound of green peppers. What is the total cost of his items?

25. How much more does a dozen eggs cost than a quart of milk?

26. When the euro became the official money of Europe, one US dollar was equal to 0.87 euros. How many euros would you have received for five US dollars?

27. **Algebra** One stamp costs 39¢. Two stamps cost 78¢. Three stamps cost $1.17. If the cost of each stamp remains the same, how much would 4 stamps cost?

28. **Think About the Process** Mrs. Neva bought two adult tickets for a movie. The cost for one adult ticket is $8.75. The cost for one child's ticket is $4.80. Which number sentence shows how to find the total cost of the tickets?

A $8.75 + $4.80 = ▢

B $8.75 × $4.80 = ▢

C 2 × $4.80 = ▢

D 2 × $8.75 = ▢

Lesson

19-5

NS 3.3 Solve problems involving addition, subtraction, multiplication, and division of money amounts in decimal notation and multiply and divide money amounts in decimal notation by using whole-number multipliers and divisors. Also NS 2.7.

Dividing with Money

How can you divide money amounts?

Edie bought 3 quarts of milk. Each quart cost the same amount. The total cost of the 3 quarts of milk was $3.45. What was the cost of each quart of milk?

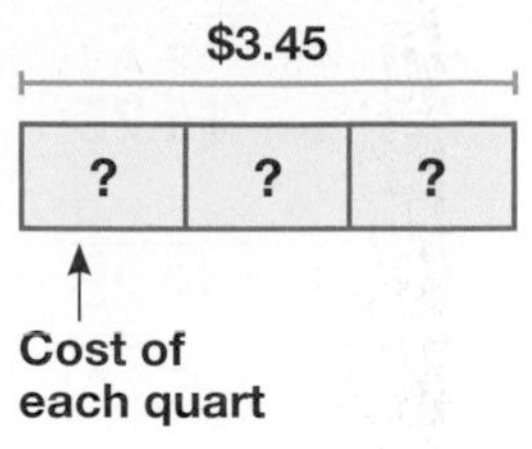

Choose an Operation $\$3.45 \div 3 = \square$

Guided Practice*

Do you know HOW?

In **1** and **2**, copy and complete.

1. $\$4.68 \div 4 = \$1.\square\square$; -4, $\square$, $-\square$, $\square\square$, $-\square\square$, 0

2. $\$2.94 \div 3 = \$0.9\square$; -27, $\square\square$, $-\square\square$, $\square$

Do you UNDERSTAND?

3. In the problem above, how can you check the quotient?

4. Clyde bought four notebooks. Each notebook cost the same amount. The total cost of the four notebooks was $4.76. What was the cost of one notebook?

Independent Practice

Leveled Practice In **5–8**, copy and complete.

5. $\$5.75 \div 5 = \$1.\square\square$; -5, $\square$, $-\square$, $\square\square$, $-\square\square$, 0

6. $\$4.76 \div 7 = \$0.6\square$; -42, $\square\square$, $-\square\square$, $\square$

7. $\$7.50 \div 6 = \$1.\square\square$; -6, $\square\square$, $-\square\square$, $\square\square$, $-\square\square$, 0

8. $\$5.92 \div 8 = \$0.7\square$; -56, $\square\square$, $-\square\square$, $\square$

In **9–12**, find each quotient.

9. $3.48 ÷ 3 **10.** $4.72 ÷ 2 **11.** $5.08 ÷ 4 **12.** $9.72 ÷ 9

*For another example, see Set D on page 435.

Step 1

Divide the same way as with whole numbers.

```
   1 15
3)$3.45
 - 3
    4
  - 3
    15
  - 15
     0
```

Step 2

Write the answer in dollars and cents.

```
  $1.15   Write the dollar sign
3)$3.45   and the decimal point.
 - 3
    4
  - 3
    15
  - 15
     0
```

Each quart of milk cost $1.15.

Problem Solving

13. Rosa bought a pack of markers. The pack had five markers. The cost of the pack was $6.85. If each marker cost the same amount, what was the cost of one marker?

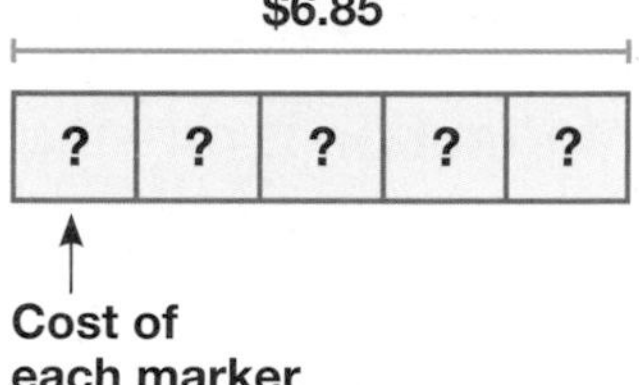

14. Rosa paid for a pack of markers with $10. The total cost of the markers was $6.85. How much change should she get?

15. Four friends made $17.56 selling used video games. They want to share the amount equally. How much should each friend get?

16. **Estimation** Nate earns about $125 doing yard work each week. Does he earn more than $400 in 4 weeks? Show how you found your answer.

17. $3.84 ÷ 3 = ▢

A $0.84 **C** $10.28

B $1.28 **D** $11.52

18. **Think About the Process** Mr. Burt bought 4 packages of stickers. Each package cost the same amount. The total cost was $4.56. Which number sentence shows how to find the cost of each package?

A $4 + $4.56 = ▢

B 4 × $4.56 = ▢

C $4.56 ÷ 4 = ▢

D $4.56 ÷ 2 = ▢

19. **Writing to Explain** Two friends each had a granola bar for a snack. Midori ate $\frac{1}{2}$ of a granola bar. Nelson ate $\frac{1}{2}$ of a different kind of granola bar. Nelson ate more than Midori. How is that possible?

Lesson

19-6

MR 1.1 Analyze problems by identifying relationships, distinguishing relevant from irrelevant information, sequencing and prioritizing information, and observing patterns. Also **NS 2.0, 3.3**

Problem Solving

Missing or Extra Information

Ruth bought one CD, one DVD, and one package of blank tapes. She spent a total of $25 on the CD and DVD. If Ruth started with $45, how much money did she have left?

Guided Practice*

Do you know HOW?

Tell what information is missing.

1. Brad bought 3 tapes for a total of $9. He also bought some CDs that cost $10 each. How much did Brad spend in all?

Do you UNDERSTAND?

2. For Problem 1, make up the missing information and solve.

3. **Write a Problem** Write a problem that has extra information about the cost of school supplies.

Independent Practice

Decide if the problem has extra or missing information. Solve if you have enough information.

4. Pablo collects coins. He has 24 coins from Mexico, 14 coins from Canada, and 6 coins from Italy. How many more coins does he have from Mexico than from Canada?

5. Meg collects stamps. She has 36 flower stamps, 24 bird stamps, and more than 20 animal stamps. How many bird and animal stamps does she have?

Stuck? Try this....

- What do I know?
- What am I asked to find?
- What diagram can I use to help understand the problem?
- Can I use addition, subtraction, multiplication, or division?
- Is all of my work correct?
- Did I answer the right question?
- Is my answer reasonable?

*For another example, see Set E on page 435.

Plan and Solve

Draw a diagram to show what you know and what you want to find.

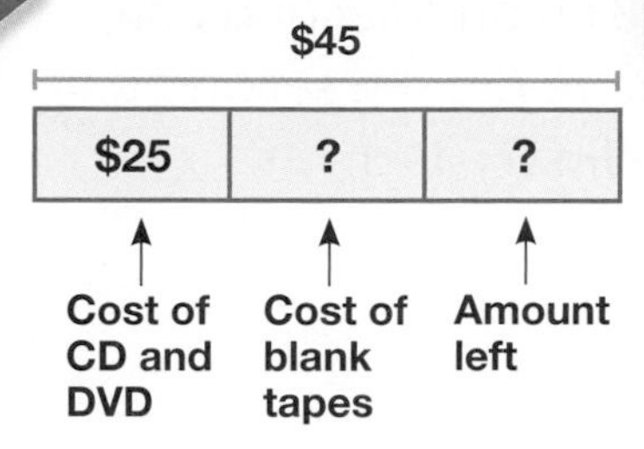

Is any information missing that you need to solve the problem?

Yes, I need to know the cost of the blank tapes so I can find the total Ruth spent. Then I can find how much she had left.

Is there extra information not needed to solve the problem?

No, there is no extra information.

For **6–9**, decide if each problem has extra or missing information. If information is missing, make up the information. Then solve.

Use the pictograph for **6** and **7**.

Trees Planted by Scouts

Oak	🌳 🌳
Maple	🌳 🌳 🌳
Walnut	🌳 🌳 🌳 🌳 🌳

🌳 stands for 3 trees

6. The scouts spent 2 hours planting oak trees and 4 hours planting maple trees. How many oak and maple trees did they plant?

7. The scouts also planted twice as many pine trees as walnut trees. How many pine trees did they plant?

8. Stacy spent $24 on 20 yards of material to make curtains. She used all of the material to make 4 identical curtains. How much material did she use for each curtain?

9. Nick is planting 36 flowers in rows in his garden. His garden is 10 feet long and 2 feet wide. How many rows of flowers can Nick plant?

10. Francis has 24 colored pencils and 14 markers. What information is needed to find the number of her pencils that are **NOT** red?

A The total number of pencils and markers

B The number of pencils that are red

C The number of markers that are blue

D The number of markers that are red

Test Prep

1. In the talent show, 6 out of the 10 acts were singing. Larry shaded $\frac{6}{10}$ in the figure. (19-1)

Which decimal equals $\frac{6}{10}$?

A 0.006

B 0.06

C 0.6

D 6.6

2. Jamison found 4 dimes under his bed. How do you write the value of 4 dimes? (19-2)

A 0.4

B 0.04

C \$0.40

D \$0.04

3. Patrice has 6 tennis balls, 12 golf balls, 2 basketballs, and some softballs in the gym closet. What other information is needed to find how many softballs Patrice has? (19-6)

A How many balls she has in all

B How many soccer balls she has

C How big the ball bin is

D How often she plays softball

4. Celia spent \$24.36 on one pair of jeans and \$28.65 on a second pair. How much more did the second pair cost than the first? (19-3)

A \$53.01

B \$5.29

C \$4.79

D \$4.29

5. What fraction and decimal represent the part that is blue? (19-1)

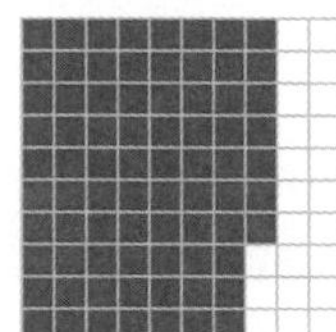

A $\frac{77}{10}$ and 0.77

B $\frac{77}{100}$ and 0.077

C $\frac{77}{100}$ and 7.7

D $\frac{77}{100}$ and 0.77

6. Jessica spent \$9.56 on four yards of material. If each yard cost the same amount, what was the cost of one yard of material? (19-5)

A \$2.39

B \$2.49

C \$37.24

D \$38.24

Test Prep

7. What is the missing number? (19-2)

$3.49 = 3 dollars + ▢ dimes + 9 pennies

3.49 = 3 ones + ▢ tenths + 9 hundredths

A 3

B 4

C 6

D 9

8. Jason wants a shirt that costs $13.89 and a CD that costs $9.95. How much is his total before tax? (19-3)

A $24.84

B $23.85

C $23.84

D $23.74

9. What is 5 × $7.68? (19-4)

A $33.00

B $38.40

C $35.40

D $3,840

10. Melissa spent $11 on a shirt, $25 on pants, $12 on a CD, and $19 on sandals. How much did Melissa spend in all on things to wear? (19-6)

A $48

B $55

C $56

D $67

11. One taco costs 79¢. Two tacos cost $1.58. If the cost of each taco stays the same, how much do 3 tacos cost? (19-4)

A $0.79

B $2.07

C $2.27

D $2.37

12. How much is $\frac{1}{4}$ of a dollar? (19-2)

A $0.25

B $0.40

C $0.50

D $0.75

13. How much change should Lucia get back from $20 if she spent $9.48? (19-3)

A $9.52

B $10.52

C $11.42

D $11.52

14. Ride tickets at the fair cost $0.75 each. Carlos used 6 tickets on the Ferris wheel. How much did the ride cost? (19-4)

A $6.50

B $4.55

C $4.50

D $4.20

Set A, pages 416–421

Tenths can be written as fractions or as decimals.

$\frac{4}{10}$ or 0.4

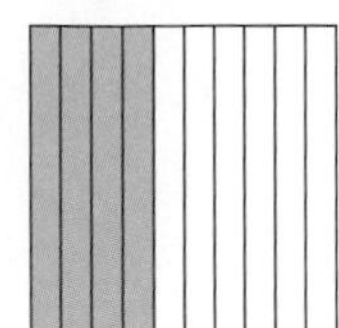

Hundredths can be written as fractions or as decimals.

$\frac{23}{100}$ or 0.23

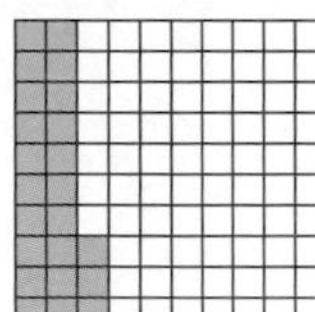

Money amounts are written as decimals.

\$3.79 = 3 dollars + 7 dimes + 9 pennies
= 3 ones + 7 tenths + 9 hundredths

Remember that tenths are 10 equal parts of a whole. Hundredths are 100 equal parts of a whole.

In **1** and **2**, write a fraction and a decimal for each shaded part.

1. 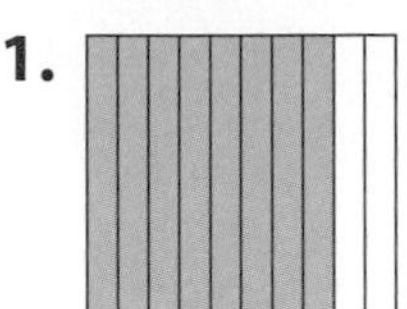

2.

In **3** and **4**, copy and complete.

3. \$5.36 = ☐ dollars + ☐ dimes + ☐ pennies
5.36 = ☐ ones + ☐ tenths + ☐ hundredths

4. \$7.04 = ☐ dollars + ☐ dimes + ☐ pennies
7.04 = ☐ ones + ☐ tenths + ☐ hundredths

Set B, pages 422–424

Find \$9.68 + \$2.75.

Add as you would with whole numbers. Write the answer in dollars and cents.

```
   1 1
  $9.68
+  2.75
 $12.43
```

Find \$10.00 − \$3.26.
Subtract as you would with whole numbers. Write the answer in dollars and cents.

```
     9  9
  0 10 10 10
 $1  0. 0  0
-    3. 2  6
    $6. 7  4
```

Remember to regroup as needed.

Find the sum or difference.

1. \$4.97 + 5.36

2. \$20.00 + 9.28

3. \$18.54 + 4.76

4. \$30.00 − 7.19

5. \$25.00 − 14.38

6. \$12.00 − 9.82

Set C, pages 426–427

Find $5 \times \$2.69$.

Multiply the same way as with whole numbers. Write the answer in dollars and cents.

$$\begin{array}{r} {}^{3\,4} \\ \$2.69 \\ \times \quad 5 \\ \hline \$13.45 \end{array}$$

Remember to add any regrouped digits.

Find the product.

1. $\begin{array}{r} \$4.96 \\ \times \quad 3 \\ \hline \end{array}$

2. $\begin{array}{r} \$8.03 \\ \times \quad 6 \\ \hline \end{array}$

Set D, pages 428–429

Find $\$4.72 \div 4$.

Divide the same way as with whole numbers. Write the answer in dollars and cents.

$$\begin{array}{r} \$1.18 \\ 4\overline{)\$4.72} \\ -\,4 \\ \hline 7 \\ -\,4 \\ \hline 32 \\ -\,32 \\ \hline 0 \end{array}$$

Remember to check your answers by multiplying.

Copy and complete. Find each quotient.

1. $\begin{array}{r} \$1.\square\square \\ 3\overline{)\$3.51} \\ -\,3 \\ \hline \square \\ -\,\square \\ \hline \square\square \\ -\,\square\square \\ \hline 0 \end{array}$

2. $\begin{array}{r} \$0.9\square \\ 9\overline{)\$8.46} \\ -\,8\,1 \\ \hline \square\square \\ -\,\square\square \\ \hline \square \end{array}$

Set E, pages 430–431

To solve a problem with a lot of information, follow these steps.

Step 1
Find the main idea, key facts, and details in the problem.

Step 2
Cross out any extra information.

Step 3
Solve the problem if you have enough information.

Remember to make sure you understand what information you need to find to solve the problem.

Decide if the problem has extra or missing information. Solve if you have enough information.

1. Three friends spent \$24 to buy lunch and \$4 for a magazine. They shared the cost of lunch equally. How much did each person spend on lunch?

Topic 20

Data and Probability

A . _
B _ . . .
C _ . _ .
D _ . .
E .
F . . _

1 How fast can a peregrine falcon fly? You will find out in Lesson 20-5.

2 In the 1800s, Morse Code used a series of dots and dashes to send messages over a telegraph or other machine. How many letters of the alphabet are sent using only dots in Morse code? You will find out in Lesson 20-2.

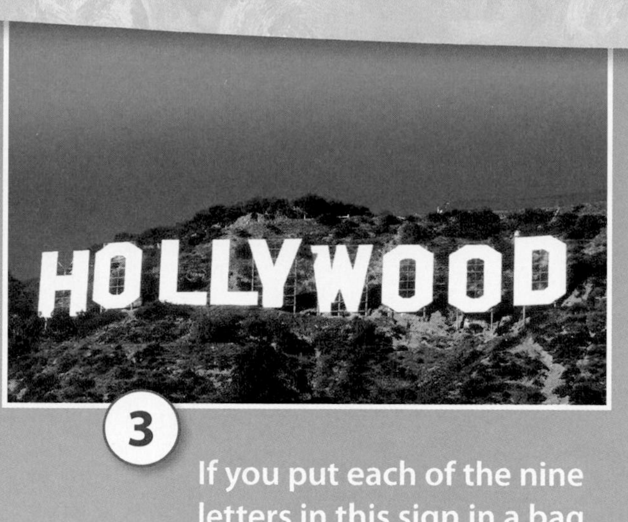

3

If you put each of the nine letters in this sign in a bag and take one out without looking, which letter are you most likely to take? You will find out in Lesson 20-3.

4

How many gold, silver, and bronze medals were won by the United States in the 2006 Winter Olympic Games? You will find out in Lesson 20-1.

Review What You Know!

Vocabulary

Choose the best term from the box.

- data
- more likely
- less likely
- tally

1. A graph can be used to compare __?__.

2. Elisa is at a library. It is __?__ that she will look at a book than eat lunch.

3. The time is 4 A.M. It is __?__ that you are playing soccer than sleeping.

Order Numbers

Write in order from least to greatest.

4. 56, 47, 93, 39, 10 **5.** 20, 43, 23, 19, 22

6. 24, 14, 54, 34, 4 **7.** 65, 33, 56, 87, 34

Skip Counting

Find the next two numbers in each pattern. Write a rule for the pattern.

8. 5, 10, 15, 20, ▢, ▢

9. 2, 4, 6, 8, ▢, ▢

10. 10, 20, 30, 40, ▢, ▢

11. 4, 8, 12, 16, ▢, ▢

Comparing

12. **Writing to Explain** Explain how to use place value to compare 326 and 345.

Lesson
20-1

SDAP 1.2 Record the possible outcomes for a simple event (e.g., tossing a coin) and systematically keep track of the outcomes when the event is repeated many times. Also SDAP 1.3.

Using Tally Charts

number cube

How can you organize data?

Theo used a cube to do an experiment about vehicles. He labeled 3 faces *SUV (Sport Utility Vehicle)*, 2 faces *Minivan*, and 1 face *Car*. Which label was tossed most often?

Data

Results of Theo's Cube Tosses		
Car	Minivan	SUV
SUV	Minivan	SUV
SUV	Car	SUV
Minivan	Car	SUV
Minivan	Minivan	SUV
SUV	Minivan	Minivan
SUV	Minivan	SUV
SUV	Car	SUV

Guided Practice*

Do you know HOW?

Use the data below to answer **1** and **2**.

Spinner Results			
Blue	Blue	Red	Green
Yellow	Green	Blue	Blue
Blue	Blue	Red	Green
Green	Blue	Green	Blue

1. Make a tally chart to show the data.

2. How many more times was green spun than red?

Do you UNDERSTAND?

3. In the example above, which outcome had the fewest cube tosses?

4. In the example above, why did Minivan have 8 tally marks?

5. **Writing to Explain** Suppose you tossed the cube 30 more times. Which kind of vehicle do you think would occur most often? Explain.

Independent Practice

In **6–10**, use the data from the experiment at the right.

6. Make a tally chart of the data.

7. How many times was the coin tossed?

8. How many times was Heads tossed?

9. How many times was Tails tossed?

10. **Writing to Explain** Why do you think these results happened?

Coin Toss Results			
Heads	Tails	Tails	Tails
Heads	Tails	Heads	Tails
Tails	Heads	Heads	Heads
Heads	Tails	Heads	Heads
Heads	Tails	Tails	Tails

For another example, see Set A on page 456.

Step 1

Make a tally chart. A tally chart is one way to record data. Data is information that is collected.

Title the tally chart. Label the columns.

Cube Toss Results

Kind of Vehicle	Tally	Number

Step 2

Make a tally mark for each outcome. A tally mark is a mark used to record data on a tally chart. An outcome is a possible result of a game or experiment.

Cube Toss Results

Kind of Vehicle	Tally	Number
SUV	卌 卌 II	
Minivan	卌 III	
Car	IIII	

Step 3

Count the tally marks. Write the number.

Cube Toss Results

Kind of Vehicle	Tally	Number
SUV	卌 卌 II	12
Minivan	卌 III	8
Car	IIII	4

SUV was tossed most often.

Problem Solving

There are 16 letter cards in a bag. The letters on the cards are A, E, N, S, or T. Elena picked a card from the bag without looking and put the card back each time. She did this 50 times. Use the tally chart at the right for **11–15**.

Letter Picked from Bag (Data)

Letter	Tally	Number
A	卌 卌 I	11
E	卌 卌 III	▢
N	卌 III	▢
S	▢	8
T	▢	10

11. Copy and complete the chart.

12. Which two letters were picked the same number of times?

13. How many more times was the letter E picked than the letter T?

14. Which letter did Elena pick most often?

15. **Reasonableness** Elena says there are 3 As, 2 Es, 4 Ns, 4 Ss, and 3 Ts in the bag. Do you agree? Explain.

16. Make a tally chart to show how many times the letters a, e, i, o, and u are used in this exercise.

17. In the 2006 Winter Olympic Games, the United States won 9 gold medals, 9 silver medals, and 7 bronze medals. Which tally chart shows these results?

A

U.S. Medals

Medal	Tally
Gold	卌 III
Silver	卌 III
Bronze	卌 I

B

U.S. Medals

Medal	Tally
Gold	卌 卌 I
Silver	卌 卌 I
Bronze	卌 III

C

U.S. Medals

Medal	Tally
Gold	卌 IIII
Silver	卌 IIII
Bronze	卌 II

D

U.S. Medals

Medal	Tally
Gold	卌 卌 II
Silver	卌 卌 II
Bronze	卌 卌

Lesson
20-2

SDAP 1.1 Identify whether common events are certain, likely, unlikely, or improbable. Also SDAP 1.0 Conduct simple probability experiments by determining the number of possible outcomes and make simple predictions.

How Likely?

Will an event happen?

An event is likely if it will probably happen. It is unlikely if it will probably not happen. An event is certain if it is sure to happen. It is impossible if it will never happen.

Think of events in a rainforest.

Certain event: seeing green plants

Impossible event: seeing a polar bear

Likely event: seeing colorful birds

Unlikely event: seeing dry soil

Other Examples

How can you compare chances?

Outcomes with the same chance of happening are equally likely.

Sometimes you compare two outcomes.
The outcome with a greater chance of happening is more likely.
The outcome with the lesser chance of happening is less likely.

The tally chart shows the results of 48 spins of the spinner above.

Which outcome is more likely than blue?

A bigger part of the spinner is red than blue. Also, the tally chart shows more red results than blue. So, red is more likely than blue.

Data

Spin Results

Outcome	Tally	Number
Red	卌 卌 卌 IIII	19
Yellow	卌 卌 III	13
Green	卌	5
Blue	卌 卌 I	11

Which outcome is less likely than blue?

A smaller part of the spinner is green than blue. Also, the tally chart shows fewer green results than blue. So, green is less likely than blue.

Which outcomes are equally likely?

The yellow and blue parts of the spinner are the same size. Also, the yellow and blue results are nearly equal. So, yellow and blue are equally likely outcomes.

Remember, a possible result of a game or experiment is called an outcome.

What are the possible outcomes of spinning this spinner?

When you spin the spinner, the outcome might be blue, red, yellow, green, or a line.

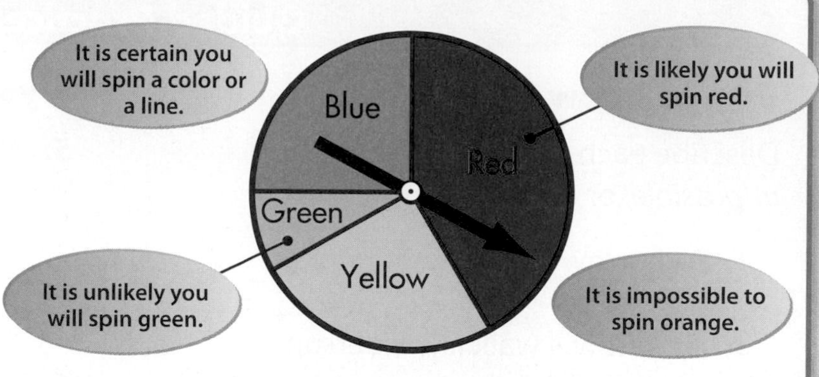

Another Example

Look at the spinner at the right. Which tally chart shows the most likely results of 25 spins?

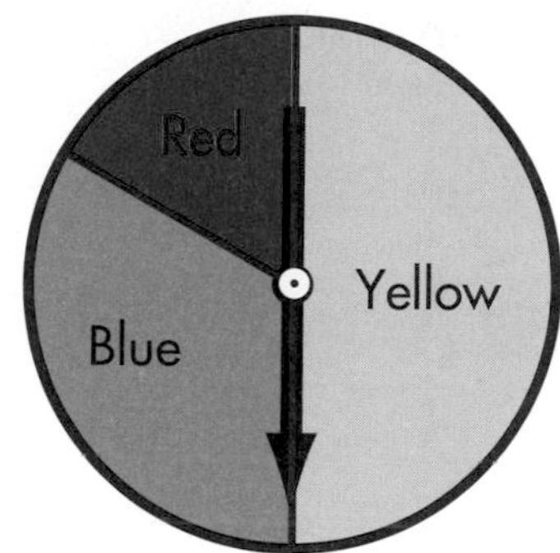

A

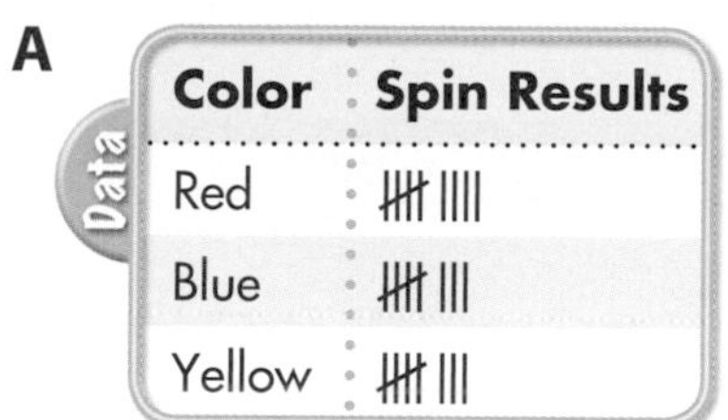

Color	Spin Results
Red	𝍸 ||||
Blue	𝍸 |||
Yellow	𝍸 |||

C

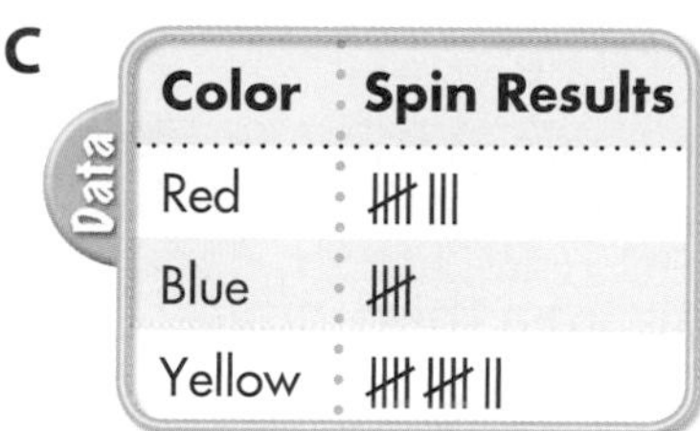

Color	Spin Results
Red	𝍸 |||
Blue	𝍸
Yellow	𝍸 𝍸 ||

B

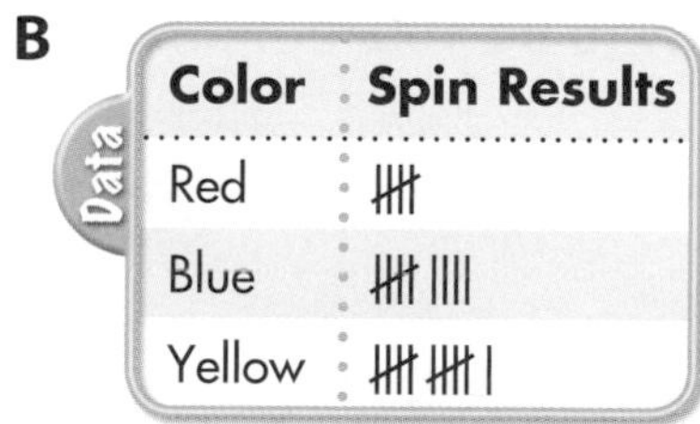

Color	Spin Results
Red	𝍸
Blue	𝍸 ||||
Yellow	𝍸 𝍸 |

D

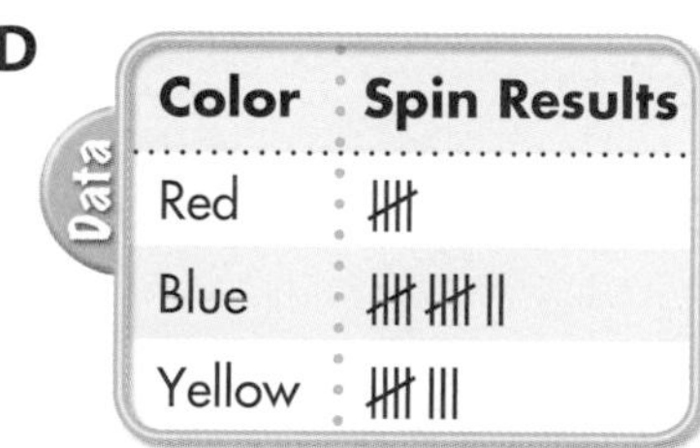

Color	Spin Results
Red	𝍸
Blue	𝍸 𝍸 ||
Yellow	𝍸 |||

Red is the smallest part of the spinner, so red should have the fewest tally marks. So, **A** and **C** are not good choices.

Look at choices **B** and **D**. The yellow part of the spinner is bigger than the blue part, so yellow should have more tally marks than blue. So, **D** is not a good choice.

Choice **B** shows the most likely results of 25 spins.

Explain It

1. Suppose a tally chart shows spin results. How can you tell if one part of the spinner is much larger than the others?

Guided Practice*

Do you know HOW?

Describe each event as *likely*, *unlikely*, *impossible*, or *certain*.

1. Tomorrow will have 24 hours.

2. A plant will walk like a person.

There are 6 white counters, 12 black counters, 2 red counters, and 6 blue counters in a bag. You take one counter from the bag without looking.

3. What outcome is more likely than blue?

4. What outcomes are equally likely?

Do you UNDERSTAND?

5. What is the difference between a certain event and a likely event?

For **6–8**, use the spinner at the top of page 441.

6. Which outcome is less likely than yellow?

7. Is purple a more likely or less likely outcome than blue?

8. Which outcome is more likely than yellow?

Independent Practice

For **9–12**, describe each event about a third-grader named Anna as *likely*, *unlikely*, *impossible*, or *certain*.

9. Anna will need food to grow.

10. Anna will grow to be 100 feet tall.

11. Anna will travel to the moon.

12. Anna will watch television tonight.

For **13–17**, use the spinner at the right.

13. What outcome is less likely than yellow?

14. What outcomes are equally likely?

15. What outcome is most likely?

16. Name an outcome that is certain.

17. Name an outcome that is impossible.

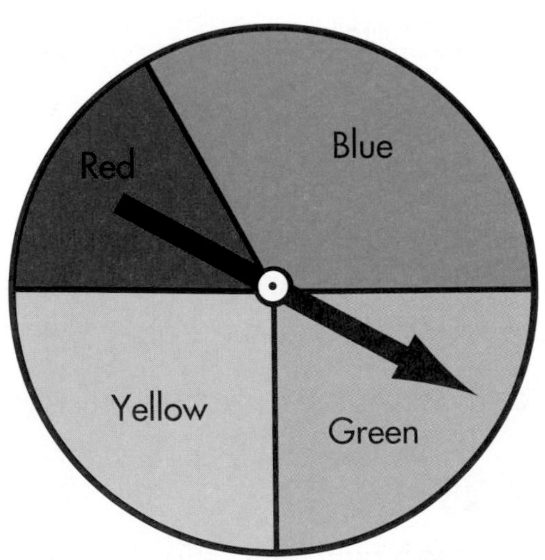

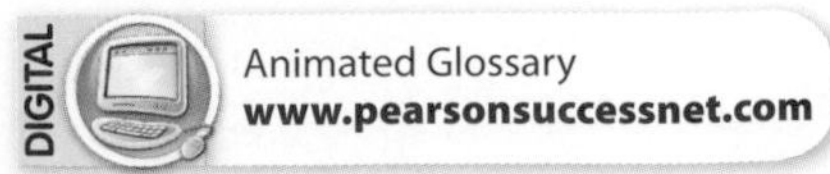

For another example, see Set B on page 456.

Problem Solving

18. The table shows which letters use only dots and which letters use only dashes in Morse Code. All the other letters of the alphabet use both dots and dashes. If you pick one letter from a bag with all 26 letters, are you more likely to pick a letter that uses dots only, dashes only, or both dots and dashes?

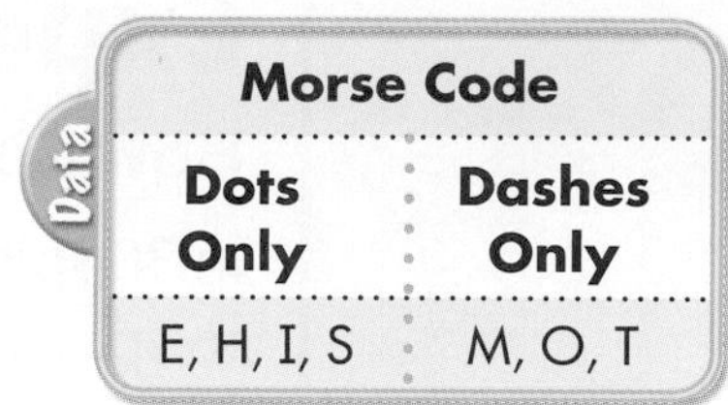

Morse Code	
Dots Only	**Dashes Only**
E, H, I, S	M, O, T

19. **Writing to Explain** How can you tell by looking at a spinner that one outcome is more likely than another?

20. There are 4 medium boxes inside a large box. Inside each medium box, there are 3 small boxes. How many boxes are there in all?

21. Look at the spinner at the right. Which tally chart shows the most likely results of 30 spins?

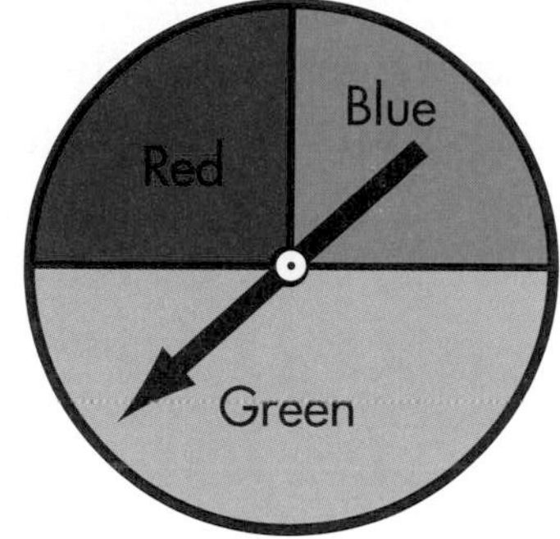

A

Color	Spin Results
Red	𝍸 ||||
Blue	𝍸 ||
Green	𝍸 𝍸 ||||

C

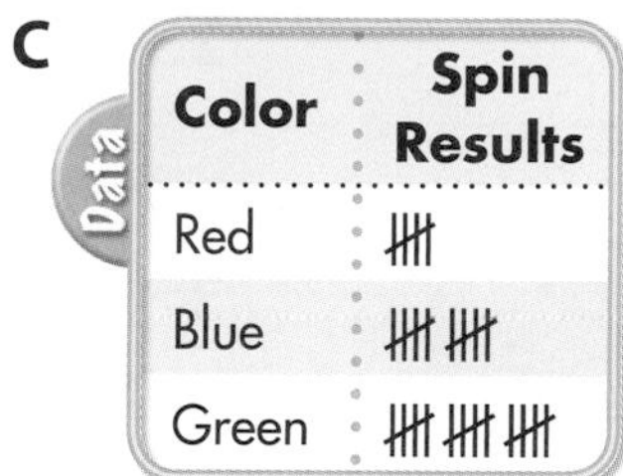

Color	Spin Results
Red	𝍸
Blue	𝍸 𝍸
Green	𝍸 𝍸 𝍸

B

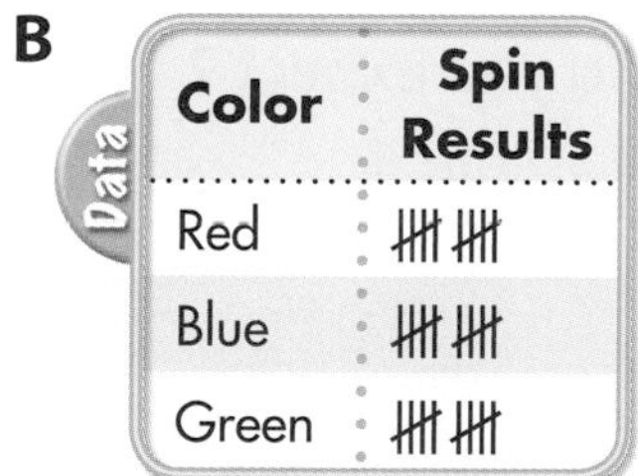

Color	Spin Results
Red	𝍸 𝍸
Blue	𝍸 𝍸
Green	𝍸 𝍸

D

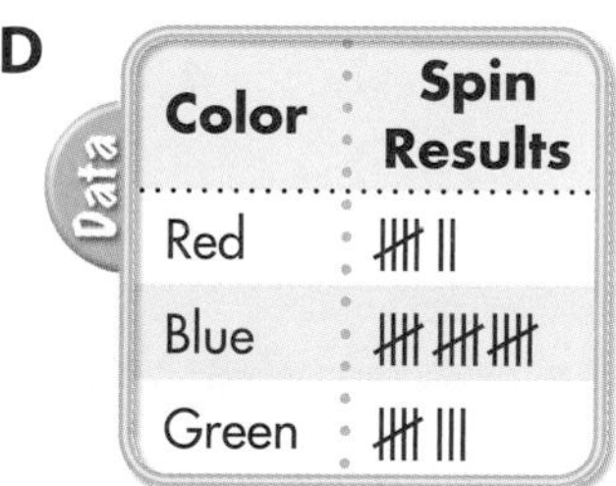

Color	Spin Results
Red	𝍸 ||
Blue	𝍸 𝍸 𝍸
Green	𝍸 |||

In **22** and **23**, use the table that shows the number of paper clips of each color in a box. Suppose Mary takes 1 paper clip out of the box without looking.

22. Which colors does she have an equally likely chance of taking?

A Green and red

B Red and blue

C Green and blue

D Red and yellow

23. Which of the four colors is she least likely to choose?

Paper Clip Colors

Color	Number in Box
Green	27
Red	38
Yellow	21
Blue	27

Lesson
20-3

SDAP 1.2 Record the possible outcomes for a simple event (e.g., tossing a coin) and systematically keep track of the outcomes when the event is repeated many times. Also **SDAP 1.4.**

Outcomes and Experiments

Hands-On
spinner

How do outcomes compare to predictions?

In 30 spins, how many times would you expect to spin red? blue?

Spin the spinner. Then compare the results to what you thought would happen.

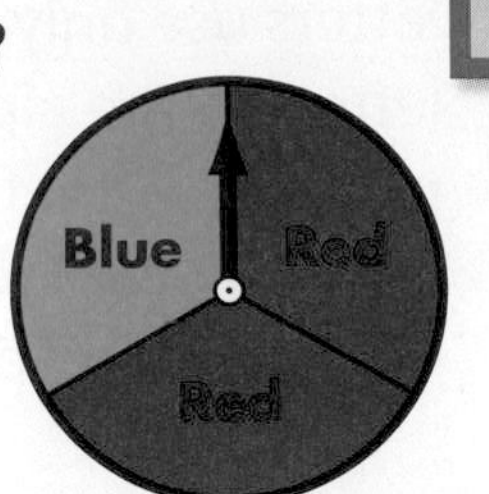

Guided Practice*

Do you know HOW?

1. Use the spinner at the right. Copy and complete the table.

Blue	2	4	6	8	10	20
Green	1	2	3	4	5	10
Red	1	2	3		5	
Total Spins	4	8	12	16		40

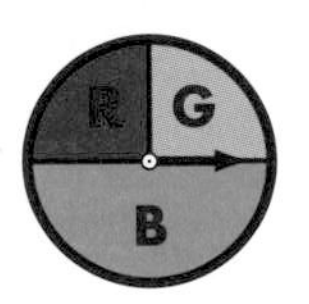

Do you UNDERSTAND?

For **2–4**, use the experiment above.

2. Predict what is likely to happen in 40 spins.

3. Do the experiment. Spin the spinner 40 times. How do the results compare to your prediction?

4. Why should you expect 2 reds and 1 blue in 3 spins?

Independent Practice

In **5–6**, use the table of letter tiles picked fom a bag.

A	5	10	15	20	25	30	35	40
B	3	6	9		15	18	21	24
C	2	4	6	8			14	
Total Picks	10	20	30		50		70	

5. Copy and complete the table.

6. Predict what is likely to happen in 90 picks.

*For another example, see Set B on page 456.

Step 1

Predict the results of 30 spins.

To predict is to tell what may happen using information you know.

Red	2	4	6	8	10	20	40	60	80
Blue	1	2	3	4	5	10	20	30	40
Total Spins	3	6	9	12	15	30	60	90	120

The prediction for 30 spins is the spinner will land on red 20 times and on blue 10 times.

Step 2

Spin the spinner 30 times. Do this test 4 times. Compare the results to what you predicted.

Test	1	2	3	4	Total
Red	22	21	21	20	84
Blue	8	9	9	10	36
Total Spins	30	30	30	30	120

When there are more tests, the results get closer to the prediction.

Problem Solving

In **7–9**, use the spinner to the right and the table below.

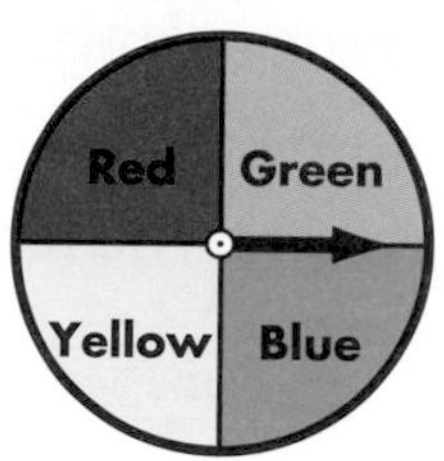

Blue	1	2	3	4		6		8
Green	1	2	3	4	5			
Red	1	2	3	4	5		7	
Yellow	1	2	3			6		
Total Spins	4	8	12	16		24		32

7. Copy and complete the table.

8. Predict the results of 40 spins. Then spin the spinner 40 times. How do the results compare to your prediction?

9. Reasonableness Danny says it is likely that in 40 spins, green will be spun more times than yellow. Do you agree? Explain.

10. Writing to Explain Suppose you put each of the nine letters in this sign in a box and take one out without looking. Which letter are you most likely to take? Explain.

11. In an experiment, the spinner results were 16 blue, 32 green, and 16 red. Which spinner most likely gave these results?

A
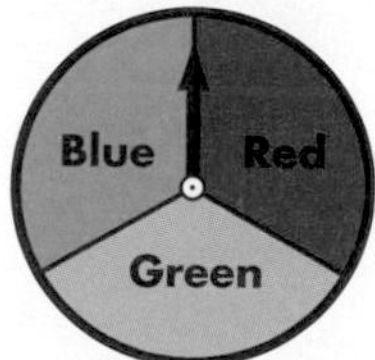

B
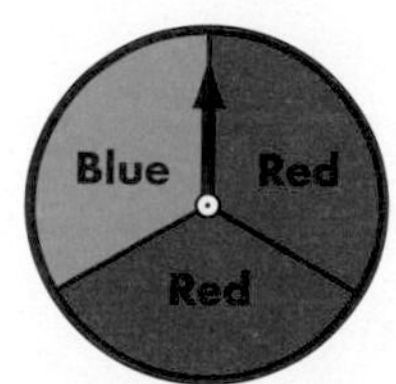

C
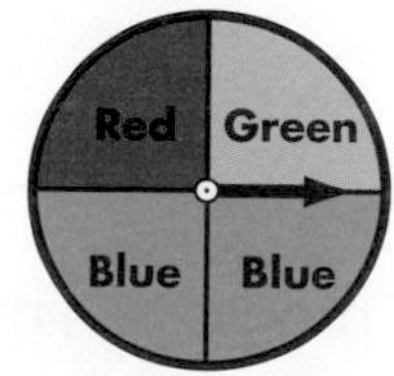

D
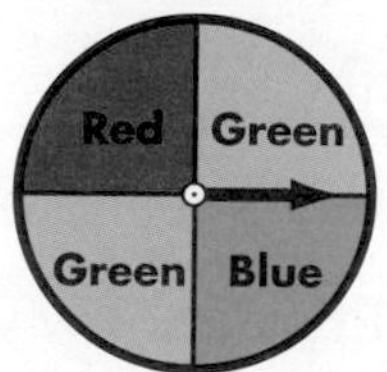

Lesson

20-4

SDAP 1.3 Summarize and display the results of probability experiments in a clear and organized way (e.g., use a bar graph or a line plot).
SDAP 1.4 Use the results of probability experiments to predict future events (e.g., use a line plot to predict the temperature forecast for the next day).

Line Plots and Probability

How can you use line plots?

For each day in April, Dara recorded the high temperature on a line plot. What temperature occurred as the high temperature most often in April?

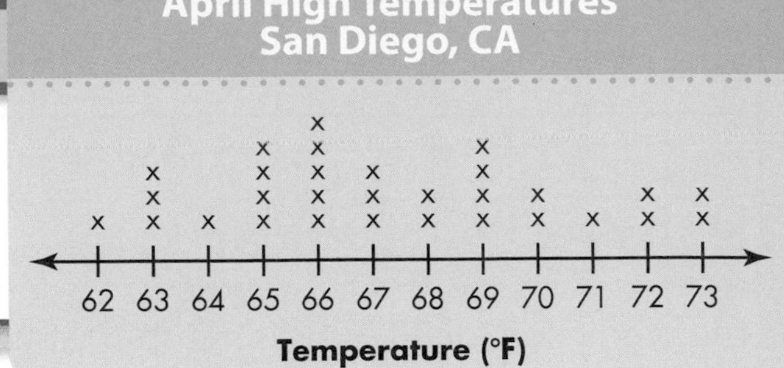

Another Example How can you make a line plot to show probability data?

Toss two number cubes with sides labeled 1 to 6. Add the numbers that you toss. The table shows the results.

Data

Results of 30 tosses

Toss	Sum	Toss	Sum	Toss	Sum	Toss	Sum	Toss	Sum	Toss	Sum
1	8	6	5	11	10	16	7	21	10	26	8
2	8	7	5	12	7	17	6	22	8	27	9
3	7	8	7	13	9	18	8	23	4	28	7
4	12	9	11	14	6	19	5	24	7	29	7
5	6	10	3	15	9	20	5	25	6	30	7

Steps to make a line plot:

- Draw a line.
- Below the line, list in order all the possible outcomes of the sum of the two number cubes.
- Write a title for the line plot.
- Use the data table. Mark an X for each time that sum was the outcome.

Toss Results

2 3 4 5 6 7 8 9 10 11 12

Sum of Numbers

Explain It

1. Use the line plot. Which sum is most likely? least likely?
2. Explain how you can predict the next sum tossed.

A line plot is a way to organize data on a line.

To read a line plot, look at the numbers below the line. Then count the Xs above each number.

On Dara's line plot, each temperature is labeled below the line. Each X represents one day.

Since there are 2 Xs above the 68, the high temperature was 68° on two days.

Which temperature has the most Xs?

There are 5 Xs above the 66, so the high temperature was 66° on five days.

The temperature that occurred as the high temperature most often in April was 66°.

Guided Practice*

Do you know HOW?

Use the data from Rob's spinner experiment for **1–3**.

Spin Results

Spin	Color	Spin	Color	Spin	Color
1	Yellow	8	Red	15	Yellow
2	Blue	9	Yellow	16	Yellow
3	Yellow	10	Yellow	17	Red
4	Red	11	Yellow	18	Yellow
5	Green	12	Green	19	Yellow
6	Blue	13	Blue	20	Blue
7	Yellow	14	Blue		

1. Make a line plot to show the data.

2. How many Xs should be drawn for the number of times that green was spun?

3. Which color do you predict will be spun next? Explain.

Do you UNDERSTAND?

4. In the example above, what was the highest temperature recorded in April?

5. Use the line plot below. Which high temperature occurred most often in August?

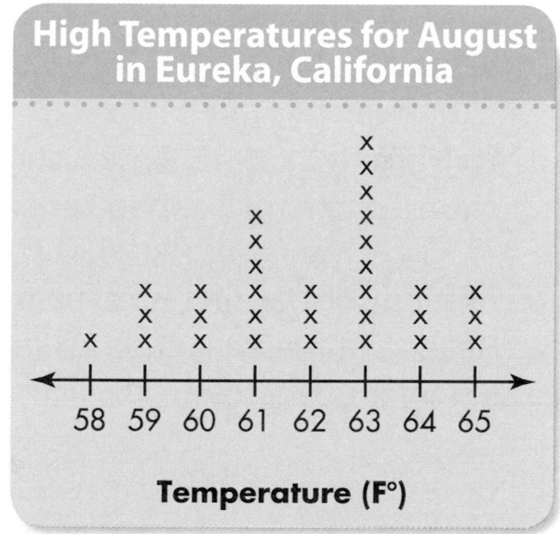

6. In Exercise 5, which high temperature occurred least often?

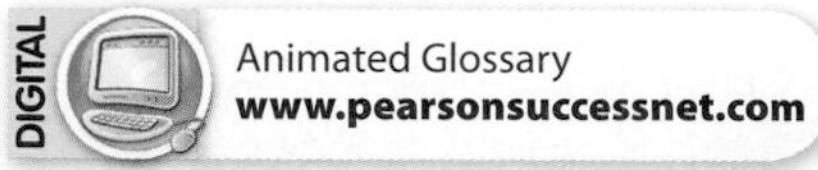

*For another example, see Set C on page 457.

Independent Practice

Amelia recorded the number of people riding in each of 30 cars that passed by. Use the data to the right for **7–11**.

7. Make a line plot to show the data.

8. How many Xs should be drawn for 3 people in a car?

9. Which number of people occurred in two cars?

10. Which number of people occurred most often?

11. What do you predict will be the number of people in the next car?

Data

Number of People in Each Car

Car	Number of People	Car	Number of People	Car	Number of People
1	2	11	3	21	1
2	3	12	1	22	2
3	2	13	2	23	2
4	1	14	4	24	4
5	4	15	1	25	1
6	1	16	3	26	3
7	1	17	1	27	1
8	5	18	2	28	1
9	4	19	6	29	5
10	1	20	1	30	2

Problem Solving

12. A spinner has two unequal parts. Janice spun the spinner 10 times. The spinner landed on Red 2 times. It landed on Green 8 times. What do you predict will be the outcome of the next spin?

13. **Writing to Explain** Which color is most likely the larger part of the spinner in Exercise 12? Explain your answer.

14. Anthony did a coin toss experiment. The coin landed on Heads 27 times. It landed on Tails 35 times. How many times did he toss the coin?

15. **Geometry** One side of a rectangle is 5 inches long. Another side of the rectangle is 7 inches long. What are the lengths of the other 2 sides of the rectangle?

16. **Algebra** One print of a photograph costs 36¢. Two prints cost 72¢. Three prints cost $1.08. If the cost of each print remains the same, how much would 4 prints cost?

Cory recorded the number of clear, partly cloudy, and cloudy days in January. He made a line plot. Use the line plot at the right for **17–21**.

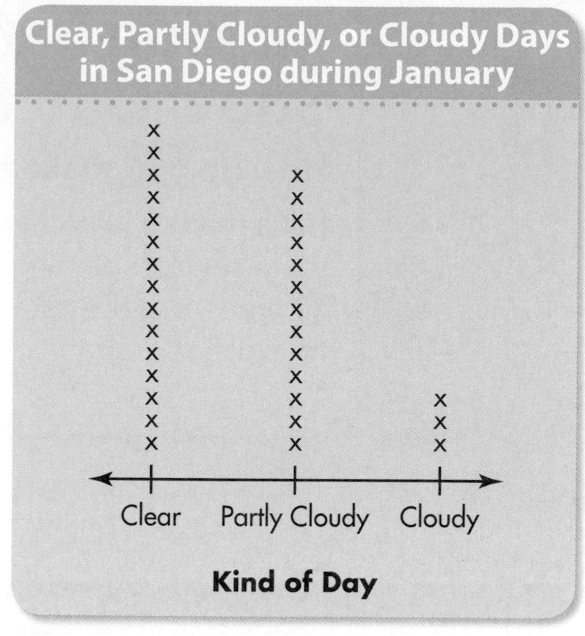

17. How many more clear days than cloudy days were there?

18. What was the total number of partly cloudy and cloudy days?

19. What kind of day occurred least often?

20. What do you predict will be the kind of day on the first day of February?

21. **Number Sense** Cory predicted that there will be 400 cloudy days this year. Is his prediction reasonable? Explain.

22. **Algebra** Copy and complete each number sentence by writing $<$, $>$, or $=$.

a $3 \times 18 \bigcirc 6 \times 9$ **b** $76 \div 4 \bigcirc 64 \div 4$

23. In an experiment, the spinner results were 3 blue, 2 green, 3 red, and 4 yellow. Which line plot matches the data?

A

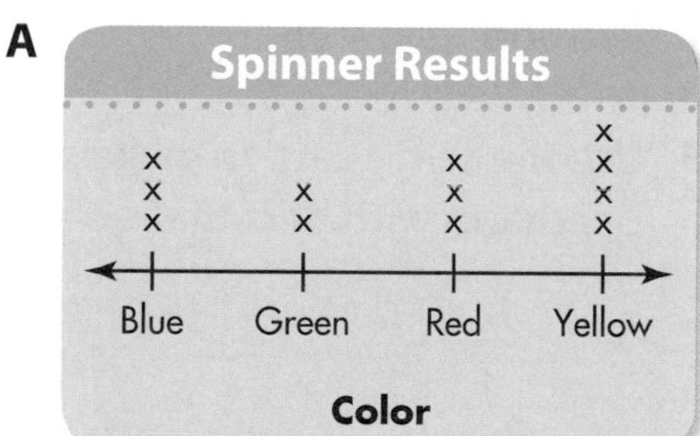

C

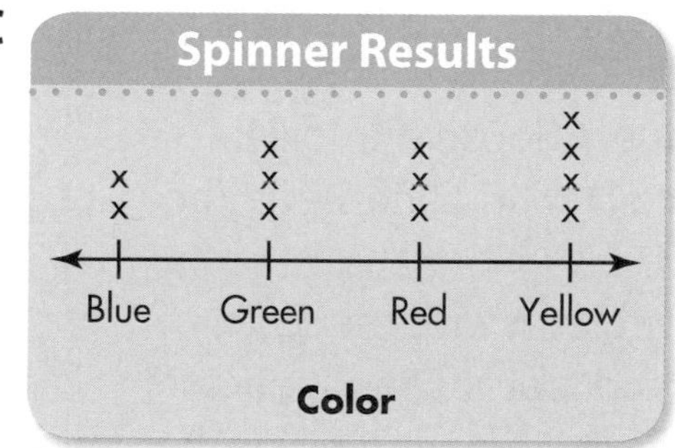

B

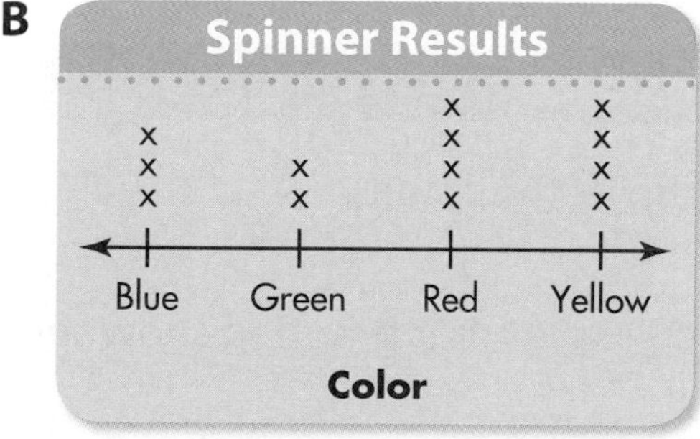

D

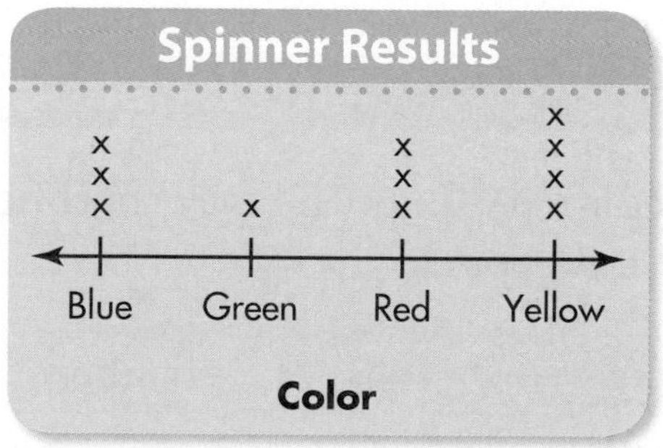

24. Which digit is used most often in whole numbers less than 20?

A 0 **B** 1 **C** 5 **D** 9

Lesson **20-5**

SDAP 1.3 Summarize and display the results of probability experiments in a clear and organized way (e.g., use a bar graph or a line plot). Also **MR 2.3**.

Making Bar Graphs to Show Outcomes

Hands-On: grid paper

How do you make a bar graph?

Hilda made a tally chart to show the results of spinning both spinners 32 times. Use the data in the tally chart to make a bar graph on grid paper.

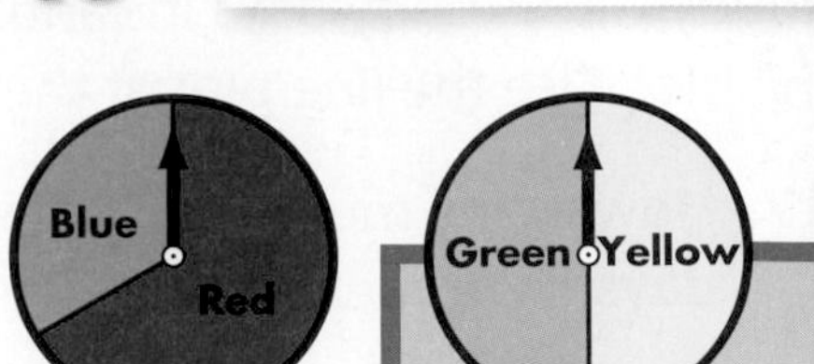

Outcome	Tally Marks
Blue and Green	卌 I
Blue and Yellow	卌 II
Red and Green	卌 卌 I
Red and Yellow	卌 III

Guided Practice*

Do you know HOW?

For **1** and **2**, use the chart below to make a bar graph.

Letter Picked from Bag		
Letter	Tally	Number
A	卌 I	6
R	卌 卌 卌	15
N	卌 卌	10

1. Write a title. Choose the scale. What will each grid line stand for?

2. Set up the graph with the scale, the title, and labels. Draw a bar for each letter.

Do you UNDERSTAND?

In **3–5**, use the bar graph above.

3. Why does the bar for Blue and Yellow end between 6 and 8?

4. Suppose the Red and Yellow outcome was spun 9 times. Between which grid lines would the bar for Red and Yellow end?

5. Use the same data to make another bar graph with bars that go across.

Independent Practice

Jan tossed 2 coins 50 times. The tally chart below shows the results. Use the chart for **6** and **7**.

Outcome	Tally	Number
Heads and Heads	卌 卌 卌	15
Heads and Tails	卌 卌 卌 卌	20
Tails and Tails	卌 卌 卌	15

6. Make a bar graph to show the data.

7. Explain how to find the outcome that occurred most often.

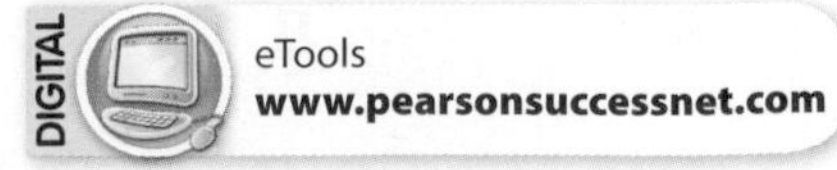

*For another example, see Set D on page 457.

Step 1

Write a title to explain what the bar graph shows.

This bar graph will be titled "Spinner Results."

Step 2

Choose the scale. Decide how many units each grid line will represent.

Each grid line will represent 2 spins.

Write the scale and the labels.

Step 3

Draw a bar for each outcome.

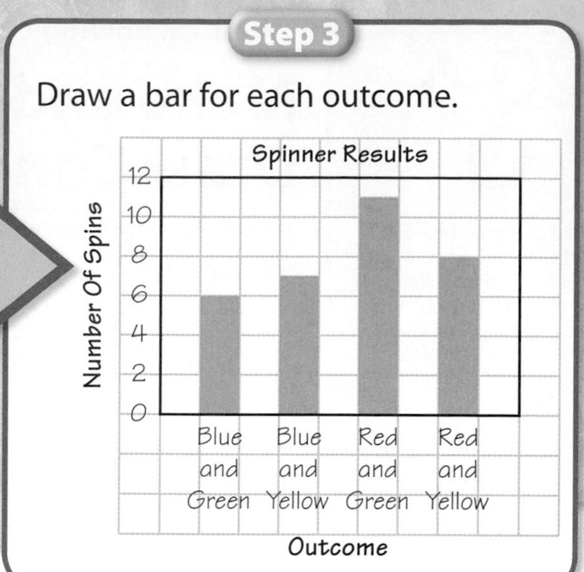

Problem Solving

Use the table for **8** and **9**.

8. Make a bar graph with bars that go across. Write a title. Choose the scale.

9. **Number Sense** Which two colors were outcomes about the same number of times?

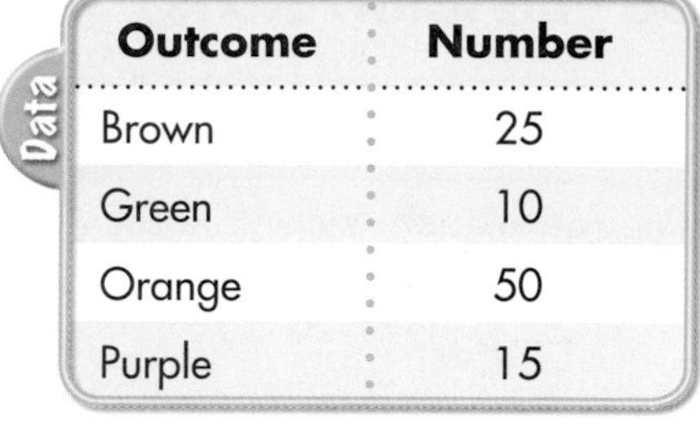

Outcome	Number
Brown	25
Green	10
Orange	50
Purple	15

In **10** and **11**, suppose you are going to make a bar graph to show the data in the table.

10. **Writing to Explain** What scale would you choose? Explain.

11. Which kind of bird would have the longest bar?

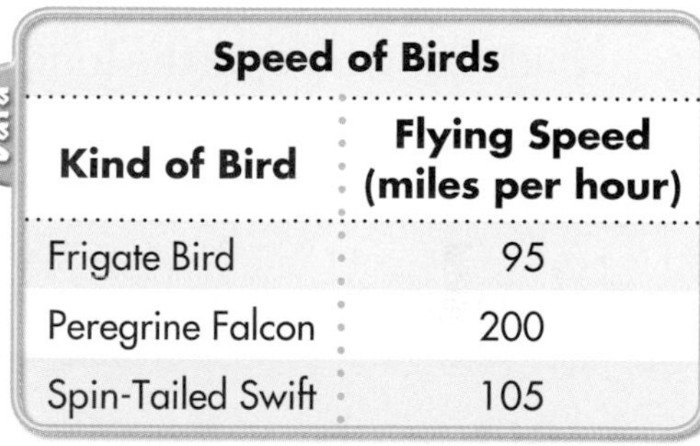

Speed of Birds

Kind of Bird	Flying Speed (miles per hour)
Frigate Bird	95
Peregrine Falcon	200
Spin-Tailed Swift	105

Use the bar graph at the right for **12** and **13**.

12. Luz picked a marble from a bag 36 times and made a bar graph of the outcomes. How many times did she pick an orange marble?

A 3 **B** 5 **C** 6 **D** 15

13. How many more times did Luz pick a green marble than a purple marble?

A 1 **B** 2 **C** 3 **D** 9

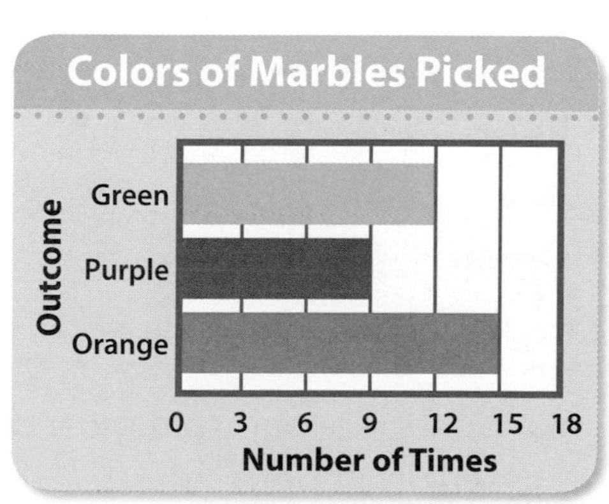

Lesson

20-6

MR 2.3 Use a variety of methods, such as words, numbers, symbols, charts, graphs, tables, diagrams, and models, to explain mathematical reasoning. Also **SDAP 1.0, Grade 4**

Problem Solving

Make and Use Graphs to Draw Conclusions

The tally chart shows data about the favorite hobbies of two Grade 3 classes. Compare the hobbies of the two classes.

Data

Favorite Hobbies

	Class A		**Class B**	
Hobby	**Tally**	**Number**	**Tally**	**Number**
Model Building	|||	3	卌	5
Drawing	卌 卌 ||	12	卌 ||	7
Rock Collecting	||||	4	||||	4
Reading	卌		6	卌 ||||	9

Guided Practice*

Do you know HOW?

Data

Bicycle Club Miles

Member	Victor	Rosita	Gary	Hal
Number of Miles	20	35	30	20

1. If you made a bar graph for this data, which bar would be the longest?

2. Who rode the same distance as Hal?

Do you UNDERSTAND?

3. How do the bars on a bar graph help you to compare data?

4. In the example above, what is the favorite hobby of Class A? of Class B?

5. **Write a Problem** Use the graphs above to write a comparison problem. Then solve the problem.

Independent Practice

For **6** and **7**, use the pictograph.

T-Shirt Sales

	Store A	**Store B**
Blue	👕 👕 ½	👕
Red	👕 👕	👕 👕 ½
Green	½	½

Each 👕 = 10 T-shirts. Each ½ = 5 T-shirts.

6. What color was sold most often at each store? equally at both stores?

7. Where was blue sold more often?

- What do I know?
- What am I asked to find?
- What diagram can I use to help understand the problem?
- Can I use addition, subtraction, multiplication, or division?
- Is all of my work correct?
- Did I answer the right question?
- Is my answer reasonable?

*For another example, see Set D on page 457.

Plan

Make a bar graph for each class.

Favorite Hobbies of Class A

Hobby: Model Building, Drawing, Rock Collecting, Reading

Number of Students: 0 2 4 6 8 10 12 14

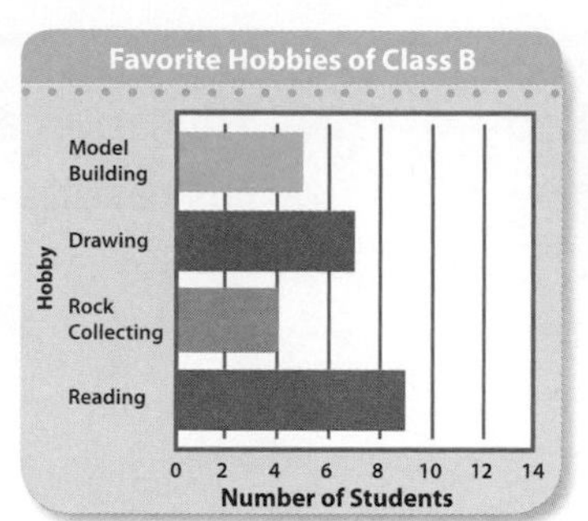

Solve

Now read the graphs and make comparisons.

- More students in Class B like model building than in Class A.
- The same number of students in each class like rock collecting.

For **8–10**, use the bar graph at the right.

8. How many people in all voted for their favorite type of exercise?

9. How many more people voted for gymnastics than for jogging?

10. **Write a Problem** Write and solve a word problem different from Exercises 8 and 9.

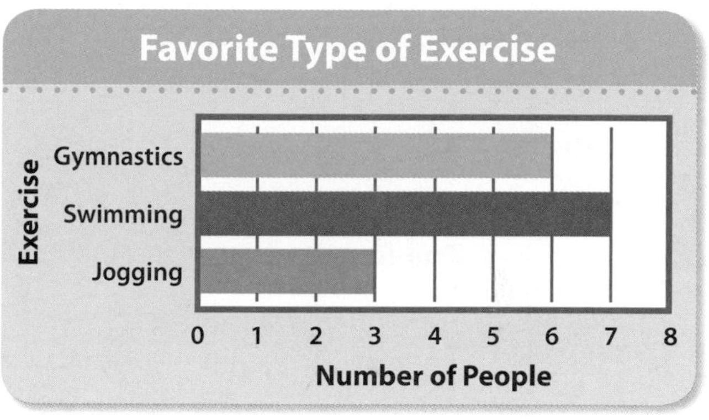

For **11–13**, use the tally chart.

11. Make a graph to show the data. Choose a pictograph or a bar graph.

12. Who read exactly ten more books than Sandra?

13. Write the members in order from most to fewest books read.

Data

Books Read by Reading Club Members

Member	Number of Books Read
Daryl	卌 卌 卌 |||
Alice	卌 卌 卌 |
Sandra	卌 |||
Helmer	卌 卌 ||||

14. **Strategy Focus** Solve. Use the strategy Make a Table.

At the farmer's market, Matt gives 2 free apples for every 6 apples you buy. If you buy 24 apples, how many free apples will you get?

15. **Writing to Explain** What kinds of comparisons can you make when you look at a bar graph or a pictograph?

Test Prep

1. As part of an experiment, Tella rolled a colored cube. She rolled "Pink" 7 times, "Purple" 3 times, and "Teal" 5 times. Which tally chart shows her results? (20-1)

A

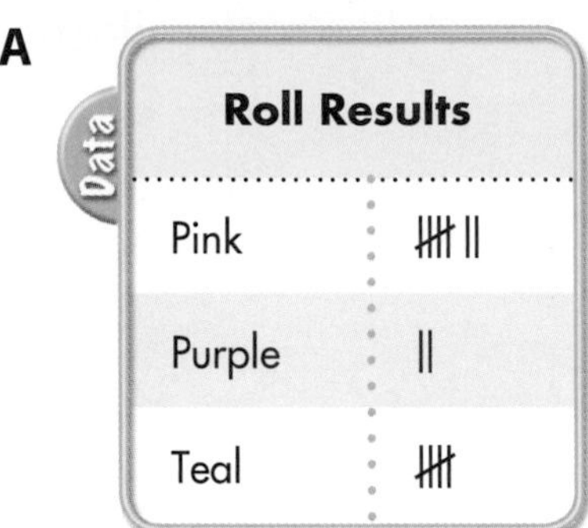

Roll Results	
Pink	𝍸 ||
Purple	||
Teal	𝍸

B

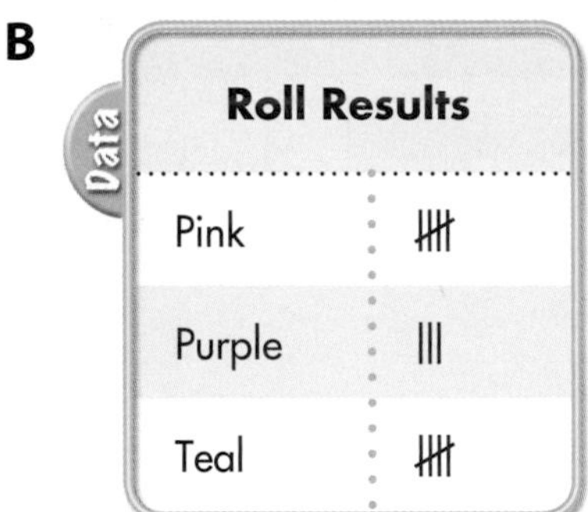

Roll Results	
Pink	𝍸
Purple	|||
Teal	𝍸

C

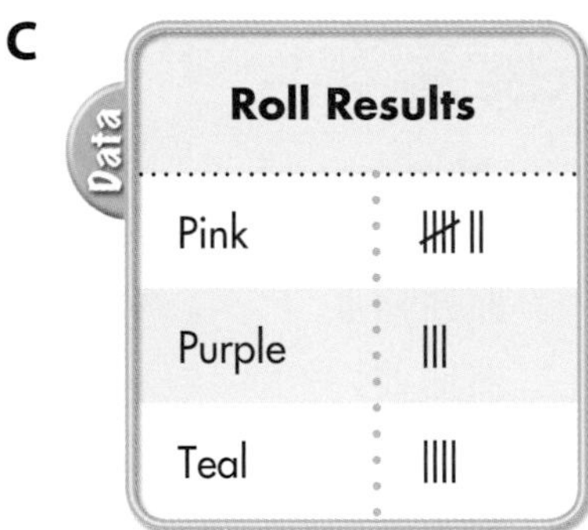

Roll Results	
Pink	𝍸 ||
Purple	|||
Teal	||||

D

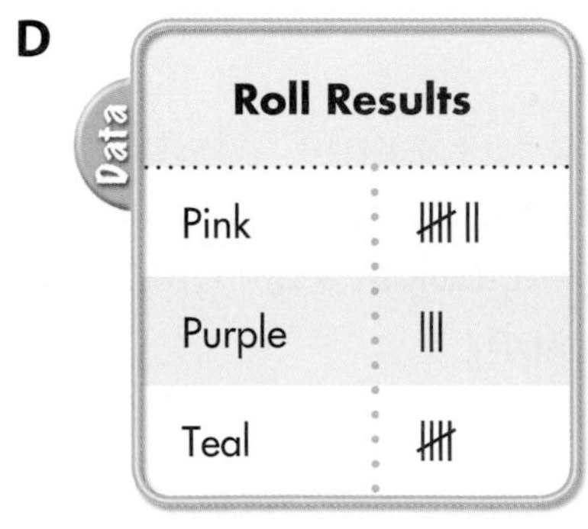

Roll Results	
Pink	𝍸 ||
Purple	|||
Teal	𝍸

2. Trey spun a spinner 23 times. His results are shown below.

Outcome	Tally
Green	𝍸 |||
Red	𝍸 |
Yellow	𝍸 ||||

Which graph matches the data in the tally chart? (20-5)

A

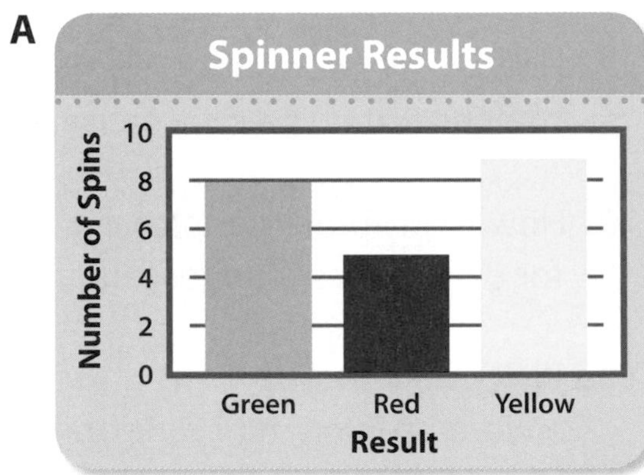

B

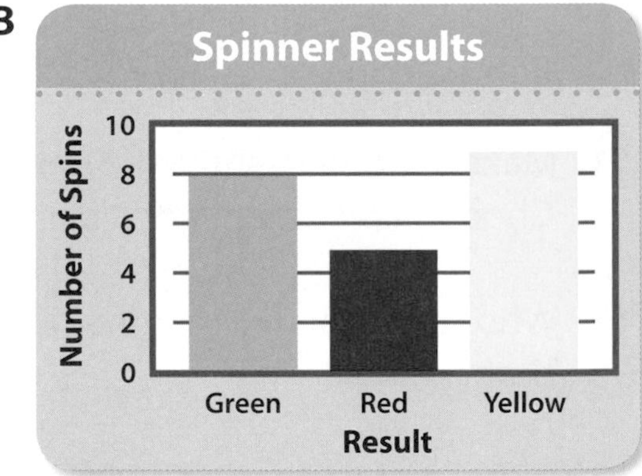

C

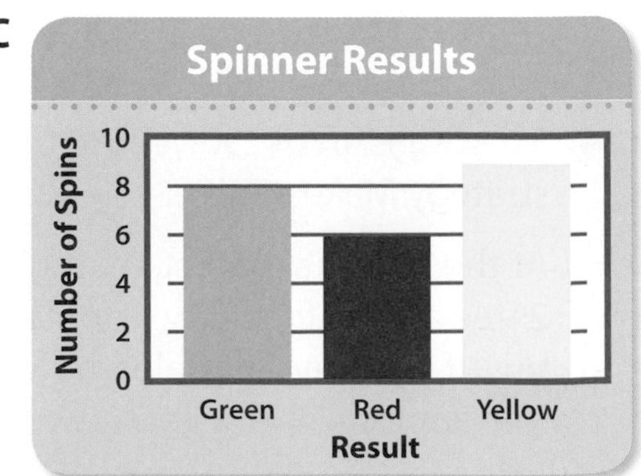

D None of them

3. Which statement is true about the data in the graphs? (20-6)

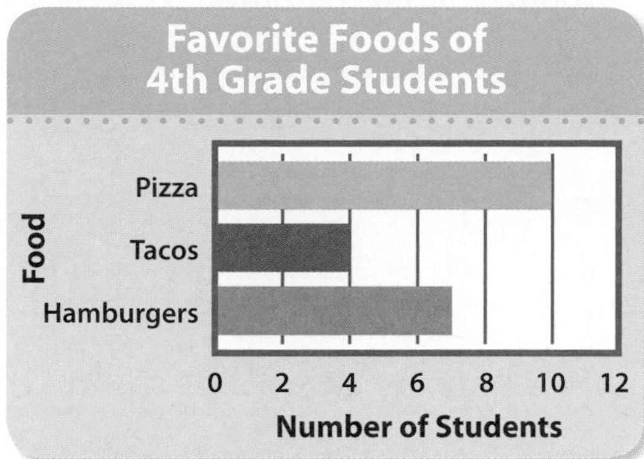

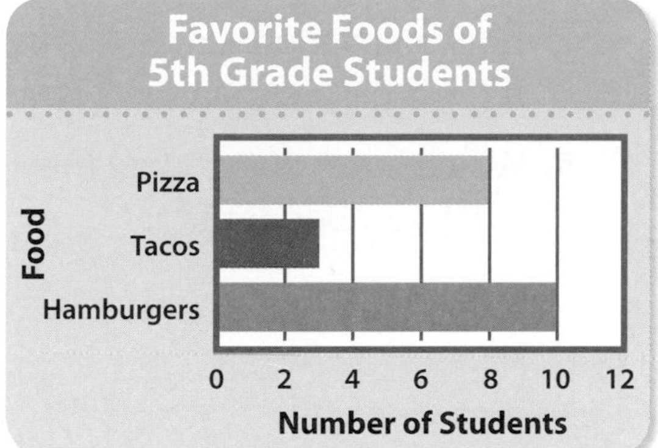

A Pizza is the favorite in both grades.

B The same number of students in both grades like tacos.

C More students in grade 4 than in grade 5 like hamburgers.

D More students in grade 4 than in grade 5 like pizza.

4. At the fair, the fish pond has 12 red fish, 9 blue fish, 10 yellow fish, and 5 orange fish. If Tammy hooks a fish without looking, what color fish is she most likely to get? (20-2)

A Red

B Blue

C Yellow

D Orange

5. Use the bag of tiles and the table to answer the question below.

Heart	3	6	9		15	
Moon	2	4	6	8		12
Star	1	2	3			6
Total Picks	6	12	18	24	30	36

Which is the best prediction for how many moons will be picked in 30 total picks? (20-3)

A 12 moons

B 10 moons

C 8 moons

D 5 moons

6. Jose spun a numbered spinner 12 times. His results are shown in the line plot below.

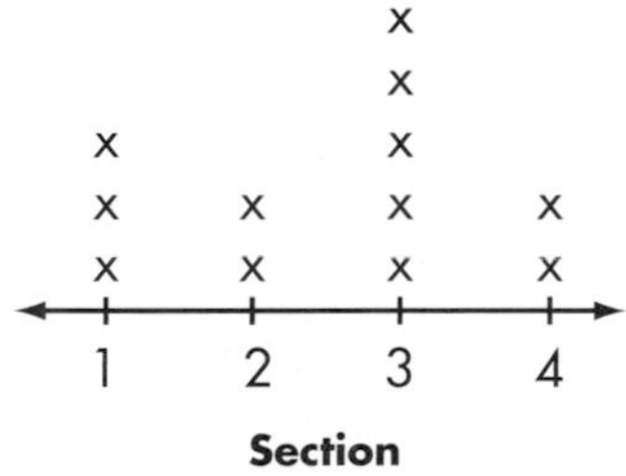

Which is the best prediction for Jose's next spin? (20-4)

A Section 1

B Section 2

C Section 3

D Section 4

Set A, pages 438–439

How many times was each color spun?

Colors Spun

Orange	Green	Blue	Orange
Green	Orange	Red	Blue
Orange	Green	Red	Orange

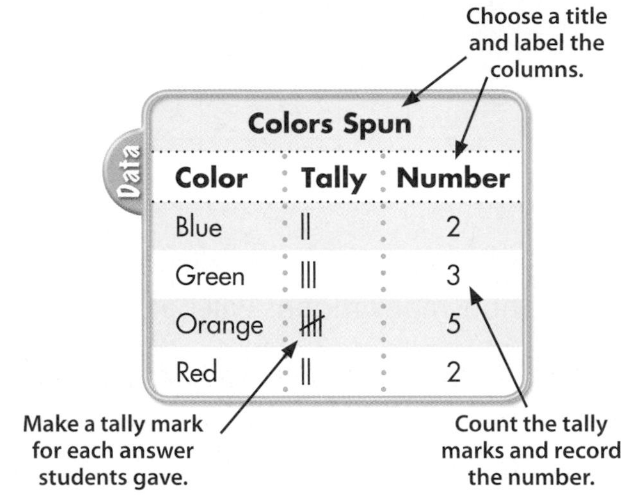

Colors Spun

Color	Tally	Number
Blue	||	2
Green	|||	3
Orange	卌	5
Red	||	2

Remember to make sure your tally marks match the data.

For **1–3**, use the data below.

Letters Picked

S	I	S	E	N
S	N	N	S	E
I	S	N	S	I
I	I	R	E	N

1. Make a tally chart for the data.

2. How many more times was the letter S picked than the letter E?

3. Which letter was picked the least number of times?

Set B, pages 440–445

When you spin this spinner, what outcome is likely? unlikely? impossible? certain?

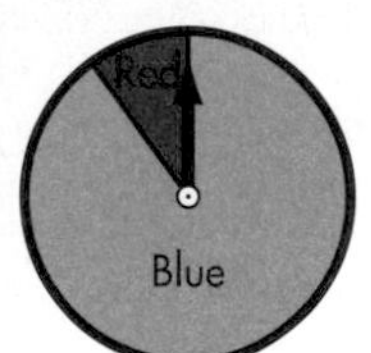

It is likely you will spin Blue.
It is unlikely you will spin Red.
It is impossible to spin Green.
It is certain you will spin a color or a line.

If you spin 40 times, how many times would you expect to spin Blue and how many Red?

Blue	9	18	27	45	54	72	90
Red	1	2	3	5	6	8	10
Total Spins	10	20	30	50	60	80	100

In 40 spins, you can expect the spinner to land on Blue about 36 times and on Red about 4 times.

Remember that you are deciding what will probably happen.

For **1–4**, use this spinner.

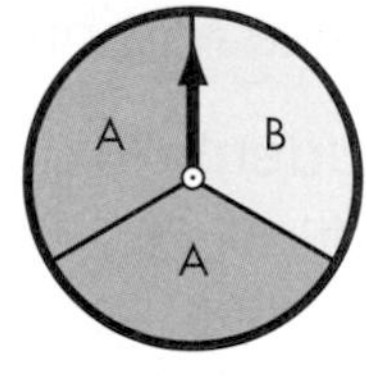

1. What outcome is likely? impossible?

2. In 3 spins, Lisa spun two As and one B. Make a prediction of what is likely to happen in 30 spins.

3. Spin the spinner 30 times. How do the results compare to your prediction?

Set C, pages 446–449

What was the high temperature in Eureka, California most often in the month of June?

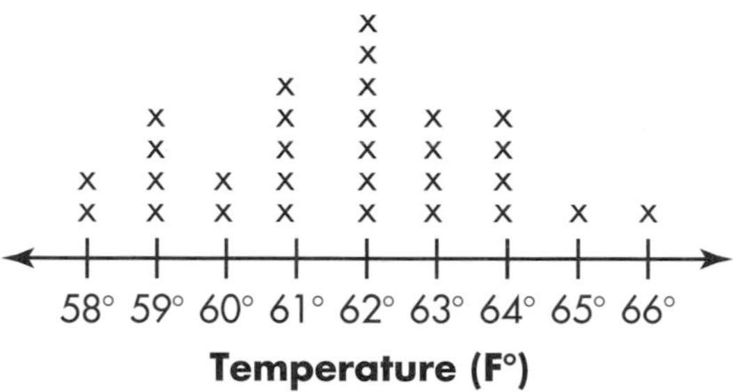

The high temperature that occurred most often was 62°.

Remember that each outcome gets an X on a line plot.

Use the data below for **1** and **2**.

Spin Results

Spin	Color	Spin	Color	Spin	Color
1	Green	6	Blue	11	Red
2	Blue	7	Red	12	Blue
3	Blue	8	Blue	13	Blue
4	Red	9	Blue	14	Blue
5	Blue	10	Green	15	Green

1. Make a line plot to show the data.
2. Which color do you predict will be spun next?

Set D, pages 450–453

How can you make a bar graph to help you draw conclusions?

Data

Color	Number of Spins
Blue	6
Green	5
Purple	11
Red	10

Use the data to choose a scale.

Choose 2 for each grid line. Odd numbers can be halfway between 2 grid lines.

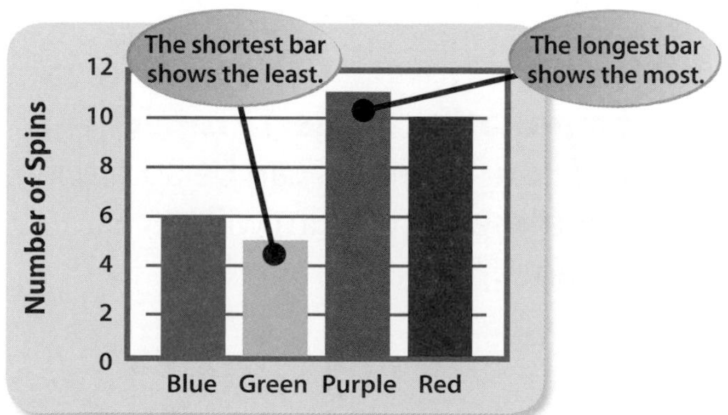

Remember that you can compare the length of the bars.

1. Choose a scale and make a bar graph to show the data below.

Data

Letter Picked from Bag		
Letter	**Tally**	**Number**
E	𝍸 III	8
S	𝍸 𝍸 IIII	14
R	𝍸 𝍸	10
T	𝍸	5

2. In the bar graph at the left, suppose a bar for Pink is as long as the bar for Red. What conclusion can you draw?

Glossary

A.M. Time between midnight and noon.

acute angle An angle that measures less than a right angle.

acute triangle A triangle with three acute angles.

addends Numbers added together to give a sum.
Example: 2 + 7 = 9
Addend (2) Addend (7)

angle A figure formed by two rays that have the same endpoint.

area The number of square units needed to cover a region.

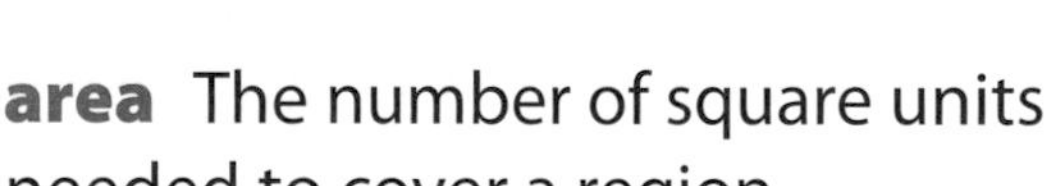

array A way of displaying objects in rows and columns.

Associative (Grouping) Property of Addition The grouping of addends can be changed and the sum will be the same.

Associative (Grouping) Property of Multiplication The grouping of factors can be changed and the product will be the same.

bar graph A graph using bars to show data.

capacity The volume of a container measured in liquid units.

centimeter (cm) A metric unit of length. 1 centimeter equals 10 millimeters.

certain event An event that is sure to happen.

Commutative (Order) Property of Addition Numbers can be added in any order and the sum will be the same.

Commutative (Order) Property of Multiplication Numbers can be multiplied in any order and the product will be the same.

compare To decide if one number is greater than or less than another number.

compatible numbers Numbers that are easy to add, subtract, multiply, or divide mentally.

cone A solid figure with a circle as its base and a curved surface that meets at a point.

congruent figures Figures that have the same shape and size.

corner Where 3 or more edges meet in a solid figure.

cube A solid figure with six faces that are congruent squares.

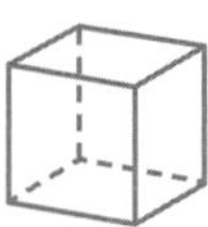

cubic unit A cube with edges 1 unit long, used to measure volume.

cup A customary unit of capacity.

cylinder A solid figure with two congruent circles as bases.

D

data Pieces of collected information.

decimal A number with one or more digits to the right of the decimal point.

decimal point A dot used to separate dollars from cents and ones from tenths in a number.

decimeter (dm) A metric unit of length. 1 decimeter equals 10 centimeters.

degree Celsius (°C) A metric unit of temperature.

degree Fahrenheit (°F) A customary unit of temperature.

denominator The number below the fraction bar in a fraction, the total number of equal parts in all.

difference The answer when subtracting two numbers.

digits The symbols 0, 1, 2, 3, 4, 5, 6, 7, 8, and 9 used to write numbers.

dividend The number to be divided.
Example: 63 ÷ 9 = 7
↑ Dividend

divisible Can be divided by another number without leaving a remainder.
Example: 10 is divisible by 2.

division An operation that tells how many equal groups there are or how many are in each group.

divisor The number by which another number is divided.
Example: 63 ÷ 9 = 7
↑ Divisor

dollar sign ($) A symbol used to indicate money.

edge A line segment where two faces of a solid figure meet.

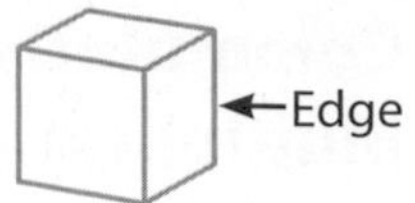

eighth One of 8 equal parts of a whole.

elapsed time Total amount of time that passes from the beginning time to the ending time.

equally likely outcomes Outcomes that have the same chance of happening.

equilateral triangle A triangle with all sides the same length.

equivalent fractions Fractions that name the same part of a whole, same part of a set, or same location on a number line.

estimate To give a number or answer that describes about how much or how many.

even number A whole number that has 0, 2, 4, 6, or 8 in the ones place; A number that is a multiple of 2.

expanded form A number written as the sum of the values of its digits.
Example: 2,476 = 2,000 + 400 + 70 + 6

face A flat surface of a solid that does not roll.

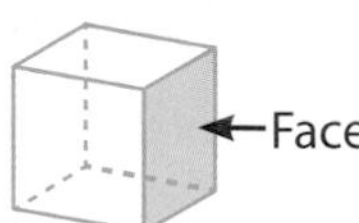

fact family A group of related facts using the same numbers.

factors Numbers that are multiplied together to give a product.
Example: 7 × 3 = 21
(7: Factor, 3: Factor)

fifth One of 5 equal parts of a whole.

foot (ft) A customary unit of length. 1 foot equals 12 inches.

fourth One of 4 equal parts of a whole.

fraction A symbol, such as $\frac{2}{8}$, $\frac{5}{1}$, or $\frac{5}{5}$, used to name a part of a whole, a part of a set, or a location on a number line.

gallon (gal) A customary unit of capacity. 1 gallon equals 4 quarts.

gram (g) A metric unit of mass, the amount of matter in an object.

half (plural, halves) One of 2 equal parts of a whole.

half hour A unit of time equal to 30 minutes.

hexagon A polygon with 6 sides.

hour A unit of time equal to 60 minutes.

hundredth One of 100 equal parts of a whole, written as 0.01 or $\frac{1}{100}$.

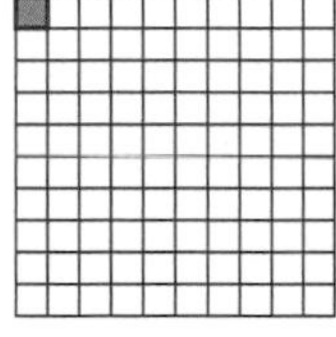

Identity (One) Property of Multiplication The product of any number and 1 is that number.

Identity (Zero) Property of Addition The sum of any number and zero is that same number.

impossible event An event that will never happen.

inch (in.) A customary unit of length.

inequality A number sentence that uses $<$ (less than) or $>$ (greater than).

intersecting lines Lines that cross at one point.

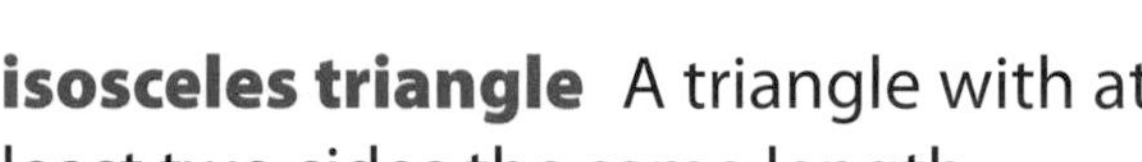

isosceles triangle A triangle with at least two sides the same length.

key Explanation of what each symbol represents in a pictograph.

kilogram (kg) A metric unit of mass, the amount of matter in an object. 1 kilogram equals 1,000 grams.

kilometer (km) A metric unit of length. 1 kilometer equals 1,000 meters.

L

likely event An event that will probably happen.

line A straight path of points that is endless in both directions.

line plot A way to organize data on a line.

line segment A part of a line that has two endpoints.

liter (L) A metric unit of capacity. 1 liter equals 1,000 milliliters.

M

meter (m) A metric unit of length. 1 meter equals 100 centimeters.

mile (mi) A customary unit of length. 1 mile equals 5,280 feet.

milliliter (mL) A metric unit of capacity. 1,000 milliliters equals 1 liter.

millimeter (mm) A metric unit of length. 1,000 millimeters equals 1 meter.

minute A unit of time equal to 60 seconds.

mixed number A number with a whole number part and a fraction part.
Example: $2\frac{3}{4}$

month One of the twelve parts into which a year is divided.

multiple The product of the number and any other whole number.
Example: 0, 4, 8, 12, and 16 are multiples of 4.

multiplication An operation that gives the total number when you put together equal groups.

N

number line A line that shows numbers in order using a scale.
Example:
0 1 2 3 4

numerator The number above the fraction bar in a fraction.

numerical expression An expression that contains numbers and at least one operation. A numerical expression is also called a number expression.

obtuse angle An angle that measures more than a right angle.

obtuse triangle A triangle with one obtuse angle.

octagon A polygon with 8 sides.

odd number A whole number that has 1, 3, 5, 7, or 9 in the ones place; A number not divisible by 2.

order To arrange numbers from least to greatest or from greatest to least.

ounce (oz) A customary unit of weight.

outcome A possible result of a game or experiment.

P.M. Time between noon and midnight.

parallel lines Lines that never intersect.

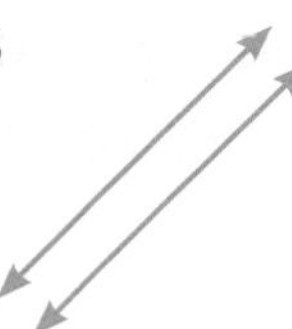

parallelogram A quadrilateral in which opposite sides are parallel.

partial product A part of a product.

pentagon A polygon with 5 sides.

perimeter The distance around a figure.

period A group of three digits in a number, separated by a comma.

perpendicular lines Two lines that intersect to form right angles.

pictograph A graph using pictures or symbols to show data.

pint (pt) A customary unit of capacity. 1 pint equals 2 cups.

place value The value given to the place a digit has in a number. *Example:* In 3,946, the place value of the digit 9 is *hundreds.*

point An exact position often marked by a dot.

polygon A closed figure made up of straight line segments.

possible event An event that might or might not happen.

pound (lb) A customary unit of weight. 1 pound equals 16 ounces.

predict To tell what may happen using information you know.

probability The chance an event will happen.

product The answer to a multiplication problem.

pyramid A solid figure whose base is a polygon and whose faces are triangles with a common point.

Q

quadrilateral A polygon with 4 sides.

quart (qt) A customary unit of capacity. 1 quart equals 2 pints.

quarter hour A unit of time equal to 15 minutes.

quotient The answer to a division problem.

R

ray A part of a line that has one endpoint and continues endlessly in one direction.

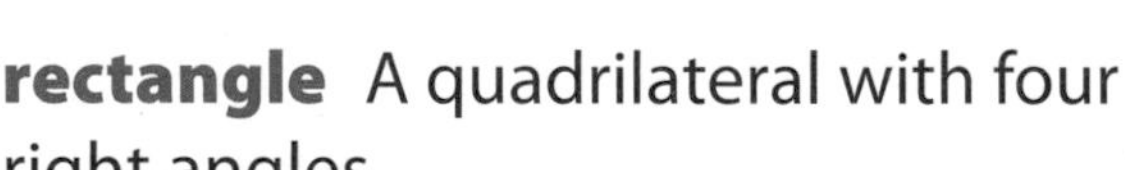

rectangle A quadrilateral with four right angles.

rectangular prism A solid figure with faces that are rectangles.

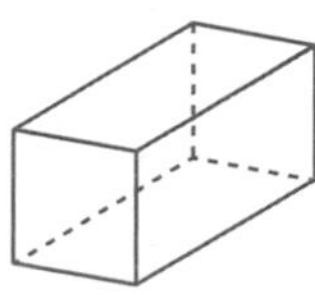

regroup To name a whole number in a different way.
Example: 28 = 1 ten 18 ones.

remainder The part that is left over after dividing.
Example: 31 ÷ 7 = 4R3

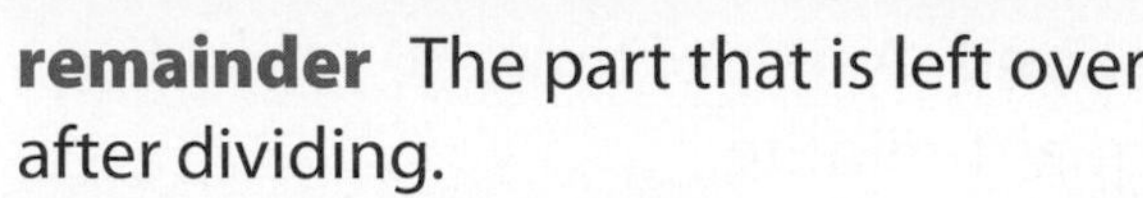

repeating pattern A pattern made up of shapes or numbers that form a part that repeats.

rhombus A quadrilateral with opposite sides parallel and all sides the same length.

right angle An angle that forms a square corner.

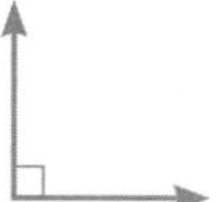

right triangle A triangle with one right angle.

round To replace a number with a number that tells about how much or how many to the nearest ten, hundred, thousand, and so on.
Example: 42 rounded to the nearest 10 is 40.

S

scale The numbers that show the units used on a graph.

scalene triangle A triangle with no sides the same length.

second A unit of time. 60 seconds equal 1 minute.

side A line segment forming part of a polygon.

simplest form A fraction with a numerator and denominator that cannot be divided by the same divisor, except 1.

sixth One of 6 equal parts of a whole.

solid figure A figure that has length, width, and height.

sphere A solid figure in the shape of a ball.

square A quadrilateral with four right angles and all sides the same length.

square unit A square with sides 1 unit long, used to measure area.

standard form A way to write a number showing only its digits.
Example: 3,845

sum The answer when adding two or more addends.
Example: 7 + 9 = 16 (↑ Sum)

T

tally chart A chart on which data is recorded.

tally mark A mark used to record data on a tally chart.
Example: 𝍸 = 5

tenth One of 10 equal parts of a whole, written as 0.1 or $\frac{1}{10}$.

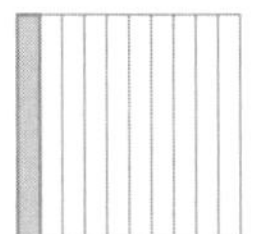

thermometer A tool used to measure temperature.

third One of 3 equal parts of a whole.

trapezoid A quadrilateral with only one pair of parallel sides.

triangle A polygon with 3 sides.

twelfth One of 12 equal parts of a whole.

twice Two times a number.

unit fraction A fraction with a numerator of 1.
Example: $\frac{1}{2}$

unlikely event An event that probably won't happen.

vertex (plural, vertices) The point where two rays meet to form an angle. The point where the sides of a polygon meet. The point where 3 or more edges meet in a solid figure that does not roll. The pointed part of a cone.

volume The number of cubic units needed to fill a solid figure.

week A unit of time equal to 7 days.

word form A number written in words.
Example: 9,325 = nine thousand, three hundred twenty-five

yard (yd) A customary unit of length. 1 yard equals 3 feet or 36 inches.

year A unit of time equal to 365 days, or 52 weeks, or 12 months.

Zero Property of Multiplication The product of any number and zero is zero.

Cover
Luciana Navarro Powell

Illustrations
Dick Gage 8, 10, 14, 46, 51, 172, 276, 376, 386; Neil Stewart 54, 82, 150, 172, 194, 255, 311, 353, 363, 377-379, 388, 426; Leslie Kell 76, 78, 87, 103, 136, 148-149, 166, 169-170, 177, 191, 193, 205, 213, 253, 267, 296, 303-304, 311, 338, 340, 370, 397, 411; Joe LeMonnier 215, 251-252

Photographs
Every effort has been made to secure permission and provide appropriate credit for photographic material. The publisher deeply regrets any omission and pledges to correct errors called to its attention in subsequent editions.

Unless otherwise acknowledged, all photographs are the property of Scott Foresman, a division of Pearson Education.

Photo locators denoted as follows: Top (T), Center (C), Bottom (B), Left (L), Right (R), Background (Bkgd).

Front Matter: xvi ©Bob Mitchell/Corbis

2 (CL) ©Roy Beusker/Weijers Domino Productions b.v., (TR) ©D. Hurst/Alamy Images; 3 ©Ron Niebrugge/Alamy Images; 6 Dave King/©DK Images; 12 (C) ©Purestock/Alamy Images, (CR) ©Brad Perks Lightscapes/Alamy, (BR) Getty Images, (BC) ©Discovery Comm/Panoramic Images; 15 (CR) Jerry Young/©DK Images, (C) ©WizData, Inc./Alamy, (CL) Dave King/©DK Images, (C) ©Kennan Ward/Corbis; 22 (TL) ©Bill Varie/Corbis, (Bkgd) Corbis, (TL) ©Paul Sakuma/AP Images; 23 ©Westend61/Alamy Images; 28 (BL) ©Westend61/Alamy Images, (CL) ©Kathleen Murtagh; 38 (C) ©Ron Watts/Corbis, (TR) ©Ken Usami/Getty Images; 39 (BL) ©Kristin Siebeneicher/AP Images, (TL) Getty Images; 43 ©Greg Vaughn/Alamy Images; 46 (CL) Getty Images, (CL) ©IT Stock Free/Jupiter Images; 48 ©Royalty-Free/Corbis; 56 (TR) ©imagebroker/Alamy, (TR) Frank Greenaway/©DK Images; 64 (CR) ©David R. Frazier Photolibrary, Inc./Alamy Images, (L) ©Joe Tucciarone/Photo Researchers, Inc., (B) Bedrock Studios/©DK Images; 65 (TL) Getty Images, (BL) NASA Image Exchange; 70 Getty Images; 73 ©David Wootton/Alamy Images; 84 ©David R. Frazier Photolibrary, Inc./Alamy Images; 98 (TL) ©Desmond Boylan/Reuters Media, (B) ©Baron Wolman/Getty Images; 99 (BL) ©Andy King/Orange Dot Productions, (TL) ©Stephen Saks/Alamy Images; 100 (BL) Jupiter Images, (BR) ©photolibrary/Index Open; 101 (BL) ©Vstock/Index Open, (BC) ©photolibrary/Index Open; 102 (C) Stockdisc, (BC, BR) Getty Images; 107 (TR, C, BR) Getty Images, (CR) Jupiter Images; 112 ©Baron Wolman/Getty Images; 115 ©Alan Weintraub/Alamy Images; 119 ©Andy King/Orange Dot Productions; 126 ©Kevin Schafer/zefa/Corbis; 127 ©Patti Murray/Animals Animals/Earth Scenes; 135 Golden Dollar Obverse ©1999 United States Mint. All Rights Reserved. Used with permission.; 137 ©Patti Murray/Animals Animals/Earth Scenes; 146 (L) ©Joe McBride/Aurora/Getty Images, (CR) ©Hulton Archive/Getty Images; 147 (TL) ©Geoff Dann/Dorling Kindersley/Getty Images, (BL) ©Bettmann/Corbis, (BC) ©Steven Puetzer/Getty Images; 159 (CL) ©Photos Select/Index Open, (C) ©ImageDJ/Index Open; 160 Getty Images; 164 (TL) ©Geoff du Feu/Alamy, (B) ©Les Chatfield, (TR) ©Joe McDonald/Corbis; 165 (B) NASA/JPL-Caltech/M. Kelley (Univ. of Minnesota)/NASA, (TL) ©George D. Lepp/Corbis; 186 (B) NASA, (TR) ©Joe McBride/Getty Images; 187 (B) ©Greg Vaughn/Alamy Images, (TL) Getty Images; 196 Getty Images; 202 (T) Getty Images, (B) ©Brad Rickerby/Getty Images; 203 (TL) ©Rubberball/Getty Images, (BL) ©Darren Baker/Alamy; 204 Getty Images; 218 (CR) Archivberlin Fotoagentur GmbH/Alamy Images, (C) Juniors Bildarchiv/Alamy Images; 224 (TR) ©Directphoto/Alamy, (CL) ©Kike Calvo/VWPICS/Alamy Images, (B) ©Panoramic Images/Getty Images; 225 Digital Vision; 229 ©Directphoto/Alamy; 230 Jupiter Images; 234 ©Alissa Crandall/Corbis; 246 (B) ©Photowood Inc./Corbis, (TR) ©Ann Flory; 247 (TL) ©Lester V. Bergman/Corbis, (BL) Dream Maker Software; 253 ©Lester V. Bergman/Corbis; 272 (CL) ©Bavaria/Getty Images, (B) ©Robert Garvey/Corbis; 273 (TC) ©WildPictures/Alamy Images, (TL) ©Ed Reschke/Peter Arnold/Alamy Images, (BL) ©Danita Delimont/Alamy Images; 279 (BL)© John T. Fowler/Alamy Images, (BC) ©David M. Dennis/Animals Animals/Earth Scenes; 292 (BL) ©Stephen Street/Alamy Images, (BC) ©Douglas Faulkner/Alamy Images, (CL) ©Mitchell Funk/Getty Images, (TL) ©Mike Hill/Alamy Images; 293 ©Jim Cummins/Corbis; 306 ©Alain Dragesco-Joffe/Animals Animals/Earth Scenes; 312 ©Bill Romerhaus/Index Open; 320 (TL) ©Tim Shaffer/Corbis, (TCL) Getty Images, (B) ©Georgette Douwma/Getty Images; 321 (BL) ©Roger Harris/Photo Researchers, Inc., (TL) ©Bill Heinsohn/Alamy Images; 323 ©Joseph Sohm/ChromoSohm Inc./Corbis; 348 (C) ©Simple Stock Shots, (C) ©Joe McDonald/Corbis; 349 (TL) ©Mary Evans Picture Library/Alamy Images, (BL) ©Gary Roberts/Rex USA; 351 Jupiter Images; 354 (CL) ©photolibrary/Index Open, (BL) Corbis, (BL) Getty Images; 355 (TR) Jupiter Images, (CL) ©Photos Select/Index Open, (B) ©Mistral Images/Index Open; 357 Getty Images; 358 (BL) ©Comstock Inc., (BC) G. Huntington, (BR) Jupiter Images, (C) ©Image Source Limited; 359 ©Simple Stock Shots; 360 (TR) ©Royalty-Free/Corbis, (BL, CL, BR) Getty Images, (BR) ©D. Hurst/Alamy, (L) Jupiter Images; 361 ©AP Images; 363 (BR) Getty Images, (BR) Richard Embery; 364 Getty Images; 371 (CR) Getty Images, (TR) ©Vstock/Index Open; 372 (TR, BR) Stockdisc, (BC) ©Photos Select/Index Open, (BL) ©DesignPics/Index Open; 374 (TR) ©Ingrid van den Berg/AGE Fotostock, (B) Digital Vision; 375 (BL) ©Wolfgang Pölzer/Alamy Images, (TL) ©Richard Cummins/Lonely Planet Images; 376 (CL) Digital Vision, (BR) ©Foodcollection/Getty Images, (TL) ©photolibrary/Index Open, (BL) Hemera Technologies; 377 (CL) ©Jim Lane/Alamy Images, (CR) ©Michele Westmorland/Corbis, (R) Jupiter Images, (BL, CL) Getty Images, (TR) ©Creatas; 380 ©PCL/Alamy Images; 382 (CL) ©photolibrary/Index Open, (BR) ©Simple Stock Shots; 383 (BR) ©Juergen & Christine Sohns/Animals Animals/Earth Scenes, (BC) Simple Stock Shots; 384 (CR) Stockdisc, (BL) Jupiter Images, (BC) Getty Images; 392 (CR) ©Mixa/Getty Images, (BR) ©photolibrary/Index Open, (BL) Getty Images; 394 (TR, CL) ©Jeff Saward/Labyrinthos Picture Library, (BL) Photo courtesy of Pleasant Time Industries; 395 (BL) ©Richard Schulman/Corbis, (TL) ©Anna Daza; 399 ©W. Blaine Pennington Photo; 414 (TL) Photo Researchers, Inc., (B) ©Phil Schermeister/Corbis; 418 ©Vstock/Index Open; 420 Getty Images; 436 (BL) ©Eric Hosking/Corbis, (TR) ©Hot Ideas/Index Open, (C) ©DK Images; 437 (BL) ©Adam Pretty/Getty Images, (TL) ©Robert Landau/Corbis; 440 ©Keren Su/China Span/Alamy Images; 445 ©Robert Landau/Corbis

Index

H

S